f you're wondering why you should buy this new edition of *Resources for Writers with Readings: From Paragraph to Essay*, here are a dozen good reasons!

1. *Resources for Writers with Readings* uses a straightforward, easy-to-comprehend **four Cs** (concise, credible, clear, and correct) **approach** that reinforces the skills needed to grasp the steps of the writing process.

2. A new highly **visual design helps you** understand the material being presented and enhances the learning process.

3. Clear, highly accessible instruction and engaging sample paragraphs, many new to this edition, enable you to more easily comprehend material and produce effective writing yourself!

4. New cultural literacy themes have been added, which not only give you interesting content about culture but also are carried throughout each chapter in illustrations, sample paragraphs, and exercises.

5. **Seventeen high-interest readings**, including ten new ones, cover a range of themes, from ethics and poverty to grades and habits. Each reading is accompanied by exercises that help you digest material and respond in writing.

6. Chapters have been combined and reorganized to make *Resources for Writers* easier to use.

7. Each chapter now includes more Writing Practice, activities giving you more ways to strengthen your writing.

8. A new chapter, "Writing from Visuals," shows you how to hone your observation skills and write about the many images you study in your academic and professional life.

9. Each photograph caption now includes a critical thinking question that asks you to practice your observation skills.

10. Exercises throughout the book have been completely revised to better reflect the chapter's content and upgraded in response to student feedback!

11. Each writing chapter now concludes with a **checklist** that helps you be sure you have fully understood the content of the chapter.

12. And now—use *Resources for Writers with Readings* alongside Pearson's unique MyWritingLab (www.mywritinglab.com) and find a world of resources developed specifically with you, the student, in mind!

If practice makes perfect, imagine what *better* practice can do . . .

PEARSON
mywritinglab™

MyWritingLab is an online learning system that provides better writing practice through progressive exercises. These exercises move students from literal comprehension to critical application to demonstration of their ability to write properly. With this better practice model, students develop the skills needed to become better writers!

When asked if they agreed with the following statements, here are how students responded:

97%
The MyWritingLab Student-user Satisfaction Level

"MyWritingLab helped me to improve my writing." **89%**

"MyWritingLab was fairly easy to use." **90%**

"MyWritingLab helped make me feel more confident about my writing ability." **83%**

"MyWritingLab helped me to better prepare for my next writing course." **86%**

"MyWritingLab helped me get a better grade." **82%**

"I wish I had a program like MyWritingLab in some of my other courses." **78%**

"I would recommend my instructor continue using MyWritingLab." **85%**

Student Success Story

"The first few weeks of my English class, my grades were at approximately 78%. Then I was introduced to MyWritingLab. I couldn't believe the increase in my test scores. My test scores had jumped from that low score of 78 all the way up to 100% (and every now and then a 99)."
—Exetta Windfield, *College of the Sequoias* (MyWritingLab student user)

TO PURCHASE AN ACCESS CODE, GO TO
WWW.MYWRITINGLAB.COM

Resources for Writers with Readings

From Paragraph to Essay

Third Edition

Elizabeth Cloninger Long
Sacramento City College

Longman

New York San Francisco Boston
London Toronto Sydney Tokyo Singapore Madrid
Mexico City Munich Paris Cape Town Hong Kong Montreal

Acquisitions Editor: Matthew Wright
Senior Development Editor: Katharine Glynn
Marketing Manager: Thomas DeMarco
Senior Supplements Editor: Donna Campion
Production Manager: Ellen MacElree
Project Coordination, Text Design, and Electronic Page Makeup: Electronic
  Publishing Services Inc., NYC
Cover Design Manager: Wendy Ann Fredericks
Cover Designer: Kay Petronio
Photo Researcher: Anita Dickhath
Senior Manufacturing Buyer: Alfred C. Dorsey
Printer and Binder: Courier/Kendallville
Cover Printer: Phoenix Color Corp/Hagerstown

For permission to use copyrighted material, grateful acknowledgment is made to the
copyright holders on pp. C-1–C-2, which are hereby made part of this copyright page.

Library of Congress Cataloging-in-Publication Data
Long, Elizabeth Cloninger.
    Resources for writers with readings: From paragraph to essay/
        Elizabeth Cloninger Long.—3rd ed.
            p. cm.
        Includes bibliographical references and index.
        ISBN-13: 978-0-205-65173-3 (student ed.)
        ISBN-10:   0-205-65173-9 (student ed.)

        ISBN-13: 978-0-205-65174-0 (annotated instructor's ed.)
        ISBN-10:   0-205-65174-7 (annotated instructor's ed.)
    1. English language—Rhetoric—Problems, exercises, etc. 2. Report writing—
Problems, exercises, etc. 3. Readers. I. Title.

PE1413.L66 2008

808'.0427—dc22   2008026164

Longman
is an imprint of

ISBN-13: 978-0-205-65173-3 (student ed.)
ISBN-10:   0-205-65173-9 (student ed.)

ISBN-13: 978-0-205-65174-0 (annotated instructor's ed.)
ISBN-10:   0-205-65174-7 (annotated instructor's ed.)

1 2 3 4 5 6 7 8 9 10—CRK—11 10 09 08

To the English Faculty and Students at Sacramento City College
and my family: Mike, Annabelle, Annelise, Susannah

Contents

CHAPTER 4   Drafting: First to Final Drafts   63

Culture Note: KNITTING   63

CHAPTER 5   Making Changes: Revision   71

Culture Note: CHOCOLATE   71

CHAPTER 6   Editing for Clarity and Correctness   90

Culture Note: WINTER HOLIDAYS   90

CHAPTER 7   Putting the Writing Process Steps Together   100

Culture Note: RUNNING   100

PART THREE
The Elements of Good Writing   109

PART FOUR
Strategies for Paragraph Development   207

CHAPTER 23   Argument   357

PART FIVE
Writing Essays   373

CHAPTER 24   The Essay and the Thesis Statement   375

PART SEVEN
Writing Correct Sentences   463

PART EIGHT
Punctuation and Mechanics 611

PART NINE
Readings for Informed Writing   705

Tips for Reading Critically   707

How We Learn   709

What We Value   738

Challenges We Face   773

Preface

Students must learn to write clearly. Even if their writing never takes them beyond composing a simple cover letter for a new job, students must understand how to craft logical, clear sentences and paragraphs if they are to be taken seriously.

Resources for Writers with Readings, Third Edition, is the second book in a three-book series designed to take students from simple paragraph construction through short essay writing. It offers students an opportunity to practice their writing-process skills while simultaneously eliminating the errors that mar their writing.

WHAT'S NEW IN THE THIRD EDITION

The third edition of *Resources for Writers with Readings* has a number of important revisions:

- **More than thirty new Writing Practice** activities give students additional relevant writing opportunities.
- **Easy-to-use checklists** summarize key concepts in every writing chapter.
- **New cultural literacy themes** revitalize critical content chapters.
- **A new chapter, "Writing from Visuals,"** teaches students to hone their critical thinking skills via observation. In addition, each photo in the book is accompanied by critical thinking questions that ask students to apply their observation skills.
- **Each writing-process chapter includes a list of Recommended Readings that are especially suited to the teaching of that chapter** and that provide suggestions for further cultural literacy and stylistic discussion.
- **Streamlined organization** helps instructors and students make logical connections between paragraph- and sentence-level writing concepts.
- **The Updated Lab Manual (both printed and online versions)** provides instructors with additional exercises designed to supplement the text.
- **New readings** represent writers from diverse backgrounds, modeling key writing styles and offering students contemporary thinking and writing opportunities.
- **A new design more effectively uses color and typography** to help students master the content of each chapter.

CONTENT OVERVIEW AND ORGANIZATION

Part One, "Getting Started," introduces the four cornerstones for good writing, which simultaneously serve as the four bases for evaluation. The four Cs—concise, credible, clear, and correct—provide students with the foundation to understand and practice the elements of good writing. Additionally, Part One teaches students to consider their audience and their purpose.

Part Two, "The Writing Process," introduces the concepts of prewriting, drafting, revising, and editing, offering students multiple opportunities for practicing each step in the writing process.

Part Three, "The Elements of Good Writing," links key writing skills to the four Cs, showing students how practicing each skill leads to the mastery of the four Cs. In addition, chapters devoted to topics including sensitive language, writing from visuals, and spelling give students specific guidance in improving their writing.

Part Four, "Strategies for Paragraph Development," gives students explanations of, examples of, and practice in writing paragraphs in nine traditional modes of paragraph development. This section includes two new themes and many new Writing Practice activities.

Part Five, "Writing Essays," introduces students to those skills necessary to writing an essay, all the while linking skills to the four Cs.

Part Six, "Writing for Different Purposes," gives students explanations, examples, and practice in writing for specific, real-life purposes.

Part Seven, "Writing Correct Sentences," provides logical, common-sense explanations of grammar with a rich array of practice and exercises.

Part Eight, "Punctuation and Mechanics," gives helpful explanations and practice, with line-by-line exercises and Editing Practice activities for each skill being studied.

Part Nine, "Readings for Informed Writing," includes seventeen high-interest readings clustered around three themes which illustrate a range of writing styles, patterns of development, and subject matter. The readings are accompanied by supplemental pre- and post-reading questions and writing assignments.

CHAPTER FEATURES OF *RESOURCES FOR WRITERS WITH READINGS*

Modular Chapter Format

The modular chapter format provides opportunities for lessons and assignments within a single chapter but allows for connections between other lessons as well. Students can read new information, receive tips for helping them integrate that new information into what they've already learned, and find cross-references to other chapters for easy reference to past and future lessons. Instructors can tailor chapter assignments to the needs of a specific class—or an individual student.

Cultural Literacy Theme

The cultural literacy component offers students easily digestible information beneficial to them in college and in contemporary society. For a variety of reasons, many beginning writing students lack basic cultural literacy; in classes that presume a certain knowledge foundation—such as history, political science, or literature—these students find themselves behind. In *Resources for Writers with Readings*, each chapter begins with a note that introduces a cultural theme; some notes are whimsical and some are serious, but all are designed to illuminate a part of the cultural heritage of the United States. Sample paragraphs and exercises in the chapter revolve around these themes, so students can see concepts illustrated with real subject matter, not just with fictionalized or overly personalized material. In addition, these themes offer students from diverse backgrounds insight into the historical bases of materials they read in their classes, and they also offer a broad range of topics students can write about.

Cultural Literacy Photos

Resources for Writers with Readings contains some three dozen full-color photographs that reinforce the cultural literacy themes in the chapters. The photos give students additional insight into our complex cultural heritage, and photo captions provide writing prompts to stimulate students' ideas.

Four Cs of Writing

Resources for Writers with Readings uses a simple mnemonic device to help students remember that their writing must be concise, credible, clear, and correct. This formula is completely integrated into text, examples, and exercises so that students learn how to check their work for the elements of good writing at every stage of development. Graphics and checklists reinforce the four Cs and provide ready reference for students.

Writing Process

Resources for Writers with Readings uses a clear, step-by-step writing process approach to guide students through the how-tos of writing a paragraph: prewriting, drafting, revising, and editing. Examples, exercises, graphics, and checklists consistently support and reinforce this paragdigm.

Writing Skills

Four basic writing skills—writing an effective topic sentence, using specific details for support and illustration, organizing and linking ideas, and writing correct sentences—are integrated into the writing process steps. The skills are also keyed to the four Cs so that students experience a coherent approach to paragraph writing. For example, students learn that writing an effective topic sentence will make their writing concise and that using specific details will make their writing credible.

Readings

Seventeen readings in the readings section illustrate a range of writing styles, development strategies, and subject matter of interest to students. Each reading is prefaced by a biographical note and prereading questions. Readings are followed by additional activities and writing exercises. Instructors can use readings in conjunction with teaching the modes they illustrate or as independent assignments.

Grammar and Language

Each chapter addressing grammar, punctuation, mechanics, word use, and other language issues is developed with the same care and creativity featured in the writing chapters. Cultural literacy themes are used so that students can see sentence-level edits in the context of real subject matter. One significant chapter, Chapter 12, "Choosing the Best Words for Sensitive Language," addresses the issue of writing for and about diverse groups in non-biased ways—a subject hardly touched on in other writing texts.

ADDITIONAL FEATURES

Resources for Writers with Readings includes a wide range of features that provide alternatives for practice and instruction.

- **Guided writing assignments** lead students through every step in the writing process for both paragraph and essay assignments.
- **Chapter exercises** give immediate reinforcement of content.
- **A wide range of writing topics** gives students relevant writing assignments to choose from.
- **A real-life writing** section in each of the modes chapters in Part Four shows students how particular strategies of development are used in educational, personal, and professional situations.

- **An individual goal sheet** template allows students to evaluate completed writing assignments and set goals for improvement in future writing assignments.

- **A peer editing worksheet** template helps students constructively evaluate each other's writing.

- **A full research and documentation chapter** is available in the printed Instructors Manual, and it helps students seek, find, evaluate, integrate, and document sources for their writing.

- **Editing exercises** in grammar and punctuation chapters give students line-by-line and whole-paragraph practice in identifying and correcting sentence-level errors.

- **A guide to reading critically and writing well** provides an overview of general writing skills.

- **Prereading critical thinking and writing exercises** allow students to consider a topic without the pressure of a formal assignment.

- **Vocabulary activities** as both pre- and post-reading activities enhance students' comprehension and sentence-variation skills.

- **Content and structure questions** for every reading give students tools for greater comprehension and analysis.

In addition, *Resources for Writers with Readings* includes the following elements:

- **Relevant writing assignments in every chapter** encourage students to practice the sentence-level skills of one chapter while further exploring the cultural literacy topic introduced in that chapter.

- **Prewriting questions** help students "warm up" to the chapter topics by thinking about academic information in an everyday context.

- **Editing exercises** in grammar and punctuation chapters give students line-by-line and whole-paragraph practice in identifying and correcting grammar errors.

- **Multiple skill level, multicultural readings** allow students to experience easy-to-follow texts as well as more complex essays by writers from diverse backgrounds.

- **Grammar tips** boxes give students assistance in remembering and mastering different grammar concepts.

- **Checklists** in every writing chapter provide students an easy reference for concepts presented in the chapter.

SUPPLEMENTS

Annotated Instructor's Edition, 0-205-65174-7
Instructor's Manual and Test Bank, 0-205-65175-5
TestGen/Electronic Testbank, 0-205-65879-2
Extra-Chapter: Conducting Research, 0-205-67425-9
Printed Lab Manual (Online Lab Manual available), 0-205-65176-3

The Pearson Student and Instructor Developmental Writing Supplements Package

Pearson is pleased to offer a variety of support materials to help make teaching developmental writing easier for teachers and to help students excel in their course work. Visit www.pearsonhighereducation.com, contact your local Pearson sales representative, or review a detailed listing of the full supplements package (including the Penguin Discount Novel Program) in your textbook's Instructor's Manual.

ACKNOWLEDGMENTS

I wish to acknowledge the contributions of my colleagues and reviewers who provided valuable advice and suggestions.

Sarah Juno Allen, Phoenix College; Mark Altschuler, Bergen Community College; Andrew S. Andermatt, Clinton Community College; Jackie Atkins, Pennsylvania State University, DuBois; Irene Anders, Indiana University–Purdue; Linda A. Austin, Glendale Community College; Liz Ann Baez Aguilar, San Antonio College; Holly Bailey-Hofmann, West Los Angeles College; Linda Barro, East Central College; Emily Blesi, Virginia Highlands Community College; Candace Boeck, San Diego State University; Vicky Broadus, Lexington Community College; Tim Brown, Riverside Community College; Dottie Burkhart, Davidson County Community College; Eileen Call, Wake Technical Community College; Patricia H. Colella, Bunker Hill Community College; Judy D. Covington, Trident Technical College; Joyce L. Crawford-Martinez, DeVry University; Dana Crotwell, El Camino College; Lillian J. Dailey, Cuyahoga Community College; Catherine Decker, Chaffey College; Ann D. Ecoff, Lambuth University; Jeannine Edwards, University of Memphis; Susan Lynne Ertel, Dixie State College of Utah; Debra Farve, Mt. San Antonio College; Laraine Fergenson, Bronx Community College, CUNY; Janice Filer, Shelton State Community College; Clarinda Flannery, Eastern Michigan University; Jane Focht-Hansen, San Antonio College; Yvonne Frye, Community College of Denver; Kathleen Furlong, Glendale Community College; Nadine Gandia, Miami–Dade College, InterAmerican

Campus; Richard F. Gaspar, Hillsborough Community College; Nicole E. Glick, Long Beach City College; Sherrie E. Godbey, University of Kentucky, Lexington Community College; Kay Grosso, Glendale Community College; Adam C. Hartmann, California State University, San Bernardino; Lauri Humberson, St. Philip's College; Laura Jeffries, Florida Community College at Jacksonville; George Z. Jiang, Riverside City College; Suzanne Joelson, Macomb Community College; Barbara Ann Kashi, Cypress College; Trudy Kirsher, Sinclair Community College; Julie Kozempel, Camden County College; Patsy Krech, University of Memphis; Sarah R. Lahm, Normandale Community College; Elizabeth Langenfeld, California State University, San Bernardino; Michael J. Lee, Columbia Basin College; Keming Liu, Medgar Evans College CUNY; John R. Lutzyk, DeVry University; Sharon Mabin, Portland Community College; Mimi Markus, Broward Community College; Elizabeth M. Marsh, Bergen Community College; Ann Marie McCarte, Lexington Community College; William S. McCarter, Eastern Shore Community College; Jason McFaul, Mt. San Antonio College; Kathy McWilliams, Cuyamaca College; Jack Miller, Normandale Community College; Theresa Mohamed, Onondaga Community College; Emily H. Moorer, Hinds Community College; Suzanne Morales, Central Texas College; Sandra Nekola, Normandale Community College; Virginia Nugent, Miami–Dade College, Kendall Campus; Tanya Olson, Vance-Granville Community College; Sam Pierstorff, Modesto Junior College; Esther Sapell Rachelson, DeVry University; Meredith Melissa Rayborn, Valencia Community College; Jeanette E. Redding, Oxnard College; Susan Reiger, Porterville College; Ruth Rhodes, College of the Redwoods; David Robinson, DeVry University; Lori J. Roth, Chicago State University; Melissa Rowland, Rock Valley College; Shannon Runningbear, Long Beach City College; William L. Ryder, West Los Angeles College, College of the Canyons, and Los Angeles Trade Technical College; Justina Sapna, Delaware Technical and Community College; David Schwankle, Riverside Community College; Laurie Sherman, Community College of Rhode Island; Maria Sortino, Sortino International Training; Debbie Stallings, Hinds Community College; Michael Stephens, Johnson & Wales University; Frances Stewart, Bessemer State Technical College; Drema Stringer, Marshall Community and Technical College; Terri L. Symonds, Normandale Community College; Michele Taylor, Ogeechee Technical College; Jennifer Berlinda Thompson, Richard J. Daley College; Suki E. Tooley, Tidewater Community College; Barbara L. Tosi, Community College of Allegheny County, Boyce Campus; Arlene Turkel, Lamar State College, Orange; Sinead Waters Turner, Wake Technical Community College; Joseph Patrick Wall, Modesto Junior College; Thurmond Whatley, Aiken Technical College; Beverly J. Wickersham, Temple Community College; Kirstin Wiley, Lexington Community College; Ellen Willard, Community College of Rhode Island; and Jacquelyn Zuromski, Valencia Community College.

The editorial staff of Longman Publishers deserves a special recognition and thanks for the guidance, support, and direction they have provided. In particular I wish to thank Matt Wright, Acquisitions Editor, for his support, guidance, and flexibility in the development of the third edition, as well as for his little league expertise. Katharine Glynn, too, offered relevant, incisive comments while always managing to be upbeat and pleasant. Haley Pero has been a goddess in her on-the-spot attention to detail and in her general assistance. Matt Harris helped immensely with the Dolphins/Patriots paragraph, while Annelise Long made a terrific suggestion for the mean teacher's name in the New York chapter. Finally, thanks to C. Emmett Mahle and Michael Beckwith for their knowledge of the federal criminal justice system in the federal crime chapter, and as always, thanks to my family—Mike, Annabelle, Lisi, and Susie—for putting up with me when I'm writing.

ELIZABETH CLONINGER LONG
SACRAMENTO, CALIFORNIA

To the Student

YOU ALREADY HAVE THE TOOLS TO WRITE WELL

Chances are, you're a better writer than you think you are. Without even realizing it, you use many essential writing and thinking skills on a daily basis. For example, you may have described what happened to make a day at work or school particularly bad, using examples to illustrate your point. You might have told your friends what you did at the mall, or you might have told them what someone or something looked like. You've probably organized your closet, drawers, or school supplies, grouping items in ways that make sense.

All these everyday tasks require skills you already possess. You'll use these same strategies, listed below, to communicate in writing.

- Illustration and example
- Narration
- Comparison and contrast
- Cause and effect
- Description
- Classification and division
- Process analysis
- Definition
- Argument

These are strategies we employ on a daily basis to make our ideas clear to other people.

WE ALL HAVE DIFFERENT EXPERIENCES AND PERSPECTIVES

Even if our ideas are clear to us, they may not always be clear to others. For example, write down the first thoughts that flash into your mind when you read the next two words shown below.

Car:_____

_____

Music:_____

_____

Now, ask two friends or classmates to write down their ideas. Compare their ideas with yours. Have any of you written exactly the same responses? Even if your ideas are similar, they very likely differ in some ways. We all most likely agree that *car* and *music* are not difficult words to define, but we all bring our own experiences and interpretations to those words. If we want people to understand and agree with our point of view, we have to learn to communicate convincingly. Since we can't assume that people automatically understand and agree with us, we must anticipate others' ideas and explain ourselves clearly.

WHAT TO EXPECT FROM THIS BOOK

Most of the examples and assignments in this textbook focus on writing a clear **paragraph.** A typical paragraph is a group of five to twelve sentences related to one idea. Paragraphs are usually around one hundred and fifty words long.

The subject matter of a paragraph is called its **topic.** The topic of your paragraphs will sometimes come from your teacher and sometimes from your own ideas. Often, your teacher will give you a general topic. Then, you can use your own experiences to narrow that topic into one that you feel familiar with and comfortable writing about.

The main idea expressed in a paragraph is called a **topic sentence.** The topic sentence is often the first sentence of the paragraph, and every other sentence in the paragraph should help support the topic sentence. A clear topic sentence helps readers understand what we're trying to communicate.

However, a clear topic sentence doesn't guarantee that we will win people to our point of view. Because no two humans think alike, we need to explain our points of view through clear examples. In other words, we need to offer proof. In writing paragraphs and essays, proof is called **support.** Your support points are the reasons you feel the way you do and thus the reasons people should believe you. Read the following paragraph to see how the support points make the topic sentence clear.

Ups and Downs

Riding the Powder Keg roller coaster at Silver Dollar City in Branson, Missouri, is a thrilling experience. First, the sounds around me build excitement. I hear a low rumbling broken up by loud squeaks and clacks which I hope are normal. I think people are screaming, but I can hardly hear anything because my heart is pounding so loudly. Next, the coaster's track makes me think twice about riding.

Its huge hills and deep plunges seem unsafe, and the track seems too skinny to hold up the cars. Then comes the scare of getting on the ride. My mouth goes dry and my hands sweat as I sit down and the lap bar locks me in. As the ride begins, an entire track section lifts up, and my stomach drops. The ride itself is a blur: we "explode" from a powder mill, climb a giant hill and then drop, race through beautiful scenery, and finish with a crazy "dragonfly" turn. As soon as I stop shaking, I step off of the waiting platform and get in line again.

The topic of "Ups and Downs" is roller coasters, specifically, the Powder Keg coaster. The topic sentence, "Riding the Powder Keg roller coaster at Silver Dollar City in Branson, Missouri, is a thrilling experience," gives the main idea of the paragraph. The writer supports the topic sentence by using words that allow the reader to experience the ride. For example, the first support point is "First, the sounds around me build excitement." To strengthen this support point, the writer gives three specific details.

Support Point	**Specific Details**
Sounds of the ride build excitement.	a low rumbling broken up by loud squeaks and clacks
	I think people are screaming
	My heart is pounding so loudly

The writer also uses **transition words,** terms that give us clues about what's coming next. In the paragraph, the transition words *first, next*, and *then* keep the support points in order.

Resources
for Writers
with Readings

PART ONE
Getting
Started

The Sphynx of Giza

FOOD FOR THOUGHT Awe-inspiring in her size—65
feet high, 241 feet long, 20 feet wide—the Sphynx in Egypt
took approximately 70 years to construct. Write a few
sentences about the most impressive human-made
structure you have ever seen.

Responding to Images. *What expression(s) does the
Sphynx seem to wear? How can you tell? Explain.*

The Bases of Good Writing:
The Four Cs

1

Culture Note

WORLD GEOGRAPHY

At a time when technology has allowed us to connect to many other people and countries of the world, knowing where places are is important. Geography—the study of the earth's surface and how it is divided into continents, countries, and cities—lets us look at how our world is organized. Geography also lets us understand our connection to other cultures and appreciate our place in the world.

GOOD WRITING IS . . .

If you've ever eaten a well-prepared meal, you know that different parts of the meal serve different functions. A light appetizer can get you ready for the main course, while a spicy sauce can tickle your tongue, and crusty bread can mellow the effects of the sauce. Finally, the perfect dessert can leave your taste buds—and your stomach—feeling just right. Even though all the parts serve different purposes, they are all necessary to create the complete effect of a satisfying meal.

Your writing is similar to such a meal. Several different elements combine to make your writing effective. Understanding what these elements are and how they work together is important. Effective writing has four characteristics. Good writing is concise, credible, clear, and correct.

RECOMMENDED READINGS

"My Mother's English," Amy Tan, *p. 773*

"'Blaxicans' and Other Reinvented Americans," Richard Rodriguez, *p. 738*

Concise. When your writing is *concise,* you have a clear point (your topic sentence) and you include only the information absolutely necessary to communicate that point. Concise writing gets to the point quickly and does not introduce unnecessary information.

Credible. When your writing is *credible,* it is believable. For your reader to believe what you say, you must offer proof—in the form of specific details—to illustrate your topic sentence.

Clear. When your writing is *clear,* it signals to your reader what points are important and how those points fit together under the umbrella of your topic sentence. **Transitional words** are essential to clear writing.

Correct. When your writing is *correct,* it is free of errors in spelling, grammar, and punctuation.

RECOGNIZING CONCISE WRITING

mywritinglab   Concise writing simply makes a point as directly as possible, without giving any information that does not support the topic sentence.

Read the following paragraphs. Then decide which one is more concise. Why?

One Continent's Contributions

Africa, the second-largest continent, has contributed much to the world. Recently, African countries such as Kenya have produced the world's best distance runners. Dominating races longer than fifteen hundred meters for twenty years, African men runners have won the Olympic gold medal in the ten thousand meter run since 1988. In addition to runners, Africa has contributed diamonds. Even though diamonds were valued long before their discovery in South Africa in 1867, no diamond deposits in other countries, such as Canada, Brazil, Russia, and Australia, were as large as those in South Africa. Even today, most of the world's diamonds come from Africa. Finally, Africa has contributed links to our past. Known as the cradle of humanity, Africa is home to Lucy, a human skeleton that is estimated to be between 3 and 3.8 million years old, the oldest human remains yet discovered. These are just some of the vast resources the African continent has given the world.

A Large Land

The African continent has made many contributions to the world. It is also the second-largest continent, big enough to contain the United States, India, Europe, Argentina, and China. One of Africa's contributions comes in the form of distance runners, particularly male distance runners. African runners have been dominant in races longer than fifteen hundred meters for many years, and they have been undefeated in the ten thousand meter Olympic race since 1988. The marathon, however, poses a greater challenge for African runners. Another African contribution comes in the form of diamonds. Diamonds are still considered an appropriate gift when two people become engaged. Since their discovery in South Africa in 1867, diamonds have been an important African product. Most importantly, Africa has provided information about human history. Lucy, the name given to the oldest human remains, was found in Ethiopia. Thus, Africa is responsible for significant human discoveries. The name *Lucy* supposedly comes from the Beatles song "Lucy in the Sky with Diamonds," which Lucy's finders sang in the evening after they made their discovery. Though Africa has made other important contributions to the world, these are a few.

The first paragraph, "One Continent's Contributions," is more *concise* and therefore more effective. It offers no information other than those details that support the topic sentence, "Africa, the second-largest continent, has contributed much to the world." Even the title "One Continent's Contributions" offers a clue as to what the paragraph will contain. In contrast, "A Large Land" contains many details that do not directly support the topic sentence, which is "The African continent has made many contributions to the world." For instance, one unnecessary detail is this:

> It is also the second-largest continent, big enough to contain the United States, India, Europe, Argentina, and China.

This detail explains how big Africa is but says nothing about the continent's contributions.

EXERCISE 1 Concise Writing

Use a pen or pencil to cross out any sentences of "A Large Land" that do not support the topic sentence.

How many sentences did you cross out? _____

You should have crossed out the following sentences:

> The marathon, however, poses a greater challenge for African runners.

> Diamonds are still considered an appropriate gift when two people become engaged.

The name *Lucy* supposedly comes from the Beatles song "Lucy in the Sky with Diamonds," which Lucy's finders sang in the evening after they made their discovery.

These details, while they might be interesting, do not help to develop the idea that "the African continent has made many contributions to the world." Thus, they need to be removed from the paragraph.

CONCISE WRITING LEADS TO UNITY

mywritinglab One important aspect of good writing is *unity*. In unified writing, all elements of a paragraph work together to communicate a single idea. By making your writing concise—and, thus, free from ideas that do not contribute to the overall message of your paragraph—you are ensuring that your writing will also be unified.

In Your Own Writing

To write concisely, you must do the following:

1. Have a clear topic sentence that states exactly what your paragraph is about.
2. Make sure every detail you use supports your topic sentence.

As you add details to your paragraph, ask yourself whether they help to explain or clarify your topic sentence. If not, take them out. For instance, suppose you are writing a paragraph on your favorite food; describing places *to find* such food would lead your reader away from your main point.

Making Sure Your Writing Is Concise

Ask yourself the following questions in order to determine whether your paragraphs are concise.

1. Do I have a clear topic sentence?
2. Does *every* specific detail support my topic sentence?

Identifying Concise Writing

Remember that everything in concise writing must connect to and support the topic sentence. For instance, in the following list, most of the items support the topic sentence, but a few do not. The items that do not support the topic sentence are crossed out.

Topic sentence: I want to visit England.

Many music groups from England

I like fish and chips and tea.

Want to see double-decker bus

~~Friend, Sam, got lost in London~~

I like rainy weather.

~~Museums are boring~~.

EXERCISE 2 Connecting Support Points with Topic Sentences

Each numbered item gives a topic sentence and list of support points. Cross out any items that do not support the topic sentence.

1. Topic sentence: Costa Rica sounds like a good place for vacation.

   a. Cool rain forests

   b. Most civilized Central American country

   c. High literacy rate in Costa Ricans

   d. Great beaches

   e. Good food

2. Topic sentence: Traveling can be uncomfortable.

   a. Stiff bus and train seats

   b. Maps are essential.

   c. Lumpy beds

   d. No ice in some restaurants

   e. Great scenery

3. Topic sentence: There are many great sights all over the world.

   a. Grand Canyon in Arizona

   b. Pyramids in Egypt

   c. Eiffel Tower in Paris

   d. Great photo opportunities

   e. Lots of exercise exploring

EXERCISE 3 Finding Sentences That Are Off-Topic

Read the following paragraphs. Then, underline the topic sentence, and cross out any sentences that do not relate to the topic sentence. The hint at the end of each paragraph will tell you how many sentences are off-topic.

A.   **Geography Is a Waste of Time**

[1]Studying geography is a waste of time for many reasons. [2]First, I'm perfectly happy here in the same neighborhood, the same city, even the same house that I grew up in. [3]My grandfather built this house with his own hands. [4]I don't need to know where Africa or China is because I will never go there. [5]Second, geography is confusing. [6]So many cities and countries sound alike that I can't keep them straight. [7]I don't know if Austria is the same place as Australia, or if the Berlin Wall was anything like the Great Wall of China. [8]Even if I wanted to know these things, I don't think I could get them right. [9]Spelling has never been my best subject. [10]Finally, it's scary to learn geography. [11]Any time some foreign country or city makes the headlines, the news is always bad. [12]Someone's been killed or trapped or bombed. [13]I don't see why I need to learn about other people's bad news when there's plenty of it right here at home. [14]I got mugged last week, and the mugger stole my watch. [15]Geography is one place I don't want to go.

Three sentences are off-topic: _____ , _____ , and _____ .

B.   **The Benefits of Studying Geography**

[1]Studying geography has many important benefits. [2]First of all, it helps me understand people better. [3]In my English class alone, there are people from Russia, Vietnam, and Ukraine. [4]Knowing that some of my classmates have had great struggles in their lives makes me admire their courage. [5]They had to leave family, friends, and home to make better lives in the United States. [6]My own family has been in the United States for more than one hundred fifty years. [7]I also like knowing where things are so that I can see why people make the choices they make. [8]For instance, some years ago, a basketball player named Steve Francis refused to play for a team in Vancouver, Canada. [9]He said that he was from Maryland and that Vancouver was too far away from his family. [10]It is pretty far away! [11]Vancouver doesn't even have a team now; the Grizzlies moved to Memphis, Tennessee.

[12]Finally, knowing geography helps me understand how much our world is changing. [13]In just the last few years, some countries such as Yugoslavia and Czechoslovakia have split up and no longer exist. [14]In fact, on the African continent, many countries have changed borders or names recently. [15]Sometimes even the newest maps don't show all the changes. [16]It's interesting to see how some places become independent and make progress while others seem to stay pretty much the same.

Two sentences are off-topic: _____ and _____.

C.   **Changing Geography**

[1]Over the last few decades, many changes in geography have taken place. [2]One of the biggest changes involves the breaking up of the USSR, or former Soviet Union. [3]The USSR used to have fourteen republics in it, ranging from Latvia to Kazakhstan. [4]Now the former Soviet Union republics run themselves as independent countries. [5]The breaking up of the USSR caused more individual countries to win medals at the Olympics. [6]Second, the borders of African nations have changed a lot in recent years. [7]A few years ago there was a country called Zaire. [8]Now there's no such place! [9]Instead, it has become the Democratic Republic of Congo. [10]This is confusing because there's also a country called the Republic of Congo. [11]Many countries throughout the world have names that are hard to spell. [12]Rhodesia has changed its name to Zimbabwe. [13]It's amazing that whole countries can just change their names like that. [14]Third, Southeast Asia has also changed a lot. [15]Cambodia is now called Kampuchea. [16]Thailand, too, had another name—Siam—and Myanmar used to be called Burma. [17]It's hard to keep up with all the changes!

Three sentences are off-topic: _____ , _____ , and _____.

D.   **Why Geography Changes**

[1]Political decisions can have long-lasting effects. [2]Borders of countries can change for a number of political reasons. [3]One reason borders change is that big nations break up into smaller ones. [4]The former Soviet Union, or USSR, is a good example of this. [5]At one point, the USSR was an extremely powerful communist nation, consisting of many different republics. [6]However, after the Berlin Wall came down in 1989, many of the former Soviet

republics wanted to govern themselves. [7]Their governments took different forms. [8]The borders of what was once the USSR are now borders between smaller countries. [9]Borders can also change when one country buys land from another. [10]In the United States, the land from the Mississippi River to the Rocky Mountains was once owned by France. [11]In 1803, the United States bought this parcel of land in what is called the Louisiana Purchase, so the borders of the United States expanded. [12]Napoleon, the leader of France at that time, was eventually banished. [13]Another reason borders change is that sometimes smaller countries are swallowed up by bigger ones. [14]The former Soviet Union is a good example of this type of change also. [15]Estonia, Latvia, and Lithuania—all Baltic countries—were originally part of the Russian empire. [16]After the Great War (World War I), they became independent nations, but during World War II they became part of the USSR. [17]Eventually, they became independent again when the USSR broke apart.

Three sentences are off-topic: _____, _____, and _____.

RECOGNIZING CREDIBLE WRITING

mywritinglab Credible writing gives your readers reason to believe you. Credible paragraphs include specific details that help convince your readers that they should believe you.

Read the paragraphs below. Then decide which is more credible. Why?

Over the River

Though the world has many rivers, three in particular—the Nile, the Amazon, and the Mississippi—are important. Located in Egypt, the Nile River is the world's longest and was important in early agriculture. Its people used its resources to master farming techniques. Not found in Egypt, another significant river is the Amazon, which carries a lot of water and has an interesting history to its name. Finally, the mighty Mississippi River is located in North America and is important for many states and two Canadian provinces.

A River Runs Through It

The world's rivers play important roles on every continent. Three rivers—the Nile, the Amazon, and the Mississippi—are worth studying. More than four thousand miles long, the Nile River flows northward through Africa to the Mediterranean Sea. Aside from being the world's longest river, the ancient Nile was significant to agriculture. Egypt's water and fertile soil presented perfect conditions for farming, and ancient people living along the Nile were some of the first to use a plow. In South America, the Amazon River is extremely powerful. It flows across northern Brazil to the Atlantic Ocean, carrying more water—184,000 cubic meters per second—than any other river. Named for legendary female warriors, the Amazon River has a mouth measuring more than two hundred fifty miles wide. Last, the mighty Mississippi River is important to many regions in North America. It acts as a watershed for—draining water from—thirty-one U.S. states and two Canadian provinces. Flowing from Lake Itasca to the Gulf of Mexico, the Mississippi River carved its upper path with the water of melting glaciers from the last Ice Age, but it is actually considered a very young river. Regardless of the continent you're on, there's probably an important river that runs through it.

The second paragraph, "A River Runs Through It," is more *credible* and therefore more effective. Both of these two paragraphs are concise and relatively easy to follow. They both have topic sentences and clear support points. The second paragraph, however, includes specific examples as proof of the writer's points. For instance, in "A River Runs Through It," the writer makes the point that the Nile is significant to agriculture and then offers a specific detail—the example of how early Nile residents were the first to use a plow—to show that the Nile is, indeed, important.

EXERCISE 4 Credible Writing

Listed below are the other support points in "A River Runs Through It." Read through the paragraph. Then underline the sentences containing specific details for these support points.

Support point 2:   In South America, the Amazon River is extremely powerful.

Support point 3:   Last, the mighty Mississippi River is important to many regions of North America.

Here are the specific details you should have found.

Specific details   It flows across northern Brazil to the Atlantic Ocean
for support point 2:   carrying more water—184,000 cubic meters per second—than any other river. Named for legendary

Specific details for support point 3: female warriors, the Amazon River has a mouth measuring more than two hundred fifty miles wide. It acts as a watershed for—draining water from—thirty-one U.S. states and two Canadian provinces. Flowing from Lake Itasca to the Gulf of Mexico, the Mississippi River carved its upper path with the water of melting glaciers from the last Ice Age, but it is actually considered a very young river.

In "Over the River," the writer makes these points: the Nile "is the world's longest river and was important in early agriculture," and "Its people used its resources to master farming techniques." However, these points are unsupported by any detail. How long is the Nile? From where does it flow? In what ways was the Nile important in early agriculture? What were its resources? How did people use them? What early farming techniques did people use? The writer answers none of these questions through examples. Thus, we are left doubting whether the writer knows much about the topic.

In Your Own Writing

To write credibly, offer specific details to show that you have reasons to back up your topic sentence. Specific examples can be the following:

1. Actual examples from your life.
2. Incidents that you've seen happen to someone else.
3. Facts that you've heard about or read, as long as you can give the source, such as a newspaper or magazine.

For instance, suppose you are writing a paragraph on your least favorite food. You could include comments describing liver as being so slimy that it kept skidding away when you tried to spear it with your fork or tell about an artichoke that stuck your hand as you tried to eat it.

Making Sure Your Writing Is Credible

Ask yourself the following questions to determine whether your paragraphs are credible.

1. Do I provide enough information so that my reader will believe me?
2. Have I made sure my reader knows what I mean?

Practicing Credible Writing

Credible writing offers enough proof for your readers to believe that you know something about your subject. Remember that in credible writing, support points are illustrated by specific details.

EXERCISE 5 Finding Support Points That Need More Detail

Read the following paragraphs. For each one, underline the topic sentence. Then write down the number of any sentence in which you think the writer needs to be more specific or provide more information. The hint at the end of the paragraph will tell you how many sentences need more detail.

A.   **Effects of Changing Geography**

   [1]Changes in geography bring about many different effects. [2]One effect of changing geography comes in the form of new names for old places. [3]Another effect is that borders change, such as in the former Soviet Union. [4]Finally, people can die. [5]In what used to be Yugoslavia, many ethnic Albanian people moved into the area called Kosovo. [6]That region was traditionally inhabited by Serbian people. [7]When the Albanians moved in, the Serbian people felt threatened. [8]Plus, the Albanians decided that they wanted the Kosovo region for themselves, and they tried to take it over. [9]This led to a huge civil war between the Albanians and the Serbs, during which thousands of people died. [10]Eventually, Kosovo became an area run mostly by the Albanians but with some input from the Serbs.

Two support points need more detail in sentences _____ and _____.

B.   **Reasons to Visit Paris**

   [1]People should visit Paris for a number of reasons. [2]First, it's beautiful. [3]All you need to do is look around. [4]Second, the food is fantastic. [5]Everywhere you go people are eating the most wonderful-looking pastries and drinking heavenly coffee. [6]The croissants and sauces alone are worth visiting Paris for. [7]Next, there's the history. [8]So many important events occurred in Paris! [9]Finally, Paris is romantic. [10]There are so many places with wonderful views, perfect for lovers. [11]If you happen to be awake late

at night, so many night sights can make you fall in love all by themselves. [12]It's a great city!

Three support points need more detail in sentences _____, _____, and _____.

C.   Reasons Not to Visit Paris

[1]Why anyone would want to go to Paris is a mystery to me. [2]For starters, it's so boring. [3]People say that there's a lot to do, but who wants to spend all day looking at museums or old buildings? [4]I heard that I should visit the Louvre museum, so I did. [5]But it was crowded and full of paintings I'd never even seen before. [6]For the whole time I was in Paris, I tried to find a good baseball game to watch, or even football highlights

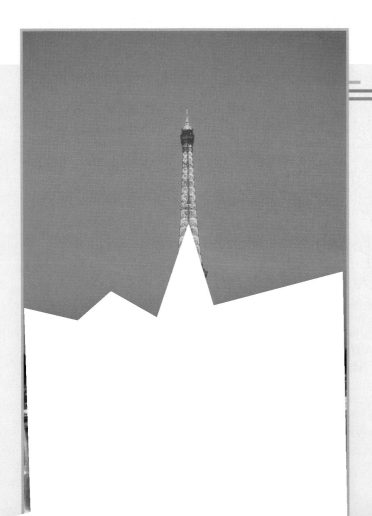

The Eiffel Tower

SURF THE NET Rising 324 meters above Paris, the Eiffel Tower has become a symbol of that city. However, the tower has not always been loved by its people. What is the tower's history? Why was it built? How did people initially react to it? Surf the Internet and write a few sentences summarizing what you learn. ***Responding to Images.*** *Paris is known as the "City of Lights." Based on the photo at left, is this an apt nickname? Explain.*

from last season. [7]I never did have any luck. [8]Next, I can't understand what the big deal is with the food. [9]I kept hearing that French food was great, but did I ever find one good French fry? [10]I never did. [11]In fact, in Paris French fries aren't even called French fries. [12]They're called *pommes frites,* and if you ask for them using any other name, people look at you as if you're from another planet. [13]That brings me to another reason Paris is no great vacation for me: the language. [14]Last but not least, Paris isn't very pretty. [15]Sure, you can look at the view from the Eiffel Tower or take a cruise down the Seine River, but there are towers and rivers everywhere. [16]I just don't understand why Paris is supposed to be so special.

One support point needs more detail beginning in sentence _____.

D.   **Climbing Mount Everest**

[1]Climbing Mount Everest is an extraordinarily difficult task. [2]One challenge climbers face is being physically fit. [3]Since Mount Everest is the world's highest peak (over twenty-nine thousand feet), teams of climbers must be in top physical condition before they can even start their trips. [4]Climbers must eat well and exercise to ensure that their hearts, lungs, and legs are in good shape. [5]Next, they must get acclimated to (used to) the thin air. [6]Usually, groups stay at what's called a base camp (located above seventeen thousand feet) for about four weeks in order to train their bodies to operate on less oxygen. [7]Another step involves dealing with physical discomfort. [8]It's so cold on Everest that toothpaste freezes, as does people's hair right after being washed. [9]Also, since the air is so thin, horrible headaches pound in people's heads, and people get terrible aches in their joints from the cold. [10]Finally, fear presents a huge challenge for the climbers. [11]No matter what, though, climbing to the summit of Mount Everest is a huge accomplishment!

One support point needs more detail beginning in sentence _____.

RECOGNIZING CLEAR WRITING

mywritinglab   Clear writing lets your readers easily follow and understand your ideas. In clear writing, information is placed in a logical order. Two common ways in which information can be ordered are chronologically and emphatically.

Transitions That Signal Chronological (Time Sequence) Order

finally	last of all
first (second, third)	next
in the first place	then
last	

In **chronological order,** also called **time sequence order,** events or steps are given in the order or sequence in which they occur. For example, suppose you are telling some friends about a terrible day that you just had. If you were following chronological order, your description of your day might go like this:

> **First,** my alarm didn't go off, so I overslept and didn't have time to take a shower. **Then,** I found out that the reason my alarm didn't go off was that the power had gone out. So, of course, I couldn't make coffee. **Next,** my boss chewed me out for being late to work and told me I needed to work on my appearance because I looked as if I had just rolled out of bed. **Finally,** my boyfriend canceled our date so he could watch the basketball game, completely forgetting that it's our anniversary.

In this example, you're telling your friends the events that happened *in the order in which they happened.* The transition words, in bold type, signal

---

Paragraph in Chronological Order

Topic sentence...
....

↓

First event or step...
.................................Specific details...........................
Second event or step..
.................................Specific details...........................
Third event or step..
.................................Specific details...........................
Last event or step..
.................................Specific details...........................

this order of events. The illustration "Paragraph in Chronological Order," on the previous page, shows this way of organizing a paragraph.

In **emphatic order,** support points are given in order of importance. You as the writer decide which points are least interesting or important and which are the most important ones. Using emphatic order, you place the points that *you think* are less important first, and you end with the points that *you think* are most important. Placing examples at the end of a paragraph often sends the message that those points are the most important, so you need to decide which points should come last. For instance, if you are telling someone why it's important to clean out a refrigerator, you might want to use emphatic order to emphasize the idea that eating spoiled food could make you sick.

> Cleaning out the refrigerator is important for many reasons. **First,** a messy fridge—one that has rotten food or spills everywhere— just doesn't help anyone's appetite. **Second,** a messy fridge makes finding things difficult. If you know you have milk but can't find it because there are so many other old containers in front of it, you can end up frustrated. **Most important,** a messy fridge can be dangerous. If you eat something that's been in the fridge awhile because it *looks* all right, you could get sick.

In this example, you're placing your reasons for cleaning a refrigerator *in order of least to most important.* The transition words in bold type signal the emphatic order used. The illustration "Paragraph in Emphatic Order," on the following page, shows the form of a paragraph organized in emphatic order.

Clear writing also includes transition words that reinforce the order of the points. In chronological order, words like *first, then, next,* and *finally* tell your reader what comes next in the sequence. In emphatic order, transitions like *above all* and *most important* tell your reader that your points are

Transitions That Signal Emphatic Order

above all	most of all
best of all	most important
finally	most significantly
first (second, third)	worst of all

Paragraph in Emphatic Order

Topic sentence...
....

↓

Least important support point....................................
..............................Specific details.........................
Important support point...
..............................Specific details.........................
Important support point...
..............................Specific details.........................
Most important support point....................................
..............................Specific details.........................

becoming more important as you go on. See Chapter 10 for more lists of transition words.

Read the paragraphs that follow. Then decide which one communicates more clearly. Why?

Sights in China

If you visit China, there is much to see. However, to hit the highlights, three sights should be on your tour route. First, you should see the Great Wall of China. Spanning more than fifteen hundred miles, the Great Wall is actually a series of walls designed over the centuries to keep enemies out. You'd think that its huge walls—some as high as twenty-five feet and fifteen to thirty feet wide at the base—would be enough to deter enemies. Another great sight is the Forbidden City, right in the center of Beijing. This enormous complex, with some eight hundred buildings and ten thousand rooms, was once the imperial headquarters. Finally, one last grand sight is Tiananmen Square, a huge plaza also in Beijing. Its gates to the north and south are impressive, as are the Monument to the People's Heroes and the mausoleum of Mao Zedong, which stand in the center of the square. This sight is significant to Americans because Tiananmen Square was the site of violent protests inspired by American democracy in 1989.

Tiananmen Square

CRITICAL THINKING Named for the Tiananmen (literally, "Gate of heavenly peace"), which sits to its north, Tiananmen Square is seen by many as the symbolic heart of China. Indeed, when Chinese students organized a pro-democracy demonstration in 1989, it was held in Tiananmen Square. What place or monument could be considered the "symbolic heart" of the United States? Write a few sentences explaining your thoughts.

Responding to Images. Based on the photo above, how disciplined or laid-back a place is China? Explain.

Seeing China

Of all the sights to see in China, three are most important. Tiananmen Square was the site of violent pro-democracy protests in 1989, so put that on your list. It also has huge monuments in the center and ancient gates to the north and south. The Great Wall of China—actually a series of shorter walls—was built to prevent enemies in Mongolia from entering China. The Forbidden City sits in the center of Beijing, and it covers an enormous area. It also has approximately eight hundred buildings and ten thousand rooms. The Great Wall has walls twenty-five feet high and fifteen to thirty feet wide at the base. Tiananmen means "Gate of Heavenly Peace." The Forbidden City was once the imperial headquarters.

The first paragraph, "Sights in China," is clearer than the second one and therefore more effective. The examples are organized in emphatic order—from least to most important. The writer also clearly signals the order of the points through the use of transitional words such as *first*.

EXERCISE 6 Clear Writing

Underline the transitional expressions in "Sights in China."

How many expressions did you find? _____

You should have underlined the following terms: _____, _____, _____, and _____.

The second paragraph, "Seeing China," is both concise and credible, but it lacks any directions for the reader to follow. The writer does not include transitional expressions. Consequently, the reader can't easily distinguish the support points or understand the reason for the order in which they are given.

In Your Own Writing

To write clearly, you must do the following:

1. Organize your ideas effectively and logically. For instance, if your topic is "The Worst Course Schedule I Ever Had," you should probably use chronological order rather than emphatic order to make your case.
2. Use transitional expressions to let your reader know when important points are coming and how important those points are.

Making Sure Your Writing Is Clear

Ask yourself the following questions to determine whether your paragraphs are clear.

1. Do I have a logical organizational format that my reader can easily follow? What is it?
2. Do I use transitional expressions to communicate what my points are and which ones are most important?

Identifying Clear Writing

Clear writing gives your reader clear signals to your support points and how important those points are.

Remember that paragraphs can be organized chronologically (according to the order in which events happened), or they can be organized using emphatic order (where points appear in order from least to most important).

EXERCISE 7 Using Emphatic Order

Read the following paragraph. Underline the topic sentence, and then answer the questions that follow.

Packing for Afghanistan

Although traveling to Afghanistan is a difficult journey, some simple tips can make the trip safer. Make sure you have the proper travel documents. Even if you have a passport, this will not be enough all by itself. Different parts of Afghanistan require different permits to enter, so you should consult a travel guide to make sure that you have the right papers. Otherwise, you might travel all that way and not be allowed into the country. Prepare yourself by dressing as the Afghans dress. Keep your arms and legs covered with long-sleeved, loose garments, and don't walk around with lots of money or valuable jewelry showing. Looking like the native people will help you move easily in crowds and stay safe. If you are a woman, make sure you are well covered as a sign of respect for the Muslim religion of the country. A little of your ankle can show, but not much else. Be respectful to the people around you. Since the terrorist attacks in the United States on September 11, 2001, the Afghan people have been sensitive about Osama Bin Laden, the man who is believed to have organized the attacks. Bringing his name up in conversation might make people angry or unhappy, so it's best not to mention him. Most importantly, you should obey the laws of the country. If you are not supposed to bring a car into the country, for instance, then find another way to travel. When the Taliban—an extreme Islamic group—was in power, its rulers did not want tourists taking pictures of the Afghan people. Travelers at that time showed respect by keeping their cameras put away. Have a good trip!

1. This paragraph should use emphatic order. Write 1, 2, 3, or 4 before each of the support points. The number 1 should represent your least important point, and the number 4 should represent your most important point.

_____ Get proper travel documents.

_____ Wear native dress.

_____ Be sensitive to people around you.

_____ Obey laws.

2. Choose an expression from the following list that could introduce the first reason given: *First, Next, In addition.*

_____

3. Choose an expression from the following list that could introduce reason 2: *Second, For Starters, Last.*

_____

4. What reason is the most important? _____

_____

5. What signal words tell you that this reason is the most important?

_____

EXERCISE 8 Using Chronological Order

Our Changing Nation

Different European nations have controlled large tracts of U.S. territory. Originally, the Spanish settled parts of what is now the United States. Spain sent explorers into what is now New Mexico as early as 1542, while in 1565 Spain established the fort of Saint Augustine in Florida. From the mid-1500s through the mid-1800s, the Spanish held vast sections of American land. In the 1600s, the English made their mark in the New World. After trying to establish a colony unsuccessfully on Roanoke Island, the English finally established thirteen colonies on the east coast of North America. The English held this large section of land until the Revolutionary War, which ended in

1783. France was another European nation that once held large areas of land in what eventually became the United States. French holdings spanned what are now the states of Louisiana, Arkansas, Missouri, Nebraska, Iowa, South Dakota, and North Dakota, as well as part of Minnesota, Montana, Colorado, Kansas, Wyoming, and Oklahoma. In 1803, Emperor Napoleon Bonaparte of France sold this tract of land to the United States for $15 million. This transaction is known as the Louisiana Purchase. Russia held different sections of American soil. Russia held Alaska and parts of northern California until 1867, when the United States bought Alaska from Russia for $7.2 million. The United States may be one nation now, but it took a lot of change to get to that point.

1. This paragraph should be organized using chronological order. Use the dates in the paragraph to guide you, numbering the support points 1, 2, 3, and 4 according to which comes first, second, third, and fourth.

_____ Russia held parts of American land.

_____ England held parts of American land.

_____ Spain explored different parts of the United States.

_____ France held land that became the Louisiana Purchase.

2. Which support point is signaled by the word *originally?* _____

_____

3. Should this point come first, second, third, or fourth? _____

_____

4. What other signal words the writer can use to introduce points 2, 3, and 4? _____

EXERCISE 9 Putting Support Points in Order

Read the paragraph on p. 24. (It is a slightly different version of a paragraph you read earlier in this chapter.) Locate the four support points. Then find the specific details for each point.

Reasons Not to Visit Paris

[1]Why anyone would want to go to Paris is a mystery to me. [2]For starters, it's so boring. [3]People say that there's a lot to do, but who wants to spend all day looking at museums or old buildings? [4]I heard that I should visit the Louvre museum, so I did. [5]But it was crowded and full of paintings I'd never even seen before. [6]For the whole time I was in Paris, I tried to find a good baseball game to watch, or even football highlights from last season. [7]I never did have any luck. [8]Next, I can't understand what the big deal is with the food. [9]I kept hearing that French food was great, but did I ever find one good French fry? [10]I never did. [11]In fact, even though I looked everywhere, I couldn't find one Denny's. [12]I looked high and low for some plain old American food, but all I found was stuff with fancy French names. [13]That brings me to another reason Paris is no great vacation for me: the language. [14]Hardly anyone speaks English at all! [15]When I asked a lady for directions, she pretended she didn't understand me. [16]Last but not least, Paris isn't very pretty. [17]Sure, you can look at the view from the Eiffel Tower or take a cruise down the Seine River, but there are towers and rivers everywhere. [18]I just don't understand why Paris is supposed to be so special.

Topic sentence: _____

Support point 1: _____

Specific details that make support point 1 clear:

_____

_____

Support point 2: _____

Specific details that make support point 2 clear:

_____

_____

Support point 3: _____

Specific details that make support point 3 clear:

_____

_____

Support point 4: _____

Specific details that make support point 4 clear:

_____

_____

RECOGNIZING CORRECT WRITING

mywritinglab   Correct writing tells your readers that you take yourself seriously and that you care about your work. In correct writing, sentences are free of errors in grammar, punctuation, and spelling.

Read the paragraphs below. Then decide which one communicates correctly. Why?

Mapping It All Out: Draft

[1]While the first map was etched on a clay tablet in the third millennium B.C.E. [2]Maps today they are drawn on paper. [3]In drawing the maps, mapmakers—called cartographers—have alot to consider. [4]First, since the earth is round and paper is flat, cartographers cant make a map that looks exactly like the earth. [5]Instead, they must think about what's called projection, or the ways there maps will differ from the earth's real shape. [6]Maybe the continents will be the right shape but the wrong size, or maybe they'll be the right size but the wrong shape, for instance these are some kinds of differences that mapmakers must show. [7]Second, cartographers deciding what kind of map to make. [8]For instance, they can make political maps which show cultural details such as the outlines of countries states and cities. [9]Showing natural features such as mountains, rivers, and oceans, cartographers can also make physical maps. [10]A road map show highways and intersections as well as tourist attractions, while a

thematic map shows information according to a theme such as population, economy, or religion. [11]Many maps are combinations of themes. [12]Who would have thought that a bunch of colored lines could be so meaningful?

Mapping It All Out: Final Version

[1]While the first map was etched on a clay tablet in the third millennium B.C.E., maps today are drawn on paper. [2]In drawing the maps, mapmakers—called cartographers—have a lot to consider. [3]First, since the earth is round and paper is flat, cartographers can't make a map that looks exactly like the earth. [4]Instead, they must think about what's called projection, or the ways their maps will differ from the earth's real shape. [5]Maybe the continents will be the right shape but the wrong size, or maybe they'll be the right size but the wrong shape, for instance; these are some kinds of differences that mapmakers must show. [6]Second, cartographers must decide what kind of map to make. [7]For instance, they can make political maps, which show cultural details such as the outlines of countries, states, and cities. [8]Cartographers can also make physical maps, which show natural features such as mountains, rivers, and oceans. [9]A road map shows highways and intersections as well as tourist attractions, while a thematic map shows information according to a theme such as population, economy, or religion. [10]Many maps are combinations of themes. [11]Who would have thought that a bunch of colored lines could be so meaningful?

The final version of "Mapping It All Out" is *correct*. It has no grammatical errors. Therefore, it is more convincing. Even if you're not sure what errors are in the final version of "Mapping It All Out," do the following: Read over both paragraphs. Put a check mark next to or underline the sections where the draft of the paragraph differs from the final version. Then do the following exercise.

EXERCISE 10 Correct Writing

Identify the types of errors in the numbered word groups in the draft paragraph of "Mapping It All Out." Circle the letter next to the type of error you see in each group of words. *Note:* Don't worry if you're unable to answer these questions. By the end of the term, you'll be answering these questions will ease.

1. In item 1, the type of error is

   a. Run-on sentence

   b. Spelling error

   c. Sentence fragment

   d. Pronoun error

2. In item 2, the type of error is

   a. Run-on sentence

   b. Nonstandard English

   c. Sentence fragment

   d. Verb tense error

3. In item 3, the type of error is

   a. Run-on sentence

   b. Pronoun error

   c. Sentence fragment

   d. Spelling error

4. In item 4, the type of error is

   a. No error. This section is correct.

   b. Apostrophe error

   c. Misplaced modifier

   d. Pronoun error

5. In item 5, the type of error is

   a. Run-on sentence

   b. Verb form error

   c. Word choice error

   d. Dangling modifier

6. In item 6, the type of error is

   a. Verb form error

b. Apostrophe error

c. Sentence fragment

d. Run-on sentence

7. In item 7, the type of error is

   a. Missing comma

   b. Sentence fragment

   c. Verb form error

   d. Subject-verb agreement error

8. In item 8, the type of error is

   a. Missing comma

   b. Sentence fragment

   c. Misplaced modifier

   d. Run-on sentence

9. In item 9, the type of error is

   a. Misplaced modifier

   b. Pronoun error

   c. Run-on sentence

   d. Apostrophe error

10. In item 10, the type of error is

   a. Sentence fragment

   b. Spelling error

   c. Pronoun error

   d. Subject-verb agreement error

You should have chosen the following answers.

1. c	**4.** b	**7.** c	**10.** d
2. b	**5.** c	**8.** a	
3. d	**6.** d	**9.** a	

In Your Own Writing

To write correctly, you must do the following:

1. Review sentence skills to avoid making errors.
2. Proofread (Chapter 6) to find and correct mistakes.

For a review of sentence-level writing, refer to Part 7, "Writing Correct Sentences" (Chapters 30–53).

Making Sure Your Writing Is Correct

Ask yourself the following questions to determine whether your paragraphs are correct.

1. Have I reviewed guidelines for grammar, punctuation, and spelling (Chapters 30–53)?
2. Have I proofread to find and correct errors (Chapter 6)?

IDENTIFYING THE FOUR CS TOGETHER

mywritinglab Understanding how each of the four Cs works by itself is important, and you have already had a lot of practice doing this. The next step is for you to practice identifying each of the four Cs as they appear together. The best writing integrates all four key elements into a unified paragraph.

EXERCISE 11   Identifying Each Element of Good Writing

Read the following paragraphs. Underline the topic sentences, and then circle the answers that best describe each paragraph.

A.   Preparing for the Sahara

[1]If you ever need to go to the Sahara—a huge desert located in northern Africa—you had better take steps to make sure you're prepared. [2]Most importantly, bring water. [3]It doesn't matter if you carry water in plastic or metal bottles; just be sure the bottles are tough. [4]You should also bring water purification tablets in case the water you drink hasn't been chemically treated. [5]One tip for desert survival is having the right clothing. [6]Though the Sahara can get extremely hot, you'll

want to stay covered up. [7]Bring loose-fitting, long-sleeved shirts and long pants. [8]If too much skin is exposed, you'll get a brutal sunburn, and you might even get sun poisoning. [9]In addition, windblown sand can become stuck to your body if you're not covered well (and probably even if you are). [10]Finally, care for your face, especially your eyes. [11]You should bring at least two pairs of sunglasses with ultraviolet protection, along with sunscreen for your face and lips. [12]Another solid piece of advice is to have good maps and guides. [13]The Sahara covers approximately 3.5 million square miles, so even if you're familiar with desert terrain, it's best to take along someone who knows the area.

1. The topic sentence is sentence _____ .

2. Circle the letters of all the answers that apply to the paragraph above. This paragraph is

a. Concise

b. Credible

c. Clear

d. Correct

3. Choose Answer a or b below. If you choose Answer b, write one of the four Cs in the blank below.

a. This paragraph is fine.

b. This paragraph would be more effective if it were more _____ .

B.   **A Meal of Geography**

[1]Geography has had a major impact on the names of food. [2]First of all, Germany has contributed the Berliner doughnut, a jelly-filled yeast doughnut named for the city of Berlin, and the Bismarck doughnut, an elongated doughnut filled with custard. [3]Sometimes a Berliner is called a Bismarck, too, which is the name of a famous German leader. [4]Two names for the same doughnut is pretty confusing! [5]My uncle Jerry often went by Jed, and that was very confusing. [6]Frankfurters, commonly called hot dogs, get their name from the German city of Frankfurt. [7]I love hot dogs with lots of mustard and pickle relish. [8]France has played a role in naming food, too.

[9]Vichyssoise, a fancy name for cold potato soup, gets its name from the French city of Vichy. [10]Supposedly, cooks should use Vichy water, which comes from springs around the city of Vichy, when making the soup. [11]I can't understand how water that comes in bottles is supposed to be better than tap water. [12]Champagne, the sparkling wine, gets its name from the French province of Champagne, where the wine is made. [13]Cities in the United States have contributed names to food as well. [14]Boston brown bread (a sweet, moist bread that comes in a can) gets its name from a geographical source. [15]Philadelphia gave us the Philly cheese steak, and New York provided the name for the New York–style cheesecake. [16]All in all, I think I eat much better thanks to geography.

1. The topic sentence is sentence _____.

2. Circle all the answers that apply to the paragraph above. This paragraph is

   a. Concise

   b. Credible

   c. Clear

   d. Correct

3. Choose Answer a or b below. If you choose Answer b, write one of the four Cs in the blank.

   a. This paragraph is fine.

   b. This paragraph would be more effective if it were more _____.

C.   **Floating in the Dead Sea**

[1]Floating in the Dead Sea, the salt lake on the border between Israel and Jordan, is an unusual experience. [2]First, the Dead Sea doesn't look like a typical sea. [3]Next, the areas around the sea look different from usual vacation resorts. [4]Third, regular swimming in the Dead Sea is impossible. [5]The buoyancy of the salt water makes diving under water almost impossible; you just pop back up to the surface like a cork. [6]Also, the water of the Dead Sea can make you very sick. [7]Finally, the name Dead Sea makes the place seem like a punishment rather than a vacation spot.

1. The topic sentence is sentence _____.

2. Circle all the answers that apply to the paragraph above. This paragraph is

   a. Concise

   b. Credible

   c. Clear

   d. Correct

3. Choose Answer a or b below. If you choose Answer b, write one of the four Cs in the blank.

   a. This paragraph is fine.

   b. This paragraph would be more effective if it were more _____ .

D.   On the Road Again

[1]Streets, roads, and highways are extremely important, no matter where you are in the world. [2]For example, in Germany, taking the autobahn is crucial if you want make good time getting around, people zip by with their horns blaring and their lights flashing if you going too slowly, you'd better get out of the way! [3]On the other hand, in paris, France, the most famous street has a slower pace. [4]The Champs Elysées, which means "Elysian Fields," or paradise, is known for its elegant shops and cafés and is a key tourist spot. [5]In addition, Khao San Road in Bangkok, Thailand, is not very pretty or very long. [6]However, it important because it gives backpackers an affordable place to stay and get used to Asia before they travel further. [7]Last but not least, Wenceslas Square in Prague, Czechoslovakia, is long and thin. [8]Even though its' name says it's square. [9]It slopes gently uphill from the streets that form the boundary of the old town and is a main road in the Czech Republic.

1. The topic sentence is sentence _____.

2. Circle the letters of all the answers that apply to the paragraph above. This paragraph is

   a. Concise

   b. Credible

   c. Clear

   d. Correct

3. Choose Answer a or b below. If you choose Answer b, write one of the four Cs in the blank.

a. This paragraph is fine.

b. This paragraph would be more effective if it were more _____ .

WRITING PRACTICE 1 Write Your Own Paragraph

In this chapter you were introduced to different places around the world and to some ideas about world geography. Your assignment is this: *Using the information on world geography that you learned in this chapter, write a paragraph on a place you would like to visit.* The place you choose can be somewhere you've heard about on the news or from a friend, or it can be a place you've read about in this chapter. Just be sure to explain why this place is somewhere you'd like to go.

Remember to do the following when you write your paragraph.

- Write your main idea in your topic sentence.
- Give support points for your topic sentence.
- Put your support points in chronological or emphatic order.
- Introduce your support points with transition words or terms.
- Offer specific examples for your support points.

Write your paragraph on a separate piece of paper.

WRITING PRACTICE 2 Write Your Own Paragraph

In this chapter, you've read people's opinions of places they would, or would not, like to visit. How would you describe your own home, neighborhood, city, region, or state to someone who has never been there? Your assignment is this: *Write a paragraph about a place you have lived.* The paragraph can praise the location you choose to write about, it can warn people against it, or it can offer the upsides and downsides to your location. Just keep in mind that your writing should be clear to someone who has not visited the place you choose. Your topic sentence may be something such as "While the Eagle Heights neighborhood does not have good places to shop, it is very affordable."

Remember to do the following when you write your paragraph.

- Write your main idea in your topic sentence.
- Give support points for your topic sentence.

- Put your support points in chronological or emphatic order.
- Introduce your support points with transition words or terms.
- Offer specific examples for your support points.

Write your paragraph on a separate piece of paper.

CHAPTER SUMMARY

Remember these important points when you write.

1. Everything in your writing should help you communicate your main idea. Your writing should be *concise*.
2. Use specific details to support your main idea and help you be *credible*.
3. Use *transitions* to make the direction of your writing *clear* to your reader, and organize your ideas logically.
4. Make sure your writing is *correct*.

MyWritingLab & Lab Activity 1

mywritinglab | For additional help with Concise, Credible, Clear, and Correct writing, go to **www.mywritinglab.com** or complete **Lab Activity 1** in the separate *Resources for Writers* Lab Manual.

Writing for a Reader and a Reason

VOTING

While not unique to the United States, the act of voting for public officials and policies remains a privilege enjoyed by relatively few people worldwide. Writer and philosopher Ralph Waldo Emerson claimed, "Those who stay away from the election think that one vote will do no good: 'Tis but one step more to think one vote will do no harm." How seriously should people take their voting responsibilities?

Exercising a Priviledge

CONDUCT AN INTERVIEW How many of your aquaintances vote or have ever voted? What motivates people to go—or stay home from—the polls? Ask at least three people about their voting habits and summarize your findings in a few sentences.
Responding to Images. How consistent or inconsistent with your idea of or experiences with voting is the photo above? Explain.

RECOMMENDED READINGS

"The Joy of Boredom," Carolyn Y. Johnson, *p. 722*

"The Price We Pay," Adam Mayblum, *p. 794*

"'Blaxicans' and Other Reinvented Americans," Richard Rodriguez, *p. 738*

WRITING FOR A READER

Though you may not have thought about it, every time you write something, you're writing for *somebody*. Even if you're just doodling before class starts, you're most likely doing that for a certain person, probably yourself.

Recognizing the person you're writing for, or your **audience,** is essential to effective writing. Writing the right thing for the right person can go a long way toward making sure you get your point across.

Look at the situations described below. Then write down the type of language you would choose for each of the following situations.

You're pointing out an error in an instructor's grading. _____

_____

You're cheering for your favorite sports team. _____

_____

You're asking someone out for a first date. _____

_____

Probably you chose different language for each situation. Discuss with a friend or classmate what would happen if you used the date language for your instructor, or yelled a rousing cheer at your potential date. Would you get the results you wanted? What did you consider when you chose the language for each situation? In writing, as in speaking, your message needs to match your audience, or you won't have much success getting your point across.

EXERCISE 1 Identifying the Audience

Read the following paragraphs. Then, choose the response that you think best describes the probable audience.

A.   Vote, Shmote: Who Really Cares?

How much good can one vote do? I know that voting is the "American way," but I really can't be bothered. First, it takes time even before you vote. You have to register to vote, and then you have to change your voter registration if you move. It's seriously inconvenient. Plus, it's not as if you can just walk up and register and *then* vote. No, you have to do things ahead of time, or you can't cast a ballot. Second, in a country of millions of people, I have a tough time believing that one vote makes much difference. Heck, when my buddy and I talk about issues (which is almost never), we have different views, so our votes would probably cancel each other out, anyway. Finally, you have to learn about the issues to vote. All the commercials sound the same—this man is evil, that woman is sneaky—and as a college student with two jobs, it's not likely that I'll do any more studying than I have to. Maybe when I'm older and have more time I'll vote, but not now.

This paragraph would be most convincing to someone who

    a. Has never voted.

    b. Has voted and has had all his or her candidates elected.

    c. Has voted and not gotten the results he or she wanted.

B.   **My Only Voice**

    While it does take some time, voting is an excellent way to make myself heard. I grew up in a very religious family, and I know what I'm supposed to think and say and do. My father doesn't understand, though, that times have changed and that I have my own ideas. When I turned eighteen, I registered as a Republican because my dad is one, but I've never voted as he does. Voting is the one time I can walk in, make my mark, and have my voice heard above (or at least in addition to) my father's. I know that my three brothers and my dad always vote differently from me, but I have to believe that other people out there think—or might someday think—as I do. Sometimes the issues I vote for go down in flames, but a few of the things I've really cared about— such as more money for schools—have passed. My little vote might not change the world right now, but it gives me hope that someday it might.

This paragraph would be most convincing to someone who

    a. is very independent.

    b. feels powerless in some way.

    c. has everything he or she wants.

    Both paragraphs in Exercise 1 are based on the same subject matter, but the messages are very different. Your own writing changes, too, depending on who your audience is. When you write for your instructor, your most common audience, you will probably pay more attention to writing with a topic sentence, specific details, and a clear organizational plan. When you write for your friends, however, you can get away with being more casual. You don't worry about getting a grade for your notes or e-mail messages to friends. Knowing your audience when you write helps you choose the best way to make your point.

WRITING FOR A REASON

In choosing language for the situations earlier in the chapter, you considered two things. First, you thought about your audience. Second, you thought about your goal, what you wanted to accomplish. Your goal might have been to get your grade raised, have fun with your friends, get to know someone better.

In your writing class, your **purpose,** why you are writing, will usually be to convince your reader that what you say is worth reading. Your purpose will often fall under one of three headings:

- To inform
- To entertain
- To persuade

Writing to Inform

When you write to **inform,** your purpose is to present information clearly and accurately. You will list causes and effects, define unfamiliar terms, and provide facts that make your point clear. For instance, if you were writing to your new doctor to tell her about your current health, you would emphasize details that describe your overall health: your eating, sleeping, and exercise routines; your professional and recreational activities; your family health history; and your current health status. You could make jokes or use slang in your letter, but that would not help your new doctor understand your overall level of health. Thus, you'd be more effective simply informing her of the facts.

EXERCISE 2 Writing to Inform

Pretend that you have to write a letter to an adult you respect. The subject of your letter is your job. Make a list of the details that best inform someone of what your home is like.

_____

_____

_____

_____

_____

Writing to Entertain

When you write to **entertain,** you want to elicit a certain reaction from your reader: laughter, anger, surprise, or fascination. Your job, then, is to include details that lead your reader to *want* to read on. Whereas writing to inform requires that you include just the facts, writing to entertain demands that you focus on the unusual, the trivial, and the unexpected elements of a situation.

For instance, if you were writing to your old roommate about how terrible your day was, you might emphasize the little details that all added up to make your day bad. You could mention your "bad hair" on that day, the spills down the front of your shirt, the way you tripped right in front of someone you wanted to impress, or the way you started drooling when you fell asleep in class. Being specific and personal will more likely be entertaining than a dry list of the events of your day.

If you were writing to inform, you might simply write that you looked bad and acted clumsily, but to entertain, you would want to exaggerate the ridiculousness of your day.

EXERCISE 3 Writing to Entertain

Write a letter to someone you know very well. The subject of your letter is an unusual person or place you know. Keeping in mind that you want to entertain your reader, make a list of the details describing that person or place.

_____

_____

_____

_____

_____

Writing to Persuade

When you write to **persuade,** you write to convince someone to accept your point of view. Writing to persuade, then, requires that you include details that appeal to emotion, reason, or both.

For instance, if you were trying to convince your parents to lend you money, you could use emotion to appeal to their sense of being good, caring parents who can help their troubled, loving child. You could also use reason to convince your parents that you are a trustworthy, hardworking person who looks upon their loan as only a temporary means of gaining money. Either way, you would want to include details that will most likely convince your reader to think as you do.

EXERCISE 4 Writing to Persuade

Write a letter to an instructor. The subject of your letter is your current grade. Include details that will best convince your instructor to give you a higher grade.

_____

_____

_____

_____

_____

All three of these purposes rely on your reader choosing to read what you have written. Your message needs to match your audience, or you won't have much chance to get your point across.

Identifying Your Audience

Ask yourself the following questions to identify your audience.

- Who will read the document I am writing—my instructor, my friend, my supervisor at work?
- How can I best appeal to my audience?
- What does my audience need to know?

Identifying Your Purpose

Ask yourself the following questions to identify your purpose.

- Do I want to inform, entertain, or persuade?
- Do I want to explain a situation, give an opinion, or suggest a course of action?

 **CHECKLIST**

Before you write, consider the following:

- Your audience is the people who will read your writing.
- Your purpose will be either to inform, to entertain, or to persuade.

WRITING PRACTICE Writing a Letter for Change

You live in a basement apartment, and the person above you left the faucet on too long and flooded the apartment above. Unfortunately, water leaked downstairs and ruined your ceiling, wallpaper, and kitchen floor. Your lease says that in situations like this, all tenants must share the repair costs with the landlords. Thus, you and your roommate, your neighbor, and the landlord are equally responsible for fixing the damage. Your assignment is this: *Write a letter to one of the following audiences*: your upstairs neighbor, your landlord, or your roommate.

First, decide what you want your letter to accomplish: to *inform* the reader of the damage, to *entertain* the reader, or to *persuade* the reader to pay his or her share of the costs. *Note*: If this were a real-life situation, you probably would not choose to entertain your reader.

If you want to *inform* your reader of the damage, begin with a topic sentence like "The water damage in my apartment is extensive." Then include details that show your reader the extent of the water damage. Some possible details are puddles in the kitchen, ruined wallpaper, sagging ceiling.

If you want to *persuade* your reader to share the costs, begins with a topic sentence like "As part of a residential community, we all should share costs of damage." Then include details that show your reader why sharing costs is important. Some possible details are that you and your neighbors are like a family; all of your apartments are affected by the damage; next time, the water damage could be in someone else's apartment.

When you finish, share your letter with your classmates and discuss the types of details you included in order to make your point.

Remember to do the following when you write your letter.

- Identify your audience through the greeting.
- Write your main idea in your topic sentence.
- Make sure your purpose is clear in your topic sentence.
- Give support points for your topic sentence.
- Offer specific examples for your support points.

Write your letter on a separate piece of paper.

CHAPTER SUMMARY

Be sure to do the following in your writing.

1. Identify your **audience,** the person, people, or organization for whom you're writing.
2. Decide on your **purpose,** either to *inform, persuade,* or *entertain.*

MyWritingLab & Lab Activity 2

mywritinglab For additional help with audience and purpose, go to **www.mywritinglab. com** or complete **Lab Activity 2** in the separate *Resources for Writers* Lab Manual.

PART TWO
The Writing Process

A Human Race

OBSERVE YOUR WORLD What kind of running do you see people do? Observe your neighbors and aquaintances and write a few sentences about people's running (even if it's just to catch a bus or escape from the rain).

Responding to Images. *What about the photo above—the bridge, the runners themselves, the fact that the runners are all in the center of the bridge— stands out to you? Explain.*

Prewriting:
Coming Up with Ideas

3

Culture Note

THE ROARING TWENTIES

Fueled with enthusiasm after helping to win World War I, Americans wanted to have fun. They experimented with new forms of music, danced new dances, and wore new fashions. Business boomed as well-employed Americans spent their money in search of entertainment and comfortable lives. Finally, major political change occurred. Women gained the right to vote, and the right to drink alcohol became a constitutional issue.

GETTING STARTED

Writer's block can happen when writers feel pressured to produce a "perfect" first draft or feel that they have nothing to say. As you follow the writing process, you will learn many techniques to help you come up with good ideas to write about. Here are some strategies to help you with **prewriting,** the first step in the writing process.

- Freewriting
- Listing
- Questioning
- Keeping a journal
- Clustering
- Outlining

Look at the diagram on the next page to see how prewriting strategies fit into the writing process. As you read about these techniques, think about how well they might work for you. Then, as you complete the exercises in this chapter, pay attention to what prewriting strategies actually do work best for you.

RECOMMENDED READINGS

"Money for Morality," Mary Aloveues, *p. 745*

"The Plot Against People," Russell Baker, *p. 779*

"The Difference Between Male and Female Friendships," Ellen Goodman and Patricia O'Brien, *p. 767*

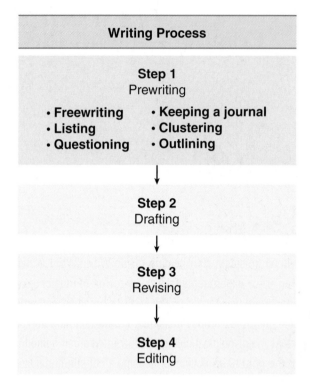

FREEWRITING

The easiest way to get started is simply to start writing, even if you feel you have nothing to say. This technique of "dumping" anything in your brain onto the paper is called **freewriting.** In freewriting you write as much as you can, as fast as you can, without stopping. Essentially, freewriting removes the factors that cause stress while you're writing. When you freewrite, you don't worry about organization, correctness, or connections between the ideas.

TIPS for Freewriting

1. Using a computer or a pen and paper, write the first word that comes into your head, and keep going.
2. If you get stuck, just keep writing the same word or group of words until something else comes to mind.
3. Don't go back to fix mistakes. Not everything you write will end up in your draft.

1920s Flapper

CRITICAL THINKING Women became active in religion and politics during the 1920s. Write a few sentences explaining how a group you know about has taken action. (Your group may be local, such as a neighborhood association, or it may be national, such as the Susan G. Komen Breast Cancer Foundation.) *Responding to Images. What mood best describes the women in the photo at left? Explain.*

Below is some freewriting by a student writer, Frida, on the topic "The Roaring Twenties." Notice that Frida's freewriting contains some grammar and spelling errors. Also, Frida writes that she is not sure about a lot of the details.

Why do we have to write on this topic? I don't no anything about the roaring twenties except that women were called flapers. Don't even know what that means, and I'm not even sure if all women were called that or just the ones who wore those funny dresses with fringe on them. I think that the roaring twenties had a lot of gangsters, too, but not the kind we have today. More like the Al Capone mobster type, and they blew things up and made people pay them for protection even though the protection was from them, I think. Man, what else? What else? What else? My mind's blank. I think my grandpa said that the twenties was a time of prohibition, but I'm not even sure what was prohibited.

Freewriting serves to give you a starting place. The point is just to get everything onto paper. Freewriting helps you generate ideas that you can redefine or develop later in your writing process. Additionally, you can note any interesting details that come to mind without forcing them to fit into a larger idea somewhere.

EXERCISE 1 Freewriting

On your own paper, freewrite for five minutes about a time in your life when a lot of changes occurred. Remember: Write as fast as you can without stopping, and don't worry about making mistakes.

LISTING

Sometimes freewriting can leave you with what seems like a mass of words that don't make sense. If freewriting doesn't work for a particular paragraph, another type of prewriting can help. **Listing** allows you the freedom of freewriting without the sense of disorganization. Simply write down everything you know about a topic, but do this in list form rather than paragraph form.

TIPS for Listing

1. On paper or on a computer, write the first word that comes into your head, and keep writing.
2. Include everything that comes to mind, even if you have no idea how it will fit with any other ideas on your list.
3. Don't go back to correct mistakes.

Below is a list that another writer, George, developed on the topic "The Roaring Twenties."

The Roaring Twenties	Major crime
Flappers	Al Capone
Women's changes	Gambling
Getting the vote	Prostitution
Prohibition	Jazz Age
Bootlegging	

In this list, George has concentrated on gathering as many ideas and details as possible on his topic. Later he will sort through his list to start developing his paragraph.

EXERCISE 2 Listing

On a separate piece of paper, make a list about a time when you had to make a big decision.

QUESTIONING

Sometimes the best place to start is with the information you *don't* have. Many times writers are unable to organize their ideas because they don't have enough specific details to use in their writing. A helpful strategy here is a technique called **questioning.** Asking and answering questions using a **T-chart** can help you identify areas where you need more information. Questioning can also help you organize the information you do have.

TIPS for Questioning

1. Divide the page vertically, with a line down the center, or use the Columns or Table feature on your computer.
2. In the left-hand column, write every question that comes to mind about your topic.
3. In the right-hand column, write any answers you have to the questions you've written on the left.
4. When you can't think of any more questions or answers, look at your chart to see what areas you have details for and what areas are lacking details.

Soua was not sure how much information she had for her paragraph on the Roaring Twenties. She did some questioning to examine her ideas.

In the T-chart on the next page, Soua has asked key questions that she needs to answer to write a detailed paragraph on the Roaring Twenties. At first, she had little information under the "Answers" heading. Through reading and research, she was able to find the answers to the questions she asked.

The Roaring Twenties

Questions	Answers
What was Prohibition?	Made alcohol production and drinking illegal.
How did Prohibition start?	Religious movement, then political.
What effects did Prohibition have?	18th Amendment passed to prohibit alcohol; 21st Amendment repealed 18th Amendment.
Why did crime increase?	Al Capone and other mobsters sold illegal alcohol, ran gambling and prostitution rings.
What changes did women experience?	Gained vote through suffrage movement (Susan B. Anthony). Dressed against convention (short hair and skirts, no corsets). Acted against convention (smoked and drank in public, ran for office).
Why were the 1920s "roaring"?	Business boomed. People had jobs in factories. People invested in stock market.

EXERCISE 3 Questioning

On your own paper, make a T-chart, writing questions in the left-hand column about the best or worst birthday you ever had. Put your answers in the right-hand column.

KEEPING A JOURNAL

The best way to improve your writing skills is to write as often as possible. Keeping a **journal**—an informal record of thoughts or ideas—is like freewriting a little bit every day. Although keeping a journal may not seem like a formal prewriting strategy, it can help you work through your ideas.

Your journal should be what *you* want it to be. Some writers use a special notebook that serves as their journal. Others use a computer to record their thoughts. The main point is to do some writing every day.

In your journal you can write ideas when they come to you. You can also ask yourself questions about topics you want to research. That way, you'll also be practicing your questioning strategy. In your journal you can even practice writing different versions of the same sentence. The more you write, the more confident you'll become.

TIPS for Keeping a Journal

1. Keep a specific notebook, folder, or computer file as your journal, and write all your entries there.
2. Write in your journal at the same time, for the same amount of time, every day.
3. Keep your journal with you if possible so you can also write ideas as they come to you.
4. Write everything that comes to mind and don't worry about making mistakes.
5. Keep all your journal entries so that you can see your progress.

Here are entries from the journal of a writer named Adam.

Monday. My instructor says I still have to write on a time called the roaring twenties even though I don't know much about it. I guess I can look it up at the library or on the Internet. In the meantime, I did learn that Prohibition made drinking alcohol illegal, but that many people still drank anyway. I also learned that only some women were flappers, but I still don't know why they were called that. I can't figure out why I have to write about something that happened almost ninety years ago. Maybe learning about the twenties will help me in history.

Wednesday. I still need help on this twenties paragraph, but Brad showed me how to do some searching on the Internet. Back to Prohibition, it started in the late 1800s. This preacher, William (Billy) Sunday, who used to be a pro baseball player (cool!), preached in favor of Prohibition, and the antidrinking idea caught on. In fact, there was even a constitutional amendment (the 18th) that made Prohibition legal, but it didn't last long. It became an amendment in 1919 but was repealed in 1933. That's all I've learned so far, but at least I've done something!

Friday. I've written a draft of my roaring twenties paragraph, but I don't like it. And I'm stuck again. I want to learn more about Al Capone, but all I can find is how bad he was. Not only was he a bootlegger (he made and sold alcohol illegally), but he also ran prostitution rings. He also ran gambling operations and made a *name for himself by being really violent. I'll work on women's rights on Monday. Nothing else to write now.*

These entries show how Adam used his journal to write about both his concerns and his progress. We learn that he is worried about not having enough information for his assignment, but these worries motivate him to gain more information.

EXERCISE 4 Keeping a Journal

Set up a journal. For one full week, write for five minutes a day about whatever comes to mind. Here are some sample topics.

- Your experiences at school, at work, or at home
- Your view of current events in the world
- Your view of what's happening in your personal relationships
- Your ideas on a subject you're studying

CLUSTERING

Another prewriting technique is **clustering,** also called **diagramming** or **mapping.** Clustering helps you organize your ideas visually and offers more structure than freewriting. It also helps you see what ideas might be off-topic when you are ready to write your draft.

TIPS for Clustering

1. Write your main idea in the center of a piece of paper.
2. Write supporting ideas around your main idea. You may want to circle your main and supporting ideas.
3. Use arrows to make connections between ideas. If all the arrows point from the same idea, that idea should probably be in your topic sentence. If no arrows point to an idea, you will probably want to omit it.

Martina made a cluster diagram around the topic "The Roaring Twenties." From her diagram, Martina can see that she knows a lot about some aspects of the Roaring Twenties. However, she has also written down

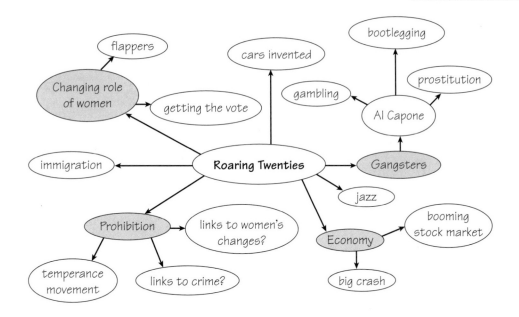

ideas—cars invented, jazz, and immigration—about which she doesn't seem to have much information. She'd do better focusing on the topics she does have information about: Prohibition, gangsters, the economy, and the changing role of women.

EXERCISE 5 Clustering

Make a cluster diagram on the topic "How Students Disrupt Classes." Use the space provided on the next page. Concentrate on clarifying connections between your ideas by using arrows and circles.

OUTLINING

Possibly the most helpful prewriting tool is outlining. **Outlining** is an effective means of organizing your ideas without actually writing sentences. Outlining also helps you see any gaps in your support because an outline is a list that organizes your whole paragraph on paper before you begin to write. In general, to outline, begin with your main idea and then add supporting points and specific details.

Topic

TIPS for Outlining

1. Write your main idea, even your topic sentence, at the top of the page.
2. Write the letter A beneath your main idea, and write your first support point next to the letter A.
3. Write the number 1 under your first support point, and add a specific detail— if you have one—to support your first point.
4. Add more support points and details.
5. When you have added all the information you know, read your outline to see which points lack specific details. These are the points that you will need to either research or omit when you write your draft.

Note: Your instructor may want you to use Roman numerals (I, II, III, etc.) for your support points and letters for your details, which follows the traditional outline format.

Minh did an outline for the topic "The Roaring Twenties" before she began her paragraph.

I. The Roaring Twenties

  A. Prohibition

    1. Temperance movement

2. Religious revival

3. Passage of 18th and 21st Amendments

B. Gangsters

1. Bootlegging

2. Gambling

3. Prostitution

4. Violence

5. Al Capone

C. Women's changing roles

1. Getting the vote

2. Flappers

3. Running for office

Minh's outline is based on information she knew and material she researched. An effective outline presents all your information in a clear, organized pattern, one that you can easily turn into a paragraph.

EXERCISE 6 Outlining

Write an outline of all the prewriting techniques covered in this chapter. Let the headings in the chapter—such as "Freewriting" and "Outlining"— serve as the headings for your outline. Refer to the tips boxes for each technique in this chapter to gather specific details for your outline. Some of the outline has already been filled in for you. *Hint*: There may be more than two details for each prewriting technique. Your job is to decide how many to include in your outline and in what order to place them.

Prewriting Techniques

A. Freewriting

1. Write without stopping.

2. Don't worry about mistakes.

B. Listing

1. Writing ideas in a list.

2. More structure than freewriting.

C. Questioning

    1. _Lets you see what information you don't have._

    2. _T-chart works well._

D. Keeping a journal

    1. _____

    2. _____

E. _____

    1. _____

    2. _____

    3. _____

F. _____

    1. _____

    2. _____

    3. _____

EXERCISE 7 Outlining for a Paragraph

On your own paper, make an outline of the steps you follow to get ready for work or school. Work on your outline for five to ten minutes. Focus on adding specific details and on organizing your ideas.

USING A COMPUTER FOR PREWRITING

If you're a fast typist, a computer is great for prewriting. Just follow these guidelines. For general information on writing with a computer, see "Tips for Using Computers in Writing" on page 68 in Chapter 4.

- Type as fast as you can to record every idea that enters your head.
- Don't stop to correct sentence-level errors.
- Try **invisible writing:** turn off the computer monitor (screen) and just type. Once you're off to a good start, turn the monitor back on.
- Turn your freewriting into a list, a question-and-answer chart, or an outline by pressing Enter to start a new line.
- Use your prewriting file when you're ready for drafting (Step 2 in the writing process).

A computer can also help you keep a journal.

- Create a file for each month. When you write in your journal, date each entry.
- Name your files so that they appear in chronological order in the directory menu: Journal 0208 (for February 2008) or Journal 1008 (for October 2008). That way, it will be easy to find specific files.

EXERCISE 8   Using Prewriting Techniques

Use these prewriting techniques to develop and organize ideas on one of the following topics. On a separate piece of paper, start by *freewriting* for a few minutes. Then do *listing, questioning*, and *clustering*. Finally, make an *outline* of your ideas. At the end of this exercise, you should have an idea of what techniques work well for you.

Topics

Tips for car maintenance

Reasons to stay in school

Tips for going backpacking

Different ways to meet members of the opposite sex

Ways to save money

Factors to consider in choosing college classes

Reasons to learn a second language

EXERCISE 9 Clustering and Outlining

Now you can use the clustering and outlining techniques to organize ideas and details that support a topic. Use your own paper to make a cluster diagram and outline for Topics A and B.

    A. Topic: Different ways to insult someone

    B. Topic: How easy it is to show affection for someone you like

EXERCISE 10 Combining Strategies

Below is a topic followed by a list of ideas to support it. In the outline that follows, the major ideas (A, B, C) have been filled in. Choose the minor ideas from the rest of the list to complete the outline. *Hint:* Check off each item on the list as you write it in the outline.

Topic: Women's changing roles in the 1920s

A. *Gained political power.* _____

    1. _____

    2. _____

B. Broke from convention in fashion. _____

    1. _____

    2. _____

    3. _____

C. Acted more independent. _____

    1. _____

    2. _____

    3. _____

Ideas

Gained right to vote.	Cut hair short.
Smoked in public.	Acted bolder, less shy.
Wore short skirts.	Refused to wear corsets.
Ran for office.	✓ Acted more independent.
✓ Broke from convention in fashion.	✓ Gained political power.
Drank in public.	

EXERCISE 11 Outlining a Paragraph

1. Read the paragraph below.

2. Identify the topic sentence and write it in the space provided.

3. Reread the paragraph and underline each support point. Check the outline that follows to see if you have correctly identified the support points (A, B, C).

4. Write the sentences containing the specific details for each support point in the spaces provided.

Hint: The purpose of this exercise is to show you how effective paragraphs are developed from good outlines.

The Many Faces of Jazz

Early jazz music (before 1960) has many different forms. The first form of jazz, called Dixieland jazz, is named for its origins in the South. Dixieland jazz often has no written music, but it does have a clear melody played on a horn and a strong beat played on the drums. One of the most famous Dixieland jazz bands was King Oliver's Creole Jazz Band, which included the famous Louis Armstrong, who played cornet. Another form of jazz music is known as swing music. Swing featured call-and-response playing, a lot of improvisation, and no written music. Duke Ellington, though, was an exception to the no-written-music rule because he wrote down the swing music he composed. A third type of jazz is bebop, or bop. This kind of jazz

Louis Armstrong (1901–1971)

FOOD FOR THOUGHT The Roaring Twenties were known for their jazz music, as played by Louis Armstrong. How do you think the early 2000s will be remembered? Write a few sentences explaining how you think the early 2000s will be characterized. Use examples from politics, sports, and entertainment.

Responding to Images. *What kind of personality do you think Louis Armstrong had, based on the photo at left? Explain.*

is a reaction to swing music. While swing music was simple, bop was complicated. While swing used big bands, bop focused on smal- lergroups. Where swing emphasized the melody, bop stressed the beat. The most famous bop musicians were Dizzy Gillespie and Charlie Parker.

Outlining

Topic sentence: Early jazz music (before 1960) has many different forms.

A.   The first form of jazz, called Dixieland jazz, is named for its origins in the South.

    1. _____

    _____

    2. _____

    _____

B. Another form of jazz music is known as swing music.

    1. _____

       _____

    2. _____

       _____

C. A third type of jazz is bebop or bop.

    1. _____

    2. _____

    3. _____

    4. _____

    5. _____

WRITING PRACTICE 1 Start Your Own Journal

Your assignment is this: With the details of keeping a journal fresh in your mind, *start your own journal*. Set aside at least five minutes today and write. You may write about academic subjects, or you may write about anything that's on your mind. The point is to begin your habit of keeping a journal today.

WRITING PRACTICE 2 Write Your Own Paragraph

You spent the last few pages reading about the 1920s. Now it's your turn to write. Use the information from this chapter or from your own life to help you find specifics. Your assignment is this: *Write a paragraph on either Topic A or Topic B below.*

Topic A: *The 1920s sound like a time in which I would (or would not) have wanted to live.*

The following steps will help you get started.

1. Use one or more of the prewriting techniques to organize your ideas.

2. Write a topic sentence like "I would have liked living in the 1920s for many reasons" or "I would not have liked living in the 1920s for many reasons."

3. Use specific details from this chapter as proof for your support points.

Topic B: *Tell about a time in your life that was particularly good or bad.*

The following steps will help you get started.

1. Use one or more of the prewriting techniques to organize your ideas.

2. Write a topic sentence like "Seventh grade was one of the best (or worst) years of my life."

3. Use specific details from your own life as proof for your support points.

CHAPTER SUMMARY

Several steps can help you with *prewriting*, the stage in writing where you come up with ideas.

1. In *freewriting*, make sure to write as fast as you can without stopping.
2. In *listing*, write as fast as you can to make a list of ideas.
3. In *questioning*, make a T-chart and write questions on the left-hand side and answers on the right-hand side.
4. In *keeping a journal*, write for a few minutes every day.
5. In *clustering*, write your main idea in the center of the page and then use arrows and circles to connect other ideas to it.
6. In *outlining*, alternate letters and numbers to develop your ideas from your main idea to your specific details.

MyWritingLab & Lab Activity 3

mywritinglab For additional practice with prewriting, go to **www.mywritinglab.com** or complete **Lab Activity 3** in the separate *Resources for Writers* Lab Manual.

Drafting:
First to Final Drafts

4

Culture Note
KNITTING

A method by which yarn may be turned into cloth, knitting consists of loops called "stitches" that are pulled through each other. Once viewed as a pastime for mothers and grandmothers, knitting has experienced a resurgence among people of different ages and backgrounds.

No Tangled Web

OBSERVING YOUR WORLD
This hand knotted net, feathered at the Guggenheim museum, reveals that hand crafts need not be limited to hand-sized items. What craft, skill, or hobby from your family could also be completed on a grand scale?

Responding to Images. *What gut reaction—such as "Wow! That's big," or "What is that?"—comes to mind when looking at the photo above? What aspects of the photo do you find most interesting?*

RECOMMENDED READINGS

"All I Really Need to Know I Learned in Kindergarten," Robert Fulghum, *p. 710*

"Manners Matter," Judith Martin, *p.758*

"My Mother's English," Amy Tan, *p.773*

READY TO PUT PEN TO PAPER

Now that you've spent some time prewriting, you're ready to move on to the next step in the writing process—drafting. **Drafting** is no more than writing a rough draft of your paragraph. In drafting, you use the information you discovered during prewriting to write sentences that flow together to convey your ideas.

ROUGH DRAFTS ARE NOT PERFECT

Some people think that they should be able to crack their knuckles, sit down at the computer or notepad, and crank out a perfect paragraph. This idea of "easy" drafting sounds wonderful, but very few writers work this way. Sometimes writing does come easily, but often it just takes time and practice. All that work has a benefit, though: the more you write, the better a writer you will become.

Some professional writers agree that writing is important. Peter Elbow writes that the way you express yourself on paper is your *voice:*

> Maybe you don't like your voice; maybe people have made fun of it. But it's the only voice you've got. It's your only source of power. . . . If you keep writing in it, it may change into something you like better. But if you abandon it, you'll likely never have a voice and never be heard.

Anne Lamott claims that writing just requires getting ideas on paper:

> The first draft is the child's draft, where you let it all pour out and then let it romp all over the place, knowing that no one is going to see it and that you can shape it later.

It's important to remember that the rough version, or **rough draft,** of your paragraph will not be perfect or finished.

- *A rough draft is not usually concise.* It may contain too many irrelevant details.
- *A rough draft is not usually credible.* It may not have enough specific detail to support its topic sentence.
- *A rough draft is not usually clear.* Its support points may not be organized logically, and it may have few or no transitional words.
- *A rough draft is not usually correct.* It may contain many errors in grammar, punctuation, and spelling.

As you work through the writing process, you'll get the chance to correct the flaws in your draft and make your paragraph more *concise, credible, clear*, and *correct*. When writing a rough draft, your goal should simply be to *get your ideas out*. Once they're on paper, you can change them, but you can't revise something you haven't written.

WRITING A ROUGH DRAFT

When you're ready to start drafting, find a comfortable space where you won't be disturbed. Don't sit down to write when you know you'll have to leave in fifteen minutes; instead, allow yourself plenty of time without deadlines. Gather your prewriting materials and any other notes, and have your writing assignment handy. Then, take a deep breath, clear your mind of outside worries as best you can, and start writing.

Your Topic Sentence

The key to writing an effective paragraph is having a clear topic sentence. The topic sentence controls the direction of your entire paragraph and represents the most important idea that you want to communicate. If your readers remember nothing else about your paragraph, they should remember your topic sentence.

Keep in mind, though, that your topic sentence may change as you discover more details and find more points that you want to explore. Coming up with your topic sentence first is often the easiest way to proceed. However, be flexible. Don't feel locked into a certain idea just because you've already written it down. You can always change it if you think of another idea that works better for you. For more on writing a topic sentence, see Chapter 8.

After thinking about an activity she was familiar with, Lina decided on the following topic sentence: "Knitting isn't just for my mom." She then started writing a rough draft. Note that Lina's draft contains several sentence-level errors.

Knitting isn't just for my mom. Sure, she's made me scarfs and socks and sweaters my whole life, I know a ton of people who have just started knitting. My brother, he knits during his "downtime" in Iraq; he makes caps for himself and his buddies out of yarn my mom and I send him. If his football buddies could see him now, I wonder what they'd say. It's pretty cool the things that you can make in a really short time. I've made wraps and cute little shrug sweaters in less than two days. Plus, there's so much to choose from in terms of yarn (but I can't think of the types now).

After writing these sentences, Lina realized that a lot of her ideas didn't directly support the idea that knitting isn't just an activity for her mother. Thus, she decided to change her topic sentence to reflect the unexpected aspects of knitting—since many of her ideas focus on them—as well as the enjoyment. Her new topic sentence is "Knitting has more to it than meets the eye." The new topic sentence more accurately states the main idea that grew from Lina's writing.

Your Support Points and Specific Details

Your prewriting is the source for support points and details for your paragraph. Once you have a topic sentence, you can identify the most convincing support points and decide on the right order for your paragraph. Using a pencil, underline support points and then number them in chronological or emphatic order. See Chapter 9 for more on choosing support points and specific details, and see Chapter 10 for more on organizing the support points in your paragraphs.

Your Rough Draft

Using the work you have done in your prewriting activities, start writing! If you are using a pen, skip lines as you write. Leaving space now will make Step 3 (revising) and Step 4 (editing) in the writing process easier to do. If you are using a computer, refer to "Tips for Using Computers in Writing" later in this chapter.

At this point, Lina has written a rough draft.

Knitting has more to it than meets the eye. First, anyone can do it. When I was little, I only saw women do it—my mom, grandma, and aunts. Now, though, I see guys at yarn stores, and I get hand-knitted presents from my brother who's stationed in Iraq. In addition to being an activity that anyone can do, knitting gets results. I could spend a few hours shopping at the mall for a little wrap, or I could spend a few hours (and less money) making a wrap myself. In a matter of hours, days, or weeks, I've made myself and others scarves, socks, wraps, and blankets. It's very rewarding to see the finished product! Finally, knitting is creative. I remember my grandma sitting with a big ball of colored yarn; she'd knit with red or blue for ages without changing color. Now I can choose from multicolored yarn with a frizzy, chunky look, so I can make something really stylish using the most basic stitches. All in all, knitting gives me more options than I ever thought possible.

Similarly, your paragraph shouldn't just stop at the end of your last specific detail. Lina's statement "All in all, knitting gives me more options than I ever thought possible" brought her writing to a natural stopping point.

Lina reminds the writer of the benefits of knitting even though she doesn't mention the word *benefit*. By including introductory and concluding statements, she helps her readers understand where the paragraph will lead and remember where it's taken them.

EXERCISE 1 Review

Fill in the blanks for the sentences below.

1. Some people believe that writing should be _____ .

2. The key to writing an effective paragraph is having a clear

_____ .

3. Staying flexible allows you to change your _____ even after you've begun writing your paragraph.

4. *Drafting* means writing more than one _____ of your paragraph.

5. Be sure to keep all your _____ from prewriting to refer to later on as you write a rough draft.

While you can follow the same steps for any kind of drafting, some specific guidelines for using a computer can make drafting easier.

Using a Computer for Drafting

Computers can help you greatly by letting you see your whole work, typed out, on the screen. Probably the greatest benefit of using a computer is *flexibility*. You can type, move, save, and generally manipulate your information before you ever print out your document. Specifically,

1. Use your prewriting to prepare more than one version of your topic sentence if you're not sure what your main idea is initially.

2. If you are thinking about using emphatic order, move your support points to different places in your draft by using the computer's Cut and Paste functions. You can decide later on the order of the support points.

3. Include illustrations or examples as you write your paragraph. Or, if ideas come to you when you're working on something else, add those examples in a separate file (or even at the very end of your draft) and then come back and insert them into your paragraph later.

4. Don't delete anything at this point! If you're not sure whether or not to keep a support point or specific detail, cut and paste it to the end of your document. Later, when you finish your draft, you can delete the extra material. Until then, you have information that may come in handy at other points in your work.

See also "Tips for Using Computers in Writing" below.

TIPS for Using Computers in Writing

1. **Save your work often.** Computer word processing programs have a Save function that allows you to update your work every time you change it.

2. **Back up your work.** Be sure to save your work to a backup drive. You can also e-mail a copy to yourself.

3. **Save different versions of your work.** Sometimes a certain sentence or piece of information doesn't seem to fit into your paragraph right away, but later on it seems perfect. Saving your various drafts allows you to refer back to earlier versions and use whatever information you need. Rename the version of your assignment that has your most recent changes.

4. **Print out your drafts.** Printing allows you to see your work in terms of length and detail.

5. **Plan for your computer time.** If you use your school's computers, make sure you leave enough time to get your work done during peak hours and around midterms.

WRITING PRACTICE 1 **Compare Writing by Hand and Writing on the Computer**

Your assignment is this: *Spend five minutes writing by hand, and then (at a later time) spend five minutes writing on the computer.* Some possible topics to write about are these:

- Health benefits of a food you've eaten
- A skill you are good at or would like to be good at (such as knitting or auto repair)
- Strategies for making friends in college

- Reasons to go to college
- Reasons to live with roommates

Then, answer these questions.

1. Which writing method is easier for you: using a pen and paper, or using a computer? Why? _____

_____

_____

_____

_____

2. What are some ways that you think using a computer can help your writing? _____

_____

_____

_____

_____

WRITING PRACTICE 2 Writing a Paragraph

Now that you've read about and practiced the first two steps in the writing process, it's time to put them together. Your assignment is this: *Write a paragraph on one of the following topics.*

Reasons a specific television program or movie is (or is not) entertaining

Reasons to eat (or not eat) a specific type of food

Reasons to get (or not get) a new pet

Benefits (or drawbacks) of staying friends with people you knew in high school

Benefits (or drawbacks) of using public transportation

Follow these steps to write your paragraph.

1. Use at least two prewriting techniques to come up with ideas.

2. Use your notes from prewriting to write a rough draft. Don't worry about making your rough draft perfect; just do your best to write down your ideas.

When you're finished, your paragraph should include these elements.

- A clear topic sentence
- Support points that relate to the topic sentence
- Specific details that give proof of your support points
- Transitions that connect your support points and examples

WRITING PRACTICE 3 Drafting with a Classmate

You will most likely have to collaborate with other students in college classes, so it's best to learn how to work effectively with your peers. Your assignment is this: *Working with a partner, write a paragraph on one of the following topics.*

Time management challenges of college students

Money management challenges of college students

Social challenges of college students

The benefits/drawbacks of asking your instructor for help

The benefits/drawbacks of taking a light/heavy academic load

CHAPTER SUMMARY

Be sure to do the following when you write your rough draft.

1. Allow yourself to write down your ideas without correcting them.
2. Write a clear topic sentence that contains your main idea and controls the direction of your paragraph.
3. Choose support points and specific details that illustrate your topic sentence.
4. Write on every other line to leave room for changes later.
5. Use a computer for additional flexibility in terms of moving and changing information in your draft.

MyWritingLab & Lab Activity 4

mywritinglab   For additional practice with drafting, go to **www.mywritinglab.com** or complete **Lab Activity 4** in the separate *Resources for Writers* Lab Manual.

Making Changes:
Revision

5

Culture Note
CHOCOLATE

One of the world's most loved sweets, chocolate has long been appreciated for its rich texture and luxurious flavor. However, despite its many admirers, chocolate also has a reputation for ruining people's waistlines. Is chocolate nutritious? Can it make you fat? Read on and see.

THINK YOU'RE DONE? TAKE ANOTHER LOOK

If you're like many people, you'd prefer writing to be more like a short-answer test: you respond with your first instincts, answer the questions, and you're done. However, good writing most often results from rewriting your paragraph until the finished product is polished. Once you've finished Step 2 of the writing process (drafting), you get many chances to improve your writing in Step 3, revising.

Revising is the process of "re-seeing" or "re–looking at" what you've already written. When you revise, you step back and try to look objectively at what you've written. The best revision is the result of many read-throughs on your part. Each time you read your paragraph, you focus on one of the first three of the four Cs—*concise, credible,* and *clear* writing—until each one is present. (You address the fourth C, *correct* writing, during the editing stage, explained in Chapter 6.)

The "Writing Process" diagram that follows illustrates how revising fits into the writing process steps. As the diagram shows, sometimes you need to go back to Steps 1 and 2 to do more prewriting and drafting before you can finish your revision.

RECOMMENDED READINGS

"Fatso," Cheryl Peck, *p. 762*
"The Joy of Boredom," Carolyn Y. Johnson, *p. 722*

71

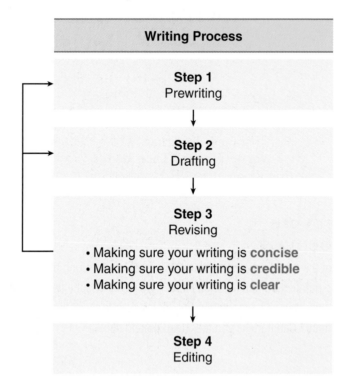

DOING STEP-BY-STEP REVISION

Read your paragraph at least one time for each characteristic of good writing listed below. As you read your paragraph, concentrate on only one area at a time. Take breaks between readings to clear your mind and help you refocus your attention. *Hint:* After making changes by hand, you can insert the changes into your computer file. Save this second draft and print it out for further revising.

MAKING SURE YOUR WRITING IS CONCISE

Check the length requirement for your assignment (if there is one) to make sure that you're not trying to do too much in your paragraph. Identify any support points that you think will need extra time and effort, and check to make sure that you have room to develop each point well. If the topic is so broad that you can't cover it thoroughly, refer to your prewriting to determine what parts of the subject interest you the most. Then focus your paragraph accordingly. Very often, after you've made changes to your draft after the first reading, the new version of your paragraph will be *shorter* than your original. Don't be alarmed. The shorter length comes from eliminating unnecessary details and repetitive sections. When you read your draft to check that it's credible and clear, you may add new information.

For instance, Jonathan wrote the following paragraph for the topic "My Favorite Flavor." Then he read through the draft to make sure his writing was concise. He crossed out every detail that did not support his topic sentence.

Chocolate is my favorite flavor for many reasons. It's my dad's favorite flavor. Ever since I can remember, I've wanted to be like my dad, and loving chocolate was an easy way. ~~One time, my dad and I went on a wilderness camping trip, just the two of us. He's a really cool dad.~~ I like chocolate because it offers a variety in flavors. ~~My sister loves vanilla, but that's no surprise since she is the most boring person on the face of the planet.~~ Chocolate is distinctive. ~~One time I ordered this huge strawberry smoothie and drank the entire thing. I had a stomachache that you wouldn't believe!~~

The details that Jonathan crossed out do not help support the idea in the topic sentence, "Chocolate is my favorite flavor for many reasons."

 ## CHECKLIST Is Your Paragraph Concise?

Ask yourself the following questions to determine whether your paragraph is concise.

- Do I have a clear topic sentence?
- Does *every detail* support my topic sentence?
- Are there any points that do not support my topic sentence?
- Are there any details that are irrelevant to my topic sentence?

EXERCISE 1 Revising to Make a Paragraph Concise

The following draft of a paragraph on chocolate needs improvement. Underline the topic sentence. Cross out any sentences that don't directly support the topic sentence. You may be tempted to make other changes in the paragraph, but *change the paragraph only to make it support the topic sentence.*

Nutritious Chocolate (Draft 1)

[1]Many myths surround chocolate. [2]The most significant myth is that chocolate makes you fat. [3]My aunt once ate too much chocolate for a whole year, and she couldn't fit into her best suit for my sister's wedding. [4]A myth surrounding chocolate is that it's unhealthy. [5]This isn't true. [6]Osteoporosis, the bone-weakening disease, runs in my family, so I make sure to get a lot of calcium in my diet. [7]I hope to keep good posture as long as I can by having strong bones. [8]One myth is that chocolate is made up only of fat. [9]Really, chocolate provides different types of calories. [10]In one ounce of milk chocolate, people get one gram of protein and fifteen grams of carbohydrates. [11]Of course, they also get nine grams of fat, that's in addition to the other types of calories. [12]Overall, chocolate is healthier than people realize.

1. The topic sentence is sentence _____.

2. Three sentences are off-topic: _____ , _____ , and _____.

MAKING SURE YOUR WRITING IS CREDIBLE

mywritinglab On your second pass through your paragraph, look for gaps in your support. Check your support points, and make sure that you have specific details to illustrate all your points. If necessary, look back at your prewriting exercises to find additional examples.

During his second reading of his draft, Jonathan noticed that he needed specific details to illustrate his support points. The specific details that Jonathan added are underlined.

Chocolate is my favorite flavor for many reasons. It's my dad's favorite flavor. Ever since I can remember, I've wanted to be like my dad, and loving chocolate was an easy way. I have great memories of the two of us licking dripping chocolate ice cream cones in summer and eating sticky chocolate candies right after Halloween. I like chocolate because it offers variety in flavors. Depending on my mood, I can choose dark chocolate, milk chocolate, white chocolate, or even a combination. I love knowing that when I walk into an ice cream parlor, I can choose from at least five different ice cream flavors that have some kind of chocolate in them. Other flavors, like vanilla, come in only one boring flavor. Chocolate is distinctive. No one could ever confuse it with another flavor like banana or strawberry, but some fruit flavors all blend together and taste the same. My mother loves to bake different kinds of fruit pies. Her pies taste great; they all taste the same, no matter what kind of fruit she uses. With chocolate, I never have any trouble knowing when someone's baking with my favorite flavor.

Now Jonathan's paragraph has plenty of examples, and they all support his topic sentence. Don't worry if you don't think of all your examples right away. As you read through your draft, just keep thinking about the best way to explain your ideas to your reader. Then add examples as they come to you.

CHECKLIST Is Your Paragraph Credible?

Ask yourself the following questions to determine whether your paragraph is credible.

- Do I provide enough information so that my reader will believe me?
- Have I made sure my reader knows what I mean?
- Do I need to review my prewriting notes to find more support for my topic sentence?
- Do I need to add more examples or specific details?

EXERCISE 2 Revising to Make a Paragraph Credible

On the next page is the corrected version of the paragraph you revised in Exercise 1. In this exercise, you need to add specific details to make the paragraph more credible. Read Specific Details A and B, which follow the paragraph. Decide where in the paragraph each belongs. Then write the number of the sentence that each specific detail should follow. You may want to make other changes in the paragraph, but don't. *Pay attention only to adding more information for support.*

Nutritious Chocolate (Draft 2)

[1]Many myths surround chocolate. [2]The most significant myth is that chocolate makes you fat. [3]A myth surrounding chocolate is that it's unhealthy. [4]This isn't true. [5]One myth is that chocolate is made up only of fat. [6]Really, chocolate provides different types of calories. [7]In one ounce of milk chocolate, people get one gram of protein and fifteen grams of carbohydrates. [8]Of course, they also get nine grams of fat, that's in addition to the other types of calories. [9]Overall, chocolate is healthier than people realize.

Specific Details

A. There are 140 calories in an ounce of semisweet chocolate and 150 calories in an ounce of milk chocolate. This might sound like a lot, but it's low compared with the number of calories in a bottle of sweetened iced tea. People get fat only if they eat too much chocolate.

This information belongs after sentence _____ .

B. Chocolate contains zinc, iron, and other nutrients that make it a good part of people's diets. Milk chocolate also contains calcium, so it helps build strong bones.

This information belongs after sentence _____ .

MAKING SURE YOUR WRITING IS CLEAR

mywritinglab On your third pass through your paragraph, check that your support points are arranged in a logical, effective order. Decide where your support points should go, and then move them around, if necessary, to create a sense of progress and balance for your reader. Make sure, too, that you signal the order of your points by using transition words like *first, second,* and *finally* in your paragraph.

During his third pass through his paragraph, Jonathan added transitions. The transitions that Jonathan added are underlined.

Chocolate is my favorite flavor for many reasons. <u>First</u>, it's my dad's favorite flavor. Ever since I can remember, I've wanted to be like my dad, and loving chocolate was an easy way. <u>In fact</u>, I have great memories of the two of us licking dripping chocolate ice cream cones in summer and eating sticky chocolate candies right after Halloween. <u>Next</u>, I like chocolate because it offers variety in flavors. Depending on my mood, I can choose dark chocolate, milk chocolate, white chocolate, or even a combination. I love knowing that when I walk into an ice cream parlor, I can choose from at least five different ice cream flavors that have some kind of chocolate in them. Other flavors, like vanilla, come in only one boring flavor. <u>Finally</u>, chocolate is distinctive. No one could ever confuse it with another flavor like banana or strawberry, but some fruit flavors all blend together and taste the same. My mother loves to bake different kinds of fruit pies. <u>Even though</u> her pies taste great, they all taste the same, no matter what kind of fruit she uses. With chocolate, <u>however</u>, I never have any trouble knowing when someone's baking with my favorite flavor.

Although a reader might have been able to figure out which details illustrated certain support points before, the transitions that Jonathan added make the connections extremely clear. Now there is no doubt as to what his support points are, what order they take, or how they relate to each other.

As a result of his three passes, Jonathan's paragraph has become concise, credible, and clear.

CHECKLIST Is Your Paragraph Clear?

Ask yourself the following questions to determine whether your paragraph is clear.

- **Do I have a logical organizational format that my reader can easily follow? What is it?**
- **Do I use transitional expressions to communicate what my points are and indicate which ones are most important?**
- **Do I need to explain any points more fully?**
- **Do I need to move or rearrange sentences to make my writing clearer?**

EXERCISE 3 Revising to Make a Paragraph Clear

On the next page is the corrected version of the paragraph you revised in Exercise 2. You need to make sure the paragraph is clear. After reading the paragraph, answer the questions about clear writing that follow it.

Nutritious Chocolate (Draft 3)

[1]Many myths surround chocolate. [2]One myth is that chocolate is made up only of fat. [3]Really, chocolate provides different types of calories. [4]In one ounce of milk chocolate, people get one gram of protein and fifteen grams of carbohydrates. [5]Of course, they also get nine grams of fat, but that's in addition to the other types of calories. [6]Another myth surrounding chocolate is that it's unhealthy. [7]This isn't true. [8]Chocolate contains zinc, iron, and other nutrients that make it a good part of people's diets. [9]Milk chocolate also contains calcium, so it helps build strong bones. [10]The most significant myth is that chocolate makes you fat. [11]There are 140 calories in an ounce of semisweet chocolate and 150 calories in an ounce of milk chocolate. [12]That might sound like a lot, but it's low compared with the number of calories in a bottle of sweetened iced tea. [13]People get fat only if they eat too much chocolate. [14]Overall, the myths are not true, and chocolate is healthier than people realize.

1. The paragraph gives support points in emphatic order (from least to most important). Write 1 before the least significant myth about chocolate, 2 before the next most important myth, and 3 before the most important myth.

    _____ Chocolate makes you fat.

    _____ Chocolate is unhealthy.

    _____ Chocolate is made up only of fat.

2. Which support point would best be introduced by the word *Finally?*
    _____

3. Which point would best be introduced by the phrase "Another myth surrounding chocolate"? _____

    _____

4. Which term shows emphasis in sentence 10? _____

    _____

5. How many times does the writer repeat the words *myth* and *myths* in the paragraph? _____

USING A COMPUTER TO REVISE YOUR DRAFT

Revision is the part of the writing process where computers really help you.

- Computers are very useful for deleting information that doesn't help you develop your topic sentence. Since your draft on the word processor looks more finished than a handwritten one, it is easier to tell what information is off-topic or unnecessary.

- You can use the Cut and Paste functions to move examples from one part of your draft to another without having to retype your whole draft.

- Word processing programs let you easily insert transitional words and phrases, so your draft becomes much more finished without a lot of effort.

- Computers give you an early sense of how your finished product will look. Instead of a messy paper with scribbled-out passages and lines with arrows pointing every which way, your writing will automatically be lined up at the margin, equally spaced, and evenly printed.

A REVISED DRAFT

The paragraph below has gone through all the necessary revisions and is now ready to be edited and handed in.

Nutritious Chocolate

Many myths surround chocolate. One myth is that chocolate is made up only of fat. Really, chocolate provides different types of calories. In one ounce of milk chocolate, people get one gram of protein and fifteen grams of carbohydrates. Of course, they also get nine grams of fat, but that's in addition to the other types of calories. Another myth surrounding chocolate is that it's unhealthy. This isn't true. Chocolate contains zinc, iron, and other nutrients that make it a good part of people's diets. Milk chocolate also contains calcium, so it helps build strong bones. The most significant myth is that chocolate makes you fat. There are 140 calories in an ounce of semisweet chocolate and 150 calories in an ounce of milk chocolate. That might sound like a lot, but it's low compared with the number of calories in a bottle of sweetened iced tea. People get fat only if they eat too much chocolate but that's true of many foods.

Overall, the myths are not true, and chocolate is healthier than people realize.

EXCHANGING HELP WITH YOUR PEERS

Working with classmates, or **peer review,** is one of the best ways to improve your writing. Working with classmates allows you to do the following:

- Receive feedback without receiving a grade.
- Receive feedback from someone who shares your experiences, at least in the classroom.
- Gain ideas for your own work by seeing how your classmates have illustrated or organized their ideas in their writing.
- Ask questions about your writing in front of a few people, not the instructor or your whole class.
- Talk about strategies that can help you improve your writing before you try them out in your paper.

Remembering the Writer's Feelings

In general, working with classmates lets you give your paper a test run before your instructor sees it. Consider the following questions before beginning your peer review workshop.

- How do you feel when someone is reading something you've written?
- How much do you value another student's opinion about your writing? Would you rather have just the instructor's comments? Explain.
- If a friend asks you to read something he or she has written, what kind of feedback do you give your friend? Does your feedback change if the friend is a co-worker or classmate? Explain.

These questions should help you remember that writing is a form of personal expression. When we comment on other people's writing, we need to be polite and careful about their feelings.

Writing as a Response

Writing is such a personal experience that sometimes it's hard to open up and let other people read what you've written. However, allowing your classmates to help you to learn about gaps in support, weak connections, and overall strengths will ultimately help you write more effectively.

Peer Review Guidelines

Use the Peer Review Worksheet on the following page and the guidelines below to give constructive feedback to your classmates. Ideally, you will work in pairs or in small groups of three or four students. Each member of your group should have a copy of every group member's paragraph and a Peer Review Worksheet.

Since some classes last longer than others, focus only on the guidelines you have time to cover. Your instructor may tell you which ones to include or ignore for a particular assignment. Additionally, the Peer Review Worksheet includes specific space for comments on the topic sentence, support points, and details. Write any other comments in the last section of the worksheet.

Follow these guidelines in evaluating your classmate's writing.

1. **Be kind.** Keep in mind that your classmates may feel nervous about letting you read their work, let alone comment on it. Therefore, do your best to be direct but kind in the comments you make to your peers. Criticism delivered with courtesy is much more likely to be helpful.

2. **Have the paragraph read aloud by someone other than the writer.** Reading along as the paragraph is read aloud forces everyone to slow down and read every word carefully. That way, people are not confused because they skipped a word or line by trying to read too quickly. Since the writers know what they mean to say, they might add emphasis or words that they think *should* be there but that end up being unclear. To best understand where the writer needs help, someone *not* familiar with the text should do the reading aloud.

3. **Tell the writer what you think the biggest strength of the paragraph is.** *Every* piece of writing has something positive about it, so work hard to find something nice to say to the writer, even if you're only complimenting the writer on the topic of the paragraph. If you think the writer has some good examples or a solid title, mention that. You may think that the paragraph is well organized or even that it has the potential to be well organized. Try very hard to find something positive to say about the paragraph you're evaluating.

4. **Write down the topic sentence on the Peer Review Worksheet.** If you can identify the writer's topic sentence, then the writer is on the right track. If you write down another sentence, or if you're not sure which sentence is the topic sentence, talk to the writer about what his or her main idea is.

Peer Review Worksheet

Reviewer's name: _____ Date: _____

Writer's name: _____

Paragraph title: _____

1. One strength of this paragraph is _____

_____

_____

2. The topic sentence for this paragraph is _____

_____

_____

3. The support points for this paragraph are _____

_____

_____

4. Write down the specific details the writer uses to illustrate each support point.

   Details for support point 1: _____

   _____

   _____

   Details for support point 2: _____

   _____

   _____

   Details for support point 3: _____

   _____

   _____

5. Overall comments on this paragraph: _____

_____

_____

5. **If there is no clear topic sentence, help the writer revise or write one.** (If the writer does have a clear topic sentence, move on to the next guideline.) Discuss what the writer wants to say, and find the best way to say it. Talk, too, about the best way to incorporate the support points and specific details the writer has already written.

6. **Write down the support points for the topic sentence.** If you can identify the support points, the writer is probably on the right track. If you're not sure what the support points are, or if your idea of the support points differs from the writer's, talk about what the writer wants to communicate and how certain points will best help support the topic sentence.

7. **Make sure that the writer has specific details that illustrate every support point.** Tell the writer if he or she needs to offer more proof of the support points. You may suggest the kinds of examples, but the writer should come up with the specific details.

8. **Make sure the writer uses a strategy (such as chronological or emphatic order) to organize the ideas in the paragraph.** The paragraph may already be organized, or partly organized, according to one of the organizational strategies. In this case, help the writer put the support points into a logical order, discussing which points should go first or last and why.

9. **Make sure the writer uses transitions to signal the order of the support points and their level of importance.** Refer to the lists of transitions in Chapter 10 in order to make the connections between ideas clear.

10. **Offer any comments not covered by the earlier guidelines.** These comments may include discussion of details that seem off-topic, places where the writer needs more detail, or places where sentence-level errors make understanding the paragraph difficult.

The Peer Review Worksheet shown on the following page has been partly filled in by one of Jonathan's classmates.

Making the Best Use of Other People's Feedback

Once we get someone's opinion of our writing, the trick becomes making good use of that opinion. The following guidelines are designed to help you make the most of other people's feedback.

Don't Expect People to Fix Everything   No one knows everything. Getting good feedback on your writing doesn't guarantee that you will improve your writing enough, say, to raise your grade from a C to an A. The

Peer Review Worksheet

Reviewer's name: Ramona _____ **Date:** 10/6/08 _____

Writer's name: Jonathan _____

Paragraph title: My Favorite Flavor _____

1. **One strength of this paragraph is** The topic choice (chocolate) is interesting. ____
   _____
   _____

2. **The topic sentence for this paragraph is** _____
   Chocolate is my favorite flavor for many reasons.
   _____

3. **The support points for this paragraph are** Chocolate is my dad's favorite flavor. ____
   Chocolate comes in a variety of flavors.
   Chocolate is distinctive.

4. **Write down the specific details the writer uses to illustrate each support point.**
   Details for support point 1: Memories of eating ice cream and Halloween chocolate with ____
   my dad. _____
   _____

   Details for support point 2: Can choose from at least five ice cream flavors with chocolate ____
   in them. _____
   _____

   Details for support point 3: All fruit pies taste alike, but chocolate is always distinctive. ____
   _____
   _____

5. **Overall comments on this paragraph:** Jonathan made his love for chocolate clear. ____
   _____

most you can expect from other people is their honest response. Then it's your job to revise your writing accordingly.

Don't Feel That You Have to Take Everyone's Advice   Even though almost every piece of writing has room for improvement, don't make changes just because someone says you should. If the suggestions make sense to you—or if *everyone* in your group says the same thing—then you should probably consider revising your draft.

Ask People to Be Specific   If you're not sure what people mean, ask them to explain further. The worst thing you can do in a peer review situation is try to revise your draft when you're not sure how to go about it. If your group doesn't make its ideas clear, ask your instructor for further clarification.

Remember: People Are Trying to Help   Even if you're disappointed that your classmates don't find your ideas as clear as you'd hoped, don't get mad. Accepting criticism from people is often difficult, so just do your best to listen and learn from your peers.

SETTING YOUR GOALS AS A WRITER

As you begin writing more frequently and for different assignments, you will discover your strengths as a writer. You may learn that you can write wonderful descriptions, that you're sharp at comparing and contrasting, or that you can make powerful argument. You will also learn what areas of your writing you need to focus your attention on.

One tool that can help you improve your writing one step at a time is a goal sheet. A goal sheet like the one on page 86 allows you to keep your topic sentence in mind at all times, emphasize what you're already doing well in your writing, and set specific goals for improvement. The goal sheet also allows you to tell your instructor and classmates—or peer reviewers—what you need from them.

The goal sheet works best if you use it right before you hand in your paper—when your ideas are fresh in your mind—and then review it when you begin another assignment. You may even want to attach it to your final draft so that your instructor can see what your goals for improvement are. Do your best to write well on your goal sheet, but don't worry if you have mistakes.

Look at the sample completed goal sheet on page 87. The student, Mario Bianchini, has written a paragraph on a challenging job he recently held.

Notice that Mario isn't always looking for hard-and-fast answers. Sometimes he simply wants suggestions. Also, he isn't afraid to ask his instructor to look at something he feels good about, in this case his use of specific detail.

Goal Sheet

Name: _____

Class: _____

1. My topic sentence for this assignment is _____
_____
_____

2. The skill I think I've improved in this assignment is _____
_____
_____

   The way I improved this skill is _____
_____
_____

3. The skill I think I still need to work on is _____
_____
_____

   I plan to improve this skill by _____
_____
_____

4. The aspect of my writing that my classmates told me to focus on is _____
_____
_____

5. What I want my instructor to notice or comment on in my writing is _____
_____
_____

Goal Sheet

Name: Mario Bianchini

Class: English 101, Section B

1. My topic sentence for this assignment is Working in a grocery store is a lot more difficult than people realize.

2. The skill I think I've improved in this assignment is the second C: credible writing. I think I've used details better in this paragraph than in my first ones.

The way I improved this skill is I did two things. I talked to my instructor about what she meant by "specific details." I also tried to use examples that relate to people's five senses. I think these steps worked.

3. The skill I think I still need to work on is the third C: clear writing. I'm still not sure how to organize ideas. Sometimes time sequence order seems right, but then I think that emphatic order seems best. I don't know which one to use.

I plan to improve this skill by I'll reread the section in the book on organization and go to the writing lab to get extra practice.

4. The aspect of my writing that my classmates told me to focus on is I want my classmates to pay attention to my organization. Maybe they can tell me if I'm organizing my ideas well or suggest ways to make my writing more clear.

5. What I want my instructor to notice or comment on in my writing is I want my instructor to notice two things. First, I want her to tell me if my examples are better, because I think they are. Second, I want her to pay attention to my organization, too, and help me decide how to organize my ideas.

WRITING PRACTICE 1 Write and Revise Your Own Paragraph

In this chapter you learned something about one food—chocolate. Your assignment is this: *Write a paragraph about a food that is or is not very good for you.* Be sure to include reasons why the food is or is not good for you. Then give specific details from your life as proof of how good or bad the food is for you.

Follow these steps to write your paragraph.

1. Use at least two prewriting techniques to come up with ideas for your paragraph.
2. Use your notes from prewriting to write a rough draft of your paragraph.
3. Revise your paragraph, reading through it to check for the first three of the four Cs: *concise*, *credible*, and *clear* writing.

When you're finished, your paragraph should include the following:

- A clear topic sentence
- Support points that relate to the topic sentence
- Specific details that give proof of your support points
- Transitions that connect your support points and specific details

WRITING PRACTICE 2 Revise a Paragraph from Another Assignment

Much of the writing you do in college will be outside your English classes. Thus, it's a good idea to practice revising your assignments for other courses as well as for English. Your assignment is this: *Choose a writing assignment from earlier in this book or from another class and revise it according to the four Cs.* You may simply reorganize or reword a history or psychology assignment, or you may turn a prewriting exercise into a paragraph.

In revising your assignment, do the following:

1. Make sure your writing is *concise*, and see that everything connects to your topic sentence.
2. Make sure you use specific details so that your writing is *credible*.
3. Make sure your writing is in a logical order so that it is *clear*.
4. Make sure your writing is error-free and *correct*.

When you're finished, your paragraph should include the following:

- A clear topic sentence
- Support points that relate to the topic sentence
- Specific details that give proof of your support points
- Transitions that connect your support points and specific details

CHAPTER SUMMARY

Remember to do the following when you revise a draft.

1. Reread your paragraph several times, revising it each time to make sure it is *concise, credible, clear*, and *correct*.
2. Ask your classmates for feedback and listen to them, but you don't have to do everything they suggest.
3. When giving feedback to your peers, help them craft a clear topic sentence, support points, and specific details.

MyWritingLab & Lab Activity 5

mywritinglab For additional practice with revising, go to **www.mywritinglab.com** or complete **Lab Activity 5** in the separate *Resources for Writers* Lab Manual.

6

Editing for Clarity and Correctness

Culture Note

WINTER HOLIDAYS

Though most people in the United States are aware of Christmas and New Year's Day, many other holidays occur during the winter months. These other holidays have varied origins—some cultural, some religious, some societal—but they all include some sort of celebration. Two of these festivals are Boxing Day and Kwanzaa.

THE IMPORTANCE OF EDITING

You've moved around, filled in, and shored up different patches of your paragraph in Step 3 of the writing process (revising). Now you're ready to polish your work. **Editing**—changing your writing to make it more effective and to correct errors—is a painstaking, but very important, part of the writing process. So don't rush! It is during this stage that you address the fourth C—*correct* writing. Look at the "Writing Process" diagram on page 91 to see how editing fits into the writing process.

Think of editing as your last mirror-check before going to an important job interview. You wouldn't show up for an interview—after carefully preparing and dressing for success—with a big piece of spinach between your teeth. Similarly, you shouldn't forget to edit your work after you've spent much time and effort writing and revising it. A well-edited, error-free paragraph shows your reader you care about your work. It makes you look smart, professional, and prepared.

RECOMMENDED READINGS

"A Homemade Education," Malcolm X p. 714

"'Blaxicans' and Other Reinvented Americans," Richard Rodriguez, p. 738

"Manners Matter," Judith Martin, p. 758

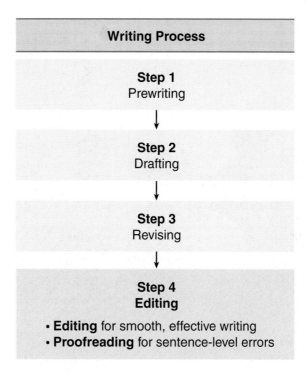

There are two parts to editing.

- Careful examination of your writing to see if you can make it smoother, more interesting, and more effective.
- Careful proofreading to catch and correct errors in grammar, punctuation, and spelling.

Notice that both steps begin with the word *careful*. Taking care at this stage—to catch, eliminate, and correct errors—will go a long way toward making a good impression on your reader.

EDITING FOR SMOOTH, EFFECTIVE WRITING

Once your paragraph is concise, credible, and clear, you need to make sure that your reader will enjoy your writing. You want your audience to read all the way to the end of the paragraph. That won't happen unless your writing is interesting and progresses smoothly. As you read your paragraph, answer the following questions.

A Kwanzaa Celebration

SURF THE NET A holiday based on African harvest festivals, Kwanzaa celebrates seven character traits emphasizing strength in community and responsibility. Search for "Kwanzaa" on the Internet, follow several links, and write a few sentences explaining what you learn.

Responding to Images. *Based on the photo above, what conclusions can you draw about Kwanzaa?*

- **Point of view.** Do I use the same pronoun throughout? Do I use the correct verb tenses throughout? (For more on using consistent verbs and pronouns, see Chapters 37–40.)

- **Appropriate language.** Do I use language that is appropriate for an academic assignment? Do I use unbiased, respectful language? (For more on sensitive language and word choice, see Chapters 12–14.)

- **Word use.** Have I chosen the best words I can? Is the writing too wordy? Are certain words repeated too often? (For more on using vivid examples and language, see Chapters 9 and 14.)

- **Sentence variety.** Have I used different kinds of sentences to keep my writing interesting? Do sentences flow logically and smoothly from one to the next? (For more on sentence variety and connecting sentences, see Chapter 52.)

You can be aware of these concerns during the drafting and revising process. However, once you reach the editing stage of the writing process, you should make sure your sentences are smooth, interesting, and effective. Look at the "Writing Process" diagram on page 91 to see how editing fits into the writing process.

PROOFREADING FOR SENTENCE-LEVEL ERRORS

Proofreading means checking your writing for errors in grammar, punctuation, and spelling. **Proofreaders' marks,** shown on this page, are a standard set of symbols used by instructors, editors, and printers to show changes in written work. Become familiar with these symbols and use them as you proofread.

By now, however, you are so familiar with your paragraph that you probably skip right over some errors without noticing them. Use the following three proofreading techniques to force yourself to read slowly so you'll have a better chance of spotting mistakes.

Mark	Meaning	Example
∧	Insert	hve
ℰ	Delete	some ~~some~~ cultural
⌒	Close up space	t̮he
∾	Transpose	some⎸of⎸sort⎹
#	Insert space	in#the
/ℓc	Make lowercase	Ørigins
≡ Cap	Capitalize	New year's Day
—	Underline (or put in italics)	all
¶	Indent paragraph beginning	¶Though

Example

¶Though pretty much everyone in#the United States are is aware of Christmas and New year's Day, many other holidays occur during t̮he winter months. Other holidays hve many different Ørigins— some ~~some~~ cultural, some religious, some societal—but they all include some⎸of⎸sort celebration two of these festivals are Boxing Day and Kwanzaa.

Proofreading Sentence by Sentence

Reading your paragraph one sentence at a time allows you to identify grammar errors like run-on sentences, sentence fragments, and mistakes in subject-verb agreement and pronoun agreement. It also helps you identify awkward sentences or poor word choices.

During your first reading, check to be sure each sentence makes sense by itself. Then make sure that each sentence leads logically into the next. Use a piece of paper to cover all but one sentence so that you can focus on that sentence alone.

Proofreading Word by Word

Slowing down and reading your paragraph word by word will allow you to find other errors—such as apostrophe or capitalization errors—that you didn't notice when reading each sentence separately. Further, reading your paragraph aloud can help you determine whether you have repeated a word one too many times or have used too many long words when you could do with shorter ones. Use a pencil or your finger to point out each word as you read it.

Reading Your Paragraph Backwards

Reading your paragraph backwards helps you find spelling errors. Use a pencil or your finger to point to the words as you read. Because your paragraph won't make sense backwards, you won't be able to anticipate—and thus skip—the upcoming errors in a sentence. You won't be able to gloss over misspellings.

USING A COMPUTER FOR EDITING

Computers can help you edit your work, but use these tools with caution.

- The spelling checker will help you find spelling errors. It will not help you find **diction** errors (mistakes in word choice), however. For instance, the following sentence makes no sense: "Their are too daze left of the big sail." The computer won't catch any of the word-choice errors, though, since all the words are spelled correctly. The correct sentence should be "There are two days left of the big sale."
- Grammar checkers should be used carefully. Sometimes a computer's explanation will point out the error but not explain it. Other times the computer will be wrong. For instance, the following sentence is correct:

"The engineer explained that that was the best method." The grammar checker marked the sentence wrong, indicating that the repetition of *that* was incorrect, but the sentence is not incorrect. To be safe, do your own proofreading when you've printed out your final draft.

To make the best use of your computer for editing, do the following:

1. Set the font on your computer to 12 point unless your instructor requests another size.
2. Set the margins to at least one inch unless your instructor recommends a different measurement.
3. Double-space your work.
4. Before you print out your draft, reread the entire piece, using the computer cursor (the blinking line that appears on the screen) to focus your attention on one line at a time. You can make changes as you go, and you will not feel overwhelmed by having to change everything at once.

EXERCISE 1 Reading Each Sentence Separately

The following paragraph contains several sentence-level errors. Read the paragraph and focus on finding errors in *sentence structure* and *punctuation*. Write the numbers of the sentences with these errors in the blanks at the end of the paragraph. Then make corrections in the paragraph. There are five sentence structure and punctuation errors in all.

Celebrate Boxing Day

[1]Many smaller holidays have interesting origins Boxing Day, for one, is a holiday in England that falls on December 26. [2]In its early years, Boxing Day was a day for people to give money to church leaders, [3]In order for them to offer prayers for people's relatives at sea. [4]The name "Boxing Day" come from the boxes that the church leaders using to collect money. [5]Later in England's history, Boxing Day served as the day that many servants received leftovers from their employers' Christmas feasts. [6]Since at that time servants are needed in large households to prepare elaborate holiday meals, the servants had to work on

Christmas day. [7]The next day, however, employers often gave their servants leftovers, which the servants could use for their own Christmas celebration. [8]The leftovers were in boxes, so the name "Boxing Day" stuck. [9]Eventually, Boxing Day becames a day for employers to tip their servants. [10]Now, however, it's just a day that most people celebrate by not having to go to work.

The following sentences contain errors: _____, _____, _____, _____, _____ .

EXERCISE 2 Reading Each Word Separately

In the following paragraph, look for errors in *capitalization*. Also look for unnecessary *repetition*. Then correct the errors you find, and answer the questions at the end of the paragraph. Errors appear in three sentences.

Celebrate Kwanzaa

[1]Kwanzaa, a holiday with contemporary origins, has its roots in African culture. [2]Founded in 1966 by Maulana Karenga, chairman of Black Studies at california State University at Long Beach at the time, Kwanzaa is one African-American festival that has become known in mainstream America. [3]It's based on African harvest festivals, and it combines symbolism with ritual as a family and community festival. [4]The seven days of the festival emphasize the values of unity, self-determination, collective work and responsibility, cooperative economics, purpose, creativity, and faith. [5]Kwanzaa begins on december 26 and ends on New Year's Day, with a festival feast on December 31. [6]Some people celebrate the festival by exchanging gifts, while others emphasize its african origins of the festival through traditional dress.

1. The following sentences contain errors: _____, _____, _____.

2. How many times is the word *festival* used? _____.

3. What are some words or expressions the writer could use in place of *festival?* _____.

EXERCISE 3 Reading a Paragraph Backwards

Read this paragraph backwards, and focus on looking for spelling errors. Write the number of the sentences containing errors and the correct spellings of the words in the blanks after the paragraph. There are five errors in all.

Celebrate St. Patrick's Day

[1]One holday celebrated in the United States is St. Patrick's Day. [2]Originating in Ireland, St. Patrick's Day honors St. Patrick, who supposedly rid Ireland of snaks. [3]On March 17, people are supposed to whear green and pinch those who don't wear it. [4]The wearing of green is in honor of "The Emerald Isle," Ireland, and the pinching represents the mouth of a snake. [5]Some people go a step ferther than just wearing green. [6]The city of Chicago, for instance, dyes its river green in honor of St. Patrick's Day. [7]Other people celebrate by marching in parades and lissening to Irish music. [8]Last of all, some people spend the day drinking green beer to toast "St. Paddy," as St. Patrick is sometimes called.

1. The following sentences contain errors: _____, _____, _____, _____, _____.

2. The following words are mispelled: _____, _____, _____, _____, _____.

WRITING PRACTICE 1 Write Your Own Paragraph

This chapter gave you some information on holidays that you might not celebrate or might not have known much about. Your assignment is this: *Write a paragraph about your most or least favorite holiday*.

Follow these steps to write your paragraph.

1. Use at least two prewriting techniques to come up with ideas for your paragraph.
2. Use your notes from prewriting to write a rough draft of your paragraph.
3. Revise your paragraph, reading through it to check for the first three of the four Cs: *concise, credible*, and *clear* writing.
4. Proofread your paragraph three times for grammar, punctuation, and spelling errors.

When you're finished, your paragraph should include the following:

- A clear topic sentence
- Support points that relate to the topic sentence
- Specific details that give proof of your support points
- Transitions that connect your support points and specific details

WRITING PRACTICE 2 Edit an Earlier Assignment and Make a List

Now that you've learned different error-finding techniques, put them to work on an earlier assignment. Your assignment is this: *Choose a paragraph, rough draft, or journal entry that you've already completed, and edit it according to the guidelines in this book*.

Be sure to do the following when you work on an assignment.

1. Read the assignment sentence by sentence.
2. Read the assignment word by word.
3. Read the assignment backwards.

When you finish, make a list of errors you found. Add to the list as the semester progresses. This list will help you avoid similar mistakes in future assignments.

CHAPTER SUMMARY

Remember to do the following when you edit your writing.

1. Read work several times to find different kinds of errors.
2. Read your work sentence by sentence for awkward wording as well as agreement or word choice errors.
3. Read your sentence word by word for repeated words as well as apostrophe and capitalization errors.
4. Read your paragraph backwards to find spelling errors.
5. Use a computer's spelling and grammar checking functions carefully, as computers cannot find and correct every error.

MyWritingLab & Lab Activity 6

mywritinglab   For additional practice with editing, go to **www.mywritinglab.com** or complete **Lab Activity 6** in the separate *Resources for Writers* Lab Manual.

7

Putting the Writing Process Steps Together

Culture Note

RUNNING

Though running has long been viewed as a punishing exercise, it has many psychological and physical benefits. As an athletic activity, running has its downside as well as its upside, from the pain of sore muscles to the runner's high.

THE WRITING PROCESS IN ACTION

Now that you have been through the writing process step by step, you'll find it helpful to see the process as a whole. This chapter will show you how a student, Sarah, worked through each stage of the writing process. Sarah's assignment was to write about an activity she *doesn't* enjoy. As she wrote her paragraph, Sarah referred to the "Writing Process Checklist" on the following page.

Step 1: Prewriting Activities

Sarah started her prewriting by doing some freewriting. Her sentence-level errors have been corrected for easier reading.

I hate to run. It makes me sweat, and it makes my muscles sore at first. It also gives me achy feet. Running makes me so hot and sweaty that

RECOMMENDED READINGS

"The Price We Pay," Adam Mayblum, *p. 794*

"The Santa Ana," Joan Didion, *p. 784*

"A Homemade Education," Malcolm X, *p. 714*

sometimes I think I can't ever be cool and clean again. My soccer coach makes us run when we show up to practice, and if we're late, we have to run extra laps. Running is punishment on our team. We have to run a lot only if we're in trouble. Running never feels good. People tell me about "runner's high," but I never feel good running. Running is the worst type of exercise I can do.

Writing Process Checklist

Step 1
Prewriting

____ Do I have enough material from my prewriting?
____ Do I need to try other prewriting techniques?
____ Do I need to talk to other people or do research?
____ Have I saved all my prewriting notes?

Step 2
Drafting

____ Have I identified a topic sentence?
____ Have I chosen support points from my prewriting?
____ have I chosen specific details from my prewriting?
____ Have I printed out my draft for revising?

Step 3
Revising

____ Have I removed details that don't support my topic sentence?
____ Do I need to develop more details to make my paragraph credible?
____ Have I made sure the support points are placed in logical order?
____ Have I added appropriate transitional words?
____ Have I printed out my draft for editing?

Step 4
Editing

____ Have I edited to make my paragraph smoother and more effective?
____ Have I proofread to catch sentence-level errors?

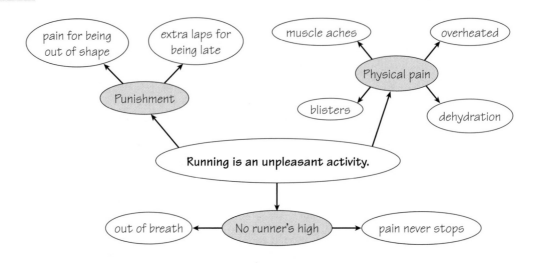

After this freewriting exercise, Sarah made a cluster diagram, shown above. She organized her ideas around the central concept of running as an unpleasant activity. Sarah's diagram includes ideas that will be her support points. She can add more specific details when she writes her rough draft.

Step 2: Drafting

Sarah now has a basic point that she wants to make: "Running is an unpleasant activity." She has also developed some support points and details. Notice that Sarah's draft contains a number of sentence-level errors, which is acceptable at this stage.

Running is an unpleasant activity. It's a painful and makes me physically sore. Every time I start running, i get sore muscles. Last soccer season, it took me two weeks before I didn't feel that my leg muscles were on fire every time I moved. I also get terrible blisters that never really went away until I stopped runing. Running is punishment. Except for our warm-ups, my soccer coach make us run only if we're in trouble for coming late to practice. Or not paying attention. He makes us run extra if we're not paying attention to him or if we do a drill wrong too many times. There is no "runner's high" for me. I've never had this feeling of "runner's high." I feel only pain when I run, and I feel only pain when I stop.

Step 3: Revising

Sarah's draft includes three support points: (1) running is painful, (2) running is punishment, and (3) there is no runner's high. It also has some good details. After taking a break, Sarah removed some unnecessary information, added extra information, and added transitional words. You'll notice that Sarah's revised draft still has some sentence-level errors.

Revised Draft

Transition added → Running is an unpleasant activity. ∧*First,* It's a painful ~~and makes me physically sore~~. Every time I start running, i get sore ← *Repetition removed* muscles. Last soccer season, it took me two weeks before I didn't feel that my leg muscles were on fire every time I moved. I also get terrible blisters that never really went away

Transition added → until I stopped runing. ∧*Second,* Running is punishment. Except for our warm-ups, ∧*and drills* my soccer coach make us run only if we're ← *Detail added* in trouble for coming late to practice. Or not paying attention. ~~He makes us run extra if we're not paying attention to~~ ← *Repetition removed* ~~him or if we do a drill wrong to many times.~~ ∧*Finally,* There is no ← *Transition added* "runner's high" for me. Ive heard that the body produces things

Detail added → called endorphins that make people feel really good when they run. Last year I ran for more than an hour waiting for the run to feel good, and it never did. ~~I've never had this feeling of "runner's~~ ~~high."~~ I feel only pain when I run, and I feel only pain when ← *Repetition removed* I stop.

Step 4: Editing

Sarah's revised draft has a clear topic sentence, support points, specific details, and transitional words. All that remains is for Sarah to edit a portion of her paragraph for smooth writing and proofread for sentence-level errors. Sarah's edited draft shows the errors she corrected.

Edited Draft

¶Running is an unpleasant activity. First, it's a painful. Every time I start

running, i get sore muscles. Last soccer season, it took me two weeks

before I didn't feel that my leg muscles were on fire every time I moved. I

also get terrible blisters that never really went away until I stopped runing.

Second, runing is punishment. Except for our warm-ups and drills, my

soccer coach make us run only if we're in trouble for coming late to

practice. Or not paying attention, or if we do a drill wrong to many times.

Finally, there is no "runner's high" for me. I've heard that the body

produces things called endorphins that make people feel really good

when they run. Last year I ran for more than an hour waiting for the run to

feel good, and it never did. I feel only pain when I run, and I feel only pain

when I stop.

HOW TO TELL WHAT COMES NEXT

Sometimes your initial freewriting or clustering may produce enough information for your whole paragraph. When this happens, you should feel free to move steps around or spend more time on one step and less on another if that's what your writing demands. Don't worry, though, if you don't have all the information you need right away. You may discover that you know more about your topic once you begin writing, or you may rediscover something you thought you couldn't use from your prewriting.

EXERCISE 1 Identifying the Next Writing Process Step

The writing samples below are at various stages of development. Choose the letter of the step that represents what the writer should do next.

1.   Runner's High

Running for exercise has many benefits. First of all, it allows me to be outside, not closed up in some gym or workout room. I get to see trees, flowers, and other people. Second, running gives me great results. I love how toned my legs get when I run regularly, and my stomach has even become more flat. People tell me that my skin seems to glow, too, maybe from improved circulation when I run. A third benefit of running is that I can eat anything I want and not gain weight. Running for just twenty-five minutes a day, four days a week, lets me eat until I'm full without worrying about whether my jeans will fit. It's great! Finally, runner's high makes running great all by itself. Even though sometimes I start my run feeling tired or achy, after a few minutes, I get the most wonderful rush. I've heard that the body releases endorphins, substances that take away physical pain and improve the mood. I believe it. When I feel the high, I don't feel any pain at all. I understand how people can get hooked on running!

The next step for the student is to

a. Write a draft.

d. Proofread and edit.

b. Revise to add detail.

e. Hand in the paragraph.

c. Revise for organization and transitional words.

2.

Questions	Answers
What results does running give?	Toned legs, flat stomach, good skin
How does running affect eating?	Eat whatever I want; clothes fit
How often should I run?	Twenty-five minutes, four days a week
What is runner's high?	Endorphin rush; pain leaves; mental lift

The next step for the student is to

a. Write a draft.

d. Proofread and edit.

b. Revise to add detail.

e. Hand in the paragraph.

c. Revise for organization and transitional words.

3. Running for exercise has many benefits. It allows me to be outside. Running gives me great results. I love how toned my legs get when I run regularly, and my stomach has become flat! I can eat what I want and not gain weight. Runner's high makes running great.

The next step for the student is to

a. Write a draft.

d. Proofread and edit.

b. Revise to add detail.

e. Hand in the paragraph.

c. Revise for organization and transitional words.

WRITING PRACTICE 1 Write Your Own Paragraph

People exercise in different ways. Some people, like the writers in this chapter, run to get in shape. Others, however, walk, swim, lift weights, play ball, ride bicycles, skate, or do any number of other activities. Your assignment is this: *Write a paragraph about an activity that you do to stay in shape.* If you don't do some type of formal exercise, then write about some other habit or activity.

Follow these steps to write your paragraph.

1. Use one or more prewriting techniques to come up with ideas.
2. Use your notes from prewriting to write a rough draft.
3. Revise your paragraph, reading through it to check for the first three of the four Cs: *concise, credible,* and *clear* writing.
4. Edit your paragraph for sentence effectiveness, word use, grammar, punctuation, and spelling.

When you're finished, your paragraph should include the following:

- A clear topic sentence
- Support points that relate to the topic sentence
- Specific details that give proof of your support points
- Transitions that connect your support points and specific details

WRITING PRACTICE 2 Write and Revise a Paragraph

In this chapter you've read about the challenges involved in running as a form of exercise. What many people don't think about, however, is how everyday activities such as doing laundry, carrying in groceries, or cleaning can also be forms of exercise.

Your assignment is this: *Write a paragraph about the activities in your life that contain "hidden" exercise.* For instance, you could write about the exercise you get in just attending school. Your topic sentence might be something like "Going to school at City College gives me some serious exercise." Your support points could be

- Walking to school (or even to class from the parking lot) gives you exercise.
- Carrying heavy books to and from classes tires your arms and back.
- Running to catch the bus (or grab the last sandwich in the cafeteria) works up a sweat.

Some other topics could be living on your own, taking care of a pet, fixing a meal for a group, or doing laundry.

Be sure to use prewriting, drafting, revising, and editing techniques. When you're finished, your paragraph should include the following:

- A clear topic sentence
- Support points that relate to the topic sentence
- Specific details that give proof of your support points
- Transitions that connect your support points and specific details

CHAPTER SUMMARY

The writing process involves four steps.

1. Use *prewriting* strategies to come up with ideas.
2. Use *drafting* techniques to begin to shape your ideas into a paragraph with a topic sentence and support points.
3. In *revising* your paragraph, move ideas around, make your language more specific, and check for connections between supporting ideas and your topic sentence.
4. In *editing*, use different methods to find and correct errors in your writing.

MyWritingLab & Lab Activity 7

mywritinglab | For additional practice with writing process steps, go to **www.mywritinglab. com** or complete **Lab Activity 7** in the separate *Resources for Writers* Lab Manual.

PART THREE
The Elements of Good Writing

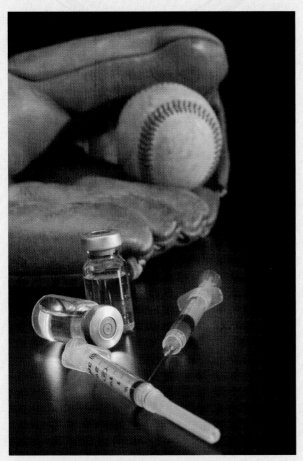

Steroids in Sports

CRITICAL THINKING Most people agree that using steroids is cheating, yet athletes continue to seek new ways to improve their performances such as swimmers wearing special swimsuits to decrease drag in water. At what point does a performance improving step—such as wearing a special suit—become cheating? Explain.

Responding to Images. Based on the positions and focus of the needles, bottles, mitt, and ball, what point do you think the photographer is trying to make? Explain.

109

Writing an Effective Topic Sentence

Culture Note

SCIENCE

Though studying physics or chemistry may seem to be of value only to people wishing to become scientists or astronauts, these subjects are an important part of our everyday lives. From the names of the planets in our solar system to the scientists who have shaped the way we think about our world, science helps us understand how and why the earth is, physically, as it is.

WHAT IS A GOOD TOPIC SENTENCE?

We've seen that the most important part of any paragraph is the **topic sentence,** which expresses the main idea. If your topic sentence is strong, you will easily find support points and specific details that offer proof for it. The result will be a concise paragraph—unified and coherent. Remember: Everything you write in your paragraph should start with and return to the topic sentence.

GUIDELINES FOR WRITING AN EFFECTIVE TOPIC SENTENCE

In academic writing, topic sentences can be long or short, and they can appear anywhere in a paragraph. This text, however, will encourage you to place your topic sentence first in your paragraph. The following simple

RECOMMENDED READINGS

"The Plot Against People," Russell Baker, *p. 779*

"Education," E. B. White, *p. 727*

"A Homemade Education," Malcolm X, *p. 714*

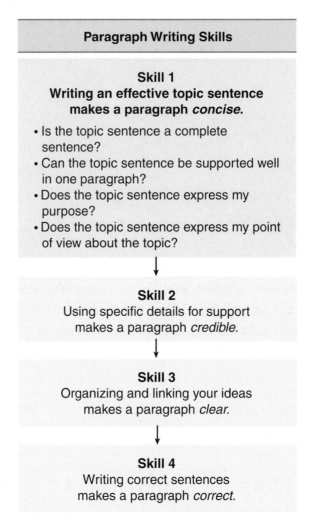

Paragraph Writing Skills

Skill 1
Writing an effective topic sentence
makes a paragraph *concise*.

- Is the topic sentence a complete sentence?
- Can the topic sentence be supported well in one paragraph?
- Does the topic sentence express my purpose?
- Does the topic sentence express my point of view about the topic?

Skill 2
Using specific details for support makes a paragraph *credible*.

Skill 3
Organizing and linking your ideas makes a paragraph *clear*.

Skill 4
Writing correct sentences makes a paragraph *correct*.

guidelines will help you craft an effective topic sentence that will help make a paragraph concise. (See the "Paragraph Writing Skills" illustration above for questions to help you evaluate your own topic sentences.)

Choose a Topic You Care About

Caring about your topic is the single most important rule you can follow in writing. If you choose a topic that does not interest you, you'll have a hard time coming up with enough support points and specific details to write a well-developed paragraph. Therefore, once your instructor has assigned a general topic, narrow it to something that interests you.

General Topic	**Narrowed Topic**
Frightening movies	*Psycho*
Contagious diseases	AIDS

EXERCISE 1 Narrowing Your Topic

Write a narrowed topic for each general topic below. An example is done for you.

General topic: ___A person you admire___

Narrowed topic: ___My father___

1. General topic: Food you don't like

Narrowed topic: _____

2. General topic: Do-it-yourself home repairs

Narrowed topic: _____

3. General topic: Cooking

Narrowed topic: _____

4. General topic: Ways to relax

Narrowed topic: _____

5. General topic: Public transportation

Narrowed topic: _____

Let Your Topic Sentence Develop Slowly

Don't feel compelled to write a perfect topic sentence on the first try. Instead, do some prewriting and see what ideas seem dominant. Don't feel as if you have to include everything. Chances are, the ideas that you really want to explore will emerge as the strongest in your freewriting, listing, questioning, clustering, or outlining in your journal. Other details can be saved for later or simply discarded as you write your rough draft.

Our Solar System

SURF THE NET Our galaxy has been the source of speculation and study for centuries. Surf the internet for information about the Milky Way or any of the planets (Mercury, Venus, Earth, Mars, Jupiter, Saturn, Uranus, Neptune, Pluto).

Responding to Images. *What terms best describe the mood or feeling—mysterious, silent, dangerous, for example—of the photo at left? Explain.*

Theo's assignment was to write about a subject he would like to know more about. He began by freewriting.

There's so much I'd like to know more about. Where do I start? I guess I'd really like to understand science and space. I've always wanted to be a pilot, so maybe learning about these areas can help me get started. I probably need to know about weather and other things if I'm going to learn how to fly a plane. I've heard that flying a plane isn't too hard but that getting to be a pilot can be challenging. That's what I'd like to learn about, though.

In this freewriting sample, Theo begins by writing that he'd like to learn more about science and space. Very quickly, however, Theo discovers what he's really interested in: becoming a pilot. Right there, Theo has found the subject that his paragraph will address. The idea "getting to be a pilot can be challenging" could very well be the main idea that he puts in his topic sentence.

Making Sure Your Topic Sentence Is a Sentence

After you have an idea that interests you, make sure to state this idea in the form of a complete sentence, not just a phrase. A **sentence** communicates a complete thought. The phrase "having a job while I was in high school" doesn't tell your readers whether you enjoyed your job in high school or hated it. If you write "Having a job while I was in high school made my life stressful," your readers will know exactly what you're going to describe to them. The following examples show how phrases can be turned into sentences.

Phrases	Sentences
Learning to become a pilot	Learning to become a pilot is a difficult process.
Children having children	Having a child before you're an adult yourself can be a huge challenge.
Getting a college degree	Earning a college degree gave my dad options.

Making Sure Your Topic Sentence Is Not Too Broad

Sometimes, having too many possibilities for development can be a problem. In a single paragraph, you should use three or four support points with specific details. If you need more examples than that to develop your idea, you should narrow your topic sentence. The following topic sentence is too broad.

Too broad: Many scientists know many things.

While you could find numerous examples to support this topic sentence, you'd have a hard time covering even a fraction of the "many" scientists it mentions. A narrowed topic sentence would work better.

Effective: Sir Isaac Newton made important contributions to the study of gravity.

Too Broad	Effective
Employment is a huge problem.	Finding a job has been hard for me.
School is important.	An education gave me career choices.

EXERCISE 2 Recognizing Overly Broad Topic Sentences

In the space before each sentence write "Too broad" if the topic sentence is too broad, or write "Good" if the topic sentence is effective.

1. _____   Many scientists have contributed much to their fields of study.

2. _____   The physicist Robert J. Oppenheimer made important contributions to atomic research.

3. _____   Scientists understand a lot about the world.

4. _____   Ancient Greek scientists were highly intelligent.

5. _____   The Greek scientist Archimedes made great advances in his studies of buoyancy.

Making Sure Your Topic Sentence Is Not Too Narrow

One danger of writing about a subject you care about is focusing too closely on one aspect of that subject. For instance, if your topic is ways your sister used to annoy you, the topic sentence "My older sister used to put soap on my toothbrush" is too narrow. While the sentence might be used as a specific detail, as a topic sentence it doesn't give you much to talk about.

A topic sentence such as "My older sister was mean" raises the questions "How was she mean?" "How often was she mean?" "In what ways was she mean?" and "Why was she mean?" You won't answer all of these questions in one paragraph, but you get to choose which ones you want to answer. This topic gives you something to argue, and it also gives you room to offer examples of how your sister was mean.

In each example below, a topic sentence that is too narrow has been broadened to allow room for the writer to add support points and specific details to develop a paragraph.

Too Narrow	Effective
I didn't get hired at the medical center.	Getting a job at the medical center is difficult.
My parents got a divorce.	People get divorced for many reasons.
My uncle, a truck driver, had an accident.	Working as a long-distance trucker can be hazardous.

A different kind of narrow topic sentence is one that leads nowhere. Watch out for topic sentences that just state what the paragraph will be about, like this one: "This paragraph will be about the scientist Benjamin Banneker." The topic may interest you, but this topic sentence does not give a way to develop a whole paragraph. The following examples show how simple statements can become effective topic sentences.

Simple Statement	**Effective Topic Sentence**
The importance of Marie Curie is the subject of this paragraph.	Marie Curie made major contributions to science.
The contributions of the ancient Greek scientist Archimedes will be discussed in this paragraph.	The ancient Greek scientist Archimedes made important discoveries about water density and volume.

EXERCISE 3   Recognizing Overly Narrow Topic Sentences

In the space before each sentence, write "Too narrow" if the topic sentence is too narrow, or write "Good" if the topic sentence is effective.

1. _____ Marie Curie was the only scientist to win a Nobel Prize in both physics and chemistry.

2. _____ Marie Curie was an important scientist.

3. _____ Benjamin Banneker taught himself to do calculus.

4. _____ Robert J. Oppenheimer is known for his work on developing the atomic bomb.

5. _____ Sir Isaac Newton was an English scientist.

Making Sure Your Topic Sentence Expresses Your Purpose

One of the purposes of writing is to inform, so you could write a paragraph informing the reader about *how* your sister sneakily put soap on your toothbrush. However, your usual purpose in writing an academic paragraph will be to persuade your audience. So in this book, we'll focus on writing topic sentences for persuasive paragraphs. Thus, your topic sentences needs to suggest that you intend to offer persuasive points—not just factual details—throughout your paragraph. Consider, for example, the following topic sentence.

Benjamin Banneker was an African-American scientist.

This topic sentence could work well as the topic sentence of an informative paragraph, but it doesn't allow for much development or discussion in a persuasive paragraph.

For an academic paragraph, a more effective topic sentence would be the following:

The African-American scientist Benjamin Banneker accomplished much in his life.

Now you not only have a topic for discussion—Benjamin Banneker— but you also have room to expand your ideas to include explanations of what his many accomplishments were.

A persuasive topic sentence (1) expresses an attitude or belief, (2) draws a conclusion, or (3) makes a recommendation. The following examples show how an informational topic sentence can be changed into a persuasive one.

Informational	**Persuasive**
Ice cream is one kind of dessert.	Ice cream makes a great dessert. (The phrase *makes a great dessert* expresses an attitude.)
Many high school students have jobs.	Having a part-time job in high school can interfere with schoolwork. (The phrase *can interfere with schoolwork* draws a conclusion for the paragraph to prove.)

EXERCISE 4 Identifying Informational and Persuasive Topic Sentences

In the blank before each sentence, write "Informational" if the topic sentence expresses the purpose of informing, or write "Persuasive" if the topic sentence suggests that the paragraph's purpose is to persuade.

1. _____ Follow these steps to download music.

2. _____ Living in this city has been an exciting and educational experience.

3. _____ Undergraduates should be required to take two semesters of science to get a degree.

4. _____ Traveling around Mexico this summer was fun.

5. _____ Playing in a band has been a gratifying experience.

Making Sure Your Topic Sentence Is Complete

One way to make sure your topic sentence is neither too broad nor too narrow is to check for two components: your *topic* and your *point of view*. These two parts work together to create an effective topic sentence. Your subject for discussion is your topic, and what you think of that subject is your **point of view** about it.

For instance, this topic sentence lacks a point of view: "Science is not well known." The subject matter—science—is clear, but what the writer thinks about science is not. Does the writer want to write about the ways that people know little about science, why people know little about science, or even the effects of people knowing little about science? Doing even one of these is a huge task for a single paragraph, but doing all of them well is nearly impossible. The incomplete topic sentence leads, in this case, to too many choices.

An easy way to complete your topic sentence—and, thus, make it more manageable—is to include a word or phrase that says what's important or what you think about your narrowed topic. This word or phrase is easy to spot because it is the part of the topic sentence that communicates the writer's point of view about the narrowed topic.

The topic sentence "Science affects people's lives in many important ways" is complete. The reader can tell both what the *narrowed topic* is (science) and what the *writer's point of view* about the topic is (that science affects people's lives).

The topic sentences below are complete because they contain both a narrowed topic and the writer's point of view.

Narrowed Topic	Point of View
Finding a job	has been hard for me.
An education	gave me options.
My friend Dolly	has a stressful job.
Getting a job at the medical center	is difficult.
Working as a long-distance trucker	can be hazardous.

EXERCISE 5 Identifying Parts of the Topic Sentence

In the topic sentences below, circle the topic and underline the word or phrase that gives the writer's point of view. An example is done for you.

(Albert Einstein's studies) have had a huge impact on our lives.

1. The French scientist Marie Curie made major contributions to physics and chemistry.

2. The scientific method helps scientists study our world.

3. The physicist Robert J. Oppenheimer made large advances in atomic research.

4. The calorie is a measurement with important uses in both science and daily life.

5. The Greek scientist Archimedes made great advances in his studies of buoyancy.

6. The Italian scientist Galileo Galilei suffered as a result of his studies.

7. Geometry, the branch of math dealing with points and lines, helps us makes sense of our world.

8. The first nuclear reactor would not exist without the work of Italian-born scientist Enrico Fermi.

9. The metric system is more logical than the English system of measurement, which is still used in the United States.

10. Memorizing the periodic table of elements can have many benefits.

11. The names of the planets in our solar system have interesting origins.

12. Studying science can have many benefits.

13. Learning about science can teach people about other subjects.

14. Science is an important part of history.

15. Scientists have paid great prices for their discoveries.

Making Your Topic Sentence the First Sentence of Your Paragraph

Placing your topic sentence first in your paragraph helps you in two ways. First, it gives you a consistent reference point to make sure you're on target with your support points and specific details. Second, it gives your reader an immediate idea of what your paragraph will be about.

Once you've become a more experienced writer, you can put the topic sentence anywhere you like—even as the last sentence in your paragraph. While you're gaining confidence in your writing through your progress in this text, however, place your topic sentence first.

 CHECKLIST Does Your Topic Sentence Give Your Point of View?

- Does your topic sentence include words that express an attitude or a belief?

  Examples   Writing a paragraph is *hard* work.

                    Cats are *easy* to care for as pets.

- Does your topic sentence include words that draw a conclusion?

  Example   My coach *helped* me make the most of my talent.

- Does your topic sentence include words that make a recommendation?

  Example   Marriage *should be* a short-term contract, not a lifetime commitment.

- Would the opposite of your topic sentence also make sense?

  Examples   Writing a paragraph is *not* hard work.

                    Cats are *not* easy to care for as pets.

                    My coach did *not* help me make the most of my talent.

                    Marriage should *not* be a short-term contract, but a lifetime commitment.

EXERCISE 6 Using Point-of-View Words or Phrases to Write a Topic Sentence

Choose five narrowed topics from the list on the next page. Then, write a word or phrase that offers your point of view about that narrowed topic. Finally, write a topic sentence using both the narrowed topic and the point-of-view words that you chose. An example is done for you.

Narrowed Topics

Spicy food	Learning another language
Video games	Hip-hop music
The benefits of exercise	Taking dance lessons
Taking care of a puppy	Deciding to buy a car
Reality television shows	Doing good deeds

Topic: _Taking care of a puppy_

Point-of-view words: _Exhausting_

Topic sentence: _Taking care of a puppy is exhausting._

1. Topic: _____

Point-of-view words: _____

Topic sentence: _____

2. Topic: _____

Point-of-view words: _____

Topic sentence: _____

3. Topic: _____

Point-of-view words: _____

Topic sentence: _____

4. Topic: _____

Point-of-view words: _____

Topic sentence: _____

5. Topic: _____

Point-of-view words: _____

Topic sentence: _____

EXERCISE 7 Identifying the Topic Sentence in a Paragraph

The following sentence groups contain the elements of a good paragraph: topic sentence, support points, and specific details. However, the topic sentence is not in the same place in both groups. Read each sentence group, and underline the topic sentence. Then fill in the blank that follows.

A.   Suffering in Science

[1]The scientist Antoine Lavoisier was beheaded during the French Revolution because the revolutionaries claimed France had "no need of scientists." [2]The American physicist Robert J. Oppenheimer lost his government security clearance because of his opposition to building of the hydrogen bomb. [3]Many scientists suffered as a result of their scientific interests. [4]The Roman Catholic Church forced Galileo Galilei to deny his belief that the earth revolved around the sun.

The topic sentence is sentence _____.

B.   Helpful Inventions

[1]In inventing the light bulb, Thomas Edison enabled us to have light at all hours, not just when the sun shines. [2]Many inventions have made our lives easier and more enjoyable. [3]Alexander Graham Bell invented the telephone, which lets us talk to people who are miles away. [4]The wireless telegraph, which was invented by Guglielmo Marconi, led to the creation of commercial radio.

The topic sentence is sentence _____.

Telegraph Machine

JOURNAL ENTRY Guglielmo Marconi's telegraph machine revolutionized the way people communicate. Write a few sentences explaining the ways–phone, email, post-it note–that you use most often to connect with other people. ***Responding to Images.*** *How easy do you think communication would be using the machine in the photo at left? Explain.*

C.   Smaller and Smaller

¹We can't see molecules with our bare eyes, but they are made up of smaller units of matter called atoms. ²Atoms contain the smaller elements called protons, neutrons, and electrons. ³ Units of matter in science seem to get smaller and smaller, the closer you look. ⁴Though protons and neutrons seem very tiny, even they are partially made of particles called quarks.

The topic sentence is sentence _____.

EXERCISE 8 Writing Topic Sentences from Details

Below are lists of specific details that can serve as the proof for a writer's topic sentence. Write a topic sentence that you think best includes all the details.

1. Topic sentence: _____

Specific details **a.** The Red Planet, Mars, is named for the Roman god of war because red is the color of the blood shed in war.

    b. Saturn, called the most beautiful of the planets, gets its name from the Roman god of agriculture.

    c. The fifth major planet from the sun is named Jupiter after the ruler of the Roman gods.

    d. Pluto, the smallest major planet and the one farthest from the sun, is named for the Roman god of the underworld.

2. Topic sentence: _____

  Specific details: **a.** The Celsius scale designates zero as the temperature at which water freezes and 100 degrees as the temperature at which water boils.

    b. The standard temperature scale in scientific work, called the Kelvin scale, measures heat starting at 273 degrees below zero on the Celsius scale.

    c. The Fahrenheit scale measures water freezing at 32 degrees and water boiling at 212 degrees, but its units of measurement are smaller than those of the Celsius and Kelvin scales.

3. Topic sentence: _____

  Specific details: **a.** The element chlorine is widely used for cleaning and sterilization.

    b. Gold, whose chemical symbol is Au, is an element that is highly valued for its beauty.

    c. The element of iron is used to make steel and has many other uses in our lives.

    d. Oxygen, one of the most important elements for humans, allows us to breathe.

WRITING PRACTICE 1 Write Your Own Paragraph

This chapter has given you information on scientific topics. Besides science, many other subjects are important—and relevant—for people to study. Your assignment is this: *Write a paragraph about a subject that you would like to study or have enjoyed studying.* If no subject interests you, write about a subject that you would not like to study or have not enjoyed studying.

Follow these steps to write your paragraph.

1. Use one or more prewriting techniques to come up with ideas for your paragraph.
2. Write a topic sentence that includes a narrowed topic and point-of-view words.
3. Use your notes from prewriting to write a rough draft of your paragraph.
4. Revise your paragraph, reading through it to check for the first three of the four Cs: *concise, credible,* and *clear* writing.
5. Edit your paragraph for sentence effectiveness, word use, grammar, punctuation, and spelling.

When you're finished, your paragraph should include the following:

- A clear topic sentence
- Support points that relate to the topic sentence
- Specific details that give proof of your support points
- Transitions that connect your support points and specific details

WRITING PRACTICE 2 Write a Paragraph About a Useful Subject

Some subjects are necessary to learn and master for daily life. Knowing how to add and subtract, say, is essential to keeping track of earnings and taxes. What other subjects are necessary? Your assignment is this: *Write a paragraph explaining how a particular subject—English, sewing, physical education, health, psychology, history, cooking, to name some—is important to know.* Your topic sentence may be something like this: "Knowing how to take care of my body, as I've learned in exercise classes, is important for many reasons."

Follow these steps to write your paragraph.

1. Use one or more prewriting techniques to come up with ideas for your paragraph.
2. Write a topic sentence that includes a narrowed topic and point-of-view words.
3. Use your notes from prewriting to write a rough draft of your paragraph.

4. Revise your paragraph, reading through it to check for the first three of the four Cs: *concise, credible,* and *clear* writing.

5. Edit your paragraph for sentence effectiveness, word use, grammar, punctuation, and spelling.

Your paragraph should include the following:

- A clear topic sentence
- Support points that relate to the topic sentence
- Specific details that give proof of your support points
- Transitions that connect your support points and specific details

CHAPTER SUMMARY

Remember the following when writing a topic sentence.

1. A topic sentence should control the direction of your paragraph.

2. A topic sentence should be broad enough to give you something to write about in an entire paragraph.

3. A topic sentence should have a narrowed topic, one that you can adequately cover in a paragraph.

4. A topic sentence should contain words that express your point of view.

MyWritingLab & Lab Activity 8

mywritinglab   For additional practice with topic sentences, go to **www.mywritinglab.com** or complete **Lab Activity 8** in the separate *Resources for Writers* Lab Manual.

9

Using Specific Examples for Support and Illustration

Culture Note

COFFEE

Though long a staple at breakfast and in boardrooms, coffee has become increasingly popular in the United States over the past few decades. A large number of coffee drinks, ranging from plain black coffee to more complicated concoctions such as café lattes and white mochas, have become a regular part of seemingly everyone's day. Coffee has also become more than just a morning habit. Nearby coffeehouses and vendors make before-work, after-lunch, and late-night coffee consumption common.

MAKING YOUR CASE

Even the most wonderful, clear topic sentences need help to be convincing. That's where specific details come in. Specific details make people believe you. If you offer proof to support your beliefs, your writing will be effective and professional. Using specific details in your writing helps you master the second of the four Cs: *credible* writing. The illustration "Paragraph Writing Skills" on page 129 shows how using specific details for support helps create an effective paragraph.

Three Types of Details

Evidence comes in many forms, and your specific details will come from different sources. Keep in mind that specific details should *add* information to support your points, not simply repeat the points. To find a broad range of information, use different types of proof. Three common types are described here.

Paragraph Writing Skills

Skill 1
Writing an effective topic sentence
makes a paragraph *concise.*

↓

Skill 2
**Using specific details for support
makes a paragraph *credible.***

- Are my specific details directly related to my topic sentence?
- Do my details give information that will persuade my reader?
- Have I told the reader the sources for my specific details?
- Are my sources reliable?
- Have I given enough specific details to be convincing?
- Have I used vivid, specific language that appeals to the senses?

↓

Skill 3
Organizing and linking your ideas
makes a paragraph *clear.*

↓

Skill 4
Writing correct sentences
makes a paragraph *correct.*

Descriptions of Objects or Events in Your Life

You have a ready-made source of information available to you: your own life. Your own experiences can serve as proof of your ideas, particularly when your experiences directly support your point.

CONDUCT AN INTERVIEW The U.S. imports millions of dollars in coffee grown in the South American countries of Brazil and Columbia. How far will people go for their coffee?
Responding to Images. *This map highlights the major South American coffee growing countries.*

For instance, Marty sent his friend the following e-mail message about a new coffeehouse that he liked.

> I love the Java Joint. The coffee is really good, and after working in the Cuppa Joe café for all those years, I know coffee. Plus, I love their selection. At Cuppa Joe, I always felt a little guilty offering customers only three coffee choices. At the Java Joint, they offer more than ten.

Marty establishes credibility by mentioning that he used to work in a coffeehouse. Thus, he has the knowledge and experience to evaluate coffee.

Accounts of Events in Other People's Lives

Sometimes the best way to learn is to listen. Your friends, family, co-workers, and classmates have likely shared experiences with you, and these experiences may have a place in your writing. For instance, if your assignment is to write about the pros or cons of having a sibling and you are an only child, talking to a friend who has brothers or sisters can be a big help. Sandy, who is an only child, wrote this about siblings.

> Having brothers is a real bonus. Even though I'm an only child, I've seen the benefits of having brothers through my best friend, Margie. Margie has three older brothers, and she always knows all the current sports facts from listening to them. She gets teased a lot, but she's learned to dish it out so that she can take an insult from anyone—and give one back—without blushing the way I do.

Sandy uses her friend's experiences to support her ideas. Even though she doesn't have firsthand experience, she offers proof to support her point.

Facts That You've Heard About or Read in Trusted Sources

Just as your friends have had experiences that you haven't shared, so have other people. Watching the news or reading a newspaper provides you with information that you might need to support your topic sentence. For instance, suppose your instructor asks you to write about the effects of a natural disaster. You might have a hard time if you've never experienced a hurricane, earthquake, or flood. However, reading about a hurricane in the Caribbean could give you information you can use in your writing.

Harry, who had never experienced a natural disaster, discussed an earthquake like this:

> Hurricanes are extremely destructive and do an incredible amount of damage. I read in the *San Francisco Chronicle* that hundreds of people were injured during Hurricane Katrina in 2005. The newspaper also explained how thousands of people were made homeless in the floods that came with the storm, and the New Orleans area, which was hit particularly hard, still hasn't completely recovered.

Possible Sources of Information

Documentary films   Reference books
Magazines   Television
Newspapers   Textbooks
Radio   Internet

When you're using information from experiences that are not your own, be sure to tell your reader where the information comes from. That way, your reader will not think you're trying to take credit for experiences you haven't had. Also, make sure that the source you use for support is credible. Stay away from unofficial documents that may not contain accurate information. See the box "Possible Sources of Information" above for a list of sources you can use.

Particularly on the Internet, make sure the sites you use as references are credible. Be especially careful of Web site addresses containing a tilde (~). This mark indicates that the site is operated by an individual, who could be anyone—including a child or a person playing online pranks. For more information on finding sources, see the chapter on Writing a Research Paper, which is online (www.ablongman.com/long).

KNOWING WHAT DETAILS TO CHOOSE

One of the most important aspects of using specific details is knowing *which* details to use. For instance, if your assignment is to write about a childhood friend, you probably won't find many helpful details in a newspaper. Similarly, if your assignment is to write about a local news issue, your childhood experiences won't do you much good. In choosing your specific details, then, *let your topic determine what kinds of details to use.* Remember: You can always find information—you just have to know where to look.

EXERCISE 1 Choosing Relevant Sources for Details

Below are possible topics for paragraphs. Decide what sources would be most helpful in finding details for a paragraph on that topic. Then write "My life," "Someone I know," or "Trusted sources" in the space after each topic. You may write more than one source for a topic. Two examples are done for you.

Benefits of owning a pet __My life_____

Hardships of homeless people __Trusted sources_____

1. Benefits of having strict parents _____

2. Downside to being a rebel _____

3. Hardships of moving around often _____

4. Success/failure of a professional athlete _____

5. Benefits/downside to taking vitamins _____

EXERCISE 2 Recognizing Credibility

The following two paragraphs address the topic of working in a coffeehouse. The writers of both paragraphs draw on their personal experiences to support their ideas. Which paragraph does a better job of credibly describing work in a coffeehouse?

The Coffee Job

[1]Working in a coffeehouse is a lot of work. [2]One part of the job that is a lot of work is making the coffee. [3]There is a lot of it to make, and it always needs to be made. [4]Making the coffee is a lot of work, too. [5]Another way that a coffeehouse job is a lot of work is in cleaning up. [6]The coffeehouse sure could get messy, and I'd have to clean it up. [7]It seemed like the cleaning never stopped. [8]Last of all, dealing with people is a lot of work. [9]I could never get used to dealing with so many people and in so many ways. [10]Just thinking about that job makes me tired.

Coffee, Anyone?

[1]Working in a coffeehouse is much more difficult than people realize. [2]First, there's so much information to keep track of. [3]Not only do you have to know many types of coffees from Brazilian to French Roast, but you also have to know all the different drinks that can be made from those coffees. [4]In my five years at the Coffee Cup, I must have made a hundred kinds of coffee drinks: espresso, latté, cappuccino, mocha, not to mention all the iced coffee drinks. [5]Thinking about all of those coffee mixtures makes my head spin. [6]In addition to learning all that information, you have a lot of hard work to do. [7]Of course, you have to make the coffee. [8]Then, there are all the tables and chairs to wipe down after sticky hands have touched them. [9]Plus, there are always dishes to do. [10]At the end of a workday, my hands would be raw from all the cleaning. [11]Finally, dealing with people is a challenge. [12]Some people are really easy to serve and just want black coffee. [13]Other people, though, have to have their coffee drinks made a different way every time. [14]One person who came to the coffeehouse loved to order a nonfat decaffeinated mocha, but then he'd have me put double whipped cream on it. [15]I never did remember every single order, but I did get better. [16]For me, a coffee break meant there was no coffee in sight.

It's easy to believe that the second paragraph, "Coffee, Anyone?" was written by someone who worked in a coffeehouse. The writer uses support points that allow the reader to understand why the job was difficult, and he then uses specific examples to *show* the reader what he means. In the first paragraph, "The Coffee Job," the writer offers very few details that let the reader see how difficult his job was. Instead, the writer simply repeats his ideas over and over, which does little to prove his point.

EXERCISE 3 Analyzing Specific Details in Paragraphs

Reread "The Coffee Job" on the previous page and "Coffee, Anyone?" on this page. Then fill in the blanks.

1. In sentence 4 in "Coffee, Anyone?" the writer explains that he

worked for _____ years at a coffeehouse called _____ .

2. Does the writer of "The Coffee Job" mention any specific

experience working in a coffeehouse? _____

3. Both paragraphs mention that cleaning is a big job in a coffee-house. Which paragraph offers more specific information about cleaning?

_____ "The Coffee Job"

_____ "Coffee, Anyone?"

4. By reading sentences 1 to 5 of "Coffee, Anyone?" you can tell that the writer knows something about coffee. List three specific details that tell you this.

a. _____

b. _____

c. _____

5. In "The Coffee Job," the writer would be more convincing if he offered more details in sentence 6. Write down one type of cleaning job that you think the writer could have used for proof.

_____

_____

WRITING VIVID DETAILS

In addition to proving your point, specific details make your writing more interesting. After all, would you want to read about a car when you could read about a gleaming, candy-apple red convertible? Use your words to paint a picture for your reader, and your reader will want to read on.

Additionally, vivid descriptions lend credibility to your writing. If you're writing about your fear of bees, for instance, but all you can say is "I'm afraid of bees," your reader can't *see* how afraid you are. If, instead, you write about your sweaty palms, pounding heart, and dizziness at the sight of a bee, your reader will most likely acknowledge your fear.

Use Words That Appeal to the Five Senses

The best way to help someone understand what you've experienced is to make your writing as close to a physical experience as possible. Using words that appeal to the **senses**—that help your reader see, hear, smell, taste, and feel what you're describing—will make your points more vivid for readers. Saying that your sweater is soft is a good start, but saying that your sweater is as soft as a kitten's fur is better. Your reader will immediately know that the sweater feels soft *and* just how soft it is.

General	Specific
The risotto was flavorful.	The risotto tasted as though twelve cloves of garlic had exploded in my mouth.
The waterfall was pretty.	Millions of crystal drops cascaded through the air, reflecting sunlight before foaming into the current below.

EXERCISE 4   Recognizing Writing That Appeals to the Senses

One of the two paragraphs below has specific details that support its topic sentence, while the other does not. Which paragraph uses specific details more effectively?

A Sense of Coffee

[1]A well-brewed cup of coffee provides a wonderful experience for all my senses. [2]First, before I even see the coffee, I can smell the aroma of specially blended Colombian coffee throughout the house. [3]It smells a little like the first campfire of the morning on a cold camping trip and reminds me of my grandmother's baking. [4]Then, still before I see the coffee, I can hear the "drip, sizzle, drip, sizzle, drip," sound that my brew makes as it drains from the water holder on my coffee machine into the coffeepot. [5]It's music to my ears. [6]The sight of fresh coffee, too, is glorious. [7]The rich brown color reminds me of deep forests or newly plowed soil just waiting to be planted with seeds. [8]Every image that comes to mind is of growing, living things, and the steam that floats up from the mug seems like a magic genie. [9]Then comes the feel. [10]I always pour it into my favorite huge mug so I can use both hands to pick it up. [11]The mug is always very warm, and on

cold mornings, the feel of the coffee mug is comforting. [12]Best of all is the taste. [13]Coffee tastes strong and gentle at the same time, like a chocolate cake made with butter. [14]Coffee also has a faint burned taste, maybe from the roasting of the coffee beans. [15]No matter how I come into contact with coffee, it's a treat.

The Coffee Experience

[1]Coffee really appeals to my senses. [2]The sight of coffee is unlike any other. [3]It just looks so inviting and delicious. [4]Then the smell of coffee is terrific, too. [5]Its smell always reminds me of so many things I like. [6]I never get tired of the smell! [7]Hearing coffee being brewed is great. [8]I can always imagine just what it sounds like, even if no coffee is being made right then. [9]Touching a coffee cup or mug makes me feel good. [10]Coffee makes me feel good even before I taste it, probably because I like the way it feels. [11]Finally, coffee tastes great. [12]It always tastes the same, but then it always tastes a little different, too. [13]I'll never forget my first cup of coffee. [14]It was great in every way.

The first paragraph, "A Sense of Coffee," uses vivid language to illustrate how coffee appeals to the writer's senses. As a result, a reader is more likely to enjoy the paragraph and also to believe that the writer knows what she's writing about. The second paragraph, "The Coffee Experience," has a clear topic sentence and is solidly organized, but it lacks detail. The reader is left wondering *what about* coffee is so "inviting and delicious," *why* it makes the writer "feel good," or *what about* coffee tastes "great."

EXERCISE 5 Analyzing Details That Appeal to the Senses

Reread "A Sense of Coffee" on pages 136–137. Then, fill in the blanks below.

1. In sentence 2, what is one type of coffee mentioned? _____

2. In sentence 3, the writer compares coffee's aroma to _____

_____ and _____

3. From sentences 12, 13, and 14 choose at least one detail that appeals to the reader's sense of taste.

_____

4. In sentence 7, the comparison of coffee's color to "newly plowed

soil" appeals to the sense of _____ .

5. One other detail from the paragraph that is effective is

_____ , and it appeals to the sense of _____ .

Use Descriptive Modifiers

Place **modifiers**—descriptive words—before nouns. Writing about a crystal-clear lake gives your reader a much better idea of what you saw than simply referring to a lake. If you're describing an action, modifiers help, too. Rather than writing that your friend was in a hurry, write that he immediately sped away from muggers.

General	Specific
Jen's fat cat moves slowly.	Jen's obese Manx moves more slowly than a snail.
The cookies made me hungry.	The warm butter cookies made my stomach growl and my mouth water.

Use Proper Names and Specific Nouns and Verbs

Often the details we use to support a point in writing could be more convincing if they were more specific. For instance, if you're writing about how fast a car is, you'll probably make your point better if you use a **proper name,** writing that the car is a Porsche or a Lamborghini. Also, instead of simply mentioning a man, write about Tran Ngyuen. Or if you're writing about your childhood bike, refer to your Trek mountain bike. Using proper names narrows your description dramatically.

Another way to make your ideas clear to your reader is to use **specific nouns.** Specific nouns offer your reader a clear view of what you are describing. The following list shows the difference between general nouns on the left and proper names and specific nouns on the right.

General Nouns	Proper Names and Specific Nouns
hairstyle	pony-tail, up-do, braid
meal	feast, breakfast, lunch, dinner
cat	Siamese, tabby, calico
sport	hockey, football, basketball, hunting

Using words that appeal to the senses, descriptive modifiers, and specific nouns and verbs can make the meaning of a sentence clear and powerful.

General Sentence	Specific Sentence
I ate a large meal.	I feasted on an elegant supper of caviar and salmon.
The song was moving.	I found myself in tears by the end of the ballad.
I want to take a trip.	I want to soak up the sun on Maui, Hawaii.
The girl on the show is good.	Felicity Huffman on the TV program *Desperate Housewives* is my hero.

EXERCISE 6 Writing Proper Names and Specific Nouns

The following list contains nouns that could be more specific. After each general detail, write a more specific version using proper names and specific nouns. An example is done for you.

dessert   *Chocolate mousse* _____

1. street   _____

2. flower   _____

3. college class   _____

4. rain   _____

5. toy   _____

Use Specific Verbs

Another way to make your language more vivid is to use **specific verbs.** Rather than write that you sang a song, write that you belted out the melody. Or, instead of saying that you relaxed, write that you sank into the couch like a cherry sinking into whipped cream. The more specific you can make your verbs, the better your reader will understand your meaning. Here are some examples.

General Verbs	Specific Verbs
sit	recline, perch, roost, lounge
spoke	whispered, muttered, yelled, screamed
hit	thrashed, punched, pummeled

EXERCISE 7 Writing Specific Verbs

The verbs in the following list could be more effective if they were more specific. In the space after each word, write a more specific verb (Example A) or the same verb with a modifier (Example B). The modifier can be either a word or a group of words.

Examples

A. write *Scrawl* _____

B. eat *Eat like a pig at a trough* _____

1. hum _____

2. walk _____

3. drive _____

4. watch _____

5. knock _____

EXERCISE 8 Writing Specific Sentences

The sentences in the following list are not very specific. Rewrite them using specific words in order to make them clearer. An example is done for you.

It was a hot day. *The sun beat down, making the asphalt shimmer in waves*

of heat. _____

1. The restaurant was dirty.

_____

_____

2. The instructor acted mean on the first day of class.

_____

_____

3. The movie had violent parts.

_____

_____

4. I hurt my hand.

_____

_____

5. Her hair looked nice.

_____

_____

6. The song sounded wonderful.

_____

_____

7. The cheese tasted terrible.

_____

_____

8. Sam helped me at home.

_____

_____

9. Jonquil treated her friend nicely.

_____

_____

10. The refrigerator needed cleaning.

_____

_____

WRITING PRACTICE 1   Write Your Own Paragraph

This chapter has given you opportunities to practice writing specific sentences. Now, you can practice turning those details into a paragraph. Your assignment is this: *Choose a topic from the following list and write a fully developed paragraph.* Concentrate on making your details as specific as possible, and use language that *shows* your reader what you mean.

Topics

Dirty restaurants	Car accidents	Exciting music
Sports injuries	Informative Internet sites	Wild clothing
Helpful friends	Relaxing weekend spots	Delicious meals

Follow these steps to write your paragraph.

1. Use one or more prewriting techniques to come up with ideas.
2. Use your notes from prewriting to write a rough draft.
3. Include details from your life, from other people's lives, or from trusted sources. Include language that appeals to the five senses.
4. Revise your paragraph, reading through it to check for the first three of the four Cs: *concise, credible*, and *clear* writing.
5. Edit your paragraph for sentence effectiveness, word choice, grammar, punctuation, and spelling.

When you're finished, your paragraph should include the following:

- A clear topic sentence
- Support points that relate to the topic sentence
- Specific details that give proof of your support points
- Transitions that connect your support points and specific details

WRITING PRACTICE 2   Write About an Extreme Situation

Oftentimes we feel most strongly when a situation is out of our everyday experiences. Getting sick, getting hired or fired, ending a relationship: these are all situations that lend themselves to powerful feelings. What types of experiences do you experience most intensely? Your assignment is this: *Write a paragraph describing a situation that caused you to feel strongly*. The feelings can be positive or negative; just be sure to use specific details to illustrate your ideas. A possible topic sentence might be something like "When Charlene broke up with me, my whole body hurt."

Follow these steps to write your paragraph.

1. Use one or more prewriting techniques to come up with ideas.
2. Use your notes from prewriting to write a rough draft.
3. Include details from your life. *Note:* Details from other people's lives and from trusted sources will not be as relevant for this assignment.
4. Revise your paragraph, reading through it to check for the first three of the four Cs: *concise, credible*, and *clear* writing.
5. Edit your paragraph for sentence effectiveness, word choice, grammar, punctuation, and spelling.

When you're finished, your paragraph should include the following:

- A clear topic sentence
- Support points that relate to the topic sentence
- Specific details that give proof of your support points
- Transitions that connect your support points and specific details

CHAPTER SUMMARY

To be *credible*, the second of the four Cs, remember to be specific. Specific details can come from a number of sources.

1. Descriptions of objects or events in your life
2. Accounts of events in other people's lives
3. Facts that you've heard or read about in trusted sources

Make sure your language is vivid and appeals to the five senses: sight, smell, taste, touch, and hearing.

MyWritingLab & Lab Activity 9

mywritinglab   For additional practice with using specific details, go to **www.mywritinglab. com** or complete **Lab Activity 9** in the separate *Resources for Writers* Lab Manual.

Organizing and Linking Your Ideas

Culture Note

INFLUENTIAL MUSICAL ENTERTAINERS, 1930–1960

Though many musicians and singers have made a difference in the way popular music has developed, some have had more influence than others. From 1930 to 1960, music in the United States changed considerably. Key musical entertainers from these years—including Benny Goodman, Ella Fitzgerald, Frank Sinatra, and Elvis Presley—had distinct styles, but each had a huge impact on popular music.

ARRANGING THE PIECES

As you've been reading examples of effective writing in this book, you've seen that the way ideas are put together is important to make the writing clear. Additionally, you've seen how transition words link ideas together, creating connections between the topic sentence, support points, and specific details. The illustration "Paragraph Writing Skills" on page 146 shows how the skill of organizing and linking your ideas helps create an effective paragraph.

ORGANIZING FOR CLARITY

When we hear someone say, "You're really great, but . . . ," we immediately know that bad news is coming. How do we know? We know because *but* is one of those words that signals a change of direction. It's one of

RECOMMENDED READINGS

"'Blaxicans' and Other Reinvented Americans," Richard Rodriguez, *p. 738*

"Working with Difficult People," Constance Faye Mudore, *p. 788*

Paragraph Writing Skills

Skill 1
Writing an effective topic sentence
makes a paragraph *concise.*

↓

Skill 2
Using specific details for support
makes a paragraph *credible.*

↓

Skill 3
Organizing and linking your ideas
makes a paragraph *clear.*

- Have I organized my ideas?
- Have I used time sequence for examples that have a specific period or for items that occur step by step?
- Have I used emphatic order to emphasize my most important point?
- Have I used transitional words and terms to link my ideas?
- Have I linked my ideas by repeating key words, using pronouns, and using synonyms?

↓

Skill 4
Writing correct sentences
makes a paragraph *correct.*

---

many transitional words that helps us show the direction we're going in our writing.

Coming up with a solid topic sentence and finding the details to support it are essential writing skills. Next, you need to practice organizing your ideas so that your reader will know just which ones are most important to you. You also need to link your ideas. Transitions help your reader understand when you're adding to a point, changing directions, or finishing up. Putting your ideas in a logical order and using transitional words to make your order clear will help you master the third of the four Cs: *clear* writing.

TWO TYPES OF ORDER

You can organize your ideas in two ways.

- Time sequence (chronological) order
- Emphatic order

Time Sequence Order

Using **time sequence (chronological) order** means organizing events in the order in which they happened. The time sequence method is especially helpful when you use examples that occur over a specific period. Time sequence is also useful for paragraphs explaining how something happened or for anything that must be explained in a series of steps. The following paragraph uses time sequence.

Ol' Blue Eyes

Known for his blue eyes and his smooth voice, the singer Frank Sinatra appealed to many audiences. In the big-band years of the 1940s, Sinatra appealed to bobby-soxers, or teenage girls, who at that time wore bobby socks. Young women screamed and fainted when he sang his hit song "This Love of Mine." In the 1950s Sinatra's career almost ended because of damage to his vocal cords, but he continued to be popular. Even when rock and roll started to dominate popular music, Sinatra's album *Songs for Swingin' Lovers* stayed on the music charts for more than a year. In the 1960s, his albums *Nice and Easy* and *Strangers in the Night* were number one hits, and he was successful singing in Las Vegas. These were the years when the "Rat Pack"—Sinatra's group of friends that included the stars Sammy Davis, Jr., and Dean Martin—was most famous. During the 1970s and 1980s, Sinatra's reputation still grew, but he performed less. In 1990, Sinatra celebrated his seventy-fifth birthday with a national tour even though his voice had faded somewhat. For all his accomplishments, Sinatra received the Legend Award at the 1994 Grammy Awards in New York. Even after his death in 1998, Frank Sinatra is loved all over the world.

EXERCISE 1 Recognizing Time Sequence Order

Reread "Ol' Blue Eyes." Then, answer the following questions.

1. The writer of "Ol' Blue Eyes" uses time, as in "the 1940s," to indicate the start of new support points. Besides "the 1940s," what six other signals does the writer use to let you know that the examples in the paragraph are organized according to time sequence?

a. _____   d. _____

b. _____   e. _____

c. _____   f. _____

2. Circle the letters of all of the following statements that are true.

a. Time sequence order shows that Sinatra had a long career.

b. Time sequence order shows some of the changes in Sinatra's audience over the years.

c. Time sequence order tells the reader which is Sinatra's most important audience.

d. Time sequence order emphasizes Sinatra's most famous songs.

Emphatic Order

Emphatic order means putting your ideas in order of *least* important to *most* important. Emphatic order allows for more flexibility than time sequence order because the writer gets to decide the importance of each point. That is, two people could organize the same subject matter differently—using emphatic order—because they see different points as being more or less important. The following paragraph is organized using emphatic order.

The King

FOOD FOR THOUGHT The first music star to blend overt sexuality into his music, Elvis wowed crowds of swooning admirers. How important is sex appeal in making singers popular? Write a few sentences explaining the importance of sex appeal in singers' popularity.

Responding to Images. *In what ways might Elvis's style as depicted in the photo at left be considered sexy or suggestive?*

Long Live the King!

Elvis Presley brought many changes to rock and roll music. First, his looks were different from those of traditional popular singers. He wore his black hair long and swept back off his face instead of short the way clean-cut young men did. He also wore tight pants and brightly colored shirts that were definitely not traditional. Second, Elvis's music had a sound all its own. Elvis combined parts of country music with rock and roll and blues. Some of his most popular songs were "Love Me Tender," "Hound Dog," and "Don't Be Cruel." Most important, Elvis made sex appeal part of his show. Instead of just standing behind his guitar and singing, Elvis moved his hips to his own rhythm. While girls in the audience swooned, other people were shocked. In fact, when Elvis first appeared on television in the 1950s, he was shown only from the waist up because his lower-body movements were considered too suggestive. With his looks, music, and sex appeal, the King changed rock and roll forever.

This writer organizes her ideas beginning with the point that is least important to her topic sentence and ending with the one that is most important. However, while *this* writer thinks that Elvis's sex appeal marked his greatest impact on rock and roll, another writer might think that Elvis's music or looks had the greatest impact.

As the writer, you rank the support points. Just be sure that your transition words and examples make clear why you've placed your support points in the order you have.

EXERCISE 2 Recognizing Emphatic Order

Reread "Long Live the King!" Then, answer the following questions.

1. What is the writer's topic sentence? _____

_____

2. What is the writer's first point? _____

_____

3. What is the second point the writer makes? _____

_____

4. What is the writer's most important point? _____

_____

5. Do you agree with the writer's idea about which point is the most important? Why or why not? _____

_____

USING TRANSITIONS

Transitions are words and expressions that organize and connect ideas. They can be placed at the beginning, middle, or end of a sentence. In the following examples, the transitions are in bold type.

To play piano well, you need to take lessons. Lessons alone, **however,** won't make you a great pianist. You have to have talent and perseverance, **too.**

To learn a new song, I read through the music **first,** humming the notes. **Next,** I pick out the notes and chords on my guitar. **Finally,** I practice playing the song over and over.

EXERCISE 3 Recognizing Transitions in Context

The paragraph below uses transitions to organize and connect ideas.

The Twist's Turn

The song called "The Twist" sung by Ernest Evans, popularly known as Chubby Checker, and the dance that went with it had a huge impact on American culture. First, the dance version of the twist revolutionized the way Americans danced. It allowed couples to break apart on the dance floor while still dancing together. Once Checker's song was played on *Dick Clark's American Bandstand* in 1961, both the song and the dance became enormously popular. Second, the song "The Twist" set a new standard for popularity in music. Once "The Twist" reached the number one spot on the *Billboard* chart in August 1961, it stayed there for eighteen straight weeks. In November of that year it reentered the charts for another twenty-one weeks. "The Twist" became the first single to appear in the number one spot in two different years. Finally, "The Twist" made its mark in advertising. In the early 1990s, for example, Nabisco borrowed the twist concept in its marketing of the Oreo cookie. Advertisements for Oreo cookies that featured Chubby Checker twisting a cookie resulted in one of the company's most successful advertising campaigns ever. Although many songs and dances have risen to popularity, few rival the twist in influence.

In "The Twist's Turn," what transitions introduce the three support points?

1. _____

2. _____

3. _____

Transitions can link ideas in several ways.

Time and time sequence:	**Later** he sang another song.
Emphatic order:	**Most importantly,** she was an exciting performer.
Addition:	They recorded the song **again.**
Space:	The recording studio is **nearby, opposite** the practice room.
Examples:	The bass is **one example of** a stringed instrument.
Change of direction:	That singer is good, **but I still** prefer Elvis.
Conclusion:	I practiced this song night and day. **As a result,** I can play it by heart.

The box on this page and the next gives lists of transition words and terms. Become familiar with these words, and use them in your own writing.

Transition Words and Terms

Words That Signal Time and Time Sequence Order

after	finally	shortly afterward
at last	first, second, third	soon
at the same time	immediately	subsequently
before	later	then
during	meanwhile	when
earlier	next	while

Words and Terms That Signal Emphatic Order

above all	first	most important
another	in the first place	most significantly
equally important	last	next

especially   least of all
even more   most of all

Words and Terms That Signal Addition

additionally	for another thing	next
again	for one thing	second
also	furthermore	then
and	in addition	third
besides	last of all	too
first of all	moreover	

Words and Terms That Signal Space

above	here	opposite
across	in back of	there
before	in front of	to the east (north, etc.)
behind	nearby	to the left
below	next to	to the right
elsewhere	on the other side	

Words and Terms That Signal Examples

an illustration of	one example of	such as
for example	particularly	that is
for instance	specifically	

Words and Terms That Signal Change of Direction

although	in contrast	regardless
but	nevertheless	still
despite	on the contrary	though
even though	on the other hand	yet
however	otherwise	

Words and Terms That Signal Conclusion

as a result	in conclusion	then
consequently	in summary	therefore
finally	last	thus

EXERCISE 4 Choosing Effective Transitions

For each underlined pair of terms, circle the correct transition for the sentences. An example is done for you.

Doris Day was a popular singer, (and)/in conclusion she was a popular actress as well.

1. The famous singer was born Doris Mary Anne von Kappelhoff, <u>finally/but</u> she changed her name to Doris Day.

2. <u>Although/In addition</u> Day first began training to be a professional dancer, a life-threatening accident prevented her from pursuing her dancing dreams.

3. <u>Finally/Instead</u>, Day began singing during her recuperation from her accident.

4. Some of her most famous hit songs are "Sentimental Journey" <u>and/last</u> "Que Sera Sera."

5. As a film star, Day made her mark playing spunky, all-American characters; <u>thus/for instance,</u> her character in *Pillow Talk* is a decorator who tries to fend off a womanizer.

6. The public believed that Day's charming, warm characters represented Day's own personality; <u>however/therefore,</u> Day's own life had its share of ups and downs.

7. <u>Alhough/Additionally,</u> Day was divorced twice early in her career, she seemed to find stability with Marty Melcher.

8. <u>Consequently/However,</u> when Melcher died in 1968, Day learned that he had left her bankrupt, and she had no prospects of work.

9. Day was awarded $22.8 million in 1974 when she won a lawsuit against her former attorney for mismanaging her affairs, <u>but/then</u> she eventually accepted $6 million.

10. In retirement from the entertainment industry, Day is a prominent activist for animal rights; <u>in fact/finally,</u> she set up her own animal rights foundation.

COMBINING ORGANIZING STRATEGIES

Sometimes your topic sentence will allow you to use both organizational strategies at the same time. For example, you can use time sequence order in your paragraph but still save the most important reason for last. Read the following paragraph to see how the two strategies can work together. The support points, arranged in emphatic order, are introduced by transitional expressions in bold type. The specific details for each support point appear in time sequence order; the transitions that introduce these are underlined.

One Good Man

The big-band leader Benny Goodman had an important effect on the music world. **First,** Goodman provided Depression-era people with fast, upbeat dance music. Goodman combined jazz with more traditional big-band sounds to make a new music for young people called swing. Even though other bandleaders started playing the same kind of music, Goodman soon became known as the King of Swing. **Second,** Goodman set a new standard for the way people played big-band music. Goodman played the clarinet, and he had excellent musical skill and style. Whenever anyone wanted to play in Goodman's band, Goodman made sure the new player also had excellent musical skills. **Most significantly,** Goodman broke through racial barriers. <u>Before the mid-1930s</u>, black and white musicians were not allowed to play on the same stage together. Benny Goodman, who was white, hired the African-American musicians Teddy Wilson and Lionel Hampton to play with his musicians. <u>Later</u>, the trumpet star Cootie Williams and the guitarist Charlie Christian, who were also African-American, became part of Goodman's band. <u>Soon</u> musicians of different races were commonly seen on stage together. After Benny Goodman entered the music scene, it was never the same again.

In this paragraph, these support points are organized in emphatic order: Goodman started playing swing music, Goodman set a new standard for musical skills, and Goodman broke through racial barriers. The paragraph places Benny Goodman's most significant effect on music last, and the writer tells us that the last point is the most important by using the term *most significantly* to lead into it.

Take a look, however, at the specific details given for the last support point. These are organized in time sequence (chronological) order. The transitions that introduce the details—"Before the mid-1930s," "Later," and "Soon"—signal the time sequence.

Ella Fitzgerald (1917–1996)

SURF THE NET Both as a singer with Chick Webb's band in the 1930s and as a soloist, Ella Fitzgerald distinguished herself as a great talent. Surf the Internet to learn about one musician mentioned in this chapter. Write a few sentences explaining what you learned about the musician you choose.

Responding to Images. *Based on the photo at left, how would you describe Ella Fitzgerald's style? Serious, elegant, relaxed, formal, content are some ideas to consider.*

EXERCISE 5 Practicing Putting Sentences in Order

The following groups of sentences make up short paragraphs. However, the sentences are out of order. Put the sentences in order by writing 1 in the space before the sentence that should come first (the topic sentence), 2 before the next sentence, and so forth.

1. a. _____ Next, she sang with Chick Webb's band.

　b. _____ The jazz singer Ella Fitzgerald accomplished much in her life.

　c. _____ Finally, she recorded many big hits, such as "A-Tisket, A-Tasket" and "Lady Be Good."

　d. _____ First, she won an amateur jazz singing contest at the Apollo theater in Harlem while she was still a teenager in 1934.

e. _____ Eventually, Fitzgerald managed Webb's band after he died in 1939.

2. a. _____ Most important, Bing Crosby was Frank Sinatra's inspiration. Sinatra heard Crosby sing in concert and decided to become a singer, too.

b. _____ Perhaps no singer has had a greater influence on popular singing than Bing Crosby.

c. _____ His biggest hit, "White Christmas," is still played often during the holidays.

d. _____ Crosby was originally known for his crooning, or low, sentimental singing.

3. a. _____ Calloway's orchestra also became famous when he broadcast its shows at the Cotton Club in Harlem over the radio during the 1930s and 1940s.

b. _____ For one, his jazz orchestra was known for being very creative in its music.

c. _____ Last, Calloway had many hit songs, including "Minnie the Moocher" and "Blues in the Night."

d. _____ The jazz singer and bandleader Cab Calloway had many successes in his life.

e. _____ Another success came when Calloway helped the jazz singers Pearl Bailey and Lena Horne become stars.

VARYING TRANSITION WORDS AND TERMS

Often writers will use many transition words in one piece of writing. Keep in mind that transitions can come in the middle of a sentence and introduce details as well as support points. The following paragraph uses a variety of transition words and terms.

A Supreme Talent

[1]The singer and actress Diana Ross has had much success. [2]First, Ross was successful as part of a group. [3]For ten years, she was the lead singer with the Supremes, the most successful female trio of the 1960s. [4]With a total of twelve number-one hits, including "Baby Love" (1964), "Stop! In the Name of Love" (1965), and "You Can't Hurry Love"

(1966), the Supremes were second only to the Beatles in record sales during the 1960s. [5]Ross was also successful as a soloist. [6]In 1970 she left the Supremes and began a career on her own. [7]Her debut single, "Reach Out and Touch," became a major hit in 1970. [8]Additionally, her second single, a new version of the Marvin Gaye–Tammi Terrell song "Ain't No Mountain High Enough," made it to number one on the pop charts. [9]Finally, Ross was successful as an actress. [10]Right after her solo debut, Ross made her acting debut, playing the legendary singer Billie Holliday in the feature film *Lady Sings the Blues*. [11]The film met with critical and popular success, and Ross earned an Oscar nomination for Best Actress. [12]Ross spent the next two decades making many albums and starring in other films. [13]No matter what Diana Ross tried, she proved to be "supremely" talented.

EXERCISE 6 Identifying Transition Words and Terms

Reread "A Supreme Talent." Then, fill in the blanks.

1. What transition word does the writer use to begin sentence 2?

_____

2. What transition word in sentence 5 shows addition?

_____

3. Write the transition words in sentences 3, 6, and 10 that show time sequence. Note that the transition terms may give years, as in the phrase *In 1980*.

a. Sentence 3   _____

b. Sentence 6   _____

c. Sentence 10   _____

4. What signal word does the writer use in sentence 8 to show

addition? _____

5. What transitions does the writer use to show that the support point

in sentence 9 is the last one? _____

OTHER WAYS TO LINK IDEAS

Aside from using transition, there are three other ways to link your ideas.

- Repeating key words
- Using pronouns
- Using synonyms

Repeating Key Words

When you repeat key words, you use important words related to your topic again and again throughout your paragraph. When not overdone, this technique can help your reader stay on track.

As you read the following paragraph, pay attention to the word *songs*. Circle it each of the eight times you find it. Notice how the repetition reinforces the use of the word in sentence 1, the topic sentence.

The Sounds of Music

[1]Singers play a large role in making songs famous. [2]In the musical drama *The Sound of Music*, the singer Julie Andrews makes many songs famous. [3]She sings "The Sound of Music," "My Favorite Things," and "Do-Re-Mi," among others. [4]Even though Andrews didn't write any of those songs, she is the one people think of when they hear those songs. [5]Another example comes from the musical *Oklahoma!* [6]In this musical play, Shirley Jones sings the songs "The Surrey with the Fringe on Top" and "People Will Say We're in Love." [7]Richard Rodgers is the one who wrote the songs, but Jones is the one people remember. [8]Finally, the songs in the movie *White Christmas* were written by Irving Berlin. [9]However, when people hear the songs—for example, "White Christmas"—they think of Bing Crosby.

Using Pronouns

Another way to help your reader stay focused on your topic is to use pronouns. Pronouns remind the reader of the name they are replacing. Using pronouns keeps you from overusing repetition.

As you read the paragraph "A Meteoric Rise," pay attention to how the pronouns *he* and *his* take the place of *Haley* and *Haley's*. Circle each of the four times the pronoun *he* appears in the paragraph. Then underline the pronoun *his* each of the eight times it appears. Notice how the pronouns remind the reader of the name that appears in sentence 1, the topic sentence.

A Meteoric Rise

[1]The singer and musician Bill Haley found his biggest success playing rock and roll. [2]Early in his career, Haley played guitar and sang for country and western groups. [3]Though he found work in bands such as the Downhomers, he became exhausted, disillusioned, and broke. [4]At the next stage in his career, Haley formed his own country and western band, called Bill Haley and His Saddlemen. [5]The group continued to play country music—they even wore white Stetson hats and cowboy boots—but they eventually adopted a new sound. [6]With this new sound came Haley's greatest success. [7]He decided to change the band's name to Bill Haley and His Comets, and with that, the group really took off. [8]Starting with songs like "Rock the Joint," which sold 75,000 copies, Haley focused on the rock and roll world. [9]In 1953 he wrote "Crazy Man Crazy," which became the first rock and roll record to make the *Billboard* pop chart Top 20. [10]Haley gained lasting fame from the recording of "Rock Around the Clock," the song that introduced rock and roll to white America. [11]It became a huge hit as the title track of *The Blackboard Jungle*, a movie about juvenile delinquents. [12]Haley's other big hit—"Shake, Rattle, and Roll"—was the first rock and roll record to sell a million copies. [13]His next big hit—"See Ya Later, Alligator"—sold a million copies within a month. [14]Though a talented country and western musician, Bill Haley's meteoric rise to success came with his Comets.

Using Synonyms

Using synonyms can help your reader follow your ideas while adding variety to your writing. A **synonym** is a word that has the same, or nearly the same, meaning as another word. For example, two synonyms for *singer* are *vocalist* and *diva*.

The following paragraph is a version of "The Sounds of Music" that appears on page 159. In that version, the word *songs* appeared eight times. In this version, however, other words replace the word *songs* in some places.

The Sounds of Music

[1]Singers play a large role in making songs famous. [2]In the musical drama *The Sound of Music*, the singer Julie Andrews makes many numbers famous. [3]She sings "The Sound of Music," "My Favorite Things," and "Do-Re-Mi," among others. [4]Even though

Andrews didn't write any of those hits, she is the one people think of when they hear those songs. ⁵Another example comes from the musical *Oklahoma!* ⁶In this musical play, Shirley Jones sings the melodies "The Surrey with the Fringe on Top" and "People Will Say We're in Love." ⁷Richard Rodgers is the one who wrote the numbers, but Jones is the one people remember. ⁸Finally, the songs in the movie *White Christmas* were written by Irving Berlin. ⁹However, when people hear the hits—for example, "White Christmas"—they think of Bing Crosby.

EXERCISE 7 Using Synonyms

Reread "The Sounds of Music." Then, fill in the blanks.

1. What word does the writer use to replace *songs* in sentence 2?

_____

2. The same word for *songs* that the writer uses in sentence 2 also

appears in sentence _____ .

3. What word does the writer use to replace *songs* in sentence 4?

_____

4. The same word that the writer uses in sentence 4 also appears in

sentence _____ .

5. How many times does the word *songs* appear in this version of the

paragraph? _____

WRITING PRACTICE 1 Write Your Own Paragraph

You've had a chance to practice recognizing transitions during this chapter. Now it's time to practice using them in your own writing. Your assignment is this: *Write a paragraph describing your going-to-bed or getting-up-in-the-*

morning routine. A possible topic sentence might be "Every night I go through the same steps before bed." Use specific times and activities that you usually follow. Use transitions to let your reader know which points come first, second, and last. After you've finished a draft, underline all the transitions you've used to link your ideas.

Use these techniques to write your paragraph.

1. Use one or more prewriting techniques to come up with ideas for your paragraph.
2. Write a clear topic sentence.
3. Use your notes from prewriting to write a rough draft of your paragraph.
4. Place your ideas in a logical order—either by time sequence order or emphatic order—and use transitions to connect them.
5. Revise your paragraph, reading through it to check for the first three of the four Cs: *concise, credible*, and *clear* writing.
6. Edit your paragraph for sentence effectiveness, word choice, grammar, punctuation, and spelling.

When you're finished, your paragraph should include the following:

- A clear topic sentence
- Support points that relate to the topic sentence
- Specific details that give proof of your support points
- Transitions that connect your support points and specific details

WRITING PRACTICE 2 Preparing for an Important Event

Though we have routines that help us organize our daily lives, often we will take special steps or precautions for a particular event. How have you prepared for a special event? Your assignment is this: *Write a paragraph describing the special preparations you have undergone for a particular occasion.* Some incidents to consider are job interviews, first dates, the first day of school, or a new job. Your topic sentence might be something like "To impress my boss on the first day of work, I made sure to prepare carefully."

Follow these steps to write your paragraph.

1. Use one or more prewriting techniques to come up with ideas.
2. Use your notes from prewriting to write a rough draft.

3. Include details from your life. *Note:* Details from other people's lives and from trusted sources will not be as relevant for this assignment.

4. Revise your paragraph, reading through it to check for the first three of the four Cs: *concise, credible,* and *clear* writing.

5. Edit your paragraph for sentence effectiveness, word choice, grammar, punctuation, and spelling.

When you're finished, your paragraph should include the following:

■ A clear topic sentence
■ Support points that relate to the topic sentence
■ Specific details that give proof of your support points
■ Transitions that connect your support points and specific details

CHAPTER SUMMARY

To make your writing *clear*, the third of the four Cs, remember to organize your ideas logically. You can use use organizing techniques to help make your point.

1. Emphatic order lets you organize your ideas from least important to the most important.
2. Chronological order lets you organize your ideas in the order in which they occurred.
3. Transitions signal to your reader the direction your writing will take.

MyWritingLab & Lab Activity 10

mywritinglab   For additional practice with organizing and linking ideas, go to **www. mywritinglab.com** or complete **Lab Activity 10** in the separate *Resources for Writers* Lab Manual.

11

Writing from Visuals

Culture Note

FREEGANISM

For most people, the idea of searching through trash cans for food is unappetizing. However, "freegans," a growing subculture of people worldwide, choose to spend as little money on food as possible. Instead, they prefer to live off consumer waste by "dumpster diving" and other practices. The term *freegan* comes from the words *free* and *vegan* (people who choose not to eat or otherwise use any animal-derived products).

Freegan Feast

FOOD FOR THOUGHT Freegans seek to decrease worldwide waste by using what others discard. What waste or excess can you eliminate in your life? Explain.

Responding to Images. *How appealing is the food in this photo? To what extent would knowing that it had come out of a dumpster make it less appealing?*

RECOMMENDED READINGS

"All I Really Need to Know I Learned in Kindergarten," Robert Fulghum, *p. 710*

PAYING ATTENTION TO WHAT YOU SEE

To write from visual sources—analyzing a painting, billboard, or photo-graph, say—you need to pay attention to detail. Whereas in daily life you might not think about every single step you take to get to the bus stop or to take out the trash, in writing, your observations are key.

EXERCISE 1 Recording Initial Observations

Before you begin this exercise, have a blank sheet of paper and a pencil ready.

Part A

1. Turn to page 170.

2. Glance quickly at the photo and return to this page.

3. Write your impressions of the photo as fast as you can on your blank paper.

Part B

1. Turn to page 170.

2. Spend a few minutes looking at the photo, taking notes about the most important details.

3. Write your impressions of the photo on your paper, taking your time in developing your ideas.

After you finish writing based on your second observation, compare your two impressions. Were your first impressions accurate? Did having more time to observe and consider the photo make a difference in your writing? Explain.

Part C

Discuss your findings with your classmates. How similar or different were your impressions of the photo? To what extent did you and your classmates pay attention to the same aspects of the photo—the lighting or people's expressions, for instance? Explain.

Hopefully, you discovered two things from Exercise 1.

1. Your initial impressions of a photograph, while needing development, were probably generally accurate.
2. Your prolonged examination of the photo provided additional evidence to support your first impressions.

Listening to Your Instincts

Your first instincts are probably right. If you've ever taken a fill-in-the-bubble test, you know that sometimes an answer just seems correct, even if you can't explain why. Similarly, if you see a front-page photo of a fire, you don't need to read the article to know that a disastrous fire is most likely burning somewhere. Trust these instincts.

After your first glance at a photo, look again and see if you can discover what about it led you to your conclusion. If you got an impression of someone suffering, for instance, look further and see if you can find details—a grieved expression, a physical pose that suggests pain, details such as filth or flood that indicate discomfort or danger—that support your initial response.

A Two-Dimensional Encounter

When you write from everyday experiences, impressions from all five senses are available to you for support. An object's or situation's smell, feel, taste, sound, and sight all contribute to your descriptions. When you write from visuals, however, you're limited to your sight. Pay special attention, therefore, to what you see since it comprises your sole source of information. Some visual aspects to consider: light, color, size, shape, expression, proportion, contrast, placement, and focus.

For instance, in the following image, the "I'm Not A Plastic Bag" slogan is at the very front of the photo, in a prominent position. If the slogan were found on a rumpled bag far in the photo's background, the photo might seem to be a statement as to people's lack fo sincerity or dedication toward environmental causes. In it's bold position however, the slogan emphasizes the importance of the anti-plastic campaign. In this case, visual clues, rather than other sensory elements, have provided all the information upon which to base an opinion.

Making a Statement

OBSERVING YOUR WORLD   Toting a brand new bag with "I'm Not A Plastic Bag" on it might seem contradictory. Write a few sentences about other environmental incongruities—trash on the ground next to, but not in, a garbage can, for instance—that you've noticed in your community.

Responding to Images.   *What is your gut reaction to the photo above? Does it inspire, amuse, irritate, or bore you? Explain.*

Writing from Instinct

A good way to begin writing about a visual source is to pay attention to your gut reaction to the photo or painting, write down that reaction, and then look for details that support your initial conclusion. For instance, Brandi viewed the photo on page 164 and initially thought that the woman going through the dumpster must be hungry and homeless. She wrote:

The woman must be poor and starving if she has to look in a dumpster for food. Being desperate is the only reason I'd *ever* get food that way.

On further examination of the photo, Brandi noticed details such as the young woman's clean face, the plastic bag, and the apparently all-vegetable contents of the bag. These elements caused Brandi to wonder if the young woman was doing something other than desperately searching for food.

It's weird that she only has vegetables (are those mushrooms?) in her bag. When I'm hungry, I want something with bread in it, and a few cloves of garlic or raw potatoes (if that's what those red things are) wouldn't do it for me. Also, she seems pretty healthy for someone going through a dumpster, not too scrawny or sick or anything. I can't think of any reason for "dumpster diving" unless she's hungry, but she just doesn't look how I think of dumpster-searchers look.

Even though Brandi doesn't know what the "freegan" movement is, she recognizes that the young woman's search for food is more deliberate that she'd initially thought.

Ask Yourself Questions

Once you've viewed a photo or painting and noted your first impression, ask yourself questions for further development.

What is the focal point, or main figure, in the picture? How can you tell this point is the most important?

What are the circumstances or setting of the primary figure? Is the central figure alone, or are there other people, animals, or objects in the picture? What role do these play?

How important is the setting—buildings, plants, vehicles—to the overall impression the picture gives?

To what extent does weather play a role?

To what extent is action important in the picture? Would the picture give the same impression if there were more or less activity?

Does everything in the picture seem to communicate the same idea, or do different sections conflict with each other? Is a homeless man sitting in front of an expensive restaurant, for instance?

What is the title of the image, if it has one? What does this title suggest to you?

The answers to these questions will give you a start toward finding specific details to support the conclusion you draw based on the photo.

Seeing What Fits

Ideally, every part of a photograph or painting will contribute something to your overall impression. For example, a news photo might show a fire engine next to a burning building, firefighters spraying water on the blaze, and the mother of a small child, looking grateful and relieved. This photo clearly demonstrates a situation that many people have seen or heard about, so it is easy to write about, however, few photos prove so cooperative.

Another photo taken at the fire might also reveal an excited little boy, gazing delightedly at the blaze. Or the same mother might well look frustrated if her child awaits attention from a paramedic. These details give a different impression of the same situation.

In your own writing, while it's important to use details from the visual source to support your conclusion, you don't need to make *everything* fit. Choose the details that best support your point, and—unless there's a glaring contradiction between details in the photo and the point you want to make—leave out the ill-fitting details.

Changing Your Mind

If too many details in the visual don't fit, you may have to revise your thinking. For instance, when Brandi wrote about the freegan woman, she initially wanted to ignore the woman's earrings, clean appearance, and vegetable findings. Brandi believed that the fact that the woman was searching for food in a dumpster must mean that she was starving. On further examination of the photo, however, Brandi realized that there were too many clues opposing her poverty idea, so she had to revise her thinking.

FOLLOWING THE IMPRESSION WITH INFORMATION

Depending on your instructor, you may be asked to write only about what you observe from a visual source. Sometimes, however, you may be expected to use a visual source as a jumping-off point for your writing. In these cases, researching additional information—if available—is a good place to start. Brandi's instructor had shown her the photo of the freegan woman, so Brandi began by asking where the photo had come from. Learning that the photo was downloaded from a freegan Web site, Brandi visited her library and searched the Internet for the photo itself and for related information. What she found was fascinating to her.

I can't believe there's a group of people (all over the world!) who make a point of eating what other people throw away. They're called "freegans," and I guess the most serious freegans don't eat or use any animal products, and they think that spending was the cause of all kinds of problems in the world: destruction of the environment, taking advantage of low-paid workers. Freegans feel that if they can use someone's leftovers rather than spend money to get what they need, then they're not part of these huge problems. I'm not sure how I feel about all this, but it's cool to know it's out there.

For more information on researching a topic, see Chapter 23, "Argument."

WRITING PRACTICE 1 Write Your Own Paragraph

Look at the photo below. Then, follow the directions.

Your assignment is this: *Write a paragraph explaining what is happening in the photo*. You may write about just what you see, or you may draw a conclusion about what is happening. Either way, follow these steps to write your paragraph.

Fine Dining

SURF THE NET Freegans argue that they can live very well on others' waste. Surf the net for examples of the abundance freegans find thrown away.

Responding to Images. *In what ways is the photo above inconsistent or contradictory? Explain.*

1. Use one or more prewriting techniques to come up with ideas.

2. Write a topic sentence that includes a narrowed topic and point-of-view words.

3. Use your notes from prewriting to write a rough draft of your paragraph.

4. Revise your paragraph, reading through it to check for the first three of the four Cs: *concise, credible*, and *clear* writing.

5. Edit your paragraph for sentence effectiveness, word choice, grammar, punctuation, and spelling.

When you're finished, your paragraph should include the following:

- A clear topic sentence
- Support points that relate to the topic sentence
- Specific details that give proof of your support points
- Transitions that connect your support points and examples

WRITING PRACTICE 2   Writing from a Visual You Choose

This chapter has given you information about freeganism and has shown you photos of different aspects of the freegan life-style and philosophy. What other messages do you *see* in your life? Your assignment is this: *Observe your neighborhood, school, or city and choose a visual source—poster, billboard, photograph, drawing, to name some.* Then, *write a paragraph about the visual source, drawing a conclusion about it and supporting your conclusion with details from the photograph.* If you see a graffiti-marked billboard advertising the local medical center, your topic sentence might be something like "People don't seem to think very highly of the local medical center." You could support your topic sentence by mentioning the scribbles covering the faces of people on the billboard, the torn edges of the billboard, and the graffiti scrawled across the words of the billboard.

When you're finished, your paragraph should include the following:

- A clear topic sentence
- Support points that relate to the topic sentence
- Specific details that give proof of your support points
- Transitions that connect your support points and specific details

CHAPTER SUMMARY

In writing from visuals, remember the following:

1. Listen to your instincts.
2. Rely on visual observation since your other senses will not be as helpful.
3. Include only those details that help you support your main idea.
4. Develop your ideas using details from outside sources, if your instructor directs you to do so.

MyWritingLab & Lab Activity 11

mywritinglab For additional practice with writing about visuals, go to **www.mywritinglab. com** or complete **Lab Activity 11** in the separate *Resources for Writers* Lab Manual.

Choosing the Best Words for Sensitive Writing

12

Culture Note

ABRAHAM LINCOLN

The sixteenth president of the United States, Abraham Lincoln led our nation through the secession of the South, the Civil War, and the beginning of Reconstruction (the process of rebuilding the post–Civil War South). Lincoln's assassination by John Wilkes Booth deprived the nation of a charitable leader whose allegiance to his country was, as Lincoln himself claimed, "registered in Heaven."

UNDERSTANDING LANGUAGE CHOICES

Very few people speak the same way all the time. The words and tone of voice you use when talking to friends probably varies greatly from the language and tone you use with your instructors. We shape our language in many ways to make ourselves understood to different groups; the key is knowing when to use which type of language.

CHOOSING LANGUAGE FOR FORMAL WRITING ASSIGNMENTS

Using informal language with someone who knows you well can communicate your ideas every bit as effectively as using formal language— maybe even better. However, it's important to understand that when *speaking,* we have certain communication aids that are missing when we

RECOMMENDED READINGS

"Money for Morality," Mary Arguelles, *p. 745*

"A Homemade Education," Malcolm X, *p. 714*

"Education," E. B. White, *p. 727*

Abraham Lincoln's Famous Fight

SURF THE NET The sixteenth president of the United States, Abraham Lincoln reunited a country divided by social and financial differences yet he was a seasoned soldier and an accomplished wrestler. Search the Internet for information on Abraham Lincoln. Write a few sentences summarizing what you learn.

Responding to Images. *How does Abraham Lincoln in the photo above differ from your other impressions of him? Explain.*

write: facial expressions, hand gestures, vocal inflection all help us communicate in person. Because these aids can't help us on paper, however, we must rely on standard forms of expression. Thus, we must make use of formal written English.

In academic writing, take care to avoid language that can interfere with, rather than assist, your communication.

- Slang
- Overly formal language
- Clichés (overused expressions)
- Wordiness

Slang

Slang is informal language, and it can be effective in spoken English. In writing, however, slang is unacceptable. In addition, slang can prevent you from communicating clearly. Though some slang expressions—such as *cool*—have stayed popular for decades, most slang words lose popularity quickly, or are known only to certain groups, so slang can leave your reader wondering what you mean. Further, slang can take the place of details necessary to communicate important ideas.

Slang: Lincoln thought the South was <u>dissing</u> the Union by seceding.

Standard: Lincoln thought the South showed disrespect for the Union by seceding.

Slang: Although Lincoln came from humble beginnings, he was <u>up for</u> being president.

Standard: Although Lincoln came from humble beginnings, he was ready to accept the challenge of being president.

Slang: Lincoln worked hard to become president; no one could call him <u>a slacker</u>.

Standard: Lincoln worked hard to become president; no one could call him lazy.

EXERCISE 1 Converting Slang to Standard English

In the following sentences, slang terms appear in italics. Rewrite each sentence using standard English expressions.

Slang: I worry that my little brother will get *caught in the crossfire* of my parents' divorce.

Standard: I worry that my little brother will suffer as a result of my parents' divorce.

1. Slang: Even after I *hit the books*, my instructor gave me a C–. *What's up with that?*

Standard: _____

2. Slang: As a result of my *lame* grade, my financial aid chances went *down the tubes*.

Standard: _____

3. Slang: When I watch television, I end up *brain dead* and *stressed out*.

Standard: _____

4. Slang: After Dino *chewed out* his girlfriend, she *bailed on* him.

Standard: _____

5. Slang: When my mother made fried chicken, I *scarfed it down*.

Standard: _____

Clichés (Overused Expressions)

Clichés are overused expressions that are ineffective because of their overuse. Like slang, use of clichés often allows writers to omit key details. Read the following sentences to see how overused language weakens them. Some clichés must be rewritten to make their meaning more specific, and some can be omitted.

Cliché: <u>In this day and age</u>, Abraham Lincoln is considered an important political leader.

Better: Today, Abraham Lincoln is considered an important political leader.

Cliché: Lincoln hoped that the Union could be preserved without civil war. However, this was <u>easier said than done</u>.

Better: Lincoln hoped that the Union could be preserved without civil war. However, this goal could not be achieved.

Cliché: <u>Needless to say</u>, Lincoln was a great president.

Better: Lincoln was a great president.

Clichés

all work and no play	hustle and bustle
at a loss for words	in the nick of time
at this point in time	in this day and age
better late than never	it dawned on me
break the ice	it goes without saying
cold, cruel world	last but not least
cry your eyes out	living hand-to-mouth
drop in the bucket	make ends meet
easier said than done	one in a million
free as a bird	on top of the world

green with envy	out of this world
had a hard time of it	sad but true
saw the light	too little, too late
short but sweet	took a turn for the worse
sigh of relief	tried and true
singing the blues	under the weather
taking a big chance	where he (she) is coming from
time and time again	word to the wise
too close for comfort	work like a dog

EXERCISE 2 Revising Overused Expressions

In the following sentences, overused expressions are in italics. Rewrite each sentence, using a less common English expression. An example is done for you.

After my nap I felt *as fresh as a daisy*.

After my nap I felt refreshed.

1. I thought I wanted to be an engineer before I became one. I guess *the grass is always greener on the other side of the fence*.

2. When my girlfriend moved to Iceland, I *cried my eyes out*.

3. When finals week was over, Jeff felt *as free as a bird*.

4. The new restaurant on Broadway is *out of this world*.

5. When I was between jobs, I *lived hand-to-mouth*.

Overly Formal Language

Sometimes writers try to sound knowledgeable or intelligent by using big, impressive-sounding words. Using such words unnecessarily, however, makes the speaker or writer sound artificial or stuffy. The best writing is as clear and direct as possible.

Stuffy:	While preparing himself for the undertaking to come, Lincoln read widely and consulted with his marital partner.
Better:	While preparing for the challenge, Lincoln read widely and talked to his wife.
Stuffy:	While the Union soldiers suffered unspeakable losses as a result of the tragedy known as the Civil War, their losses were but a fraction of those experienced by the downtrodden Confederate soldiers.
Better:	While the Union soldiers suffered greatly from the Civil War, the Confederate soldiers suffered far more.

EXERCISE 3 Overly Formal Language

In the following sentences, overly formal language appears in italics. Rewrite the sentences, using clear, direct language. An example is done for you.

Stuffy: Lincoln *acquired the skill of comprehending the written word* as a result of reading the Bible.

Better: Lincoln learned to read by reading the Bible.

1. I had an idea at work, but I was *terrified to communicate* it to my boss.

_____

2. Tom thought Susanne wore an *overabundance of cosmetics*.

_____

3. *Ron lost a battle to extreme exhaustion while attending a class.*

_____

4. *As a result of the failure of my chronological device to hasten my departure from slumber*, I am late to class.

_____

5. Whoever made these brownies is a *culinary expert of the first order*.

_____

Wordiness

Wordy writing contains unnecessary words or sentences. Getting to the point quickly will save you and your reader time and energy. The sentences below contain unnecessary words or phrases that add length but nothing else. You don't need to write all simple sentences that follow the same pattern, but you should always use the fewest words possible to get your ideas across.

Wordy:	Lincoln was <u>of the opinion</u> that the secession of the South had many <u>negative drawbacks</u>. (*Of the opinion* is a longer way to say *thought*; a drawback is something negative, so writing *negative* is redundant.)
Better:	Lincoln thought that the secession of the South had many drawbacks.
Wordy:	It <u>seems to me in my opinion</u> that Lincoln <u>really and truly</u> worked hard <u>over the course of the many years that he served as president</u>. (The writer doesn't need to say "it seems to me" or "in my opinion." *Over the course of many years that he served as president* is a long way to say "during his presidency.")
Better:	Lincoln worked hard during his presidency.

EXERCISE 4 Eliminating Wordiness

Underline the wordy sections in the sentences on the following page. Then, rewrite the sentences to eliminate wordiness. An example is done for you.

Wordy: Abraham Lincoln's accomplishments are his legacy <u>to the people who lived after him</u>.

Better: Abraham Lincoln's accomplishments are his legacy.

_____

1. Wordy: Although Lincoln had a great influence over many people, he came from humble beginnings.

Better: _____

2. Wordy: His first home was a cabin of just one room in an area with a sparse population of settlers.

Better: _____

3. Wordy: To attend school as a boy, Lincoln walked two miles to his destination of the schoolhouse each day.

Better: _____

4. Wordy: In school, Lincoln learned the elementary basic rudiments of reading, writing, and arithmetic.

Better: _____

5. Wordy: When Lincoln was only nine years of age, his mother died.

Better: _____

Alternatives to Wordy Expressions

Wordy Expression	Shorter Expression	Wordy Expression	Shorter Expression
a large number of	many	for the reason that	because
a period of a week	a week	four in number	four
arrive at an agreement	agree	in every instance	always
at all times	always	in my own opinion	I think
at an earlier point in time	before	in order to	to
at the present time	now	in the area of	around
at this point in time	now	in the nature of	like
because of the fact that	because	in the neighborhood of	around
big in size	big	in the event that	if
by means of	by	in the near future	soon

circle around	circle	in this day and age	today
connect together	connect	is able to	can
due to the fact that	because	large in size	large
during the time while	while	owing to the fact that	because
for the purpose of	for	past history	history
plan ahead for the future	plan	true fact	fact
positive benefit	benefit	until such time as	until
postponed until later	postponed	white in color	white
return back	return		

EDITING PRACTICE 1

The following paragraph contains italicized examples of slang, overused expressions, and wordy and overly formal language. In the spaces following the paragraph, identify the poor language choices: S for "slang," C for "cliché," F for "formal language," or W for "wordy." On the lines provided, rewrite the section of the sentences containing poor word choices to make them more readable. The first item has been done for you.

Lincoln's Legacy

[1]Although members of the Confederacy detested Abraham Lincoln, *he rocked*. [2]*First, he acquired his education from the informal sources provided him at home.* [3]*His mother kicked the bucket* when he was nine years old, so Lincoln didn't have the chance to learn from her. [4]Lincoln claimed that he wasn't sure how he learned to read and write, but *whether he had to beg, steal, or borrow his education, he got one*. [5]*Second, Lincoln worked like a dog*. [6]*He held many positions in a wide spectrum of workplaces*: he worked on a farm, split rails for fences, and managed a store in New Salem, Illinois. [7]He was also a captain in the Black Hawk War, so *people should have known not to mess with him*. [8]Lincoln also spent eight years in the Illinois legislature and worked in the courts *forever and a day*. [9]*His partner in law was said to say* of him, "His ambition was a little engine that knew no rest." [10]Finally, *Lincoln was of a charitable mindset*. [11]Although he did send troops to *take down* the Confederacy and bring the southern states back into the Union, he wanted the defeated Confederacy treated with "malice toward none and charity for all." [12]However, before his Reconstruction

plans were carried out, *the breath of life was snatched from him at Ford's Theater in Washington.* [13]*Thus ended the presidency of Abraham Lincoln and the life of Abraham Lincoln.*

Sentence 1: _____S_____   Lincoln was a great president. _____

Sentence 2: _____   _____

Sentence 3: _____   _____

Sentence 4: _____   _____

Sentence 5: _____   _____

Sentence 6: _____   _____

Sentence 7: _____   _____

Sentence 8: _____   _____

Sentence 9: _____   _____

Sentence 10: _____   _____

Sentence 11: _____   _____

Sentence 12: _____   _____

Sentence 13: _____   _____

WRITING PRACTICE 1 Revise a Paragraph for Effective Language

Now that you can identify ineffective language, it's time to revise a paragraph to eliminate slang, clichés, overly formal language, and wordiness. Read the following paragraph, a reworded version of Lincoln's famous Gettysburg Address, which was delivered at the dedication of a Civil War cemetery. As you read, take care to mark the twelve instances of ineffective language. Then, rewrite the speech on another piece of paper.

Way back when, our esteemed and notable fathers created a new country based on the idea that all men are created equal.

Now we are fighting, fighting, and fighting in a violent, bloody,

and murderous civil war, which is testing our ability to

stick together. We're here, in this place, to dedicate this ceme-tery, and it's totally cool that we're doing this. But actually, those who have willingly and unsparingly given their worthy lives for us, the living, have already dedicated this field with their blood. Most folks ain't gonna remember what I say, but they'll remem-ber the tried and true men who died. So let's pull together and keep trying to work things out so that this government of the people, by the people, for the people, shall not perish from the earth.

WHAT IS SENSITIVE LANGUAGE?

You probably know that some language—such as profanity or slang—is inappropriate in certain situations. Using a four-letter word during a job interview, for instance, would not make a good impression on most employ-ers. Similarly, using a derogatory or insulting term to refer to a woman when talking to a friend might offend him or her. By using **sensitive lan-guage** that is free from stereotypes and ethnic or gender slurs, you can make your point effectively while keeping your readers open to what you have to say.

USING SENSITIVE LANGUAGE

Most people have heard stories about "ditzy blonds" or "dumb jocks." Generalizations like these can be very hurtful. Follow these guidelines in your writing.

- Don't exclude people.
- Don't make assumptions about groups of people.
- Don't call people by names they do not choose for themselves.
- Don't assume that all members of a group are the same.
- Don't mention a person's race, sex, age, sexual orientation, disability, or religion unnecessarily.

Don't Exclude People

In the past, the pronouns *he, his,* and *him* were used to mean "he or she," "his or her," and "him and her." Similarly, writers would write *man* and mean "all human beings." While most men had no trouble with these terms, many women came to feel excluded by them. In the past few decades, writers have become more sensitive to gender. Now, instead of writing "Man has made great progress," writers say, "People have made great progress." Thus, women are represented as well as men. You can use the following methods to include both genders in your writing.

1. Use *he or she* or *she or he* (and *his or her, her or his, him or her, her or him*).

Insensitive: Every member of the Underground Railroad jeopardized <u>his</u> safety. (Was it only men who participated in the Underground Railroad?)

Better: Every member of the Underground Railroad jeopardized his <u>or her</u> safety. (Both men and women are included.)

2. Use a plural noun, such as *people, persons,* or *humans*.

Insensitive: Even a <u>person</u> with children had to risk <u>her</u> life while escaping or helping others to escape. (Is every person with children female?)

Better: Even <u>people</u> with children had to risk <u>their</u> lives while escaping or helping others to escape.

Don't Make Assumptions About Groups of People

It's easy to make assumptions about groups or individuals—but it's insensitive and unfair to do so. For instance, assuming that only mothers are interested in a new playground leaves out the possibility that fathers are interested, too. To avoid making assumptions about groups of people, ask yourself the following questions.

- Does my description apply to everyone in the group?
- Could someone feel offended because he/she does not fit my description?

If you can answer "yes" to the first question and "no" to the second, your language is probably safe. Otherwise, think of ways to change your language.

Insensitive: <u>Mothers</u> who take their children to the park are lobbying for a new playground.

Better: <u>Parents</u> who take their children to the park are lobbying for a new playground.

Names of Groups

The following terms are generally considered acceptable by the groups they refer to. Keep in mind that the more specific the term, the better. For instance, referring to a group of Southeast Asian people as *Vietnamese, Hmong*, or *Laotian* is better than simply calling them *Asian*.

African-American *or* black

Asian

Caucasian or white

disabled (*not* handicapped)

Indian (for people from India)

Latino/Latina

Native American (*not* Indian)

Don't Call People by Names They Do Not Choose for Themselves

The key to using sensitive language is to let people choose what they wish to be called. Letting people choose their own names applies to groups as well as individuals. For instance, *Oriental* is no longer the term of choice to identify people of Asian descent. Instead, the term *Asian* is generally considered to be respectful, but as noted earlier, more specific terms such as *Laotian* or *Vietnamese* may be even better. Follow these guidelines to avoid offending people.

■ Find out what members of a group prefer to be called. If you're not sure whether to use *Hispanic* or *Latino*, for example, do some research or ask your instructor for the preferred term. Note that preferences can vary from group to group and from place to place. The point here is that some thought and research may be needed.

■ Pay attention to how people are addressed. If everyone calls your supervisor Ms. Smith, for instance, you should call her that, too, unless she tells you otherwise.

■ Sometimes members of a particular group will call themselves a name that they do not wish others to call them. For example, a man might talk about going to "boys' night out," but that doesn't mean he wants to be called "boy." Pay attention to what people *prefer* to be called even if that isn't what they call themselves.

Don't Assume That All Members of a Group Are the Same

It's unfair and inaccurate to assume that members of a group are all the same. To avoid stereotyping, on p. 186 do the following:

- Look for exceptions to the claim you want to make. If even one person doesn't fit the description you offer, don't use it.

  Insensitive: Teenagers are emotional and irritable.

  Better: Teenagers may sometimes express volatile emotions.

- Avoid using absolute labels such as *all, none, always,* and *never.* A single exception renders them false.

- Avoid generalizations involving personal characteristics, attitudes, and achievements. Even something that seems complimentary, such as "Asian students are good at math," may offend a Vietnamese student who writes poetry or has no interest in math class.

Don't Mention a Person's Race, Sex, Age, Sexual Orientation, Disability, or Religion Unnecessarily

Being specific is important in writing because it helps your readers understand your ideas. However, describing someone in terms of race or gender can send an unspoken message of criticism.

If you're writing about someone who cut you off on the freeway, for instance, the only details you need to mention are those relevant to the other person's *driving*. Saying that "some jerk" cut you off isn't passing judgment on any particular group of people. Writing that the person who cut you off is a woman, for instance, implicitly states that all women are bad drivers. The driver's race, gender, age, disability, religion, and sexual orientation are irrelevant; talking about those factors only serves to communicate bad feelings about a particular group of people.

To avoid mentioning race, gender, or other characteristics unnecessarily, ask yourself the following questions.

- In the same situation, would I want to be described in terms of my race, gender, or any other characteristic? If the answer is "no," omit using such details.

- Could my reader think that I am biased against a certain group of people because of the details I include? If the answer is "yes," omit such details.

EXERCISE 5 Identifying Insensitive Language

Write OK by each sentence that isn't offensive and I by each sentence that contains insensitive language. Rewrite the sentences that contain insensitive language on a separate piece of paper. An example is done for you.

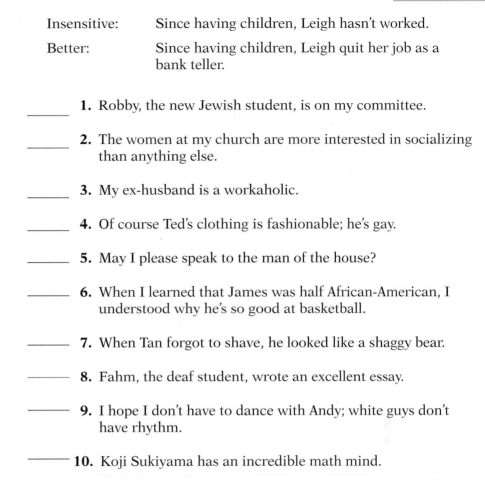

Insensitive: Since having children, Leigh hasn't worked.

Better: Since having children, Leigh quit her job as a bank teller.

_____   **1.** Robby, the new Jewish student, is on my committee.

_____   **2.** The women at my church are more interested in socializing than anything else.

_____   **3.** My ex-husband is a workaholic.

_____   **4.** Of course Ted's clothing is fashionable; he's gay.

_____   **5.** May I please speak to the man of the house?

_____   **6.** When I learned that James was half African-American, I understood why he's so good at basketball.

_____   **7.** When Tan forgot to shave, he looked like a shaggy bear.

_____   **8.** Fahm, the deaf student, wrote an excellent essay.

_____   **9.** I hope I don't have to dance with Andy; white guys don't have rhythm.

_____   **10.** Koji Sukiyama has an incredible math mind.

EXERCISE 6 Finding Bias in Writing

The following paragraph contains six instances of insensitive language. In the spaces at the end of the paragraph, write the numbers of the sentences containing insensitive language. Then, briefly explain why that language is insensitive. The first item has been done for you.

Abe Lincoln: Tough as Nails

[1]One story about Abraham Lincoln's physical toughness deals with him taking on the town bully. [2]The leader of the local young <u>white</u> men, the "Clary's Grove boys," were high-spirited and sometimes reckless like all boys but good-natured despite their rowdy reputation. [3]The owner of the town store boasted that his clerk, Lincoln, could whip

even the best fighter in the bunch. [4]Hearing this, the group leader, Jack Armstrong, challenged Lincoln to a wrestling match, and Lincoln accepted, like any red-blooded American man would. [5]Lincoln was 6 feet 4 inches tall and weighed 185 pounds, but Jack Armstrong was a knowledgeable and powerful fighter. [6]At first, the two wrestlers circled around, each waiting for the other to make a move. [7]As the tension built, I'm sure all the women cowered and cried. [8]The wrestlers tried to throw each other to the ground, which seems a kind of sissy move, but neither could. [9]Little by little, Lincoln began to get the best of Armstrong, and the Clary's Grove boys seemed as if they might all attack Lincoln. [10]Backed up against the town store, Lincoln challenged the group, saying he'd take them on one at a time. [11]At this point, that wimpy Armstrong came forward and offered his hand to Lincoln, which ended the match and began a friendship. [12]"Honest Abe" may be how most of us think of Abraham Lincoln, but underneath his integrity he was as tough as they come.

Sentence ___2___   It's unnecessary to mention that the men where

white; if racial reference is necessary, "Caucasian"

would be better.

Sentence _____   _____

Sentence _____   _____

Sentence _____   _____

Sentence _____   _____

Sentence _____   _____

EDITING PRACTICE 2

Rewrite the following sentences to make them free of insensitive language of the kind indicated before each sentence.

1. Don't exclude people: When man invented the wheel, he made his

life much easier. _____

_____

2. Don't make assumptions about groups of people: When Kyle and Jane

had their baby, of course Jane quit her job and stayed home. _____

_____

3. Don't call people names they don't choose for themselves: Those
geeks made it impossible for the rest of us to get a good grade in the

class. _____

_____

4. Don't assume that all members of a group are the same: Heidi
would make a perfect cheerleader; she's a natural blonde, you

know. _____

_____

5. Don't mention a person's race, sex, age, sexual orientation, disability, or religion unnecessarily: A rude Asian woman ran over my toe

with a shopping cart. _____

_____

WRITING PRACTICE 2   Writing About a Delicate Matter

Many times in life you will be called to deliver unpleasant news to someone.
The news may be about yourself—you spent too much on a new stereo, say,
or forgot to do something for a friend or family member. The news might also
be about someone else: telling your neighbor that her dogs have once again
used your yard as a toilet. In any case, you will need to choose your words
carefully. Your assignment is this: *Write a letter in which you deliver unwanted
news to someone.* The news may be about a situation where you have made
a mistake, or it may be about a time when you are displeased with someone
or something. You may decide the purpose–to inform or persuade–of your
writing. The point is to communicate your message without offending your
reader. A possible topic sentence might be something like "I really don't think
it would be a good idea for us, as friends, to work at the same store."

Follow these steps to write your paragraph.

1. Use one or more prewriting techniques to come up with ideas.

2. Use your notes from prewriting to write a rough draft.

3. Include details from your life. *Note:* Details from other people's lives and from trusted sources will not be as relevant for this assignment.

4. Revise your paragraph, reading through it to check for the first three of the four Cs: *concise, credible,* and *clear* writing.

5. Edit your paragraph for sentence effectiveness, word choice, grammar, punctuation, and spelling.

When you're finished, your paragraph should include the following:

- A clear topic sentence
- Support points that relate to the topic sentence
- Specific details that give proof of your support points
- Transitions that connect your support points and specific details

CHAPTER SUMMARY

Although informal language such as slang or clichés can be effective in speaking, it is unacceptable in formal writing assignments. Thus, you should remember the following:

1. Avoid slang, or informal language; it can be unclear and dated.
2. Clichés, or overused expressions, are ineffective because they can cause you to leave out key details.
3. Overly formal writing sounds artificial or stuffy; thus, you should avoid it.
4. Avoid wordy writing; it dilutes your meaning by using too many words to make a point.

Remember to use sensitive language when writing to make your point clearly without offending your readers. Use the following guidelines.

5. Don't exclude people or make assumptions about people.
6. Don't call people by names they do not choose for themselves.
7. Don't assume that all members of a group are the same.
8. Don't mention a person's race, sex, age, sexual orientation, disability, or religion unnecessarily.

MyWritingLab & Lab Activity 12

 For additional practice with sensitive writing, go to **www.mywritinglab. com** or complete **Lab Activity 12** in the separate *Resources for Writers* Lab Manual.

Improving Your Spelling

Culture Note

TOMATOES

Because it is a member of the same family as the deadly nightshade, an extremely poisonous plant also known as belladonna, the tomato was once thought to be deadly. However, far from being harmful to humans, tomatoes are an excellent source of nutrition. Additionally, tomatoes don't lose their nutrients through the high-heat cooking process, so canned tomatoes are as healthy as their fresh counterparts.

UNDERSTANDING YOUR SPELLING HABITS

The key to spelling well is *paying attention to words* as you read and write. How do you figure out how to spell words? Do you guess? Do you ask someone? Do you use a dictionary? Paying attention to your spelling habits—what types of words you typically spell correctly and what types you have trouble with—can help you make fewer errors and correct the errors that do appear in your papers.

IMPROVING YOUR SPELLING

You may not think you're a "natural" speller, but you can improve your spelling if you take the initiative. Here are some methods that can help you.

- Reading
- Using a dictionary

RECOMMENDED READINGS

"The Plot Against People," Russell Baker, *p. 779*

"The Santa Ana," Joan Didion, *p. 784*

- Creating your own spelling list
- Understanding basic spelling rules
- Memorizing words that look or sound alike
- Using a computer's spelling checker

Reading

The easiest way to improve your spelling is to read more. Reading from a variety of sources—newspapers and magazines, novels, self-improvement books, even cookbooks or music books—greatly increases your chances of seeing new words. Additionally, reading words in context—as opposed to studying a list or reading a dictionary—can help you learn the meanings of words, which will help you remember their spellings.

Using the Dictionary

Any time you read or write for college, keep a dictionary at your side. Looking up words in the dictionary takes very little time, but it can bring great rewards.

Creating Your Own Spelling List

Every time you misspell a word or read a word that is spelled differently from how you expected, add the correct spelling to your list. This list should include all the words you misspell now and in the future. Once you've identified the words that give you trouble, review your list regularly and practice using the words.

- **Say the words out loud.** Pronounce a word, spell it out loud to yourself, and say it again. Hearing the words and letters spoken may help you remember the correct spelling.
- **Give yourself hints.** Breaking a word into individual syllables can help you remember how to spell it. For instance, you might think of the word *together* as three short words: *to, get, her.* Similarly, *attendance* is made up of three short words: *at, ten, dance.*
- **Become an active reader.** When you're reading—for pleasure, for research, for class—keep your spelling list handy. Whenever you come across a word that's on your list, highlight it (unless it's in a borrowed book, of course). Seeing the word in context can help you remember its correct spelling.

■ **Make flash cards.** Pull out your cards and read through them while you're waiting to see an instructor or at the bus stop; soon you'll master your list.

Understanding Basic Spelling Rules

Learn the three basic spelling rules about adding endings such as *-ed* or *-ing* to words ending with vowels versus consonants. (Vowels are the letters *a, e, i, o, u,* and sometimes *y.* Consonants are all other letters.)

■ **Double the final consonant** if (1) the last three letters follow the pattern of consonant, vowel, consonant; (2) the word's accent or stress is on the last syllable or the word has only one syllable; and (3) the ending begins with a vowel.

begin + ing = beginning	occur + ing = occurring
brag + ed = bragged	omit + ing = omitting
commit + ing = committing	slim + est = slimmest
drop + ed = dropped	stun + ing = stunning

■ **Change the final *y* to *i*** if the letter before the *y* is a consonant.

The *y* becomes *i*:	dry + ed = dried
	heavy + er = heavier
Keep the *y*:	dismay + ed = dismayed
	obey + ing = obeying

■ **Drop the final e** if the ending begins with a vowel.

Drop the *e*:	bite + ing = biting
	care + ing = caring
Keep the *e*:	home + less = homeless
	care + ful = careful

EXERCISE 1 Adding Word Endings

Add the endings to each word shown. An example is done for you.

play + ed = *played* _____

1. sure + ly = _____

2. marry + ed = _____

3. shop + ing = _____

4. love + able = _____

5. love + ly = _____

6. have + ing _____

7. try + es _____

8. rip + ed _____

9. travel + ing _____

10. deny + es _____

Memorizing the Meanings of Words That Look or Sound Alike

Recognizing homonyms and other words that look or sound alike is one more way to improve your spelling. (Review Chapter 51 for a solid understanding of homonyms.)

Using a Computer's Spelling Checker

The spelling checker on a computer can be a great help in locating and correcting typing and spelling errors. However, an electronic spelling checker will find only misspelled words, not misused words. For instance, in the sentence "Their is a knew dress on the stares," three words are used incorrectly—*their, knew,* and *stares*—but none is misspelled, so a spelling checker would miss the errors. The sentence should read "There is a new dress on the stairs."

For further assistance, ask someone (a friend, parent, or tutor) who spells better than you do to proofread your writing. *Do not* let that person make corrections, however. Instead, ask your proofreader to make a check mark in the margins of the lines that include spelling errors. Then you can locate the errors and correct them.

FREQUENTLY MISSPELLED WORDS

Study the list of commonly misspelled words on the next page and memorize the words. For extra practice, add the words that give you the most trouble to your own spelling list or make flash cards for them.

ache	doesn't	opinion
address	dozen	opportunity
all right	eighth	optimist
a lot	embarrass	original
amateur	enough	ounce
among	environment	particular
answer	exaggerate	people
anxious	familiar	perform
argument	fascinate	perhaps
athlete	February	personnel
August	finally	possess
autumn	foreign	possible
beginning	government	potato
behavior	grammar	prefer
brilliant	height	prejudice
business	horse	prescription
calendar	illegal	privilege
career	immediately	probably
careful	important	psychology
cereal	integration	pursue
college	intelligent	quarter
competition	interest	reference
condition	interfere	rhyme
conscience	jewelry	ridiculous
crowded	knock	separate
daughter	knowledge	similar
definite	library	since
deposit	maintain	sincerely
describe	mathematics	soldier
desperate	meant	speech
develop	minute	strength
different	necessary	studying
disappoint	nervous	success
disapprove	occasion	surprise
disease	omit	taught

(continues)

temperature	touch	villain
tenant	Tuesday	Wednesday
thorough	until	weight
thought	unusual	window
tired	variety	writing
tongue	vegetable	young

EXERCISE 2 Identifying Correctly Spelled Words

Circle the correctly spelled words in the sentences below. An example is done for you.

A few years ago, I planted my first (tomatoe, tommato, (tomato)) garden.

1. I had done careful research in (Febuary, February, Februrary).

2. In fact, I read all the gardening books at my local (library, libary, libbrary).

3. The first book (discribed, describbed, described) how to turn the soil in my garden after the long winter.

4. Another book told me how to place the (yung, young, yong) tomato plants into small holes in the dirt and then carefully cover the roots with more dirt.

5. I also learned that snail bait is (impotant, importent, important) when the tomato plants are small. Later, the plants grow small spikes that protect them from snails.

6. Throughout the summer, I (maintained, mantained, maintened) my garden by watering it every day, sometimes twice.

7. As the plant stalks grew taller, I tied them to wooden stakes, being (carful, careful, carefull) to prevent the tomato fruit from sitting on the ground where it could rot.

8. The result was tall, green stalks bearing (brilliant, briliant, brillient) red and orange tomatoes.

9. I felt so good every time I looked out my (wendow, windo, window) and saw my thriving garden.

10. Now, every fall I mark my (calender, calendar, callendar) to begin planting in the spring.

EDITING PRACTICE

The following paragraph contains twenty-two spelling errors. Cross out each misspelled word and write the correct spelling above it. Use a dictionary and the list of commonly misspelled words in this chapter if you need help. (All the health-related words, such as vitamin names, cancer-related terms, and *lycopene*, are spelled correctly.)

You Say Tomato

Though tomatoes were once thoght to be harmful to peple's health, they are actualy a healthy food. Tomatos contain large amounts of vitamin C. They also contain vitamin A, potassium, and iron. The red pigment containd in tomatoes is called lycopene. Studys have shown that the lycopene in tomatoes is a definit health benefit and can reduce the risk of develping prostate cancer. New research is begining to indicate that tomatoes may help prevent other types of cancer. When choossing tomatoes, pick those with the most briliant shades of red. These have the hiest amounts of lycopene. Altho raw tomatoes are great, cooking them—especialy in a litle bit of olive oil—releases even mor benifits. Even better, tomatoes don't lose their nutrishinal value in high-heat procesing, makeing caned tomatoes and tomato sause just as beneficial as

fresh tomatoes.

WRITING PRACTICE   Improve Your Spelling in an Earlier Assignment

Now that you're familiar with various techniques for improving your spelling, you can put them into action in your own writing. Your assignment is this: *Choose a paragraph or homework assignment that you've already completed for this or another class, and read through it.* Pay special attention to your spelling throughout the assignment, marking any words you think might be misspelled. Then, using a dictionary or the list of commonly misspelled words on pages 196–197, *correct any spelling errors you find.* If you find no errors, experiment with different wordings for sentences in your assignment, paying attention to spelling as you make substitutions.

CHAPTER SUMMARY

The following activities can help you improve your spelling.

1. Reading
2. Using a dictionary
3. Creating your own spelling list
4. Understanding basic spelling rules
5. Memorizing words that look or sound alike
6. Using a computer's spelling checker

MyWritingLab & Lab Activity 13

mywritinglab   For additional practice with spelling, go to **www.mywritinglab.com** or complete **Lab Activity 13** in the separate *Resources for Writers* Lab Manual.

14

Expanding Your Vocabulary

Culture Note

STEROIDS

Tainting nearly every sport, anabolic steroids increase protein synthesis within cells, which in turn leads to cellular tissue build-up, especially in muscles. From sprinter Ben Johnson's disgrace at the Seoul Olympics in 1988 to cyclist Floyd Landis's 2006 controversy in which he was stripped of his Tour de France title, few sports remain free from the steroid controversy. The word *anabolic* comes from the Greek *anabole*, "to build up."

UNDERSTANDING THE VALUE OF A WIDE VOCABULARY

Being able to explain your ideas in different ways gives you options in your speech and writing. If one explanation doesn't convince your reader, another one, written using different expressions, just might. Give yourself every chance to succeed in your communication efforts by expanding your vocabulary.

RECOMMENDED READINGS

"The Ways We Lie," Stephanie Ericsson, *p. 750*

"Money for Morality," Mary Arguelles, *p. 745*

"All I Really Need to Know I Learned in Kindergarten," Robert Fulgham, *p. 710*

STRETCHING YOUR VOCABULARLY

You can try four specific strategies to build a larger vocabulary.

- Reading for pleasure and education
- Using a dictionary
- Using a thesaurus
- Keeping a personal vocabulary journal

Marion Jones

CRITICAL THINKING Taking vitamins to improve one's health is considered fair, yet taking steroids is not. At what point do an athlete's actions become cheating?

Responding to Image. *What is the mood of the photo above? Consider the expressions or posture of everyone visible as well as the weather.*

Study aids such as vocabulary workbooks can also help if you use them regularly. However, the tips listed in this chapter can help you build your vocabulary using the materials you already have: readings for class, paper to write on, and a writing instrument.

Reading for Pleasure and Education

Reading is the best way to build your vocabulary. Reading introduces you to new words and gives you the chance to learn their meanings from the context. The more you read, the more new words you'll learn. Ask your instructor or a school librarian for suggestions of books you might enjoy, or read magazines (available free in most libraries) on topics that appeal to you.

Using a Dictionary

Perhaps the best way to learn the meanings of new words is to look them up in a dictionary as you encounter them. Keep a small dictionary with you when you're reading, and look up the meanings of any words that aren't familiar to you. That way, you'll know the meaning of that word for the sentence you're reading, and you'll also know the word's definition when you come across that word again.

Using a Thesaurus

A **thesaurus** is a book of **synonyms,** or words with similar meanings. When you're writing your college papers, keep a thesaurus handy. After you've used the same word two or three times, check the thesaurus for other words with similar meanings. Then, substitute a word from the thesaurus for the one you've been using.

For example, Mark wrote the paragraph below about steroids, but he noticed that he had used the word *steroids* over and over.

Electronic thesauruses can provide you with synonyms. However, use suggested words only if they are familiar to you; look up others in a dictionary first. Here's Mark's original paragraph, with synonyms inserted.

> Athletes who use steroids don't realize the price they pay for using them. First, athletes must break the law to use steroids. Since steroids are banned by major sports organizations such as the NBA and NFL, people who want to use steroids must get them from

Popular Magazines That Can Help Build Your Vocabulary

Bon Appetit	Muscle and Fitness
Cooking Light	Newsweek
Essence	People
Family Fun	Popular Mechanics
Field and Stream	Redbook
GQ (Gentleman's Quarterly)	Savoy
Good Housekeeping	Self
In Style	Sports Illustrated
Marie Claire	Time

black-market sources. If the athletes are caught using steroids, as sprinter Marion Jones and baseball player Jason Giambi were, they face penalties such as forfeiting their awards, records, and prize money. Second, steroids hurt athletes' health. According to the head trainer at my gym, steroids cause a lot of health problems, ranging from premature balding and acne to higher cholesterol levels and heart disease. Finally, steroids hurt sports. Every time an athlete uses steroids and wins, he or she makes it harder for the honest athletes to succeed. Even if the steroid users eventually get caught, as in the case of cyclist Floyd Landis, people remember only that the winner cheated, not who the real victor is.

In the nine sentences above, Mark uses the word *steroids* ten times. Although *steroids* has no true synonyms in a thesaurus, Mark had heard steroids referred to by different names (*performance-enhancing substances,* *"juice," and "'roids"*) as well as their different forms (pills, patches, and injectibles). Mark's revised paragraph reads as follows:

Athletes who use steroids don't realize the price they pay for using them. First, athletes must break the law to use <u>performance-enhancing substances</u>. Since steroids are banned by major sports organizations such as the NBA and NFL, people who want to use <u>them</u> must get them from black-market sources. If the athletes are caught using any of the *pills, patches, or injectibles,* as sprinter Marion Jones and baseball player Jason Giambi were, they face penalties such as forfeiting their awards, records, and prize money. Second, steroids hurt athletes' health. According to the head trainer at my gym, <u>"juice"</u> causes a lot of health problems, ranging from premature balding and acne to higher cholesterol and heart disease. Finally, steroids hurt sports. Every time an athlete uses a <u>banned substance</u> and wins, he or she makes it harder for the honest athletes to succeed. Even if the <u>users</u> eventually get caught, as in the case of cyclist Floyd Landis, people remember only that the "winner" cheated, not who the real victor is.

Mark still used the word *steroids* four times, but he also used the terms, *performance-enhancing substances, them, pills, patches, or injectibles, juice,* and *banned substance.* He also omitted the word *steroid* from the term *steroid users* in order to avoid repetition. This variety of words makes Mark's writing more interesting to read. Note that when Mark uses the terms "juice" and "'roids," he puts them in quotation marks. For more information on correct quotation mark usage, See Chapter 47.

TIPS for Using a Thesaurus

Keep in mind that not every word you find in the thesaurus will suit your purpose. If Mark had substituted the term *Equipoise*—a word also found on a steroid information Web site—his paragraph would have had a very different meaning since this word refers to a veterinary steroid, or one meant for animals. Remember: Use only the words that you recognize in the thesaurus. If you're not sure about a word, use a dictionary to double-check its meanings.

EXERCISE 1 Using a Thesaurus

Look up each word below in a thesaurus. Then, write down three possible synonyms for each word. An example is done for you.

Word: house

Synonyms: _____*home*_____ _____*place*_____ _____*abode*_____

1. Word: tree

Synonyms: _____ _____ _____

2. Word: car

Synonyms: _____ _____ _____

3. Word: music

Synonyms: _____ _____ _____

4. Word: child

Synonyms: _____ _____ _____

5. Word: doctor

Synonyms: _____ _____ _____

Keeping a Personal Vocabulary Journal

A personal vocabulary journal will help you improve your vocabulary. Every time you read something, highlight the words whose definitions you don't know. Then, either while you're reading or after you've finished, write those words in your personal vocabulary journal. Include the correct spelling of the word, its pronunciation, its parts of speech, and its most important meanings. For instance, if you added the word *labile* to your vocabulary journal, your entry might look like this.

Personal Vocabulary Journal

Word: labile   Pronunciation: `lā-bīl   Part of speech: adj.

Meanings: 1. Readily or continually undergoing chemical, physical, or biological change or breakdown. 2. Readily open to change.

Sentence: When Marcella turned thirteen, she became labile, changing from smiling to tearful in a few seconds.

EXERCISE 2 Starting Your Personal Vocabulary Journal

In a notebook, start a personal vocabulary journal. Look up five words that you would like to know better, and write their definitions in your list. Include the pronunciation and part of speech, and write a sentence that shows what the word means and how to use it. Follow the model given above.

TIP

Visit www.ablongman.com/vocabulary, www.vocabulary.com, or www.freerice.com for additional opportunities to build your vocabulary.

CHECKLIST

To improve your vocabulary, do the following:

- Read for pleasure and education.
- Use a dictionary.
- Use a thesaurus.
- Keep a personal vocabulary journal.

EDITING PRACTICE

Read the following essay, which contains words you may not know. Choose five words that you would like to understand better, and add them to your personal vocabulary journal. Use the same format you followed in Exercise 2.

Cheaters Never Prosper, or Do They?

While athletes are penalized for using steroids, many still benefit from their use, even after they get caught. Take Mark McGuire, for instance. In 1998 Mark McGuire of the St. Louis Cardinals and Sammy Sosa of the Chicago Cubs contended for the all-time home run record, which Mark McGuire won with an astonishing seventy homers. Though McGuire was widely thought to have used performance-enhancing substances, he was still showered with the respect, admiration, and endorsements of a hero. Competitive cyclist Floyd Landis is another example. Though he was stripped of his 2006 Tour de France victory, he still had the delectation of riding into Paris wearing the famed yellow jersey of the leader. Few people remember Óscar Pereiro, the cyclist who supplanted Landis as the winner, but people remember Landis finishing first. Last is sprinter Marion Jones. In 2007 Jones was found to have prevaricated concerning her own steroid use and was stripped of her five medals in the 2000 Olympics. Even though she was disgraced and imprisoned, she still had the thrill of crossing the finish line first, setting records, and standing on the Olympic podium with the gold medal around her neck. She may have to return the $700,000 prize money she earned, but she can never return her glorious moments to those from whom she stole them.

WRITING PRACTICE   Improving Vocabulary in Your Own Writing

You've learned and practiced different strategies for varying and expanding your vocabulary in your own writing. Now it's time to use these skills in a paragraph that you've written. Your assignment is this: *Revise an assignment you completed earlier in the term. Use a dictionary and thesaurus to expand your vocabulary in the assignment, and take care to delete repetitive words and terms.*

MyWritingLab & Lab Activity 14

mywritinglab   For additional practice with vocabulary expansion, go to **www.mywritinglab. com** or complete **Lab Activity 14** in the separate *Resources for Writers* Lab Manual.

PART FOUR
Strategies
for Paragraph Development

A Mighty Roar

JOURNAL ENTRY How much do you think people's actions change when they are in group situations? Write a few sentences explaining how your own actions are or are not influenced by others'.

Responding to Images. *What feelings does this photo inspire? Consider color, facial expressions, and body language.*

Illustration and Example

WHAT IS AN ILLUSTRATION AND EXAMPLE PARAGRAPH?

Suppose you want to set your friend up with your brother, but she remembers growing up with him and seeing him do things like make prank phone calls that didn't impress her. You think he has changed, and you offer the following examples to illustrate your brother's adult behavior.

- He gave your mother flowers just for being a great mom.
- He attends the community college while holding down a job.
- He has apologized for the way he acted when you were children.

Providing illustrations and examples is one of the simplest and most effective writing strategies. In an illustration and example paragraph, you offer specific details that fit logically into the larger picture.

RECOMMENDED READINGS:

"The Plot Against People," Russell Baker, p. 779

"The Price We Pay," Adam Mayblum, p. 794

"Manners Matter," Judith Martin, p. 758

New York City Skyline

FOOD FOR THOUGHT Impressive for its landmark structures, New York City boasts such attractions as the Statue of Liberty, the Empire State Building, and the Chrysler Building. What impressions do you have of New York City? Write for ten minutes about what you know, think, or imagine about it. ***Responding to Images.*** *How prominent is the Statue of Liberty in this photo? Write about how it's placement, the light, and it's surroundings communicate how important–or unimportant–the statue is.*

Examples and illustrations can come from three sources.

■ Descriptions of objects or events in your life
■ Accounts of events in other people's lives
■ Facts that you've heard about or read in trusted sources

REAL-LIFE WRITING

In real-life writing, writers use the strategy of providing illustrations and examples in a number of important settings.

For College
■ Use illustrations and examples on placement or assessment tests.
■ Use illustrations and examples on in-class essay exams—such as in history, English, or art courses—when you need to show your instructor that you know certain information.

In Your Personal Life

■ Use specific examples in a letter to a friend to convince her that a new restaurant is worth trying.

■ Use examples and illustrations in an e-mail to your friends to show them that an apartment is a good place to live.

At Work

■ Cite examples of other stores to convince your boss to update your store's window displays.

■ Give examples of the additional work you've done so that your boss might give you more responsibility and a raise.

A MODEL PARAGRAPH: ILLUSTRATION AND EXAMPLE

To use illustration and example, follow the basic format shown in the "Illustration and Example Paragraphs" diagram on page 212.

In the following paragraph, the writer has developed a topic sentence and provided illustrations and examples that prove the support points.

Big-City Life

Living in New York is exciting for many reasons. For instance, I have many different travel options. When I lived in other, smaller cities, I drove my car to work. I always took the same route and never saw much that was different. In New York, however, I can take the subway and see people from all over the city who ride in the same train car, or I can take a taxi (if I can afford it) and watch people out the windows. If the weather is nice, I can even walk. No matter which way I choose, I always see something new. Another illustration of New York's excitement is its architecture. Just walking down the street is like being in a museum. I can see the Chrysler Building, with its grimacing gargoyles, or the Empire State Building, rising up like a giant. I can also see the narrow, twisting streets of the Wall Street area, with famous buildings such as the New York Stock Exchange and Fraunces Tavern. Walking through New York is like taking secret passageways to new and wonderful places. A last example of New York's exciting life is the food. I can find pretty much any kind of food I'm in the mood for. Sometimes I want an Italian meal, so I head down to Little Italy. If I'm in the mood for

---

Illustration and Example Paragraphs

Topic sentence....*Stating the main idea*..
....

↓

Support point 1...
......................Example or illustration......................
......................Example or illustration......................
Support point 2...
......................Example or illustration......................
......................Example or illustration......................
Support point 3...
......................Example or illustration......................
......................Example or illustration......................

Japanese food, there's always great sushi to be found. Sometimes, I just want a hot dog, and then I can find a vendor on a street corner who gives me my perfect lunch. Living in New York is never boring.

The writer's topic sentence is "Living in New York is exciting for many reasons." The following support points show how living in New York is exciting.

1. Different travel options

2. Great architecture

3. Different foods

The writer uses these transitions to link the three support points: *for example, another illustration, a last example*. The transitions tell the reader to expect examples and illustrations.

EXERCISE 1 Finding Examples in a Paragraph

Some of the details from "Big-City Life" on page 211 are filled in on p. 213. Write in the remaining details that the writer uses to illustrate her support points.

Support point 1:   Different travel options

Examples: Subway ride

_____

_____

Support point 2:   Great architecture

Examples: Chrysler Building

_____

_____

Support point 3:   Different foods

Examples: Italian food in Little Italy

_____

_____

CHOOSING A GOOD TOPIC FOR DEVELOPMENT

Sometimes your instructor will give you a topic, but other times you'll choose your own. One way to find a topic that works well for using illustrations and examples is to do some prewriting. For instance, Eva wondered if she could write an effective paragraph about her neighborhood as a place to be a single, aspiring artist. She made a cluster diagram to help her find examples. Nearly everything in the diagram supports the idea that her neighborhood is a good place to be a single artist.

WRITING AN EFFECTIVE TOPIC SENTENCE

Eva organized her examples and illustrations according to the support points they illustrate.

Support point 1: The neighborhood is convenient to museums and parks for inspiration.

Support point 2: The neighborhood is well lighted and safe for a single woman.

Support point 3: There are many other single artists for social and moral support.

After identifying support points from her cluster diagram, Eva wrote her topic sentence: "The Oak Grove neighborhood is a good place to live and work as an aspiring artist." When she writes her rough draft, Eva can eliminate two examples—the absence of an art supply store nearby and the lack of pets—since they don't illustrate any of her support points. Another point—about the neighborhood watch program—had potential for development, but since Eva found fewer details supporting that idea, she decided not to include it.

DEVELOPING SPECIFIC DETAILS

When you have experience in the subject you're writing about, using examples from your own life will be most effective. However, if your topic is one that you know less about, you can use examples from other people's experiences or from trusted sources such as a magazine or newspaper.

Some of the examples Eva developed during clustering came from her personal experience: "near grocery store" and "close to public transportation." Other examples came from Eva's discussion with others in the neighborhood: "other artists nearby" and "artists I can ask for advice." However, one illustration was a fact that Eva read in the local newspaper: "near new health clinic."

For most of the assignments in this book, examples from your own life or from the lives of people you know will be adequate for support. When you write for more complicated assignments, however, you will need to use examples from additional sources. In many college courses, you'll need to read about a specific event or topic, learn about it, and then write what you've learned in an essay or report.

Read the paragraph that follows. Then read the outline that the writer used to develop the paragraph. How do you think the writer got his information for the examples in the paragraph? Do the examples come from his own life? Pay attention to the specific details that the writer chose.

On with the Show!

[1]Probably no other city has been a greater subject for artists and entertainers than New York, New York. [2]A case in point comes from the hundreds of songs about the city. [3]In the 1930s the songwriter Cole Porter wrote "I Happen to Like New York," and then Frank Sinatra made the song "New York, New York" famous by singing about "the city that never sleeps." [4]Further, in the 1980s, Billy Joel's "New York State of Mind" and Grand Master Flash and the Furious Five's song "New York, New York" became hits even though their messages about New York were less happy than the ones in earlier songs. [5]Movies are another example of how New York has influenced entertainment. [6]The movie *An Affair to Remember* featured the Empire State Building as a meeting place for lovers, and then both *Love Affair* and *Sleepless in Seattle* used the same romantic setting. [7]*King Kong* was an adventure movie set in New York, and *Enchanted* showed fairy-tale characters all over the Big Apple. [8]Even the *Spider-Man* movies and *The Devil Wears Prada* were set in New York, too. [9]A final example of how New York is a subject for entertainment comes from television shows.

[10]Many recent television programs, including *30 Rock* and *Law and Order*, are all set in New York. [11]In fact, it seems hard to find TV series that are *not* set in New York City. [12]All in all, New York is a big star!

Topic sentence: Probably no other city has been a greater subject for artists and entertainers than New York, New York.

A. Songs
   1. Cole Porter, "I Happen to Like New York"
   2. Frank Sinatra, "New York, New York"
   3. Billy Joel, "A New York State of Mind"
   4. Grand Master Flash, "New York, New York"

B. Movies
   1. *An Affair to Remember*   **5.** *Enchanted*
   2. *Love Affair*   **6.** *Spider-Man* series
   3. *Sleepless in Seattle*   **7.** *The Devil Wears Prada*
   4. *King Kong*

C. Television programs
   1. *30 Rock*   **2.** *Law and Order*

EXERCISE 2 Providing Specific Details

Each sentence below is a support point in a paragraph. Provide at least three examples that support each point.

Support point: Many people are interested in buying a hybrid car.

Examples: Hybrids use a combination of gasoline and electric power.

   Their motors efficiently provide plenty of power.

   They usually get better than forty miles per gallon.

1. Support point: Reality TV shows are actually carefully staged.

Examples: _____

   _____

   _____

2. Support point: There are several ways to deal with a roommate who snores.

Examples: _____

_____

_____

3. Support point: Computer blogs give everyone the ability to be "published."

Examples: _____

_____

_____

4. Support point: Space exploration is (or is not) important to the future of our country.

Examples: _____

_____

_____

5. Support point: History's most influential written works illustrate the saying "The pen is mightier than the sword."

Examples: _____

_____

_____

ORGANIZING AND LINKING YOUR IDEAS

Once you've come up with a topic, written a topic sentence and support points, and supported those points with details, you're ready to organize your ideas using either time sequence (chronological) order or emphatic order. Writing an illustration and example paragraph gives you some freedom in organizing your ideas.

Transition Words and Terms That Signal Examples

an illustration of	particularly
for example	specifically
for instance	such as
one example of	that is

In "Big-City Life," on page 211, the writer loosely uses emphatic order. Even though she doesn't say she thinks that food is the most important aspect of living in New York City, her placement of "different foods" as the last support point makes that an important point. In "On with the Show!" on page 215, the writer uses a loose form of time sequence order. He doesn't say that his points occur in chronological order, but he begins with singers from the 1930s in his first support point, and he ends with television programs that still air today.

To introduce examples and link ideas, writers use **transitional expressions.** In the sentences that follow, the underlined transitional expression signals that an example or illustration is being introduced.

> Another reason this is a good neighborhood for an aspiring artist is that there are many arts resources nearby. <u>For example</u>, an art supply store is right around the corner.

EXERCISE 3 Following the Four Cs

Read the paragraph below. Then, answer the questions that follow.

New York City: The Ultimate Survivor

[1]After the terrorist attacks of September 11, 2001, New York seemed to be reeling. [2]I know I was. [3]The New York Stock Exchange (NYSE) suffered its biggest-ever one-day losses, businesses fled Manhattan, and an enormous mound of rubble marked the spot where the World Trade Center had been. [4]It didn't look good. [5]In spite of all this, New York is making a comeback. [6]One example of New York's recovery has come in the financial world. [7]The stock market has rallied, rebounding from under 9,000 points in September 2001 to over 12,000 points in 2008. [8]Another illustration of New York's rebounding ability comes in the fact that people have returned to the city for business. [9]According to a report by the Russell Sage Foundation, people's need for face-to-face contact is the cause. [10]Finally, the new 7 World Trade Center office building, completed in 2006, stands on the site of one of the demolished buildings, while the Freedom Tower is under construc-

Building a Future

SURF THE NET Beginning with the beam at left, the Freedom Tower's construction continues. Surf the Internet for details about the building's construction program.

Responding to Images. *How important is the placement of the initial beam of the Freedom Tower, as depicted in this photo, to building freedom? Explain.*

tion. [11]At 1,776 feet (541 meters) upon completion, the tower will become the tallest building in North America and one of the tallest in the world. [12]I've heard that people who worked in the Sears Tower in Chicago were afraid they might be attacked, too, because that building is so tall. [13]No one can forget the attacks of 2001, and few people would say that New York now is better for having endured the plane crashes. [14]However, as people do their business, stay in the city, and watch the Freedom Tower rise, it's impossible not to see New York, New York, as the survivor it is.

Concise

1. What two sentences are off-target and should be removed?

_____ , _____

2. What is the topic sentence? _____

Credible

3. What are the three ways in which New York has come back since the 9/11 attacks, according to "New York City: The Ultimate Survivor"?

    a. _____

    b. _____

    c. _____

4. What is one example that you think is particularly effective?

_____

Clear

5. What important signal words does the writer use to introduce support points?

    a. _____

    b. _____

    c. _____

6. a. What is the most positive sign of New York's comeback that the writer mentions? _____

_____

b. Why do you think the writer put this reason last? _____

_____

_____

Correct

The sentences in this paragraph are all correct. To check for correctness in your own writing, go to Part 7, "Writing Correct Sentences."

WRITING PRACTICE 1 Develop Details for a Topic Sentence

Below are five topic sentences that need support. For each topic sentence, provide one well-developed illustration. An example is done for you.

Topic sentence:	Modern music includes many different sounds.
Support point:	*Some songs even use sounds that aren't really musical.*
Example:	*In the Bahamian song "Who Let the Dogs Out," for instance, the regular musical sounds of a melody and a beat are highlighted by the barking of a dog throughout the song.*

1. Topic sentence: Sharing a room with two siblings taught me how to get along with other people.

Support point: _____

Example: _____

_____

2. Topic sentence: Working as a pool cleaner for the summer was a hard job.

Support point: _____

Example: _____

_____

3. Topic sentence: Taking risks is necessary for success.

Support point: _____

Example: _____

_____

4. Topic sentence: Sometimes good things happen to you when you least expect them.

Support point: _____

Example: _____

_____

5. Topic sentence: Television shows rarely have stars that look like everyday people.

Support point: _____

Example: _____

_____

WRITING PRACTICE 2 Write an Illustration and Example Paragraph

Now write an illustration and example paragraph of your own.

Prewriting

1. Choose one of the following topics for your illustration and example paragraph.

An exciting sport or activity

A funny television show or movie

A frustrating or satisfying job

A funny person

An irritating person

A famous person

A place from your childhood

2. Freewrite for five to ten minutes on the topic. Then, use at least one other prewriting technique—listing, questioning, keeping a journal, clustering, or outlining—to come up with more descriptive details.

If you need help coming up with a topic and doing prewriting, use the outline below. (Write your own topic sentence to reflect your ideas on a funny person you know.) Add your own specific details to complete the outline.

Topic sentence: My uncle is very funny. _____

A. Always has a new joke

1. _____

2. _____

3. _____

B. Performs a stand-up comedy routine at a local club

   1. _____

   2. _____

   3. _____

C. Helps lighten up family dinners

   1. _____

   2. _____

   3. _____

Another helpful prewriting technique for writing an illustration and example paragraph is asking questions. To develop ideas about the topic "a place from my childhood," Henry used this technique.

Fourth-Grade Classroom

What was my teacher like?	Mrs. Roberts was tough, strict, not always nice.
Who were my classmates?	Big kids picked on me.
What was the classroom like?	Too much chalk dust

Drafting

3. Write a topic sentence. Draw on your prewriting to find a point to develop through an entire paragraph. For instance, the answers to Henry's questions are all negative. Thus, a workable topic sentence could be "Thinking about my fourth-grade classroom can still make me nervous."

4. Choose support points and specific details. Henry wrote down the reasons thinking about his fourth-grade classroom makes him nervous.

Mean teacher

Big kids

Chalk dust allergy

Then, choose the details that you think best illustrate your support points and will make your paragraph believable. Henry chose the following details.

Support Point	Specific Details
Mean teacher	Mrs. Roberts gave me detention for tapping my finger on the desk.
Big kids	Sam and Al picked on me during recess; Marc stole my lunch.
Chalk dust allergy	Constant sneezing, itchy skin

5. Arrange your support points using time sequence (chronological) or emphatic order. Decide which order works better by examining your details. If all of Henry's negative fourth-grade experiences occurred simultaneously throughout the school year, he should probably use emphatic order. However, if the negative events in fourth grade occurred one after another, Henry could use time sequence order. As you're organizing your ideas, be sure to eliminate details that don't fit.

6. Now write a draft of your paragraph using the topic sentence, your support points, and your specific details. Feel free to do more prewriting if you need additional specific details.

Revising

7. Check for the first three of the four Cs: *concise, credible*, and *clear* writing. Make any necessary changes to your draft.

Editing

8. Check your paragraph for the fourth C: *correct* writing. Proofread your paragraph to make sure you have used correct spelling, punctuation, and grammar.

WRITING PRACTICE 3 Write a Paragraph About a Person

Write about a person who has had an impact on your life. Choose Topic A or Topic B to write your paragraph. Remember to include a topic sentence, support points, and examples. If you need help, refer to Writing Practice 2 on pages 222–224.

Topic A

Write a paragraph about a person who has had a positive influence on you. This person can be someone you know well, or someone you've only seen on television. (A person does not need to be an active part of your life in order to have a positive influence on you.)

Possible Topics

Someone who encouraged you	Someone who taught you
Someone who disciplined you	Someone who rewarded you
Someone who set a good example for you	Someone who inspired you

Topic B

Write a paragraph about someone who has had a negative effect on your life. Again, this person does not need to be someone you know well. Use examples to show how the person influenced your life.

Possible Topics

Someone who embarrassed you	Someone who hurt your feelings
Someone who set a poor example	Someone who lied to you
Someone who discouraged you	Someone who cheated you

CHAPTER SUMMARY

To develop your ideas using illustration and example, remember the following:

1. Choose a topic that lends itself to illustration and example.
2. Use examples from your own experiences, your observations of others' experiences, and trusted sources.
3. Signal your examples to your reader by using relevant transitions.

MyWritingLab & Lab Activity 15

mywritinglab For additional practice with providing illustrations and examples, go to **www.mywritinglab.com** or complete **Lab Activity 15** in the separate *Resources for Writers* Lab Manual.

Narration

Culture Note

FAIRY TALES

As stories of good and evil, reward and punishment, fairy tales have been told for centuries. Though part of their appeal is entertainment, fairy tales were also used to show people the difference between right and wrong. In the twentieth century, fairy tales came under attack for emphasizing beauty and virtue above other qualities in women, but some tales have messages that everyone can appreciate.

WHAT IS A NARRATIVE PARAGRAPH?

If you've ever sat down after a long day and explained to a friend just what happened to make that day rotten—your alarm clock didn't go off, your boss got mad at you, your car broke down, and your coffee spilled down the front of your white shirt—you've already practiced the art of narration, or of telling a story.

Narration is a paragraph development strategy that involves writing about events in the order in which they occur (time sequence order). Narration's purpose is to tell a story, so it works particularly well when you are writing about events that happen one after another.

RECOMMENDED READINGS

"A Homemade Education," Malcolm X, *p. 714*

"The Price We Pay," Adam Mayblum, *p. 794*

"My Mother's English," Amy Tan, *p. 773*

REAL-LIFE WRITING

In real-life writing, we use narration frequently to provide "the whole story" or to give our readers a context for our arguments. Here are some situations in which you might use the strategy of narrating an event.

A Modern Prince Charming

JOURNAL ENTRY What Fairy Tale heroes or villains do you find particularly interesting or realistic in terms of their personalities or actions? Explain in a few sentences.

Responding to Images. *What about this photo seems out of place or contradictory? Explain.*

For College

- Use narration in history or political science exams or papers. Narrating events—especially those based on a timeline—can ensure that you include all the necessary details in the correct order.
- Use narration for recounting events that occurred in your life.

In Your Personal Life

- Use narration in a letter or in your own journal to describe an event or a series of events.

- Use narration when writing a letter to a business to explain your experience with the customer service department.

At Work

- In a memo, narrate your week-by-week interaction with a client during a project.
- In a job application, offer a brief narrative that illustrates your qualifications for a job. For instance, tell step by step how you solved a particular problem.

A MODEL PARAGRAPH: NARRATIVE

To write a narrative paragraph, follow the basic paragraph format, shown in the "Narrative Paragraphs" illustration on page 229. The writer has developed a topic sentence and included details in time sequence order.

The Price for a Prince

[1]In the Hans Christian Andersen's tale "The Little Mermaid," the youngest daughter of the Sea King pays a great price for an attempt to win a prince. [2]The little mermaid loves a young human prince whom she has seen. [3]The prince has no idea of the little mermaid's existence, and even when she saves him from drowning, he believes another girl to be responsible. [4]The little mermaid decides to try to become human. [5]First, she approaches the sorceress of the sea and asks for her help. [6]Just finding the sorceress is unpleasant because the sorceress's captives try to grab and keep the little mermaid. [7]Next, the sorceress gives the little mermaid frightening news about the price she will have to pay. [8]Even after drinking the potion, the little mermaid can become human only if the prince marries her. [9]If the prince marries anyone else, the little mermaid must die. [10]Additionally, once the little mermaid becomes human, every time her feet touch the ground, she will feel as if she is walking on sharp knives. [11]The fee the sorceress requires is the little mermaid's lovely voice. [12]In exchange for a magic potion, the sorceress cuts out the little mermaid's tongue. [13]Eventually, the little mermaid drinks the potion, grows legs that feel piercing pain, and meets her prince. [14]He is enchanted with her, even allowing her to sleep on a cushion outside his bedroom door. [15]However, he marries another princess. [16]The little mermaid has given everything for someone who will not return her love.

Narrative Paragraphs
Topic sentence.....*Stating the event or story*...
↓
Event 1.. ....Details about the event........................ Event 2.. ....Details about the event........................ Event 3.. ....Details about the event........................ Event 4.. ....Details about the event........................ Event 5.. ....Details about the event........................

EXERCISE 1 Identifying the Elements of a Narrative Paragraph

Reread "The Price for a Prince." Then, answer the questions and fill in the blanks that follow.

1. What is the starting point for the story?_____

_____

2. What is the ending point for the story? _____

_____

3. What steps does the little mermaid take to become human?

    a. _____

    b. _____

    c. _____

4. How does the prince react to the little mermaid? _____

_____

5. What transitions does the writer use in the following sentences that help the reader move from one event to another?

Sentence 5: _____	Sentence 7: _____
Sentence 8: _____	Sentence 10: _____
Sentence 11: _____	Sentence 13: _____

CHOOSING A GOOD TOPIC FOR DEVELOPMENT

Sometimes your instructor will give you a topic, but when you have to choose your own, make sure your topic lends itself to telling a story. Many topics can be organized according to time sequence, but some are easier to write about than others.

Topics That Work Well for Narration	**Topics That Don't Work Well for Narration**
How you decided to try skydiving	The importance of preparing for skydiving
The first time you cried at a movie	Why movies make you cry

Topics that work well are limited to a certain event or time period. Topics that don't work have points that might not necessarily occur in chronological order. For instance, if movies make you cry because the screen images are large and because you are an emotional person, you might have a difficult time deciding which one of those points comes first according to time sequence order. Thus, explaining *why* you tend to cry is not the best choice for a narrative paragraph.

One way to tell if your topic will work well for narration is to *make a list of all the events that your paragraph will cover*. Listing will help you keep your facts in order and eliminate facts that are irrelevant.

For instance, in "The Price for a Prince" on page 228, the writer never mentions the other story line: that the little mermaid also wants to become human so that she can have an immortal soul. The writer also leaves out the details that the little mermaid has the chance—on the prince's wedding night—to kill him and become a mermaid again, but that she can't bring herself to harm him. While these details are interesting, they don't help the writer develop the idea in the topic sentence, that the little mermaid paid a great price for an attempt to win her prince. Notice, too, how the writer "hurries" through longer periods of time—for example, the little mermaid's whole life until she meets the sorceress—to focus on the events that matter most.

Dean's assignment below was to write a paragraph on a particularly good or bad event in his life. He began by making a list of events that occurred the day his high school soccer team won a championship.

Winning the big game
Lost to Seahall Spartans for past two years.
They played dirty (we could, too).
We knew we were better.
Clear fall day.
Good smell of newly mown grass.
Won the coin toss at midfield.
Coin glimmered as it fell.
Coin seemed to fall in slow motion.
Kicked off, passed to Andre, and scored in first five minutes.
Other team scored in first half, too, but we dominated play.
Coach was nervous.
Ron, Steve, and Franco almost scored, but their goalie was awesome.
Second half started badly (I slipped and missed a scoring chance).
Shoe came untied.
Got an assist for passing to Pablo for his header in.
Thought we'd won for sure, but then Carlos fouled their striker in the penalty box.
They shot a penalty kick and missed.
Bobby and Jim controlled the ball for the last two minutes.
We won.
First time Grant High School won a soccer title.

Most of Dean's details show a progression from the start of the game through to the end. However, some details—the coach's nervousness and the fact that this was the high school's first soccer title—can be omitted from the paragraph because they don't lead to the winning moment of the game.

WRITING AN EFFECTIVE TOPIC SENTENCE

After making his list, Dean realized that he mentioned the names of several teammates. This told him that their victory was a team effort. Thus, his topic sentence became "Winning the section title in varsity soccer was a complete team effort."

DEVELOPING SPECIFIC DETAILS FOR NARRATION

To add information and interest to your narrative paragraphs, you can use three types of details.

- Background details
- Action details
- Sensory details

Background Details

Background details give information about other events that may have occured at the same time as the main event of your paragraph or earlier. The following background details come from Dean's prewriting list.

> Lost to Seahall Spartans for past two years.
>
> They played dirty (we could, too).
>
> We knew we were better.

These details don't tell anything about the championship game. However, they help the reader understand why this game is so important to the writer.

Action Details

Action details move your story along from one point to the next. In a narrative paragraph, the writer doesn't use formal support points. Dean referred to his prewriting list to find the action details that served as important place markers for his information. Thus, he knew he would write about the following parts of the game.

> Early scoring by his team
>
> Missed shots and assists during the game
>
> Possible tie when Carlos was called for a foul

Dean decided that these were the pivotal action details he *had* to include.

Sensory Details

Sensory details add information that makes your paragraph more vivid and thus more interesting. For instance, Dean described the start of the soccer game using these details. He added sensory details to give the reader a better feel for the day.

> Clear fall day.
> Good smell of newly mown grass.
> Coin glimmered as it fell.
> Coin seemed to fall in slow motion.

In Dean's paragraph, the phrase "smell of newly mown grass" and the description of the coin as it "caught the sun and glimmered as it fell—as if in slow motion" paint a picture for the reader. Even if the reader isn't a soccer fan, by including these sensory details, Dean hopes to make sure that the reader will *want* to read his paragraph. Here is Dean's final draft.

A Team Effort

Winning the section title in varsity soccer was a complete team effort. On the day of the big game—a bright, clear fall day—we all felt nervous. We had come up against the Seahall High School Spartans for the last two years, and we'd lost both times. They played dirty, but we knew we were the better team, so we were prepared to take elbows to the head (and maybe give a few back) in order to win the game. The smell of newly mown grass hit me as I stepped onto the field for the coin toss. I called "heads," and as the coin fell, it caught the sun and glimmered—as if in slow motion—to land in the heads-up position. We chose to go with the wind first. As Seahall kicked off, I stole the ball, sprinted up the side, and centered to Andre, who scored. We dominated play during the first half—Ron, Steve, and Franco came really close to scoring—but Seahall's goalie was awesome. By halftime, the Spartans had managed to score, too. The second half started badly because I slipped and missed what should have been an easy goal. Then my shoe came untied, and I almost missed trapping a key pass. We hit our stride, however, as I passed to Pablo. He had a great header in, and I got the assist. With a few minutes to go, we were starting to get excited, but then Carlos fouled their striker in the penalty box. Luckily, their kicker missed the penalty shot, and Bobby and Jim controlled the ball for the last two minutes. The only thing better than winning the game was knowing that we all had contributed.

Dean uses all three types of details—background, action, and sensory—to provide a context for his event, move the action along, and vividly illustrate the events leading up to the big win.

EXERCISE 2 Analyzing a Paragraph for Good Narration Strategy

Read the paragraph below. Then, answer the questions that follow.

A Fairy Tale for Today

[1]The life and marriage of Lisa Halaby, an American, are a modern-day fairy tale. [2]Lisa Halaby was born in 1951 to an important Arab-American family that was involved in politics. [3]She grew up attending excellent private schools, and in 1969 she enrolled in Princeton University as part of the first coed class. [4]At Princeton, Halaby studied architecture and urban planning. [5]After she graduated, she took a job in the country of Jordan. [6]Since her father worked in politics in Jordan at that time, he introduced her to the King of Jordan, King Hussein I. [7]Halaby and King Hussein became friends, and later their friendship developed into a romance. [8]They were married in 1978, and Halaby became the first American-born queen of an Arab nation. [9]She took the name Noor al-Hussein, which means "Light of Hussein," and converted to the Muslim faith. [10]For the next twenty years, Queen Noor lived happily with King Hussein, and they had four children. [11]Even though she was a queen and did not need to work for a living, Queen Noor worked hard to improve the lives of women and children in Jordan. [12]In particular, she worked to give women employment options without criticizing women who chose not to work for religious reasons. [13]King Hussein died in 1999, but Queen Noor continued to live in Jordan with her children. [14]Though many would say that Queen Noor is like a fairy-tale princess, she has done so much for others that she is also like a fairy godmother.

1. Make a list of events in the paragraph. The first two items are done for you.

    a. Lisa Halaby was born in 1951 to an important Arab-American family that was involved in politics.

    b. She grew up attending excellent private schools.

    c. _____

    d. _____

    e. _____

    f. _____

g. _____

h. _____

i. _____

j. _____

k. _____

l. _____

m. _____

n. _____

2. The beginning of the paragraph contains many background details. Write down one background detail from the paragraph.

_____

_____

3. Write two action details from the paragraph.

a. _____

b. _____

ORGANIZING AND LINKING YOUR IDEAS

One way to organize your ideas before writing them in a paragraph is to make a timeline. This horizontal list allows you to place events in the order in which they occurred, along with times or dates. That way, you can map out all the events you're writing about before you start drafting.

Unlike other kinds of paragraphs you've seen in this text so far, narrative paragraphs don't necessarily contain obvious individual support points. Also, they often don't use transitions such as *for one, another point,* or *finally* to introduce individual points. Still, you need to make sure that each event is clearly connected to the events before and after it.

But instead of writing *one example* or *another instance when,* you will use transitions that show time sequence order, such as the ones listed in "Transitions That Show Time Sequence" on page 239. These transitions will keep your reader on track.

EXERCISE 3 Following the Four Cs

Read the paragraph below. Then answer the questions that follow.

Lessons from Loss

[1]Until I "invested" my measly savings in a "can't miss" business opportunity, I thought Jack from "Jack and the Beanstalk" wasn't too smart when he traded the family cow for some beans. [2]However, after I made the mistake of listening to my sister's boyfriend Hank, I learned a number of lessons about money. [3]One lesson was to learn about what I put my money in. [4]Right when I started back to school after working to save money, Hank told me about a new computer company that would pay me triple whatever I put in. [5]Since I still needed money for school, I gave Hank my hard-earned cash even though I knew nothing about computers. [6]Like Jack's magic beans, my investment—I was sure—would bring me great profits. [7]I was wrong. [8]I never saw a penny of profit, or of my original money. [9]I also learned to be persistent when I was expecting a payment. [10]After Hank missed the first three payment deadlines—offering flimsy excuses about how "complicated" the business was—I should have demanded my money back, but I didn't. [11]After six months I realized that my money—and my sister's—was gone for good, and by then so was Hank. [12]Because I'd lost my college money, I had to hustle around to get whatever loans I could from the school, the state, and my parents. [13]Luckily, I pieced together enough money to pay for school, and I read *Investing for Dummies* and learned how to make money grow. [14](Investing in my sister's boyfriend's "great opportunity" was not in the book.) [15]I still have some loans to pay back, but the lessons I learned from the experience were worth the price I paid. [16]Maybe Jack benefited from trusting someone for a few beans, but I wasn't so lucky.

Concise

1. What is the topic sentence of the paragraph "Lessons from Loss"?

_____

_____

2. What are some of the lessons that the writer learned about investing?

_____

_____

Credible

3. What are some specific details the writer uses to show how his situation is similar to Jack's?

_____

_____

4. What are some specific details the writer uses to show how his life is different from Jack's?

_____

Clear

5. What transitions does the writer use in the following sentences to indicate when certain events occurred?

Sentence 2:   _____

Sentence 4:   _____

Sentence 11:   _____

6. What transitions does the writer use in sentences 2, 5, 10, 11, and 12 that show a change of direction in the writer's ideas? (Feel free to check the list of transitions in Chapter 10.) _____, _____, _____, _____, _____

EXERCISE 4 Providing Details for a Narrative Paragraph

The following are possible topic sentences for narrative paragraphs. For each one, write four events that could help develop the topic sentence. An example is done for you.

Topic sentence: My sixteenth birthday proved to be one of the happiest days of my life.

Events: **a.** I passed my driver's test. _____

b. I drove myself to best friend's house. _____

My best friend organized a "Sweet Sixteen/Happy
c. Driving" party for me. _____

d. My workaholic dad took time off to come to the party. ___

1. Topic sentence: My little brother learned an important lesson
when he _____.

Events: **a.** _____

b. _____

c. _____

d. _____

2. Topic sentence: Sometimes even a little gesture of kindness can
go a long way.

Events: **a.** _____

b. _____

c. _____

d. _____

3. Topic sentence: From the first moment I saw _____,
I knew we would be good friends.

Events: **a.** _____

b. _____

c. _____

d. _____

4. Topic sentence: My first day of college proved to be ———————.

Events: **a.** _____

b. _____

c. _____

d. _____

5. Topic sentence: On my first day at _____,
I definitely got off on the wrong foot.

Events: **a.** _____

b. _____

c. _____

d. _____

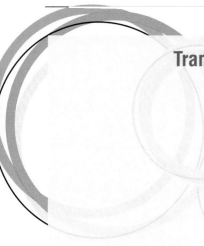

Transitions That Show Time Sequence

after	finally
as	later
as soon as	next
at last	now
at the same time	soon
before	then
during	upon
earlier	when
first	while

WRITING PRACTICE 1   Write a Narrative Paragraph

Now write a narrative paragraph of your own.

Prewriting

1. Choose a topic for your narrative paragraph.

Possible Topics

Your first day at a new job or at college

Moving to a new home

An experience that made you sad

How a historical event affected you

A personal triumph or success

A family celebration

2. Freewrite for five to ten minutes on your topic. Then, use at least one other prewriting technique—listing, questioning, keeping a journal, clustering, or outlining—to see what information you have and where possible gaps are.

For narrative paragraphs, the prewriting technique of listing is very useful because it helps you keep important events in order. For example, here is a sample list on the topic "moving to a new home."

Moving Day

Woke up rested.

Called friends to make sure they could still help me.

Labeled boxes.

Loaded truck.

Steve broke my one good chair.

Sonya brought a great lunch (roast beef sandwiches).

Unloaded truck.

Started unpacking kitchen boxes.

Realized that boxes were labeled incorrectly.

Gave up for the day and just talked about old times.

Drafting

3. Write a topic sentence that includes a topic and point-of-view words. For example, here is a topic sentence for the listing done above.

Topic:	Moving to a new home
Point of view:	Friends can make a hard day good.
Possible topic sentence:	Moving to a new home showed me that friends can make even a hard day a good day.

4. Choose the support points (if your topic lends itself to using formal support points) and specific details. For instance, in the list above, the writer has already identified many details he wants to include in his paragraph. Some of these details address the moving process: "Labeled boxes," "Loaded truck." Other details emphasize the role his friends played in the moving process: "Steve broke my one good chair," "Sonya brought a great lunch."

5. Organize your details according to when they occurred, getting rid of irrelevant information. In other words, make sure all the details serve some purpose in your paragraph: background detail, action detail, or sensory detail. Remember to add transitions that express time sequence order.

6. Now write your draft. Do your best, but don't worry if your paragraph is not perfect the first time around.

Revising

7. Check for the first three of the four Cs: *concise, credible,* and *clear* writing. Make any necessary changes to your draft.

Editing

8. Check your paragraph for the fourth C: *correct* writing. Proofread your paragraph to make sure you have used correct spelling, punctuation, and grammar.

WRITING PRACTICE 2 **Write About an Important Day**

Choose either Topic A or Topic B. Write a paragraph about a day that stands out in your mind, either for positive or negative reasons. Think about the overall impression you have of that day, and then decide which events helped to make that day stand out.

Topic A

Write a paragraph about a day in your life that you would like to experience again. These are some days that may stand out in your mind.

A day when you proved you were right about something

A day when you tried something new and it worked

A day when you discovered that you were good at something new

A day when you solved a problem for someone else

Topic B

Write a paragraph about a time in your life that you are glad is over. Make sure that the time you write about is fairly short—a few hours, a day, or a week. Also, make sure that that period of time has a definite beginning and end. You might consider the following times in your life for this topic.

A time when you were sick or injured

A time when you had to admit that you were wrong

A time when you had to make a tough decision

A time when you were worried that you might fail

Once you have chosen a topic, listed some possible reasons for support, and written a possible topic sentence, try to think of details that will make your paragraph believable for your reader. For instance, if your topic sentence is "My high school graduation day was one of the best days of my life," write down all the events that made that day special. Use your list of events to help you write a draft of your paragraph. Make sure that you include only those details that support your topic sentence. Then, when you have a draft, revise for the four Cs: *concise, credible, clear*, and *correct* writing.

WRITING PRACTICE 3 Sell Yourself in Your Writing

Your assignment is this: *Write a paragraph in which you "sell yourself" to a coach, an instructor, or an employer.* Your purpose is to use narrative to persuade your reader to act: give you a starting position on the team, raise your grade in class, or give you a promotion at work. By narrating an event about yourself, your paragraph shows your reader that you have the necessary experience to succeed. However, you need to limit your paragraph to a short period in time: one practice, one day, or one specific period of time.

CHAPTER SUMMARY

When writing a narrative paragraph, remember the following:

1. Narratives involve telling a story in time sequence order.
2. You may not have formal support points in narrative paragraphs.
3. Support your main idea with three different types of specific ideas: background details, action details, and sensory details.

MyWritingLab & Lab Activity 16

mywritinglab For additional practice with writing a narrative paragraph, go to **www. mywritinglab.com** or complete **Lab Activity 16** in the separate *Resources for Writing* Lab Manual.

Description

WHAT IS A DESCRIPTIVE PARAGRAPH?

If you've ever tried to tell someone what an incredible sunset over the ocean looked like, you know that description is important and challenging. Descriptions of the colors, the color changes, and the reflection of the sun on the water are all essential to helping someone else see what you saw.

Description is a paragraph development strategy in which you tell about a person, place, or object so clearly that your reader can form a mental picture from your words. Being able to describe something vividly comes in handy for any type of writing.

REAL-LIFE WRITING

In real-life writing, description helps us make our ideas clear and helps us communicate what we want.

Pablo Picasso, *Guernica*, 1937

CRITICAL THINKING Pablo Picasso's painting *Guernica* portrays the brutality of war. Can a painting like *Guernica* get people to change their minds about war? Can you think of a work of art, such as a song or photo, that has affected what you think about a subject? Explain in a few sentences.

Responding to Images. *What Feelings do you think Picasso is trying to elicit from viewers? Explain Using details from the painting above.*

For College

- Use descriptive writing in a history essay to show that you know how an important city looked or how people dressed.
- Use descriptive language in a science report to show that you understood the results of an experiment.

In Your Personal Life

- Use descriptions for romantic gestures, such as writing poetry about the one you love.
- Describe your apartment to a potential roommate, your car to a potential buyer, or a medical problem to your doctor.

At Work

- Use description on order forms and in reports to help make your requests clearly understood.
- Describe a product—or the benefits of a product—to make that product more appealing and, thus, help you sell it.

A MODEL PARAGRAPH: DESCRIPTION

Details in a descriptive paragraph may not be grouped into individual support points. Instead, every detail works to support the topic sentence. The key to writing a solid descriptive paragraph is to make your reader *see* whatever it is you're describing. Look at the "Descriptive Paragraphs" illustration below to see how one is organized. Then, read the following paragraph, paying attention to the way the writer describes the work of art.

Descriptive Paragraphs
Topic sentence.. *Setting the scene* ....
↓
Sensory detail 1 ....
Sensory detail 2 ....
Sensory detail 3 ....
Sensory detail 4 ....
Sensory detail 5 ....

Gory *Guernica*

In the painting *Guernica* by the Spanish painter Pablo Picasso, the many strange images portray the violence of war. My high school history teacher, Mr. Pazzoni, thought it would be a good idea for us to see some art that had political messages, so he brought in a photograph of Picasso's *Guernica*. I had to look at it for a few minutes to take it all in. Even though I saw just a photo of the painting, I could tell that the painting is huge, like a mural, and that it uses all kinds of shapes mixed up together. Then, I noticed all the weird body parts in the painting. Heads, feet, arms, and hands of both people and animals appear at odd angles throughout the painting. What's even stranger, though, is that the body parts are twisted and are not attached to full bodies. Even the animal heads seem to be screaming, and everyone in the painting seems to be in pain. Mr. Pazzoni explained that Guernica was a small town in Spain that Germany bombed during the Spanish Civil War and that Picasso was so upset by the bombing that he painted *Guernica* for the World's Fair in Paris in 1937. When I looked at the painting again, I could see the war signs. Flames and smoke seem to come out of nowhere, and broken knives, or swords, show up, too. The worst part, though, is the place where a howling woman is holding a dead baby. It's awful! The painting was a protest against the violence of war, and it definitely makes its point.

The writer's topic sentence is "In the painting *Guernica* by the Spanish painter Pablo Picasso, the many strange images portray the violence of war." The writer supports his topic sentence by identifying these main characteristics of the painting.

- Many kinds of shapes mixed together
- Images of twisted, unattached body parts
- Images that portray people and animals in pain
- Flames, smoke, and weapons emphasize the awfulness of the scene

The writer connects his points by using transitions such as *then, what's even stranger, when,* and *though*.

EXERCISE 1 Identifying Descriptive Details in a Paragraph

The writer of "Gory *Guernica*" describes the painting as being both violent and strange. Reread the paragraph to find details that illustrate each of the following ideas. Then, fill in the blanks below.

1. Write three details that develop the idea of violence in the painting.

a. _____

b. _____

c. _____

2. Write three details that develop the idea that the painting is strange.

a. _____

b. _____

c. _____

CHOOSING A GOOD TOPIC FOR DEVELOPMENT

Sometimes your instructor will assign a topic, and other times you will choose your own. For a descriptive paragraph, choose something that you find interesting to look at or think about. You don't need to choose an artistic or complicated topic as long as you're interested in it. For instance, Leo is interested in construction, and he wants to see if he has enough information to write a descriptive paragraph. He begins by freewriting.

It's so cool to see a new building going up. I love the way the bulldozers have to make sure that the ground is level before anyone can start building. Watching the shiny (but sometimes dirty) machines push the dirt this way and that, smoothing out piles of soil, is hypnotizing. I could watch it all day. Then I love to see the foundation being poured, though my sister thinks I'm nuts. Something about all that heavy gray liquid concrete makes me want to press my hands into it. It always looks as if it'll feel cool, even on a hot day. I also love seeing the frame go up, with the wood boards and planks making the outline of a house begin to seem real.

Leo has plenty to say about construction, so he decides to use this topic for his paragraph.

WRITING AN EFFECTIVE TOPIC SENTENCE

To write an effective topic sentence for a descriptive paragraph, think about how you want the reader to experience your topic. Leo needs to think about what he might say about construction, so he refers to his freewriting. He's particularly fascinated by the early stages of the building process; thus, his topic sentence is "The early stages of the building process are fascinating to watch." With that, he identifies three stages that he'll describe in his paragraph.

- Leveling the ground
- Pouring the foundation
- Erecting the frame

DEVELOPING SPECIFIC DETAILS

Specific details are extremely important in descriptive paragraphs because they often make up the *entire* paragraph. Thus, it's essential to make every detail count. When choosing details for your paragraph, make sure to use the ones that most vividly bring your topic to life.

What Are Sensory Details?

To develop your descriptive paragraph, use **sensory details**—details that appeal to your reader's five senses.

- **Sight.** Use words that help your reader see colors, light, shadow, shapes, and textures: "The light in the old library streamed down the rows of books from large windows, making a checkerboard of light and shadow at the end of the aisles."
- **Smell.** Use words that let your reader associate what you're describing with specific, familiar scents: "The odors of gasoline, window cleaner, and bug spray reminded me of every family summer trip I ever took as a child."
- **Taste.** Words that remind your reader of powerful flavors are especially effective in describing taste: "Every ingredient Maria added to the bowl made my mouth water—potent cinnamon, moist brown sugar, creamy butter."
- **Touch.** Use words that help your reader feel the textures of what you're describing: "The grooves of the tree's bark felt like a cheese grater; they seemed as though they could scrape the skin off tender little fingers."
- **Hearing.** Use words that let your reader hear the sounds—and the quality of sounds—that you hear: "The screeching of birds before dawn—like a thousand poorly played violins—pierced my eardrums and woke me."

The Benefits of Sensory Details

Using sensory descriptions in your writing offers two main benefits. First, clear descriptions give you credibility. For instance, here are some details that could help your reader believe you have ridden in a hot-air balloon.

Sensory Details

The lurching sensation that you felt when the balloon began to rise

How much greener the ground looked when you could see the treetops instead of the dry grass

The whooshing sound the wind made as it blew past you in the balloon

Second, sensory details make your writing enjoyable to read. Think about a time when a friend has described dinner at a restaurant: "It began with sharp cheese and fresh tomatoes on crispy crackers. Next followed a succulent steak surrounded by lightly browned potatoes and tender young vegetables. And the whole meal was topped off by a pie of sweet-tart black-berries in the flakiest pie crust ever." You can understand the restaurant's appeal because the sensory details are so vivid.

The paragraph that follows describes a room in a way that allows the reader to picture it.

The Studio of Secrets

My uncle Phil's art studio seems filled with secrets. Even before I'm actually inside the room, I feel a prickly sensation at the back of my neck because I'm never sure exactly what I'll find inside the spe-cial room. Just opening the heavy wooden door is a treat since my uncle almost always keeps it locked. Inside, the first thing I notice is the smell. The aromas of paint, paint thinner, and my uncle's day-old bologna sandwiches mingle together to create a scent that I've never smelled anywhere else. The smell is so strong that sometimes I feel as if I'm tasting the air, which is a strange sensation. Probably because it is so unusual, the combination of smells seems like a secret mixture of my uncle's. Next, the cloth-covered chairs, easels, and covered shapes always catch my attention. Uncle Phil never knows exactly what figure or scene he wants to paint next. Conse-quently, he keeps almost everything in the room covered with sheets so that nothing gets paint on it while he's deciding. When he has made up his mind about his next work, he unveils whatever figure or object he needs to work with and begins. Before he removes the sheet, though, the studio looks like a room filled with ghosts. Addi-tionally, the sound of the room makes me think of secrets. The studio is so quiet that it seems as if the room must be hiding some-thing. Really, though, I know that it's quiet because it's at the very top of the house, away from the noisy kitchen. I guess the part of the room that's the most mysterious is the feeling. Just standing in that quiet studio makes me feel creative, as if I could pick up my uncle's brushes and paint a masterpiece. Of course, he definitely would not like my touching his artist's tools, so I am content just to look around at Uncle Phil's mysterious studio.

EXERCISE 2 Identifying Sensory Details in a Paragraph

Below is a list of details from "The Studio of Secrets." Write down the sense that the detail appeals to: sight, hearing, smell, taste, or touch. An example is done for you.

1. Detail: "I feel a prickly sensation at the back of my neck . . ."

Sense: Touch

2. Detail: "The aromas of paint, paint thinner, and my uncle's day-old bologna sandwiches mingle together to create a scent . . ."

Sense: _____

3. Detail: "I feel as if I'm tasting the air . . ."

Sense: _____

4. Detail: ". . . cloth-covered chairs, easels, and covered shapes . . ."

Sense: _____

5. Detail: "The studio is so quiet that it seems as if the room must be hiding something."

Sense: _____

EXERCISE 3 Practice Writing Sensory Details

Below is a list of support points from a variety of essays. For each one, write three descriptive details that appeal to the senses: sight, hearing, smell, taste, and touch. An example is done for you.

Support point: It's easy to tell when my mother is angry.

Details: **a.** Deep wrinkles in her forehead

   b. Mouth becomes puckered up

   c. Right index finger points menacingly

1. Support point: Mark always looks happy when he watches a
                        NASCAR event.

Details: **a.** _____

           b. _____

           c. _____

2. Support point: Samantha dressed as if she wanted to be a
                        pop singer.

Details: **a.** _____

           b. _____

           c. _____

3. Support point: Tom always looks so healthy after a good
                        workout.

Details: **a.** _____

           b. _____

           c. _____

4. Support point: Ray's house needs new plumbing.

Details: **a.** _____

           b. _____

           c. _____

5. Support point: Sondra built a snowman with her children.

Details: **a.** _____

           b. _____

           c. _____

ORGANIZING AND LINKING YOUR IDEAS

Once you have written a topic sentence, identified any support points, and come up with vivid, specific details to illustrate your ideas, you're ready to organize your paragraph. Emphatic order works well for descriptive paragraphs since many descriptions do not contain events that can be ordered chronologically. **Emphatic order** lets you organize your ideas from least to most important.

Words and Terms That Signal Emphatic Order

above all	last
another	least of all
equally important	most important
especially	most of all
even more	next
first	significantly
in the first place	

Words and Terms That Signal Space

above	near
across	next to
around	on a diagonal (catercorner)
before	on the other side
behind	opposite
below	outside
beyond	over
elsewhere	there
farther away	to the east (north, etc.)
here	to the left
inside	to the right
in back of	under
in front of	underneath
in the middle (center) of	

With descriptive paragraphs, you also have the option of using **spatial** organization—describing something in terms of its shape or layout. The writer of "The Studio of Secrets" on pages 249–250 for instance, moved randomly around the art studio as he developed the paragraph. The writer could, however, have started with details to the left of the door and worked his way around the room, ending with details to the right of the door. If you choose to use transitions that signal space, be sure you have a plan. Move through the place you're describing, from nearest to farthest, or from one side to the other.

EXERCISE 4 Following the Four Cs

Read the paragraph below, keeping in mind how good description includes details that appeal to the senses. Then, answer the questions that follow.

Unhappy Vincent van Gogh

[1]While he was alive, the Dutch painter Vincent van Gogh was the portrait of a tortured artist. [2]Because he suffered from mental illness, van Gogh's life contained few of the comforts that many people take for granted. [3]His appearance reflected his pain. [4]Upon meeting him, van Gogh's contemporaries noticed his tattered shoes and filthy clothing. [5]Though he had been raised by a loving family, van Gogh lived in a little hut near a sewer. [6]Consequently, his possessions—down to his undergarments—smelled as though they had never been clean. [7]In addition to his clothing, van Gogh's habits were very rough. [8]When he said prayers, he often knelt in mud or dirt, and he slept in straw. [9]His own parents, not understanding that their son was unwell, were a little afraid of him because they thought he lived like a beast. [10]Van Gogh's face showed pain and neglect, too, in its untrimmed beard and bloodshot eyes. [11]The rest of his head revealed the real shock. [12]One of his ears was missing because when he was very depressed after an argument with another artist, van Gogh had cut it off and given it to a prostitute. [13]Arguments or rejections affected van Gogh greatly because his illness caused him to react in irrational ways. [14]Above all, van Gogh felt tortured by what he viewed as his career failures—as an art dealer, in the ministry, and as an artist. [15]Even his artwork seems to reflect his personal misery, with its almost painfully intense colors against dismal backgrounds set down by short, stabbing brushstrokes. [16]Van Gogh's mental illness tortured him daily, making him very unhappy. [17]His unhappiness took the

ultimate, final form of suicide when he shot himself at the age of thirty-seven. [18]In an ironic twist, people today believe that van Gogh's personal torture may have contributed to his excellence as an artist. [19]If only van Gogh could have known how significant and beloved his work would become, perhaps he would not have suffered so greatly.

Concise Writing

1. What is the topic sentence for "Unhappy Vincent van Gogh"?

_____

2. List three aspects of van Gogh's appearance that show that he was "tortured."

a. _____

b. _____

c. _____

Credible Writing

3. What detail do you think is most effective in illustrating the topic sentence?

_____

4. Write down two more details that develop the idea that van Gogh was a tortured artist. Be sure to identify the sense that the detail appeals to.

_____

_____

Clear Writing

5. How many times does the writer use some form of the word *torture* in the paragraph? _____

6. What transitions does the writer use in sentences 6, 7, and 14?

Sentence 6: _____

Sentence 7: _____

Sentence 14: _____

Correct Writing

The sentences in this paragraph are all correct. To check for correctness in your own writing, go to Part 7, "Writing Correct Sentences."

WRITING PRACTICE 1 Write a Descriptive Paragraph

Now write a descriptive paragraph of your own.

Prewriting

1. Choose a topic for a paragraph describing your favorite character from television, comic books, or the movies. Your character should *not* be a real person.

Fictional Characters

King Kong	Wicked Witch of the West
Santa Claus	Shrek
Spider-Man	Lisa Simpson

2. After you've decided on a character, freewrite for five to ten minutes. Then, use at least one other prewriting technique—listing, questioning, keeping a journal, clustering, or outlining—to come up with more descriptive details. When you are writing a descriptive paragraph, two specific prewriting techniques can be especially helpful. Listing can help you see all your details together in one place, and outlining can help you group your details together logically. Here is a sample list on the topic "Batman."

Batman

Seems to have everything	Strong
Intelligent	Tortured
Perfectly fitting armor	~~Gotham resembles NYC~~
Wealthy	Loyal servant Alfred
Great car	~~Real identity is Bruce Wayne~~
Cool bat cave	

Read over your prewriting and eliminate any details that do not seem to help describe your topic. In the previous list, the writer has crossed out "Gotham resembles NYC" and "Real identity is Bruce Wayne" because they don't directly describe Batman.

Drafting

3. Write a topic sentence if you haven't done so already. One possible topic sentence for the previous list is "Batman seems to be the perfect modern superhero."

4. Choose the support points and/or specific details for your paragraph, taking care to appeal to the reader's senses. Making an outline from your first list can help you plan your paragraph. A possible outline of the "Batman" paragraph follows.

Topic sentence: Batman seems to be the perfect modern superhero.

    A. Seems to have everything

        1. Wealthy

        2. Handsome

        3. Loyal servant Alfred

    B. Powerful

        1. Physically strong

        2. Tortured (drives him to succeed)

        3. Intelligent (brain power)

    C. Great accessories

        1. Great car

        2. Cool bat cave

        3. Multiple handy gadgets

5. Arrange your support points and details in a logical order. The outline above groups the details under three main support points, but you don't need to do that. Just make sure that your details have some logical connection to each other.

6. Now write a draft of your paragraph. Do your best to include important details and transitions, but don't worry if the paragraph is not perfect.

Revising

7. Check for three of the four Cs: *concise, credible,* and *clear* writing. Make any necessary changes to your draft.

Editing

8. Check your paragraph for the fourth C: *correct* writing. Proofread your paragraph to make sure you have used correct spelling, punctuation, and grammar.

WRITING PRACTICE 2 Describe a Place

Write a paragraph about a place on your campus. Make sure you choose a place that you are familiar with, and include details that appeal to the senses. Here are some suggestions.

Places on Campus

A classroom	The cafeteria
The library	An instructor's office
The gymnasium	The bookstore

Do some prewriting, as usual, to get your ideas on paper. Then think about your opinion of the place you want to focus on, and write your topic sentence. Remember that your topic sentence controls the direction of your paragraph. Possible topic sentences are these:

My math classroom is filled with tension.

The school cafeteria is a place that is bustling with activity.

The school library is a peaceful place.

My English instructor's office is cheerful.

The school gymnasium is a healthy place to spend time.

Consider *what about* the place you chose makes it special or distinctive to you. Does it have certain smells that you associate with it? Is there a particular feeling that you're aware of when you enter this place? Does the place have an unusual layout that stands out in your mind? These are the types of questions to ask yourself to find the details to support your topic sentence.

Once you have your topic sentence and some specific details, write your draft. In describing a place, use transitions that signal spatial order to direct your reader. (See "Words and Terms That Signal Space" on page 252.) These transitions direct your reader to mentally look around the place you're describing.

Revise your paragraph as necessary to make sure it's concise, credible, and clear. Proofread your paragraph for sentence-level errors.

WRITING PRACTICE 3 Describe an Object

Study any painting or photograph in this textbook.

How does it affect you?

Look at the painting for at least five minutes, paying attention to the people and the setting. Then, freewrite for five to ten minutes on what your overall impression of the painting is. Your topic sentence can be something like: "The photograph of tourists on the Great Wall of China communicates a feeling of _____."

Some terms to fill in the blank are these:

lasting strength   curiosity

timelessness   people connecting with nature

Write a paragraph describing the photograph according to your topic sentence. Be sure to list details that appeal to the senses.

- How do people or objects in the photograph look?
- How does the setting look?
- How do you think it feels to be in that photograph?
- What does the setting in the photograph smell like?
- What do you think it sounds like in the photograph?
- What tastes do you think you'd experience in the photograph?

For this assignment, not all the senses may be relevant.

CHAPTER SUMMARY

When you write a descriptive paragraph, remember the following:

1. Description helps a reader *see* the object being described.
2. To make your descriptions vivid, use details that appeal to the five senses: sight, smell, taste, touch, and hearing.
3. Descriptive paragraphs may not contain formal support points.
4. Descriptive paragraphs may be organized emphatically or spatially.

MyWritingLab & Lab Activity 17

mywritinglab   For additional practice with descriptive paragraphs, go to **www.mywritinglab. com** or complete **Lab Activity 17** in the separate *Resources for Writers* Lab Manual.

Classification and Division

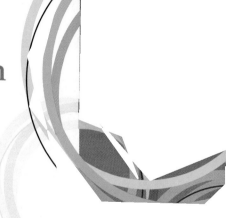

Culture Note

FINANCIAL HABITS

The American Dream includes a home of our own, independence, and—of course—financial security. But how do we achieve this kind of security? Particularly in a time when corporate greed and an unstable stock market make the news daily, it's hard to know the best way to manage our financial futures. More than ever, now it's important to know about sound spending, saving, and investing practices.

WHAT ARE CLASSIFICATION AND DIVISION PARAGRAPHS?

If you've ever shopped on the day before Thanksgiving, you know how important organization is. With so many people trying to get their groceries purchased, even the most organized market can seem like chaos. Some steps on the part of store management, however, make the shopping experience easier: having products classified into sections, having items grouped according to size and quantity, having sale items brightly marked. All these practices show an awareness of what the customer needs.

In your writing, too, organization is critical. Classification and division skills help you make your method of organization clear. **Classification** means grouping similar items together. On your shopping trip to the supermarket, suppose you visit the dairy section. In this section, you find milk, cheese, yogurt, butter, and cream—all dairy products. These foods

RECOMMENDED READINGS

"The Ways We Lie," Stephanie Ericsson, p. 750

"The Plot Against People," Russell Baker, p. 779

"'Blaxicans' and Other Reinvented Americans," Richard Rodriguez, p. 738

New York Stock Exchange

JOURNAL RESPONSE The New York Stock Exchange serves as the hub of the world's financial center. How do you handle your finances? How did you form your financial habits? Write for ten minutes about the kind of spender or saver you are.

Responding to Images. What kind of an atmosphere does the stock exchange, as it appears in this photo, have? Explain. Serious, Stressful, or thoughtful are some ideas to consider.

have been grouped, or *classified*, as dairy products. **Division** means breaking down breaking down a single specific thing into its separate parts. The supermarket itself, for instance, has been *divided* into sections. Meat, produce, and frozen foods all have their sections. Similarly, areas like the checkout lanes, the storage area, the employees' area, and the offices represent other examples of the store's division.

For classification, ask "What idea can I use to group these items together? What do these items have in common?" For division, ask "What parts can I break this item into? What pieces is this item made up of?" Classification and division require similar skills, so you can think of them as a single strategy for developing a paragraph. To see how these paragraphs are organized, look at the "Classification and Division Paragraphs" illustration on page 261 and the example tables that follow.

Classification and Division Paragraphs
Topic sentence.....*Stating the categories*........................
↓
Category 1 ....
Category 2 ....
Category 3 ....

Classification

Pets	News Media	Music
Dogs	Newspapers	Classical
Cats	Television	Jazz
Birds	Internet	Rock and roll

Division

My Family	A Department Store	A Computer System
My mother	Women's clothing	Monitor
My father	Men's clothing	Keyboard
My brother Jon	Shoes	Mouse

REAL-LIFE WRITING

In real-life writing, classifying and dividing help us organize and keep track of our ideas.

For College

- Use division in a sociology paper to explain the structure of a society.
- Use classification in an anthropology essay to identify characteristics that groups have in common.

In Your Personal Life

- Divide your household chores and list them in categories: daily, weekly, monthly, seasonal.
- Make a list organizing your finances by classifying expenses in a budget.

At Work

- Make a list classifying supplies needed during your annual inventory.
- Make a list dividing your job into different tasks: working the cash register, helping customers, organizing store products.

A MODEL PARAGRAPH: CLASSIFICATION AND DIVISION

Read the following paragraph to see classification and division at work.

So Many Spenders

[1]Spenders can be divided into three types. [2]First are the "super spenders." [3]Super spenders spend money as soon as they get it. [4]Keeping money around, unspent, is impossible for super spenders, as is waiting for the big sale. [5]Unfortunately, super spenders also spend money they don't have. [6]They use credit cards to increase their spending power, which often leads them into trouble. [7]Super spenders definitely live on the edge, from paycheck to paycheck, waiting for the next thing to buy. [8]"Simple spenders" are the second type of spender. [9]Simple spenders are careful about the ways they part with their hard-earned cash. [10]They shop at outlets, wait for sales, and scan the sale racks at big stores in order to find the best deal. [11]Simple spenders always make sure they save a little bit of each paycheck so that they have a cash cushion to protect them from unexpected expenses such as

a broken pipe or car repairs. [12]Simple spenders occasionally buy things simply for pleasure, but only if they can afford them. [13]The last group of spenders is "pretend spenders." [14]This group of spenders has little extra cash, so they just don't spend money unless they absolutely have to. [15]Rent, food, gas, and doctor bills all get paid, but a new stereo or dinner out has to wait until more money comes in. [16]However, even though pretend spenders don't spend much money, they do have a guilty secret: they love to shop. [17]Pretend spenders read mail-order catalogs and wander through the malls for hours, just looking at things. [18]Sometimes they even fill up shopping carts, but they never check out. [19]Pretend spenders who have access to the Internet also spend time "shopping" online, but they never push the last button to submit an order. [20]Thus, even though pretend spenders don't really buy much, they act as if they do.

EXERCISE 1 Analyzing a Classification and Division Paragraph

Reread "So Many Spenders." Then, answer the questions below.

1. What is the topic sentence of "So Many Spenders"? _____

_____

2. What are the three types of spenders that the writer describes?

a. _____

b. _____

c. _____

3. Give three specific details for super spenders.

a. _____

Detail 1: _____

Detail 2: _____

Detail 3: _____

b. _____

    Detail 1: _____

    Detail 2: _____

    Detail 3: _____

c. _____

    Detail 1: _____

    Detail 2: _____

    Detail 3: _____

4. What kinds of transitions does the writer use to signal a change from one support point to another?

    Sentence 2: _____

    Sentence 9: _____

    Sentence 13: _____

CHOOSING A GOOD TOPIC FOR DEVELOPMENT

Sometimes your instructor will give you a topic, but other times you'll choose your own. If you're asked to develop a classification or division paragraph, make sure you pick a topic that can be (1) broken down into smaller groups or (2) grouped according to a broader idea. One way to find a topic that works well for using classification or division is to prewrite.

Geraldine wondered if she could write an effective paragraph about the types of people who live in her neighborhood. She used listing to help her decide, making a general list first, and then making more specific lists for each category she identified. Her first list looked like this:

My neighbors

Families with young children   Invisible professionals   Elderly

After coming up with a general way to divide her neighbors, Geraldine began thinking of specific examples that illustrated each type of neighbor. She outlined her ideas.

A. Elderly neighbors
  1. Mrs. Platt is out walking or sitting in early morning and early evening.
  2. Mr. Tocterman sweeps constantly.
B. Families with young children
  1. Mrs. Taylor goes out walking with her kids late morning and late afternoon, between naps.
  2. The Hendricks family is always equipped with kid stuff (stroller, toys, snacks).
C. Invisible professionals
  1. Marla leaves before dawn and gets home after dark.
  2. Todd has several people working for him (gardener, housekeeper, shoppers).

In this case, the connecting idea among all the people Geraldine writes about is that they are her neighbors. Within that category, three subcategories—elderly neighbors, families with young children, and invisible professionals—provide Geraldine with opportunities to develop her paragraph. Geraldine was happy that she had noticed so much about her neighbors, and she felt she had enough information to write an effective classification and division paragraph.

WRITING AN EFFECTIVE TOPIC SENTENCE

Geraldine organized her categories according to how they came to her in her prewriting.

Category 1:	Elderly neighbors
Category 2:	Families with young children
Category 3:	Invisible professionals

After identifying these categories from her listing, Geraldine wrote her topic sentence: "Each of my neighbors in the Sierra Pines neighborhood seems to be one of three types." When she writes her rough draft, Geraldine can decide whether she has enough details for each type of neighbor or she needs to do more prewriting. Geraldine's key to writing a clear topic sentence was to identify her topic—her neighbors—and state how the topic will be discussed (categorizing by type). Thus, her reader knows exactly what to expect from the rest of Geraldine's paragraph.

EXERCISE 2 Classifying Topics for Writing

Look at the topics given below. Then, decide what classification to use and what subcategories each topic should be divided into. Finally, write a topic sentence that best communicates your classification and division strategy for each topic. An example is done for you.

Topic	**Classified by**	**Subcategories**
Friends	Neediness	Independent
		Need you sometimes
		Need you constantly

Topic sentence: _Friends can be classified into three groups according to how much they need you._

1. Topic	**Classified by**	**Subcategories**
Music		

Topic sentence: _____

2. Topic	**Classified by**	**Subcategories**
Study habits		

Topic sentence: _____

3. Topic	**Classified by**	**Subcategories**
Cooking		

Topic sentence: _____

DEVELOPING SPECIFIC DETAILS

In some of your classes, you may write paragraphs or essays requiring you to research your topic using sources other than your own life. However, the classification and division paragraphs you'll write when using this book will ask you to draw on your own experiences for support.

For Geraldine to discover details about the types of neighbors on her block, she only had to think of the people she knew. Details like "Mr. Tocterman sweeps constantly" or "equipped with kid stuff" came from Geraldine's observations. Only the information about the "invisible professionals" came from another source—her early-rising neighbors—since the professionals were almost always gone to work before Geraldine was up.

Here's some freewriting that another writer, Chuck, did in order to determine whether he had enough examples to write a full paragraph. His topic is "types of cooking."

How can I write about types of cooking? The only cooking I really like is my mom's, and she's a full-on American cook. She uses lots of beef in her stews and casseroles, and she loves to make creamy "hot dish" meals using can after can of cream of mushroom soup. She also makes great Jell-O treats: finger Jell-O, Jell-O parfaits—with whipped topping and canned fruit layered with the Jell-O—and Jell-O salads. I love Jell-O! Why do I have to write about other types of cooking? Mom's is good enough for me. She always has a lot of food, too, so if I want to bring a buddy (or three) home for dinner, that's no problem. Last week, she had so much meatloaf that half the football team came over after practice. Wait a second . . . I wonder if I can write about the types of Mom's cooking? Gotta ask my instructor about that.

Without realizing it at first, Chuck divides his mother's cooking into three categories: hot dishes, Jell-O dishes, and multiserving dishes. Chuck discovers that he has enough information to write about the type of cooking he loves, his mom's.

ORGANIZING AND LINKING YOUR IDEAS

The key to classification and division paragraphs is to have a strong topic sentence. It should tell your reader how you will divide your topic into smaller parts, or subcategories, or classify all the subcategories through a connecting idea. **Emphatic order,** organizing your ideas from least to most important or interesting, is a good way to arrange your support points. Since you get to decide which points are most—or least—important when you're using emphatic order, pay attention to how much detail you derive from your prewriting. Chances are, the points that have the most detail will be the ones that matter the most to you, and those should be the ones you save for last.

Use transitional words and expressions to introduce specific details and link ideas. In the sentences that follow, the underlined transitional expressions signal that a specific detail is being introduced.

<u>One more type of high-risk investment</u> is international stocks.

Anxious bankers make up <u>the second group</u> of investors.

<u>The last group</u> of spenders is "pretend spenders."

Read the paragraph below, paying attention to how the topic sentence serves as a unifying concept for the entire paragraph.

The Ways We Save

People who save their money can be divided according to how much they trust others to handle it. First are easy investors, people who have great faith in financial institutions such as brokerage houses and financial consultants. These people have no problem writing out a check to a stockbroker every month and letting the broker invest their funds in stocks, bonds, or mutual funds. If the stock market goes down and these people lose money, they just figure that the market will go back up sometime. Anxious bankers make up the second group of investors. These people trust banks and credit unions and save their money in savings accounts and certificates of deposit (CDs). Anxious bankers don't move their money around as much as easy investors, and if interest rates on their savings go down, they become nervous. Last come the self-help savers. These people don't trust anyone else to handle their money. They don't trust stockbrokers, banks, or even each other. Consequently, self-help savers take care of their money themselves. They buy safes for their valuables, and some have been known to stuff large amounts of cash into their mattresses. People in this third group never worry about the stock market or about interest rates because all their cash is right at their fingertips.

EXERCISE 3 Analyzing a Paragraph for Support Points and Details

Fill in the outline for "The Ways We Save." The first item is done for you.

Types of Savers

A. Easy investors

    1. Trust others to manage their money.

    2. Invest in stocks, bonds, and mutual funds.

    3. Don't worry if they lose some money.

B. _____

   1. _____

   2. _____

   3. _____

C. _____

   1. _____

   2. _____

   3. _____

"The Ways We Save" classifies people according to how much they trust others to handle their money. It could also have been organized, with some revision, by financial strategies or by the amounts of money that people invest. Often, information can be organized a number of ways. The writer's job is to choose the best idea to unify the paragraph. An alternative way of organizing the information from "The Ways We Save" follows.

Financial Strategies

A. Investment markets
   1. Stocks
   2. Bonds
   3. Mutual funds

B. Federally insured savings institutions
   1. Banks
   2. Credit unions

C. Home security
   1. Safes for valuables
   2. Stuffing money into mattresses

If you want to write about a certain topic but are having a hard time classifying it in one way, there may be another way to organize your ideas.

EXERCISE 4 Classifying Topics Different Ways

Below are five groups. Write down two ways you can classify each group. An example is done for you.

Topic	Classification
Instructors	**a.** How much work they give
	b. How nice they are
1. Students	**a.** _____
	b. _____
2. Cars	**a.** _____
	b. _____
3. Books	**a.** _____
	b. _____
4. Diets	**a.** _____
	b. _____
5. Gardens	**a.** _____
	b. _____

EXERCISE 5 Following the Four Cs

Read the following paragraph, noting that the writer classifies investments according to their level of risk. Then, answer the questions that follow.

Risky Business

Financial investments can be classified according to how risky they are, or how likely they are to cause the investor to lose money. High-risk investments are the first category. Firms that are brand-new fall into this category because they're too new to guarantee success to their investors. Technology stocks are also considered high-risk since they, too, are new and their products often have no track record of success. One more type of high-risk investment is international stocks because foreign companies' success depends on factors that U.S. citizens can't control, such as foreign governments. People invest in these high-risk stocks because they offer the chance to make a lot of money. Medium-risk investments make up the second type of investments. Companies that have operated successfully for a long time are considered medium-risk. Companies such as General Electric and Boeing generate less money for investors than the high-risk stocks, but with less risk. These companies are sometimes called "blue chip" corporations, and they are considered fairly safe investments. The last type of investment is low-risk. Banks and bonds are low-risk investments. People can put their money into savings accounts or CDs at low interest rates and almost no risk because banks are insured by the federal government. People can also buy bonds from a company or a government, and the money they invest helps the company or government run. Bonds may not pay as much interest as stocks, but they're usually less risky. Government bonds are considered especially safe.

Concise Writing

1. What is the writer's topic sentence? _____

_____

2. What are the three categories of financial investments that the writer covers?

a. _____

b. _____

c. _____

3. What concept are the categories classified by?

_____

Credible Writing

4. What is one type of high-risk investment?

_____

5. What is a name for a safe investment in a traditionally successful company? _____

6. Name two types of investments that are considered low-risk.

a. _____

b. _____

Clear Writing

7. How many times does the writer use some form of the word *risk* (including in the title)? _____

8. What are two other words that the writer uses frequently throughout the paragraph?

a. _____

b. _____

9. What three transitions does the writer use to introduce each new type of investment?

a. _____

b. _____

c. _____

Correct Writing

The sentences in this paragraph are all correct. To check for correctness in your own writing, go to Part 7, "Writing Correct Sentences."

WRITING PRACTICE 1 Identify a Connecting Idea in Details

Below are short outlines of ideas. The general topic heads the list, followed by details that relate to that topic. Your job is to identify what the details have in common and write down the connecting idea that ties all the details together. An example is done for you.

General topic: Shoes
Details: Sandals, galoshes, snow boots
Connecting idea: _Seasonal shoes_____

1. General topic: Desserts
   Details: Frozen, baked, whipped
   Connecting idea: _____

2. General topic: Cities
   Details: Crime, traffic, pollution
   Connecting idea: _____

3. General topic: Computers
   Details: Help keep track of finances, help with school-work, help design party invitations and notes
   Connecting idea: _____

4. General topic: Books
   Details: Have to read them for college, want to read them for pleasure, should read them for information
   Connecting idea: _____

5. General topic: Neighborhoods
   Details: High crime rate, low crime rate, medium crime rate
   Connecting idea: _____

WRITING PRACTICE 2   Write a Classification and Division Paragraph

Now write a classification and division paragraph of your own.

Prewriting

1. From the list below, choose a topic that you think lends itself to being divided into separate parts or classified according to an over-riding principle.

Topic

Parents	Cars	Travel
Doctors	Hobbies	School courses
People's manners	Entertaining	Movies

2. Freewrite on the topic of your choice for five to ten minutes. What are your initial ideas about classifying your topic? What details have you written that will work in a paragraph? One writer, Miranda, chose to freewrite on the topic "manners."

> My mother always wanted me to have good manners, but sometimes I think I'm the only one who cares. Everyone I know either pays so much attention to manners that they seem phony, or else they ignore manners completely. My friend Janey always wants her manners to be perfect, but then I worry when I'm around her that I'll say the wrong thing or use the wrong fork or something. But then Pete, my brother's buddy, says he doesn't care about manners at all, and he's always belching right when I'm about to start eating. I guess people just have to find manners that work well for them.

Miranda places people into at least two groups according to the kinds of manners they use. One group cares very much about manners, while the other group doesn't care at all. A third group could be people who care just enough about manners, and the connecting idea could be how much people care about manners.

After you've finished freewriting, use another prewriting technique—listing, questioning, keeping a journal, clustering, or outlining—to see other specific details you can develop. Outlining can be especially effective in planning classification and division paragraphs.

Drafting

3. Write a topic sentence that clearly divides or classifies your topic. For example, here is a topic sentence for Miranda's topic: "People can be classified into three groups according to how much they care about good manners."

4. Choose the subcategories and specific details for your topic. In her outline Miranda identified three groups of people to discuss, and she offered some specific details for each group.

5. Arrange your support points—in this case, your subcategories—using a logical order, most likely emphatic order.

6. Write a rough draft of your paragraph, using details and transitions as best you can. Don't worry about making your paragraph perfect at this point; just get your ideas down in a basic order.

Revising

7. Check for the first three of the four Cs: *concise, credible*, and *clear* writing. Make any necessary charges to your draft.

Editing

8. Check your paragraph for the fourth C: *correct* writing. Proofread your paragraph to make sure you have used correct spelling, punctuation, and grammar.

WRITING PRACTICE 3   Use Classification and Division in Real Life

Classifying and dividing ideas can be helpful in everyday life. Choose either Topic A or Topic B below and write a paragraph.

Topic A

You have volunteered to be a student orientation counselor at your college, and you are telling a group of new students about the types of instructors on campus. *Write a paragraph dividing your college's instructors into types*. Your purpose is to prepare new students for a variety of experiences with instructors, so you must offer specific details about each type of instructor. Following are some possible ways to classify instructors.

How much work they give

How strict they are about attendance

How much they value in-class participation

How hard their tests are

How much out-of-class help they give

Topic B

You have volunteered to serve on a committee that helps instructors understand students. Your job is to tell the instructors how to recognize signs that students in their classes need help. *Write a paragraph classifying students who need help in their classes*. Make sure you use specific details about types of students to make your ideas clear. Following are some possible ways to classify students who need help.

How often they miss class

How often they do the homework

How well they perform on tests

How interested they seem in their test or class performance

How prepared they are for class (supplies, books, class handouts)

CHAPTER SUMMARY

When writing classification or division paragraphs, remember the following:

1. Classification paragraphs group similar items together.
2. Division paragraphs break down a single specific idea into its separate parts.
3. Choose topics that lend themselves to being grouped or broken down easily.

MyWritingLab & Lab Activity 18

mywritinglab For additional practice with classification and division paragraphs, go to **www.mywritinglab.com** or complete **Lab Activity 18** in the separate *Resources for Writers* Lab Manual.

Explaining a Process

Culture Note

RECYCLING

As people deplete more of our planet's natural resources, the act of recycling—the reprocessing of materials into new products—becomes increasingly important. Arguing the downsides of recycling—that the recycling process often involves large amounts of water, for instance, and that waste pickup involves carbon emissions from vehicles—critics reveal that recycling is not a perfect process. However, in reducing landfill and saving energy and resources, recycling seems to be a permanent part of our lives.

Cooking Up A Cleaner Planet

CONDUCT AN INTERVIEW In what ways do people recycle? Ask at least three people you know about their recycling habits.

Responding to Images. Describe what you see in this photo in a few sentences.

WHAT IS A PROCESS PARAGRAPH?

If you've ever tried to show someone how to do something, you know how important specific instructions are. **Explaining a process** means describing how to do something or how something works, step by step. This chapter will focus on two kinds of process paragraphs.

- How-to paragraphs
- Explanation paragraphs

How-To Paragraphs

How-to paragraphs tell a reader how to complete some action step by step. For instance, to tell a friend how to find your new apartment, you might write down instructions like this:

First, take I-5 South.

Second, take the Cabrillo Avenue exit.

Next, turn left onto Blossom Road.

Turn into the parking lot at 5226 Blossom Road.

Go left to apartment 3A.

In this process, the order is particularly important. The process determines the success of your friend's travel.

Explanation Paragraphs

The second kind of process paragraph is the explanation paragraph. **Explanation paragraphs** explain how something works, such as how a DVD player operates or how salmon swim upstream. Similarly, explanation paragraphs can explain historical events. In presenting an event such as a war or a political movement to your class, your instructor may talk in terms of a process, as though one step led to the next. However, often these "steps" became apparent only after the end result was achieved. For instance, in the paragraph on pages 279 to 280 in this chapter, you will read about how paper is recycled.

After being collected and sorted, paper goes through five main steps to be recycled.

First is pulping, where the paper is soaked with water and chemicals and mixed around to break up the fibers.

Next comes filtering, which is the step during which the pulp is then sifted through large screens that remove further contaminants.

Third is the de-inking or "floating" step which involves putting the pulp into a floatation device and mixed with several different kinds of "soapy" chemicals to separate the ink from the pulp.

After that, the mixture is kneaded to remove additional particles.

Finally, water is passed through the pulp during the washing step.

REAL-LIFE WRITING

In real-life writing, we explain processes all the time in order to teach people skills or explain how consequences came about.

For College

- In a biology class, write about the process of meiosis.
- In a history class, write about how women gained the vote or how the French Revolution came about.

In Your Personal Life

- Write notes to roommates or repair people about how you want something done.
- Write recipes or directions for a friend.

At Work

- Write directions explaining how to use a piece of equipment.
- Write notes to a new employee explaining office procedures.

A MODEL PARAGRAPH: EXPLAINING A PROCESS

To explain a process, follow the basic paragraph format shown in the illustration "Process Paragraphs" on page 280. The writer of "Two Points for Me, Two Points for Trees" has developed a topic sentence and then explained different steps that make up the process of recycling paper.

Process Paragraphs

Topic sentence...Naming the process....................................
....

↓

Step 1 ....
.....................Details about Step 1...........................
Step 2 ....
.....................Details about Step 2...........................
Step 3 ....
.....................Details about Step 3...........................
Step 4 ....
.....................Details about Step 4...........................
Step 5 ....
.....................Details about Step 5...........................

Two Points for Me, Two Points for Trees

Pretty much every time I write a paragraph for English class, I get frustrated, wad up my draft, and toss it (for two points, like in basketball) into the recycling can in my apartment. As the trash overflows, I often wonder what happens to the paper after it leaves me. I learned from my uncle, who works for Waste Connection, that paper goes through a process by which it becomes new paper. The first step is pulping, where water is added and mechanical action separates paper fibers from each other. Next, the mixture is screened with either slots or holes to remove contaminants that are larger than pulp fibers. What's left, the pulp slurry, is spun in the cleaning step to remove unusable materials, and then in the de-inking step, air bubbles are passed through the slurry to help remove ink. During the kneading step, mechanical action further breaks up particles of unwanted substances so they can be removed during the washing step—where water is passed through the pulp. If the recycled paper will be white, the pulp is bleached to remove color. The clean fiber is then made into "new" paper products in the same way that paper is made. I read online that in 2006, more than half of the waste paper was recycled in the United States, which seems pretty good to me. So the next time I "swish" my homework, I'll remember what a difference recycling makes.

EXERCISE 1   Analyzing a Process Paragraph for Steps and Details

Now you can analyze a process paragraph.

1. Write down the topic sentence of "Two Points for Me, Two Points for Trees."

_____

_____

2. What steps are involved in the process above? *Note:* Some sentences contain more than one step, so read carefully.

Step 1: _____

Step 2: _____

Step 3: _____

Step 4: _____

Step 5: _____

Step 6: _____

Step 7: _____

Step 8: _____

CHOOSING A GOOD TOPIC FOR DEVELOPMENT

Sometimes your instructor will assign you a topic, but often you will get to choose your own. When you choose your own topic, make sure that it has distinct stages or steps that work together as part of a process. Many topics can seem like they work well for explaining a process, but some are easier to write about than others. Some examples of topics that do and do not work well for process paragraphs follow.

Good Topics for Explaining a Process	Hard Topics for Explaining a Process
How to drive a car	The ways people learn to drive
How to use a computer program	Benefits of computers
How bees pollinate flowers	Qualities of bees

Each of the good topics for a process paragraph deals with a skill or activity. While the topics that do not work as well for process paragraphs are related themes, they do not offer the same opportunities for explaining step by step how to complete a process or how a process works.

One way to tell whether your topic will work well for narration is to *make a list of all the steps that your process involves*. Listing will help you keep your facts in order and eliminate facts that are irrelevant.

For instance, in "Two Points for Me, Two Points for Trees," the writer focuses on the steps in the paper recycling process. He does not, however, include such details as how the water used in the pulping and washing steps (steps 1 and 6) is cleaned for reuse, or how the waste material from the process is disposed of. While these details are interesting, they do not help explain the process of recycling the paper. Thus, the writer excludes such details.

Yolanda was asked to write a paragraph explaining a process she had recently learned. She began by making a list of events that occurred the first time she made pancakes.

Making Breakfast on Mother's Day
Never made pancakes before but had watched Mom.
Turned on electric frying pan.
Put bacon strips in pan.
Bacon grease spattered on me.
Flipped bacon when it started to curl up.
Bacon smells so good.
Stirred pancake mix with milk and eggs.
Took bacon out of pan when crispy.
Poured out grease (left some to cook pancakes).
Poured batter into hot pan.
Flipped pancakes when bubbles appeared on top.
Took pancakes out when they were brown on bottom.
Served pancakes and bacon with butter, syrup, and milk.

These details show a progression from the start of the cooking process through the end. Some details—like Yolanda getting spattered with bacon grease and bacon smelling so good—can be omitted because they don't act as steps in the process.

WRITING AN EFFECTIVE TOPIC SENTENCE

After looking over her list, Yolanda realized she had a complete account of how to make bacon and pancakes. She wrote the following topic sentence: "Making a bacon and pancake breakfast involves a number of simple steps."

DEVELOPING SPECIFIC DETAILS

Sometimes the steps in a process include all the details necessary to communicate a point. For instance, as one step in making pancakes, Yolanda listed "Put bacon strips in pan." Some readers might want to know how many strips Yolanda put in, how far apart the strips were, and whether the strips were all the same size. If she had been writing for someone not familiar with cooking, she would have included more details to make the steps in the process clear.

Another important aspect of including specific details is choosing relevant steps in your process. Make sure, then, that *you include only those steps essential to the process you're explaining.* For instance, in almost any human process, breathing is necessary. When writing about a process, however, you ordinarily leave out breathing as a step since it's something, we do without thinking. When writing your process paragraphs, make sure you focus on the steps most necessary to complete the task at hand.

EXERCISE 2   Identifying Unnecessary Steps in a Process

Read the list of steps in the processes below. Cross out the unnecessary steps in each. An example is done for you.

Building a fire in the woods requires following a number of steps.

a. First, gather dry pine needles, small twigs and sticks, and some small logs.

b. Next, make a small pyramid of pine needles and twigs.

c. ~~Use your fingers to take a match out of the box.~~

d. Then, light the pyramid on fire.

e. As the flames grow, gradually add larger twigs and sticks until the fire is strong enough to burn logs.

1. Dressing to exercise requires some important steps.

    a. First, put on comfortable clothing.

    b. Put your left foot through the left pant leg, followed by the right foot through the right pant leg.

    c. Next, put on exercise shoes with good arch support.

    d. Then, put sweatbands on your head and wrists.

2. Taking an engaging photograph involves a number of essential steps.

    a. Think ahead of time about how you want the final picture to look.

    b. Choose the main subject of the photo.

    c. Consider placing the main subject away from the center of the photo, for added visual interest.

    d. Think about the best photos you have seen in books and museums.

    e. Focus carefully so the main subject will be sharp.

    f. Hold your hands rock steady as you press the shutter button.

3. There are several easy steps in making a delicious vinaigrette salad dressing.

    a. Open the refrigerator and take out some garlic.

    b. Mince finely one or two cloves of garlic and put the garlic into a small bowl.

    c. Cut a fresh lemon in half, and squeeze the juice from one half into the bowl.

    d. Run the cold water and with your hand sprinkle three quick bursts of water into the bowl, then triple the amount of liquid in the bowl by adding high-quality olive oil.

    e. Add salt and pepper to taste, and mix with a whisk.

4. You can prepare for most tests by following some important steps.

    a. First, take good notes in the days leading up to the test, and highlight the points your instructor emphasizes.

    b. Second, do any required reading early, so that you can give the text a second and third look before the test.

    c. Third, pretend you are the instructor, and ask yourself what you think would be challenging test questions; then, answer the questions.

    d. Fourth, review your answers and intensively study the areas in which you need to brush up.

    e. Finally, have a good dinner the night before the test, making sure that it includes plenty of protein.

5. Changing the oil in a car is not difficult if you follow a few simple steps.

    a. Crawl under the car and locate the bolt on a fairly large tank; this is the discharge bolt.

    b. Go to wherever you store your tools and find a wrench to remove the bolt.

    c. Place under the discharge bolt a shallow pan that is wide enough to hold four or five quarts.

    d. Remove the bolt with a wrench, let the oil drain into the pan, and then screw the bolt back in.

    e. Check your owner's manual for the proper amount of oil for your tank, normally four to five quarts, then pour the new oil into the proper spout in your engine.

ORGANIZING AND LINKING YOUR IDEAS

Process paragraphs, like narrative paragraphs, do not contain specific support points. Instead, the steps or stages in the process act as markers for your readers. Thus, one of the most important factors in writing a process paragraph is *keeping your steps in order*. Using time sequence order keeps you and your reader on track. For example, if you are explaining to someone how to make ice cream, you will most likely include the steps of getting the proper ingredients, mixing the ingredients, and freezing the liquid ice cream. Forgetting to tell someone, for instance, to mix all the ingredients before freezing them could result in a finished product that you're not happy with.

In a how-to process paragraph, transitions are particularly important. If you don't tell your readers when to perform certain steps, you run the risk of confusing them. Consult the box on page 286 for transitions that are useful in writing a process paragraph.

Transition Words and Terms That Are Useful in Process Paragraphs

Transitions That Signal the Start of a Process

at first	first
begin by	initially

Transitions That Signal That the Process Is Still Going On

after	during	second, third, etc.
afterward	later	until
as soon as	meanwhile	when
before	next	while

Transitions That Signal the End of a Process

at last	finally
at the end	last

EXERCISE 3 Putting Details in Order

Below are short outlines for possible process paragraphs. The details listed are not in time-sequence order. Put the details in order by writing the number 1 in front of the detail that should come first, 2 in front of the detail that should come second, and so on.

1. Topic sentence: "Recycling" leftover food is an easy process.

    a. _____ Next, mash or grind up things that could go together: cooked meat, potatoes, carrots.

    b. _____ First, search the fridge for meals made within the last few days.

    c. _____ Finally, heat up the mixture, and you have "recycled" hash!

    d. _____ Third, place the mashed mixture in pan.

2. Topic sentence: Recycling aluminum products involves some effort.

a. _____ Last, getting paid for your efforts—the deposit on the cans—is the step that makes the others worthwhile!

b. _____ Bringing your cans to the center is the third step.

c. _____ Collecting empty aluminum cans in a large bag or box marks the first step.

d. _____ Second comes locating a recycling center near your home.

3. Topic sentence: Breaking down kitchen scraps through composting is easy.

a. _____ First, put all your uneaten fruit and vegetable parts—skins, leaves, stems, for instance—in a closed container near your sink.

b. _____ Last, mix the crumbly black compost back into the soil as fertilizer.

c. _____ Next, find a patch of soil—in a community garden, say—where you can dump your kitchen scraps.

d. _____ Third, use a shovel or pitchfork to turn the pile periodically and speed up the decomposition process.

4. Topic sentence: Clothes recycling in our home involves a few simple steps.

a. _____ Last, Grandma goes through the "renewal" process again for my younger brothers.

b. _____ Initially, my oldest brother outgrows his shirts, shoes, and pants.

c. _____ Third, I wear the clothes until I have outgrown them.

d. _____ Then, my grandma "renews" them with new buttons, zippers or laces, reinforced seams, and sometimes patches.

5. Topic sentence: Recycling cullet, which is broken or refuse glass, involves a number of specific steps.

a. _____ Finally, the crushed glass is blown or molded into new shapes.

b. _____ After being sorted, the cullet is crushed.

c. _____ Next, the crushed cullet is mixed with raw materials in a melting furnace.

d. _____ First, the cullet is picked up from curbside containers and taken to a recycling plant.

Read the following paragraph to see how the writer explains the process by which solid waste is dealt with at the dump. Note how the writer uses transitions to link one step to the next.

A Way Out of This Dump

[1]Discarded goods that are not recycled often find their way to a local landfill, more commonly known as a dump. [2]Here, people's garbage is dealt with methodically. [3]First, the waste collection vehicles are weighed on arrival, and their loads are inspected for unacceptable wastes. [4]Then, the waste collection vehicles make their way to the "tipping face" or working front, the place where they dump their contents. [5]After loads are deposited, compactors or bulldozers are used to spread and compact the waste. [6]Typically, what comes next is that the compacted waste is covered daily with soil, sprayed-on foam products, or temporary blankets, which can be lifted into place with excavators and then removed the following day prior to waste placement. [7]The fact that millions of tons of garbage are removed so efficiently every day is amazing, but how much more amazing would it be if it weren't so necessary?

EXERCISE 4 Analyzing a Completed Process

Reread "A Way Out of This Dump." Then, answer the questions that follow.

1. What is the topic sentence?

_____

2. What process is being explained in this paragraph?

_____

3. List each of the four steps involved in the process explained in "A Way Out of This Dump."

   a. _____

   b. _____

   c. _____

   d. _____

4. What words signal the introduction of new steps in the process?

   a. _____

   b. _____

   c. _____

   d. _____

EXERCISE 5 **Following the Four Cs**

Read the following paragraph, paying attention to how the writer instructs the reader in how to practice home recycling.

Recycling at Home

A number of simple steps can help you recycle at home. Your first step should be to call your local recycling centers to determine what types of materials they accept, if they do curbside pickup, and if they provide recycling bins. Second, make or get recycling bins for the different types of materials you will recycle (for example, one bin for cans, one bin for plastics, one bin for glass). After getting the bins, set aside a place for kitchen recyclables (jars and cans). Then, once a day (or more often if needed), rinse and crush the kitchen recyclables. After the rinsing, sort the items and place them in the appropriate bins. Your last step is to remove the items from your home. If you have curbside pickup, remember to put the bins out on the assigned day. If you must take your recyclables to the recycling center, choose a regular day. Just a few minutes here and there can drastically reduce the quantity of your household garbage.

Concise Writing

1. What is the writer's topic sentence?

_____

2. What should you be able to do after you finish reading this paragraph?

_____

3. Write down the six steps involved in the process of recycling.

a. _____

b. _____

c. _____

d. _____

e. _____

f. _____

4. Which step can potentially involve more than one action? List the

steps. _____

Credible Writing

5. What are some specific types of materials that can be recycled?

_____

6. Which steps do you think are less necessary in the recycling

process? _____

Clear Writing

7. What words does the writer use to indicate each step in the process of recycling at home?

    a. _____

    b. _____

    c. _____

    d. _____

    e. _____

    f. _____

8. How many times does the writer use a form of the word *recycle*?

_____

Correct Writing

9. The sentences in this paragraph are all correct. To check for correctness in your own writing, go to Part 7, "Writing Correct Sentences."

WRITING PRACTICE 1 Write Steps in a Process

Below are topic sentences for paragraphs that explain a process. Write down three to five steps that are involved in each process.

1. By completing a number of steps, I improved my appearance.

    a. _____

    b. _____

    c. _____

    d. _____

    e. _____

2. I plan to vote knowledgably in the next election.

    a. _____

    b. _____

    c. _____

    d. _____

    e. _____

3. For me, writing a paragraph works the best if I follow this routine.

    a. _____

    b. _____

    c. _____

    d. _____

    e. _____

4. It's easy to get books from the library.

    a. _____

    b. _____

    c. _____

    d. _____

    e. _____

5. Learning how to _____ is a process involving many steps.

    a. _____

    b. _____

    c. _____

    d. _____

    e. _____

WRITING PRACTICE 2 Writing a Paragraph Explaining a Process

Now write your own paragraph explaining a process.

Prewriting

1. Below is a list of topics for paragraphs that can be developed using the process strategy. Choose one topic that you have experience with, or select any other task you enjoy or do well.

Possible Topics

Losing weight

Studying for an exam

Learning to drive a car

Ironing a dress shirt

Getting your hair straightened or colored

Making a cup of tea

Taking a dog for a walk

Going fishing

Downloading files from the Internet

Stringing a guitar

2. Freewrite for five to ten minutes. In prewriting for a process paragraph, listing can be useful because a list helps you keep steps in order. Below is a sample list on the topic "ironing a dress shirt."

Ironing a Dress Shirt

Set up ironing board.

Fill iron with distilled water.

Plug in iron.

Spray starch onto collar, yoke, and cuffs of shirt.

Iron collar, yoke, and cuffs.

Spray sleeves with starch.

Iron sleeves.

Spray starch onto button side of shirt.

Iron button side of shirt.

Spray back of shirt with starch.

Iron back of shirt.

Spray buttonhole side of shirt with starch.

Iron buttonhole side of shirt.

Hang up shirt.

Drafting

3. Write a topic sentence if you haven't done so already. Don't worry if it's not exactly what you want for now. You can always revise it. A possible topic sentence for the topic above is "Ironing a dress shirt is one of the most repetitive processes I can think of."

4. Choose the steps in the process and the specific details relating to those steps that are the most important to explaining the process.

5. Organize your steps in time sequence order, using transitions to introduce new steps and link your ideas.

6. Write your draft. Include as many details and transitions as you can, but don't worry about making the draft perfect at this point.

Revising

7. Check for three of the four Cs: *concise, credible,* and *clear* writing. Make any necessary changes to your draft.

Editing

8. Check your paragraph for the fourth C: *correct* writing. Proofread your paragraph to make sure you have used correct spelling, punctuation, and grammar.

WRITING PRACTICE 3 Write to Teach Someone

Writing to explain a process can be useful when you are teaching someone how to do something or explaining a series of events. Choose Topic A, Topic B, or Topic C below and write a paragraph.

Topic A

You have volunteered to do community service to teach local youth how to do specific tasks connected with getting and keeping a job. Choose one topic from the list below. *Then, write a paragraph explaining how to perform the task you've chosen.*

How to prepare a résumé

How to write a cover letter

How to find the best organizations to which to apply

How to dress for the job interview

How to dress while on the job

How to negotiate your salary

How to act businesslike while on the job

How to make yourself valuable to your supervisor

Topic B

You have volunteered to talk to a group of high school students about the experiences that led you to go to college. Your purpose is to show these students that they, too, can attend college even if they're having trouble in high school. *Write a paragraph explaining the steps you follow to be a successful student.* You can include details about how you choose your classes, how you do or do not talk to a counselor, how you study, or how you budget your time.

Topic C

Because you have demonstrated excellent writing skills, you have been asked to teach your fellow students how to write a narrative paragraph. Your purpose is to show students that knowledge of certain methods and a little hard work can make the task go smoothly. *Write a paragraph explaining the steps you follow in writing a narrative paragraph.* You can include details about how you choose a good topic, prepare an effective topic sentence, develop specific details for your narration, or organize and connect your ideas. Feel free to consult Chapter 16 for information about narrative writing.

CHAPTER SUMMARY

When you are explaining a process, keep the following points in mind:

1. Process paragraphs explain step by step how to do something, how something works, or how something happened.

2. Only those steps essential to communicating how the process works should be included in your explanation.

3. Time sequence order and transitions are necessary in process paragraphs to keep a reader on track.

MyWritingLab & Lab Activity 19

mywritinglab For additional practice with explaining a process go to **www.mywritinglab. com** or complete **Lab Activity 19** in the separate *Resources for Writers* Lab Manual.

Comparing and Contrasting

Culture Note

FLORIDA

The Sunshine State has long been famous for its beautiful beaches, wild weather, and fresh oranges. Recently, however, Florida has gained notoriety as an athletic powerhouse, boasting successful football, basketball, and baseball teams at both the college and professional levels. Even as its cities and shores have served as safe havens for Cuban and Haitian refugees, Florida's political pull came into the spotlight when its electoral votes determined victory in the 2000 presidential election.

Number 1

CRITICAL THINKING Athletes' victory expressions—such as dancing—have been limited by sporting authorities in an effort to reduce bad sportsmanship. At what point does an athlete's celebrating become unsportsmanlike? Explain.

Responding to Images. *What about the player (#1) in the photo indicates that he is celebrating? Explain.*

WHAT IS A COMPARISON OR CONTRAST PARAGRAPH?

It's easy to notice the contrast, or difference, that one red shirt makes in a crowd of black-clad dancers. Just as we admire the main dancer's skill, we also marvel at the dance group whose members are so similar, so "in step," that each seems hardly separate from the others. However, how much do people really pay attention to differences and similarities? How much should they?

The answers to these questions are important. Comparing and contrasting are skills that help us make well-informed, intelligent decisions. Comparison is the development strategy involving finding similarities between two things. The following sentences show comparison between two subjects.

> My brother and my father are two of the most stubborn men I know.
>
> Although their areas of expertise are different, both Yo-Yo Ma and Wynton Marsalis are excellent musicians.

Contrast is the development strategy focusing on the differences between two things. Below are examples showing contrast.

> My friends Paula and Charlene couldn't be more different in their fashion styles if they tried.
>
> History and science classes require very different skills for success.

REAL-LIFE WRITING

Comparison and contrast enter into our daily lives often without our awareness. Consider the following instances in which you might use these development strategies.

For College

- In literature classes, you compare or contrast two writers for their content or style.
- In science class, you contrast the results of two experiments to learn about a compound you are testing.

In Your Personal Life

- You write a note to a friend, contrasting two iPods to decide which one is the better choice for your needs.

- You write a note to your roommate comparing your new rental agreement with your previous agreement to make sure you will keep all your privileges in your apartment complex.

At Work

- You write a memo to your boss contrasting your current performance with last year's performance to show your boss you deserve a raise.

- For a brochure, you contrast your company's product to your competitor's to show how yours is superior.

A MODEL PARAGRAPH: CONTRAST

Read the following paragraph. Pay attention to how the writer focuses on the differences between two football teams yet makes the point that the differences are significant because both teams have tremendous success in common.

Perfection Is Hard to Come By, Or Is It?

[1]Few things in life are perfect. [2]Two professional football teams, however, have shown that they can be perfect, or undefeated, over the course of one season. [3]Although both the Miami Dolphins of 1972 and the New England Patriots of 2007 went undefeated during the regular season, they were very different teams. [4]One key difference lies in their quarterbacks. [5]The Patriots' Tom Brady started every game of the 2007 season and led the team to each of its wins. [6]The Dolphins, on the other hand, relied on backup quarterback Earl Morrall when starter Bob Griese went out with a broken ankle in the fifth week of the season. [7]Griese returned for the AFC playoffs and the eventual Super Bowl win, but it was a dual effort that kept the Dolphins' winning streak intact. [8]Another key difference between the teams is their defense. [9]While Patriots' players Mike Vrabel, Rodney Harrison, and Teddy Bruschi had played for the Pats for a few seasons, several new players began playing with the Patriots only in 2007. [10]These players included Adalius Thomas, Tory James, and Eddie Jackson, among others. [11]In contrast, the Dolphins' defense—nicknamed the no-name defense—was made up of players who had played together for years. [12] Bill Stanfill, Manny Fernandez, Dick Anderson, and Jake Scott had all played together for at least three seasons. [13]Finally, the Dolphins and the Patriots

used very different offensive strategies. [14]The Patriots primarily passed the ball to score, and Tom Brady and wide receiver Randy Moss worked together to set passing and receiving records. [15]The Dolphins, however, were both a passing and running team, making use of receiver Paul Warfield and running backs Mercury Morris and Larry Csonka for their points. [16]Even though both the Patriots and the Dolphins ended up at the same destination—the Super Bowl—their differences show that there is more than one way to be a winner.

EXERCISE 1 Analyzing a Contrast Paragraph

Reread "Perfection Is Hard to Come By, or Is It?" Then, answer the questions that follow.

1. What two football teams are being contrasted? _____

_____

2. What is the writer's topic sentence? _____

_____

_____

3. List the differences between the two groups contrasted.

a. _____

b. _____

c. _____

4. What transitions show that the writer is switching from an example of one team to an example of another?

Sentence 6: _____

Sentence 11: _____

Sentence 15: _____

5. What does the writer conclude after detailing the differences between the two teams?_____

_____

A MODEL PARAGRAPH: COMPARISON

Read the following paragraph to see how the writer uses comparison to draw a conclusion.

Blown Away

My cousin and I recently debated which weather systems were more damaging: hurricanes or tornadoes. Growing up in Florida, I've definitely seen more than I want of wild, wet, and dangerously windy weather. My cousin, a longtime resident of Oklahoma, argues that his tornadoes are more dangerous. When we factor in winds, size, and damage, however, I know hurricanes are worse. According to the dictionary, a hurricane is a tropical storm with a low-pressure center that has high winds (74 miles per hour or greater) and flooding rains. Tornadoes—funnel-shaped clouds reaching to the ground—offer strong winds, too, sometimes topping 110 miles per hour, so in this area they are "tougher" than hurricanes. However, in size, hurricanes are the champions. Tornadoes usually span a mere 250 feet, though they sometimes cover up to a mile, but hurricanes on average are 200 to 300 miles across and can span up to 700 miles. It's clear which is more impressive in the size category. Finally, hurricanes are far more destructive than tornadoes. While the biggest tornado outbreak in the last hundred years (the "super outbreak" of April 3–4, 1974, which included 148 tornadoes across thirteen states and caused damage in excess of $600 million), a single hurricane—Hurricane Andrew in 1992—wreaked more than $36 billion in damage. Damage totals from Hurricane Katrina, by far the worst hurricane in North American history, have yet to be determined. Overall, hurricanes have to be considered the most severe type of bad weather. My cousin and I have pointless competitions about things such as weather types, and we both love to win. When it comes to damage and death, however, tornadoes and hurricanes have us all beat.

EXERCISE 2 Analyzing a Comparison Paragraph

Reread "Blown Away." Then, answer the questions that follow.

1. What is the topic sentence?_____

_____

2. What aspects of tornadoes and hurricanes does the writer compare?

a. _____

b. _____

c. _____

3. What details does the writer use to show the strength or "tough-ness" of each weather type?

a. _____

b. _____

c. _____

4. The writer concentrates on the similarities between tornadoes and hurricanes. What differences can you think of?

a. _____

b. _____

5. What ultimate conclusion does the writer draws as a result of his

comparison? _____

CHOOSING A GOOD TOPIC FOR DEVELOPMENT

One challenge in writing a comparison or contrast paragraph is finding a topic that will allow you to say something interesting about both subjects. For instance, choosing two subjects such as a winter vacation and a sports car might give you enough to write about for a comparison or contrast paragraph, but it's more likely that you'll have a tough time finding common areas to discuss for both subjects. Comparing or contrasting a winter vacation and a summer vacation instead will offer you differences—the times of year of the vacations—but enough similarities to serve as common ground between the subjects. Thus, you should choose two items that have something in common, such as two friends, two classes, or two desserts.

Once you've decided on your two items for comparison or contrast, you need to decide *what aspects of the two items you wish to focus on*. If you're writing about two types of dogs, for example, what about them do you want to compare or contrast? You could mention their intelligence, friendliness, aggressiveness, cost, overall health, and indoor and outdoor habits. The point is to decide ahead of time, before writing a draft, just what areas you want to discuss.

Some examples of strong and weak topics for comparison and contrast follow.

Strong Topics for Comparison/Contrast	**Weak Topics for Comparison/Contrast**
Comparing *Casablanca* and *The Maltese Falcon*	Comparing *Casablanca* and *Bambi*
Comparing the Honda Accord and the Toyota Prius	Comparing the Honda Accord and a semi truck
Comparing Dan Marino and Bob Griese	Comparing Dan Marino and Hillary Clinton
Contrasting eating dinner at home with having a picnic	Contrasting eating dinner at home with fasting

Freewriting on possible comparison or contrast topics is a good way to determine whether you have enough information to develop a paragraph. Rosie was looking for a new job, and she thought that contrasting her top two choices might make her decision easier. Her freewriting ended up looking like this:

I really need a job. School's costing too much, and my rent just went up, but I can't work too much or my grades will go down. There's an assisted living senior place near the college, so that would be convenient, but taking the bus downtown for a kid's day-care job wouldn't take too long, either. I keep hearing that the seniors are a lot nicer to the staff than the little kids are, and I bet I wouldn't have to pick up after them as much. The day-care job pays a little more, but I could get more hours at the senior complex. What else? What else what else? Oh, yeah. I hear that the seniors are sometimes lonely and want to talk, but I think I'd like that better than crabby kids. No more time!

In just a few minutes of freewriting, Rosie identifies three possible areas for development: location, pay, and potential downsides. While she may discover even more areas of contrast, these three make a good start to her paragraph.

EXERCISE 3 Developing Topics for a Contrast Paragraph

The following list contains topics for contrast. Below each topic, write down three differences between the two subjects. An example is done for you.

Topic: A children's movie and an R-rated movie

Differences: **a.** Amount of violence

b. Amount of profanity

c. Amount of nudity

1. Topic: Your friend's car and your father's car

Differences: **a.** _____

b. _____

c. _____

2. Topic: Your first haircut and your current haircut

Differences: **a.** _____

b. _____

c. _____

3. Topic: Your study habits in high school and your study habits now

Differences: **a.** _____

b. _____

c. _____

4. Topic: Your taste in music and your parents' taste in music

Differences: **a.** _____

b. _____

c. _____

5. Topic: A vacation in the snow and a vacation at the beach

Differences: **a.** _____

b. _____

c. _____

EXERCISE 4 Developing Topics for a Comparison Paragraph

The following list contains topics for comparison. Below each topic, write down three similarities between the two subjects. An example is done for you.

Topic: Two friends, ___Susannah___ and ___Cindy___

Similarities: **a.** Both are friendly. _____

b. Both are hard workers. _____

c. Both have serious boyfriends. _____

1. Topic: Two college teachers, _____ and _____

Similarities: **a.** _____

b. _____

c. _____

2. Topic: Two neighborhoods, _____ and _____

Similarities: **a.** _____

b. _____

c. _____

3. Topic: Two holiday celebrations, _____ and _____

Similarities: **a.** _____

b. _____

c. _____

4. Topic: Two television programs, _____ and _____

Similarities: **a.** _____

b. _____

c. _____

5. Topic: Two sports, _____ and _____

Similarities: **a.** _____

b. _____

c. _____

WRITING AN EFFECTIVE TOPIC SENTENCE

Once you've done some freewriting and identified some possible areas for development, write your topic sentence. Ideally, your topic sentence will identify the two subjects that you are comparing or contrasting, and it will state whether or not you'll be finding similarities or differences between these two subjects. For instance, Rosie wrote the following topic sentence.

The job at the senior living complex is very different from the job at the children's day-care center.

Right away, Rosie lets her reader know that she will concentrate on the *differences* between two jobs: one working with elderly people and one working with small children. Some other effective topic sentences are these:

Eating dessert is a lot like getting a massage.

Watching television and playing computer games have many aspects in common.

My history instructor and my English instructor are very different in their teaching styles.

Fixing a car and planting a garden require very different skills.

DEVELOPING SPECIFIC DETAILS

Many comparison and contrast paragraphs will require details from your own experience and observations. As you write longer, more involved assignments, you will need to consult other sources for information. An important characteristic of comparison and contrast paragraphs is *balance*. Make sure you include approximately the same amount and type of information about both subjects. For instance, if Rosie writes seven or eight lines discussing the job at the senior complex, but only two sentences discussing the job at the day-care center, the reader might think Rosie hasn't learned much about the day-care job. A reader could also conclude that Rosie isn't really interested in contrasting these subjects. Neither conclusion is beneficial to Rosie in terms of making her point.

One way to make sure you include adequate details for both subjects being discussed is to use the prewriting technique of questioning. Below is an example of questioning that Rosie used to see where she needed more information.

Question	Answer (senior complex)	Answer (day-care center)
Location of job	Near college	Downtown
Pay rate	Minimum wage, but some tips	More than minimum?
Downsides	Lonely people?	Changing diapers; crying kids; constant picking up

From this chart, Rosie can see that she needs more information about the downsides of the senior complex job and about the day-care pay scale. Once she adds information where the question marks are, she can begin another round of questioning to find specific details.

ORGANIZING AND LINKING YOUR IDEAS

Just as you have different options for organizing a narrative paragraph, you have options here. Two types of organizational strategies work best for writing a comparison or contrast paragraph.

All-of-One-Side Approach

In the all-of-one-side approach, you write down all the details about one subject in your paragraph first, and then write down all the details about the other subject. The benefit of this type of organization is that it's easier for you, the writer, to remember all the details and examples about each side, since they all go together in a paragraph. Another plus is that using transitions can be a bit easier, since you're not jumping back and forth between two separate subjects. The challenge of this strategy, however, is keeping your reader from forgetting your first subject by the time you finish discussing the second one. The illustration "All-of-One-Side Paragraph" shows how this approach is organized.

Comparison and Contrast Paragraphs:
Whole-to-Whole Approach

Topic sentence....*Stating the main idea*.............................
....

↓

Subject A ....
............Support point 1 and specific details.............
............Support point 2 and specific details.............
............Support point 3 and specific details.............
Subject B ....
............Support point 1 and specific details.............
............Support point 2 and specific details.............
............Support point 3 and specific details.............

Rosie's outline used the all-of-one-side approach. Filled in, it looks like this.

The jobs at the Jefferson Senior Complex and the Sunshine Day-Care Center have many differences.

A. Jefferson Senior Complex

1. Close to college
2. Minimum wage
3. Can't always get work done if lonely people want attention

B. Sunshine Day-Care Center

1. Downtown
2. $9.50 per hour
3. Demanding little kids

Point-by-Point Approach

The point-by-point approach alternates details from each subject for discussion, offering a detail from one side, then the other side, then back to the first side, and so on. Both subjects are integrated throughout the entire paragraph. The benefit of this type of organization is that your reader can see details from both subjects side by side and, thus, see the comparison or contrast more easily. One challenge of point-by-point organization is making sure your transitions keep your reader on track at all times. Going back and forth between two ideas can be confusing if you don't give your reader good, clear directions through your transitions. The illustration "Point-by-Point Paragraph" shows this approach.

**Comparison and Contrast Paragraphs:
Point-by-Point Approach**

Topic sentence...*Stating the main idea*...
....

↓

Support point 1 ....
........................Subject A...
........................Subject B...
Support point 2 ....
........................Subject A...
........................Subject B...
Support point 3 ....
........................Subject A...
........................Subject B...

Transitions That Work Well to Show Comparison

Comparison		Contrast	
and	just as . . . so, too, is . . .	although	on the other hand
also	like	but	unlike
both	neither	conversely	whereas
each of	similarly	despite	while
in addition	too	however	yet
in the same way		in contrast	

If Rosie had chosen to use the point-by-point method, her outline would have looked like this.

The jobs at the Jefferson Senior Complex and the Sunshine Day-Care Center have many differences.

    A. Location

        1. Senior center is close to college.

        2. Day-care center is downtown.

    B. Pay scale

        1. Senior center pays minimum wage.

        2. Day-care center pays $9.50 per hour.

    C. Challenges of the job

        1. Sometimes hard to get work done

        2. Demanding little kids

Notice that in this form of Rosie's outline, she must identify the three areas of comparison that will eventually become her support points.

Some transitions that work very well in comparison and contrast writing are shown in the box at the top of this page.

Read the following paragraph, noting how the writer organizes her ideas and keeps them connected by using transitions.

A Real Blast

[1]Of the more than 150 piloted space flights sent up by the National Aeronautics and Space Administration (commonly known as NASA), those from the Apollo and Space Shuttle programs have been

particularly significant. [2]However, they are quite different in their goals, costs, and results. [3]The Apollo program was created to put people on the moon, but each vessel could be launched only once. [4]Astronaut Neil Armstrong's words, "One small step for man, one giant leap for mankind," remind us of the Apollo's successes even though the spacecraft Armstrong flew was never launched again. [5]To develop the Apollo space program, NASA spent between $20 and $25 billion. [6]The results of the Apollo program were largely positive: human presence on the moon, significant scientific data, and nearly 400 kilograms of lunar samples. [7]Even the "successful failure" of *Apollo 13*, which was damaged in an explosion, did not result in any loss of life during flight. [8]In contrast, the Space Shuttle program had different goals, budgets, and results. [9]The intended benefit of the program was to create a reusable means of human space travel. [10]Indeed, unlike the Apollo rockets, the shuttle *Columbia* flew twenty-eight flights! [11]These flights were not cheap, however. [12]Costing four times more than the Apollo flights, the Space Shuttle program topped the $100 billion mark. [13]The results of the shuttle program were mixed. [14]The shuttle did

Shuttle Streak

SURF THE NET Seen from Earth, the speeding space shuttle appears more shooting star than streaking ship. How fast and how high—or far—does the space shuttle go? Surf the Net for answers.

Responding to Images. *What words or ideas best describe this photo? Explain. Mysterious, Scientific, celestial, or grand are some ideas to consider.*

allow such projects as the Hubble telescope and the shuttle-*Mir* connections—in which the U.S. Space Shuttle docked at the Russian *Mir* space station—to be successful. [15]Unfortunately, two Space Shuttle missions—those of *Challenger* in 1986 and *Columbia* in 2003—ended in disaster as the shuttles disintegrated and their crews were killed. [16]Though both the Apollo and Space Shuttle programs contributed greatly to scientific knowledge, the shuttles—in terms of both dollars and lives lost—have proved much more expensive.

EXERCISE 5 Analyzing a Paragraph for Elements of Contrast

Reread "A Real Blast." Then, answer the questions that follow.

1. Is the purpose of this paragraph to compare or contrast two spacecraft programs? _____

2. What is the topic sentence? _____

_____

3. The writer looks at different aspects of each space program. What types of information does the writer use to evaluate each program?

   a. _____

   b. _____

   c. _____

4. What specific details does the writer give for each program?

   a. Apollo: _____

   _____

   b. Space Shuttle: _____

   _____

5. What strategy does the writer use to organize her ideas, all-of-one-side or point-by-point? _____

6. What transitions does the writer use to signal that she is starting a discussion of the Space Shuttle program? _____

7. The writer directly contrasts the two space programs in three sentences. What four sentences mention both? *Hint:* Look at the very beginning and very end of the paragraph.

Sentence _____   Sentence _____

Sentence _____   Sentence _____

EXERCISE 6 Outlining a Contrast Paragraph

Make an outline of the paragraph "A Real Blast." The first few items have been done for you.

Space Program Differences

A. Apollo program

1. Goal: to put humans on the moon _____

2. Cost: $20–25 billion _____

3. _____

4. _____

5. _____

B. Space Shuttle program

1. _____

2. _____

3. _____

4. _____

EXERCISE 7 Following the Four Cs

Read the paragraph below. Then, answer the questions that follow. Pay close attention to the areas of comparison that the writer has chosen to write about.

A Great Read About the Greatest Show

[1]I grew up in Sarasota, Florida, near where the Ringling Brothers Circus stops for the winter. [2]Consequently, I've been to the Ringling circus museum and to shows so often that I thought noth-

ing could amaze me, and certainly not a circus book. [3]When I had to read Sara Gruen's novel *Water for Elephants* last year for a class, I prepared to yawn. [4]Boy, was I surprised! [5]Everything about the book reminded me of an actual circus. [6]For one thing, both the real circus and the book circus stimulated my senses. [7]Real circuses are larger than life: bright colors, pungent smells, and brassy noises. [8]The *Water for Elephants* details were larger than life, too: shimmering pink sequins on costumes, powerful popcorn-animal-hay smells, and clanging music. [9]In addition, the circus animals were exciting. [10]In the real circus, the horses are graceful and elegant, moving to the music or to the sound of their trainers' voices, even as the big cats are sleek and terrifying. [11]The story animals were thrilling: the elegant Liberty horses performed in perfect time, and the elephant Rosie made my heart stop as she balanced on her ball. [12]Finally, *Water for Elephants* was as heart-stopping as a real circus. [13]In a circus show, there's always a "Can they really do this?" element when the trapeze artists or other thrill seekers perform their dangerous stunts. [14]Reading the novel, I never worried about whether an act would be performed well, but my mouth went dry when the bad guys started "red-lighting" (getting rid of) some of the circus workers and others sought revenge. [15]Even though I knew that I was only reading a story, I still felt nervous until I knew how it ended. [16]Opening *Water for Elephants* was like going into the big top: I couldn't believe how well the novel captured my circus experience.

Concise Writing

1. Is the purpose of this paragraph to compare or contrast two experiences? _____

2. What is the topic sentence?

_____

_____

3. What three areas of comparison, or support points, does the writer offer?

a. _____

b. _____

c. _____

Credible Writing

4. What details does the writer offer to support each support point?

   Details illustrating support point 1:

   a. _____

   b. _____

   c. _____

   Details illustrating support point 2:

   a. _____

   b. _____

   Details illustrating support point 3:

   a. _____

   b. _____

5. What details does the writer offer which show that she knows about circuses?

   a. _____

   b. _____

   c. _____

Clear Writing

6. What transitions does the writer use to signal the start of each support point?

   Sentence 6: _____

   Sentence 9: _____

   Sentence 12: _____

7. How many times does the writer use some form of the word
*circus?*____

Correct Writing

The sentences in this paragraph are all correct. To check for correctness in
your own writing, go to Part 7, "Writing Correct Sentences."

WRITING PRACTICE 1

Below are five topics that can be compared or contrasted. Write two topic
sentences for each topic, one that shows a comparison relationship and one
that shows a contrast relationship. An example is done for you.

Topic: Two books, _Gone with the Wind_ and _The House of Mirth_

Topic sentences:

Comparison: _Gone with the Wind and The House of Mirth are alike in
terms of how the main women characters are prepared
for lives of wealth._

Contrast: _Gone with the Wind and The House of Mirth show many
differences in how women deal with adversity._

1. Topic: Two sports stars, _____ and _____

Topic sentences:

Comparison: _____

_____

Contrast: _____

_____

2. Two musical or fashion styles, _____ and _____

Topic sentences:

Comparison: _____

_____

Contrast: _____

_____

3. Two ways to commute to work or school, riding the bus and driving

Topic sentences:

Comparison: _____

_____

Contrast: _____

_____

4. Two stages of life, being a student and being an employee

Topic sentences:

Comparison: _____

_____

Contrast: _____

_____

5. Two types of relationships, being just friends and being romantically involved

Topic sentences:

Comparison: _____

_____

Contrast: _____

_____

WRITING PRACTICE 2 Writing a Paragraph Step by Step

Now it's time to write your own paragraph.

Prewriting

1. Choose a topic for your paragraph. On the next page is a list of different topics for paragraphs that compare or contrast two items. Read the list, and think about whether you can find more similarities or differences between the paired items in the list. Then, choose a topic, and decide on comparison or contrast.

Two different romantic relationships

Two different family relationships

Two different work relationships

Two entertainers

Two problems in your life

Two happy times in your life

Two friends

Two meals at the same restaurant

Your school at two different times of day

Your place of work at two different times of day

A shopping mall at different times of year

Your appearance as a child and your appearance now

Your home as a child and your home now

Studying for an easy test and studying for a difficult test

A chore or task you enjoy and a chore or task you dislike

2. Questioning is a very helpful type of prewriting for comparison and contrast because it allows you to focus on the same areas for each subject in your paragraph. Look at the sample question-and-answer list below. This writer has chosen to contrast the shopping mall in July with the shopping mall in December.

Question	Answer (July)	Answer (December)
Who is at the mall?	People looking for summer clothing: swimsuits, shorts	People looking for everything: clothing, holiday gifts, holiday decorations
What does the mall look like?	Decorations of suns, sand, beaches	Decorations of snow, Christmas, Hanukkah, New Year's Eve, Kwanzaa
How crowded is it?	Not crowded at all, especially in morning	Extremely crowded all the time
How do store clerks act?	Bored but friendly	Hyper, stressed, too tired, not friendly

Drafting

3. Write a topic sentence. Make sure that the relationship you're writing about—comparison or contrast—is clear in your topic sentence.

Possible topic sentence: It's amazing how different the mall can be at two different times of the year.

4. Choose support points—the areas of comparison—and specific details.

5. Organize your ideas using the all-of-one-side or the point-by-point strategy.

6. Write your draft. Use freewriting to fill in the gaps with details, and keep checking to make sure your organization is consistent throughout your paragraph.

Revising

7. Make sure all the details in your list directly advance your topic sentence. Eliminate any details that do not show a similarity or difference between your two items. Check again to see that you have included all the necessary details. Make sure your details are organized and connected through clear transitions that let your reader know where every step in the process comes.

Editing

8. Proofread your paragraph to make sure you have used correct spelling, punctuation, and grammar.

WRITING PRACTICE 3 Comparing or Contrasting in Real Life

Deciding between choices can be very difficult, particularly when many choices exist. The situations below outline real-life situations requiring comparison or contrast as part of a decision-making process. Use your comparing or contrasting skills to help a friend make an important decision.

Topic A

Your friend is trying to decide which television programs to let her twelve-year-old daughter watch. You have volunteered to view various television programs and report back to your friend. You have come across two television shows that you think might be suitable for your friend's daughter. *Write a paragraph comparing or contrasting two television programs.* Be sure to focus on support points that let you consider both programs, such as characters, educational value, entertainment value, and music.

Topic B

Your friend is trying to decide between two instructors for a class he has to take, and you have taken classes taught by both instructors. *Write a paragraph comparing or contrasting two instructors*. Think about what areas of comparison or contrast you want to focus on: how "hard" the instructors are, how much they value attention in class, how much work they give, how approachable they are, how much feedback they give. Then, include specific details from your own experiences and observations in order to make your points convincing.

CHAPTER SUMMARY

Remember the following in writing a comparison or contrast paragraph:

1. Comparing two things involves finding similarities between them.
2. Contrasting involves focusing on the differences between items.
3. Good topics for comparison and contrast have some common areas for comparison.
4. Comparison or contrast paragraphs can be organized using the all-of-one-side approach or the point-by-point approach.

MyWritingLab & Lab Activity 20

mywritinglab For additional practice with comparing and contrasting, go to **www.mywritinglab.com** or complete **Lab Activity 20** in the separate *Resources for Writers* Lab Manual.

Cause and Effect

Culture Note

HEALTH AND FITNESS

Many people have heard the expression "If you don't have your health, you don't have anything," but how many take it seriously? Health clubs and organic foods are the rage across the country, yet junk food sales remain high. Further, while Americans spend hours at the gym, they also spend hours in front of the computer or television. Are Americans healthy, and what are the consequences if they aren't?

Stepping Up

OBSERVE YOUR WORLD In what ways could you add physical activity to your life? Try something new—such as walking up stairs rather than riding in an elevator for a week and write about your finding.
Responding to Images. *What is this man's attitude toward his exercise? Explain.*

RECOMMENDED READINGS

"Fatso," Cheryl Peck, *p. 762*

"The Santa Ana," Joan Didion, *p. 784*

The Joy of Boredom," Carolyn Y. Johnson *p. 742*

WHAT IS A CAUSE-AND-EFFECT PARAGRAPH?

Every day we attempt to explain, predict, and control situations in our lives: why we were late, how we'll save enough money to buy holiday presents, how we can lose weight. Though these situations are very different, they all have one thing in common: the element of cause-and-effect reasoning.

In the cause-and-effect paragraph development strategy, you explain why something occurred by identifying the reasons it happened (**causes**), the outcome of certain actions (**effects**), or both.

Some sentences focusing on the *causes* of an event follow.

Moving back in with your parents as an adult can cause tension in the house.

Many factors contribute to a couple's decision to get a divorce.

A number of happy surprises in his life have caused John to have a sunny outlook on life.

Some sentences focusing on the *effects* of an event follow.

Following a daily exercise program can have many positive effects.

Taking on additional responsibilities at work can have a great effect on your career.

Failing to study for final exams can have a disastrous effect on a student's grades.

EXERCISE 1 Finding Causes

Provide a cause for each of the following effects. An example is done for you. *Note:* There are many possible correct answers.

Cause: *Eating too many candy bars before bed* Effect: Bad teeth

1. Cause: _____ Effect: Oversleeping

2. Cause: _____ Effect: Getting a promotion

3. Cause: _____ Effect: Sunburn

4. Cause: _____ Effect: Car breaks down

5. Cause: _____ Effect: Holiday weight gain

EXERCISE 2 Finding Effects

Provide an effect for each of the following causes. An example is done for you. *Note:* There are many possible correct answers.

Cause: Running a red light   Effect: *Crashing your car* _____

1. Cause: Not brushing your teeth   Effect: _____

2. Cause: Exercising every day   Effect: _____

3. Cause: Doing your homework   Effect: _____

4. Cause: Taking on more responsibility
   at work   Effect: _____

5. Cause: Cheating on a quiz   Effect: _____

REAL-LIFE WRITING

Cause-and-effect reasoning enters into real life daily. Here are some examples that show how cause-and-effect thinking plays significant roles in real-life activities.

For College

- In science classes, writing about the causes of chemical reactions help you identify unknown compounds.
- In history class, writing about the causes and effects of an event help you understand it better.

In Your Personal Life

- Restore your credibility with a loan officer by explaining the causes for some late payments noted on your credit rating.
- Try to convince your father to stop smoking by explaining the effects of that habit on his health.

At Work

- Convince your boss to promote you by predicting the effects of your leadership in a new job.
- Explain to your boss the causes for a shipment being late.

A MODEL PARAGRAPH: CAUSE AND EFFECT

Read the sample paragraph below. The writer uses cause-and-effect reasoning to explain why he is out of shape.

One Step at a Time

[1]Never one to put myself down, I frequently described myself as "big-boned" or "sturdy" with a "relaxed" (that is, nonexistent) fitness schedule. [2]According to my doctor, however, I am unhealthy. [3]My wake-up call as to my health came when my physical revealed high weight (220 pounds on my five foot nine inch frame), high blood pressure (160/110), and high cholesterol (230). [4]The doctor says many factors have contributed to my current poor health. [5]For one thing, I don't eat well. [6]I've heard of the "five servings a day" fruits and vegetables recommendation, but there's not much green stuff that I like, so I pretty much consider French fries and ketchup my salad. [7]The doctor said that the lack of nutrients, the high fat and salt content of my diet, and the high calories all contribute to my problems with weight, cholesterol, and blood pressure. [8]For another thing, my job is stressful. [9]I answer phones for a credit card company, and people who call me (usually because they haven't paid their bills) are never happy. [10]I have to be polite, but inside I'm all wound up. [11]The doctor said the stress sends my blood pressure up. [12]A third cause of my poor condition is my inactive lifestyle. [13]I take the bus to work, but my stop is only two buildings down from my apartment, and then I sit at a desk all day. [14]I always take the elevator, and I eat lunch in the break room on my floor, so I do no walking then, either. [15]According to the doctor, I'm not giving my heart (or any part of me) enough exercise, and I don't burn enough calories; consequently, I'm overweight. [16]I know I need to make changes, but all I've done so far is start walking up the stairs to my third-floor cubicle. [17]It's not much, but it's a step in the right direction.

EXERCISE 3 Analyzing a Cause-and-Effect Paragraph

Reread "One Step at a Time." Then, answer the questions that follow.

1. What is the topic sentence?

2. What causes does the writer offer for his poor physical condition?

a. _____

b. _____

c. _____

3. What three transitions does the writer list to introduce the support points?

Sentence 3:   _____

Sentence 5:   _____

Sentence 8:   _____

CHOOSING A GOOD TOPIC FOR DEVELOPMENT

In writing a cause-and-effect paragraph, be sure to choose a topic that allows you to show how one event caused another to happen. For instance, writing about the causes of some types of cancer is tricky since even medical experts don't have the answers. A better topic, then, would be how smoking causes lung disease since there is a clear, medically supported link between these two.

Once you've chosen a topic, make sure you narrow it down so that you can cover it in a paragraph. Writing about the causes of World War II, for instance, could lead you to write an entire book! A better topic might be writing about the reasons a particular soldier chose to enlist in the armed forces to fight in that war, or three effects of the United States dropping the atom bomb on Hiroshima.

Once you've narrowed your topic to an event that works well for cause-and-effect development, *decide whether the cause or the effect is more significant to write about*. Many topics can be argued from either the cause or effect viewpoint, but usually one perspective—the cause or the effect—is stronger.

For instance, while exploring the causes of the invention of the automobile—needs for transportation and comfort—could make an interesting paragraph, these concerns applied to horse and train travel, too. However, the *effects* of the invention of the car are so far-reaching that we are seeing them a century later. Thus, writing about the effects of the automobile's invention is a better choice.

Martha wasn't sure what to write about, but she wanted to explore ways to prevent herself from getting sick so often. After reading some health magazines, Martha did some freewriting on the subject.

> I am so sick of being sick! Every time I go to work or school or pick my kids up from day care, I feel like I'm catching some new virus. I read that touching things like doorknobs, computer keyboards, and desktops is a sure way to become infected with a virus, and even shaking hands can spread illness. Since I work in a restaurant, I'm always touching things that other people have already touched. I know I don't wash my hands enough. I also learned that not getting enough sleep can break down my immune system and make it really easy for me to get sick. Whoever wrote that must not have kids! I wish I could get more sleep.

In this freewriting sample, Martha identifies two *causes* of getting sick: touching things that sick people have touched and not getting enough sleep. Even though she knew she needed more information to write a whole paragraph, Martha decided that she had enough ideas to start writing.

WRITING AN EFFECTIVE TOPIC SENTENCE

After you have chosen your topic, make sure you identify what aspect—cause or effect—you plan to write about. In general, put the area of focus for your paragraph at the end of your topic sentence. For instance, writing "Many people drink and drive with disastrous results" *could* lead readers to expect a paragraph on the reasons people drink and drive. However, since "disastrous results" comes at the end of the sentence, it's more likely that the writer plans to explain the *effects* of drinking and driving. Some other possible topic sentences follow.

Sandy was pleased that all her overtime paid off at work.

In this sentence, the reader expects to learn about the ways Sandy's overtime paid off, or the *effects* of her overtime.

Many factors eventually led Mark to cheat on a quiz.

Here, the reader expects to learn more about what *caused* Mark to cheat.

Different Names for Causes

basis   motive
cause   reason
factor

Different Names for Effects

consequence   outcome
effect   result

After Martha finished her freewriting, she identified two possible support points.

Support point 1:   Touching things that sick people have touched

Support point 2:   Not getting enough sleep

Since both of these points deal with *causes* of illness, Martha came up with this topic sentence.

Especially during cold and flu season, several factors contribute to people getting sick.

From this topic sentence, a reader expects to learn *causes* of illness, which is exactly what Martha wants to write about.

EXERCISE 4 Identifying Causes and Effects

In each sentence below, identify the cause and the effect. An example is done for you.

Many people sitting in the shade were sunburned as a result of the sun's glare off the white sand.

Cause: Sun's glare

Effect: Sunburn

1. Road construction led to a three-hour delay on the highway.

Cause: _____

Effect: _____

2. Studying hard for finals paid off for Shauna when she earned three Bs and an A.

Cause: _____

Effect: _____

3. A good vocabulary starts with reading.

Cause: _____

Effect: _____

4. My headaches all seem to come from watching too much television.

Cause: _____

Effect: _____

5. Knowing Carlos likes the color red, I bought a dress that color.

Cause: _____

Effect: _____

6. Smoking cigarettes causes lung disease.

Cause: _____

Effect: _____

7. Since we ate too much turkey, we fell asleep immediately.

Cause: _____

Effect: _____

8. Babies often stop crying when they're rocked.

Cause: _____

Effect: _____

9. Drinking coffee makes me nervous.

Cause: _____

Effect: _____

10. When the Twins lost their playoff game, Mike slipped into depression.

Cause: _____

Effect: _____

DEVELOPING SPECIFIC DETAILS

Using prewriting techniques such as freewriting or clustering, make a list of support points for each part of your argument. Then decide whether focusing on causes or on effects is better for your topic. After freewriting, Martha identified "touching things that sick people have touched" and "not getting enough sleep" as two causes of illness. She knew she needed more information, so she used a cluster diagram to see where she could fill in details.

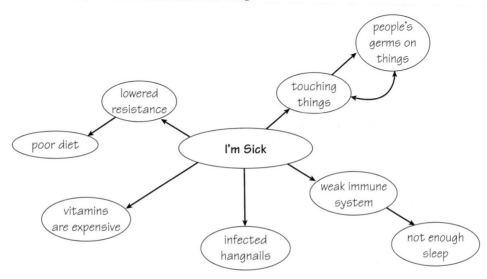

Some details—such as the high price of vitamins and an infected hangnail—are generally related to Martha's topic. However, since they don't actually support the idea of Martha being sick, she omits them. Martha remembers reading about poor diet being a cause of poor health, so she includes that in her cluster diagram. Thus, she ends up with three solid points to develop in her paragraph. Sometimes specific details illustrating causes or effects will come from your own experiences, but if you have trouble thinking of enough detail to support your topic sentence, refer to other sources, such as talking to people or reading trusted publications.

ORGANIZING AND LINKING YOUR IDEAS

Emphatic order—organizing your support points from least to most important—works well for cause-and-effect paragraphs. Remember that you, as the writer, get to decide which points are most—or least—important, and order them accordingly. Even though Martha's first cause of illness was "touching things that sick people have touched," she decided to place that point last in her paragraph. For her, the idea that just touching a doorknob that a sick person had touched could make her sick was so unsettling that she wanted to make sure other people knew they should wash their hands frequently. This is the final order for Martha's support points.

Support point 1: Not getting enough sleep
Support point 2: Not eating well
Support point 3: Touching things that sick people have touched

Words and Terms That Signal Emphatic Order

above all	last
another	least of all
equally important	most of all
especially	most importantly
even more	most significantly
first	next
in the first place	

EXERCISE 5 Analyzing a Paragraph for Causes and Effects

Read the following paragraph. Determine what the causes and effects are for the situation under discussion. Then, answer the questions that follow.

More Than Just Muscles

¹I got a new job as a part-time package handler at a shipping company, so I figured I should get in better shape. ²The job description said I'd be lifting packages that weigh about thirty pounds continually for four hours, and I worried about my back. ³Once I started a weight training class at school, however, I noticed several positive changes. ⁴First, I could do the job without injury. ⁵My co-workers all complained of low-back pain, and some even missed work for it. ⁶Even though I was sometimes achy and always tired at the end of a shift, my low-back exercises and ab work kept me from hurting myself. ⁷A second benefit of lifting weights was that I looked better. ⁸I didn't really lose weight, but my clothes fit better, and I didn't have a "muffin top," that roll of flab over the top of my jeans, anymore. ⁹Most important, I felt better about myself. ¹⁰I've never considered myself athletic, and I still won't join the other workers to play basketball after work, but I'm a lot stronger than I ever thought I could be. ¹¹Some days I lift thousands of pounds' worth of parcels, but I never have to quit working. ¹²I know now I can do physical work for hours and not stop, and that's a great feeling.

1. What is the topic sentence? _____

_____

2. From your reading of the topic sentence, do you think this paragraph will focus on the causes or the effects of taking a weight

training class? _____

3. List three effects of the weight training class:

   a. _____

   b. _____

   c. _____

4. In the writer's view, what effect is the most important? How can

you tell? _____

_____

5. How does the writer signal the start of support points?

Sentence 4: _____

Sentence 7: _____

Sentence 9: _____

EXERCISE 6 Following the Four Cs

Read the paragraph below. Then, answer the questions that follow.

Baby Steps

[1]After I finished high school and didn't play sports every day anymore, I gained a lot of weight. [2]Between school and my two jobs, I had no time to work out, and soon all my clothes were tight. [3]After my sister had a baby, she heard about a step-counting fitness program that has people wear step counters (called pedometers) and try to walk ten thousand steps a day for fitness (about five miles) or twelve thousand steps (about six miles) for weight loss. [4]I took the idea and ran (or walked) with it, and I immediately lost weight, even without the step counter. [5]Three aspects of the program were primarily responsible for my weight loss. [6]Probably the most significant aspect of the program for me was that I started walking everywhere to get more steps in. [7]Instead of cutting across an empty lot to get to the market, I went around the corner and added five hundred steps. [8]Another factor in my weight loss was how I walked. [9]I figured that going fast would burn more calories than going slowly, so I made a point to speed-walk whenever possible. [10]My friends teased me about how silly I looked, weaving through crowds at the mall, but even they couldn't deny I was losing weight. [11]A final factor in my weight loss came with the realization that just being active played a big role in my overall fitness. [12]Now I always try to be

moving—tapping my foot in class, stepping back and forth while I fold laundry, lifting my legs one at a time when I'm sitting on the couch—and I've noticed that I'm staying thinner with less effort. [13]I'm not really sure how many steps I walk each day, but it's more walking than I used to do, and my body can tell the difference.

Concise Writing

1. What is the topic sentence? _____

_____

2. How many reasons does the writer of the paragraph give to support

the main idea? _____

3. What points does the writer offer in support of the topic sentence?

a. _____

b. _____

c. _____

Credible Writing

4. What are some examples of how the writer became more active?

a. _____

b. _____

c. _____

5. What other details does the writer give about her activity level?

a. _____

b. _____

Clear Writing

   6. What are four important transitions the writer uses to direct
   the reader?

   Sentence 6: _____

   Sentence 8: _____

   Sentence 11: _____

   7. What does the writer think is the most significant cause of her

   weight loss? _____

   8. This paragraph is organized according to which ideas are least
   or most important, but how is it different from typical emphatic
   paragraphs?

   _____

   9. Why do you think the writer chose this form of organization?

   _____

   _____

Correct Writing

The sentences in this paragraph are all correct. To check for correctness in
your own writing, go to Part 7, "Writing Correct Sentences."

WRITING PRACTICE 1 **Providing Details for "Effect" Paragraphs**

Below is a list of possible topic sentences for cause-and-effect paragraphs.
Choose a topic that appeals to you. Then, write one well-developed example that illustrates the cause of the effect listed. The effect is underlined in
each case. An example is done for you.

Effect: Exercising regularly helps <u>improve my mood</u>.

Cause: *Whenever I go for a long run, for instance, I feel relaxed and ready*

            for the rest of the day. Even if I still have a lot of work to do, just

            getting to blow off some steam through exercise helps me feel

            ready to meet the challenge.

1. Effect: Having an after-school job can cause <u>major stress</u> for teenagers.

    Cause: _____

    _____

    _____

2. <u>Being healthy</u> comes from a variety of factors.

    Cause: _____

    _____

    _____

3. Effect: <u>Students cheat in school</u> for many reasons.

    Cause: _____

    _____

    _____

4. Effect: You can try several techniques to earn a <u>promotion at work</u>.

    Cause: _____

    _____

    _____

5. Effect: <u>Divorce</u> is caused by a number of factors.

Cause: _____

_____

_____

WRITING PRACTICE 2 Providing Details for "Cause" Paragraphs

Below are five other topic sentences for cause-and-effect paragraphs. For each case, write one well-developed example that illustrates an effect of the cause listed. The causes are underlined.

Cause: <u>Getting too much sun over long periods of time</u> can ruin your skin.

Effect: _____

_____

_____

1. Cause: <u>Spending more than you earn</u> can have serious consequences.

Effect: _____

_____

_____

2. Cause: <u>Volunteering to do community service</u> can be very rewarding.

Effect: _____

_____

_____

3. Cause: <u>Accepting dares from your friends</u> can be dangerous.

   Effect: _____

   _____

   _____

4. Cause: <u>Treating people with respect</u> brings about positive changes in your life.

   Effect: _____

   _____

   _____

5. Cause: <u>Not knowing how to read</u> can make life difficult in many ways.

   Effect: _____

   _____

   _____

WRITING PRACTICE 3   Writing a Paragraph Step by Step

Now you have the chance to write a paragraph of your own.

Prewriting

1. Choose a topic for your paragraph from the list below.

   Causes of overcrowding in schools

   Causes of people taking the bus or subway

   Causes of people taking yoga

   Causes of living a long life

Causes of road rage

Effects of a new pet/roommate/baby on the household

Effects of alcohol or drugs

Effects of taking steroids

Effects of treating people with respect

Effects of being a vegetarian

2. Freewrite for ten minutes to come up with details for support. Try to think of details that will make your paragraph believable for your reader. For instance, if your topic is "effects of treating people with respect," list all the different times you can think of when being nice brought about beneficial changes in your life and what those changes were. A sample list follows.

Happy girlfriend (picked daisies in the park)

Promotion at work (smiled at customers and thanked them for coming in)

Happy roommates (cleaned apartment when it wasn't my turn)

Good friends (listen to them, offer advice when they want it)

Big tips at work (bring extra napkins with pizza)

Drafting

3. Write your topic sentence, making sure to emphasize either the cause or the effect of the situation you're discussing.

4. Choose the support points and details that you think best illustrate your topic sentence.

5. Rearrange your support points and details so that they come in the order you want them. If some details don't fit as well as others, leave them out.

6. Write a draft of your paragraph using the topic sentence, support points, and details from the list you've chosen.

Revising

7. Make sure all the details in your paragraph make the causes or effects of the situation being discussed clear. Make sure your details are organized and connected through clear transitions that let your reader know where every step in the process comes.

Editing

8. Proofread your paragraph to make sure you have used correct spelling, punctuation, and grammar.

WRITING PRACTICE 4 Explaining the Causes or Effects of a Situation

Cause-and-effect reasoning often helps us explain, predict, or control situations in our lives. Before beginning this assignment, think about how much influence you have over the lives of people you love.

Topic A

You have lived at home your whole life, but now it's time to get your own place. You have a good relationship with your parents, but you fear you will hurt their feelings. *Write a letter to your parents explaining the changes in your life that have led you to make this decision.* Explain, for instance, how working and saving money has made it possible for you to support yourself or how two friends are looking for a roommate now. You could also explain how your desire for more privacy has led you to seek independence now. Be sure to use specific details to support your topic sentence.

Topic B

You work for a business that requires detailed documentation for all personnel matters, and you have just promoted another employee to be shift manager. *Write a letter for the employee's file explaining what, specifically, the employee did to earn the promotion.* You might explain that the employee's habit of always arriving early led him or her to receive additional opportunities or how the employee's willingness to do more than is necessary led him or her to be considered for the job. Be sure to use specific details to support your topic sentence.

CHAPTER SUMMARY

When you write a paragraph explaining a cause or an effect, remember the following points:

1. Cause-and-effect reasoning helps us explain, predict, and control various aspects of our lives.

2. In choosing a topic for a cause-and-effect paragraph, look for a situation in which one event caused another.

3. Your topic sentence should make clear whether your paragraph focuses on the causes or the effects of a situation.

4. Using emphatic order works well for organizing cause-and-effect paragraphs.

MyWritingLab & Lab Activity 21

mywritinglab For additional practice with cause and effect, go to **www.mywritinglab. com** or complete **Lab Activity 21** in the separate *Resources for Writers* Lab Manual.

Definition

Culture Note

BASEBALL, THE AMERICAN PASTIME

Long considered the "American pastime," baseball is the great American sport. Its history is a mix of victory, change, and conflict. From the creation—and, later dismantling—of baseball leagues such as the Negro league and women's league, the history of baseball reflects the history of the American nation. Baseball itself has also undergone changes, from the installation of artificial turf, domes, and an altered pitcher's mound to labor strikes by both players and umpires.

WHAT IS A DEFINITION PARAGRAPH?

We are constantly defining terms to better understand others and be understood ourselves. In the **definition** strategy of paragraph development, the writer explains one specific word or idea so that other people can understand it. Definition may be one of the most valuable skills a writer can master.

REAL-LIFE WRITING

Defining terms is important in everyday communication. Here are some real-life uses of definition.

For College
- For a history exam, you are asked to define *imperialism* in terms of your country's growth.
- In biology class, you are asked to define *pistil* on an exam.

RECOMMENDED READINGS

"'Blaxicans' and Other Reinvented Americans," Richard Rodriguez, p. 738

"What is Intelligence Anyway?" Isaac Asimov p. 718

"The Ways We Lie," Stephanie Ericsson, p. 750

In Your Personal Life

- You and your partner continually redefine *discipline* in terms of raising your children.
- You and your friends define *honesty* and *trust* when you have conflicts.

At Work

- For a job application, you are asked to define yourself in one word.
- For an employee handbook, you define *responsibility*.

TYPES OF DEFINITIONS AND MODEL PARAGRAPHS

You can define terms in a number of ways.

- Formal definition
- Definition by class the item belongs to
- Definition by negative example
- Definition by extended example

Formal Definition

A **formal definition** usually takes no more than two or three sentences. It's similar to what you might find in a dictionary. Here are three examples.

A *bicycle* is a vehicle that has only two wheels.

Intelligence is the ability to learn or understand from experience.

Vivacious means "spirited and full of life."

Formal definitions quickly and accurately tell us what a word means. However, formal definitions are generally not the type of definition required for college writing.

EXERCISE 1 Finding Formal Definitions

You may already know the formal definition of some of the words below; others may be unfamiliar to you. Write a formal definition for each word, using a dictionary if you need to. Then, provide a sentence that illustrates the definition of the word. An example is done for you.

Word: Loneliness

Formal definition: Feeling of being alone when you don't really want

to be

Sentence: Coming home to an empty house every day after

my mom died filled me with loneliness.

1. Word: Friendly

Formal definition: _____

Sentence: _____

_____

2. Word: Boyfriend (or girlfriend)

Formal definition: _____

Sentence: _____

_____

3. Word: Escape

Formal definition: _____

Sentence: _____

_____

4. Word: Relaxation

Formal definition: _____

Sentence: _____

_____

5. Word: Exciting

Formal definition: _____

Sentence: _____

_____

Definition by Class

The type of definition that is more common in college writing is **definition by class.** Definition by class involves two main steps.

Step 1: Place the term you're defining into a general category, or class.

The following examples illustrate the first part of definition by class. The term being defined is in italics; the general category, or class, is in bold print.

A _smooth talker_ is a **person** . . .
Fear is the **feeling** . . .
A _hot rod_ is a **car** . . .

In the above examples, _smooth talker_ is placed into the general category _person_, while _fear_ is labeled a _feeling. Hot rod_, finally, is put in the class _car_. In all cases, the definition places the term in a broad category before giving any other details.

Step 2: Offer details to further clarify the term.

Begin a definition paragraph with a topic sentence that includes your general category or class, and then add details to make the meaning of your term clear. Your topic sentence will end up having two parts: the general category and some details.

Asking questions about the term you want to define can help you find examples for your definition. In the examples below, the term being defined is in italics, the general category is in bold print, and the defining details are underlined.

For _smooth talker_, ask yourself _what kind_ of person is a smooth talker. What makes such a person _different from_ other people?

A _smooth talker_ is a **person** who can get out of any problem simply by using slick words, winks, and sly smiles.

For *fear,* ask yourself *what kind* of feeling fear is. What about it is *different from* any other type of feeling?

Fear is the **feeling** that <u>something bad is about to happen</u>.

For *hot rod,* ask yourself *what kind* of car a hot rod is. How is it *special,* or *different from* other cars?

A *hot rod* is a **car** that has been <u>specially altered for power and speed</u>.

**Definition Paragraphs:
Definition by Class**

Topic sentence giving defined term, general category, and some specific details ....
....

↓

Specific detail 1 ....

Specific detail 2 ....

Specific detail 3 ....

Specific detail 4 ....

Specific detail 5 ....

The answers to the questions about the general terms provide details that complete the definition by class. The question "What kind?" is helpful in defining terms. Asking it throughout your writing process will help you find details to illustrate your term.

Definition-by-class paragraphs often contain support points and specific details to support their topic sentences. The model paragraph shown on page 346, "An Ace," does just this. However, another way to write a definition-by-class paragraph is to list a series of details without any formal support points. The paragraph "Play Ball!" on pages 351–352 offers a model of this kind of definition-by-class paragraph. See the illustration "Definition Paragraphs: Definition by Class" above for an idea of how to write this type of paragraph.

A Model Paragraph: Definition by Class

Read the paragraph below to see how definition by class works.

An Ace

[1]In baseball, an *ace* is a pitcher who is extremely skilled. [2]An ace is able to throw a range of pitches. [3]Throwing "heat" means pitching fastballs that batters have a hard time hitting. [4]An ace can also throw balls that don't just make a straight line from the pitcher's mound to home plate. [5]Instead, a curve ball from a true ace can move any number of ways: breaking away from the batter, into the batter, or downward. [6]A knuckleball, thrown with the fingertips and a stiff wrist, moves very slowly, dancing around, making it unpredictable and very hard to hit. [7]Further, an ace can throw sliders, which are pitches that have speed like a fastball and movement like a curveball or knuckleball. [8]An ace also knows how to work with the catcher (the player who crouches behind home plate and catches the pitches) to mix up the pitches and the location of the pitches in order to confuse batters. [9]In addition to knowing how to throw different pitches, an ace knows when to let batters hit the ball. [10]An ace knows how to throw pitches that cause batters to pop the ball up into the air. [11]Those balls can be easier for a fielder to catch. [12]An ace also knows how to hurl pitches that batters hit downward—with luck, straight into the mitt of an infielder. [13]An ace is a valuable player for any team.

EXERCISE 2 Analyzing a Definition Paragraph

Reread "An Ace" above. Then, answer the questions that follow.

1. What is the general class, or category, for *ace?* _____

2. In sentence 1, what information does the writer provide that shows that an ace is different from other pitchers?

_____

3. What are some skills the writer says an ace has?

a. _____

b. _____

c. _____

4. What are some specific pitches that the writer names?

a. _____

b. _____

c. _____

d. _____

5. What transitions in sentences 4, 7, 8, 9, and 12 does the writer use to show addition, or more of the same type of information?

Sentence 4: _____

Sentence 7: _____

Sentence 8: _____

Sentence 9: _____

Sentence 12: _____

6. What other word does the writer use in place of *ace?* _____

Definition by Negative Example

In **definition by negative example,** you state what a term is *not* and then state what the term *is*. An easy way to begin a paragraph that uses definition by negative example is to use a stereotype as the "negative" part of the definition and then add what the term *is* later in the sentence. In the following example, the negative part of the definition is in italics.

> In baseball, an ace is *not simply a pitcher* but one who is extremely skilled.

Definition by Extended Example

In **definition by extended example,** a writer uses a single example throughout the entire paragraph. In this case, the paragraph begins with a one-sentence explanation of the term—the topic sentence. However, after the topic sentence comes one detailed example. This detailed example illustrates the term being defined. To get an idea of how to write this kind of paragraph, see the illustration "Definition Paragraphs: Definition by Extended Example" on page 348.

A Model Paragraph: Definition by Extended Example

Read the paragraph below to see how the writer uses definition by extended example.

A Great Milestone

A milestone is a significant or important event in history. The inclusion of the baseball player Jackie Robinson in major league baseball is a milestone in baseball and American history. Right after the Civil War, black players were allowed to play on teams with white players. However, after Jim Crow laws restricting the rights of African-Americans were implemented in the late 1880s, black players were barred from professional baseball, so they formed their own teams. In 1920, the Negro National League was founded by Rube Foster, a talented African-American player. In 1945, when the general manager for the Brooklyn Dodgers saw Jackie Robinson play for a Negro league team, the Kansas City Monarchs, things started to change. In 1947 the Dodgers signed Robinson, who broke down the color barrier and became the first African-American player in the major leagues. Since then, major league baseball has included players of many backgrounds, including Latinos, Asians, African-Americans, and Caucasian players.

Definition Paragraphs: Definition by Extended Example
Topic sentence giving defined term and example to be extended ....
↓
Specific detail 1 ....
Specific detail 2 ....
Specific detail 3 ....
Specific detail 4 ....
Specific detail 5 ....

EXERCISE 3 Analyzing a Definition by Extended Example

Reread "A Great Milestone" on page 348. Then, fill in the blanks below.

1. What is the formal definition of *milestone*?

_____

2. What example does the writer use throughout the paragraph to

define the word *milestone?* _____

3. What historical situation prevented black players from playing

major league baseball? _____

4. What method of organization—time sequence (chronological)

order or emphatic order—does the writer use? _____

Jackie Robinson

FOOD FOR THOUGHT Jackie Robinson's talent and strength of character helped him break through the color barrier to play professional baseball. What barriers in sports still exist? Write a few sentences explaining how some groups may or may not still be left out in the professional sports world.

Responding to Images. What about Jackie Robinson's posture or expression in the photo at left indicates that he was a serious competitor? Explain.

5. Aside from *baseball*, what three other words does the writer repeat throughout the paragraph?

a. _____   **b.** _____   **c.** _____

CHOOSING A GOOD TOPIC FOR DEVELOPMENT

Choosing a good topic for a definition paragraph will largely depend on what kind of definition paragraph you're writing. Most commonly, your instructor will assign you a definition-by-class paragraph and give you a topic to develop. In general, terms that mean different things to different people are suitable for development in a definition-by-class paragraph.

Emotions:	love, hate, happiness, loneliness, fear, sadness, joy, excitement
Family:	mother, father, sister, brother, grandmother, uncle, family, home
Stereotypes:	know-it-all, bad boy, Goody Two-shoes, nerd, jock, bully

Notice that all these terms allow for a range of explanations. Even terms such as *mother* or *father*—terms that most people understand—let you write about *what aspects* of motherhood or fatherhood mean the most to you.

In preparing to write a definition paragraph, do some prewriting to see what ideas come to mind on your topic. One student, Devon, decided to freewrite for ten minutes on the topic "know-it-all."

My sister Paula is a know-it-all. No matter what people are talking about, Paula is in on the conversation. Last week my buddies and I were talking about cars, and even though Paula is only fourteen and has never driven <u>anything</u>, she had an opinion about how to fix up an old Camaro. Besides that, she comes up with theories that no one else believes but that she swears are fact. One time she told me that if I put soap on my toothbrush before brushing my teeth, I'd get fewer cavities. She swore she'd heard it from the dentist, but he told me it was totally false information. Oh! Paula also is <u>never</u> wrong, even when she is.

Devon has identified three possible ways to define the term *know-it-all*: such a person is in on every conversation, has wacky theories, and is never wrong.

WRITING AN EFFECTIVE TOPIC SENTENCE

As with choosing a topic, writing an effective topic sentence depends on the type of definition paragraph you're writing. When Devon analyzed the three points that surfaced in his freewriting, he realized that they all involved his sister claiming to know something that she didn't know. Thus, Devon's topic sentence was "A know-it-all is someone who claims to know things even if she doesn't know them."

If Devon were writing a definition-by-negative-example paragraph, his topic sentence might be "A know-it-all is not only someone who gets on your nerves but someone who claims to know things she doesn't know." For a paragraph using definition by extended example, Devon could use the same topic sentence that he used for his definition-by-class paragraph.

DEVELOPING SPECIFIC DETAILS

The details you use will depend on the kind of definition paragraph you're writing. For instance, the paragraphs "An Ace" (page 346) and "Play Ball!" (below) are definitions by class. However, while the details in "An Ace" could all apply to a single type of player, the details in "Play Ball!" read more like a list of details than a single extended example. Whatever kind of details you use, draw from your own experiences, other people's experiences, and trusted sources as necessary in defining your term.

ORGANIZING AND LINKING YOUR IDEAS

Definition paragraphs can be organized in several ways. Generally, if your paragraph uses an extended example, time sequence (chronological) order—giving events in the order in which they happened—works well, since you'll be relating details of one occurrence. If you're writing a definition-by-class or definition-by-negative-example paragraph, your topic and examples will dictate the best order to use. For some paragraphs, emphatic order—from least to most important—might be most effective.

EXERCISE 4 Following the Four Cs

Read the paragraph below. Then, answer the questions that follow.

Play Ball!

Baseball is many experiences rolled into one. It is a day with your dad or your best friend under a blue sky. Baseball is the smell of hot dogs, popcorn, grass, and leather all mingled into one scent that surrounds you. It is the glory of seeing your team win the World Series, and it is the agony of watching as your favorite hitter strikes out with bases loaded. Baseball is having your own language, using expressions such as *RBI, K'd, double play, strike out, full count,* and *home run.* It is a feeling of pride, knowing that people like Jackie Robinson fought for racial equality while people like Lou Gehrig fought for their lives. Baseball is a feeling of history, knowing that the same number of games, the same number of players, and the same number of innings have been part of the game since the beginning. It is also a feeling of camaraderie as the faces of baseball become increasingly diverse: Japanese, Dominican, Cuban, and American. Baseball is the feeling of rage when the umpire calls a ball on what you knew was a strike, and it is jubilation when your team's shortstop makes an impossible catch to get your pitcher out of the inning. Baseball is sometimes confusion, when the announcer talks about a "six-to-four-to-three" double play and you're not sure what that means. Above all else, though, baseball is the sport that Americans claim as their own.

Concise Writing

1. What is the topic sentence for "Play Ball!"? _____

_____

2. What single idea do all of the examples in the paragraph relate to?

_____

Credible Writing

3. Give three examples the writer uses to illustrate her topic sentence.

a. _____

b. _____

c. _____

4. List one example from the paragraph that you find particularly

interesting or effective. _____

Clear Writing

    5. How many times does the writer use the word *baseball* in this paragraph? _____

    6. What pronoun does the writer uses in place of *baseball?* _____

WRITING PRACTICE 1   Write a Definition Paragraph

Now write a definition paragraph of your own.

Prewriting

    1. Choose a topic. Below is a list of topics for paragraphs that allow you to use definition to develop your ideas. This list contains labels, many of which are slang terms, for people with certain characteristics. Read the list, and think about the people you know who fit one of these labels. Feel free to choose a term not on the list.

    Topics

bookworm	sports fan	salesman
workaholic	procrastinator	hypochondriac
worrywart	crybaby	grouch
perfectionist	optimist	bleeding heart
control freak	fussbudget	bad boy

    2. Freewrite for five to ten minutes on your topic. Below is an example of freewriting by a student, Brian, on the term *hypochondriac*. Brian has been assigned a definition-by-class paragraph.

> A hypochondriac is a person who thinks he or she is sick all the time. Hypochondriacs are always looking for the smallest symptom of sickness and are actually disappointed if they don't find it. True hypochondriacs are excited to go to the doctor and seem sad if they're found to be totally healthy. Hypochondriacs seem to think that being ill makes them more interesting, which I think is bogus.

    In writing a definition paragraph, the prewriting technique of questioning can be helpful. Look at the following question-and-answer list for the term *hypochondriac*.

Question	Answer
What is the formal definition of *hypochondriac?*	Extreme depression often centered on imaginary physical ailments
What is the general category for *hypochondriac?*	Person
What are some ways to recognize a hypochondriac?	Always has appointments with doctors; always brings up latest illness; subscribes to health-related magazines; takes herbal remedies

Drafting

3. Write your topic sentence. Your topic sentence should include a definition of your term, but this definition will vary depending on the kind of definition paragraph you're writing. Since Brian's paragraph is a definition-by-class assignment, his topic sentence places the term *hypochondriac* in a general category. Here's his topic sentence: "Hypochondriacs are people who think they are sick all the time."

4. Choose support points—if necessary—and specific details to develop your definition. If you want to use several short examples, do more freewriting to come up with them. If you want to use a single extended example, consider making a list or an outline to keep the points of your extended example in order.

5. Organize your ideas using emphatic order or time sequence (chronological) order. Keep in mind that time sequence order works very well for an extended-example paragraph.

6. Write your draft. Check to make sure your organization is consistent throughout your paragraph. Make sure all the details define your term. If any details do not, remove them.

Revision

7. Check your paragraph for the first three of the four Cs: *concise, credible,* and *clear* writing. Make any necessary changes to your draft.

Editing

8. Check your paragraph for the fourth C, *correct* writing. Proofread your paragraph to make sure you have used correct spelling, punctuation, and grammar.

WRITING PRACTICE 2 Define an Emotion or a Quality

Write a paragraph defining one of the terms below. If you need help getting started, follow the steps you used in Writing Practice 1 on pages 353–355.

kindness	sensitivity	strength	fear
power	confidence	anger	sorrow

WRITING PRACTICE 3 Define *Family*

Over the past fifteen years, the definition of the word *family* has caused politicians and religious leaders to debate each other and themselves, seeking to find one meaning for the term that everyone can agree on. Choose Topic A or Topic B and write a definition paragraph.

Topic A

In politics today, many leaders propose laws and bills that affect families. However, with changes in people's lifestyles, the definition of *family* has become unclear in many cases. *Write a paragraph defining the term* family. Use several examples to define your term, as opposed to a single extended example, in order to make the meaning of *family* clear.

Topic B

Using the same background information as in Topic A, *write a paragraph defining the term* family *but using a single extended definition*. You may use an example from your own family or friends, or you may use an example from television or the movies to illustrate your ideas.

CHAPTER SUMMARY

Remember the following when you write a definition paragraph:

1. Definition-by-class paragraphs offer a one-sentence definition as the topic sentence and many examples to illustrate the concept.

2. A definition by negative example shows what the term is *not*.

3. A definition by extended example uses a single example throughout the paragraph.

4. Your topic sentence, examples, and organization will vary depending on the type of definition paragraph you write.

MyWritingLab & Lab Activity 22

mywritinglab For additional practice with definition, go to **www.mywritinglab.com** or complete **Lab Activity 22** in the separate *Resources for Writers* Lab Manual.

Argument

Culture Note
CIVILITY

Civility is politeness; it means acting in ways that show consideration for others. Most of us know that it's courteous to say "please" and "thank you," and many of us are aware that in American culture, handshakes and eye contact are signs of respect. Many other areas of civility, however, such as cell phone etiquette, are still unclear.

WHAT IS AN ARGUMENT PARAGRAPH?

The term *argument* usually implies something unpleasant: a combative discussion in which two people are tense and upset or a situation in which a group of people are yelling back and forth without listening to each other. For writers, however, to **argue** a position is simply to give reasons to back up your point of view. An **argument** is an exchange of ideas in which two sides attempt to persuade each other. The following sentences represent different sides of an argument. Each sentence also could be a topic sentence for a paragraph with support points and details.

Drunk driving penalties are unreasonably tough.
Drunk driving penalties need to be tougher.

The key to writing an argument paragraph is understanding that people do not necessarily start out agreeing with your point of view. Your job as a writer is to present enough information and explanation to persuade your reader of your main point. The illustration "Argument Paragraphs" on the next page gives you an idea of how to write this type of paragraph.

RECOMMENDED READINGS

"Manners Matter," Judith Martin, *p. 758*

"All I Really Need to Know I Learned In Kindergarten," Robert Fulghum, *p. 710*

"Money for Morality," Mary Arguelles, *p. 745*

Argument Paragraphs
Topic sentence stating the argument ....
↓
Support point 1 ....Details from experience or ....facts from trusted sources................. Support point 2 ....Details from experience or ....facts from trusted sources................. Support point 3 ....Details from experience or ....facts from trusted sources................. Support point 4 ....Details from experience or ....facts from trusted sources.................

REAL-LIFE WRITING

Argument is relevant in many aspects of daily living. Read the examples below to see how argument skills are especially helpful in real-life situations.

For College

■ Write a persuasive paper for a composition, rhetoric, or speech course.
■ Write a letter to an instructor to persuade her that you deserve a higher grade.

In Your Personal Life

■ Write an e-mail to a friend to dissuade him from making a poor choice.
■ Write a letter to the city council, arguing that you need a stop sign on your corner.

At Work

■ Write a memo to your boss to convince her to carry a new product. Offer factual reasons for its superiority.
■ Write a memo to your boss to convince him to give you a raise. Clearly state your reasons for deserving it and your evidence for those claims.

A MODEL PARAGRAPH: ARGUMENT

Read the following paragraph to see how offering support points and examples makes an argument.

No Need for Manners

^{1}Manners are more trouble than they're worth. ^{2}Ever since I was a little girl, my mom has tried to teach me that manners are important. ^{3}I've said "please" and "thank you," I've written thank-you notes until doomsday, and I've stood up when people my parents' age enter the room. ^{4}No good has come from all my efforts. ^{5}First, manners are phony. ^{6}Last year I wrote thank-you notes to all of my friends when they gave me a surprise birthday party. ^{7}It took me hours to think of different ways to say thank you, and I used a lot of paper. ^{8}When my friends read my notes, they asked me if I was trying to be high-class. ^{9}They said they knew I wrote them only because I "had to." ^{10}My friends and I know each other well enough to tell whether we like each other's gifts; writing notes just puts pressure on the rest of us to do something we don't believe in. ^{11}Second, manners cause confusion. ^{12}My mom always taught me to be polite to people even if I didn't like them. ^{13}However, more than one boy has told me I've sent the wrong message because I was nice when I really wasn't interested. ^{14}If only I'd been honest and told the guys that I didn't want to go out with them, I'd have saved them—and myself—a lot of trouble. ^{15}Most important, manners are tricky. ^{16}My mother taught me never to eat with my hands, but using a fork, knife, and spoon isn't normal everywhere. ^{17}My friend Prassana is from Sri Lanka, and at dinner people in his family take food from a large bowl in the center of the table and eat it with their hands. ^{18}The first time I ate with Prassana's family, I asked for a fork. ^{19}I thought I was using good manners, but I felt so uncomfortable being the only one with silverware that I decided to eat with my hands, too. ^{20}Then I felt uncomfortable because I knew my mother would disapprove. ^{21}I couldn't win! ^{22}All in all, I think that if people just treat one another as adults, there's no need for manners.

EXERCISE 1 Analyzing an Argument Paragraph

Reread "No Need for Manners" above. Then, answer the questions below.

1. What argument (or point) is the writer making?

Fender Bender

CRITICAL THINKING According to civility expert P. M. Forni, anonymity—or feeling that no one knows who we are—contributes to incivility on the road. To what extent is this true? Write a few sentences explaining whether or not people are more likely to be rude if they don't know the people they're being rude to, or if they're unlikely to be caught.

Responding to Images. *What about the photo at left communicates stress or tension? Explain.*

2. In which sentence is the argument stated? _____

3. What three reasons does the writer give to support her topic sentence?

a. _____

b. _____

c. _____

4. List three examples the writer gives to illustrate her support points.

a. _____

b. _____

c. _____

5. What three transitions does the writer use to signal the start of each support point?

Sentence 5: _____

Sentence 11: _____

Sentence 15: _____

6. How does the writer organize her ideas, in time sequence (chronological) order or emphatic order? _____

CHOOSING A GOOD TOPIC FOR DEVELOPMENT

For the most part, arguments don't occur over topics that people agree on. If people are of one mind about an issue, there isn't much to say about it. Thus, in choosing a topic, follow these guidelines.

- Choose a topic you believe in.
- Choose a topic that has two sides.
- Choose a topic you know something about.

Choosing a Topic You Believe In

It's possible to write good paragraphs about issues you don't support, but it's much easier to write about topics that you believe in. Think about what's going on in your life right now—work, school, family responsibilities, relationships—and choose a topic that is relevant to your life. For instance, Guillermo was frustrated that his college provided so few student parking spots and that the spaces available were often dangerous after dark. Guillermo did some freewriting to see if he could write an argument in favor of expanding the student parking lot at his school.

I can't believe my stereo got stolen out of my car again! It's not right that I have to park off campus where there is no security and no lighting, and I bought a parking pass. If I buy a pass, I should be able to park on campus, but I can never find a spot even if I'm thirty minutes early to class. Also, there's room to park in the empty lot right next to the student parking area. The college president has been saying for two years that the lot is going to be paved over and made into faculty parking spots, but I don't see my instructors parking off campus. Students should be able to use that lot for parking.

Guillermo was happy to see that his frustrations could work as support points for an argument, so he decided to develop his topic further.

WRITING AN EFFECTIVE TOPIC SENTENCE

In his freewriting, Guillermo identified these points for development.

Point 1: Students who buy parking passes should get to park on campus.

Point 2: Parking off campus is unsafe.

Point 3: There's room to park on campus.

At first, Guillermo thought that each point should be developed into a paragraph of its own, but then he realized that a solid topic sentence could tie them all together. He wrote this topic sentence: "Hopkins College needs more on-campus student parking spaces." Guillermo can use his three points from freewriting as support points in his paragraph, adding details to develop his ideas.

DEVELOPING SPECIFIC DETAILS

Just by making and supporting a point in other kinds of paragraphs, you've been sharpening your argument skills. Two additional techniques can help you make your argument paragraph even more effective.

- Making your side stronger
- Making the other side weaker

Making Your Side Stronger

You already know that once you find support points to back up your topic sentence, you need to use specific details to illustrate them. Specific details fall under the three categories listed below.

- Descriptions of objects or events in your life
- Accounts of events in other people's lives
- Facts that you've heard or read about from trusted sources

(For more information on types of specific details, see Chapter 9.)

Consulting Experts An **expert** is someone who has special skills or knowledge in a certain field. Organizations such as the American Medical Association and the Better Business Bureau, and the people who work there, are expert sources in their fields. Consulting and quoting experts can make your argument stronger. There are ways to get expert opinions even when you can't talk face-to-face with an authority.

- Read articles written by experts.
- Read articles that quote experts.
- Watch television interviews with experts.
- Listen to radio interviews with experts.

Seeing, hearing, or reading about experts' ideas can help you make your side of an argument stronger. For instance, since Guillermo is trying to convince his reader that Hopkins College needs more on-campus parking spaces, consulting the campus police reports helps him make his point.

Topic sentence:	Hopkins College needs more on-campus parking spaces.
Expert support:	According to Hopkins College campus police reports, 45 percent of students who park off campus suffer from some crime to themselves or their cars.

Reading Up on Your Subject　Reading about your topic is a great way to expand your knowledge and make your argument stronger. Newspapers and magazines often carry general information on subjects of public interest. Books, although possibly useful, may contain more information than you need for a single paragraph.

Topic sentence:	Writing thank-you notes is important.
Expert support:	In her newspaper column *Miss Manners*, the etiquette expert Judith Martin writes that there is no excuse for failing to write a thank-you note.

Surfing the Net　Credible Web sites, such as those operated by schools and respected organizations, can give you information to use in your argument. Online databases provide a huge amount of reliable information as well. With so many places to find information, however, you need to judge which sources are really helpful. For instance, if you wanted to know the health risks associated with smoking, you probably wouldn't want to read a report sponsored by a tobacco company. Make sure that the sources you use are ones you can trust. Talk to your school librarian about distinguishing reliable sources from unreliable ones.

If you're writing to convince a reader that smoking is unhealthy, for example, consulting the American Lung Association's Web site can help you make your point.

Topic sentence: Smoking is harmful to your health.

Expert support: According to the American Lung Association's Web site, smoking not only causes lung disease but also weakens your immune system.

Making the Opposing Side Weaker

As you've seen, every argument has an opposing one. To strengthen your own argument, you must understand the opposing one. That way, you can target the gaps in its information or logic.

Finding Incorrect Information in the Opposing Argument   One of Pamela's friends told her she should exercise every day, without taking a day off. Pamela researched the issue and learned that people should *not* exercise strenuously every day, and that the human body needs rest after a hard workout. Pamela's findings are easy to see in the list she wrote.

Other Side	My Side	Expert Opinion
Exercise daily.	You need some rest days.	The body needs rest days.
Only strenuous exercise promotes fitness.	Many kinds of exercise promote fitness.	Varying strenuous exercise with less strenuous exercise is best.

Looking for Unsupported Claims in the Opposing Argument   Even if an argument sounds logical or true, make sure the claims can be verified. For instance, if a friend says that a herbal remedy for a particular illness works because "everyone says so," you should ask who "everyone" is. Chances are, the number of supporters for the remedy is fewer than your friend claims.

ORGANIZING AND LINKING YOUR IDEAS

Once you have come up with a topic, written a topic sentence and support points, and supported those points with details, you're ready to organize your ideas. Using emphatic order—giving points from least to most important—works particularly well for argument paragraphs, since it lets you save your best argument for last.

Remember that Guillermo identified three support points (page 362).

- Students who buy parking passes should get to park on campus.
- Parking off campus is unsafe.
- There's room to park on campus.

Even though "Parking off campus is unsafe" was Guillermo's second point in his freewriting, he decided that it was the most important reason for needing more on-campus parking. Thus, he placed it last. Guillermo's final paragraph, with transitions in bold type, is below.

The Right to Park

Hopkins College needs more on-campus parking spaces. **First of all,** students pay for a parking permit. After spending $28 each semester, students should be able to find an on-campus parking space, even if it's way out by the stadium. If the college chooses to accept students' money for parking spaces, it should provide parking. **Second,** the college has additional, unused room for more parking spaces. According to the college facilities manager, Bob Reardon, the empty lot next to the main student parking lot is not being used. Even though the school president has been saying for two years that more faculty parking is going to be built on the empty lot, Mr. Reardon claims that he has heard nothing of this. Since I have never seen any of my instructors driving around off campus trying to find parking spaces, I assume that faculty already have sufficient parking. **Most important,** parking anywhere but on campus is unsafe. According to Hopkins College campus police reports, 45 percent of students who park off campus suffer from some crime to themselves or their cars. If almost half the students who park off campus are victims of crime, something needs to be done. Adding more parking spaces for students seems a logical solution.

Guillermo uses emphatic order to organize his ideas, using the transitions *first of all, second,* and *most important* to let his reader know which points are most significant.

EXERCISE 2 Following the Four Cs

Read the paragraph below. Then, answer the questions that follow.

Benefits of Polite Behavior

[1]Treating people with respect has many benefits. [2]First, being polite can create employment opportunities. [3]Two years ago I worked as a receptionist at a doctor's office and was urged by the office manager to be helpful and kind to the patients. [4]One patient, Ms. Simmons, was always difficult. [5]She never remembered my name and always showed up late for her appointments. [6]It took quite an effort to be polite to her. [7]However, six months ago, I applied for a job at a large office with many doctors. [8]The big surprise was that Ms. Simmons worked there, and she was doing the hiring! [9]She told me in the interview that she remembered me and was always impressed with how courteous I had been. [10]A second example of how manners can have benefits is in personal relationships. [11]According to the nationally known marriage counselors Judith Wallerstein and Sandra Blakeslee, married people who treat each other with respect often have a healthy relationship. [12]The marriage counselors claim that if people listen to each other and try to be considerate, everyone is happier. [13]Another area where being polite pays off is in business. [14]Sean Nguyen, a business owner in Minneapolis, Minnesota, claims that making his employees comfortable leads to a happier, better work force. [15]He pays them good wages, gives them health benefits, and has a policy of rewarding courteous and helpful behavior. [16]According to an article in *Money* magazine, his company became a multimillion-dollar company because of how hard its employees worked. [17]One last important area where manners can have benefits is at home. [18]To save money, my friend Jason lives with three other people in a small apartment. [19]They all go to school and have jobs, so they're often tired. [20]Because they want to get along, they have some unspoken rules. [21]No one drinks the last of the milk unless he can replace it, and no one plays loud music if someone else wants to sleep or study. [22]Even though the apartment still feels crowded, the roommates get along because they treat each other with respect. [23]Manners make life better in so many ways.

Concise Writing

1. What is the writer's argument? _____

2. What four areas does the writer identify for support?

a. _____

b. _____

c. _____

d. _____

Credible Writing

3. Each sentence listed below marks the beginning of an example in "Benefits of Polite Behavior." Write down the four examples the writer offers to illustrate each area of support as well as the *type* of examples used (personal experience, friend's experience, reputable source, or expert opinion).

	Example	Type of Example
Sentence 7:	_____	_____
Sentence 11:	_____	_____
Sentence 14:	_____	_____
Sentence 18:	_____	_____

Clear Writing

4. What transitions signal the beginning of new support points?

Sentence 2:	_____
Sentence 10:	_____
Sentence 13:	_____
Sentence 17:	_____

5. a. What organizational strategy—time sequence (chronological) order or emphatic order—does the writer use? _____

b. Which point does the writer consider the most important?

_____

c. How can you tell? _____

Correct Writing

The sentences in this paragraph are all correct. To check for correctness in your own writing, go to Part 7, "Writing Correct Sentences."

WRITING PRACTICE 1 Provide Support for Arguments

Each of the following sentences makes an argument. For each argument, write one well-developed sentence, backed up by a specific detail. An example is done for you.

Argument: Health care insurance should be provided for everyone.

Support: Not being able to afford health care isn't necessarily anyone's fault. For instance, my neighbors have a little girl, Peggy, who has a rare illness. Peggy's medications are so expensive that my neighbors have hit the limit of their insurance coverage. They need help.

1. Argument: Penalties for parking tickets should be stronger.

   Support: _____

   _____

2. Argument: Any professional athlete who breaks the law should be banned from the sport.

   Support: _____

   _____

3. Argument: Honesty is the best policy.

   Support: _____

   _____

4. Argument: Honesty is *not* the best policy.

   Support: _____

   _____

5. Argument: Attendance should count toward college students' grades.

   Support: _____

   _____

WRITING PRACTICE 2   Write an Argument Paragraph

Now write your own argument paragraph.

Prewriting

1. Choose a topic for development. Here is a list of possible topics for argument paragraphs.

Topics

Age as a factor in setting car insurance rates

Lighter sentences for criminals who have been abused by their parents

Prosecuting nursing home workers who abuse elderly residents

Allowing condom machines on campus

Automatically passing students with perfect attendance

Requiring military service for all eighteen-year-olds

Gay marriage

Affirmative action in college admissions

Requiring a second language for high school graduation

2. Freewrite on your topic for five to ten minutes. Outlining can be effective because it helps you keep track of both your supporting reasons and your specific details.

Below is a sample outline based on one of the topics from the list above, "requiring a second language for high school graduation."

Requiring a Second Language for High School Graduation

A. Helpful for daily life in United States

   1. Mechanic speaks Japanese

   2. Mail carrier speaks Spanish

   3. Plumber speaks Russian

B. Helpful in getting a job

   1. Employees may need to communicate with non-English-speaking customers

   2. Improves opportunities of working for non-English-speaking employers

C. Other advantages

   1. Using vocabulary from two languages

   2. Better understanding of English language

Drafting

3. Write a topic sentence. A possible topic sentence for the topic "requiring a second language for high school graduation" would be "High school students should be required to study a second language in order to graduate."

4. Choose your support points and specific details. For this step, you may need to learn more about your topic. Notice that the outline in Step 2 above has many reasons that support the topic sentence, but it lacks specific details. In writing an argument paragraph, you may sometimes find details more easily after you've outlined your general points. Make sure all the details in your draft come from trusted sources.

5. Organize your points in a logical order, remembering that emphatic order works well for argument paragraphs. Add transitions that connect your ideas.

6. Now write your draft. Do your best, but don't worry if it's not perfect the first time around.

Revising

7. Check your paragraph for the first three of the four Cs: *concise*, *credible*, and *clear* writing. Make any necessary changes to your draft.

Editing

8. Check your paragraph for the fourth C: *correct* writing. Proofread your paragraph to make sure you have used correct spelling, punctuation, and grammar.

WRITING PRACTICE 3 Write to Effect Change

Having sharp argument skills can be a great benefit in life. Choose Topic A or Topic B below, and write an argument paragraph.

Topic A

Your neighbor has two dogs that bark loudly. Because the dogs sleep outside, they frequently keep you awake at night or wake you up early. You do not want to antagonize your neighbor, but you want her dogs to stop barking. *Write a paragraph persuading your neighbor to solve the barking-dog problem.* You might suggest that the neighbor train the dogs, let the dogs sleep inside, buy the dogs antibarking collars, get the dogs debarked through an operation, or move away from you. If you do not know how expensive or time-consuming one of the suggestions is, do some research to learn more about your topic. Keep in mind that your goal is to live without having to put up with the dogs' barking at inconvenient hours. A Web page that might prove helpful in learning about your topic is at http://www. sfspca.org/behavior/dog_library/barking.pdf.

Topic B

Because of all the crime stories broadcast on the news and written about in the newspaper daily, you want to organize a neighborhood watch program to protect your street from burglary and other crime. This program entails having all the neighbors on your street agree to post "Crime Watch" posters, exchange phone numbers, and look out for each other's property. *Write a letter to your neighbors convincing them to participate in a neighborhood watch program.* You may argue the benefits of participating in such a program, or you may argue the dangers of not having such a program in your neighborhood. Either way, learn about neighborhood watch programs in order to make your writing more convincing. Some possible places to find information are your local police department, neighborhoods with programs already in place, local community centers, and local schools. Your goal is to encourage as many of your neighbors as possible to join a program with you. A Web site that might prove helpful in learning about your topic is at http://www.ncpc.org/.

CHAPTER SUMMARY

When writing an argument, remember the following:

1. Choose a topic that you know and feel strongly about.
2. Use examples from your own experiences, other people's experiences, and trusted sources.
3. Develop your argument by making your side stronger or the other side weaker.
4. Emphatic order works well for argument paragraphs.

MyWritingLab & Lab Activity 23

mywritinglab   For additional practice with argument, go to **www.mywritinglab.com** or complete **Lab Activity 23** in the separate *Resources for Writers* Lab Manual.

PART FIVE
Writing
Essays

Far From Freedom

CRITICAL THINKING Fingers of inmates poke through penitentary fences emphasizing how near to—and far from—freedom these people are. In what way(s) do you feel trapped in some aspect of your life? Explain. ***Responding to Images.*** *What emotions does this photo stir in you? Explain, citing details from the picture.*

The Essay and the Thesis Statement

WHAT IS AN ESSAY?

Good news! Writing an effective essay involves the same skills that you've already practiced by writing effective paragraphs. In fact, you should make a point to keep using the same skills that you've been practicing throughout this text. Just as a paragraph is a group of sentences that work together to communicate an idea, an **essay** is a group of *paragraphs* working together to communicate an idea. An essay's purpose can be to persuade, to inform, or to entertain, and an essay's audience, at least when you're a student, will usually be your instructor.

Paragraphs and essays differ, however, in length and development. Whereas a paragraph might include only one or two specific details to support each point, an essay can devote a whole paragraph to developing a single support point. And where paragraphs can usually get by with a transition word to make connections clear, essays often use entire sentences to help keep the reader on track. While both paragraphs and essays concentrate on making a point, essays can contain many more subpoints, all of which need development. Finally, while a paragraph contains a topic sentence, an essay uses a **thesis statement** to give the essay's main idea, state the writer's purpose and point of view, and tell the reader what to expect.

RECOMMENDED READINGS

"Money for Morality," Mary Arguelles, *p. 745*

"The Ways We Lie," Stephanie Ericsson, *p. 750*

"The Price We Pay," Adam Mayblum, *p. 794*

Five-Paragraph Essays

Introduction
Opening: Gets reader's attention.
Thesis statement: Gives the writer's main idea, point of view, and purpose; tells the reader what to expect.

↓

Body Paragraphs
Body paragraph 1
Topic sentence
  Specific details

Body paragraph 2
Topic sentence
  Specific details

Body paragraph 3
Topic sentence
  Specific details

↓

Conclusion
Final thoughts: Adds something new that is closely related to the essay's main idea.
Summary: Repeats briefly the main idea and support points.

ESSAY FORM

The five-paragraph essay is the most basic form. The illustration "Five-Paragraph Essays" above gives a visual representation of the essay. Notice how the body paragraphs follow the same format while the first and last paragraphs (the introduction and conclusion) are different.

A MODEL ESSAY

Read the following essay, paying attention to the way the writer develops his body paragraphs.

Sierras 1

Raul Sierras

Professor Harris

English 50

12 September 2008

Offensive Behavior

Any time I see Tommy Lee Jones in a movie, it seems he's wearing his U.S. Marshals outfit, chasing some fugitive from the law. If Tommy isn't working that day, some FBI person is on the trail of a serial killer, or a Secret Service agent is tracking down counterfeiters. All three of these situations focus on a different type of federal crime, but there are other types that are more common. Though federal criminal law covers many areas, three of the biggest categories of federal crime are theft and fraud crimes, immigration offenses, and drug violations.

One large area of federal crime is theft and fraud, which involves taking something from someone. Not long ago, according to federal defense attorney C. Emmett Mahle, a ring of postal workers was arrested. These workers intercepted other

Sierras 2

people's mail, opened it, stole personal
information, and created new identities
using the information. The workers then
used the new identities themselves and
also sold them to others for huge
profits. When they were finally stopped--
only because of a traffic violation--the
police officer noticed a duffel bag in
the backseat of the car they were
driving. The bag contained hundreds of
fake identification cards made from the
stolen information. The workers were
sentenced to five years in federal
prison, not a light sentence for a first-
time offender.

A second, and growing, area of federal
crime is immigration offenses. For example,
Mr. Mahle tells of a woman and her husband
who, in 2005, were stopped from selling
fake visas to people who wanted to enter
the United States but did not qualify for
entry. Working at U.S. embassies in Fiji,
Sri Lanka, and Vietnam over the course of
ten years, the couple used contacts in the
United States to produce the visas. In

Sierras 3

exchange for an "approved" entry visa, each
potential immigrant had to pay thousands
of dollars. Eventually, the couple was
caught when an audit of approved visas
showed many Vietnamese nationals were
getting visas not from the U.S. embassy in
their home country but from the embassy in
Sri Lanka. The couple received eight years
in federal prison and had to forfeit the
hundreds of thousands of dollars they had
been paid.

One final large--and certainly the
most severely punished--area of federal
crime is drug offenses. An example of drug
crime comes from U.S. Assistant Attorney
Michael Beckwith. Two Latino men were
hired, they believed, to be *piñeros*
(people who care for trees in national
forests). The two men were offered jobs
tending pine trees in an old forest and
were offered transportation to the site.
The men became suspicious when they
overheard their employers talk about
harvesting crops, but they still stayed on
the job. Once in the middle of a remote

forest, they were told the truth about their job: cultivating marijuana. Finding themselves in the middle of nowhere and still in need of work, the men stayed. Two weeks after they arrived, the would-be *piñeros* were caught and arrested after agents in helicopters noticed the marijuana plots. Even though their crime lasted less time than either the identity thieves or the immigration felons, the *piñeros* were given the stiffest sentence: ten years in federal prison, the minimum sentence if at least a thousand plants were being cultivated, even for first-time offenders.

Everyone makes mistakes, and many people even break the law. Both Mr. Mahle and Mr. Beckwith agree that no person is perfect and everyone has the right to a fair trial. However, breaking federal law-- unlike what many people think about "getting a slap on the wrist" or "getting off on a technicality"--is a way to get in a lot of trouble that doesn't go away for a long time.

WRITING AN EFFECTIVE THESIS STATEMENT

The thesis statement is the most important part of an essay because it determines how you organize your ideas, what kind of specific details you use, and what kind of transitions you use. A thesis statement has the following characteristics.

- It usually comes in the first paragraph—the introduction—of an essay.
- It contains a narrowed topic and gives the writer's point of view on the topic.
- It must be at least one complete sentence, although it may be more than one sentence.
- It states the writer's purpose.
- It controls the direction of the essay.

See the Checklist for Writing a Thesis Statement below.

 CHECKLIST Writing a Thesis Statement

- Does my thesis statement give the main idea of my essay?
- Does my thesis statement give my point of view?
- Does my thesis statement state my purpose?
- Does my thesis statement tell the reader what to expect?
- Is my thesis statement arguable?
- Is my thesis statement at least one complete sentence?

Don't feel compelled to write a perfect thesis statement immediately. Use prewriting activities, both for your essay and for your thesis statement, and see what ideas seem strongest. Chances are that you will want to explore the ideas that emerge as the strongest in your freewriting, outlining, or clustering. For example, the topic "drunk driving" could suggest several ideas: the damage it causes, the cost to taxpayers, and the danger to the driver, him- or herself.

Making Sure Your Thesis Statement Is a Complete Sentence

After you've come up with an idea that interests you, make sure to state it in a complete sentence. A thesis statement such as "Drunk driving penalties should be stiffer" gives you not only something to argue but also different ways to develop your ideas. Thesis statements can be more than one sentence, but for the essays you'll write using this text, it's a good idea to write thesis statements of a single sentence. Later, as you write longer, more complex essays, your thesis statement can take different forms. The examples below show how phrases fail to communicate the complete idea that you need from a thesis statement.

Not a sentence:	The need for longer school breaks
Sentence:	Full-time students need longer school breaks to perform their best.

Writing "The need for longer school breaks" will leave your reader wondering why you want to write about school breaks and what your position is on the subject. Instead, if you write "Full-time students need longer school breaks to perform their best," readers might disagree with you, but at least they will be clear as to what you're arguing.

Avoid starting your essay with comments such as "The purpose of this essay is to show that . . ." or "This essay will show the differences between. . . ." Introductory phrases such as these don't provide any essential information about your topic. A clear thesis statement will tell your readers all they need to know about what's to come in your essay.

Avoid:	In this essay, I will discuss how studying hard in college pays off.
Good:	Studying hard in college pays off.

The writer simply eliminated the "announcement" to end up with an effective thesis statement.

Making Sure Your Thesis Statement Is Broad Enough

The first thesis statement below would be hard to develop because it simply gives a fact. Restated, it is broad enough for an essay.

Not broad enough:	Top-of-the-line cell phones are expensive.
Broad enough:	Cell phones are not worth the money people pay for them.

If a thesis statement begins with "I think," the reader has a tough time arguing with *anything* the writer says.

| Not broad enough: | I think that taxes are too high. |
| Broad enough: | Payroll taxes are too high for people who earn minimum wage. |

People can believe or think whatever they choose. No one could reasonably argue that you *don't* think taxes are too high. Thus, avoid expressions such as *I think*, *In my opinion*, or *I believe* because these statements throw the focus of your writing onto *your* thoughts instead of the issue under discussion.

Making Sure Your Thesis Statement Is Narrow Enough

After you've crafted a thesis statement that can lead you in multiple directions, you face a new task: you must narrow your thesis statement to make it manageable. One way to narrow your thesis statement is to include a point-of-view phrase or clause, the way you use point-of-view words in a topic sentence. This lets your reader know the scope of your argument.

Don't feel compelled to sit down, face a blank page or computer screen, and write a perfect thesis statement on the first try. Remember, the thesis statement will determine everything else that comes in your essay, so give yourself time to come up with one that works for you. Use prewriting activities, both on your essay and on your thesis, and see what ideas seem strongest. Chances are, the ideas that emerge as the strongest in your freewriting, outlining, or clustering will be those ideas that you really want to explore. Trim your ideas down into a sentence or two and you'll most likely have a working thesis statement that you can use throughout the drafting process.

Making Sure Your Thesis Statement Is Arguable

Just as you take care to narrow the scope of your thesis, be sure that your thesis can be argued, that it is a topic people can have different opinions about. Having a definite opinion gives you momentum for writing a persuasive essay, and it lets your reader know where you stand. The following thesis statement is unclear; does the writer want tougher drunk driving laws or not?

| Not arguable: | We need tougher drunk driving laws, but we need to make sure they're not *that* tough. |

Recognizing a problem with his thesis statement, the writer revised it to say that the laws need to be even tougher than they already are.

Better: Even though drunk driving laws are tough, we need them to be tougher.

Sometimes, as in an informative essay, your thesis statement may not appear to be arguable. For instance, the thesis statement "Coach Fowler's guidance taught me the value of hard work, teamwork, and perseverance" expresses an opinion based on the writer's experience. However, the writer's job is still to use details to illustrate the thesis, thus creating a convincing essay.

Making Sure You're Clear on the Purpose of Your Thesis Statement

Perhaps the most important part of your thesis statement is its purpose, the reason you're writing it, yet this is often unstated. Although your purpose can be to inform or entertain, most academic essays you write will be *persuasive*; they will try to convince your reader of your point of view. Your thesis statement needs to show that purpose.

Unclear purpose: I don't understand how movie stars can look the same year after year.

Here the writer's point is unclear. Is the writer arguing that movie stars look eternally young? Or is the writer critical of movie stars? The writer doesn't make a particular point, so the purpose of the thesis statement is unclear.

Better: Movie stars have to work too hard to stay young-looking.

Here the writer has a clear point: to convince readers that movie stars put in too much time and effort on their looks. Even if you disagree with the writer's claim, you know what the point of the essay is and that the writer cares about the topic.

Consider Offering a "Map" of Your Essay

Some topics are easy to organize into general support points. For such topics, it is useful to mention your **map**—how you plan to organize your essay. For instance, in the essay "Offensive Behavior," Raul mentions the three areas of federal crime that he will discuss: theft and fraud, immigration offenses, and drug violations. Although his thesis statement could have worked without this map, telling his readers the specific items he'll discuss lets his readers know exactly what to expect from his essay. Additionally, a map gives him a plan to refer back to as he writers his essay.

EXERCISE 1   Identifying Effective Thesis Statements

Read the sentence pairs below. Next, circle the letter of the sentence that is an effective thesis statement. Then, write a brief explanation of why the sentence you chose is the better thesis statement. An example is done for you.

a. My dog is a great pet for me.

b. Dogs make great pets.

The second sentence works better as a thesis statement because it gives the reader something to argue. It's hard to argue "Your dog is not a good pet for you" because the person making the claim will know the subject (her own dog) better than a reader.

1. a. Cooking is a helpful skill for students living on their own.

   b. Cooking is good.

   _____

   _____

   _____

2. a. In the next few pages, I will explain why joining the military is a good option for young adults.

   b. Joining the military is a good option for young adults.

   _____

   _____

   _____

3. a. I am not sure why my job requires me to have a physical examination before starting work.

    b. My job's physical examination requirement is a waste of time, effort, and money.

_____

_____

_____

4. a. Tuition at my school is too high.

    b. My school raised its tuition last semester.

_____

_____

_____

5. a. Living in a city is exciting for a single person.

    b. I'm not sure why people can't enjoy living in a city.

_____

_____

_____

DEVELOPING THE PARAGRAPHS IN AN ESSAY

Paragraphs can serve different functions. Some paragraphs grab your attention while others simply convey information. Still others condense or summarize the content of the whole essay. As you saw in the illustration on page 376, an essay has three main types of paragraphs.

- Introductory paragraph
- Concluding paragraph
- Body paragraphs

INTRODUCTORY PARAGRAPH

Think about a time when you've given someone unexpected news. Did you just plunge in, or did you lead up to it in steps? An **introductory paragraph,** or **introduction,** provides background information and sets the tone for your essay. A good introduction has two components.

- An **opening** that catches the reader's attention.
- A **thesis statement,** which gives the main idea of the essay, states the writer's purpose and point of view, and tells the reader what to expect.

An introduction may also contain a **map** of your essay, a statement that shows your reader what your essay will cover or how it will be organized. In the thesis statement from his essay "Offensive Behavior," Raul mentions the three areas he plans to develop—his map—at the end: "Though federal criminal law covers many areas, three of the biggest categories of federal crime are theft and fraud crimes, immigration offenses, and drug violations."

Writers can draw from a number of techniques to craft an effective opening.

Providing Background Information

One of the writer's most important jobs is making the essay relevant, or meaningful, to a reader.

Using a Personal Anecdote

Telling a **personal anecdote,** a story from your personal experience, is another good way to catch your reader's attention.

When I was a little girl, every room in our home felt cheerful and alive because of the living things my mother helped to grow. She had a gift for nurturing plants, and I vowed that my first home on my own would feel as cheerful as my childhood home had. Also, I wanted to show my mother that I had learned from her and that I, too, had a "green thumb" which would help me grow things. However, I was in for a horrible shock. **After making many mistakes, I learned that taking care of plants requires proper light, the right amount of water, and plant food.**

This writer begins her essay with a story that lets the reader know how she's connected to her topic. Explaining her mother's talent for gardening lets us see why the writer cares about gardening.

Beginning with a Quotation

Beginning your essay with a quotation is a good way to focus your reader's attention on a particular aspect of your topic.

> Gloria Steinem said, "A pedestal is as much a prison as any small, confined space." Arguing that women want to be taken seriously as equals, not simply dolled up to accessorize men, Steinem faced the challenge of being a young, attractive woman in a male-dominated world. However, she rose to this challenge admirably. **Because of her efforts, women now have many more options in their personal and professional lives.**

The quotation in this paragraph focuses the essay's topic (and the reader's attention) on women's roles. Arriving at the thesis statement (in bold print), the reader understands both the meaning of the quotation and the relationship between the quotation and the thesis statement.

Using Opposites

Using an example that contrasts with your thesis can be an effective and attention-grabbing way to begin your essay.

> "A friend is a present you give yourself." This quotation was printed on a pink coffee mug that my friend Pamela gave me in high school. At the time I received the mug, I was delighted with both the gift and my friendship. As time went on, however, I began to wish I could return the "gift." **Through Pamela's unkind put-downs, disloyal gossip, and unreliable behavior, I learned that not all friendships are positive.**

By opening with a quotation about friendship, the writer leads the reader to expect an essay on the virtues of the writer's friend Pamela. When the thesis statement (in bold print) switches perspective, the reader is intrigued by the contrast.

Asking Questions

Beginning your essay with a question forces the reader to think about responses.

> Have you ever thought about running away and joining the circus? Or have you thought that maybe your destiny in life is to

become famous? How do you find out the answers to these questions? And once you find out the answers, how do you decide whether to act on them? **I learned in the eighth grade that running away to try to become famous is a hard way to live.**

The writer uses a number of questions to work his way to his thesis statement (in bold print), but the thesis statement itself is not a question.

EXERCISE 2 Recognizing Introduction Strategies

Read each of the following paragraphs, which use different introduction strategies. Then, circle the letter that corresponds to the introduction strategy used.

1.   "To thine own self be true." For as long as I can remember, my father has told me this, explaining that if I'm not true to myself, then I can't be true to anyone else, either. For years, I believed this quotation, too. However, in my high school English class, my teacher pointed out that Polonius—a crafty, sneaky character in Shakespeare's *Hamlet*—said this. I figured that if someone who is not entirely honest gives this advice, then it can't be all good. Since then, I've changed my attitude. Though I try to be true to myself, sometimes my ideas have to come second to other people's.

    a. Background information   **b.** Personal anecdote

    c. Quotation   **d.** Opposites

    e. Questions

2.   I've often heard the saying "Nice guys finish last." For most of my life, I've tried to be a good guy—being a team player in sports, having a good attitude in school, respecting my girlfriends. You'd think, from that saying, that I'd be a loser without any future or any friends. Actually, being a nice guy has brought me rewards in my athletic experiences, in my professional and academic experiences, and in my personal life.

    a. Background information   **b.** Personal anecdote

    c. Quotation   **d.** Opposites

    e. Questions

3.   What inspires people to meet great challenges such as climbing Mount Everest? What goes through the minds of the climbers as they trudge, climb, and pull themselves through oxygen-poor air to the summit? Are they trying to meet death head-on, or are they simply bored with their lives? *Into Thin Air: A Personal Account of the Mount Everest Disaster*, by Jon Krakauer, reveals the challenges and consequences of climbing Mount Everest.

a. Background information   **b.** Personal anecdote

c. Quotation   **d.** Opposites

e. Questions

BODY PARAGRAPHS

The **body paragraphs** of an essay perform two main functions.

1. They make connections to the thesis statement.
2. They give support points and specific details that support the thesis statement.

Making Connections to the Thesis Statement

Each body paragraph must echo some part of the thesis statement. The easiest place to connect a body paragraph to the thesis is in the paragraph's topic sentence.

In his essay "Offensive Behavior" on pages 377–380, Raul uses key terms from the thesis statement in each topic sentence to show the reader how the body paragraphs relate to the thesis statement.

Thesis statement:	Though federal criminal law covers many areas, three of the biggest categories of federal crime are theft and fraud crimes, immigration offenses, and drug violations.
Topic sentence of first body paragraph:	One large area of federal crime is theft and fraud, which involves taking something from someone.

Giving Support Points and Specific Details That Support the Thesis Statement

All your evidence comes in the body paragraphs. In "Offensive Behavior," Raul provides specific details to show how much trouble people can get into if they commit a federal crime.

CONCLUSION

A **concluding paragraph,** or **conclusion,** finishes your essay in one of these ways.

- It ends with a question.
- It adds final thoughts.

Adding Final Thoughts

Though "Offensive Behavior" could have ended with a summary, Raul chose instead to add a few final thoughts.

> Everyone makes mistakes, and many people even break the law. Both Mr. Mahle and Mr. Beckwith agree that no person is perfect and that everyone is entitled to a second chance. However, breaking federal law—unlike what many people think about "getting a slap on the wrist" or "getting off on a technicality"—is a way to get in a lot of trouble that doesn't go away for a long time.

This paragraph provides some new information about Raul attitude toward punishment of federal crimes. However, the information is closely related to the rest of the essay, so the reader stays on track.

Ending with a Question

Just as starting your essay with a question can be a great way to catch your reader's attention, ending with a question focuses your reader as well. Consider another version of the conclusion for "Offensive Behavior."

> Everyone makes mistakes, and many people even break the law. Both Mr. Mahle and Mr. Beckwith agree that no person is perfect and that everyone is entitled to a second chance. However, breaking federal law—unlike what many people think about "getting a slap on the wrist" or "getting off on a technicality"—is a way to get in a lot of trouble that doesn't go away for a long time. Who could possibly think that breaking federal law is a good idea?

In this conclusion, Raul ends his essay by asking a question. But the reader already knows the "answer" because Elijah has explained the consequences of these crimes in his essay.

EXERCISE 3 Writing a Conclusion

Read "A Gardener at Heart," below. This essay has no conclusion. Write a conclusion for the essay, using one of the development strategies outlined in this chapter.

A Gardener at Heart

I grew up in an apartment, so whenever I'd see people mowing lawns or planting gardens on TV, it always looked like fun. Secretly, I wondered if I could be a good outdoor gardener. Last summer, I found out. I spent the summer with my grandparents, and they "let" me take care of their yard. I learned that even though gardening seems easy, it requires patience, consistency, and creativity.

My first lesson in yard work was a lesson in patience. I had always thought that I'd simply whip out a lawn mower, race up and down the yard a few times, and be done with it. I was so wrong. My grandfather showed me how to "edge" his front yard, pushing this spiky ball on the end of a stick along the border between the grass and the driveway. It was exhausting. Every time I'd seem to get going, I'd hit a big weed clump that would block the edging tool. I'd have to stop, pull the clump off the edger, and resume my work. Even though my grandparents' lawn is tiny, it took me an hour to do a satisfactory job.

My second lesson in lawn care—consistency—came in the area of spreading fertilizer. My grandfather explained that his lawn looked much nicer if he treated it with fertilizer every month during the growing season (spring and summer). He showed me how to pour fertilizer into the spreader and then walk up and down the lawn to distribute the fertilizer evenly. I did my best to walk in straight lines, up and down the grass, to make sure I didn't miss any spots. When I'd get hot, I'd take a break. Then I'd try to pick up where I'd left off. Unfortunately, I never remembered quite where that was, so I'd just start over at the beginning of the lawn. Within a week, I saw that being inconsistent had ruined my grandparents' yard. The place where I'd begun was "burned" dark brown from being overfertilized, while the other side of the lawn was the same weak green color it had always been. If I had spread the fertilizer in a consistent manner, the lawn wouldn't have looked so awful.

My only positive lesson in gardening—creativity—came when I decided to plant some flowers to surprise my grandmother. I had always thought that there were rules about what plants you could put in certain places. Well, the man at the garden store told me that as long as plants were planted in places where they could survive— with the right amount of light and water—then there was no rule against planting whatever I liked. I went crazy. My grandmother loves bright colors, so I planted bright red impatiens and yellow primroses in the shady places, orange pansies in the partial sun, and some wild-looking purple flowers (I never did learn their name) in the sun. I followed no rules, but I felt like an artist, adding splashes of color all over the place. Grandma loved the flowers.

Conclusion: _____

_____

_____

_____

_____

_____

The strategy I used in writing the conclusion to "A Gardener at Heart" is

_____

_____

WRITING PRACTICE 1 Turning a Paragraph into an Essay

For this assignment, choose a paragraph that you think you can develop further to write a complete essay. Then, follow the guidelines below.

For the assignment, Raul decided to expand a paragraph he'd written for a criminal justice class into an essay. His original paragraph focused only on theft and fraud, so he had to interview his instructor for information on other types of crime.

Prewriting

1. Ask yourself questions about your paragraph. Some helpful questions are:

Will my topic sentence work as a thesis statement?

How can I change it, if necessary, to be an effective thesis statement?

Can I use my paragraph support points as essay support points?

Do I need more short examples for each support point, or more development in the examples I have?

What kinds of transitions do I need to make the connections to my thesis statement clear?

2. Freewrite for five to ten minutes in response to the questions that most apply to your writing. Pay attention to any new support points or specific details that arise during your freewriting.

Raul did some freewriting to see how he could come up with more information about his topic.

OK, what else can I say about federal crime? I know that drug crimes are big because Mr. M mentioned it, but I really don't know what other areas of federal crime are big. I also keep worrying that no one is going to care about this topic, but I think it's important, so I guess I just need to make other people see why. What else? What else? I think I'll ask Mr. M about serial killers and see if that's a good direction to go in.

Raul realizes that his topic might not seem relevant to another person, so he resolves to make its importance clear. He also needs to decide what other areas to focus on, but he knows that he must first talk to his criminal justice teacher to find out what areas would be best.

3. Modify topic sentence into thesis statement, using "map" of support points.

Topic Sentence for Original Paragraph:

Theft and fraud crimes happen in many places.

Thesis Statement for Essay:

Though federal criminal law covers many areas, three of the biggest categories of federal crimes are theft and fraud crimes, immigration offenses, and drug violations.

Now Raul can develop two other support points that—along with theft and fraud—show what areas of federal crime are particularly large.

4. Make an outline of your essay to see where you need more information. When first starting to plan his essay, Raul's outline looked like this:

Offensive Behavior

A. Introduction
   1. TV and movies seem to focus on serial killers and other, less common criminals.
   2. FBI, Secret Service, U.S. Marshals are federal law enforcement.
   3. Thesis statement: Though federal criminal law covers many areas, the three biggest categories of federal crime are theft and fraud crimes, immigration offenses, and drug violations.

B. Body paragraph 1
   1. Topic sentence: One large area of federal crime is theft and fraud.
   2. Example illustrating topic sentence: One example of federal fraud happened when a ring of postal workers opened people's mail, stole personal information, and created new identities, which they sold.

C. Body paragraph 2
   1. Topic sentence: A second, and growing, area of federal crime is immigration offenses.
   2. Example illustrating topic sentence: Employees at an embassy sold fake visas to people wanting to enter the United States.

D. Body paragraph 3
   1. Topic sentence: One final large—and certainly the most severely punished—area of federal crime is drug offenses.
   2. Example illustrating topic sentence: One local case dealt with two men who were told they would be *piñeros* tending a forest, but were really hired as marijuana growers.

E. Conclusion
   1. Summary: It's not hard to find a way to break federal law.
   2. Final thoughts: Though people might think they carry light penalties, federal offenses can guarantee you serious punishments.

Notice that Raul narrowed his discussion of federal crime to three major areas of federal crime.

Raul's outline is complete, so he does not need to add information. Often, however, outlines are incomplete, thus revealing where additional details or topic sentences should be added. Although Raul has chosen topics, the outline helps him see how he will develop his ideas. He may need to do more prewriting to come up with specific details. Like Raul, you may need to do more freewriting to get enough material for your outline. Remember also to add transitions.

Drafting

5. Modify your topic sentence into a thesis statement, using a map of support points.

6. Choose more specific details.

7. Organize your essay by making an outline to see how your ideas fit together and where you need more information. A completed outline of "Offensive Behavior" appears below.

8. Write a draft of the essay, using your outline as a guide.

Revision

9. Check your essay for the first three of the four Cs: *concise, credible*, and *clear* writing. In particular, check to see that the topic sentence of each paragraph echoes the thesis statement in some way. Make any necessary changes to your draft.

Editing

10. Check your essay for the fourth C: *correct* writing. Proofread your essay to make sure you have used correct spelling, punctuation, and grammar.

WRITING PRACTICE 2 Write an Introductory Paragraph

Follow the guidelines below to write an introductory paragraph for an essay.

1. Choose one paragraph that you've already written for your English class, or select a topic from the list below.

Possible Topics

Compare two movies.

Contrast two people.

Explain the reasons that caused you to make a particular change in your life.

Explain the effects of a decision you made.

Argue for a change in your home, job, or school.

2. Freewrite for five to ten minutes to discover what comes to mind first about your topic.

3. Use one of the techniques mentioned in this chapter for writing an introduction.

- Background information
- Quotation
- Questions

- Personal anecdote
- Opposites

4. Write a clear thesis statement as the last sentence in your introductory paragraph. Make sure your thesis sentence includes a point-of-view word, and make sure it includes a map of your essay, if that seems appropriate.

WRITING PRACTICE 3 Write an Essay

Now it's your turn to write an essay. Follow the guidelines below.

Prewriting

1. Choose a topic for your essay. As a starting point for your essay, you may use the topic from a paragraph you've already written, or you may choose from the list below to write an essay from scratch.

Topics

A movie worth seeing

A decision someone made that helped your community

A place worth visiting

A candidate who should or should not be elected

Challenges of attending college

Benefits or drawbacks to buying a car

2. Freewrite for five to ten minutes on the topic of your choice. Then, use at least one other prewriting technique—listing, questioning, keeping a journal, clustering, or outlining.

If you need help coming up with a topic and doing prewriting, use the topic a "movie worth seeing" and fill in the scratch outline below. Add your own specific details to complete the outline, but don't feel that you have to fill in every space.

Topic: Strengths of *No Country for Old Men*

   A. Exciting action scenes

      1. _____

      2. _____

      3. _____

   B. Excellent acting

      1. _____

      2. _____

      3. _____

   C. Great use of setting

      1. _____

      2. _____

      3. _____

Drafting

3. Write a thesis statement. Draw on your prewriting to find a point that you can develop through an entire essay. For instance, in the outline above, the details show why the writer thinks that *No Country for Old Men* is a movie worth seeing. Thus, a workable thesis statement could be *"No Country for Old Men* is worth seeing for its exciting action scenes, excellent acting, and great use of setting."

4. Choose support points and specific details. For instance, if your thesis statement is *"No Country for Old Men* is worth seeing for its exciting action scenes, excellent acting, and great use of setting," write down all the examples of the three support points that come to mind. Choose the details that you think best illustrate your

support points and will make your essay believable. For instance, for the support points listed previously, you might choose the following details.

Support Point	Specific Details
Exciting action scenes	Suspenseful chase and hiding scenes; gruesome murders
Excellent acting	Javier Bardem as terrifying, evil murderer; Tommy Lee Jones as third-generation sheriff; Josh Brolin as cross between good guy and outlaw
Great use of setting	Chase scenes move over barren West Texas borderland

Remember that in an essay, one support point will take up an entire paragraph, so think of enough details to develop each support point throughout a paragraph.

5. Organize your support points using time sequence (chronological) or emphatic order. Examine your details to decide which order works better. If all of the examples from *No Country for Old Men* occurred simultaneously in the movie, the writer should probably use emphatic order. However, if the examples occurred one after another, the writer could use chronological order. As you're organizing your ideas, eliminate details that don't fit. Use transitions that make your organization clear.

6. Now write a draft of your essay using the thesis statement, your support points, and your specific details. Remember that an essay includes an introductory paragraph with the thesis statement, body paragraphs with support points and specific details, and a concluding paragraph. Feel free to go back and do more prewriting if you need more information for specific details.

Revising

7. Make any necessary changes to your draft. Check for the first three of the four Cs: *concise*, *credible*, and *clear* writing.

Editing

8. Check your essay for the fourth C: *correct* writing. Proofread your essay to make sure you have used correct spelling, punctuation, and grammar.

CHAPTER SUMMARY

Remember the following in writing an essay:

1. An essay differs from a paragraph in length and development.
2. The thesis statement, which controls the direction of the paragraph, is crucial to essay development.
3. Essays contain three types of paragraphs: introductory, body, and concluding.

MyWritingLab & Lab Activity 24

mywritinglab   For additional practice with writing essay paragraph, go to **www.mywritinglab.com** or complete **Lab Activity 24** in the separate *Resources for Writers* Lab Manual.

Prewriting for and Drafting an Essay

Culture Note

RUNNING REVISITED

While running is widely recognized as good exercise, not everyone understands the excitement of seeing a competitive track race. Understanding both the everyday benefits of running and the special thrill that watching a race gives sports fans and couch potatoes alike a reason to appreciate this simple sport.

USING THE WRITING PROCESS WITH ESSAYS

A typical essay has five paragraphs: an introduction, three body paragraphs, and a conclusion. The opening and the thesis statement—which give the main idea of the essay, state the writer's purpose and point of view, and tell the reader what to expect—appear in the introduction. The body paragraphs contain support points and specific details. Finally, the conclusion gives a summary or adds final thoughts to the essay. For more information on the thesis statement and the parts of an essay, see Chapter 24.

The same writing process steps that helped you write an effective paragraph can help you write an effective essay.

Step 1: Prewriting—coming up with ideas

Step 2: Drafting—writing a rough draft

Step 3: Revising—making changes in your draft

Step 4: Editing—checking for correctness

In this chapter, you can practice using prewriting and drafting to start an essay. Chapter 26 shows you how to use revising and editing to finish your essay. The illustration "Writing Process for Essays" on page 402 will also help you see how the writing process can be used for essays.

RECOMMENDED READINGS

"All I Really Need to Know I Learned in Kindergarten," Robert Fulghum, *p. 710*

"How to Write with Style," Kurt Vonnegut, Jr. *p. 732*

"The Joy of Boredom," Carolyn Y. Johnson, *p. 722*

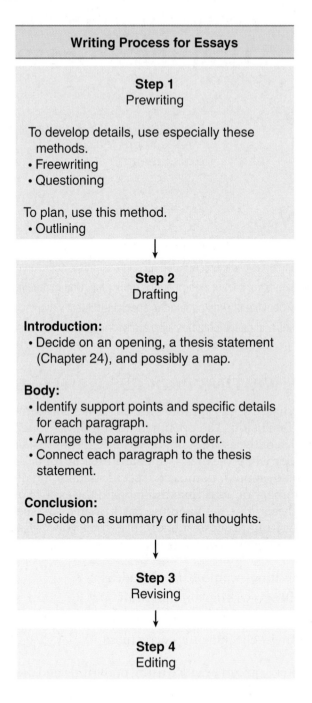

Writing Process for Essays

Step 1
Prewriting

To develop details, use especially these methods.
• Freewriting
• Questioning

To plan, use this method.
• Outlining

Step 2
Drafting

Introduction:
• Decide on an opening, a thesis statement (Chapter 24), and possibly a map.

Body:
• Identify support points and specific details for each paragraph.
• Arrange the paragraphs in order.
• Connect each paragraph to the thesis statement.

Conclusion:
• Decide on a summary or final thoughts.

Step 3
Revising

Step 4
Editing

A MODEL ESSAY

In the model essay that follows, the thesis statement is in bold print and the body paragraph topic sentences are in italics.

A Miler's Style

Introduction

I grew up watching the "classic" sports: football, basketball, and baseball. My whole family thought that individual sports didn't really count, and that competitive track runners—people who ran in circles for their races—were just crazy people who couldn't make the football team. Watching the state track and field finals, however, changed my mind about track. **Specifically, I discovered that competitive milers must use strategy, efficiency, and speed to win.**

Body
paragraph 1

A miler's strategy is important right from the beginning. The fastest runners get to start closest to the inside of the track, so right from the beginning of the race, everyone is elbowing each other, trying to get in close to the middle. Watching people jostle each other as they try to pass—or fend passers off—makes the race seem like a fight. The first lap of the mile is fast because people want good positions on the track and because they're not yet tired. However, some runners deliberately hang back and wait to make their move. They hope that the "rabbits"—the runners who go out too fast—will burn out quickly so that the rest of the pack can set a more natural pace. Sometimes waiting like this works, but sometimes the patient runners get left behind and can't catch up. Knowing how fast to go— and when to go fast—is a huge part of a miler's success.

Body
paragraph 2

Another part of a miler's success is efficiency. After the first lap (and often sooner), the runners start feeling tired. Some of them have run the first lap in under sixty seconds, a very fast pace, so they have to settle into a pace that they can maintain for the next three laps. The runners lengthen their strides, relax their shoulders, and pump their arms as fluidly as possible, trying to be efficient to save energy. At the start of the third lap, many runners are fading. The strongest, however, continue their mechanical motions in an effort to maintain speed without exerting themselves more. Because the racers slow down as they get tired, they must exert more energy just to maintain the same pace. Being efficient is the key here. If runners use extra energy to flail their arms or keep their shoulders hunched up, they won't be strong enough to keep up the pace. Many runners even try to "make a move" and pass people at the start of the third lap so that they can have a good position for the final turn around the track. Pushing to speed up or maintain a fast pace—when half of the race remains—requires ultimate efficiency. After seeing runners fight to maintain their pace, I figured they would be too exhausted for any kind of big finish.

Body
paragraph 3

A big finish, however, is exactly what I saw. *One more quality that milers possess is speed.* Even though the mile is considered a distance race, its racers must be fast to win. As the racers approach the start of the last lap, also known as the bell lap or gun lap because a bell or gun is sounded at its start, some of them begin to accelerate. They shorten their strides, digging in around the turn, speeding up all the way. The fly down the backstretch, trying to catch others or not be caught themselves, and head into the final turn. The real speedsters make their moves here, starting a sprint at the top of the turn and barreling down the last straightaway. Sometimes the speedsters pass people and win. Often, however, the gutsy runners who started fast or sped up earlier will be too far away for them to catch. Either way, it's exciting to see long, lanky runners speeding toward the finish.

Conclusion   It took seeing a top-notch mile race to make me appreciate the excitement of track and field. Since that track meet, I've brought my father and my brothers to the track to see meets, and while they're not as impressed as I am, they don't consider runners "wanna-be" athletes any more. After all, anyone who can combine strategy, efficiency, and speed deserves a little respect.

PREWRITING FOR YOUR ESSAY

While writing an essay may seem more intimidating than writing a paragraph, it's not really more difficult—just a bit more time-consuming. The trick is to plan your essay so that it includes the key support points and specific details it needs to be effective.

All the prewriting techniques covered in Chapter 3 can help you start your essay. Three are especially helpful: freewriting, questioning, and outlining.

- **Freewriting.** Freewriting is helpful in beginning an essay because it allows you to get ideas on paper without worrying about whether or not your writing is "right." Plan to freewrite frequently.

- **Questioning.** Asking questions can help you focus on the information you need to write a well-developed essay. For instance, in "A Miler's Style," Raoul had a pretty good initial idea why track meets didn't seem interesting. However, he needed information to support the idea that a mile race could require qualities he admired in other athletes. Asking questions helped him focus his writing on the areas that needed attention.

- **Outlining.** Raoul developed enough details from his freewriting and questioning to write a possible thesis statement. Then he started to plan his essay.

Writing an outline is often the single most helpful way to plan your essay. Begin with a simple outline—sometimes called a **scratch outline**—that contains few, if any, details. Look at the one on the next page for "A Miler's Style."

A Miler's Style—Informal Outline

Possible thesis statement: Milers must use strategy, efficiency, and speed to win.

1. Milers must use strategy.
2. Milers need efficiency.
3. Milers need speed.

For an initial outline, this is enough. Raoul has added a possible thesis statement. Finally, he has put his support points in order. Raoul then wrote a second outline, after he did some thinking and research on the topic. This detailed outline helped him plan and organize his essay when he started drafting.

A Miler's Style

A. Introduction
  1. My family liked "classic" sports but not track.
  2. I saw state track and field finals and changed my mind about track.
  3. Thesis statement: Milers must use strategy, efficiency, and speed to win.
B. Milers use strategy.
  1. "Elbow" for good position.
  2. Go out fast.
  3. Hang back and wait.
C. Milers use efficiency.
  1. Milers are tired after a lap.
  2. Try to save energy in running style.
  3. Must try harder just to keep same pace.
D. Milers use speed.
  1. Some runners speed up during third lap.
  2. "Dig in" to speed up.
  3. Pass people on last lap.
E. Conclusion
  1. Seeing a track meet changed my mind about runners.
  2. My family watched meets and changed their minds, too.

Use the Essay Planning Form on page 408 to create an informal outline.

EXERCISE 1 Outlining to Plan an Essay

Choose a thesis statement from the list below. Then, use the outline form that follows to plan an essay based on that thesis statement. You may substitute your own words for the underlined terms in the thesis statements, or you may write your own thesis statement.

1. In order to be successful in school, students must <u>study</u>, <u>ask for help</u>, and <u>go to class</u>.

2. *Sweeney Todd* is an excellent movie because of its <u>music</u>, <u>costumes</u>, and <u>story</u>.

3. The <u>Kings</u> are a great team because of their <u>talented players</u>, <u>good coaching</u>, and <u>generous owners</u>.

4. Getting fired from a job is easy if you <u>come late</u>, <u>don't do your work</u>, and <u>act rude to the boss</u>.

5. Using a computer is helpful for <u>completing schoolwork</u>, <u>staying organized</u>, and <u>tracking finances</u>.

Thesis statement: _____

A. Introduction

    1. _____

    2. _____

    3. _____

B. Body paragraph 1 support points

    1. _____

    2. _____

    3. _____

C. Body paragraph 2 support points

1. _____

2. _____

3. _____

D. Body paragraph 3 support points

1. _____

2. _____

3. _____

E. Conclusion

1. _____

2. _____

3. _____

DRAFTING YOUR ESSAY

When you're ready to start drafting, gather your assignment, your prewriting results, your outline, and any other information you will need. You can draft by hand or on a computer (see Chapter 5 for tips on using a computer).

Writing a Strong Introduction

The thesis statement is the most important part of your introduction. It controls the direction of your entire essay and states the main idea that you want to communicate.

For "A Miler's Style" on pages 403–404, the writer modified his possible thesis statement to fit smoothly into his introduction and clarify his point of view.

Possible thesis statement:	Milers must use strategy, efficiency, and speed to win.
Final thesis statement:	Specifically, I discovered that competitive milers must use strategy, efficiency, and speed to win.

Essay Planning Form

Title: _____

Introduction

Opening: _____
_____

Thesis statement (with map, if needed): _____
_____

Body

Support point for paragraph 1: Topic sentence _____
_____
_____

    Specific details: _____
_____
_____

Support point for paragraph 2: Topic sentence _____
_____
_____

    Specific details: _____
_____
_____

Support point for paragraph 3: Topic sentence _____
_____
_____

    Specific details: _____
_____
_____

Conclusion

Summary or final thoughts: _____
_____
_____

Organizing and Connecting the Body Paragraphs Effectively

Use your outline to decide the order of your paragraphs. Think about whether time sequence order (chronological) or emphatic order (least to most important) is more effective for your purpose and reader. Pay particular attention to connecting your ideas. Four key strategies can help you connect your ideas effectively.

Repeating Key Words from the Thesis Statement   In "A Miler's Style," Raoul uses the word *miler* in the topic sentence of all three body paragraphs, so the reader can easily see how the body paragraphs are connected to his thesis statement.

Repeating Key Words from the Preceding Paragraph   At the end of body paragraph 1 in "A Miler's Style," Raoul states:

> Knowing how fast to go—and when to go fast—is a huge part of a miler's success.

He then begins body paragraph 2 with this statement:

> Another part of a miler's success is efficiency.

By repeating the words *miler's success*, Raoul connects the two paragraphs for the reader.

Using Transitional Terms to Signal Paragraphs   In "A Miler's Style," Raoul begins each body paragraph with a transition that signals a new point. He begins body paragraph 1 by writing this:

> A miler's strategy is important right from the beginning.

He begins body paragraph 2 like this:

> Another part of a miler's success is efficiency.

He begins body paragraph 3 this way:

> One more quality that milers possess is speed.

By using the transitions *from the beginning, another,* and *one more,* Raoul lets the reader know that the essay is connected and moving along.

Using Transitional Sentences to Connect Paragraphs   In "A Miler's Style," Raoul ends body paragraph 2 by writing this:

> After seeing runners fight to maintain their pace, I figured they would be too exhausted for any kind of big finish.

Instead of jumping into his next support point—that milers have speed—Raoul uses a transitional sentence at the beginning of body paragraph 3 to continue the idea of a "big finish."

> A big finish, however, is exactly what I saw.

This sentence links the ideas in body paragraphs 2 and 3.

Writing a Sharp Conclusion

In your conclusion, you have the chance to reinforce your thesis. Using your outline, write a brief summary or add some final thoughts that will help convince your readers. For more on writing an effective conclusion, see Chapter 24.

EXERCISE 2 Following the Four Cs

Sarah based the following essay on a paragraph she wrote. Read "Runner's High," below, and answer the questions that follow.

Runner's High

[1]For years when my three older brothers would come back from football practice, I would hear about how awful running was. Their coaches made them run for punishment, for instance, if they showed up late to practice, and my brothers ran only if they absolutely had to. Before I tried it for myself, I had a horrible impression of running. However, since I wasn't any good at softball or soccer, I tried out for the high school cross-country team. Soon I discovered that many positive changes were occurring in my life. I was enjoying my time outside, my new fit body, my faster metabolism, and the "runner's high" that comes with exertion. In fact, through my experience as a runner, I've learned that running for exercise has many benefits.

²First of all, running allows me to be outside, not closed up in some gym or workout room. I get to see trees, flowers, and other people. I've read a lot of fitness magazines, and one article says that outdoor exercise gives people more of a mental lift than indoor exercise. I believe that. Even on days that are cold and rainy, when I don't want to run, within five minutes outside, I'm happy that I've started. There's just nothing like feeling cold air—or even cold rain—on my face as I run around the park. That's an experience I definitely can't get at a gym.

³Another benefit of running is the physical change my body undergoes. Within two weeks of regular running, my legs started looking more toned and my stomach became flatter. People tell me that my skin seems to glow, too, maybe from improved circulation when I run. I also notice that when I walk up a flight of stairs, I don't even get out of breath. When I don't run, however, I'm huffing and puffing by the tenth step. After a few weeks off, it takes me a while to get back in shape, but the benefits of running are always worth the effort.

⁴A third benefit of running is that I can eat anything I want and not gain weight. Just running for half an hour a day, four days a week allows me to eat until I'm full and not worry about whether or not my jeans will fit. I've learned from my coach that when I run, my metabolism speeds up, so I burn calories faster than when I'm not exercising. Even better, my metabolism stays faster for hours after my run, so my body keeps burning food even after my workout. I almost feel as if I'm cheating by getting the extra hours of additional calorie burning, but I love it.

⁵Finally, "runner's high" makes running great all by itself. Even though sometimes I start my run feeling tired or achy, after a few minutes, I loosen up and get the most wonderful rush. I've heard that the body releases endorphins, substances that take away physical pain and improve the mood. I've even heard that endorphins are actually addictive, so people can get physically hooked on them. It's true that when I feel the "high," I don't feel any pain at all, and I start feeling edgy if I can't run for a few days. I never thought I would be happy to be hooked on something, but I'm glad that running is my habit.

⁶All in all, though the sore muscles and sweat might turn people off, I understand how people can get hooked on running. Aside from the pounding my joints take from putting in miles each week, there is no downside to running for exercise. It's a habit that has so many benefits.

Concise Writing

1. Which of the following details does the writer use to introduce her topic? Circle all that apply.

   a. She ran with her dog.

   b. Her football-playing brothers hated running.

   c. She ran to win a bet with her brothers.

   d. She ran to lose weight after the holidays.

   e. She started running after finding she was not good at softball or soccer.

2. What is the thesis statement in paragraph 1 of "Runner's High"?

   _____

   _____

3. What are the four support points the writer makes? *Hint:* Look at the map before the thesis statement, or look at the topic sentences in paragraphs 2 through 5.

   a. _____

   b. _____

   c. _____

   d. _____

Credible Writing

4. What details does Sarah use in paragraph 3 to show the physical benefits of running?

   a. _____

   b. _____

   c. _____

   d. _____

5. What two experts (in paragraphs 2 and 4) does the writer cite to support her examples?

Paragraph 2: _____

Paragraph 4: _____

6. What details does Sarah use in paragraphs 1 and 6 to show that she understands that not everyone likes running?

a. _____

b. _____

c. _____

Clear Writing

7. What key word from the thesis statement does the writer repeat in

her topic sentences for paragraphs 3 and 4? _____

8. What transitions does the writer use to introduce each support point?

Paragraph 2: _____

Paragraph 3: _____

Paragraph 4: _____

Paragraph 5: _____

How many times does the writer use a form of the word *run* (including in the title)? _____

Correct Writing

The sentences in this paragraph are all correct. To check for correctness in your own writing, go to Part Seven, "Writing Correct Sentences."

WRITING PRACTICE 1 Write About a Personal Relationship

Write an essay about a relationship that has had a strong effect on you. The relationship may be positive or negative; it may be a current relationship or one in your past.

Prewriting

1. Choose a relationship for your essay topic. Here are some possibilities.

A parent	A sibling	A friend
An instructor	A counselor	A coach
An employer	A neighbor	A teammate

2. Begin by freewriting about the relationship for ten minutes.
3. Make an informal outline of your essay. Use more prewriting strategies to add specific details to your brief outline. Asking questions can help you get started.

Drafting

4. Write a thesis statement. Make sure it includes your main idea, your point of view, your purpose, and possibly a map of your essay to let readers know what to expect.
5. Choose support points and specific details that you think best illustrate your thesis and that will make your essay believable.
6. Organize your support points using time sequence (chronological) or emphatic order. You may create a detailed outline to help you or use the outline you developed during prewriting. Decide which order works better by examining your details. As you're organizing your ideas, eliminate details that don't fit.
7. Now write a draft of your essay. Remember that essays include an introductory paragraph with a thesis statement, body paragraphs with support points and specific details, and a concluding paragraph. Do more prewriting if you need more information for specific details.

Revising

8. Check your essay for the first three of the four Cs: *concise*, *credible*, and *clear* writing. Make any necessary changes to your draft.

Editing

9. Check your essay for the fourth C: *correct* writing. Proofread your essay to make sure you have used correct spelling, punctuation, and grammar.

WRITING PRACTICE 2 Write About a Personal Goal

Write an essay explaining how you have achieved, or will achieve, a personal goal. Your goal can be one that you have achieved already, or it can be one that you have set and are still working toward.

Prewriting

1. Choose a topic that interests you.

Possible Topics

College graduation	Getting in shape
Passing a class	Buying a car
Getting a job	Buying a house
Getting a promotion	Moving out on your own

2. Freewrite on your topic for ten minutes.

3. Make an informal outline using your topic or a possible thesis statement. A sample outline follows.

Thesis statement: Getting into shape involved more self-discipline than I ever thought I had.

A. Gave up sweets.

B. Made myself eat healthy foods.

C. Made myself exercise regularly.

Drafting

4. Write a thesis statement. Make sure your thesis includes your main idea, your point of view, your purpose, and possibly a map of your essay to let readers know what to expect.

5. Choose support points and specific details that you think best illustrate your thesis and will make your essay believable.

6. Organize your support points using chronological or emphatic order. Decide which order works better by examining your details. As you organize your ideas, omit unnecessary details. You may create a detailed outline to help you or use an outline you developed during prewriting.

7. Now write a draft of your essay. Remember that essays include an introductory paragraph that includes the thesis statement, body paragraphs that include support points and specific details, and a concluding paragraph. Feel free to do more prewriting if you need more information for specific details.

Revising

8. Check your essay for the first three of the four Cs: *concise, credible,* and *clear* writing. Make any necessary changes to your draft.

Editing

9. Check your essay for the fourth C: *correct* writing. Proofread your essay to make sure you have used correct spelling, punctuation, and grammar.

WRITING PRACTICE 3 Write About a Current Event

Every day the newspapers report local, statewide, nationwide, and international news. Often, the events they cover span several months. Spend a few weeks reading and clipping articles from the newspaper (or downloading them from a news Web site), and then write an essay about the event you've studied. Begin your writing process *after* you've read and learned something about your topic.

Prewriting

1. Choose an event from current news stories that interests you. Some possible topics follow.

A war or conflict overseas

An issue that affects the country (homelessness, taxes, immigration, drug testing at work)

An issue that affects your state, county, or city (weather crises, education policies, crime)

An election race

2. Freewrite for ten minutes about your topic. Focus your freewriting not only on what you know about your topic but also on what you'd like to know. An example of freewriting by one writer, Marty, follows.

It really bothers me that this driver lost his temper and rammed his car into a family's van. The little girl in the family may never walk again, and the police aren't even sure if they arrested the right guy. I can't believe anyone would get so mad about not getting a parking space that he'd try to hurt someone, but that's what this guy did (or it looks like that anyway). Out-of-control driving can hurt people! What's worse is that then the guy drove away and didn't even see if he'd hurt anyone. It's lucky that a woman in the parking lot saw the whole thing and got part of his license plate; I hope the police found the right guy. I hope, too, that the little girl will be OK. People need to make sure they're under control when they drive.

Marty's freewriting reveals that he has been following the news story. Additionally, Marty identifies a possible thesis statement in his last sentence.

3. Make an informal outline of your essay. After rereading articles about his topic, Marty came up with support points that he could use for his essay. His outline looked like this:

Possible thesis statement: People need to make sure they're under control when they drive.

- A. Introduction
  1. Comments about injuries from car accidents
  2. Comments about frustrations arising from driving
  3. Thesis statement
  4. Essay map: Accidents cost money; accidents cause stress; people get hurt.

- B. Body paragraph 1: Accidents cost money.
  1. Example from articles about how much car damage costs
  2. Example from articles about how much injuries cost
  3. Get details on legal fees?

- C. Body paragraph 2: Accidents cause stress.
  1. Example from articles about how the accident affected other drivers

- D. Body paragraph 3: People get hurt.
  1. Example from articles on young girl's injuries
  2. Example from articles on both drivers' injuries

- E. Conclusion
  1. Comments about the cost—money, stress, health—of losing control behind the wheel
  2. Comment about how public transportation is a good idea?

Drafting

4. Write a thesis statement. Make sure your thesis includes your main idea, your point of view, your purpose, and possibly a map of your essay to let readers know what to expect. Marty already had a possible thesis statement: "People need to make sure they're under control when they drive." But his outline showed him that he was focusing most specifically on the costs—or consequences—of driving while out of control. Thus, Marty revised his thesis statement: "Driving while out of control has serious consequences."

This new thesis statement accurately reflects the content of Marty's essay. Then Marty decided to include a map to keep himself and his reader on track. His thesis statement eventually read as follows:

> Driving while out of control has serious consequences, including loss of money, increased stress, and injury.

From this thesis statement, a reader knows exactly what Marty is arguing and how he plans to develop his argument.

5. Choose support points and specific details that best illustrate your support points and will make your essay believable. Marty used the support points he had included in his outline. Then, from the articles he had read, he gathered specific details for his support points.

6. Organize your support points using time sequence (chronological) or emphatic order. Examine your details to decide which order works better. As you're organizing your ideas, eliminate details that don't fit.

7. Now write a rough draft of your essay. Remember that essays include an introductory paragraph with an attention-getting opening and a thesis statement; body paragraphs with support points and specific details; and a concluding paragraph with a summary or final thoughts. Feel free to do more prewriting if you need more information for specific details.

Revising

8. Check your essay for the first three of the four Cs: *concise*, *credible*, and *clear* writing. Make any necessary changes to your draft.

Editing

9. Check your essay for the fourth C: *correct* writing. Proofread your essay to make sure you have used correct spelling, punctuation, and grammar.

CHAPTER SUMMARY

Remember the following in writing an essay:

1. As in paragraph writing, use prewriting and drafting techniques.
2. Include an introduction with your thesis statement.
3. Write body paragraphs that include your support points and specific details.
4. Echo key words from the thesis, and use transitional expressions to keep your reader on track.

MyWritingLab & Lab Activity 25

mywritinglab   For additional practice with essay planning, go to **www.mywritinglab.com** or complete **Lab Activity 25** in the separate *Resources for Writers* Lab Manual.

Revising an Essay

Culture Note

PROCESSING CHOCOLATE

While people might think that chocolate is naturally delicious, chocolate actually must undergo many steps before becoming edible. From picking the cocoa bean through the roasting, grinding, and mixing processes, chocolate changes greatly before taking the forms we recognize and appreciate.

RECOMMENDED READINGS

"Fatso," Cheryl Peck, *p. 762*

"How to Write with Style," Kurt Vonnegut, Jr. *p. 732*

"The Plot Against People," Russell Baker, *p. 779*

Far From The Bar?

CRITICAL THINKING Seemingly a river of chocolate, this sweet stream will eventually take forms we recognize, such as bars or chips. Write a paragraph explaining how one food—such as an egg—can be used to make another, such as cookies.

Responding to Images. *What about this photo appeals to or repulses you? Explain.*

REVISING YOUR ESSAY

One of the greatest challenges in revising an essay is getting yourself to take apart, or adjust, something that already may look quite good. Essays, however, need even stronger connections than paragraphs, so revising for the four Cs is vital. Revising—making changes in your draft—is a creative process in which you unify your writing, add information, and strengthen connections between ideas, using all the skills you used in writing your rough draft. Look at the illustration "Writing Process for Essays" below to see where revising and editing fall in the writing process.

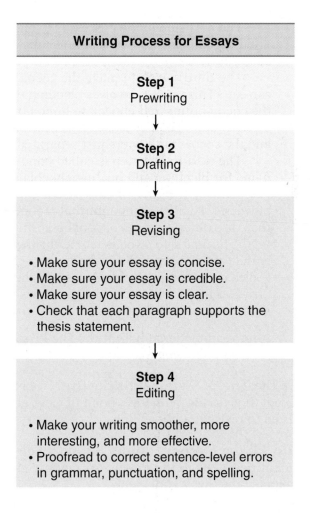

Writing Process for Essays

Step 1
Prewriting

↓

Step 2
Drafting

↓

Step 3
Revising

• Make sure your essay is concise.
• Make sure your essay is credible.
• Make sure your essay is clear.
• Check that each paragraph supports the thesis statement.

↓

Step 4
Editing

• Make your writing smoother, more interesting, and more effective.
• Proofread to correct sentence-level errors in grammar, punctuation, and spelling.

Making Sure Your Essay Is Concise

Sergei has chosen to write about the process by which cocoa beans become edible chocolate. He has already done some reading on the subject of processing chocolate and written a rough draft. Now he's ready for revision. As you read Sergei's essay, think of ways in which it can be made more concise.

The Process of Making Chocolate—Rough Draft

Introduction

[1]The cocoa bean must go through many steps to become the kind of chocolate we can buy in stores and eat.

Body paragraph 1

[2]The first step is harvesting the cocoa pods containing the beans and fermenting them for about six days. [3]Then, the cocoa beans are split from the pods and dried. [4]I never thought that a bean could end up being so delicious.

Body paragraph 2

[5]The next step in the process is to change the beans from plain, dried cocoa beans to two separate substances—cocoa powder and cocoa butter.

Body paragraph 3

[6]The third step is to make the cocoa powder into chocolate we can eat. [7]This process involves blending the cocoa powder back with the cocoa butter and chocolate liquor that was pressed out of the dried, ground beans. [8]This seems like a silly step since the powder and the cocoa butter were just separated from each other.

Body paragraph 4

[9]The next-to-last step is called conching, which is just a fancy name for blending and heating chocolate a special way. [10]A conch is a heated container filled with the blended, liquefied chocolate powder. [11]I'd always thought that a conch was a shell, but I guess there are different types of conches.

Body paragraph 5

[12]The final step involves tempering the chocolate. [13]All this means is that after the conching process, the chocolate is heated up and cooled down carefully to achieve the right texture and appearance.

Conclusion

[14]All in all, the chocolate we eat is very different from what nature starts out with.

After reading Sergei's draft of "The Process of Making Chocolate," ask yourself the following questions to determine whether it is concise.

Is the Thesis Statement Effective?   Sentence 1 is Sergei's thesis statement. It gives his main idea, point of view, and purpose, so Sergei does not need to revise it at this point.

Do All the Support Points Support the Thesis Statement?   Sergei identifies steps in the process of making chocolate. These steps directly support the thesis statement.

Do All the Specific Details Support the Thesis Statement?   Sergei includes some good specific details that illustrate the process of making chocolate, but he also has some sentences that are off-topic.

Read his essay again, and cross out the sentences that do not support the thesis statement. (You should cross out sentences 4, 8, and 11.)

Making Sure Your Essay Is Credible

Now Sergei needs to provide more details to illustrate the ideas in his body paragraphs. Reread "The Process of Making Chocolate," keeping the following two questions in mind.

Is There Enough Information?   Body paragraphs 1 and 2 contain very little information other than their topic sentences. Body paragraphs 3 through 5 offer some details, but not enough for the reader to understand the entire process of making chocolate. Thus, all of the paragraphs need additional details.

Is More Support Needed?   Sergei already included everything he had from his prewriting, so he needs to gather more information for his essay. After reading an article about the drying process, Sergei revised body paragraph 1 as follows:

> The first step is harvesting the cocoa pods containing the beans and fermenting them for about six days. Then, the cocoa beans are split from the pods and dried. The best-quality chocolate is produced when the drying process is done by the sun for about seven days. Speeding up the drying process using artificial methods may be faster, but the chocolate doesn't end up nearly as good.

Going forward with his revision, Sergei adds details to support his thesis and make his essay credible. In addition, he does the following:

- Adds an attention-getting opening to his introduction
- Changes his thesis statement slightly to fit in the new introduction
- Adds some sentences and words to his body paragraphs
- Adds some final thoughts to his conclusion

These changes are underlined in his revised draft, which follows.

The Process of Making Chocolate—Revised Draft

Introduction

I've always had a sweet tooth, and I've especially loved choco-late. In fact, whenever I've ordered an ice cream cone, my only deci-sion has been what kind of chocolate to get. I've always assumed that since chocolate was so easy to find, it must also be easy to make. However, according to my nutrition instructor, this isn't the case. From the time it's harvested until it appears in stores, the cocoa bean must go through a process of many steps to become the kind of chocolate we like to eat.

Body paragraph 1

The first step in the cocoa bean's journey to becoming chocolate is harvesting the cocoa pods containing the beans and fermenting them for about six days. Then, the cocoa beans are split from the pods and dried. The best-quality chocolate is produced when the drying process is done by the sun for about seven days. Speeding up the drying process using artificial methods is faster, but the choco-late doesn't end up nearly as good.

Body paragraph 2

The next step in the chocolate process is to change the beans from plain, dried cocoa beans to two separate substances—cocoa powder and cocoa butter. This process of separation involves roast-ing the cocoa beans, grading them according to how good they are or what type of flavor they have, and grinding them up. This three-step process results in a powder. The powder is then pressed to remove the cocoa butter, or the fat, which leaves cocoa powder.

Body paragraph 3

The third step in transforming the cocoa bean begins to make the cocoa powder into chocolate we can eat. This process involves blending the cocoa powder back with the cocoa butter and choco-late liquor that was pressed out of the dried, ground beans. Adding different amounts of cocoa butter, cocoa liquor, and other ingredi-ents to the cocoa powder determines the type of chocolate you end up with. For instance, plain chocolate consists of cocoa powder, cocoa liquor, cocoa butter, and sugar. Milk chocolate, however, has milk or milk powder in it in addition to the cocoa powder, cocoa liquor, cocoa butter, and sugar. White chocolate is different, too. It contains cocoa liquor, cocoa butter, milk or milk powder, and sugar, but it has no cocoa powder. At this point, after all the ingredients have been added, the chocolate looks finished.

Body paragraph 4

However, to be truly finished, the chocolate still has two steps to go. The next-to-last step is called conching, which is just a fancy name for blending and heating chocolate a special way. A conch is a container filled with the blended chocolate powder and kept heated to keep the blended chocolate in liquid form. The length of time given to the conching process determines the final smoothness and quality of chocolate. The finest chocolate is conched for at least a week. After the process is completed, the chocolate is stored in heated tanks, ready for the final step.

Body paragraph 5   The final step involves tempering the chocolate. All this means is that after the conching process, the chocolate is heated up and cooled down carefully to achieve the right texture and appearance. Tempering the chocolate starts with cooling it in stages and then warming it up to liquid form again. Then the chocolate is cooled down one more time, so it ends up in a solid form.

Conclusion   All in all, the chocolate we eat is very different from what nature starts out with. From the bean to the bar, making chocolate involves far more effort than we make in just going to the candy section of the supermarket and choosing a brand. Even though I don't see myself making any chocolate from scratch, I really appreciate my candy bar a lot more now that I know how it's made.

Making Sure Your Essay Is Clear

Sergei's essay has an effective thesis statement, solid support points, and credible specific details. Now he needs to make sure that his connections are as strong as possible.

Are Key Words Repeated?   In his revised draft, Sergei's thesis statement says, in part, that "the *cocoa bean* must go through a process of many *steps* to become the kind of *chocolate* we like to eat." In the topic sentence of body paragraph 1, Sergei now repeats the words *step*, *cocoa bean*, and *chocolate*. Sergei passes the first test of clarity—repeating key words from the thesis statement—with flying colors.

Sergei states at the end of body paragraph 4 that the chocolate is ready for "the final step." He then begins body paragraph 5 with "The final step," connecting the two paragraphs for the reader. An added bonus is that the word *steps* appears in the thesis statement. Thus, Sergei makes connections between the two paragraphs *and* the thesis statement by repeating key words.

Do Transitional Expressions Signal the Support Points?   Sergei begins body paragraph 1 by writing "The *first* step in the cocoa bean's journey. . . ." In the next body paragraph, he begins with "The *next* step," and he uses similar terms to introduce each remaining support point. By using the transitions *first, next, third, next-to-last*, and *final*, Sergei makes the time sequence (chronological) order of the support points clear.

Are Transitional Sentences Used to Connect Paragraphs?   Sergei ends body paragraph 3 by writing that "the chocolate looks finished." But instead of jumping into his next support point—that chocolate needs to go through the conching process—Sergei uses a transitional sentence to move from the possibility of the chocolate being "finished" to the next step in processing chocolate. He writes, "However, to be truly *finished*, the chocolate still has two steps to go." This sentence links body paragraphs 3 and 4, successfully connecting the ideas of both paragraphs.

EXERCISE 1 Analyzing an Essay for Organization and Support

Reread "The Process of Making Chocolate—Revised Draft" on pages 424–425. Then, answer the questions below.

1. What kinds of details does Sergei offer in his introduction to lead up to the thesis statement?

   a. _____

   b. _____

   c. _____

2. What is the thesis statement? _____

   _____

3. Write down the steps explained in each of the body paragraphs.

   Body paragraph 1: _____

   Body paragraph 2: _____

   Body paragraph 3: _____

   Body paragraph 4: _____

   Body paragraph 5: _____

4. Which step required the most specific detail as explanation of the

   process? Why? _____

   _____

5. What key words does Sergei echo throughout his essay?

a. _____

b. _____

c. _____

d. _____

Checking Each Paragraph Individually for the Four Cs

Reading each paragraph in your essay one at a time lets you check the paragraphs individually for the first three of the four Cs. As you read each paragraph of your essay, look for the following components.

- A clear topic sentence that connects the paragraph to the thesis statement
- Clear support points, if appropriate, that support the topic sentence
- Relevant specific details that illustrate both the paragraph's topic sentence and the essay's thesis statement.

EDITING YOUR ESSAY

Just as essays include more information than paragraphs, they can also—simply because they are longer—include more errors. Thus, **editing**—working on your writing to make it more effective and to correct errors—is essential. There are two parts to editing.

- Making your writing smoother, more interesting, and more effective
- Proofreading to correct sentence-level errors in grammar, punctuation, and spelling

Making Your Writing Smoother, More Interesting, and More Effective

After checking that your essay is concise, credible, and clear, you need to make sure that your reader will enjoy your writing. As you read your essay, answer the following questions.

- **Point of view.** Do you use the same pronoun throughout? Do you use the correct verb tenses? (For more on using consistent verbs and pronouns, see Chapters 38 and 39.)

- **Appropriate language.** Do you use language that is appropriate for an academic assignment? (For more on sensitive language and word choice, see Chapter 12.)

- **Word use.** Have you chosen the best words? Is the writing too wordy? Are certain words repeated too often? (For more on using vivid examples and language, see Chapters 9 and 14.)

- **Sentence variety.** Have you used a variety of sentences to keep your writing interesting? Have you made sure that one sentence flows logically and smoothly into the next? (For more on sentence variety and connecting sentences, see Chapter 32.)

These are points you will address first during drafting and again during revising. When you reach the editing stage of the writing process, you have another chance to make sure your writing is smooth, interesting, and effective.

Proofreading to Correct Sentence-Level Errors

During proofreading, you check your writing for errors in grammar, punctuation, and spelling. As you find errors, you might want to mark your corrections using **proofreaders' marks,** a standard set of symbols used by instructors, editors, and printers to show changes in written work.

You can use three techniques to proofread your essay.

- Proofreading sentence by sentence. This step will help you find errors such as run-on sentences, sentence fragments, incorrect subject-verb agreement, and incorrect pronoun agreement.

- Proofreading word by word. This step will help you find apostrophe and capitalization errors and other errors that you might miss during the sentence-by-sentence proofreading.

- Reading your essay backwards. This step can help you find spelling errors.

For each of these steps, read your essay over one more time, focusing on the task at hand. When you've finished editing your essay, read it again, just to be sure it is free of errors.

WRITING PRACTICE 1 Write About Giving Advice

We've all had successes and made mistakes in our lives, and sometimes we've benefited from what others have told or shown us. Write an essay in which you give advice to someone just entering high school.

Prewriting

1. Choose an advice topic based on your own experiences and observations.

Possible Topics

Be friendly to everyone.

Choose your friends carefully.

Work hard.

Don't work too hard.

Try hard to be well liked.

Don't worry about what people think of you.

Get a part-time job.

Focus only on school.

2. As always, freewrite for ten minutes about your topic, paying careful attention to the experiences that led you to hold your opinion on this kind of advice.

3. Make an informal outline to clarify your support points.

Possible thesis statement: Because it's impossible to please everyone, it's better to keep to yourself.

A.   You're less likely to get put down by peers.

B.   You're less likely to get called on in class.

C.   You don't have to worry about being phony when you feel like being alone.

Question	Answer
How does keeping to yourself keep you from being put down?	People don't notice you, don't seek you out, don't make trouble for you.
How does keeping to yourself keep the instructor from calling on you?	Being quiet means you won't call attention to yourself; the instructor might not notice you if you're quiet.
How does keeping to yourself keep you from being phony?	Not as many people to talk to, so you can act naturally.

Remember that all prewriting strategies can be used effectively through-out the writing process. Even if you're almost finished with a draft of your essay, it's not too late to go back and ask questions or freewrite to come up with more details. For this essay, asking questions can help fill in the details to support the thesis.

Drafting

4. Write a thesis statement. Make sure your thesis includes your main idea, point of view, purpose, and possibly a map of your essay.

5. Choose support points and specific details that best illustrate your support points and that will make your essay believable.

6. Organize your support points using time sequence (chronological) or emphatic order. Examine your details to decide which order works better. As you're organizing your ideas, eliminate details that don't fit.

7. Now write a draft of your essay. Remember that essays include an introductory paragraph with the thesis statement, body para-graphs with support points and specific details, and a concluding paragraph. Feel free to do more prewriting if you need more infor-mation for specific details.

Revising

8. Check your essay for the first three of the four Cs: *concise, credible,* and *clear* writing. Make any necessary changes to your draft.

Editing

9. Check your essay for the fourth C: *correct* writing. Proofread your essay to make sure you have used correct spelling, punctuation, and grammar.

WRITING PRACTICE 2 Write About a Favorite Activity

Write an essay about an activity you enjoy. Begin by offering a brief overview of the activity, and use the body paragraphs to explain what you enjoy about the activity.

Prewriting

1. Choose a topic that interests you.

Possible Topics

Eating dinner at a favorite restaurant

Going to the movies

Hiking

Going to the beach

Participating in a sport

Relaxing at home

2. Freewrite on your topic for ten minutes to find details that will help you explain your enjoyment of this activity.

3. Make an informal outline or ask questions in order to organize your ideas. For her thesis statement, "My idea of heaven is eating dinner in a restaurant," the writer has written complete topic sentences for the outline below.

Cooking Out at the Park

   A. Introduction

      1. Story about disaster preparing dinner

      2. Comments about getting out of the house

   B. Body paragraph 1 topic sentence: My favorite thing about cookouts is that everyone can help.

      1. _____

      2. _____

      3. _____

   C. Body paragraph 2 topic sentence: Second, nobody cares whether we are dressed casually.

      1. _____

      2. _____

      3. _____

D. Body paragraph 3 topic sentence: Another plus is that I can enjoy talking to different people.

1. _____

2. _____

3. _____

E. Body paragraph 4 topic sentence: Finally, clean-up is easy—we just put out the fire and gather up the trash.

1. _____

2. _____

3. _____

F. Conclusion
1. Cooking out at the park is a nice break.
2. Cooking out makes me appreciate cooking at home.

Notice that the writer has developed many important parts of her essay—including transition words at the start of her topic sentences—but still needs specific details.

Drafting

4. Write a thesis statement that includes your main idea, point of view, your purpose, and possibly a map of your essay.

5. Choose support points and specific details to illustrate your support points and make your essay believable.

6. Organize your support points using time sequence (chronological) or emphatic order. Examine your details to decide which order works better. As you're organizing your ideas, eliminate details that don't fit.

7. Now write a draft of your essay. Remember that essays include an introductory paragraph with the thesis statement, body paragraphs with support points and specific details, and a concluding paragraph. Feel free to do more prewriting if you need more information for specific details.

Revising

8. Check your essay for the first three of the four Cs: *concise, credible,* and *clear* writing. Make any necessary changes to your draft.

Editing

9. Check your essay for the fourth C: *correct* writing. Proofread your essay to make sure you have used correct spelling, punctuation, and grammar.

WRITING PRACTICE 3 Write About an Issue That Matters to You

Every day we encounter situations we wish we could change. We also encounter situations that—through other people's time and effort—have changed for the better. Think about what changes you have made or would like to make in your life. Choose either Topic A or Topic B below for your essay.

Topic A

Write an essay about a change that has occurred in your school, neighborhood, or city and that you feel good about. Your change may be as simple as adding speed bumps to a street where children play, or it may be as complex as the decision to elect a new mayor. Choose a topic that you can find information about in the newspaper or online, and *write about why the change you've noticed is positive.* Your thesis statement may be something like "Electing Mayor Johnson has proved to be beneficial to families, students, and the homeless." Then, follow the steps in Writing Practice 2 to develop your essay. Be sure to use specific details from written sources such as newspapers and from your own experiences and observations.

Topic B

Write an essay about a change in your school, neighborhood, or city that you think was a mistake. For instance, you can write about how making a two-way street into a one-way street has inconvenienced bicyclists and drivers. You can also write about how a new policy of keeping city parks open all night has led to more violence in your neighborhood. Your thesis statement may be something like "Making 21st Street into a one-way street has inconvenienced bicyclists and drivers alike." Then, follow the steps in Writing Practice 2 to develop your essay. Be sure to use specific details from written sources such as newspapers and from your own experiences and observations.

CHAPTER SUMMARY

Remember the following in revising an essay:

1. Make sure to connect your support paragraphs to the thesis statement and eliminate unnecessary information to make your essay concise.

2. Include specific details to support and illustrate your ideas.

3. Echo key words from the thesis, use transitional expressions, and use transitional expressions to keep your reader on track.

4. Be willing to read your essay several times, checking for each of the four Cs individually.

MyWritingLab & Lab Activity 26

 For additional practice with revising an essay, go to **www.mywritinglab.com** or complete **Lab Activity 26** in the separate *Resources for Writers* Lab Manual.

PART SIX
Writing for
Different Purposes

SWEENEY TODD
DRIVEN BY
REVENGE

JOHNNY DEPP
HELENA BONHAM CARTER

SWEENEY TODD
THE DEM ER OF FLEET STREET

COMING SOON

Bloody Barber

CONDUCT AN INTERVIEW
Fueled by revenge, barber Sweeney Todd slaughters his customers and has them made into meat pies. Ask two or three people what actions, if any, warrant revenge.

Responding to Images. *What about the photo at left contributes to its overall "creepy" feeling? Explain.*

Essay Exams

Culture Note

HORROR FILMS

Designed to tap into our worst, often hidden, fears, horror films stalk, stab, and slash their way into our emotions. While director Alfred Hitchcock—widely considered the master of suspense—believed that true horror comes in the anticipation of a horrifying act rather than the act itself, millions disagree and flock to see "victims" scream and bleed on screen.

Keeping Watch

JOURNAL RESPONSE Why do you think people watch horror movies? Explain the appeal of such films.

Responding to Images. *What elements make this photo frightening? Explain.*

WHAT'S GOOD ABOUT AN ESSAY EXAM?

No matter how prepared students are, many still panic at the idea of the essay exam. Somehow, sitting down *in class* and facing a blank page seems like a terrifying experience. Since essay exams become more common as you pass through college classes, knowing how to excel on them is crucial. A bright spot, however, is that essay tests—ones written in your classroom during an allotted amount of time—have many advantages. They allow you to do the following:

- Present information in a format chosen by *you*, not the instructor.
- Use whatever details and information *you* think best address the exam questions.
- Organize your information in the way *you* think most effective.
- Add a little style and spice that *you* think makes the essay more interesting.

In short, writing an essay exam gives you power. As long as you've learned the material and become comfortable writing essays, you have an opportunity to show your instructor how much you know and how well you can express that information.

DEVELOPING A PLAN

The key to writing a strong essay for an exam is preparation. The following tips can help you prepare for the challenge of writing an in-class essay.

Before the Exam

Know Your Subject Matter   The first step to writing a good in-class essay is to study your subject. Read everything the instructor has assigned, and memorize key names, places, and dates. The more information you know, and the better you know it, the better your chances of writing a strong essay exam will be.

Predict the Future   Wouldn't all tests be easier if we knew the test questions in advance? Paying attention in class can help you figure out what you need to know. Listen to what information the instructor emphasizes, and notice what information your book develops most. Chances are, an essay question will be on a topic that your textbook or instructor has emphasized.

For instance, Shani, a student in a film history class, prepared for her essay exam by highlighting in her notes the topics that her instructor had spent the most time talking about. Shani also made notes around the topics that were covered the most thoroughly in her textbook. After reviewing her notes, Shani figured that the topic of horror films—among other topics—had a good chance of showing up on her test. To prepare for the test, she wrote out every question she could think of that related to the subject of horror films. Some of her questions were these:

What makes up a horror film?
How long have horror films been around?
What are the different types of horror films?
Which films are considered to be the scariest horror films?
Are the scariest films always the most popular ones?
How have horror films changed since their creation?

Asking questions gives you a chance to focus your studying and organize the information you learn. Asking and then answering questions before the exam also helps you make connections between ideas, which will help you explain key concepts on the test.

Answer Your Questions About the Subject   After you identify possible questions for the exam, make sure you know the answers. Some questions are more likely to end up on an essay exam than others. Questions like "How long have horror films been around?" don't give students much to write about, but the answers are necessary background information for a response to almost any other question. Therefore, Shani made sure she knew the answers to every question she made up. Other questions—such as "What makes up a horror film?"—could definitely end up as essay topics. So understanding the subject—not just memorizing it—is essential to preparing for an essay exam. In fact, one skill that essay exams let you show is the skill of *analysis*, the process of breaking down information and making connections where there might not seem to be any.

Make a Memory Plan   After you've identified possible test questions and answers, think of a one- or two-word term that helps you remember the information. For instance, Shani made the following list in response to the question "What are the different types of horror films?"

1. Monster
2. Slasher
3. Science fiction

Shani made a note that there were more than three different types of horror films, but these were the three that her instructor focused on. Shani decided to memorize the terms *monster, slasher*, and *science fiction*. Those terms triggered her full responses to the exam question.

Other students simply remember the first letter of each word and associate those letters with a saying easy for them to remember. An example of this type of memory device would be remembering MSS, or "Mom Says So."

M = monster
S = slasher
S = science fiction

| **M**om | **S**ays | **S**o |
| **M**onster | **S**lasher | **S**cience fiction |

The point is to find some technique that helps you remember the information you need for the exam.

During the Exam

Read the Instructions   Before you begin writing, *read the directions on the test*. Some students are so eager to start writing that they ignore this step. Following the directions is important because they tell you *how* the instructor wants you to present the information. For instance, if the directions say to compare early horror films to contemporary ones, you could make a huge mistake by focusing on current movies. The box on the next page lists some key terms to keep in mind.

Shani's test question was this:

Discuss and give examples of three main types of horror films.

The key terms for Shani to pay attention to are *discuss, give examples*, and *three*. These terms give her more directions.

- They tell how to approach the topic (*discuss* it and *give examples* of it).
- They tell what aspects of the topic to focus on (the *main three*).

Budget Your Time   Students' greatest fear in writing an essay exam may be that they'll work hard to learn the material and prepare their ideas only to run out of time during the test itself. Never fear! Once you've read the directions, figure out how much time you have to plan, write, and proofread. Suppose you have 50 minutes for the exam, for instance. You could decide to spend your time like this:

10 minutes planning

35 minutes writing

5 minutes proofreading

Chances are, if you're well prepared, you can spend less time planning, but it's better to have a good plan than to forge ahead writing a disorganized essay that may leave out key details. Allotting time for proofreading, even if you don't actually get to read over your essay, gives you options.

Make a Writing Plan   Making a list or an outline is an excellent way to plan your essay. Once you've read the instructions, write out the main concepts you want to include in your response. For instance, when Shani read that she was to discuss three main types of horror films—a question she had anticipated and prepared for—she quickly wrote out her memory tool.

MSS for monster, slasher, science fiction

These terms triggered her memory, and she was able to start planning her essay.

Key Terms for Essay Exams

Analyze means to break something into parts and make connections between those parts. Analysis includes explaining why something happened or why you feel as you do. Other terms indicating analysis include **examine** and **explain.**

Argue means to take a stand on some aspect of the topic (see Chapter 23). Other words indicating that you should take a stand include **defend** and **justify.**

Classify means to group items into subcategories (see Chapter 18).

Compare means to show similarities between things (see Chapter 20).

Contrast means to show differences between things (see Chapter 20).

Define means to state the meaning of a term clearly and completely (see Chapter 22).

Describe means to offer details (see Chapter 17).

Discuss means to carefully look at and present a subject through examples and illustrations.

Discuss causes means to talk about the causes of something (see Chapter 21).

Discuss effects means to talk about the effects or consequences of something (see Chapter 21).

Divide means to break down something into its parts (see Chapter 18).

Evaluate means to talk about a subject's advantages and disadvantages.

Illustrate means to give examples and illustrations (see Chapter 15).

Narrate means to tell how something has developed, step by step (see Chapter 16).

Summarize means to give a brief version of events or ideas (see Chapter 28).

Next, Shani made an outline. She wrote a tentative thesis statement and jotted down details that supported the key terms that she had remembered. Shani's outline looked like this:

Thesis statement: Three types of horror films—monster, slasher, and science fiction—remain popular.

A. Monster—grotesque villain stalks victims; villain can be beast, demon, vampire, mummy, or combination; monsters can be sympathetic but are still frightening

  1. Early monster movies: Nosferatu (1922), early vampire flick; Frankenstein (1931), also on science fiction list; The Mummy (1932); I Was a Teenage Werewolf (1957)

  2. Modern monster movies—Nightmare on Elm Street series (monster Freddie Krueger), Friday the 13th series (monster Jason), Halloween series (monster Michael Myers)

B. Slasher movies—where lots of blood and gore are present

  1. Early slasher films: Tobe Hooper's Texas Chainsaw Massacre (1974) and John Carpenter's Halloween (1978): crazed killer murders everyone in sight, for reasons no one understands

  2. Modern slasher films: Saw (I–III), See No Evil, Hostel

C. Science fiction movies—technology interwoven with evil, leading to terrifying consequences; knowledge taken too far; planets, gadgets, robots, and scientific developments are all part of science fiction horror

  1. Early science fiction horror films—Frankenstein (1931), Invasion of the Body Snatchers (1956), The Fly (1958)

  2. Modern science fiction horror films:—Alien series, The Thing, The Fly (1986)

This rough outline (which is really just an organized list) provides Shani with the structure needed to write her essay. Each type of horror movie could be a support (body) paragraph in her essay; she needed only to add an introduction and conclusion in order to have a complete essay. Shani's completed essay appears on page 443.

Relax By the time you begin writing, you may be so eager to get your ideas down that you may find it hard to relax. Many different techniques can help you remain calm: take a few deep breaths, loosen the muscles in your neck, or think a happy thought. All these methods can help you get beyond the heart-pounding first few minutes of the exam and make a strong start to your essay. Then, once you've begun writing, you can concentrate fully on your response.

Write Neatly on Every Other Line   Rarely will you have the time to copy your essay over to make it neat. You'll need to make sure you get everything on paper, and this process may take up most of your time. It's a good idea, then, to write neatly on every other line of your paper or exam booklet. Writing neatly ensures that your instructor can read your writing on your first draft. Writing on every other line gives you the flexibility to go back and insert information or cross out a misspelled word and write it in above the mistake.

Write a Clear, Organized Essay   You've studied, planned, and relaxed. Now you're ready to write. Begin your essay test just as you begin any other essay.

- Write your introduction with a clear thesis statement.
- Connect your paragraphs to your thesis statement.
- Use the specific details you've learned from your studies to support your ideas.
- Do your best to include transitions and details, but concentrate on following your plan and getting your information down in essay form as quickly as possible.

Remember that the primary purpose of an essay exam is to draw out your knowledge. Therefore, don't worry about having an attention-getting opening or a dramatic conclusion. While these traits are effective tools (and important ones in an out-of-class essay), they are less important than the facts you are writing to show your instructor how much you know.

Here is Shani's completed essay exam.

A Horrible Way to Go

Horror films are made to scare us through just about any means possible on film. Three types of horror films—monster, slasher, and science fiction—are consistently popular with moviegoers.

One type of popular horror film is the monster movie, which features a terrifying, grotesque creature that sets out to capture or kill its ~~victom~~ victim. Sometimes the monster's evil isn't his fault: in Frankenstein's case it comes from the criminal brain that was salvaged for use in him, and in <u>The Phantom of the Opera</u> the monster is a deformed person who has known very little human kindness. Still, both these monsters do scary things. Modern movie monsters seem more evil. Michael Myers in the <u>Halloween</u> movies killed his sister, but he returns to his hometown after escaping from an asylum and resumes his slashing activities and Freddie Krueger in the <u>Nightmare on Elm Street</u> movies is as evil as he is creepy.

In slashers, a newer type of horror film, people are as scared as in monster movies, but they end up "slashed" (like Jason does with a big hunting knife) and dead. <u>Black Chrismas</u>, in which a killer lurks in a sorority house, is considered the but Alfred Hitchcock's <u>Psycho</u> (1960), where Janet Leigh is famously slashed in the shower, inspired the modern slasher first real slasher movie, ~~but there were slashing scenes in earlier movies~~. Another early slasher movie is <u>Texas Chainsaw Massacre</u> (1974), where the killer uses a chainsaw to "slash" and kill his victims. Current slashers include the <u>Saw</u> and <u>Hostel</u> series, which involve torture as well as simple slashing murder.

One last type of horror film is the science fiction horror blend. This type is very popular, but fewer movies make its list than the other two. In science fiction horror, knowledge is often taken too far so that technology is corrupted. Space travel, gadgets, robots, and experiments all appear in science fiction horror films. Early examples include <u>Frankenstein</u> (1931), in which a scientist brings to life a monster he made from various body parts; <u>Invasion of the Body Snatchers</u> (1956), in which strange pods appear on earth and begin "growing" duplicates of people (which means that the original people need to be killed); and <u>The Fly</u> (1958), in which a scientist mixes up his DNA with a fly's. More recently, the <u>Alien</u> series features a seemingly indestructible space creature that devours humans.

Even though each type of horror movie has specific features that classify it as monster, slasher, or science fiction, some movies end up on more than one list. Both Freddie Krueger and Jason, for example, slash their victims, and both seem to be monsters. At the end of each movie, however, all that really matters is whether you were scared, and monsters, slashers, and science fiction horror movies are just the ticket to do that.

EXERCISE 1 Analyzing an Essay Exam

Reread "A Horrible Way to Go." Then, answer the questions that follow.

1. What is the thesis statement? _____

_____

2. List the three types of horror movies that Shani discusses.

a. _____

b. _____

c. _____

3. What transitions does the writer use to signal the start of each new point in the body paragraphs?

a. _____

b. _____

c. _____

4. In the topic sentence for each body paragraph, the writer echoes the same key words from the thesis statement. What are these

words? _____

5. What are the three sentence-level revisions the writer makes?

Paragraph 2: _____

Paragraph 3: _____

_____

_____

EXERCISE 2 Analyzing Essay Exam Questions for Key Terms

The groups of sentences below are possible essay exam questions. Underline the key words in the sentences. An example has been done for you.

> The Civil War had a huge effect on the entire U.S. economy. Write an essay discussing the most important economic effects of the Civil War.

1. Both Marley the dog in *Marley and Me* and Rosie the elephant in *Water for Elephants* prove themselves to be independent thinkers. Write an essay comparing the main animal characters in these two novels.

2. How are soccer and hockey different? Write an essay contrasting the two sports.

3. How can a disorganized student make better use of his or her time? Write an essay explaining what steps a person can take to become more organized.

4. If passed, the Equal Rights Amendment would prohibit denial of rights on the basis of gender. Do you think the Equal Rights Amendment should be added to the Constitution? Write an essay arguing your position on this issue.

5. Many people debate whether public funds should be used to start independent charter schools as an option parents choose for their children. Write an essay agreeing or disagreeing with this concept.

 CHECKLIST Developing an Essay Exam

Before the Exam

- Study the material you will be tested on.
- Practice asking and answering questions you think may appear on the exam.
- Use memory plans to help you remember important details.

During the Exam: Prewriting

- Read the exam directions carefully, identifying key words.
- Budget your time, allowing for planning, writing, and proofreading.
- Use prewriting strategies to get your ideas on paper.

Drafting

- Write a thesis statement that addresses the exam question.
- Select convincing support points and specific details based on your exam preparation.
- Organize your ideas, using transitions to connect your support points for your reader.
- Write neatly on every other line of the paper or exam booklet.

Revising

- If time permits, revise your work, as necessary, according to the first three of the four Cs: *concise*, *credible*, and *clear* writing.

Editing

- If time permits, proofread your work for sentence-level errors to address the fourth C: *correct* writing.

WRITING PRACTICE 1 Preparing for an Essay Exam

Pretend you are taking an essay exam in one of your classes. Now, follow the instructions below.

1. Make up three questions that your instructor could ask you to write an essay about.

    a. _____

    b. _____

    c. _____

2. Then, study the material to find where you can find answers to your questions.

    Question   **Answer**

    a. _____   **a.** _____

    b. _____   **b.** _____

    c. _____   **c.** _____

3. Make an outline of your response to one of the questions, complete with a working thesis statement.

    A. _____

        1. _____

        2. _____

        3. _____

    B. _____

        1. _____

        2. _____

        3. _____

    C. _____

        1. _____

        2. _____

        3. _____

WRITING PRACTICE 2 Writing an Essay Exam in Response to a Reading

Follow the guidelines below to write an essay based on one of the readings in this book.

1. Choose any reading from Part 9, "Readings for Informed Writing."
2. Read the selection you have chosen.
3. Follow the steps outlined in this chapter to prepare yourself to write an essay exam on that essay. Be sure to include a list of possible essay questions about the reading.
4. Write a response to one of the essay questions you wrote, following the steps in the checklist on page 446 and allowing yourself only 30 minutes to complete your essay.

WRITING PRACTICE 3 Writing an Essay Exam on a General Interest Topic

Without realizing it, we are frequently affected by situations and decisions that may seem removed from us. Questions involving some everyday situations are listed below. Choose an essay question from the list of topics below. Then, write an essay exam in response to the question. Follow the steps outlined in the checklist on page 446 when you are planning and writing your essay.

Topic A

Pet overpopulation is a problem that concerns many people. Though many domestic animals are well cared for, others are homeless. Should pet owners be forced to have their pets spayed or neutered in order to cut down on the number of unwanted animals? *Write an essay discussing the benefits or drawbacks of forcing pet owners to spay or neuter their pets*.

Topic B

Movies and advertising make light of rude passengers disrupting airline flights. Should the airlines be allowed to take steps to control or punish people who are rude, for the sake of their other passengers? *Write an essay arguing that airline personnel should or should not be allowed to take steps to control the behavior of rude travelers for the sake of their other passengers*.

Topic C

Many contemporary movies are remakes of movies made years ago. Many movies also explore the same material that earlier movies explored. *Write an essay comparing or contrasting two films that focus on the same time period, conflict, or person*. Some movie pairs to consider are these:

There Will Be Blood and *No Country for Old Men*

Ocean's Eleven (with George Clooney) and *Ocean's Thirteen*

Chicago and *Sweeney Todd*

Hostel and *Saw*

Waitress and *Chocolat*

Enchanted and *Cinderella* (Disney version)

Spider-Man and *Batman Begins*

King Kong (1933 or 1976 version) and *King Kong* (2005)

Atonement and *Pride and Prejudice* (2005 version)

Chronicles of Narnia: Prince Caspian and *The Golden Compass*

Collateral and *Minority Report*

Topic D
Many parents are concerned that CDs with certain lyrics are inappropriate for their children. Should local governments be able to forbid the sale of CDs whose lyrics they consider offensive? *Write an essay explaining why local governments should or should not be able to forbid the sale of CDs whose lyrics they consider offensive.*

Topic E
Many schools raise money for academic and extracurricular activities by having their students sell products—candy, magazines, entertainment guides—door to door. Should people support their neighborhood schools by purchasing these items, even if they don't need the items being sold? *Write an essay arguing that people should or should not support their neighborhood schools by buying things they don't necessarily need.*

CHAPTER SUMMARY

Follow these guidelines for writing in-class essays:

- Study and memorize the material, trying to imagine what questions will be asked.
- Be sure you understand the directions.
- Budget your writing time, allowing yourself to get organized.
- Write neatly on every other line.
- Review your work if time permits.

MyWritingLab & Lab Activity 27

mywritinglab   For additional help with essay exams, go to **www.mywritinglab.com** or complete **Lab Activity 27** in the separate *Resources for Writers* Lab Manual.

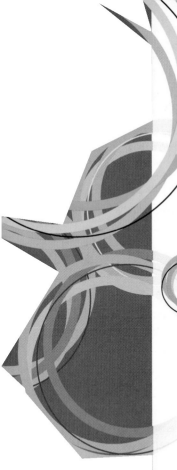

Writing Summaries

SUMMARIES ARE USEFUL

A **summary** concisely restates a longer document—such as an essay, an article, or a book—emphasizing the key points and eliminating the less important details. When you write a summary, follow these guidelines.

- Use your own words, though you may want to borrow key phrases from the original.
- *Do not add your opinions or views of the material you're summarizing.*
- Present only what the original writer had to say.
- Give only the main points of the original but not the specific details unless one or more of them is unusually important.

Malcolm X (1925–1965)

FOOD FOR THOUGHT One of the civil rights movement's greatest advocates, Malcolm X preached ideas that did not initially include racial harmony. Malcolm X's message was not always heard favorably, but he was extremely influential. Who today speaks a message that people may not always want to hear? ***Responding to Images.*** *Based on the photo [at left], what can you conclude about Malcolm X?*

WRITING AN EFFECTIVE SUMMARY

A good summary presents the main support points without misrepresenting the original text.

Step 1: Look Over the Document for Clues About What's Most Important   The most important ideas in a reading will stand out in some way: in the title, the thesis statement, the introductory paragraph, the topic sentences of body paragraphs, or the conclusion. Important ideas may also be identified through headings, italicized words, or words in bold print.

Step 2: Read the Entire Document   To summarize a reading accurately, you must understand it completely. Read the entire document to get a general idea of what the writer is saying.

Step 3: Reread the Document and Mark the Important Ideas   The more you work with the material you're summarizing, the better you will understand and remember it. Rereading and underlining or highlighting key ideas is a good way to proceed. If you're not sure whether to underline an item, mark it and move on.

Step 4: Write a Rough Draft Using Your Own Words Give the information in your summary in the same order that the writer uses in the original document. Do not use expressions such as "the author claims" or "the writer points out," which are unnecessary and make the summary longer than it has to be.

Step 5: Check Your Summary Against the Original After you've drafted your summary, make sure that you have included the important details and omitted secondary or irrelevant details. Your summary should devote the same percentage of space to key points as the original does. Additionally, make certain that the information in your summary is accurate. Don't exaggerate or downplay details; simply restate the facts as they appear in the original.

Step 6: Revise Your Draft for Concise, Credible, and Clear Writing Remember: The benefit of a summary is its brevity, so omit anything not absolutely essential to communicating the points of the original. Also, make sure that the connections between ideas are clear and logical.

Step 7: Proofread Your Summary Correct any errors in spelling, punctuation, and grammar, following the editing tips from Chapter 6 for help with proofreading.

Step 8: Document Your Source At the end of the summary, include information about the source—the author's name and the title and publication information the book, magazine, journal, newspaper, or online database or Web site where you found the original article.

A MODEL SUMMARY

The following is a summary of an essay. The original article is approximately 900 words long, but the summary is about 150 words. Note how the writer includes some quotations from the article but few specific details.

In the essay "A Homemade Education," Malcolm X writes about how reading and copying the dictionary helped him discover the "freedom" of learning. Malcolm X writes that he started trying to improve his writing skills to communicate better with Elijah Muhammad. Malcolm X also explains how he wanted to build up his "stock of knowledge" to be able to contribute more to conversations. However, reading proved frustrating because he didn't understand many words. Malcolm X requested a dictionary from prison officials and began copying it to improve his penmanship as well as his reading and writing abilities. Malcolm X compares the dictionary to an encyclopedia, and he says that as his knowledge of words broadened, he was able "for the first time to pick up a book and read and now begin to understand what the book was saying." He became fascinated with books, which led to a feeling of freedom even while he was in prison.

—Malcolm X, "A Homemade Education," in *The Autobiography of Malcolm X.*

EXERCISE 1 Analyzing a Summary

Reread the summary on pages 452–453. Then, answer the questions below.

1. What is the thesis of the article being summarized? _____

_____

2. What motivates Malcolm X to improve his reading and writing?

_____

3. What does Malcolm X do to improve his reading and writing?

_____

4. To what does Malcolm X compare the dictionary? _____

5. What is one result of Malcolm X's copying the dictionary?

_____

WRITING PRACTICE 1 Write a Summary of a Chapter

Write a one-paragraph summary of a chapter from a book you are reading for another class. Concentrate on including those ideas that you think you'll need to remember for an exam. Follow the guidelines for writing a summary.

WRITING PRACTICE 2 Write a Summary of an Article

Read an article from a magazine or newspaper. Then, write a one-paragraph summary of it. Make sure you include only those details communicating the main point of the article. Include a copy of the article when you hand in your summary.

WRITING PRACTICE 3 Write a Summary of an Oral Presentation

Watch a television program, or listen to an interview on the radio. Then, write a one-paragraph summary of the program or interview. Begin your summary by stating the name and date of the program or interview you're summarizing.

CHAPTER SUMMARY

Remember the following in writing a summary:

- Look for clues as to the document's overall meaning.
- Read the entire document.
- Reread and highlight the document.
- Write a rough draft in your own words.
- Check your summary against the original.
- Revise your draft for concise, credible, clear writing.
- Proofread your summary.
- Document your source.

MyWritingLab & Lab Activity 28

mywritinglab For additional help with writing summaries, go to **www.mywritinglab. com** or complete **Lab Activity 28** in the separate *Resources for Writers* Lab Manual.

Writing to Get a Job

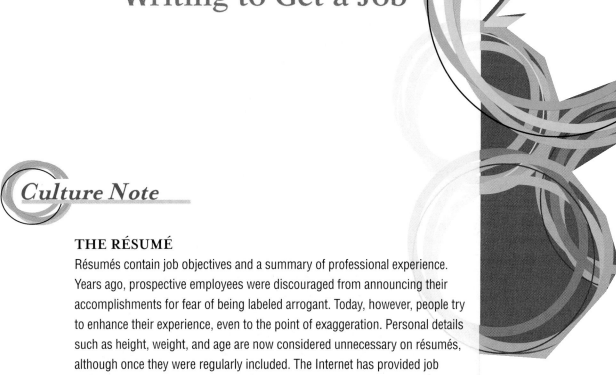

EMPLOYERS VALUE GOOD WRITING SKILLS

For most people, writing is a necessary skill throughout life. Even people in careers that seem to require little writing—plumbers and mechanics, for instance—need to keep records, fill out order forms, track inventory, and apply for bank or credit accounts to keep their businesses running smoothly. Whatever career you want to pursue, learning to write well can give you an edge in the job market.

CRAFTING A RÉSUMÉ

A **résumé** is a brief summary (usually one page) of your work qualifications. It is a record of your education, training, and job experience. The purpose of a résumé is to introduce you to a potential employer and get you an interview. The model below shows what one type of résumé looks like. The guidelines that follow it will help you create a résumé.

A Model Résumé

Your name, full address, and phone number

Jane Michaels
1750 43rd Avenue Sacramento, CA 95823 (916) 555-2388

Items listed from most to least recent

EXPERIENCE:

Sales Associate, Grand Department Store, 8/05–present
I was trained to work in the Infants and Toddlers Department, but I have worked in many different areas when they needed help.

Sales Clerk, Monroe's Department Store, 7/03–7/05
I was primarily responsible for working in the Children's Department, but I also covered the teen and misses sections.

Job title, employer, and dates employed

Brief description of job

Diploma, educational institution, and year graduated

EDUCATION:

Bachelor of Arts, Fashion Merchandising, California State University, Stockton, 6/08

Associate of Arts, English, Sacramento City College, Sacramento, 6/03

Diploma, Hiram Redding High School, Sacramento, 6/00

SPECIAL SKILLS:

Through my work in retail clothing stores, I have developed organizational skillls. I have also become proficient at using both cash registers and adding machines.

Relevant skills

Significant volunteer activities

ACTIVITIES:

Volunteer Story Reader for Children's Program, Belle Rivers Public Library, 8/05–present
I spend two hours a month reading stories to visiting children.

Availability of references

REFERENCES:

Available on request.

Making Your Résumé Look Professional

Print your résumé on good-quality paper, with a one-inch margin on all sides. Use an easy-to-read format, and always send a clean copy.

Emphasizing Your Good Points

While we're often taught not to brag about our accomplishments, a résumé is the place to emphasize your qualifications and skills. Mention any relevant extracurricular or volunteer activities you've been involved in. Don't, however, mention grades—unless they're Bs or better—or hobbies or personal interests. Always be honest on your résumé; exaggerating or fibbing about your accomplishments or responsibilities in previous jobs can have negative consequences.

Following a Logical Format

It's usual to start with your work experience. If you have no work experience, you can start with your education. Use a form of organization that's easy for an employer to follow. List experiences and educational activities in *reverse order*, starting with your most recent experience and working your way backward.

Be Brief

Chances are, an employer has limited time and many applications to read. Keep your résumé to a single page.

Omitting Unnecessary or Negative Details

Don't list your age, marital status, height, weight, health, or other personal details. Additionally, don't mention your previous salaries or reasons why you left your last job. These details say nothing about your qualifications for the job, and they may unfairly bias an employer against you.

Proofread, Proofread, Proofread!

A potential employer may interpret errors on your résumé as a sign that you are careless or sloppy. Ask a friend to read your résumé, too.

Mention That References Are Available

Do not write the names of your **references** (people who can vouch for you as a responsible employee) on your résumé. However, keep a list of names, addresses, and phone numbers that you can provide if the prospective employer asks for references. Make sure you've asked the people you're claiming as references for their permission to do so.

EXERCISE 1 Planning Your Résumé

Use the form below to organize the information for your résumé. Be sure your information is accurate and clearly stated.

Résumé Outline Form

Name: _____

Address and phone number: _____

_____

E-mail address: _____

_____

_____

Experience: _____

_____

_____

Education: _____

_____

_____

Special skills: _____

_____

Activities: _____

_____

References: _____

_____

WRITING A LETTER TO APPLY FOR A JOB

In addition to preparing a clear, error-free résumé, you must also write a **cover letter,** also called a **letter of application,** to a potential employer. The purpose of this letter is twofold: to introduce you to the employer and to highlight your skills.

When you write your cover letter, follow these guidelines.

- Make your letter look professional.
- Emphasize your good points.
- Follow a logical format.
- Be brief.
- Omit unnecessary or negative details.
- Proofread for accuracy.

Also follow these additional guidelines, illustrated in the model cover letter on page 460.

Give Your Address and the Date   Place your full return address and the date at the top of the letter.

Address the Letter Correctly   This step is very important. Make sure that the inside address (the address of the person you are writing to) appears *exactly* as it does in the advertisement for the job. Double-check the spelling of any contact names or addresses so that they are correct in your letter.

Begin with a Greeting   Part of making a good impression, even on paper, is being polite. If you know the name of the person who will read your application, use it. If not, you may open your letter with the greeting "Dear Sir or Madam."

Clearly State Your Purpose   In the first paragraph, tell the employer that you are writing to apply for a job, and explain how you heard about the job.

State Your Qualifications for the Job and Willingness to Be Interviewed   Briefly and clearly say why you are qualified for the job, and direct the reader to your résumé. Tell the employer that you are ready and willing to meet for an interview. Emphasize your enthusiasm for the job.

End Your Letter with a Closing Expression   Offering an appropriate closing will make a positive final impression on an employer. Be sure to sign

A Model Cover Letter

Your return address	1750 43rd Avenue Sacramento, CA 95823
Date	November 15, 2008
Inside address	Ms. Rachel Nguyen Manager Belle Femme Clothing Store 6601 Fourth Avenue Sacramento, CA 95864
Greeting	Dear Ms. Nguyen:
Your purpose	I am writing to apply for the job of assistant manager of the Fourth Avenue Belle Femme Clothing Store as advertised in the <u>Sacramento Gazette</u>.
Your qualifications	In addition to completing my associate of arts degree from Sacramento City College, I am on my way to achieving a bachelor of arts degree in Fashion Merchandising from California State University in Stockton. I have learned about retail clothing stores both from my course work and from my two positions at Grand Department Store and Monroe's. As my résumé indicates, I am well qualified to work in your store.
Your availability for an interview	I am very interested in working for you and would be more than willing to come for an interview. I am a high-energy employee who works hard and eagerly takes on responsibility. I have confidence that I can make a positive difference in your store.
Closing	Sincerely,
Your signature and typed name	*Jane Michaels* Jane Michaels
Enclosure notation	enc.

your name in addition to typing it. A polite closing expression is "Sincerely" or "Sincerely yours."

Enclose Your Résumé   Put your résumé in the same envelope with your cover letter. Add the notation "enc." opposite your typed name to show that an item is enclosed.

WRITING AND SENDING E-MAIL

Thanks to the Internet, people can be in touch quietly, easily, and immediately. E-mail also has the added benefit of not needing to be "answered" right away; you can send a message, and your recipient can read and respond when there's time. Be careful, however: just as there are rules for how to write business letters or how to properly address people on the telephone, there are also rules for e-mail. Consider the following list.

Avoid Sending Potentially Offensive Messages. Think twice before sending an e-mail message that could even remotely be considered offensive. Particularly at the office—where employers have a legal right to read your (even deleted) messages—what you think is a good joke might result in a bad ending. A good rule of thumb is never to send a message via e-mail that you wouldn't want someone besides your intended recipient to read.

Avoid Sending Sensitive Messages. Even if you're dying to communicate something sensitive, don't do it through e-mail. For sensitive information, give people the courtesy of addressing them face-to-face, if possible; a phone call should be your next attempt. Sending e-mail, especially anonymous e-mail, to deliver a message that someone might not want to hear is unprofessional and impolite.

Avoid Sending Spam or Chain E-mail. There's little worse than opening an e-mail from a friend only to find that it contains a long, boring message or one that urges you to send copies of the e-mail to five people. While a few people might enjoy such messages, most do not. If you really think people will be interested in a forwarded message, do the following: make sure the message is legitimate, and ask potential recipients for permission before you send it.

Avoid Sending Unedited Messages. Even though e-mail is an informal way to communicate, sending a misspelled, error-ridden message is a sure way to confuse your reader and diminish your credibility. Most e-mail software can check grammar and spelling. If yours doesn't, cut and paste your message into a word processing program that has these functions, and then run a check.

Respond Quickly. Waiting too long to answer someone's e-mail sends a message of disrespect to that person. Even if you're too busy to answer an e-mail fully, sending a quick message—such as "I got your message and will get back to you by tomorrow"—will pay the sender the courtesy of a response. In general, you should answer e-mail messages within one day.

WRITING PRACTICE 1 Write a Cover Letter

Advertisements for three jobs appear below.

Dental—Registered Dental Assistant (RDA)

Seeking highly motivated RDA to join our practice. No experience necessary. Computer experience helpful. Many perks and great benefits. Send résumé and cover letter to Ruth Watkins, 72 Florence Boulevard, Fair Park, IL 60617.

Grocery—Section Manager

Now accepting applications for Bakery/Deli Plaza Manager. Great opportunity to work in our chain's nationally recognized flagship store in Northern Arizona. Send application, résumé, and cover letter to Aaron Greentree, 3315 Canyon Avenue, Flagstaff, AZ 43201.

Mechanic—Lawn Equipment

Established turf equipment company is seeking mechanics to work in our La Salle Island repair and new equipment preparation facility. The ideal candidate will have experience in electrical and hydraulic operations. Lawn equipment repairs experience a plus. This is an excellent career position. E-mail résumé and cover letter to Tomtruman@Elkke.com or send to Tom Truman, 4537 Lawn Lane, Atlanta, GA, 77089.

Pretend that you are applying for one of these jobs. Write a rough draft of a letter of application, following the guidelines in this chapter. Concentrate on writing a strong opening paragraph. If possible, ask your instructor or current employer for tips on how to make your opening paragraph more effective.

WRITING PRACTICE 2 Respond to a Help Wanted Ad

Read the advertisements for jobs in a local newspaper or magazine. Then, prepare your résumé as if you were applying for one of the jobs. Next, write a letter of application with clear opening and closing paragraphs, a detailed middle paragraph, and a polite greeting and closing expression. Take care to type the correct contact information in your letter.

CHAPTER SUMMARY

In applying for a job, remember the following:

- Write a résumé that is concise, positive, and professional.
- Write a cover letter that includes your purpose and qualifications.
- Proofread any document sent for professional purposes, even e-mail.

MyWritingLab & Lab Activity 29

mywritinglab For additional help with writing to get a job, go to **www.mywritinglab.com** or complete **Lab Activity 29** in the separate *Resources for Writers* Lab Manual.

PART SEVEN
Writing
Correct Sentences

Fallen Giants

OBSERVE YOUR WORLD How important are large structures in creating a feeling of pride or significance about a place? Pay attention to the eye-catching buildings or monuments in your area and write about how important they are to your area's image.

Responding to Images. *What is your gut reaction to the photo at right? Explain, making note of the loss associated with the picture.*

463

Prepositional Phrases

30

Culture Note

FABLES

In a fable, a fictitious story meant to teach a lesson, the characters are usually talking animals whose actions mirrors human behavior. Fables often combine entertainment with education and are an important part of folklore.

THE HARE AND THE TORTOISE

The Tortoise and the Hare

WRITE A PARAGRAPH

Despite the fast-paced, high-tech lifestyle of many Americans, the lessons from Aesop's fables, such as "The Tortoise and the Hare," still hold meaning. What childhood lessons still hold meaning for you? Write a paragraph discussing which lessons learned in childhood are important to you.

Responding to Images. What indication is there in the photo to the left that the tortoise is the unexpected victor of the race?

IDENTIFYING PREPOSITIONAL PHRASES

A **phrase** is a group of related words lacking a subject and a verb. A **prepositional phrase** is a phrase beginning with a preposition. Many prepositional phrases show spatial and time relationships between ideas. Recognizing prepositional phrases can help you identify the subject and verb of a sentence, as you will see later in this chapter.

The easiest way to identify prepositional phrases is to look for prepositions (see the box below). **A preposition** shows the relationship between a noun or pronoun and the rest of a sentence. The prepositions are underlined in the following examples.

<u>in</u> the house   <u>with</u> her sister
<u>after</u> the game   <u>for</u> breakfast

Some of the words listed in the box below can also function as other parts of speech, such as conjunctions.

The words *to* and *through* are common prepositions. Here, *to* and *through* begin two prepositional phrases.

The way <u>to</u> a man's heart is <u>through</u> his stomach.

Common Prepositions

aboard	between	out
about	beyond	outside
above	by	over
according to	concerning	than
across	despite	through
after	during	throughout
against	except	to
along	for	toward
along with	from	under
among	in	underneath
around	inside	until
at	into	up
before	like	upon
behind	near	with
below	of	within
beneath	off	without
beside	on	
besides	onto	

To determine the end of a phrase, remember that *every preposition asks a question*. The noun that answers the question is the end of the prepositional phrase. When you see the word *to* in a sentence, ask yourself "To what?" When you see the word *through*, ask yourself "Through what?" In the example above, the nouns that answer those two questions—*heart* and *stomach*—mark the ends of the prepositional phrases.

There is no shortcut to learning the prepositions. You simply need to learn the list on page 466.

EXERCISE 1 Writing Prepositional Phrases

Write two prepositional phrases using each of the prepositions below. Practice answering the question that the preposition asks. An example is done for you.

Over	**a.** _Over the rainbow_	**b.** _Over the telephone_
1. After	**a.** _____	**b.** _____
2. Below	**a.** _____	**b.** _____
3. Toward	**a.** _____	**b.** _____
4. Until	**a.** _____	**b.** _____
5. Without	**a.** _____	**b.** _____

Using Prepositional Phrases to Identify the Subject and Verb of a Sentence

After you have identified the prepositional phrases in a sentence, cross them out. For example:

The way ~~to a man's heart~~ is ~~through his stomach~~.

You're left with *The way is*. These remaining words are the subject and verb of the sentence: *The way* is the subject, and *is* is the verb. By eliminating the prepositional phrases, you've made the job of identifying the subject and verb much easier.

Watching Out for Infinitives

An **infinitive** is a verb form that looks like a prepositional phrase but isn't. The infinitives underlined below are made up of the word *to* plus a verb— for example, *to run*.

> Henry ran fast <u>to escape</u> the school bully.
> <u>To get</u> good grades, Marian studied hard every night.
> Before I could ask <u>to go</u> to the concert with Ben, he invited me.

Note that the infinitive in each sentence is *not* the verb.

EXERCISE 2 Identifying Prepositional Phrases

Identify the thirty-six prepositional phrases in the following sentences. Underline the prepositional phrases, and circle the prepositions. An example is done for you.

> "The Grasshopper and the Ants" is a fable (by) Aesop.

1. One day in winter some ants were drying their supply of food.

2. The food was lying in a pool of water after a long rain.

3. A hungry grasshopper approached them and asked for a few grains of corn.

4. The grasshopper appeared to be weak from hunger.

5. The ants kept working at their drying for a long time until a few of them turned to the grasshopper.

6. The ants asked the grasshopper why she had no food of her own.

7. The grasshopper first turned away and then turned back to the ants with a tear in her eye.

8. The grasshopper complained that during summer she had had no time for gathering food.

9. "What," asked the ants, "kept you from finding food until winter?"

10. The grasshopper's tears flowed to the ground as she thought about her sad plight.

11. She said she was singing underneath a shady leaf and had no time left for work.

12. The ants went back to their hardworking sisters and discussed the matter concerning the hungry grasshopper.

13. Coming to an agreement among themselves, the ants all turned back toward the grasshopper.

14. "If you spent the days of summer singing, then you can spend the nights of winter dancing," said the ants, sending her away without a bite.

15. The moral of the story is "It is best to prepare today for the needs of tomorrow."

EDITING PRACTICE

Identify the thirteen prepositional phrases in the following paragraph. Underline the prepositional phrases, and circle the prepositions. There may not be a prepositional phrase in every sentence.

The North Wind and the Sun: A Fable

The North Wind and the Sun each claimed to be stronger than the other. Finally they agreed to test their powers on a traveler to see who could get him to remove his coat. The North Wind tried first, whirling furiously around the man, grabbing at his coat in a burst of power. But the harder the wind blew, the more closely the man wrapped his coat around himself. Next, it was the Sun's turn. First, the Sun beamed gently upon the traveler, who unbuttoned his coat and strolled with it loosely hanging open. Then the Sun shone brightly in full strength, and when the man had gone only a few steps, he was happy to take off his coat and continue without it. The moral of the story is this: Gentle persuasion works better than force.

WRITING PRACTICE

Choose one lesson from the fables of this chapter and explain how it is meaningful for you. Explain, for instance, how the lesson of preparing for the future has meaning for you. Circle the prepositional phrases when you finish.

MyWritingLab & Lab Activity 30

mywritinglab For additional help with prepositions, go to **www.mywritinglab.com** or complete **Lab Activity 30** in the separate *Resources for Writers* Lab Manual.

31

Subjects and Verbs

THE MAIN PARTS OF A SENTENCE

Subjects and verbs are the basic units of sentences. In fact, a group of words can't be a sentence unless it includes both a subject and a verb. Some sentences also have **objects,** words that receive the action or direction of another word such as a verb or preposition.

IDENTIFYING VERBS

Verbs tell us what's going on in a sentence. They express any action or change in time and condition that takes place. **Main verbs** communicate the primary action or state of being in a sentence while **helping verbs** let us know when and under what conditions the action of the main verb took place. **Linking verbs** connect the subject to words that identify or modify it. Read the sentences below, and for each sentence, ask "What's going on?"

Poor Richard's Almanack

FOOD FOR THOUGHT   Known for its inventions and pithy sayings, Ben Franklin's book *Poor Richard's Almanack* contains expressions we still hear today, such as "Haste makes waste." Write a few sentences explaining how certain expressions—heard from people you know—are meaningful for you.

Responding to Visuals. *Just from observing the photo above, what can you tell about people's feelings toward Ben Franklin (the one holding the paper)?*

A rolling stone <u>gathers</u> no moss. (The stone is *gathering* no moss.)

Silence <u>is</u> golden. (Silence is identified as *being* golden.)

Still waters <u>run</u> deep. (Waters are *running* deep.)

Note that for the sentence containing *is*, the explanation of what's going on includes the word *being*: silence is *being* golden. Some verbs, such as the verb *to be*, do not show overt action so much as a state of being. Forms of the verb *to be* (*am, is, are, was, were, be, being, been*) can act as the main verb of a sentence.

Complete Verbs

Helping verbs work with main verbs to communicate *when* an action took place or the *conditions* under which it took place. The **complete verb** in a sentence includes helping verbs and main verbs. In order to fully understand the rules of grammar and punctuation, you need to be able to identify *all parts of the verb*.

The complete verbs are underlined in the following sentences. The helping verbs (in bold print) tell *when* the action of the main verb takes place.

> A man **is** known by the company he keeps. (*Is* indicates when someone is known by his company: now, not in the past or future.)

> The chickens **have** come home to roost. (*Have* indicates when the chickens came home: some time before now.)

In the following sentences, the helping verbs indicate *condition*. The helping verbs qualify whether or not the action of the main verb will actually take place.

> I **would** try harder to memorize proverbs if I had help. (*Would* makes it clear that the writer will try harder only after receiving help.)

> Julia **may** read the book you lent her. (*May* indicates a possibility that Julia will not read the book.)

Sometimes both types of helping verbs—those indicating time and those indicating condition—are used together in a sentence. The complete verbs in the following sentences are underlined.

> She may have heard the news. (*May* casts doubt as to whether she has heard the news; *have* indicates that the news was received sometime before now.)

> You should be going to work. (*Should* communicates a recommendation that someone go to work; *be* indicates that the action of *going* takes place now, not in the past.)

Linking Verbs

Linking verbs, which link the subject to words that identify or modify it, often indicate action that can't be seen.

> Tom appears happy to be home.

> Shaunte feels better about her decision to stay in school.

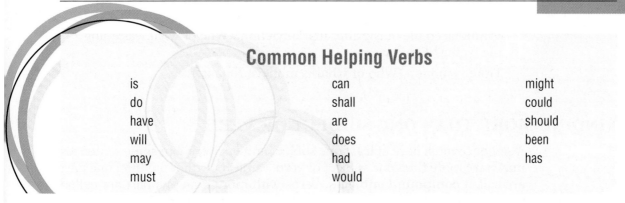

Common Helping Verbs

is	can	might
do	shall	could
have	are	should
will	does	been
may	had	has
must	would	

Think of linking verbs as equal signs when they are used as the main verb in a sentence. For instance, you could think of "Natalie is my best friend" as "Natalie = my best friend." Other linking verbs that act as equal signs are *appear*, *be* (*am*, *is*, *are*, *was*, *were*), *become*, *feel*, *look*, and *seem*.

EXERCISE 1 Identifying the Complete Verb

Underline the complete verb in each sentence below. *Hint:* Cross out any prepositional phrases first. The first one is done for you.

1. Certainly that new kid ~~at school~~ will be a thorn ~~in my side~~.

2. I have learned to take my grandmother's advice with a grain of salt.

3. Nicola is falling for the salesman's pitch hook, line, and sinker.

4. I would have gone skiing if not for my conscience.

5. Tonight at seven o'clock I will be off to the land of Nod.

IDENTIFYING THE SUBJECT

The **subject** of a sentence says what the sentence is about. Once you've identified the verb, you can find the subject by asking yourself *who* or *what* is performing the action of the verb. The subject of a sentence is often a **noun**—the name of a person, place, thing, or idea. In the following sentences, the subjects are in bold print and the verbs are underlined.

Simple **conversation** breaks the ice at a party. (Who or what is doing the breaking? A *conversation* is.)

Frank <u>faced</u> the music after his conviction. (Who or what was doing the facing? *Frank* was.)

Time <u>is</u> money. (Who or what is money? *Time* is.)

FINDING MORE THAN ONE SUBJECT OR VERB

A sentence must have at least one subject and one verb, but some sentences may have more than one subject or verb. Subjects with more than one part are called **compound subjects.** Verbs with more than one part are called **compound verbs.** Finding subjects and verbs involves finding *all* subjects and verbs in a sentence.

<u>John</u> and <u>Jane</u> cut a rug at the dance. (*John* and *Jane* are the subjects of the sentence.)

John and Jane <u>danced</u> and <u>sang</u> until the cows came home. (Danced and sang are the verbs of the sentence.)

EXERCISE 2 Identifying Subjects and Verbs

Read the following sentences. Underline the subjects once and the complete verbs twice. Some sentences contain more than one subject or verb. *Hint:* Cross out any prepositional phrases first.

1. Tad and Rhea do things by the book.

2. When the cat is away, the mice will play.

3. You can never teach an old dog new tricks.

4. The grass is always greener on the other side of the fence.

5. Absence makes the heart grow fonder.

6. Jill does not judge a book by its cover.

7. Lightning never strikes twice in the same place.

8. Too many cooks spoil the broth.

9. You can't unscramble an egg.

10. One good turn deserves another.

WHAT TO WATCH OUT FOR

Finding subjects and verbs is often an easy process. However, some sentence elements can look like subjects and verbs and, thus, make the identification process more difficult. Some of the most common causes for confusion are explained below.

Nouns That Follow the Verb

Marco still <u>carries</u> a torch for Francine.

In the sentence above, you might have been tempted to choose *torch* as the subject of the underlined verb. This word isn't part of a prepositional phrase, and it is a noun. However, *torch* is not the subject of the sentence. Ask yourself who or what does the carrying. You can see that Marco, not the torch, is performing the action of the verb. Thus, *Marco* is the subject.

The subjects are underlined in the sentences below, and any nouns following the verb are in italics.

<u>Mom</u> baked a *cake* for my birthday. (*Mom*, not *cake*, is doing the baking.)

<u>Ana</u> found a gold *watch* near her *house*. (*Ana*, not *watch* or *house*, did the finding.)

Pronouns

A **pronoun** is a word that can take the place of a noun. Pronouns as well as nouns can be subjects. Watch for the following pronouns as the subjects of sentences.

I	it	you	we
he	they	she	

Treat pronoun subjects exactly the same way that you would treat any other subjects.

<u>I</u> went to the store.   <u>She</u> reads frequently.

Commands

Sometimes the subject of a sentence will be the pronoun *you*, but the word *you* will not appear in the sentence. For instance, in the saying "Don't burn your bridges behind you," the subject is actually *you*. Written out completely, the sentence is "(You) don't burn your bridges behind you." Because the sentence is a **command**—an order to do something—the writer doesn't need to include the subject specifically. Keep in mind that if a sentence appears to be giving an order, the subject is probably *you*. Each pair of sentences below contains one sentence where *you* is not written and one sentence where *you* is written in parentheses.

Wait for me after the game.   Don't go near the fire!

(You) wait for me after the game. (You) don't go near the fire!

Understanding Objects

- A **direct object** is a noun or pronoun that receives the action of the verb.
  Ed drove his <u>car</u> too fast.
- An **indirect object** is a noun or pronoun that receives the direct object.
  I made <u>Alan</u> a sandwich.
- The **object of a preposition** is the noun or pronoun introduced by a preposition.
  The devil can cite scripture for his <u>purpose</u>.

No, Not, and *Always*

Watch out for words such as *no, not, never, always, still, very*, and *just*. These words are **adverbs,** words that describe verbs. They often sit right next to the verbs, but they are *not* part of the verb.

Marian <u>was</u> **always** <u>acting</u> like a prima donna. (*Was acting* is the verb; *always* is not part of the verb.)

Peter <u>would</u> **never** <u>steal</u> his sister's thunder. (*Would steal* is the verb; *never* is not part of the verb.)

The Word *Not* in Contractions

The word *not* can be especially tricky when it's attached to a verb in a contraction. Remember, however, that the *n't* (as in *can't*) is not a part of the verb.

Words Ending in *-ing*

Words ending in *-ing* are never the verb of a sentence all by themselves. (An *-ing* word can be part of the verb, but only if a helping verb is in front of it.)

Incorrect: Gary <u>driving</u> Maria crazy with his practical jokes. (*Driving* is not a complete verb. Thus, the group of words does not form a complete sentence.)

Correct: Gary <u>is driving</u> Maria crazy with his practical jokes. (*Is driving* is the whole verb, so the sentence is complete.)

Infinitives

Verbs with *to* in front of them are never the verb of the sentence.

Wilma <u>wanted</u> **to bury** the hatchet with Reni. (*Wanted*, not *bury*, is the verb.)

EXERCISE 3 Finding Complete Subjects and Verbs

In the following sentences, underline the subjects once and the verbs twice. Some sentences contain more than one subject or verb. Be sure to underline all parts of the verb. *Hint:* Cross out any prepositional phrases first.

1. Actions speak louder than words.

2. Beggars can't be choosers.

3. The early bird catches the worm.

4. Yolita can't hold a candle to her mother.

5. After breaking up with his girlfriend, Leon felt down in the dumps.

6. A stitch in time saves nine.

7. It never rains but it pours.

8. A leopard can't change his spots.

9. (You) give him enough rope and he will hang himself.

10. Though he looked scruffy, my puppy proved to be a diamond in the rough.

EDITING PRACTICE

In the italicized section of each sentence below, underline the subjects once and the verbs twice. *Hint:* Cross out any prepositional phrases first. An example is done for you.

When his sister totaled his car, *Joe hit the ceiling.*

1. *Hiro hoped that his hit album* would make him more than a flash in the pan.
2. Coming home late from work five nights in a row, *Jana was in the doghouse with her husband.*
3. *Sarah figured that after two weeks on the job,* she would know the ropes.
4. Juan wanted his promotion to be a secret, but *his boss let the cat out of the bag.*
5. By the time the electricity came back on at the end of the power blackout, *I was at the end of my rope.*
6. After her job interview, *Shawna waited on pins and needles.*
7. When the scandal grew out of proportion, *the company president passed the buck to the vice president.*
8. After his boss hired a new assistant, *Robert believed himself to be a fifth wheel at the office.*
9. *Plain old elbow grease caused Terry* to get the job done.
10. Though Tom had feet of clay, *he seemed perfect at first impression.*

WRITING PRACTICE

Read the explanations of the proverbs and idioms in the box on pages 479–480. Then, choose one of the topics below and write a paragraph.

Topic A
   Explain how one proverb's or idiom's meaning seems especially strange or surprising to you.

Topic B
   Explain the meaning of a current expression, such as "one-hit wonder." Underline the subjects and verbs when you finish.

Proverbs and Idioms Explained

These expressions appear in examples in this chapter.

"A rolling stone gathers no moss" means that (1) something or someone on the move will pay the price of never putting down permanent roots; (2) people who are always on the move avoid responsibility; or (3) people who stay active will also stay vital.

"Silence is golden" means that silence is even better than speaking.

"Still waters run deep" means that a person who is quiet can have great depth of character.

"The chickens have come home to roost" indicates that the consequences of earlier actions or mistakes are being felt.

A "thorn in one's side" is something that gives constant irritation or pain.

To take advice "with a grain of salt" is to give it little credit.

To "fall for something hook, line, and sinker" means to believe it completely.

To go "off to the land of Nod" means to go to sleep.

To "break the ice" means to improve an awkward situation, often through conversation.

To "face the music" is to accept unpleasant consequences.

"Time is money" means that wasting time will lead to losing money.

To "cut a rug" means to dance enthusiastically.

"Until the cows came home" means that something happened for a long time, usually all night.

To do something "by the book" is to follow established rules.

"When the cat is away, the mice will play" means that when the person usually in authority is gone, subordinates will act more freely.

"You can't teach an old dog new tricks" means that people who have done things the same way for a long time will not change.

"The grass is always greener on the other side of the fence" means that no matter what people have, they always want something different.

"Absence makes the heart grow fonder" means that we value things more when we are away from them.

"You can't judge a book by its cover" means that you can't always tell what something is like just by looking at it.

"Lightning never strikes twice in the same place" means that the same misfortune cannot happen to the same person twice. (In real life, however, lightning often strikes the same object again.)

"Too many cooks spoil the broth" means that when too many people work on the same thing, they ruin the results.

"You can't unscramble an egg" means that some processes are irreversible.

"One good turn deserves another" means that we should return favors people do for us.

To "carry a torch" for someone is to have romantic feelings toward that person.

(continued)

"The devil can cite scripture for his purpose" means that even good things can be used for evil ends.

A "prima donna" is (1) the lead woman singer in an opera; (2) a demanding, hard-to-please person, usually a woman.

To "steal someone's thunder" means to take attention away from someone who has earned it.

To "drive someone crazy" means to irritate someone.

To "bury the hatchet" means to forgive and forget disagreements.

A "flash in the pan" is something that makes a brief but not lasting impression.

To be "in the doghouse" is to be in trouble.

To "know the ropes" is to be familiar with the way things are done.

To "let the cat out of the bag" is to tell a secret.

To be "at the end of one's rope" is to be out of patience.

To be "on pins and needles" is to be anxious about the outcome of something.

To "pass the buck" means to blame someone else instead of accepting responsibility.

To be a "fifth wheel" is to feel out of place.

"Elbow grease" means physical effort.

A person with "feet of clay" has character flaws that are not immediately obvious.

MyWritingLab & Lab Activity 31

mywritinglab   For additional help with writing correct sentences, go to **www.mywritinglab. com** or complete **Lab Activity 31** in the separate *Resources for Writers* Lab Manual.

Clauses **32**

BREAD

Although food varies from culture to culture, almost every type of cuisine includes some type of bread. From naan in India and tortillas in Mexico to croissants in France, bread plays a major role in many cultures' meals.

CLAUSES AND SENTENCES

In almost every area of life, some elements of an object or a situation are more important than others. For instance, in a car, the fuel pump is more important than the audio components. Different sections of sentences are more important than others, too. One important aspect to writing well involves knowing how to emphasize the ideas that you think are the most important through their placement in a sentence.

WHAT IS A CLAUSE?

The basic unit of a sentence is the **clause,** which is a group of related words having a subject and a verb that work together to communicate an idea. The first two word groups below are examples of short clauses. Some examples of longer clauses follow.

Birds fly. (*Birds* is the subject; *fly* is the verb.)

Go! (*You* is understood to be the subject; *go* is the verb.)

Every season we bake a different type of bread to accompany our meals. (*We* is the subject; *bake* is the verb.)

If we ever had to give up eating bread, we would starve. (*We* is a subject, and *had* is a verb; *we* is a subject, and *would starve* is a verb.)

EXERCISE 1 Identifying Clauses and Phrases

Read the sentences below. Then, identify the italicized section of each sentence group as either a **phrase** (a group of related words that doesn't have a subject and a verb) or a clause. Write P for a phrase and C for a clause. *Note:* Crossing out the prepositional phrases and underlining the subjects and verbs may help you determine whether a group of words is a clause. An example is done for you.

_____C_____ I have worked hard to learn how to bake San Francisco sourdough bread *because it is my favorite type of bread.*

_____ **1.** Sourdough starter, the most important ingredient in baking authentic San Francisco sourdough bread, is *a simple mixture of yeast, flour, and water.*

_____ **2.** You cannot bake authentic San Francisco sourdough bread *with just any sourdough starter*, nor can you bake it with starter that doesn't contain San Francisco yeast culture.

_____ **3.** The starter will take at least twenty-four hours before it is ready to be used, so *you should plan ahead.*

_____ **4.** *Stir the mixture for a few minutes* using a wooden spoon; never use metal bowls or utensils.

_____ **5.** The starter should end up *having the consistency of thick gravy or runny pancake batter*, but don't worry if there are a few lumps in the mixture.

_____ **6.** You need to place the starter in a dark, warm place to promote the fermentation process—*a good place is the oven.*

_____ **7.** Do not actually turn on the oven because *even the lowest setting will be too hot for the starter.*

_____ **8.** The starter needs *to ferment for about eight hours*, but there's no need to worry if you wait a little less or a little more time.

_____ **9.** *After eight hours or so*, add one cup of bread flour and one cup of water to the starter. You can also wait until the starter has reached its peak, when it becomes bubbly.

_____ **10.** Mix this additional flour and water into the starter. *Return the starter to the oven* and let it sit for another eight hours or so.

INDEPENDENT CLAUSES

A clause that makes sense all by itself is an **independent clause.** An independent clause is a complete sentence. In the sentence "Birds fly," you may wonder why someone is giving you this piece of information, but you probably understand what the speaker is talking about without further explanation. The following sentences are examples of longer independent clauses.

Manuel retired from his job as a baker after forty-three years of service. (*Manuel* is the subject; *retired* is the verb.)

After returning home from the bakery, he decided to fix a snack. (*He* is the subject; *decided* is the verb.)

He piled meat, cheese, peppers, and tomatoes on some bread. (*He* is the subject; *piled* is the verb.)

DEPENDENT CLAUSES

A group of words that has a subject and a verb but doesn't make sense all by itself is a **dependent clause.** When a dependent clause is not attached to an independent clause, it is a **fragment.** The dependent clauses are underlined in the sentences below.

<u>Because she was shy</u>, Mary never spoke up in class.

<u>Although I love music</u>, I prefer peace and quiet in the morning.

Each of the dependent clauses has a subject (*she, I*) and a verb (*was, love*). Remember that for a group of words to be a clause of any kind, it must have a subject and a verb. A dependent clause, however, has another element: a

Common Dependent Words

after	although	because
before	even though	how
if	in order that	since
so that	that	though
unless	until	what
whatever	when	whenever
whenever	whether	which
whichever	while	who
whoever	whose	

dependent word. Note that *a clause with a dependent word cannot be a sentence*. In the following clauses, dependent words are underlined. Cover the dependent words and read the clauses that remain.

<u>Because</u> she was shy

<u>Although</u> I love music

Dependent clauses are so named because they *depend* or *rely* on an independent clause to make sense. Without the dependent words, the clauses are *independent* and make sense all by themselves. With the dependent words, the clauses do not make sense on their own and are therefore *dependent* clauses. You'll need to memorize the list of dependent words in the box above.

EXERCISE 2 Identifying Clauses

Read the clauses below. If a clause is independent, write IC in front of it, and if a clause is dependent, write DC. *Hint:* If you're not sure whether a clause is independent or dependent, read the clause aloud. If it sounds as if it needs more information to make sense, most likely it's a dependent clause.

_____DC_____   Because she was going to the store.

_____   **1.** When Christmas draws near.

_____   **2.** My grandmother always makes her famous stollen, a German Christmas bread.

_____   **3.** Stollen is a slightly sweet raised bread made with mashed potatoes.

_____ **4.** Because the bread is baked at festive times.

_____ **5.** It is decorated with raisins, candied fruits, and
slivered almonds.

SENTENCES BUILT WITH CLAUSES

Independent clauses are important to recognize because they serve as the
building blocks for longer, more complicated sentences.

Simple Sentences

A single independent clause is also called a **simple sentence.** The following independent clauses are simple sentences.

I love to eat bread for every meal. (*I* is the subject; *love* is the verb.)

Bread with jam remains my favorite food. (*Bread* is the subject;
remains is the verb.)

Compound Sentences

A sentence containing two or more independent clauses joined together
using a semicolon or a comma and a coordinating conjunction is called a
compound sentence. Because every clause in a compound sentence is an
independent clause, every part of the sentence is equally important. In the
following compound sentences, brackets surround each independent clause.
Notice that the comma and the conjunction are not part of either clause.

[I love to eat bread for every meal], and [I usually do].

[Without some kind of bread, a meal is incomplete], so [I always
have rolls, whole loaves, and slices of bread on hand].

EXERCISE 3   Identifying Clauses in a Compound Sentence

Each of the sentences on the following page is a compound sentence.
Place brackets around the two independent clauses. *Hint:* Look for the
comma and conjunction as a clue to where the clauses are separated.
An example is done for you.

[Making yeast bread dough from scratch can be complicated] but [it's also very satisfying].

1. First, you need to combine dry yeast with warm water , but don't use hot water .

2. Hot water will kill the yeast , and then your bread is doomed .

3. Sift flour into a bowl , so you can add it to the yeast mixture later .

4. Mix together milk, butter, and maybe some sugar , or heat these together on the stove .

5. Mix everything together except the flour , and then add the flour one cup at a time .

Complex Sentences

A sentence that combines at least one independent clause with at least one dependent clause is a **complex sentence.** Even though the word *complex* can make these sentences seem tricky, they're not difficult to write. Brackets surround each clause in the following complex sentences. Notice that when the dependent clause comes first, you must use a comma to separate the two clauses. However, if the independent clause comes first, you do not need a comma.

dependent clause independent clause

Comma needed: [Before you go], [I want your keys].

dependent clause

[Whenever I feel blue about having to get out of bed

independent clause

in the morning], [I remember being unemployed].

independent clause dependent clause

No comma: [I worry about you] [because I love you].

independent clause

[I'm definitely glad to have a job]

dependent clause

[even though I wouldn't mind sleeping in now and then.]

The important part of recognizing and writing compound and complex sentences is being able to identify the clauses in each sentence. Remember to find the subjects and verbs in compound and complex sentences because they will help you identify each clause.

EXERCISE 4 Identifying Clauses in Complex Sentences

The following items are complex sentences. Place brackets around the two clauses in each sentence, and write DC above or below each dependent clause and IC above or below each independent clause. *Hint:* Look for the dependent word as a clue to the start of the dependent clauses. An example is done for you.

                     DC   IC
[Even though bread seems to be a basic food] [people find interesting ways to eat it].

1. In Italy, stale bread becomes a delicious mush   when people

    dampen it with water .

2. When children eat bread , they often tear off the crusts .

3. The "one-eye" is another tasty way to use bread   although this

    dish involves more than bread .

4. If you tear out the center of a piece of bread and fry an egg in

    the hole, you have a one-eye .

5. One of the most popular ways to eat bread is as turkey stuffing

    when the holidays roll around .

EDITING PRACTICE

In the following sentences, identify each italicized word group: for a phrase, write P; for an independent clause, IC; and for an dependent clause, DC. *Hint:* Cross out prepositional phrases and underline subjects and verbs to help you determine whether or not a word group is a clause.

Tortillas in the Making

WRITE A PARAGRAPH The process for making authentic tortillas can be quite difficult. The recipes or methods for making many foods have been handed down through generations. What foods does your family make? Write a paragraph explaining how to prepare one of your traditional family foods.

Responding to Images. How difficult does the tortilla-making process seem to be, according to your observations of the photo above? Explain.

_____ **1.** *Making tortillas* is a difficult process.

_____ **2.** To make tortillas, first, *get some white corn grain* and boil it in a covered pot with some crumbled lime or wood ashes.

_____ **3.** *This cooking process loosens the skins of the kernels*, which will be floating at the top of the liquid the next morning.

_____ **4.** Next, discard the skins and liquid *before washing the remaining kernels*.

———— **5.** *Then, start grinding the cooked corn with a grinding stone and pestle*, and remember that the dough dries out easily, so you need to keep a jug of water nearby.

———— **6.** Next, work the dough into small balls for *shaping tortillas*; this step requires the greatest skill.

———— **7.** Try to create as thin and round a patty *of the dough as possible*, being careful not to lose too much moisture in this step.

———— **8.** Finally, fry both sides *of the tortilla for thirty to sixty seconds on a hot griddle* so that the resulting product is soft and pliable.

———— **9.** *If the tortilla is either too dry or too wet* when you put it on the griddle, it will be ruined.

———— **10.** Mexican women who make tortillas three times a day don't have to think about baking time or moisture content because *they simply know* when the dough is ready and how long they should fry it.

WRITING PRACTICE

Write a few sentences or short paragraph explaining the role of bread in your life, consider the types of bread you eat, the occasions on which you eat it, and the process—shopping or baking, say—by which you acquire bread. Put brackets around your clauses when you finish.

MyWritingLab & Lab Activity 32

mywritinglab For additional help with clauses, go to **www.mywritinglab.com** or complete **Lab Activity 32** in the separate *Resources For Writers* Lab Manual.

Run-On Sentences

Culture Note

WILLIAM SHAKESPEARE

Perhaps the world's most famous writer, William Shakespeare is known for his range of works. From tragic plays such as *Romeo and Juliet* and *Hamlet* to comedies such as *A Midsummer Night's Dream* and *As You Like It*, Shakespeare continues to move audiences with his wit and sense of drama. His poems, too, stand as tributes to both love and heartache. Even today, movies, plays, and novels based on Shakespeare's works make their way into popular culture.

WHAT IS A RUN-ON SENTENCE?

One of the most common mistakes in writing is the run-on sentence. Run-ons take two forms: the fused sentence and the comma splice. Both types of run-on sentences attempt to combine two independent clauses without proper conjunctions or punctuation. The result is a sentence that tries to do too much, thus confusing the reader.

Fused Sentences

A **fused sentence** is one in which the writer tries to join two independent clauses without any connecting words or punctuation.

Fused: William Shakespeare was an English playwright he is considered the greatest of writers in English.

Fused: Shakespeare's most famous works include plays he wrote many poems as well.

The writer has placed one independent clause after another without any connecting word or punctuation, thus creating a fused sentence.

Comma Splices

Comma splices are the most common type of run-on sentence. **Comma splices** join two independent clauses with a comma. A comma is not a strong enough punctuation mark to connect two independent clauses.

Comma splice: Many famous sayings have come from Shakespeare's plays, some sayings are so common that people don't even know they come from Shakespeare.

The writer has attempted to connect the two independent clauses with a comma. However, the connections need to be stronger and clearer.

EXERCISE 1 Identifying Run-On Sentences

Read the sentences below. Then, write F for a fused sentence, CS for a comma splice, or C for a correct sentence.

_____ **1.** Many of Shakespeare's poems were sonnets the sonnet format is a fourteen-line verse.

_____ **2.** Sonnets originated in Italy, and they often contain rhyming lines.

_____ **3.** Shakespeare's sonnets contained a couplet as the last two lines, a couplet is a pair of rhyming lines in a poem.

_____ **4.** In fact, Shakespeare's sonnets became famous, his type of sonnet is known as a Shakespearean sonnet.

_____ **5.** Many of Shakespeare's sonnets are well loved one of his most famous sonnets is "Shall I Compare Thee to a Summer's Day?"

FIXING RUN-ON SENTENCES

There are four ways to correct run-on sentences.

- Make the run-on into two separate sentences.
- Use a comma and a coordinating conjunction.
- Use a semicolon.
- Create a dependent clause.

Making the Run-On into
Two Separate Sentences

To change a run-on into two separate sentences, place a period at the end of the first independent clause and capitalize the first letter of the second independent clause. Here's how to use this method to fix the last fused sentence on page 490.

Correct: Shakespeare's most famous works include <u>plays. He</u> wrote many poems as well.

The trick to using this method effectively is determining where one clause (or complete idea) ends and the other begins. If you're not sure where to place the period and begin a new sentence, try reading the run-on out loud. Chances are, your voice will drop when you come to the end of the first clause.

Modern Othello

SURF THE NET Like his Shakespearean counterpart (Othello), fictional basketball star Oden, above, is torn apart by jealousy in the movie "O". Surf the net for modern movies based on Shakespeare's plays. Summarize your findings in a few sentences.

Responding to Images. *What conclusion can you draw about the basketball player's state of mind in the photo above? Explain in a few sentences.*

EXERCISE 2 Correcting Run-On Sentences

Each of the following sentences is a run-on. Some of the run-ons are fused sentences, and some are comma splices. Determine where the two clauses meet, and correct the run-ons using a period and a capital letter. Rewrite the sentences in the blanks. An example is done for you.

Run-on: One of Shakespeare's most famous plays is *Romeo and Juliet* it tells the story of two "star-crossed" lovers.

Correct: One of Shakespeare's most famous plays is Romeo and Juliet.
It tells the story of two star-crossed lovers.

1. "Star-crossed" means unlucky, few people have luck as bad as Romeo and Juliet's. _____

_____

2. Romeo Montague and Juliet Capulet were the children of rival families the two families didn't get along. _____

_____

3. Romeo meets Juliet at a Capulet party to which he was not invited, he and Juliet fall in love immediately. _____

_____

4. Romeo and Juliet decide very quickly to get married, they keep their marriage a secret. _____

_____

5. Tybalt, Juliet's hotheaded cousin, doesn't like Romeo he picks a fight with Romeo. _____

_____

6. During the fight, Romeo's friend Mercutio fights Tybalt, Romeo gets in the way, and Mercutio is killed. _____

_____

7. Tybalt tries to kill Romeo, he ends up getting killed by Romeo. ____

_____

8. Tybalt's death leads to Romeo being banished from Verona, Juliet is inconsolable over his departure. _____

_____

9. Not knowing about the secret marriage, Juliet's mother arranges for Juliet to marry someone else, a friar and Juliet plan to reunite her with Romeo outside the city. _____

_____

10. Juliet plans to drink a sleeping potion to fake her own death, her friend the friar writes a letter to Romeo telling him of the plan.

_____

_____

11. The letter does not reach Romeo, so he buys poison, he commits suicide in Juliet's tomb. _____

_____

12. Juliet's sleeping potion wears off, she wakes up to find Romeo dead beside her. _____

13. Juliet is devastated by finding Romeo dead, using Romeo's dagger, she kills herself. _____

_____

EXERCISE 3 Correcting Run-Ons in a Paragraph

The following paragraph has five run-on sentences. Some of the run-ons are fused sentences, and others are comma splices. Find each run-on and correct it using a period and a capital letter.

Romeo's Everywhere

[1]*Romeo and Juliet*, the tragedy by William Shakespeare, has been performed in many modern ways. [2]The musical play and movie *West Side Story* may be the most famous version its main characters are from rival gangs—the Jets and the Sharks—rather than rival families. [3]In this story, the lovers, Maria and Tony, sing songs and dance as part of their tale their story ends as unhappily as Romeo and Juliet's does, however. [4]Another movie version of Shakespeare's play was directed by Baz Luhrmann in 1996 the stars are Leonardo DiCaprio and Claire Danes. [5]This movie uses loud, almost violent music and gaudy makeup and costumes to portray the two families only the characters of Romeo and Juliet seem innocent in any way. [6]Of course, they both die in this movie, too. [7]Finally, the movie *Shakespeare in Love*, directed by John Madden in 1998, contains yet another version of Shakespeare's "star-crossed lovers" theme. [8]In this movie, the lovers—played by Joseph Fiennes and Gwyneth Paltrow—are supposed to be the characters of Shakespeare himself and the lovely Viola. [9]Shakespeare is having trouble writing his latest play, and Viola inspires him. [10]Their love can never be the lovely Viola is pledged to marry wealthy Lord Wessex. However, at least no one dies in this version.

The sentences with errors are these: _____, _____, _____, _____, _____.

Using a Comma and a Coordinating Conjunction

The second way to correct run-ons is by using a comma and a coordinating conjunction. **Coordinating conjunctions** are words that join elements of equal importance, such as two independent clauses. *Tip:* An easy way to remember the coordinating conjunctions is to think of FANBOYS, an acronym from the words *for, and, nor, but, or, yet*, and *so*.

Although all the coordinating conjunctions serve the same function, they mean different things, so choose your conjunction carefully. For instance, the fused sentence below can be corrected in a number of ways.

Fused: *Macbeth* is my favorite Shakespearean play the "tomorrow and tomorrow and tomorrow" speech is incredibly sad.

Common Coordinating Conjunctions

Word	Meaning	Example
for	because	William Shakespeare is one of the world's famous playwrights, for he has written many well-known plays.
and	in addition	Shakespeare was an excellent playwright, and he was a talented poet, too.
nor	an addition of negative ideas	Not all of Shakespeare's works are easy to under stand, nor are all of them enjoyable.
but	indicates opposition or change; means *however* or *except*	Shakespeare's tragedies are extremely sad, but they contain humor, too.
or	a choice	Many of Shakespeare's heroes face evil villains, or they face evil in themselves.
yet	same as *but*	Shakespeare's heroes usually have a major character flaw, yet playgoers still want them to succeed.
so	therefore; indicates a result	Shakespeare isn't always easy to read right away, so students need to practice reading his works.

This sentence contains two independent clauses, but the reader cannot easily tell how the two ideas are related. Using a comma and a coordinating conjunction can help make this connection clear.

Correct: *Macbeth* is my favorite Shakespearean play, and the "tomorrow and tomorrow and tomorrow" speech is incredibly sad. (This combination explains two things: first, *Macbeth* is the writer's favorite play; second, the speech is sad.)

Correct: *Macbeth* is my favorite Shakespearean play, but the "tomorrow and tomorrow and tomorrow" speech is incredibly sad. (This combination explains that, although the speech is sad, *Macbeth* is still the writer's favorite play.)

Both corrected sentences make sense, and both are grammatically correct. However, the simple switch in coordinating conjunction—from *and* in the first sentence to *but* in the second—radically alters the meaning of the sentence.

EXERCISE 4 Correcting Run-Ons Using Commas and Conjunctions

Correct the following comma splices by inserting an appropriate coordinating conjunction. An example is done for you.

People often think Shakespeare wrote only sad stories, ^for^ he did write many tragedies.

1. William Shakespeare wrote many tragedies, he wrote many comedies as well.

2. *A Midsummer Night's Dream* is one of Shakespeare's most famous comedies, many people think it is one of his funniest.

3. In *A Midsummer Night's Dream*, confusion is a huge cause of humor, many characters have spells placed on them or wear disguises.

4. Love is another source of humor in *A Midsummer Night's Dream*, at least love causes people to do silly things.

5. All the characters eventually end up as their normal selves and in

love with the "right" people, this play has a happy ending.

EXERCISE 5 Joining Independent Clauses Using Coordinating Conjunctions

Read the sentences below. Then, add an idea that logically follows from
the first sentence. Use a comma and each of the coordinating conjunctions listed here to join the two ideas (*and, but, so, for*). An example is
done for you.

I secretly want to learn to understand Shakespeare better,

but I'm afraid my friends will think I'm weird. _____

1. I always look forward to the end of the school semester _____

_____

2. Tran seems to keep himself busy _____

_____

3. Latrice loves being a bartender _____

_____

4. I was tired after work _____

_____

5. Jesse wants to get a dog _____

_____

6. I want to sleep in on Saturday _____

_____

7. Maria loved being in school during the day _____

_____

8. I saw each *Star Wars* movie five times _____

_____

9. Pablo wanted to ask Rita out on a date _____

_____

10. My house was dirty after a party _____

_____

Using a Semicolon

A third way to fix run-ons is to link the two independent clauses with a semicolon. Essentially, if you can use a period to separate two clauses, you can use a semicolon instead; using semicolons as well as periods will give your sentences more variety.

Using a Semicolon to Separate Independent Clauses   If you discover a fused sentence or comma splice in your writing, simply place a semicolon between the two clauses.

Run-on:	The Shakespearean hero Macbeth thought he could escape destiny, he was wrong.
Correct:	The Shakespearean hero Macbeth thought he could escape destiny; he was wrong.
Run-on:	Not many parents choose the names of Shakespeare's heroines for their daughters few women today are named Desdemona or Ophelia.
Correct:	Not many parents choose the names of Shakespeare's heroines for their daughters; few women today are named Desdemona or Ophelia.

EXERCISE 6 Using a Semicolon to Correct Run-ons

Insert a semicolon between the two clauses in each of the following run-on sentences. An example is done for you.

Watching plays in Shakespeare's day was physically uncomfortable

;
people had to stand throughout the play.
^

1. Modern entertainment has been influenced by Shakespeare the singer Sting named one of his albums *Nothing Like the Sun,* after one of Shakespeare's sonnets.

2. The movie *Ten Things I Hate About You* is based on Shakespeare's *The Taming of the Shrew* both stories deal with the conflicts of love.

3. The actor Kenneth Branagh did some of his best acting in Shakespearean plays he even starred in a movie version of *Henry V.*

4. The story of *Othello* was made into the movie *O* the main character in the movie is a high school basketball star.

5. Even one of *People* magazine's "sexiest men alive" starred in a Shakespearean movie Mel Gibson played the role of Hamlet on the big screen.

Using Semicolons with Transitions   Another way to use a semicolon is with a transitional word or phrase. These words can tell your reader how the two ideas linked by the semicolon are related. The most common transitions (also called **conjunctive adverbs**) that are used with semicolons are listed in the box below.

Common Transitional Phrases (Conjunctive Adverbs)

Word/Phrase	Explanation
also	and
furthermore	and
in addition	and
moreover	and

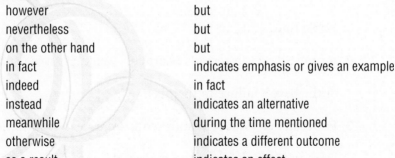

however	but
nevertheless	but
on the other hand	but
in fact	indicates emphasis or gives an example
indeed	in fact
instead	indicates an alternative
meanwhile	during the time mentioned
otherwise	indicates a different outcome
as a result	indicates an effect
thus	indicates an effect
consequently	indicates an effect
therefore	indicates an effect

In the following examples, the corrected sentences use a transition with a semicolon to link two ideas.

Run-on: I read *Julius Caesar* twice, I did really well on my English exam.

Correct: I read *Julius Caesar* twice; consequently, I did really well on my English exam.

Run-on: I'm glad I had to read some Shakespeare for class I might never have done it.

Correct: I'm glad I had to read some Shakespeare for class; otherwise, I might never have done it.

Notice that you need to place a comma after the transition when it follows a semicolon.

EXERCISE 7 Using Semicolons and Transitions to Fix Run-Ons

Join the two clauses below using a semicolon and a transition from the list above. Be sure to choose a transition that makes sense in your sentence. Several different transitions may work equally well in a sentence. Remember to include a comma after the transition. An example is done for you.

I'd like to be an English major ; therefore, I should read Shakespeare.

1. Many of Shakespeare's heroes have noble qualities they also have a tragic flaw.

2. A tragic flaw is a serious character weakness it is usually the cause of the hero's failure in the play.

3. For instance, Macbeth suffered from excessive ambition he died from trying to become too powerful.

4. One Shakespearean hero, Othello, was a great military leader he had a serious problem with jealousy.

5. Othello's jealousy caused him to lose his wife it caused him to lose his life.

6. If Othello had been able to see through his lieutenant's lies, he could have had a happy marriage he loved Desdemona.

7. Hamlet is another hero with many positive qualities he possessed the flaw of indecision.

8. Because he couldn't make up his mind, Hamlet missed his chance for triumph he and most of his friends and family died.

9. King Lear was a noble leader and loving father he suffered from vanity.

10. He gave his kingdom to his two lying, immoral daughters without considering the consequences even his loving, third daughter Cordelia was too late to save him.

Common Dependent Words

after	before	since	until
although	even though	though	when
because	if	unless	while

Creating a Dependent Clause

The last way to fix a run-on sentence is to use a dependent word to make one of the clauses in a run-on subordinate to the other. **Subordination** means making one idea weaker, or less important, than the other one. That way, your reader can easily tell which one is the focus of the sentence. A list of common dependent words appears in the box above.

Look at how the run-on sentences below have been rewritten so that one idea is less important than the other. Each new sentence contains a dependent clause and an independent clause. The dependent words are in bold print.

Run-on:	I read Shakespeare, I was afraid I wouldn't understand him.
Correct:	**Before** I read Shakespeare, I was afraid I wouldn't understand him.
Run-on:	I read *Romeo and Juliet* I was surprised at how exciting it was.
Correct:	**After** I read *Romeo and Juliet*, I was surprised at how exciting it was.
Run-on:	Now I know to give plays a chance, I might like them.
Correct:	Now I know to give plays a chance **because** I might like them.

Note: When the *dependent* clause comes first, a comma comes between the clauses. However, when the *independent* clause comes first, you don't need a comma.

EXERCISE 8 Correcting Run-Ons Using Dependent Words

Correct the run-on sentences on page 504 by using the dependent word given to make one of the ideas less important than the other. Remember to place a comma between the two clauses if the dependent clause comes first. An example is done for you.

even though
even though   Shakespeare can be fun to read ˄ readers find him challenging.

1. although   Most people read from left to right across the page

poetry often requires a different reading strategy.

2. since   Reading one line at a time can be confusing, it is

easier to read Shakespeare one sentence at a time.

3. because   Some lines contain the end of one sentence and the

beginning of another Shakespeare wanted every line

to have the same number of syllables.

4. if   You get confused, you can read aloud from the start

to the end of each sentence.

5. even though   Reading plays can be interesting they were meant to

be performed.

EXERCISE 9 Using Dependent Words for Subordination

Fill in each blank with an appropriate dependent word from the box on page 503.

1. _____ you are interested, we can rent *Shakespeare in Love*.

2. We can order a pizza _____ we start the movie.

3. _____ you want to wait till the weekend, we can watch it tonight.

4. _____ you see the movie, you'll recognize some of the lines from Shakespeare's works.

5. _____ we watch the film, we can imagine Shakespeare writing his plays.

EDITING PRACTICE

Use one of the four methods of correcting run-ons to fix each fused sentence or comma splice below. Use each correction method at least twice. Rewrite the corrected sentences.

1. Women in Shakespeare's plays have many different roles almost

every role is significant. _____

_____

_____

_____

2. Some women are strong-willed and powerful, Lady Macbeth

in *Macbeth* and Viola in *Twelfth Night* are two of these. _____

_____

_____

_____

3. Lady Macbeth pushes her husband to commit murder her ambition

causes her great unhappiness. _____

_____

_____

_____

4. Viola is a strong woman of action she gets what she wants in the

end. _____

_____

_____

5. Other women, such as Ophelia in *Hamlet*, are unstable they are

important to the story. _____

_____

_____

_____

6. The witches in *Macbeth* possess magical powers, the ways they use

their powers bring tragedy to humans. _____

_____

_____

_____

7. The witches use their power to tempt Macbeth their mysterious

language makes him believe he cannot be killed. _____

_____

_____

_____

8. Titania, the queen of the fairies in *A Midsummer Night's Dream*,

is affected by magic she is placed under a spell. _____

_____

_____

_____

9. Desdemona from *Othello* and Juliet from *Romeo and Juliet* are

both beautiful, they are both innocent as well. _____

_____

_____

_____

10. Shakespeare does not spare these innocent women they both suffer

and die. _____

_____

_____

WRITING PRACTICE

Shakespeare's works include themes of love, ambition, jealousy, revenge, and indecision, among others. Write a paragraph explaining which one of these feelings—or another that you choose—can lead to the greatest trouble. Check your work to eliminate run-on sentences.

MyWritingLab & Lab Activity 33

mywritinglab▌ For additional help with clauses, go to **www.mywritinglab.com** or complete **Lab Activity 33** in the separate *Resources for Writers* Lab Manual.

Fragments

Culture Note

MARVELS OF MODERN CONSTRUCTION
From the Golden Gate Bridge in San Francisco to the Empire State Building in New York City, examples of amazing construction abound in the United States. Some structures are triumphs of function, while others enhance the beauty of their settings.

WHAT IS A FRAGMENT?

A sentence **fragment** is an incomplete idea that tries to stand alone as a sentence. Because fragments don't communicate a complete idea, they can be confusing. Even though we use sentence fragments all the time in speaking, fragments are unacceptable in standard written English. There are three major types of fragments.

- Dependent clause fragments
- Phrase fragments
- Missing-information fragments

RECOGNIZING AND CORRECTING DEPENDENT CLAUSE FRAGMENTS

A **dependent clause fragment** is a dependent clause that is not attached to an independent clause. These fragments are easy to recognize because they begin with a dependent word or term. A list of dependent words and terms follows on the next page.

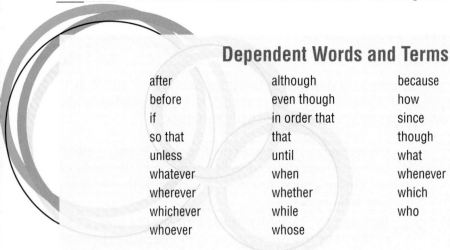

Dependent Words and Terms

after	although	because
before	even though	how
if	in order that	since
so that	that	though
unless	until	what
whatever	when	whenever
wherever	whether	which
whichever	while	who
whoever	whose	

The dependent words are in bold print in the following dependent clause fragments.

Fragment: **Even though** people said the Brooklyn Bridge couldn't be built. The engineer J. A. Roebling knew he could do it.

Fragment: Building the Brooklyn Bridge involved a great commitment by the construction crews. **Because** the work was so dangerous.

Fragment: **After** many people gave their lives to the bridge. It was finally built.

The fragments above contain a subject and a verb, so at first glance, they look like sentences. However, the presence of a dependent term—*even though, because,* or *after*—turns each statement into a dependent clause. (Try reading each dependent clause by itself, and you'll hear that it seems incomplete.) Because each dependent clause lacks an independent clause, it is a fragment.

There are two primary strategies for eliminating dependent word fragments.

- Attach the fragment to another sentence.
- Turn the fragment into a complete sentence.

Attaching the Fragment to Another Sentence

The easiest way to correct a dependent word fragment is to attach it to another sentence. If a dependent clause comes before an independent clause, you must separate the two clauses with a comma.

Correct:	**Even though** people said the Brooklyn Bridge couldn't be built, the engineer J. A. Roebling knew he could do it. (The fragment has been attached to the sentence that follows it.)
Correct:	Building the Brooklyn Bridge involved a great commitment by the construction crews **because** the work was so dangerous. (The fragment has been attached to the sentence that precedes it.)
Correct:	**After** many people gave their lives for the bridge, it was finally built. (The fragment has been attached to the sentence that follows it.)

Eliminating the Dependent Word

A second way to correct dependent clause fragments is this: eliminate the dependent word in the dependent clause and let the clause stand alone as a complete sentence.

~~Even though people~~ *People* said the Brooklyn Bridge couldn't be built. The

engineer J. A. Roebling knew he could do it.

Building the Brooklyn Bridge involved a great commitment by the

construction crews. ~~Because it~~ *The work* was so dangerous.

~~After many~~ *Many* people gave their lives for the bridge. It was finally built.

In each of these sentences, the fragment has been corrected by eliminating the dependent word. While eliminating the dependent word is an effective way to correct fragments, it can make your writing choppy. Use this technique sparingly.

The Brooklyn Bridge

JOURNAL RESPONSE At one time considered the eighth wonder of the world, the Brooklyn Bridge remains a construction marvel. What interesting buildings have you noticed in your neighborhood or city? Write for ten minutes about any buildings or structures in your area that you find interesting or unusual.

Responding to Images. *Based on the photo at left, what about the Brooklyn Bridge do you think people find interesting or impressive?*

EXERCISE 1 Attaching Dependent Clauses to Independent Clauses

Correct the dependent clause fragments on p. 512 by attaching them to sentences that you write. Some require a sentence before the dependent clause and others require it after. Write your new sentence in the space provided. An example is done for you.

Because Amanda was wonderful with children , she was in constant

demand as a baby-sitter.

1. When the snow falls heavily _____

_____

2. Who is my best friend _____

_____

3. Before I can answer your question _____

_____

4. Where the deer and the antelope play _____

_____

5. Until we elect a new governor _____

_____

6. If the bus comes late one more time _____

_____

7. Whenever Tanya needed to do laundry _____

_____

8. As far as you can see _____

_____

9. The place where people come together to sing _____

_____

10. So that Tim could pay his bills _____

_____

EXERCISE 2 Correcting Dependent Clause Fragments in a Paragraph

The paragraph on the next page contains five dependent clause fragments. Correct each fragment by using one of the techniques you learned in this chapter. Be sure to use each technique at least once.

Bridging the Gap

¹The completion of the Brooklyn Bridge in 1883 was considered a miracle of modern construction. ²It was built from 1869 to 1883 in New York City. ³Where buildings were no more than five stories tall and transportation was by horse and buggy. ⁴Because it was the world's longest suspension bridge at the time of its completion. ⁵It was called the eighth wonder of the world. ⁶The bridge was the first steel-wire suspension bridge in the world. ⁷The bridge links lower Manhattan to Brooklyn and spans 1,595.5 feet (487 meters) across the East River. ⁸The bridge is also a marvel of human commitment. ⁹Engineer J. A. Roebling battled against the elements, corrupt politicians, and scientists. ¹⁰Who claimed the massive bridge would collapse in the first strong wind. ¹¹Because he was so dedicated. ¹²Roebling was involved in many aspects of construction, including diving to check the massive bases of the bridge. ¹³These dives resulted in Roebling's death. ¹⁴Before the bridge was completed. ¹⁵Roebling's son had to finish the project.

The fragments are found in these word groups: ____, ____, ____, ____, ____.

RECOGNIZING AND CORRECTING PHRASE FRAGMENTS

Phrase fragments are the most common type of fragments. Phrase fragments come in three major forms.

- *-ing* word fragments
- *to* fragments
- Extra-information fragments

Correcting *-ing* Verb Fragments

An *-ing* word fragment is a phrase that begins with the *-ing* form of a verb.

> Fragment: Every year, thousands of tourists visit the Empire State Building. **Hoping** to see the stunning view.

Notice that the phrase containing the *-ing* word does not make sense all by itself. There are two ways to correct a fragment beginning with an *-ing* word.

- Attach the *-ing* phrase to the sentence before or after it or build it into one of those sentences.
- Turn the *-ing* phrase into a sentence.

Attaching the *-ing* Phrase to a Sentence   An easy way to correct a phrase fragment is to attach it or build it into a nearby sentence. For example, the fragment in the preceding example can be corrected as follows.

> Correct: Every year, thousands of tourists visit the Empire State Building, **hoping** to see the stunning view. (The fragment has been attached to the sentence that precedes it.)
>
> Correct: Every year, thousands of tourists hop**ing** to see the stunning view visit the Empire State Building. (The fragment has been built into the sentence that precedes it.)

Turning the *-ing* Phrase into a Sentence   Another way to correct an *-ing* word phrase fragment is to turn the phrase into a sentence. Do this by (1) adding a subject to the *-ing* phrase and (2) changing the *-ing* word to the correct verb form. In the examples that follow, the added subject is underlined once, and the new verb is underlined twice.

> Fragment: The Empire State Building is the tallest building in New York City. **Having** regained that title because the World Trade Center was destroyed in 2001.

Correct:	The Empire State Building is the tallest building in New York City. <u>It has regained</u> that title because the World Trade Center was destroyed in 2001. (*Having* has been changed to *It has regained*.)
Fragment:	The Empire State Building has 102 floors and is 1,250 feet high. It **being** the workplace for 25,000 tenants.
Correct:	The Empire State Building has 102 floors and is 1,250 feet high. <u>It is</u> the workplace for 25,000 tenants.

The two methods do not work equally well for all fragment corrections. In particular, it's often more effective to turn a fragment with the verb *being* into a sentence with *is* or *are*.

EXERCISE 3 Correcting *-ing* Fragments

The following passages contain *-ing* fragments. Rewrite each to eliminate the fragment.

1. Skyscrapers are buildings of great height. Being constructed on a

steel skeleton. _____

_____

_____

2. Originating in the United States in the late 1800s. The skyscraper

soon became a common sight in large American cities. _____

_____

_____

3. Originally, the bottom floors of tall buildings had very thick walls.

Holding up the higher floors. _____

_____

_____

4. Builders soon found ways to strengthen the structure of tall

buildings. Using cast iron along with masonry. _____

_____

_____

5. Next came the invention of a metal framework to support the walls and the floors. Allowing buildings to use floor space efficiently.

_____

_____

Correcting *to* Fragments

To fragments, also called **infinitive fragments,** are easy to recognize. They begin with an infinitive—the word *to* followed by a verb. Correct such a fragment by attaching it to the sentence before or after it, just as you would do to correct an *-ing* fragment.

Fragment	A person must be very fit. To walk down the stairs of the Empire State Building.
Correct:	A person must be very fit <u>to walk</u> down the stairs of the Empire State Building.

EXERCISE 4 Correcting *to* Fragments

Rewrite each of the following passages, correcting the *to* fragments.

1. The Golden Gate Bridge is a beautiful landmark. To see in California.

_____

_____

2. Not only is it lovely, but it is also an amazing construction work. It stretches 9,266 feet in length between San Francisco and Marin County. To make it the longest suspension bridge in the world.

_____

_____

3. Built from 1933 to 1937, the bridge seemed an impossible achievement. There were too many obstacles, such as the wide bay, steep banks, and turbulent tides. To allow the bridge to be built.

_____

_____

_____

4. However, the plans of the engineer Joseph B. Strauss were a masterpiece. In four years, the longest, highest, most spectacular suspension bridge on earth was completed. To become one of the greatest symbols of American ingenuity.

_____

_____

_____

5. The Golden Gate Bridge continues. To inspire people through its beauty and strength. It stands as a triumph in engineering.

_____

_____

_____

Correcting Extra-Information Phrases

A third type of phrase sometimes ends up as a fragment. The **extra-information phrase** contains details that contribute meaning to a subject covered in another sentence, usually the previous sentence. See the following box for a list of words that often begin the extra-information phrases.

A fragment that begins with the word _including_ is an _-ing_ fragment as well as an extra-information fragment. You can correct these two types of fragments in the same way, so don't worry about deciding which type of fragment an _including_ fragment is.

The information provided in the fragment that follows is interesting and necessary for specific communication. However, because these details

Words and Terms That Often Begin Extra-Information Phrases

also	for instance	like
especially	for one	such as
except	from	
for example	including	

appear in a fragment, the reader will have difficulty understanding how they relate to the rest of the information provided.

> Fragment: Many jobs are required to keep the Empire State Building in good shape. <u>Including</u> updating the elevators, cleaning, doing preventive maintenance, washing windows, and adding high-speed Internet connections.

Two main strategies can correct extra-information fragments.

- Attach the fragment to the sentence before or after it.
- Turn the fragment into a sentence by (1) adding a subject and verb or (2) revising it so that it makes sense on its own.

Attaching the Fragment to the Sentence Before or After It   When attaching an extra-information fragment (such as the one in the preceding example) to the previous sentence, remember to use a comma.

> Correct: Many jobs are required to keep the Empire State Building in good shape, <u>including</u> updating the elevators, cleaning, doing preventive maintenance, window washing, and adding high-speed Internet connections. (The fragment is attached to the previous sentence.)

Turning the Fragment into a Sentence   You can correct an extra-information fragment by turning it into a sentence on its own. You can do this either by (1) adding a subject and a verb to the fragment or (2) revising the fragment to make it a sentence.

> Fragment: Most people don't realize how much work is involved in maintaining the Empire State Building. <u>Especially</u> how long it takes to wash all the windows.

Correct: Most people don't realize how much work is involved
             in maintaining the Empire State Building. <u>Especially
             surprising is how long it takes to wash all the windows.</u>

Correct: Most people don't realize how much work is involved
             in maintaining the Empire State Building. <u>Washing the
             windows, for instance, takes a long time.</u>

EXERCISE 5 Correcting Extra-information Fragments

Rewrite each of the following passages to correct the extra-information
fragments.

1. Many masterpieces of engineering and construction exist in the
   United States. Especially those built in the past century.

   _____

   _____

   _____

2. Some building masterpieces help preserve the environment. Such

   as the Alaska pipeline. _____

   _____

   _____

3. The Alaska pipeline allowed oil to be transported hundreds of

   miles. From Prudhoe Bay, Alaska, to the port of Valdez. _____

   _____

   _____

4. After oil was discovered in Prudhoe Bay in 1968, construction was
   delayed by environmentalists who feared negative effects from the
   pipeline. Especially the disruption of Alaskan ecosystems.

   _____

   _____

5. However, a benefit of the Alaska pipeline is that it prevents oil spills

in the ocean. Such as the one by the *Exxon Valdez* in 1989. _____

_____

_____

RECOGNIZING AND CORRECTING
MISSING-INFORMATION FRAGMENTS

The last type of fragment is the **missing-information fragment.** This type of fragment leaves out an essential part of a sentence. The result is an incomplete idea. Missing-information fragments usually lack the subject of a sentence. Sometimes, however, missing-information fragments lack a verb.

Fragment:	Another marvel of construction is the Transcontinental Railroad, which linked both coasts in 1869. And made settlement of the West occur much more quickly. (The fragment contains no subject for the verb *made*.)
Incorrect:	The Union Pacific Railroad Company built from the east. And the Central Pacific Railroad Company from the west. (The fragment contains no verb for the subject *Central Pacific Railroad Company*.)

Missing-information fragments are easy to correct. Simply use the same techniques that you've used throughout this chapter to correct other types of fragments.

- Attach the fragment to the sentence before it.
- Add the missing information to the fragment and turn it into a complete sentence.

Attaching the Fragment to the
Sentence Before It

Attaching the fragment to the preceding sentence brings about the following results.

Correct: Another marvel of construction is the Transcontinental Railroad, which linked both coasts in 1869 <u>and made settlement of the West occur much more quickly</u>.

Correct: The Union Pacific Railroad Company built from the east <u>and the Central Pacific Railroad Company from the west</u>.

Turning the Fragment into a Sentence

You can also provide the missing information to turn the fragment into a complete sentence.

Correct: Another marvel of construction is the Transcontinental Railroad, which linked both coasts in 1869. <u>The railroad made settlement of the West occur much more quickly</u>. (The subject *the railroad* makes the sentence complete.)

Correct: The Union Pacific Railroad Company built from the east. <u>The Central Pacific Railroad Company built from the west</u>. (The verb *built* makes the fragment a complete sentence.)

Tip: While turning fragments into sentences can correct an error, it can also make your writing choppy or listlike, so be careful not to overuse this technique.

EXERCISE 6   Correcting Missing-Information Fragments

Rewrite the following passages to correct the missing information fragments. Use each technique at least once.

1. One criticism of the transcontinental railroad construction concerns its employment practices. The Central Pacific Railroad employed Chinese immigrants. And let them do the hardest labor.

_____

_____

_____

2. The Union Pacific hired Irish immigrants to do the backbreaking work. And thus ensure that the railroad was completed.

_____

_____

_____

3. These men were forced to work long hours under horrible

conditions. And were not treated well. _____

_____

_____

4. Some historians have claimed that the Chinese workers were

treated like slaves. And the Irish, too. _____

_____

_____

5. The workers made the meeting of the two lines possible. And completed an important link across the United States.

_____

_____

EDITING PRACTICE 1

Each of the following passages contains at least one fragment. Underline each fragment. Then, rewrite the passage to correct it using one of the techniques from this chapter.

1. High-speed elevators have made indoor travel fast, but some people will climb the outside of a building. Even though that's extremely dangerous.

_____

_____

2. Some years ago, a French daredevil was caught. Trying to scale a tall building in Singapore. He had climbed several buildings before.

_____

_____

3. Other daredevils enjoy the ride down. Some residents of Seattle, Washington, have parachuted from the Space Needle. Which is sixty stories high.

_____

_____

4. Another building targeted by daredevils is the Sears Tower in Chicago, Illinois. It being the third tallest building in the world at 1,454 feet.

_____

_____

5. Finally, the Golden Gate Bridge is a favorite among a special group of daredevils. People who scale the cables to the top.

_____

_____

EDITING PRACTICE 2

Read the paragraph below and identify the seven fragments. Then, correct the fragments using the techniques you learned in this chapter. Do not use the same technique for every correction.

Sad Stories

[1]Though engineering masterpieces such as the Golden Gate Bridge and the Eiffel Tower fill us with awe. [2]They also have many sad stories attached to them. [3]One type of sad story comes from the

workers who die during construction of these wonderful structures. [4]Though statistics are not often kept on the people who die during construction, there are rough records for places like the Brooklyn Bridge. [5]Some twenty-seven people died during the construction of the Brooklyn Bridge. [6]Either by falling from a great height or meeting with some other misfortune. [7]Another type of sad story comes from attacks on tall buildings. [8]Such as the attack on the World Trade Center on September 11, 2001. [9]Thousands of people died in the attacks. [10]Even though they had nothing to do with the cause of their own death. [11]Just the grandeur and height of the buildings made them targets. [12]Probably the saddest story comes from people who commit suicide from beautiful bridges or buildings. [13]Such as the Empire State Building in New York City or the Space Needle in Seattle. [14]Authorities try their best to patrol these buildings. [15]In order to prevent more deaths. [16]However, those determined to end their lives can be difficult to stop. [17]More than a thousand lives have ended from the Golden Gate Bridge alone. [18]The beauty of magnificent buildings and bridges draws people there. [19]For their last view.

Fragments are found in these word groups: ____, ____, ____, ____, ____, ____, ____.

WRITING PRACTICE

This chapter has presented you with some examples of impressive modern construction. Write a paragraph explaining whether natural sites or wonders—such as the Grand Canyon or a sunset—are more or less impressive than human-made ones such as the Empire State Building.

MyWritingLab & Lab Activity 34

mywritinglab For additional help with fragments, go to **www.mywritinglab.com** or complete **Lab Activity 34** in the separate *Resources for Writers* Lab Manual.

Regular Verbs

Culture Note

PSYCHOLOGY

Psychology deals with mental processes. Psychologists study emotions, intelligence, consciousness, and perception as well as how these processes are connected. Though psychology experts agree on the importance of their field, they approach it with a wide variety of philosophies and practices.

THE PRINCIPAL PARTS OF REGULAR VERBS

Most verbs in English are **regular verbs,** which means they follow the same pattern in their principal parts. For instance, you form the past tense of regular verbs by adding *-d* or *-ed* to the present tense. All verbs have four **principal parts:** present, past, past participle, and present participle. These four parts help us create all the verb tenses—the **forms** of the verb—which tell us the time and condition under which the action of the verb takes place. For example, for the verb *to love*, the principal parts are *love, loved, loved,* and *loving.* The box below shows some examples of the four verb forms.

Principal Parts of Regular Verbs

Present	Past	Past Participle	Present Participle
search	searched	searched	searching
play	played	played	playing
travel	traveled	traveled	traveling

The Present Tense

The **present tense** of a verb is the form seen in the dictionary: *love, jump, pick*. The present tense allows us to communicate actions that occur *now*, that are ongoing, or that are generally true.

Action occurs now:	I <u>love</u> you.
Action is ongoing:	I <u>jump</u> to reach the high shelves in my closet.
Action is generally true:	Small children <u>pick</u> ladybugs from my rose bush.

The Past Tense

The **past tense** indicates actions that occurred before now. The past tense consists of the present plus *-d* or *-ed: loved, jumped, picked*.

Action occurred before now:	I <u>loved</u> you.
Action occurred before now:	In my old house, I <u>jumped</u> to reach the shelves in my closet.
Action occurred before now:	Small children <u>picked</u> ladybugs from my rose bush.

The Past Participle

The **past participle** is often the same as the past tense form, and indicates actions that occurred before now. It consists of the present plus *-d* or *-ed: loved, jumped, picked*. It works with forms of the helping verbs *have* or *be* or can be used alone as a modifier.

Past participle with form of *be*:	I <u>was loved</u> by my parents.
Past participle with form of *have*:	I <u>have jumped</u> to reach high shelves in my closet.
Past participle as modifier:	The <u>picked</u> roses soon began to droop.

The Present Participle

The **present participle** consists of the present tense plus *-ing: loving, jumping, picking*. It works with forms of *be* as a verb, works as a modifier, or works as a noun.

Present participle with form of *be*:   I <u>am loving</u> my time in New York.

Present participle as modifier: The <u>jumping</u> lizards can be dangerous.

Present participle as noun: <u>Picking</u> an outfit for school can take forever.

FORMING THE TENSES OF REGULAR VERBS

Knowing when things happen is important. If you're explaining to your boss on Friday that you need a day off to study for an exam but then say, "My test was Thursday," your boss will wonder why you need time to study for a test that already occurred. The simple switch from *is* (present tense) to *was* (past tense) can radically alter your meaning. Thus, understanding the verb tenses—and knowing how to form them—is crucial to your success as a writer.

Present Tense

The **present tense** of a verb tells a reader that an action is going on right now, as opposed to sometime in the past or future. Form the present tense of regular verbs as follows:

- Use the simple present form with *I, you, they*, and other plural subjects (*the man, the buildings*).

  I **look** for a pot of gold at the end of every rainbow.

  You **search** for your own treasure wherever you want.

  They **discover** over and over again that fool's gold is worthless.

- Add *-s* or *-es* to the present form if the subject is *he, she, it*, or any singular name. For instance, the following sentences contain verbs ending in *-s* or *-es*. Each action below is going on right now.

  Mary **talks** constantly about her problems. (The subject is *Mary*; the present tense verb ends in *-s*.)

  It **bothers** Mary to think of others. (The subject is *It*; the verb ends in *-s*.)

  My counselor **preaches** to me about moving on with my life. (The subject is *counselor*; the verb ends in *-es*.)

  My husband **tries** not to be bothered by my annoying laugh. (The subject is *husband*; the verb ends in *-es* after the *y* is changed to an *i*.)

EXERCISE 1 Forming the Present Tense of Regular Verbs

Fill in the blanks with the correct present tense form of the verb in parentheses.

1. My brother (want) _____ to change his personality.

2. My brother (seem) _____ very angry whenever the things in his life don't work.

3. In fact, usually he (ruin) _____ things like his computer or his bicycle if they act strangely.

4. I (explain) _____ to him that he should be more like me,

but this only (cause) _____ him to get angry.

5. I also (recommend) _____ my school counselor to him,

but he (refuse) _____ to talk to her.

6. He (desire) _____ to solve his problems himself.

7. He (believe) _____ that psychology (solve) _____ all problems.

8. Thus, he (study) _____ many books on the subject.

9. He also (watch) _____ old tapes of the television show *Frasier* even though the doctors on that show are psychiatrists, not psychologists.

10. My parents (hope) _____ my brother (change) _____

before he (wreck) _____ something else!

EXERCISE 2 Using the Present Tense of Regular Verbs

Each of the sentences on p.530 contains an error in a standard present tense verb. In the italicized section of each sentence, cross out any incorrect present tense verbs and write in the correct verb form. An example is done for you.

seems

Psychology ~~seem~~ to have many different ways to explain behavior.

1. *One popular theory of behavior originate* from the psychologist B. F. Skinner.

2. *Skinner's theory emphasize the connections* between animal and human behavior.

3. *The theory state that behavior* can be modified or conditioned.

4. Skinner is famous for developing a box where *an animal push a button to get food or water*.

5. Supposedly, *the animal learn that* certain actions bring about certain results.

6. This process of associating the result with an action is a type of "conditioned response" experiment. *A conditioned response experiment try* to see if animals will act differently to get what they want.

7. The so-called *Skinner box support Skinner's ideas* that animals can be conditioned to act a certain way.

8. *The box reveal effectively* that behavior can be modified.

9. However, critics of Skinner's ideas claim that *not all behavior change with conditioning*.

10. *Some behavior start from the way* people or animals are.

EXERCISE 3 Correcting Present Tense Verb Errors in a Paragraph

The following paragraph contains six errors in present tense verbs. Correct these errors.

Terms of Psychology

[1]In my introductory psychology course, I've learned many interesting terms. [2]For instance, a *compulsion* is an inner force that lead people to act against their will. [3]A compulsive gambler, for one, believe that he or she must gamble. [4]I've also learned that *charisma* is a strong personal power that appeals to others. [5]A great leader benefits from charisma. [6]Many U.S. presidents have had charisma.

7Another term I've learned is *brainwashing*. 8Brainwashing force people to abandon their beliefs in favor of another set of beliefs. 9My mother brainwash   people into thinking they need to eat vegetables. 10All in all, psychology offer me a lot!

Verb errors occur in these sentences: ____ , ____ , ____ , ____ , ____ , ____ .

Past Tense

The **past tense** of a verb indicates that an action occurred at some time in the past. For regular English verbs, the past tense form (in the principal parts) ends in *-d* or *-ed*. In the sentences below, each verb communicates that the action has already happened.

Last year, <u>I</u> **convinced** myself to overcome my fears.
My <u>friends</u> all **watched** me struggle.

To create the past tense verbs, the writer added *-d* or *-ed* to the present tense form.

EXERCISE 4 Using the Past Tense Form of Regular Verbs

Fill in each blank with the past tense of the verb in parentheses.

1. I (start) _____ working on my fear of heights.

2. I (climb) _____ the fire escape to the top of my apartment building.

3. My mother (look) _____ up at me and (yell) _____ for me to come down.

4. When I (reach)_____ the top, I (lift) _____ my hands over my head.

5. All my friends (applaud) _____ .

6. Sigmund Freud, an Austrian doctor, (learn) _____ about medicine in the late 1800s and early 1900s.

7. He also (gain) _____ knowledge about the way the mind works.

8. Freud (develop)_____ a study of the mind (call) _____ psychoanalysis.

9. According to Freud, psychoanalysis (provide) _____ patients with a way to understand their mental illnesses.

10. Freud (believe) _____ that most mental illnesses

(originate) _____ in childhood traumas.

Participles

Even though the term *participle* refers to a verb form, participles can be used as adjectives.

Past Participles as Adjectives   The past participle verb form can serve as an adjective if it follows a linking verb or comes before a noun.

Sigmund Freud (1856–1939)

JOURNAL RESPONSE Although many psychologists today view Sigmund Freud's psychological theories as outdated or unsupported by scientific evidence, his ideas have had a profound impact on the study of behavior. What is your attitude toward therapy or counseling? Write for ten minutes, explaining your experiences and attitudes.

Writing from Visuals. Write a paragraph drawing a conclusion about Freud—that he is serious, intense, unhappy, or scary, say—based on your observations of the photo at left.

Words with Multiple Personalities

- Sometimes a word that looks like a verb serves as a different part of speech. When a present participle acts as a noun, it is called a **gerund.**

  <u>Running</u> is my favorite form of exercise. (The word *running* is a noun and is the subject of a sentence.)

- A present participle that ends in *-ing* or *-ed* can be used as an adjective.

  The <u>running</u> water felt icy cold. (The adjective *running* modifies the noun *water.*)

- A present participle acts as a verb only if a helping verb accompanies it.

  Angelo <u>was running</u> after the bus. (Here *running* is the action verb of the sentence. The word *was* is the helping verb.)

The psychologist appeared <u>surprised</u> by my condition. (The adjective *surprised* describes the subject, *psychologist.*)

The <u>depressed</u> patient felt better after telling his story. (The adjective *depressed* describes the subject, *patient.*)

Remember that a participle acts as a verb only if it is accompanied by a helping verb.

My instructor <u>is pleased</u> when our class remembers his lessons. (The subject, *instructor*, performs the action *pleased*, which is accompanied by the helping verb *is*.)

Present Participles as Adjectives and Nouns   **Present participles—** verb forms ending in *-ing*—can also be used as adjectives.

My favorite <u>walking</u> stick is made from cherry wood. (The participle *walking* modifies the noun *stick*.)

EDITING PRACTICE 1

For each sentence, write the correct present or past tense form of the verb in the blank. The tense needed is given in parentheses after the sentence. You may need to add *-s, -es, -d,* or *-ed* to make the verb form correct.

1. Many people (suffer) _____ from the mental disorder depression.

Depression (express) _____ itself in many forms. (present tense)

2. My friend Randy (exhibit) _____ depression by feeling anxious.

He (act) _____ as if the world might end at any time; he

(seem) _____ worried. (present tense)

3. He (appear) _____ better when he (walk) _____

outside. The fresh air (help) _____ clear his mind. (present

tense)

4. Last semester, Randy (watch) _____ television twenty hours

a day. (past tense)

5. Last month he (learn) _____ to do yoga. He (stretch)

_____ and (exhale) _____ his way back to feeling

better. (past tense)

EDITING PRACTICE 2 Correcting Regular Verb Tense Errors

Read the paragraph below. Then, edit any incorrect verbs by adding -s or -es
for the present tense or -d or -ed for the past tense. There are ten verb errors
in all.

Maniacs in Action

[1]A mania is abnormal or impulsive behavior. [2]When I was grow-

ing up, I often wonder if the people in my family had certain manias.

[3]For instance, my aunt Margie certainly suffer from kleptomania, or

the impulse to steal. [4]She could never leave a shopping mall without

putting something she didn't buy into her pocket. [5]She always said,

"I have to have a little gift for myself," even if no one want to give her

anything. [6]The mall security officers arrest her three times before

she change her behavior. [7]She still takes things without paying, but

only the free magazines by the entrance to the stores. [8]My cousin

Freddy had problems, too. [9]He was a pyromaniac, or someone obsessed with fire. [10]He constantly start fires in inappropriate places, such as his parents' bedroom. [11]The higher the flames rose, the more he celebrate. [12]One time he even burned a hole in the kitchen table. [13]He had to go to counseling for a long time after that, but to this day he still like to light matches. [14]Finally, my stepsister Clara showed signs of being a megalomaniac, or someone who has delusions of grandeur. [15]She stood in front of her stuffed animals for hours, bossing them around and acting like a dictator. [16]She even try to train her goldfish. [17]Actually, she ended up being successful. [18]She manage a bank, and everyone there is afraid of her. [19]They do anything she wants. [20]Maybe being a maniac isn't always a bad thing.

WRITING PRACTICE

You've learned about different psychological theories and different types of abnormal behavior. Write a paragraph describing someone you know who exhibits intense or unusual behavior. Check your work to correct errors in regular verb usage.

MyWritingLab & Lab Activity 35

mywritinglab   For additional help with regular verbs, go to **www.mywritinglab.com** or complete **Lab Activity 35** in the separate *Resources for Writers* Lab Manual.

36 Irregular Verbs

Culture Note

EUROPEAN EXPLORERS

Few places on earth remain unexplored. However, despite the fact that our maps are now crammed with names and symbols, there was a time when vast stretches of land and sea were undiscovered by any except those who lived there. Christopher Columbus, James Cook, and Sir Walter Raleigh are some of the explorers who mapped our world.

THE PRINCIPAL PARTS OF IRREGULAR VERBS

Most English verbs are regular; those whose parts are always formed the same way. English also has many **irregular verbs,** which use unpredictable forms for the different tenses. For example, the past tense of *choose* is *chose*, and the past participle is *chosen*.

  The list below shows the principal parts of the most common irregular verbs. If you're not sure what the past or past participle of a verb is, check this list below or look in a dictionary.

Principal Parts of Irregular Verbs

Present	Past	Past Participle	Present Participle
am (are, is)*	was (were, was)	been	being
arise	arose	arisen	arising
awake	awoke *or* awaked	awoke *or* awaked	awaking

*The infinitive ("to" form) is *to be*.

(*continued*)

Principal Parts of Irregular Verbs *(continued)*

Present	Past	Past Participle	Present Participle
become	became	become	becoming
begin	began	begun	beginning
bend	bent	bent	bending
bid	bid	bid	bidding
bite	bit	bitten	biting
blow	blew	blown	blowing
break	broke	broken	breaking
bring	brought	brought	bringing
build	built	built	building
burst	burst	burst	bursting
buy	bought	bought	buying
catch	caught	caught	catching
choose	chose	chosen	choosing
come	came	come	coming
cost	cost	cost	costing
cut	cut	cut	cutting
dive	dived *or* dove	dived	diving
do (does)	did	done	doing
draw	drew	drawn	drawing
drink	drank	drunk	drinking
drive	drove	driven	driving
eat	ate	eaten	eating
fall	fell	fallen	falling
feed	fed	fed	feeding
feel	felt	felt	feeling
fight	fought	fought	fighting
find	found	found	finding
flee	fled	fled	fleeing
fly	flew	flown	flying
forget	forgot	forgot *or* forgotten	forgetting
freeze	froze	frozen	freezing
get	got	got *or* gotten	getting
give	gave	given	giving
go (goes)	went	gone	going

(continued)

Principal Parts of Irregular Verbs *(continued)*

Present	Past	Past Participle	Present Participle
grow	grew	grown	growing
hang (suspend)	hung	hung	hanging
have (has)	had	had	having
hear	heard	heard	hearing
hide	hid	hidden	hiding
hold	held	held	holding
hurt	hurt	hurt	hurting
keep	kept	kept	keeping
know	knew	known	knowing
lay	laid	laid	laying
lead	led	led	leading
leave	left	left	leaving
lend	lent	lent	lending
let	let	let	letting
lie	lay	lain	lying
lose	lost	lost	losing
make	made	made	making
meet	met	met	meeting
pay	paid	paid	paying
ride	rode	ridden	riding
ring	rang	rung	ringing
rise	rose	risen	rising
run	ran	run	running
say	said	said	saying
see	saw	seen	seeing
sell	sold	sold	selling
set	set	set	setting
send	sent	sent	sending
shake	shook	shaken	shaking
shrink	shrank	shrunk	shrinking
shut	shut	shut	shutting
sing	sang	sung	singing
sink	sank *or* sunk	sunk	sinking
sit	sat	sat	sitting

Principal Parts of Irregular Verbs *(continued)*

Present	Past	Past Participle	Present Participle
sleep	slept	slept	sleeping
slide	slid	slid	sliding
speak	spoke	spoken	speaking
spend	spent	spent	spending
spring	sprang *or* sprung	sprung	springing
stand	stood	stood	standing
steal	stole	stolen	stealing
stick	stuck	stuck	sticking
sting	stung	stung	stinging
swear	swore	sworn	swearing
swim	swam	swum	swimming
swing	swung	swung	swinging
take	took	taken	taking
teach	taught	taught	teaching
tear	tore	torn	tearing
tell	told	told	telling
think	thought	thought	thinking
throw	threw	thrown	throwing
wake	woke *or* waked	woken *or* waked	waking
wear	wore	worn	wearing
win	won	won	winning
write	wrote	written	writing

EXERCISE 1 Writing the Correct Form of Irregular Verbs

In each blank, write the correct past tense form of the irregular verb. If you're not sure of the correct verb form, check the list on pages 536–539. An example is done for you.

The Italian-born Christopher Columbus (be) was_____ a famous explorer in the 1400s.

1. Christopher Columbus tried to find new lands that (hold) _____ treasures.

2. If he (find) _____ the right treasures, he could make a fortune selling them in Europe.

3. Columbus (swear) _____ that there were undiscovered lands across the ocean.

4. He (know) _____ , however, that getting money for his journey would be hard.

5. King Ferdinand and Queen Isabella of Spain (lend) _____ him the money for his journey.

6. Columbus (buy) _____ three ships: the *Niña*, the *Pinta*, and the *Santa Maria*.

7. He (take) _____ a new route toward China by sailing across the Atlantic Ocean.

8. Upon landing in the New World, Columbus (meet) _____ the people we know as Native Americans.

9. He (think) _____ he was in India, so Columbus called the people of the New World Indians.

10. Columbus's discoveries (lead) _____ to changes that affected people throughout the world.

EXERCISE 2 Choosing Correct Irregular Verb Forms

In each blank provided, write the correct form of the irregular verb shown. The tenses are indicated in parentheses. Check the list of irregular verbs on pages 536–539 if you need help. An example is done for you.

think   Many people (present) *think* that being an explorer of new lands sounds exciting. At one time, I (past tense) *thought* so, too. My friend Andy (present) *thinks* that sailing around the world sounds great. However, he has never (past participle) *thought* that danger might be part of an explorer's job.

1. come   When a big storm (past)_____, sailors had to be
           ready. Foul weather was a sure sign that danger had
           (past participle)_____ .

2. catch   Another danger came from pirates that were trying to
           catch explorers' ships. In many cases, pirates (past)
           _____ explorers' ships in the hopes of robbing them.
           If explorers were (past participle) _____, they could
           lose everything: their cargo, their supplies, even their lives.

3. drink   Running out of fresh water to drink was a third danger.
           Sailors (past) _____ water daily, so they had to
           carry fresh water in barrels on the ship. Once the sailors
           had (past participle) _____ the last of the water,
           they were in trouble unless they found a port quickly.

4. get   Yet another danger came if a sailor could not get enough
           vitamin C. Without vitamin C from fresh fruits and
           vegetables, sailors often (past) _____ scurvy, a
           serious disease that caused people to feel weak and have
           spongy gums. Once a sailor had (past participle)
           _____ scurvy, he could lose his teeth and
           get nosebleeds.

5. leave   Dangers in exploring came as soon as the ship left port.
           When they (past) _____, sailors knew that they
           might never come back. They could get lost, get attacked,
           or die from hunger or thirst. Thus, once a sailor had
           (past participle) _____, his family knew he might
           never come home again.

THE BIG THREE: *TO BE, TO DO,* AND *TO HAVE*

The irregular verbs that routinely give writers the most trouble are three of the most common verbs: *to be, to do*, and *to have*. To avoid errors with these three verbs, memorize their correct forms.

Principal Parts

Once you've memorized the correct verb forms of *to be, to do*, and *to have*, you will be surprised at how often they appear in your writing.

Verb	Present	Past	Past Participle	Present Participle
to be	am, is, are	was, were	been	being
to do	do, does	did	done	doing
to have	have, has	had	had	having

Tenses

The verbs *to be, to do*, and *to have* are irregular: their tenses take unpredictable forms. For *to be*, the past tense changes depending on the subject.

To Be

Present Tense		Past Tense	
I	am	I	was
You	are	You	were
He, she, it	is	He, she, it	was
We	are	We	were
You (plural)	are	You (plural)	were
They	are	They	were

To Do

Present Tense		Past Tense	
I	do	I	did
You	do	You	did

He, she, it	does	He, she, it	did
We	do	We	did
You (plural)	do	You (plural)	did
They	do	They	did

To Have

Present Tense		**Past Tense**	
I	have	I	had
You	have	You	had
He, she, it	has	He, she, it	had
We	have	We	had
You (plural)	have	You (plural)	had
They	have	They	had

Avoiding Common Errors

People often use incorrect verb forms when speaking informally. Using the incorrect forms of the verbs *to be, to do,* and *to have* can hurt your credibility as a speaker and as a writer, so be careful to avoid them.

Incorrect	**Correct**
~~I be.~~	I am.
~~He don't.~~	He doesn't.
~~She have.~~	She has.

EXERCISE 3 Using *To Be, To Do,* and *To Have* Correctly

Circle the correct form of the verbs *be, do,* and *have* in each sentence.

1. Leif Ericson (was, were) a Norwegian explorer of about the year 1000.

2. He (is, be) known for the Viking discovery of North America.

3. Vinland (be, is) a place that Ericson supposedly discovered.

4. The location of Vinland (has, have) been in dispute since Ericson found it.

5. Some places said to be Vinland (are, is) the Canadian province of Newfoundland and the New England region of the United States.

6. Though Columbus is credited with being the first European to discover America, some people say Ericson (is, was).

7. Ericson's travels, however, (are, is) not documented as thoroughly as Columbus's.

8. Also, Ericson's exploration (did, done) not result in continuous colonization of America, as Columbus's did.

9. Ericson's discoveries (did, done), however, inspire others to explore.

10. If nothing else, Ericson's travels (was, were) the foundations for great tales of travel.

Viking Ships

CRITICAL THINKING The eldest son of Eric the Red, the Viking Leif Ericson was the first European to discover and settle Greenland. Explorers' travels have brought people from all parts of the world together. Do you think people are better off living near others of different backgrounds? Explain in a few sentences.

Responding to Images. Write a few sentences describing the mood—excitement, anger, joy, say—in the photo above, based on your observations.

EXERCISE 4 Using the Past Tense of *To Be*, *To Do*, and *To Have*

Fill in each blank with the correct form of *be, do,* or *have.*

1. Captain James Cook _____ an English explorer of the 1700s.

2. Few explorers accomplished as much as he _____ .

3. Australia _____ its first European colony as a result of Cook's voyages.

4. Cook _____ the first European to visit Hawaii.

5. Some people claim that the *Star Trek* character James T. Kirk _____ meant to be a modern version of James Cook.

6. One reason for this _____ the similarity of their names: James Cook and James Kirk.

7. Their ships _____ similar names, too.

8. Cook's ship _____ the *Endeavor*, and Kirk's ship was called the *Enterprise*.

9. Finally, Cook supposedly made the statement that he wanted to "go boldly" where no one had gone before. Kirk made almost the same statement that Cook _____ .

10. Kirk claimed he wanted to "boldly go" where no man had gone before. Though he lived centuries ago, James Cook _____ a significant influence on the world.

EXERCISE 5 Writing Sentences Using Irregular Verbs

Write a sentence for the verb form given below using the tense shown in parentheses. See the list on pages 536–539 if you need help. An example is done for you.

lie (past tense) *Yesterday, I lay down for a nap after lunch.* _____

1. *swim* (past) _____

2. *make* (past participle) _____

3. *bring* (past participle)_____

4. *wear* (past)_____

5. *hide* (past) _____

6. *draw* (past participle) _____

7. *freeze* (past) _____

8. *fly* (past) _____

9. *begin* (past participle) _____

10. *eat* (past) _____

EDITING PRACTICE

Circle the correct verb forms in the paragraph below.

A Gentleman and Explorer

Sir Walter Raleigh (was, were) an English explorer of the late 1500s and early 1600s. His expeditions (took, taking) him on voyages to the Americas, and he (made, making) great profits on his ventures. He (did, done) a great service to England by introducing two popular products from the New World: the potato and tobacco. His fame, however, (come, comes) largely from his good manners. Even today, Sir Walter Raleigh (be, is) an excellent example of a gentleman. People (think, thought) that he (went, going) to great lengths to treat others with courtesy. One well-known tale of his courtesy (tells, tell) of a time he (comes, came) across a mud puddle when the queen was near. Sir Walter Raleigh (lay, laid) his coat over the puddle so that Queen Elizabeth would not have to walk through the mud.

WRITING PRACTICE Write About a Place You've Explored

In this chapter you've read about some people who helped map the modern world. What is the closest you've come to "exploring" someplace? For instance, as a child did you ever search behind bushes in the park, or peek into unfamiliar alleys? Write a few sentences or short paragraph about a time when you investigated a new place. Check your writing for correct irregular verb use.

MyWritingLab & Lab Activity 36

For additional help with irregular verbs, go to **www.mywritinglab.com** or complete **Lab Activity 36** in the separate *Resources for Writers* Lab Manual.

37

Subject-Verb Agreement

Culture Note

CLASSICAL MUSIC AND MUSICIANS

Although it is a large part of our culture, classical music remains a mystery to many people. The names of the "three Bs" of classical music—Bach, Beethoven, and Brahms—may sound familiar, but their contributions aren't always fully understood.

UNDERSTANDING SUBJECT-VERB AGREEMENT

For sentences to make sense, subjects and verbs have to agree with each other. This means that if the subject is **singular,** then the verb should be singular. Also, if the subject is **plural,** then the verb must be plural. The subjects and verbs in the following sentences reflect the same numbers.

Brahms was a great conductor.

(Here the subject *Brahms* indicates a single person, while the verb *was* also indicates action by one person. If the subject were plural, the verb would be *were*.)

Classical music conductors often master many instruments.

(The plural subject *conductors* matches the plural verb form *master*. If the subject were *A conductor*, the verb would need to be *masters*.)

Subject-verb agreement—where the subject and verb reflect the same number—is one of the most important grammar skills you can master. The good news is that subject-verb agreement is usually simple to get right if the subject and verb are close to each other. However, errors in subject-verb agreement can happen in the following cases.

- Words come between the subject and the verb.
- The verb comes before the subject.
- The subject has two or more parts.
- The sentence contains an indefinite pronoun.

AGREEMENT WHEN WORDS COME BETWEEN THE SUBJECT AND THE VERB

Sometimes when words come between the subject and verb, it's hard to decide what the subject of a sentence is. In the sentences below, a prepositional phrase comes between the subject (underlined once) and the verb (underlined twice). Remember that a prepositional phrase is *not* the subject.

Musical compositions by Johann Sebastian Bach offer a music lover many choices.

(The subject *compositions* is plural, so the verb *offer* must also be plural.)

One of Bach's most famous pieces is "Jesu, Joy of Man's Desiring."

(The subject *One* is singular, so the verb *is* must be singular too.)

The sentences are much easier to check for subject-verb agreement when the prepositional phrases are eliminated.

Musical compositions ~~by Johann Sebastian Bach~~ offer a music lover many choices.

One ~~of Bach's most famous pieces~~ is "Jesu, Joy of Man's Desiring."

EXERCISE 1 **Checking for Subject-Verb Agreement When the Subject Is Separated from the Verb**

In the following sentences, circle the correct forms of the verbs in parentheses. *Hint:* Cross out the prepositional phrases to help you identify the subject and verb.

1. The career moves in Johann Sebastian Bach's life (was, were) many.

2. Even now, Bach's first opportunity in his professional life (seem, seems) exciting. Here's how things happened.

3. A church in Arnstadt, Germany, (offer, offers) him a job as organist and choirmaster.

4. The job in the church (pays, pay) well.

5. Bach's duties at the church (demand, demands) little time and energy.

6. One of Bach's weaknesses (is, are) the desire to attend concerts.

7. Music in many forms (inspires, inspire) Bach, so his superiors let him go to some concerts.

8. Bach's enthusiasm for concerts (keep, keeps) him away from the church too much.

9. The leaders in the church (scold, scolds) Bach for being away at concerts too often.

10. The conflicts between Bach and his superiors (drive, drives) him away to look for another job.

AGREEMENT WHEN THE VERB COMES BEFORE THE SUBJECT

Sometimes the verb in a sentence comes before the subject. In the following sentences, the subjects are underlined once and the verbs twice.

In Bach's collection of compositions are many fugues.

(The plural subject *fugues* comes after the verb *are*.)

What is a fugue?

(The singular subject *fugue* comes after the verb *is*.)

With the feelings of flight or escape come the different parts of the fugue.

(The plural subject *parts* agrees with the verb *come*.)

To find the subject, first eliminate prepositional phrases. Then ask yourself what the action of the sentence is and then *who* or *what* is performing that action. *Just because a word comes first does not mean it's the subject.*

**EXERCISE 2 Checking for Subject-Verb Agreement
When the Verb Comes Before the Subject**

In the sentences below, circle the correct form of each verb in parentheses.

1. Among Bach's works (exist, exists) many fugues.

2. From Latin (come, comes) the term *fugue*, which means "to chase" or "to escape."

3. All through a fugue (are, is) the sounds of three voices.

4. Expressed in the pattern of a fugue (are, is) the concept of three voices "chasing" each other.

5. At different points in the music (come, comes) the three voices.

6. In a later part of the fugue (come, comes) a second voice.

7. What (do, does) this second voice bring to the music?

8. Through the second voice (echoes, echo) the first voice's theme.

9. Into the music, but many notes higher, (sings, sing) a third voice.

10. What (is, are) the job of the third voice? It echoes the first theme yet again.

AGREEMENT WHEN THE SUBJECT HAS TWO OR MORE PARTS

Subjects with two or more parts are called **compound subjects.** Generally, these subjects are plural and require a plural verb.

Bach, Beethoven, and Brahms all come from Germany.

(The compound subject has three parts—*Bach, Beethoven,* and *Brahms*—so the verb *come* is plural.)

When the verb has both a helping verb and a main verb, the helping verb changes to agree with the subject.

People who study classical music have learned much about the music they love.

(The subject *People* is plural, so the helping verb *have* is plural.)

Beethoven's *Moonlight Sonata* is considered one of his finest works.

(The singular subject *Moonlight Sonata* agrees with the helping verb *is*.)

When subjects are joined by *either . . . or, neither . . . nor,* or *not only . . . but also,* the verb must agree with the subject that is closest to it.

Not only Beethoven and Brahms but also Bach was from Germany.

(Even though *Beethoven* and *Brahms* are part of the subject, *Bach* is the one the singular verb agrees with because it's closer.)

EXERCISE 3 Making Verbs Agree with Compound Subjects

In the sentences below, circle the correct form of each verb in parentheses.

1. Many complicated terms and expressions in classical music (has, have) simple meanings.

2. A *virtuoso* and a person with great technical skill (is, are) the same.

3. Not only Bach and Beethoven but also Brahms (was, were) a virtuoso on several instruments.

4. The Italian terms *cantata* and *sonata* (mean, means) pieces to be performed, usually as solos accompanied by an orchestra.

5. Not only fugues but also the cantata (is, are) music meant to be sung.

6. On the other hand, the term *sonata* or *concerto* (indicate, indicates) music meant to be played on an instrument, not sung.

7. *Allegro* and *allant* (mean, means) that music should be played in a "bright" or "lively" way.

8. *Andante* and *lento* (indicate, indicates) a slower tempo.

9. Finally, the term *symphony* and the term *concerto* (have, has) similar original meanings.

10. Now, though, neither a symphony nor a concerto (is, are) the simple instrumental combination it once was.

AGREEMENT WHEN THE SUBJECT IS AN INDEFINITE PRONOUN

An **indefinite pronoun** does not refer to a specific person or thing. The indefinite pronouns listed below require singular verbs, even when they refer to more than one person.

anyone	anybody	anything	each
everyone	everybody	everything	either
no one	nobody	nothing	neither
someone	somebody	something	one

Tip: Make sure not to use the pronoun *they* to agree with *everyone* and *everybody*. Even though these words sometimes seem as if they should be plural, they are singular. For more on pronoun agreement, see Chapter 40.

Everyone listening to Bach was in a peaceful mood.

(The subject *everyone* takes the singular verb *is*.)

No one admits to taking my Brahms CD.

(The subject *no one* takes the singular verb *admits*.)

The indefinite pronouns listed below require plural verbs.

both	many
few	several

Both of my parents love hearing Beethoven.

(The subject *both* requires the plural verb *love*.)

EXERCISE 4 Making Verbs Agree with Indefinite Pronouns

In the following sentences, circle the correct form of each verb in parentheses.

1. Anything related to classical music (is, are) intimidating to me.

2. Everything on classical CDs (sounds, sound) perfect.

3. Nevertheless, something (make, makes) me want to play in the school orchestra.

4. However, something (appears, appear) to be wrong with me when I try to understand or play classical music.

5. First, nothing about the sheet music (looks, look) as if it could ever sound pretty.

6. Second, classical music has different parts, and each (have, has) a tricky name such as *overture, coda*, or *air*.

7. In the orchestra, if people beside me (play, plays) off-key, no one seems to notice.

8. In fact, nobody else (admits, admit) to being out of tune or making mistakes.

9. Instead, everyone in the orchestra (blames, blame) me for making the music sound bad.

10. Neither of my parents (encourage, encourages) me to continue playing.

Ludwig van Beethoven (1770–1827)

FOOD FOR THOUGHT Despite being completely deaf by the end of his career, Beethoven composed pieces expressing the full range of human emotion. Should college students be required to learn about classical music? Write a few sentences explaining whether or not colleges should require this type of instruction. ***Responding to Images.*** *How does Beethoven, in the illustration at left, feel about his music? Explain in a few sentences based on your observations.*

EDITING PRACTICE 1

In the sentences below, circle the correct form of each verb in parentheses.

1. The mood swings and personality of Johannes Brahms (is, are) a contradiction.
2. Nobody (disagree, disagrees) that Brahms was full of bad humor and criticism.
3. People (claim, claims) that Brahms was prickly and kept to himself.
4. "The Outsider" (remain, remains) a name that Brahms even gave himself.
5. That said, more than one person (tell, tells) of his sociable side.
6. The content of many letters (reveal, reveals) that Brahms had a large circle of friends and acquaintances.
7. Everyone who was an important part of his life (write, writes) of Brahms' wide range of interests.
8. Brahms' love interests or even his true love (remain, remains) a mystery.
9. From pages of letters and books (speak, speaks) colleagues and friends of Brahms about his love interests.
10. People claim that either his genius or his weaknesses (play, plays) a large role, even today, in understanding Johannes Brahms.

EDITING PRACTICE 2

The following paragraph contains ten errors in subject-verb agreement. Cross out the incorrect verbs, and write in the correct forms.

Lend an Ear to Beethoven

Many people considers Ludwig van Beethoven the greatest of all composers. First, Beethoven's music cover the range of human emotions. His Third Symphony, "Eroica," express ideas of heroism while the *Moonlight Sonata* is sad. Another reason people finds Beethoven so great is that his music show the talent of combining skills to write orchestral movements. For instance, Beethoven's famous Fifth

Symphony reveal his mastery of timing, writing chords, and mixing the sounds of different instruments. One more reason people find Beethoven such a powerful composer are his effort to create flawless work that would last forever. Thousands of pages of drafts of his music lets the world know how hard Beethoven tried to make his work perfect. His goal to be perfect were even more difficult since he became totally deaf by the end of his career. From his first published composition at the age of twelve to his moving Ninth Symphony, Beethoven stand the test of time.

WRITING PRACTICE

Classical music was once heard more often than it is today. Cartoons and movies, for instance, used classical—rather than popular—music for their scores. Write a paragraph explaining what kind of popular music (R & B, rock, or hip-hop, to name a few) you think will last and why. Check your writing for subject-verb agreement errors.

MyWritingLab & Lab Activity 37

mywritinglab For additional help with subject-verb agreement, go to **www.mywritinglab.com** or complete **Lab Activity 37** in the separate *Resources for Writers* Lab Manual.

Verb Tense and Tense Consistency

38

Culture Note

AMERICAN LEGENDS

Although the United States is young compared with many other countries, its history is rich in legends, which are stories handed down through generations and based in truth. Legends are similar to myths in that their central characters are usually larger than life.

CONSISTENCY IN VERB TENSE

Consistency in verb tense simply means using the same verb tense throughout your writing. If you start a story or example in the past tense, for instance, then you must write your entire paragraph or essay in the past tense. Otherwise, your *inconsistent* verb tenses will send a confusing message to your reader.

Sometimes longer works require the use of different verb tenses. In these cases, it is important to make sure your verbs are consistent through each section of your work rather than throughout the entire piece.

The following sentence sends an unclear message to the reader, who will not know whether the action is taking place now or has already taken place.

Incorrect: Paul Bunyan was a giant lumberjack who carries a huge axe. (The verb <u>was</u> is past tense, and the verb <u>carries</u> is present tense.)

The sentence can be revised in two ways.

■ Revise to put both verbs in the present tense.

Correct: Paul Bunyan <u>is</u> a giant lumberjack who <u>carries</u> a huge axe.

■ Revise to put both verbs in the past tense.

Correct: Paul Bunyan <u>was</u> a giant lumberjack who <u>carried</u> a huge axe.

EXERCISE 1 Using Consistent Verb Tense in Sentences

The following sentences contain verb tense errors. Write the correct verb forms in the blanks. Use the underlined verb in the first part of each sentence as a clue to the correct verb tense. An example is done for you.

When I <u>was</u> a child, my mother (tuck) _tucked_____ me into bed every night. (The first verb of the sentence—*was*—is past tense, so the verb later in the sentence must also be past tense.)

1. She <u>sat</u> on my bed and (tell) _____ me stories about historical Americans.

2. Some of the stories <u>were</u> true, and some of them (be) _____ fiction.

3. I especially <u>loved</u> the story of Paul Bunyan, who (travel) _____ around Minnesota with his blue ox, Babe.

4. I also <u>enjoyed</u> the story of Rip Van Winkel, who (love) _____ to sleep.

5. Now, however, I <u>am</u> an adult, so I rarely (listen) _____ to bedtime stories.

6. Instead, I <u>tell</u> stories to my children, who (be) _____ very young.

7. They <u>like</u> to hear about Johnny Appleseed because they (love) _____ to eat apples.

8. Although they never <u>get</u> to eat apples during the story, they still (hope) _____ that they might get to sometime.

9. My children <u>used</u> to like the story about John Henry because they (want) _____ to hear about the race of a man against a machine.

10. Now, however, they know that story, so they (ask) _____ to hear others.

G-9—Paul Bunyan and Babe, The Blue Ox

8A-H899

Paul Bunyan and Babe the Blue Ox

JOURNAL RESPONSE Known for his huge appetite and gigantic stature, Paul Bunyan is a favorite American legend. Should stories like this be taught in school? Write for ten minutes discussing whether or not American legends such as Paul Bunyan or John Henry should be taught in schools.

Responding to Images. *Based on the picture above, do Paul Bunyan and Babe the Blue ox appear menacing or friendly? Explain in a few sentences.*

EXERCISE 2 Choosing the Correct Verb Tense for Consistency

In the sentences below, circle the correct verbs in parentheses. An example is done for you.
Note: Not every sentence begins in the same tense.

Even when he was first born, Paul Bunyan (gives, gave) his parents a challenge.

1. Many stories tell about Paul Bunyan's adult life, and a few (describe, described) his early years.

2. When Paul Bunyan was born, it (takes, took) five storks to deliver him to his parents.

3. At birth Paul weighed eighty pounds, and he (is, was) driven home in a lumber wagon.

4. In fact, the lumber wagon (becomes, became) his baby carriage.

5. Young Paul's appetite is incredible; he (eats, ate) forty bowls of oatmeal as the *start* to his breakfast.

6. Paul grows so fast that he (wears, wore) his father's clothes just one week after being born.

7. Paul's baby teeth were so big that he (has, had) to use a log as a teething toy.

8. Some people describe baby Paul's voice as a buzz saw, and others (say, said) it sounds like a bass drum.

9. In fact, his voice was so loud that he (empties, emptied) a pond of frogs with one yell.

10. Paul Bunyan is certainly tall, but the tales about him (are, were) taller.

Tip: Verb tense inconsistencies often creep into pieces of writing that are a paragraph or longer. When proofreading your work, pay close attention to verb tense in your paragraphs or essays.

CHANGING VERB TENSE

Generally, you should keep your verb tense consistent throughout your sentence, paragraph, or essay. However, there are some instances when you may need to switch tenses.

When you want to indicate different times in one sentence, use different verb tenses.

Last fall I <u>panicked</u> during finals week, but this semester I <u>feel</u> more relaxed.

The verb *panicked* indicates an action that took place in the past, and the verb *feel* communicates another action that is taking place right now.

You may need to change verb tenses when you discuss the ongoing influence of people or events from the past. For example, the people who

Verb Tense in Stories

In writing about literature (poetry, stories, and novels), use the present tense to discuss the action and to talk about an author's writing style and technique. For instance, write, "William Shakespeare *explores* themes of love and revenge in his play *Othello*." Even though Shakespeare lived centuries ago, we still write about his works in the present tense.

the legends in this chapter are based on lived hundreds of years ago. To tell their stories straight through, we could use the past tense. However, even though the tales occurred in the past, their influence on us is ongoing. Thus, discussions of Paul Bunyan, John Henry, and Johnny Appleseed may begin in the present tense. For instance, the first two sentences in the paragraph "Man Versus Machine" below have different verb tenses.

One of the greatest legends in American history is the tale of John Henry.

John Henry was born a slave in the 1840s or 1850s in the American South.

The present tense verb *is* in the first sentence tells us that the influence of John Henry is still present, while the past tense verb *was* in the second sentence indicates an event that occured in the past: John Henry's birth.

EXERCISE 3 Using Consistent Verb Tense in a Paragraph

Circle the correct verbs in the paragraph below.

Man Versus Machine

One of the greatest legends in American history is the tale of John Henry. John Henry was born a slave in the 1840s or 1850s in the American South. After the Civil War, he (is, was) hired as a steel driver for the C&O Railroad. Steel drivers (spend, spent) their work-days driving steel drills or spikes into rock. John Henry (uses, used) a fourteen-pound hammer to drill ten to twenty feet in a twelve-hour day, the best of any man on the rails. The C&O's new line was moving along quickly until Big Bend Mountain (blocks, blocked) its path. The mountain was too vast to build around, so the men (have, had) to drive their drills through its belly. It (takes, took) a thousand men three years to finish the treacherous work. Visibility was poor, and the air inside the tunnel (is, was) thick with black smoke and dust. One day, a salesman (comes, came) to camp, boasting that his steam-powered machine could work faster than any man. A race was set: man against machine. Although John Henry (wins, won), he (dies, died) shortly after the contest, some say from exhaustion, some say from a stroke.

EDITING PRACTICE

Rewrite the following paragraph to use past tense verbs consistently. There are five errors in verb consistency in all.

Planting the Seeds of a Legend

Johnny Appleseed is an American folk hero during the late 1700s and early 1800s. His real name was John Chapman, and he lived in New England. He travels through Pennsylvania, Ohio, Indiana, and Illinois. At a time when frontier settlers have little fruit to eat, he planted apple seeds. He also starts an apple tree nursery in Pennsylvania and encourage settlers to plant orchards of their own. Johnny Appleseed became famous through the telling of his story. He is also the subject of a ballad by W. H. Venable and of many poems by Vachel Lindsay including one titled "In Praise of Johnny Appleseed."

WRITING PRACTICE

Few people today speak of Paul Bunyan, John Henry, or Johnny Appleseed, yet children and adults alike refer to legends. Choose one of the following topics, and write a paragraph.

Topic A

Write a paragraph explaining the kind of person people today view as a legend.

Topic B

Choose one person and explain how he or she is a legend. Be sure to offer an explanation of what you mean by *legend*.

MyWritingLab & Lab Activity 38

mywritinglab   For additional help with correct and consistent verb tense, go to **www. mywritinglab.com** or complete **Lab Activity 38** in the separate *Resources for Writers* Lab Manual.

39 Pronoun Types

Culture Note

THE OLYMPIC GAMES

Even when world politics seem about to explode in violence or mistrust, the Olympic Games usually bring countries and cultures together in peace. Modeled after the games begun in ancient Greece, the modern Olympics consist primarily of athletic contests.

RECOGNIZING PRONOUNS

Pronouns are words that take the place of nouns. They are essential to clear, concise communication because they allow us to substitute a short, easily recognizable word for another word or phrase.

> The Olympic Games were held in honor of Zeus; the Olympic Games included athletic games and contests in dance and poetry.

In the preceding sentence, the subject *the Olympic Games* is written out twice. The sentence is shorter when it contains a pronoun instead. The pronoun *they* allows us to avoid repeating the subject *the Olympic Games*.

> The Olympic Games were held in honor of Zeus; they included athletic games and contests in dance and poetry.

There are many types of pronouns. In this chapter, we focus on the five most common types.

- Subject pronouns
- Object pronouns
- Possessive pronouns
- Reflexive pronouns
- Demonstrative pronouns

SUBJECT PRONOUNS

A **subject pronoun** is the subject of a sentence or clause.

Singular Subject Pronouns	**Plural Subject Pronouns**
I, you, he, she, it	we, you, they

The subject pronouns are underlined once in the sentences below; verbs are underlined twice.

They competed to honor the god Zeus, ruler of Olympus. (*They* is the subject of the verb *competed*.)

We have modeled our current Olympic games after those in ancient Greece. (*We* is the subject of the verb *have modeled*.)

Using a Subject Pronoun as Part of a Compound Subject

A **compound subject** is a subject with more than one part.

Incorrect: ⌐ compound subject ¬
Olympic athletes and me share an interest with my brother.

Correct: ⌐ compound subject ¬
Olympic athletes and I share an interest with my brother.

Incorrect: compound subject
Them and him are dedicated to sports.

Correct: compound subject
They and he are dedicated to sports.

If you're not sure which pronoun to use, try reading the sentence using the pronoun by itself as the subject. "Me share an interest" doesn't sound right, so you know to use the pronoun *I*.

Using a Subject Pronoun After Forms of *To Be*

The forms of the verb *to be* are *am, is, are, was, were, has been,* and *have been*. Subject pronouns are used following any form of the verb *to be*.

Correct: It was she who won the gold medal in 1964.

It may have been they who boycotted the Olympics that year.

The sentences above may sound strange or artificial, but they are grammatically correct. Even though you can make your point in conversation by using expressions such as "It was her" or "It may have been them," these uses of pronouns are incorrect in standard written English. They should not appear in your writing. If you're not comfortable using subject pronouns after forms of the verb *to be*, revise your sentences.

> Correct: She won the gold medal in 1964.
>
> They boycotted the Olympics that year.

Using a Subject Pronoun After *Than* and *As*

When a clause starts with *than* or *as*, use the subject pronoun.

> Correct: The Kenyans typically have faster distance runners *than* we.
>
> Although Dara Torres won many Olympic medals, swimmer Michael Phelps won more gold medals *than* she.

You can tell that the subject pronoun is correct by silently adding the verb that came earlier in the sentence.

> The Kenyans have faster distance runners than we (have).

> Although Dara Torres won many Olympic medals, swimmer Michael Phelps won more gold medals than she (won).

> If your sentence doesn't make sense when you silently add the verb, you probably need to change your pronoun.

EXERCISE 1 Choosing the Correct Subject Pronoun

In the following sentences, circle the correct subject pronouns in parentheses.

1. Though the Greek Olympic team is relatively small when compared with other teams, (it, he) is symbolically very important.

2. The ancient Greeks started the tradition of laying aside political and religious differences. (We, They) held the Olympic Games as a time of celebration.

3. It was (they, them) who began the custom of holding the Olympics every four years.

4. The Greeks value the modern Olympics as much as (us, we).

5. Greece is still the source of the Olympic flame. (She, It) is lit by the sun's rays at Olympia, Greece, and then carried to the site of the Olympics.

6. Lighting the Olympic flame is no easy task. (It, You) must be lit using only a parabolic mirror and the sun's rays.

7. Once the flame is lit, many hands carry the torch. (Them, They) ensure that the flame reaches the country of the Olympic Games safely.

8. In 1976, technology helped transport the flame to Canada. A satellite transmitted the flame from Athens, Greece, to Ottawa, Canada, where (it, he) was carried to the Olympic site.

9. During the Montreal Olympic Games in 1976, an official relit the sacred Olympic flame with a cigarette lighter after it was drenched by a rainstorm, but (he, him) was not supposed to do that.

10. The Olympic organizers had kept a reserve flame—originally lit at Olympia—on hand. (We, They) extinguished the "fake" flame and replaced it with an authentic Olympic one.

OBJECT PRONOUNS

An **object pronoun** is used as the object of a verb or preposition. (**Prepositions** are words such as *about, for, behind*, and *to* that relate a noun or pronoun to the rest of a sentence.) An object pronoun can never be the subject of a sentence.

Singular Object Pronouns	**Plural Object Pronouns**
me, him, her, you	us, them, you

In the sentence below, the underlined object pronoun is the object of the preposition in italics.

After the American Nastia Luikin won the all-around gymnastics title, the Olympic official awarded a gold medal *to* <u>her</u>. (*Her* is the object of the preposition *to*.)

In the following sentence, the underlined pronoun is the object of the verb in italics.

My coaches *told* <u>me</u> about the Olympics after their visit to the Beijing games. (*Me* is the object of the verb *told*.)

Sometimes writers aren't sure whether to use a subject pronoun or an object pronoun.

Incorrect:	*For* Rob and <u>I</u>, this Olympic event was the most meaningful.
Correct:	*For* Rob and <u>me</u>, this Olympic event was the most meaningful.

Incorrect:	The sports commentators *praised* <u>he</u> and <u>she</u> after their races.
Correct:	The sports commentators *praised* <u>him</u> and <u>her</u> after their races.

If you can't decide which pronoun to use, try saying the sentence aloud with each pronoun by itself. The pronoun that sounds correct will most likely be the right choice. For instance, "For *I* (drop the *Rob*), this Olympic event was the most meaningful" sounds awkward, but "For *me*, this Olympic event was the most meaningful" does not.

If a pronoun follows a preposition, it's likely to be an object of the preposition. If a pronoun follows a verb, it's likely to be an object of the verb.

EXERCISE 2 Using the Correct Object Pronouns

In the sentences below, circle the correct pronouns in parentheses.

1. The Olympic Games include many sports for (we, us) to view.

2. Running, jumping, and throwing are the first events my brother and (I, me) want to watch.

3. If the ancient Greeks didn't perform a feat for survival—such as throwing a spear to get meat or defend a village—then it was not an Olympic sport for (they, them).

4. My brother and (I, me) love to watch the track and field competitions.

5. My sister tells (we, us) about her favorite event: synchronized swimming.

6. There's a pact between (she, her) and my mother to watch every synchronized swimming event they can find.

7. Those events give my mother and (she, her) great thrills.

8. My cousin Eugenia loves synchronized swimming even more than (they, them).

9. Synchronized swimming, however, with all the sequins and makeup and gelled hair, just doesn't seem like a sport to my brother or (I, me).

10. However, my brother is like (I, me). We try to appreciate the athleticism required for synchronized swimming.

POSSESSIVE PRONOUNS

A **possessive pronoun** shows that something belongs to someone or something. A list of possessive pronouns follows.

Possessive Pronouns

my, mine	our, ours
your, yours	your, yours
his, her, hers, its	their, theirs

The possessive pronouns are underlined in the sentences below.

Randy's television broke during the Olympics, so I let him watch my TV. (*My TV* means "The TV that belongs to me.")

Even though athletes win medals at the Olympics, the winners' countries claim the medals as theirs. (*Theirs* means "the medals that belong to the winners.")

Never use an apostrophe with a possessive pronoun. For more on apostrophes, see pages 625–635.

Incorrect:	The Olympic spirit will always have it's roots in Greece.
Correct:	The Olympic spirit will always have its roots in Greece.
Incorrect:	The five Olympic rings communicate a message that is uniquely their's.
Correct:	The five Olympic rings communicate a message that is uniquely theirs.

EXERCISE 3 Using Possessive Pronouns Correctly

Correct the pronoun error in each sentence below. An example is done for you.

Of all the symbols associated with the Olympics, none is so widely

recognized as ~~it's~~ *its* flag.

1. On it's white background, the Olympic flag has five different-colored rings.

2. The five continents each have a ring on the flag that is their's.

3. This flag and the games it represents have helped build goodwill among nations, including our's.

4. Even when countries have boycotted Olympic competition, the flag has flown proudly over it's events.

5. A symbol of hope for worldwide peace, the flag makes the statement "The games are everyone's, mine and your's ."

PRONOUNS ENDING IN -*SELF* OR -*SELVES*

Two kinds of pronouns end in -*self* or -*selves*.

- Reflexive pronouns
- Intensive pronouns

Reflexive Pronouns

A **reflexive pronoun** indicates that someone performed an action himself or herself. The reflexive pronouns are underlined in the following sentences.

In addition to the pride their countries feel for them, Olympic athletes feel proud <u>themselves</u>. (*Themselves* refers to *Olympic athletes*.)

The experienced athlete may train <u>himself</u>. (*Himself* refers to *experienced athlete*.)

Do not use a reflexive pronoun as the subject of a sentence.

    Incorrect: My mother and <u>myself</u> proudly watched the opening ceremonies of the Olympic Games.

    Correct: My mother and <u>I</u> proudly watched the opening ceremonies of the Olympic Games.

Tip: Think of a reflexive pronoun as a *reflection* of the subject. Thus, if the subject is *I*, the correct reflexive pronoun is *myself*. Since you can't have a reflection of an object without the object itself, you shouldn't use a reflexive pronoun—the *reflection* of the subject—unless the subject is present.

Intensive Pronouns

An intensive pronoun is used for emphasis. It always directly follows the word it refers to.

She <u>herself</u> was pleased with her win in the hundred-meter dash. (*Herself* emphasizes that she—in addition to others—was pleased with her win.)

EXERCISE 4 Using Reflexive and Intensive Pronouns Correctly
In the sentences below, write the correct reflexive or intensive pronoun in each blank.

1. Many Olympians _____ themselves have reason to feel pride.

2. For instance, Shaun White earned _____ an Olympic gold medal in 2006.

3. The United States softball team played _____ into history by losing three games and then winning the gold medal.

4. Jamaica's Usain Bolt distinguished _____ by winning two gold medals in the sprints.

5. China _____ felt pride at having hosted an impressive Olympic Games.

DEMONSTRATIVE PRONOUNS

A **demonstrative pronoun** singles out a specific item or person.

Singular Demonstrative Pronouns   **Plural Demonstrative Pronouns**

this   these
that   those

In general, use *this* and *these* to indicate something or someone nearby, and use *that* and *those* to indicate something farther away. The demonstrative pronouns are underlined in the sentences below.

<u>This</u> is a great event.

<u>These</u> are some of the finest athletes I have ever seen.

An Olympic official would never overlook <u>that</u>.

His medals are <u>those</u> in the cabinet.

Demonstrative pronouns can be used as adjectives, too.

<u>This</u> year's Olympics included baseball and softball for perhaps the last time.

Men have competed in the hammer throw for decades, but the 2000 Olympic Games marked the first time women competed in <u>that</u> event.

<u>These</u> days, training for the Olympics is a full-time job.

Approximately 11,000 athletes competed in <u>those</u> events in Beijing.

Avoid using the expressions *this here* and *that there* in your writing. They are not acceptable in standard written English.

EXERCISE 5 Using Demonstrative Pronouns Correctly

In the following sentences, write the correct demonstrative pronouns in the blanks.

1. _____ days, people are interested in the money they can make from Olympic gold medals.

2. For _____ purpose, in 1994, the American figure skater Tonya Harding arranged to have another skater, Nancy Kerrigan, attacked.

3. In the national championships leading up to _____
Olympic Games, Harding thought she could win the gold medal if
Kerrigan was out of the way.

4. However, while Harding did win _____ skating
competitions, she did not win Olympic gold.

5. To _____ day, Harding is known for her dishonest plot.

EDITING PRACTICE

Circle the correct pronouns in the paragraph below.

Misleading Names

The summer Olympic Games contain many events with misleading names. For instance, the triple jump is a track and field event.
The name implies that the event includes three jumps, but (it, they)
is made up of a hop, a skip, and a jump. The athletes who compete
in (this, these) event look as if (they, them) are doing a dance as (he
or she, they) bounce down the runway. Not everyone is as coordinated as (them, they). Another event is the hammer throw. (These,
This) event's name is misleading because the hammer looks nothing like a carpenter's tool. The hammer in the Olympic event is a
metal ball that hangs from a wire handle. The athlete holds the handle with both of (his or her, their) hands, spins around to build
momentum, and then releases the hammer into the air. Even though
hammer throwers might not be as famous as other athletes, they
earn (theirselves, themselves) pride through their Olympic accomplishments. It is (they, them) who propel the weight over seventy
meters. A favorite Olympic contest of (my, mine) is the butterfly
stroke in swimming. Swimmers in (this, these) events must thrust
(his or her, their) arms out at the sides at the same time and then
bring (they, them) forward out of the water and down in a circular

A Gold-Medal Reaction

SURF THE NET Swimmer Michael Phelps won a record eight gold medals at the 2008 Olympic Games. How did his swimming career begin? Surf the Net for answers.

Responding to Images. *From the photo above, what would you guess the athletes are feeling? Explain.*

motion. Even though (that, those) stroke is called the butterfly, the swimmers look more like dolphins than butterflies. All in all, a sport can look very unlike what (its, it's) name suggests.

WRITING PRACTICE

Although many original contests of speed and, remain part of the Olympics, new events—the triathlon, snowboarding, and aerial ski jumping, to name some—have become part of the games. Should they? Write a paragraph explaining why the Olympics should change with the times or remain true to tradition. Check your writing for pronoun errors.

MyWritingLab & Lab Activity 39

mywritinglab For additional help with pronoun types, go to **www.mywritinglab.com** or complete **Lab Activity 39** in the separate *Resources for Writers* Lab Manual.

40

Pronoun Agreement, Pronoun Reference, and Point of View

Culture Note

TEXAS

The second-largest state geographically (the largest is Alaska), Texas has a rich, rough history intertwined with the history of the entire United States. From its Lone Star State heritage to its variety of cultures, Texas has made its mark on many aspects of American life.

The Alamo

FOOD FOR THOUGHT Although Texans lost the battle of the Alamo, "Remember the Alamo!" became a rallying cry for Texans throughout the war they won against Mexico. What examples of positive results from negative situations can you think of? Write a few sentences about how a negative situation produced positive results.

Responding to Images. *What kind of place—serious, pleasant, forbidding, safe—does the Alamo appear to be in the photo above? Write a few sentences based on your observations.*

PRONOUN AGREEMENT

Pronouns must be consistent in number with their **antecedents,** the word or words they replace. Singular antecedents require singular pronouns, just as plural antecedents require plural pronouns. In the examples that follow, the pronouns are underlined and their antecedents are in italics.

Correct: *Texans* swell their chests when talking about their state. (*Their* refers to *Texans* in both cases.)

Correct: The *flag* of Texas has undergone many changes throughout its life. (*Its* refers to *flag*.)

Correct: One *resident* of Texas claims he could never live anywhere else. (*He* refers to *resident*.)

Make sure that the pronouns you use in your writing always agree with their antecedents.

Incorrect: Texas is one place where a *person* can feel good about their life. (*Person* is singular, but the pronoun *their is* plural; the pronoun does not agree with its antecedent.)

Correct: In Texas, a *person* can feel good about his or her life.

In Texas, *people* can feel good about their lives.

Incorrect: *Each* of the three All-Pro Dallas Cowboys gave their autograph to the sick child. (*Each* is singular, but *their* is plural.)

Correct: *Each* of the three All-Pro Dallas Cowboys gave his autograph to the sick child.

Personal Pronouns

A **personal pronoun** refers to a specific person or thing.

Personal Pronouns

I, me, my, mine, myself	we, us, our, ours, ourselves
you, your, yours, yourself	they, them, their, theirs, themselves
he, him, his, himself	
she, her, hers, herself	
it, its, itself	

EXERCISE 1 Practicing Pronoun Agreement

Read the following paragraph, in which twelve pronouns are underlined. Fill in the chart that follows with each pronoun's antecedent (the word the pronoun refers to). The first one has been filled in for you.

Six Flags over Texas

¹Though Texas has long been part of the United States, <u>it</u> has been a part of other countries, too. ²The expression "six flags over Texas" refers to the different countries that Texas has been part of. ³The first flag to fly over Texas was the Spanish flag. ⁴The Spanish claimed what is now Texas for <u>their</u> own from 1519 to 1685 and from 1690 to 1821. ⁵In 1685, under the Frenchman René-Robert Cavelier de La Salle, France claimed the eastern part of Texas near the Gulf Coast. ⁶La Salle called <u>his</u> claim Fort St. Louis. ⁷Though the fort was an important settlement for the French, <u>it</u> was doomed by bad luck. ⁸The French claim ended when La Salle was murdered by one of <u>his</u> own men. ⁹The third flag to fly over Texas was Mexican; <u>it</u> features an eagle, a snake, and a cactus on bars of red, green, and white. ¹⁰However, Texans revolted against Mexican rule and won <u>their</u> independence in 1836 when the Mexican general Antonio López de Santa Anna declared <u>himself</u> dictator. ¹¹From 1836 to 1845, Texas was <u>its</u> own republic, and during this time much of Texans' pride in <u>their</u> region developed. ¹²The Lone Star flag, the fourth to fly over Texas, still flies nearly everywhere in Texas today. ¹³The fifth flag to fly over Texas kept the red, white, and blue of the Lone Star flag, but <u>it</u> included a circle of stars for the Confederacy, which Texas joined from 1861 to 1865. ¹⁴Last but not least, Texas flew the flag of the United States from 1845 to 1861 and has flown <u>it</u> from 1865 to the present.

	Pronoun	**Antecedent**
Sentence 1	it	Texas
Sentence 4	their	_____
Sentence 6	his	_____
Sentence 7	it	_____
Sentence 8	his	_____

Sentence 9	it	_____
Sentence 10 (two pronouns)	their	_____
	himself	_____
Sentence 11 (two pronouns)	its	_____
	their	_____
Sentence 13	it	_____
Sentence 14	it	_____

Indefinite Pronouns

Indefinite pronouns are pronouns that do not refer to any specific person or thing. Make sure that when you use an indefinite pronoun as the subject of a sentence, the verb agrees with it.

The pronouns that agree with these must also be singular: *he, him, his, she,* or *her.* If you don't know the gender of *everyone* or *anyone* in a sentence, use the expressions he or she or him or her to include both sexes.

Everyone loves his football team in Texas.

Among Texan women, no one knows whether she will become a football widow in the fall.

However, since Texan women are football fans, too, somebody usually has a party to watch the game in his or her home.

PRONOUN REFERENCE

Sometimes the antecedent to a pronoun is unclear. The following sentences contain unclear **pronoun references,** pronouns that do not seem to refer to anything in particular.

Unclear: When I called the University of Texas admissions office, they told me to send in an application. (The pronoun they doesn't refer to anyone specific; there is no plural word to act as an antecedent.)

To make the sentence clear, substitute a specific person for *they.*

Clear: When I called the University of Texas admissions office, the admissions clerk told me to send in an application.

Unclear:	Kathy told Rhonda that <u>her</u> Texas accent was fading. (In this sentence, the reader wonders whose accent—Kathy's or Rhonda's—was fading.)
Clear:	Kathy told Rhonda that <u>Rhonda's accent</u> was fading.
Clear:	Kathy told Rhonda, "Your Texas accent is fading."
Unclear:	I decided to move to Austin, <u>which</u> is great. (In this case, is the decision to move great? Or is Austin?)
Clear:	I decided to move to <u>the great city of Austin</u>.
Clear:	I made a <u>great decision</u> to move to Austin.

EXERCISE 2 Making Clear Pronoun References

Rewrite the following sentences to correct each unclear pronoun reference in italics.

1. In *The History of Texas, it* says that few men are as important as

Sam Houston. _____

_____

2. Sam Houston led *them* in their struggle to win Texas's independence

from Mexico. _____

_____

3. He served as president of the Republic of Texas and senator to the

United States Senate. *It* required a lot of work. _____

_____

_____

4. He was elected governor of Texas just before the Civil War; *they*

really wanted him to be their leader. _____

_____

5. However, Houston opposed the Confederacy's president, so *he* was removed from office. _____

_____

PRONOUN CONSISTENCY AND POINT OF VIEW

Good writing is clear and consistent in **point of view.** Point of view refers to the perspective of the writer: whether the writer is telling his or her own story (first person), giving directions or speaking directly to someone else (second person), or telling a story *about* someone else (third person).

First person:	I was upset when my flight was canceled.
Second person:	You should try to get another flight as soon as possible.
Third person:	He decided to skip his trip completely.

Pronouns should be consistent throughout your writing. For instance, if you start a paragraph using *I*, don't suddenly switch to using *you*. Such shifts can be confusing to your reader.

The pronoun *one* is usually used to mean a single, unspecified person.

Walking through the Dallas–Fort Worth airport, <u>one</u> could get lost.

Shifting to *you* is an easy error to make because we use *you* to mean *one*.

Point of View	Pronouns	
	Singular	Plural
First person	I (me, my, mine, myself)	we (us, our, ourselves)
Second person	you (your, yours, yourself)	you (your, yours, yourselves)
Third person	he (him, his, himself)	they (them, their, theirs, themselves)
	she (her, hers, herself)	
	it (its, itself)	
	one (one's, oneself)	

Incorrect: When <u>I</u> got off the plane in Dallas, <u>you</u> could feel the humidity.

Revised: When <u>I</u> got off the plane in Dallas, <u>I</u> could feel the humidity.

Incorrect: When <u>visitors</u> see the Alamo for the first time, <u>you</u> get goosebumps.

Revised: When <u>visitors</u> see the Alamo for the first time, <u>they</u> get goosebumps.

A pronoun used as a subject must agree in number (singular or plural) with its verb in the sentence.

<u>He</u> <u>is</u> from Texas. (Both *he* and *is* are singular.)

<u>They</u> <u>know</u> their way around the city. (Both *They* and *know* are plural.)

Sometimes changing a pronoun requires you to change the verb in a sentence. When the subject of the sentence changes point of view, the verb must reflect that change.

<u>They</u> <u>want</u> to stay here in San Antonio. (The plural subject *They* requires a plural verb, *want.*)

<u>He</u> <u>wants</u> to move to Austin. (The singular subject *He* requires a singular verb, *wants.*)

EXERCISE 3 Keeping Point of View Consistent

In the following sentences, correct any problems with inconsistent pronouns. Change the verb form if necessary. An example is done for you.

When visitors see the Alamo for the first time, ~~you~~ *they* get goosebumps.

1. When parents bring their families to the Alamo, one must teach

the children to appreciate it.

2. For instance, when parents tell their six-year-olds about the men

who died defending the Alamo, you often start by explaining

who Davey Crockett was.

3. If a parent wants to make seeing the Alamo a memorable experience, they should tell the child about it ahead of time.

4. When children understand how "Remember the Alamo" became a rallying cry for Texans, one takes pride even in the loss.

5. All in all, when parents prepare children to appreciate the Alamo, you are giving the youngsters an unforgettable lesson.

EDITING PRACTICE 1

Circle the correct pronouns in parentheses below.

Texans: Rich in More Than History

[1]Texans have gained prosperity from two main sources. [2]After the Civil War, (he or she, they) profited from longhorn cattle. [3](They, He or she) not only provided food for the growing United States but also gave many people work. [4]People had to raise, breed, and then herd the cattle. [5]The American cowboy was born from the longhorn business, and (his, their) work on the range has been romanticized for decades. [6]The legendary cattle drives that people read about in books and see in movies also received (his or her, their) start from cowboys' work on the range. [7]Another natural source of wealth for Texas is (their, its) oil resources. [8]Not far into the twentieth century, great oil gushers were discovered across Texas. [9]Like the longhorns, oil brought prosperity not just to the people who discovered (it, them) but also to those who worked on drilling and processing (it, them). [10]The oil business attracted additional businesses into oil communities to support the oil workers.

EDITING PRACTICE 2

In the sentences below, cross out the incorrect pronouns and write in the correct nouns. Then, circle the type of pronoun error made in each sentence. An example is done for you.

> The image of the Texas cowboy has left ~~their~~ *its* mark on American culture.
>
> (a.) Pronoun agreement   b. Pronoun reference   c. Point of view

1. When people see a cowboy in American movies, for instance, you often also see scenes that resemble the plains of Texas.

   a. Pronoun agreement   b. Pronoun reference   c. Point of view

2. A lone man on his trusty horse, Rusty shows his profile to the camera as the sun sets.

   a. Pronoun agreement   b. Pronoun reference   c. Point of view

3. When the cowboy speaks, their Texas accent comes through clearly in the greeting "Howdy, ma'am."

   a. Pronoun agreement   b. Pronoun reference   c. Point of view

4. When a cowboy speaks to his partner, his expression and tone of voice are always serious.

   a. Pronoun agreement   b. Pronoun reference   c. Point of view

5. When we see advertisements, too, you often see cowboy images.

   a. Pronoun agreement   b. Pronoun reference   c. Point of view

6. For years, one cigarette company has used a cowboy figure to promote their products.

   a. Pronoun agreement   b. Pronoun reference   c. Point of view

7. Every ad features a rugged, handsome cowboy smoking a cigarette or holding one in their hands.

   a. Pronoun agreement   b. Pronoun reference   c. Point of view

8. Certain clothing lines and car companies also show cowboys in its ads.

   a. Pronoun agreement   b. Pronoun reference   c. Point of view

9. In fact, when you watch cowboys on television, one can almost imagine being out on the range.

   a. Pronoun agreement   **b.** Pronoun reference   **c.** Point of view

10. Everyone who watches television must recall some time when they saw a cowboy.

    a. Pronoun agreement   **b.** Pronoun reference   **c.** Point of view

WRITING PRACTICE

Texas has been portrayed in fiction and in movies as a rugged land, full of rough beauty and tough, independent people. Write a paragraph about another place that you think has been stereotyped by the entertainment industry. Consider places with urban appeal (such as Manhattan or Chicago) or natural appeal (such as Florida or Colorado). Check your writing for pronoun agreement errors.

MyWritingLab & Lab Activity 40

mywritinglab For additional help with pronoun agreement, go to **www.mywritinglab. com** or complete **Lab Activity 40** in the separate *Resources for Writers* Lab Manual.

Adjectives and Adverbs

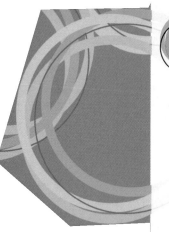

Culture Note

SLEEP

Though we often take sleep for granted, it is necessary for good physical, mental, and emotional health. Sleep is the rest period that allows our bodies and minds to "reset" themselves so we can think and act clearly and effectively.

WHAT IS AN ADJECTIVE?

An **adjective** describes a noun (person, place, or thing) or a pronoun. An adjective answers the question *which one, what kind*, or *how many*. Adjectives usually come before the word they describe, but they can come after forms of the verb *to be* (*am, is, are, was, were, have been*). Adjectives can also come after **linking verbs** such as *look, appear, become, feel, seem, smell, sound*, and *taste*. The adjectives are underlined in the following sentences, and the words they describe are in italics.

A dark *room* works best for sleeping. (The adjective *dark* describes *which* room the writer means.)

When my room feels cool, I always sleep well. (The adjective *cool* also describes *what kind* of room the writer means.)

Counting fifty *sheep* puts me to sleep. (The adjective *fifty* describes *how many* sheep the writer means.)

TYPES OF ADJECTIVES

People often think of adjectives as words that provide details appealing to the five senses—sight, sound, taste, touch, and smell—and often adjectives do just that. However, adjectives' primary job is to **modify,** or help identify, nouns or pronouns. Under that definition, several groups of words must be included as adjectives: articles, possessive and demonstrative pronouns, and numbers.

- **Articles**—the words *a, an*, and *the*—are adjectives that answer the questions *which one* and *how many*.
- **Possessive pronouns** show ownership or possession: *my, mine, your, yours, his, her, hers, its, our, ours, your, yours, their*, and *theirs*. These adjectives answer the question *which one*.
- **Demonstrative pronouns**—*this, that, these*, and *those*—introduce a specific person, place, or thing. These adjectives answer the question *which one*.
- **Numbers** answer the question *how many* and, thus, are adjectives.

EXERCISE 1 Identifying Adjectives

Circle the adjectives in the following sentences. Remember to circle articles, possessive pronouns, demonstrative pronouns, and numbers.

1. Depriving weary people of sleep does not sound as though it would help people sleep better.

2. However, the process has had excellent results.

3. Rest therapy begins by having people keep a log of their nightly sleep.

4. After a set amount of time, the patients calculate their average amount of sleep.

5. Some people average five hours a night, and others sleep seven glorious hours.

6. Then, these same people allow themselves only that amount of sleep.

7. If a person must get up for work at 6:00 a.m. and her average sleep time is six hours, then she cannot go to bed until midnight.

8. The idea behind the program is that people will come to view their beds as places where they get to sleep rather than as places where they only try to sleep.

9. Although they are skeptical, people who have tried this program say it works to help them sleep without waking up.

10. Their bodies become so tired that they are desperate for every minute of slumber they can get.

USING ADJECTIVES FOR COMPARISON

An important use for adjectives is making **comparisons,** the process of finding similarities or differences between two things. In the following examples, the adjectives are underlined and the words they describe are in italics.

My husband needs less *sleep* than I do.

In fact, I need the most *sleep* of anyone I know.

Comparative adjectives are used to compare *two* things. You can change most one-syllable adjectives and some two-syllable adjectives by adding -*er* to the end.

Sleeping in a tent is harder for me than for my brother.

The *pillow* on my bed is softer than the one in the guest room.

Superlative adjectives are used to compare three or more things. You can change most one- or two-syllable adjectives by adding -*est* to the end.

Of all my friends, Su has the nicest *bed*.

Kazuko and Margaret have warm comforters, but Su's is the warmest *comforter* of all.

Adjectives ending in *y*, however, must change the *y* to *i* before adding -er or -*est*.

I was sleepier after lunch than I was right before bed. (*Sleepy* becomes *sleepier*.)

For longer adjectives, add *more* when comparing two things or *most* when comparing three or more things.

The *mountains* are <u>more restful</u> than the city, but the *ocean* is the <u>most restful</u> place of all.

To make negative comparisons, use *less* when comparing two items and *least* when comparing three or more items.

Our *apartment* next to the rock band was <u>less restful</u> than our room at my parents' house.

Our apartment next to the fire station was the <u>least restful</u> *place* I ever lived.

Two points are important to keep in mind when using adjectives for comparison.

■ Use either *-er/-est* or *more/most* in making a comparison. Using both is incorrect.

Incorrect:	*I* was the <u>most sleepiest</u> I've ever been during my math class.
Correct:	*I* was the <u>sleepiest</u> I've ever been during my math class.
Incorrect:	*He* was <u>more happier</u> than I was after he took a nap.
Correct:	*He* was <u>happier</u> than I was after he took a nap.

■ Some adjectives have irregular comparative and superlative forms that you will have to memorize.

Adjective	Comparative	Superlative
bad	worse	worst
good	better	best
little (amount)	less	least
many	more	most
much	more	most
well	better	best

EXERCISE 2 Using the Correct Forms of Regular Adjectives

In each sentence, write the correct form of each adjective in parentheses in the blank. You may need to add -er or -est, more, or most. Two examples are done for you.

Of all the habits that can negatively affect sleeping, drinking alcohol

is one of the _most harmful_____. (harmful)

I try to stay up _later_____ on Friday nights than on Monday nights. (late)

1. Last night, I felt _____ than I usually do. (sleepy)

2. I wanted to go to bed _____ than usual, but I had work to do. (early)

3. In fact, the project I was working on is my _____ task for my job. (important)

4. I made myself comfortable, hoping to feel _____ about working late than I usually do. (positive)

5. However, making myself comfortable was the _____ mistake I could have made. I fell asleep and accomplished nothing. (big)

EXERCISE 3 Using the Correct Forms of Irregular Adjectives

In each sentence, write the correct form of each adjective in parentheses in the blank. You may need to add -er or -est, more, or most. An example is done for you.

I always sleep _better_____ on hard mattresses than on soft ones. (good)

1. Many tips can help people get a _____ night's sleep than they have gotten in the past. (good)

2. Getting of exercise makes people feel _____ than if they simply sit in a chair all day. (relaxed)

3. Exercising early in the day or just before sundown gives the _____ benefits. (good)

4. One of the _____ mistakes people can make is using the bedroom to do work. (bad)

5. Working in the bedroom trains many people to think of their rooms as a place of business, not of rest; thus, getting to sleep is

_____ than if they only slept in their rooms. (hard)

WHAT IS AN ADVERB?

An **adverb** can describe a verb, an adjective, or another adverb. Many adverbs end in -*ly*. Adjectives answer the questions *how, when, where*, and *to what extent*. The adverbs in the following sentences are underlined and the words they describe are in italics.

After a lot of exercise, I *fall asleep* easily. (The adverb *easily* describes *how* the writer falls asleep.)

I *will get up* at the same time tomorrow as I do every day. (The adverb *tomorrow* describes *when* the writer will get up at the same time.)

My math teacher's lecture made me feel extremely *sleepy*. (The adverb *extremely* describes *to what extent* the writer felt sleepy.)

Tip: Never, no, not, and *very* are also adverbs.

EXERCISE 4 Identifying Adverbs

Circle the adverbs in the sentences below.

1. Different strategies help me wake up easily each morning.

2. At night I set my clock radio to my favorite station and turn the volume up so that the music plays loudly the next day.

3. In the morning I brew a cup of very strong tea.

4. Before I take an extremely hot shower, I do my yoga exercises.

5. I've learned that doing things I enjoy when I wake up helps me not to dread getting out of bed.

CORRECTING COMMON ERRORS WITH ADJECTIVES AND ADVERBS

Writers sometimes incorrectly use adjectives when they should use adverbs, especially after a verb. Adding *-ly* to the underlined adjectives makes them adverbs.

Incorrect: My roommate *sleeps* sound.
Correct: My roommate *sleeps* soundly.

Incorrect: To wake myself up, I *sing loud*.
Correct: To wake myself up, I *sing loudly*.

EXERCISE 5 Choosing Between Adjectives and Adverbs

Circle the correct modifiers in each sentence below. Remember that adjectives describe nouns and pronouns while adverbs describe verbs, adjectives, and other adverbs.

Important Sleep

People need to be (serious, seriously) about their sleep habits. When a person becomes (over, overly) tired, body and mind crave sleep (desperate, desperately). Rapid eye movement (REM) sleep is easy to recognize by the (quick, quickly) movements the sleeper's eyes make beneath the eyelids. Although it is (usual, usually) for REM sleep to come every ninety minutes or so during the night, REM sleep happens more (frequent, frequently) toward morning. A person who sleeps only a few hours misses the (real, really) important REM sleep periods when the brain restores itself most (efficient, efficiently). Brain connections can grow (noticeable, noticeably) during REM sleep, too. People should be (careful, carefully) in planning their sleep times so they can get enough rest.

Good and *Well*

The two words *good* and *well* are often confused. These words may seem to have the same meaning, but *good* is an adjective, which describes nouns and pronouns, while *well* is an adverb, which describes verbs, adjectives, and other adverbs. *Well* can also be used as an adjective to describe someone's health.

My new puppy is a good *sleeper*. (The adjective *good* modifies the noun *sleeper*.)

In fact, she has *slept* well from the moment I brought her home from the pound. (The adverb *well* modifies the verb *slept*.)

Aside from occasional indigestion, *she* is generally well. (The adjective *well* modifies the pronoun *she*.)

EXERCISE 6 Using *Good* and *Well* Correctly

Circle the correct modifiers in parentheses below.

1. I suffer a lot if I don't sleep (good, well).

2. For instance, if my sleep isn't (good, well), I feel stiff in the morning.

3. The stiffness causes me to hunch over, which causes me not to drive (good, well).

4. Then, even if I wake up in a (good, well) mood, I always get a headache.

5. The headache ruins any chance I have of performing (good, well) at work.

EDITING PRACTICE

The following paragraph contains ten adjective and adverb errors in bold print. Cross out the incorrect word or words and write in the correct modifier.

How to Wreck Your Sleep

If you want to get a poor night's sleep, you can do that **easy**. First, make sure you never go to bed or get up at the same time, and you will keep your body **real** confused. Another trick that works **good** is drinking caffeinated beverages. Coffee, tea, and soft drinks are some of the **more good** sleep wreckers. If that doesn't do the job, drinking alcohol will **sure** get in the way of your slumber. Alcohol makes people **more sleepier** than not drinking, but it also interferes with the sleep cycle. You might fall asleep **quick** after drinking alcohol, but you're likely to wake up after a few hours. One more way to make sure you don't sleep **good** is to think about your worries just as you're trying to drift off. This method is guaranteed to keep your eyes open for the **most longest** time. Finally, sleeping in a hot room is a sure way to make sleep come **slow**.

WRITING PRACTICE

This chapter has presented information on how to sleep well. Write a paragraph explaining any tips or tricks you use to fall asleep. If you don't use any specific tricks to fall asleep, write the steps you follow to get ready for bed. Check your writing for adjective and adverb errors.

MyWritingLab & Lab Activity 41

mywritinglab For additional help with adjectives and adverbs, go to **www.mywritinglab. com** or complete **Lab Activity 41** in the separate *Resources for Writers* Lab Manual.

Misplaced Modifiers

TORNADOES

The subject of movies and a cause of great damage, tornadoes are formed from a combination of weather conditions. Some people make a career out of "chasing" tornadoes, but most residents of areas they affect find them more frightening than fascinating.

Tornado

JOURNAL RESPONSE Common in the midwestern United States, tornadoes are both powerful and terrifying. What is the most dramatic natural disaster or occurrence that you've experienced? Write for ten minutes about the most powerful storm, drought, earthquake, or other natural occurrence of your life.

Responding to Images. *What about this photo communicates impending danger? Write a few sentences to explain.*

WHAT IS A MISPLACED MODIFIER?

Modifiers (adjectives and adverbs) clarify our ideas and make them more vivid. However, just as a well-placed adverb or adjective can help us communicate our ideas, a misplaced modifier can confuse our readers. A **misplaced modifier** is a word or group of words in the wrong place. A misplaced modifier sends an incorrect message to the reader. In the sentences below, the misplaced modifiers are underlined and the words being modified are in italics.

Misplaced modifier: During the *rain* my brother stayed dry under his umbrella, which was soaking everyone.

(The modifier *which was soaking everyone* describes *rain*. However, the placement of the modifier makes it seem as if the modifier is describing *umbrella*.)

Misplaced modifier: *Jim* had always wanted to see a tornado growing up in California.

(Here *growing up in California* really modifies *Jim*, but the placement of the modifier makes it seem as if he wanted to see a *tornado* growing up in California.)

EXERCISE 1 Interpreting Misplaced Modifiers

Underline the misplaced modifiers in the following sentences. On the lines below, write (a) what the writer means and (b) what the sentence actually says. An example is done for you.

I saw the tornado blow over a huge tree watching from the window.

a. I was watching from the window.

b. The tree was watching from the window.

1. Tornadoes give me "bad hair" days blowing through the sky.

a. _____

b. _____

2. In fact, my permanent waves—that I nearly paid fifty dollars for—were blown right out!

a. _____

b. _____

3. I even prepared for tornadoes wearing a hair net.

a. _____

b. _____

4. It didn't matter; the twister destroyed my "up-do" with dangerous gusts.

a. _____

b. _____

5. I looked at my disheveled appearance in the mirror with an angry expression.

a. _____

b. _____

6. My brother almost spent thirty dollars on his own twister problem.

a. _____

b. _____

7. He is addicted to watching tornado movies with nacho cheese tortilla chips.

a. _____

b. _____

8. He's nearly seen *Twister* twenty times.

a. _____

b. _____

9. He also loves to watch the movie from the sofa with the flying monkeys in it.

a. _____

b. _____

10. Last fall, he watched every movie, documentary, and news show using a special setting on TiVo.

a. _____

b. _____

CORRECTING MISPLACED MODIFIERS

Most misplaced modifiers are simply too far away from what they're describing. Thus, the easiest way to fix a misplaced modifier error is to move the modifier as close as possible to what it's describing.

Misplaced modifier:	During the rain my brother stayed dry under his umbrella, which was soaking everyone.
Correct:	During the rain, which was soaking everyone, my brother stayed dry under his umbrella.
Incorrect:	Jim had always wanted to see a tornado growing up in California.
Correct:	Growing up in California, Jim had always wanted to see a tornado.

EXERCISE 2 Identifying and Correcting Misplaced Modifiers

Underline the misplaced modifiers below. Then, rewrite each sentence so that the modifier is placed correctly. An example is done for you.

Misplaced modifier: Many movies feature tornadoes that are quite popular.

Revised: Many movies that are quite popular feature tornadoes.

1. Misplaced modifier: In one film, a tornado picks up a house called *The Wizard of Oz*.

Revised: _____

_____

2. Misplaced modifier: The main character, Dorothy, was blown around by the tornado, who was asleep in the house.

Revised: _____

_____

3. Misplaced modifier: Another movie features tornadoes made in 1996.

Revised: _____

4. Misplaced modifier: This film has many impressive special effects, called *Twister*.

Revised: _____

_____

5. Misplaced modifier: The tornadoes in *Twister* make a house roll, a semi truck drop from the sky, and cows fly, which are scary and dangerous.

Revised: _____

_____

WRITING PRACTICE

Wild weather always gets our attention, yet tornadoes appear to hold a special fascination for people. Write a paragraph explaining *what about* tornadoes people find particularly interesting. *Note:* If you don't find tornadoes fascinating, write about some natural occurence—such as earthquakes—that you do find interesting. Check your writing to eliminate misplaced modifiers.

MyWritingLab & Lab Activity 42

mywritinglab For additional help with misplaced modifiers, go to **www.mywritinglab. com** or complete **Lab Activity 42** in the separate *Resources for Writers* Lab Manual.

Dangling Modifiers

WHAT IS A DANGLING MODIFIER?

A **dangling modifier** is a group of words that opens a sentence but does not modify the noun following it. Most dangling modifiers contain a verb form, and often the words they are meant to modify do not actually appear in the sentence. In the following sentence, the underlined dangling modifier sends the wrong message.

Incorrect: <u>Packed with nine vitamins and minerals</u>, my teeth grow stronger from milk.

Read literally, this sentence says that someone's *teeth* are packed with vitamins and minerals. But the writer means to say that something else—*milk*—is packed with those nutrients.

CORRECTING DANGLING MODIFIERS

The writer has three options for revision to correct a dangling modifier.

- Put the word being described right after the dangling modifier as the subject of the sentence.

> Correct: Packed with nine vitamins and minerals, *milk* makes my teeth grow stronger.

■ Make the word being described part of the modifier.

> Correct: Because *milk* is packed with nine vitamins and minerals, my teeth grow stronger from it. (The reader now has no doubt that milk is what contains the nutrients.)

■ Move the dangling modifier close to the word being described.

> Correct: My teeth grow stronger from *milk*, which is packed with nine vitamins and minerals. (The writer adds *which is* before the moved modifier in order to make the meaning clear.)

Cows Being Milked

CONDUCT AN INTERVIEW Having advanced beyond hand-milking for greater productivity, dairies use automated milking machines to milk cows. How much milk do your friends drink? Interview two friends to learn about their typical milk consumption. Write a few sentences summarizing your findings.

Responding to Images.   Write a few sentences describing the photo above as if you didn't know what it was. What does the photo make you think of?

EXERCISE 1 Interpreting Dangling Modifiers

Underline the misplaced modifiers in the sentences below. Then, on the following lines, explain (a) what the writer means and (b) what the sentence actually says. An example is done for you.

<u>Taking twenty-four hours to be processed</u>, cows provide milk.

a. Writer's meaning: The milk takes twenty-four hours to be

processed.

b. Sentence meaning: The cows take twenty-four hours to be

processed.

1. Milked with automated milking equipment, no human hands are used.

a. Writer's meaning: _____

_____

b. Sentence meaning: _____

_____

2. Cleaned thoroughly before being attached to the milking machines, the milking process takes place on many cows at once.

a. Writer's meaning: _____

_____

b. Sentence meaning: _____

_____

3. Stored in giant, chilled holding tanks, the cows give up to seven gallons of milk each.

a. Writer's meaning: _____

_____

b. Sentence meaning: _____

_____

4. Delivered to a processing plant, special trucks arrive each day.

a. Writer's meaning: _____

_____

b. Sentence meaning: _____

_____

5. Flowing through stainless steel pipes into the processing plant, modern equipment helps make many dairy products.

a. Writer's meaning: _____

_____

b. Sentence meaning: _____

_____

EXERCISE 2 Identifying and Correcting Dangling Modifiers

Underline the dangling modifiers below. Then, rewrite each sentence to correct the error. An example is done for you.

Dangling modifier: <u>Filled with bacteria</u>, the French chemist Louis Pasteur discovered a way to "clean" raw milk.

Revised: The French chemist Louis Pasteur discovered a way to "clean"

raw milk, which is filled with bacteria.

1. Dangling modifier: Heating milk at 161.5 degrees for fifteen seconds, the federal government requires raw milk to be pasteurized.

Revised: _____

_____

2. Dangling modifier: Coming straight out of the cow, dairy farmers work hard to prevent germs and bacteria from growing.

Revised: _____

_____

3. Dangling modifier: Making it safe to drink and fresh for long periods of time, pasteurized milk is a healthy food.

Revised: _____

_____

4. Dangling modifier: A great favorite around the world, dairies always use pasteurized milk for ice cream.

Revised: _____

_____

5. Dangling modifier: Making sure it is safe to be turned into products such as yogurt and cottage cheese, milk is tested by quality control labs.

Revised: _____

_____

WRITING PRACTICE

Milk not only comes from different sources, but it also comes in different forms: nonfat, low fat, or buttermilk, for instance. Write a paragraph about another food (such as tomatoes) or beverage that takes many forms. Check your writing to eliminate dangling modifiers.

MyWritingLab & Lab Activity 43

mywritinglab For additional help with dangling modifiers, go to **www.mywritinglab.com** or complete **Lab Activity 43** in the separate *Resources for Writers* Lab Manual.

Errors in Parallelism

WHAT IS PARALLELISM?

Clear, consistent writing requires parallel, or balanced, sentences. In **parallelism,** or **parallel structure,** two or more related words or groups of words have the same structure. The following sentences contain faulty parallel sentence structure.

Faulty parallelism: Cookies come in many shapes, sizes, and are of different flavors.

                       (The first two items in the series are nouns, but the third—*are of different flavors*—is not.)

Faulty parallelism: People enjoy eating cookies for snacks and when they want dessert.

                       (The first item in the series is a prepositional phrase, but the second is a clause.)

Read the corrected, parallel versions of the same sentences.

Revised: Cookies come in many <u>shapes</u>, <u>sizes</u>, and <u>flavors</u>.
(The three items in the series are all plural nouns.)

Revised: People enjoy eating cookies <u>for snacks</u> and <u>for dessert</u>.
(The two prepositional phrases *for snacks* and *for dessert* are parallel.)

Parallel structure gives your writing consistency and strength. The repetition of structures helps your reader anticipate points in your writing.

RECOGNIZING SPECIAL SENTENCE STRUCTURES

Some sentence structures require parallelism. The following terms contain two parts that are used to link words or word groups. The words or word groups following each part must be parallel.

Terms Needing Parallel Structure

both . . . and   neither . . . nor
either . . . or   not only . . . but also

The underlined words or word groups in each sentence below are parallel.

Peanut butter cookies are *both* <u>tasty</u> and <u>filling</u>.
(*Tasty* and *filling* are both adjectives.)

People either <u>enjoy baking</u> *or* <u>dislike it</u>.
(*Enjoy baking* and *dislike it* are both verb phrases.)

I love *not only* <u>chocolate chip cookies</u> but also <u>brownies</u>.
(*Chocolate chip cookies* and *brownies* are both nouns.)

You can create parallel sentences using a variety of structures. Nouns, verbs, prepositional phrases, adjectives, and clauses can all help you make sentences parallel. The following example uses verbs to create parallel structure.

Rather than writing "measured ingredients," "creaming butter and sugar," and "roll dough," write, "My favorite cookies involve *measuring* the ingredients, *creaming* the butter and sugar, and *rolling* the dough."

All three verbs have *-ing* endings, which makes the sentence parallel.

EXERCISE 1 Correcting Faulty Parallelism

The sentences below contain errors in parallelism. Rewrite each sentence using parallel structure. An example is done for you.

Faulty parallelism: Cookies resulted first from a test, then from an experiment, and finally someone made a decision.

Revised: *Cookies resulted first from a test, then from an experiment,*

and finally from a decision.

1. Faulty parallelism: Originally, cooks wanted to test oven temperature, batter flavor, and that the consistency of the batter was good.

   Revised: _____

   _____

2. Faulty parallelism: Baking small amounts of batter not only told the cooks whether the temperature was correct but also it created a new treat.

   Revised: _____

   _____

3. Faulty parallelism: Significant factors were color, shape, and how big the batter bits were.

   Revised: _____

4. Faulty parallelism: These features told the cooks both whether the oven was hot enough and the cooked batter's flavor.

   Revised: _____

   _____

5. Faulty parallelism: The test cakes became known either as *koekje* in Dutch and *cookies* in English.

   Revised: _____

EXERCISE 2 Writing Parallel Sentences

The sentences below are incomplete. Finish each sentence using parallel structure. An example is done for you.

My favorite things about going to a <u>Chinese restaurant are having great food, eating with chopsticks, and</u> *getting fortune cookies*_____.

1. I like not only breaking the fortune cookies open _____.

_____

2. Fortune cookies are usually light brown, crunchy, _____.

3. I find that the fortunes within the cookies are usually either

educated _____.

4. After reading many, many fortunes from these cookies, I am

convinced that they are neither wise _____

5. Nevertheless, the fortunes are often both clever _____.

BALANCED WORD ORDER

Sometimes using the same word order in two clauses creates a more effective sentence.

Unbalanced: One <u>type</u> of cookie is the drop cookie; using a mold for cookies makes another <u>type</u>.

(Although *type* is repeated, it has a different role in each clause.)

Balanced: One <u>type</u> of cookie is the drop cookie; another <u>type</u> is the molded cookie.

(Here, *type* is the subject of both clauses.)

A series of balanced sentences can make it easier for a reader to anticipate the writer's meaning.

Balanced: One <u>type</u> of cookie is the drop cookie. Another <u>type</u> is the molded cookie. A third <u>type</u>, my favorite, is the rolled cookie, which can be cut into shapes.

(Here, *type* is the subject of three sentences in a series.)

EXERCISE 3 Writing Balanced Sentences

Each of the following sentences will become the first of two balanced statements. Write your own second sentence with a structure that is parallel to, or balanced with, the first. *Hint*: You might find it helpful to start your sentence with a topic or situation that contrasts with the one given. An example is done for you.

Drop cookies are dropped onto a cookie sheet and then baked.

Bar cookies are baked in a pan and then cut into bars.

1. During vacation, I love to sleep in. _____

_____

2. My boyfriend thinks that women should work outside the home.___

_____

3. When it's rainy, I feel like being lazy._____

_____

4. My study habits include drinking a lot of coffee. _____

_____

5. The flower under the tree is lovely._____

_____

EDITING PRACTICE

The following paragraph contains five errors in parallelism. Cross out the sections containing errors, and replace them with parallel constructions.

The Toll House Cookie: An American Treat

Not only was the invention of cookies an accident, and the invention of the Toll House cookie was a surprise, too. In Massachusetts in the 1930s, Ruth Wakefield, an innkeeper, was baking cookies. Because she ran out of nuts, she needed a substitute. Either she could use nothing or use some chocolate. She read the recipe, looked around her kitchen, and a bar of baking chocolate ended up being cut for her dough. The now-famous batter was made of flour, butter, and it also had a fair amount of brown sugar. Sure enough, the "accidental" cookies were a hit. They were named Toll House cookies after the inn. The cookies became famous, the Nestlé chocolate company heard about them, and asked Ms. Wakefield for permission to print the recipe on its chocolate wrappers. Saying yes, Ms. Wakefield requested only a lifetime supply of chocolate in return.

WRITING PRACTICE

This chapter has provided information about cookies, a common treat. Write a paragraph discussing an unusual aspect of a food you enjoy. For instance, write about how some cheeses contain mold.

MyWritingLab & Lab Activity 44

mywritinglab For additional help with parallelism, go to **www.mywritinglab.com** or complete **Lab Activity 44** in the separate *Resources for Writers* Lab Manual.

Punctuation and Mechanics

Tied in Knots

OBESERVE YOUR WORLD With gas prices skyrocketing, many drivers claim to be turning to alternative methods of transportation, such as buses or bicycles. Is it helping? Write a few sentences about how traffic in your area seems to be improving or worsening.

Responding to Images. *What are the most or least appealing aspects of the photo above? Explain.*

Commas

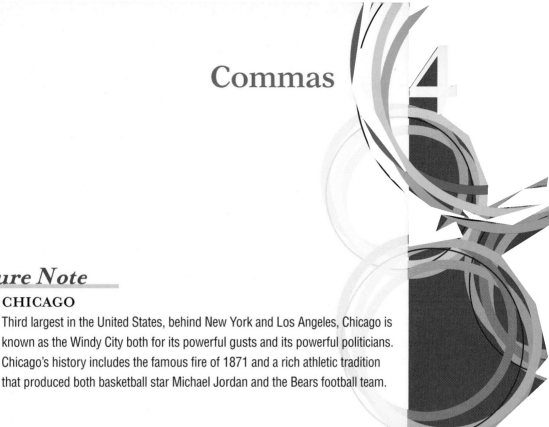

UNDERSTANDING COMMAS **,**

Commas separate items in a sentence. It's easy to leave out commas by mistake or put them in where they don't belong, but a misplaced comma can radically alter the meaning of your sentence. Knowing how to use commas properly is essential to keeping your writing clear and easy to read. Commas have six main uses.

- Setting apart items in a series
- Setting off introductory material
- Setting off information that interrupts the main ideas in a sentence
- Joining two independent clauses also linked by a coordinating conjunction (*for, and, nor, but, or, yet,* or *so*)
- Setting off direct quotations from the rest of the sentence
- Clarifying everyday information such as dates, addresses, and numbers

You may have been taught that a comma signals a pause in a sentence, but this guideline can lead to mistakes. Commas actually direct the reader to *keep reading*. To signal a pause or break, writers use a semicolon, a colon, or a period.

SETTING ITEMS APART IN A SERIES

Use commas to set apart, or separate, items in a series. A **series** is two or more items—for example, two or more adjectives—in a row.

Chicago is known for its cold, gusty winds.

Also famous are its politics, the Sears Tower, and the Great Lakes.

Comma Before a Conjunction in a Series

In a series of three or more items joined by a conjunction, the final comma helps clarify meaning.

Confusing: I ordered three deli sandwiches: tuna salad, ham and cheese and pastrami on rye.

Clear: I ordered three deli sandwiches: tuna salad, ham and cheese, and pastrami on rye.

Commas in a Series of Adjectives

Use a comma between adjectives in a two-item series only if the word *and* can logically be substituted for the comma.

Chicago is known for its cold, gusty winds.

Chicago is known for its cold and gusty winds.

If the word *and* sounds strange between two adjectives, do not use a comma.

Chicago's mayor received a big fat raise.

(Saying "a big *and* fat raise" would sound strange, so omit the comma.)

EXERCISE 1 Using Commas in a Series

Add commas where necessary in the following sentences.

1. Some well-known Chicago figures include Al Capone,Richard J. Daley,Harold Washington,and Oprah Winfrey.

2. All these people are known for their influence,intelligence,and success in their chosen areas.

3. Al Capone, however, chose to make his mark through illegal activities, such as gambling,prostitution,and bootlegging.

4. Richard J. Daley, on the other hand, was a charismatic,focused mayor who was known for his "machine" politics.

5. The first African-American mayor of Chicago, Harold Washington, was a decorated veteran of World War II,a member of the Illinois House and Senate,and a member of the U.S. House of Representatives.

Chicago Skyline

CRITICAL THINKING As the third largest city in the United States, Chicago, Illinois, boasts an impressive skyline. After looking at the photo above, what do you think is the city's mood? Write a few sentences describing the mood of Chicago, using specific details from the photo to support your ideas.

Responding to Images. *What conclusion can you draw about a city that places pleasure boats, ferris wheels, and skyscrapers close together? Write a few sentences explaining why you think this.*

SETTING OFF INTRODUCTORY MATERIAL

Use commas to set off introductory material in a sentence.

Though famous for its sports and politics , Chicago is also famous for serving excellent steaks.

Different from steaks elsewhere in the country , Chicago steaks are sometimes served "blue."

In fact , the term "blue" for meat comes from the fact that the steak is so rare that it is still cool in the middle.

If the introductory phrase is very short and describes *when* or *where*, the comma is sometimes omitted.

In 1902 Richard J. Daley was born.

EXERCISE 2 Using Commas to Set off Introductory Material

Add commas where necessary in the following sentences.

1. A number of years ago Chicago hosted an unusual art display.

2. Featuring life-sized cow sculptures all over the city the display titled "Cows on Parade " met with mixed reactions.

3. Unlike their counterparts in the field these cows were not simply black, brown, or spotted.

4. Instead the Chicago cows were decorated in almost every way imaginable.

5. In designs from florals to plaids the cows in Chicago made their own statement in the art world.

SETTING OFF INFORMATION THAT INTERRUPTS THE MAIN IDEAS IN A SENTENCE

One of the most important uses of the comma is to set off, or highlight, information that interrupts the main ideas in a sentence. Such information is often interesting and colorful, but it is usually not essential to understanding the main ideas.

Interruptions in the Middle of a Sentence

Use two commas to set off information that interrupts the middle of a sentence.

> Legend has it that the Great Fire , one of Chicago's most famous tragedies , had a humble beginning.

> Mrs. O'Leary's cow , not concerned with fire safety , kicked over a lantern in the barn.

> Thus, the Great Chicago Fire of 1871 , which claimed thousands of lives , may have been started by a cow.

Essential and Unessential Information

Use commas to separate information from the rest of the sentence *only if that information is not essential to the sense of the sentence*. For instance, if you leave out the information between the commas, the sentences above about the Great Chicago Fire still make sense. Thus, the commas are necessary.

In the following sentence, the underlined information is necessary for the sentence to make sense. Therefore, no commas should be used.

> The cow that supposedly started the Great Chicago Fire belonged to Mrs. O'Leary.

Leaving out the information *that supposedly the Great Chicago Fire* would make the full meaning of the sentence unclear. Readers would not know *which* cow the writer is referring to. Similarly, the following sentence requires no commas.

> The barn belonging to the O'Learys was close to downtown Chicago.

The information *belonging to the O'Learys* is necessary to identify the barn. Without this information, the reader has no idea *which* barn the writer means.

Often you can tell whether commas are necessary by reading a sentence out loud. You can hear whether a piece of information is necessary to the meaning of the sentence. If the information is necessary, do not use commas. If the information is *not* needed for a full understanding of the sentence, use commas.

Additional Material at the End of a Sentence

Use commas to separate added material at the end of a sentence.

> Oprah Winfrey has made the most of her education and experience**,** becoming one of the most successful businesswomen in America.

In this case, *becoming one of the most successful businesswomen in America* could have come at the beginning or in the middle of the sentence instead of at the end.

> Becoming one of the most successful businesswomen in America**,** Oprah Winfrey has made the most of her education and experience.

> Oprah Winfrey **,** becoming one of the most successful businesswomen in America**,** has made of the most of her education.

Regardless of where it appears, the phrase provides extra information that is not essential to the meaning of the sentence. Thus, it must be set off from the rest of the sentence by a comma or commas.

Direct Address

When people are being **addressed**—spoken or written to—their names should be set off from the rest of the sentence.

> Jed **,** which way is Chicago?

> I know **,** Ronald **,** why you are doing this.

EXERCISE 3 Using Commas to Set Off Extra Information

Add commas where necessary in the following sentences.

1. Oprah Winfrey one of Chicago's most famous residents has done much to benefit other people.

2. Winfrey's proposal to require that convicted child abusers register in a national database signed into law by President Clinton in 1994 shows her dedication to children's causes.

3. Reading another interest of Winfrey's is promoted by Oprah's Book Club.

4. Books that Winfrey presents on her show often become best-sellers. Thus, unknown writers who might not otherwise receive much public exposure are given an opportunity for success.

5. Finally, Oprah Winfrey has done much to promote women's issues. One of Winfrey's companies Oxygen Media is dedicated to producing Internet and cable programming for women.

JOINING TWO INDEPENDENT CLAUSES LINKED BY A COORDINATING CONJUNCTION

One of the most important comma uses is joining two independent clauses. When two independent clauses are joined *without* a comma, the result is a run-on sentence—a common error.

Keep in mind, too, that standard written English requires a coordinating conjunction (one of the FANBOYS: *for, and, nor, but, or, yet, so*) along with the comma.

The highs and lows of Chicago politics are famous **,** and many powerful Chicago politicians are Democrats.
independent clause

The aldermen of Chicago are one reason for Chicago's political fame **, for** aldermen are extremely powerful in the city's daily functions.

An alderman is like a city council member **, but** he or she is responsible for city regions known as wards.

The sentences contain two complete ideas in the form of two independent clauses. Thus, they also contain a conjunction and a comma.

Tip: Do not use a comma when a sentence has one subject but two verbs. In the following sentences, the nouns are underlined once and the verbs twice.

Aldermen address city issues and solve problems for their wards.

They listen to their ward residents and act according to the needs of

the people.

EXERCISE 4 Using Commas to Join Independent Clauses

Add commas where necessary in the following sentences.

1. Unlike many other large cities, Chicago is run by aldermen but the mayor has influence as well.

2. Chicago aldermen are elected officials but the mayor may appoint an alderman if someone retires or resigns.

3. Chicago is divided up into fifty districts known as wards and an alderman is responsible for the issues of his or her ward.

4. Every ten years the wards are reorganized for some wards become more heavily populated than others.

5. Reorganization gives the wards equal population so they also have equal power.

6. Some wards are miles long but others are only one-half mile long.

7. Residents can seek help from city agencies or they can approach their alderman with their concerns.

8. Chicago aldermen have great power for Chicago has great resources in terms of people and money.

9. In Chicago, the aldermen are more important than state senators for aldermen are the ones to whom most people turn.

10. Garbage collection is an important issue in urban areas but aldermen have to solve other problems as well.

SETTING OFF DIRECT QUOTATIONS

Use a comma to signal the start, and sometimes the end, of a quotation. In most cases, you should place periods and commas *inside* the quotation marks.

The actor Gary Cole said , "I miss everything about Chicago except January and February." (The comma indicates the start of the quotation.)

"Chicago will give you a chance , "the writer Lincoln Steffens states. "The sporting spirit is the spirit of Chicago." (The comma indicates the end of a quoted sentence.)

"I set foot in this city , " Oprah Winfrey claimed , "and just walking down the street, it was like roots, like the motherland. I knew I belonged here." (The paired commas signal an interruption in the quotation.)

EXERCISE 5 Using Commas to Set Off Direct Quotations

Add commas to set off the quotation in each sentence below.

1. As Frank Sinatra sang in a great song "Chicago is my kind of town."

2. "I wrote about Chicago after looking the town over for years and years "said the poet Carl Sandburg.

3. Former Vice President Dan Quayle made a mistake when he said "It is wonderful to be here in the great state of Chicago."

4. "Anywhere in the world you hear a Chicago bluesman play "said former Congressman Ralph Metcalfe "it's a Chicago sound born and bred."

5. "I give you Chicago " stated the writer H. L. Mencken. "It is not London and Harvard. It is not Paris and buttermilk. It is American in every chitling and sparerib. It is alive from snout to tail."

CLARIFYING EVERYDAY INFORMATION

Commas help us make sense of and organize everyday information. Use commas in the following situations.

■ **Dates**

The Great Fire of Chicago , which began on October 8 , 1871 , was a catastrophe.

■ **Addresses**

My brother used to live at 9 Belden Avenue , Chicago , Illinois 60614.

■ **Greetings and Closings of Letters**

Dear Mom ,

Dear Professor Chen ,

Sincerely ,

Note: In business correspondence, use a colon (*Dear Sir:* or *Dear Madam:*) instead of a comma.

■ **Numbers**

When a Chicago millionaire made $2,500,368 in one year, he paid taxes in excess of $1,003,000.

EXERCISE 6 **Using Commas to Organize Everyday Information**

Add commas where necessary in the following sentences.

1. Chicago is the home of more than 2 800 000 people.

2. My favorite store is located at 450 Michigan Avenue Chicago Illinois.

3. September 4 1983 was the day Oprah Winfrey came to Chicago.

4. Since that date, Oprah Winfrey has received praise from more than 100 000 fans.

5. I was sad to leave Chicago, but I love my beautiful house at 4500 J Street Sacramento California where I live now.

EDITING PRACTICE 1

Add commas where necessary in the following paragraph. You will need to add twenty-two commas in all.

A Taste of Chicago

Because of its ethnic diversity Chicago has much to offer in terms of food. From its Irish population Chicago offers corned beef hash and green beer especially on St. Patrick's Day. From its residents with a German heritage Chicago gets wonderful beef sausage called bratwurst and sauerkraut. In fact one of Chicago's most famous restaurants is the Berghoff Restaurant located at 17 West Adams Street. This restaurant was the first to get a liquor license after Prohibition was repealed. People with Russian roots also have contributed to Chicago's food choices. At Russian Tea Time also located on Adams Street more than 10 000 people have been served vodka beef stroganoff and borscht. In the area of Chicago known as

Greektown one of the city's most famous restaurants is Pegasus Restaurant and Taverna. It is known for its fresh fish, authentic atmosphere and flaming Greek cheese called *Saganaki*. Perhaps the most famous Chicago food is the Chicago-style pizza. Deeper than regular pizzas Chicago-style pizza has a thick crust. On top of the crust are piled layers of cheese sauce meat and other assorted toppings. Two famous pizza restaurants in Chicago are Gino's East and Giordano's. These types of food and others are celebrated at the annual Taste of Chicago festival which brings Chicago residents together to try wonderful food.

EDITING PRACTICE 2

Add commas as necessary to the following letter. You will need to add twenty commas in all.

Faye Johnson
53001 East Portola Avenue
Santa Ana CA 92701

August 23 2005

Dear Mom

I'm having a great time here in Chicago! Every day Monte and I do something different. Yesterday we visited the Art Institute took a sky-line cruise on Lake Michigan and saw a Cubs game. Even though the Cubs lost the game was a lot of fun. I'm exhausted but it's great to be here. Monte's family his dad in particular likes to eat as much as I do so we've been trying new food every day. So far we've had pizza hot dogs at the game and steaks. I think I've gained 1 000 pounds. By the time I get home, I probably won't fit through the front door so you should get the diet food ready for me. Actually I'm not eating that much; it's so humid that I'm sweating off whatever I gain. Over the next few days I plan to visit the Northwestern University campus (actually in Evanston Illinois) along with the University of Chicago. Maybe that will get me motivated to fill out those college applications when I get home. Well we're going to walk down Michigan Avenue to find souvenirs for you and Dad so I need to end here.

Love

Terrell

WRITING PRACTICE

This chapter has introduced interesting details about Chicago. What is interesting about where you live? Write a paragraph discussing aspects of your home, neighborhood, city, or state.

MyWritingLab & Lab Activity 45

mywritinglab For additional help with commas, go to **www.mywritinglab.com** or complete **Lab Activity 45** in the separate *Resources for Writers* Lab Manual.

Apostrophes

VIRUSES

Though almost everyone has suffered from the common cold, few people understand how colds come about or, more important, how they can be treated. From the sniffles to more dangerous strains, viruses affect us almost daily.

UNDERSTANDING THE APOSTROPHE'

One of the great time-savers in punctuation, the **apostrophe** allows us to omit letters and even whole words. The apostrophe has two main uses.

- Showing the omission of letters
- Showing possession or ownership

SHOWING THE OMISSION OF LETTERS

An apostrophe allows us to leave out letters in a **contraction,** one word that results from the combination of two words. Here are some common contractions.

can + not = can't	he + is = he's
I + am = I'm	she + is = she's
I + have = I've	who + is = who's
I + had = I'd	could + not = couldn't
I + will = I'll	did + not = didn't

I + would = I'd   do + not = don't

it + is = it's   is + not = isn't

it + has = it's   will + not = won't

they + are = they're   would + not = wouldn't

you + are = you're

Note that some contractions can be used for two different word combinations. For example, *I'd* can mean "I had" or "I would." You can tell the meaning of the contraction from its use in the sentence.

I'd thought the common cold was just one virus. (*I'd* means "I had.")

I'd go if you invited me. (*I'd* means "I would.")

EXERCISE 1 Forming Contractions

Combine the following words into contractions. An example is done for you.

here + is = _____here's_____

1. he + would = _____

2. there + would = _____

3. we + will = _____

4. you + have = _____

5. let + us = _____

EXERCISE 2 Changing Contractions into their Original Word Pairs

Change the following contractions into their original word pairs. If a contraction has two possible word pairs, write them both. An example is done for you.

you'd = _____you had_____   _____you would_____

1. we'll = _____

2. he'd = _____   _____

3. she's = _____   _____

4. there's = _____   _____

5. they're = _____

EXERCISE 3 Forming Contractions in Context

Combine the words in parentheses into contractions.

1. (I have) _____ had a cold for three weeks.

2. (You had) _____ better hope you (do not) _____
get it.

3. The first symptom (you will) _____ notice is a tickle in
your throat.

4. This might be all (you will) _____ get. If so, (you are)
_____ lucky!

5. (I am) _____ beginning to think (I will) _____
never recover.

6. (It is) _____ no fun to have cold symptoms.

7. (I have) _____ had all of these: runny or stuffy nose, sneezing,
sore throat, cough, headache, mild fever, fatigue, muscle aches, and
loss of appetite. Good health to you!

SHOWING POSSESSION OR OWNERSHIP

Many expressions can show ownership or possession—for example, *owned
by, possessed by, belongs to*, and *of*.

the medicine <u>owned by</u> the drug store

the main entrance <u>of</u> the hospital

There is another, faster way to show the same thing: use an apostrophe, as
explained in the following sections.

Singular Nouns

Add an apostrophe and -*s* (*'s*) to show possession or ownership if a noun is singular.

the drug store's medicine   the hospital's main entrance

If the noun is singular and already ends in -*s*, follow the same rule; add an apostrophe and -*s* to show possession.

Marcus's virus took a month to run its course.

EXERCISE 4 Using Apostrophes to Show Possession or Ownership

Rewrite the underlined portion of each sentence to show possession or ownership. An example is done for you.

The health of Ron is a concern to us all. Ron's health

1. The sign owned by the pharmacy lists common illnesses.

_____

2. Last year Ron had the telltale signs belonging to the flu.

_____

3. The friends belonging to Ron noticed his low energy level.

_____

4. The concern of people for Ron has led them to drop hints.

_____

5. At the office of the doctor, Ron saw notices for flu shots.

_____

6. A bulletin from the office of the nurse urged people to get flu shots.

_____

7. Even the boss of Ron offered Ron time off to get a flu shot.

_____

8. However, these hints failed to sink into <u>the brain possessed by Ron</u>.

_____

9. He insists that <u>the office of the doctor</u> is too expensive and that the school nurse just wants to bother people. _____

10. I guess we'll all have to live with <u>the poor health of Ron</u>.

_____

EXERCISE 5 Showing Possession or Ownership Through Apostrophes

Rewrite the underlined portion of each sentence to show possession or ownership.

One Bad Virus

The rare but deadly Ebola virus is named for <u>the river belonging to Zaire</u> . Although the <u>source of the virus</u> is unknown, monkeys and humans may become the <u>carriers of the virus</u>. The <u>symptoms of the disease</u> include fever, headache, and joint and muscle pain. As the disease progresses, <u>the symptoms of Ebola</u> include vomiting, diarrhea, abdominal pain, sore throat, rash, and chest pain. The disease may also affect internal organs and the <u>ability of blood</u> to clot. When the blood fails to clot, the <u>bleeding of the patient</u> may extend into internal organs and from body openings. In most of <u>the outbreaks belonging to Ebola</u>, the majority of cases occurred in hospital settings. In such cases, <u>the main problem of the facility</u> was inadequate medical supplies leading to poor infection control. <u>The presence of Ebola</u> has not been confirmed in any humans in the United States.

Plural Nouns

If a plural word already ends in -s, add an apostrophe to the word to show possession or ownership. Do not add another -s.

My *doctors'* offices are large and cheerful. (The offices belong to more than one doctor.)

My *friends'* flu bug has kept them sick for two weeks. (The illness affects more than one friend.)

For plural nouns not ending in -s, add 's to show possession or ownership.

the toys belonging to the children = the *children's* toys

the concern of the people = the *people's* concern

EXERCISE 6 Using Apostrophes to Show Possession in Plural Nouns

In each blank, write the plural of the noun in parentheses. Then, rewrite the sentence to include the possessive plural form of the word. An example is done for you.

Sentence: The (drug) effects are still unknown.

Plural: drugs

Revised: The drugs' effects are still unknown.

1. Sentence: Several (disease) cures are derived from common sources.

Plural: _____

Revised: _____

2. Sentence: (Medication) benefits are variable, but the benefit of rest is well-known.

Plural: _____

Revised _____

3. Sentence: Some (cold remedy) benefits can be the relief of symptoms.

Plural: _____

Revised: _____

4. Sentence: However, some (medicine) side effects, such as drowsiness, make them poor choices.

Plural: _____

Revised: _____

5. Sentence: (Nap) benefits, though, are undeniable.

Plural: _____

Revised: _____

UNNECESSARY APOSTROPHES

Be careful not to misuse or overuse apostrophes. Avoid using apostrophes in two areas, in particular.

- No apostrophes with possessive pronouns
- No apostrophes with simple plurals

Do Not Use Apostrophes with Possessive Pronouns

Never use an apostrophe with a possessive pronoun (*his, hers, theirs, yours,* and so on).

Incorrect: Their's is the house next to the hospital.

Correct: Theirs is the house next to the hospital.

Incorrect: Your's is the face I love most.

Correct: Yours is the face I love most.

Incorrect: I am more worried about his health than about her's.

Correct: I am more worried about his health than about hers.

Do Not Use Apostrophes with Simple Plurals

To make most nouns plural, add an -s to the end of the word. Plural nouns that end in -s are **simple plurals.** Never add an apostrophe to a simple plural. For instance, if you want to discuss more than one symptom, write *symptoms*. Do not write *symptoms'* or *symptom's* for the plural—both are incorrect. Keep in mind that the apostrophe shows possession or ownership.

Veronica's watery eyes showed that she had a cold.

In this sentence, the only word requiring an apostrophe is *Veronica*. The -*'s* attached to *Veronica* shows that the eyes *belong to* Veronica. The -*s* on the word *eyes* simply shows that Veronica has more than one eye.

EXERCISE 7 Using Apostrophes Correctly

In the following paragraph, rewrite the five words that require apostrophes. Then, make a list of all the simple plural nouns.

Be Clean, for Health's Sake

[1]Washing your hands can keep you from getting sick. [2]Because many people rub their eyes or touch their mouths with their hands, germs can spread to things they touch. [3]Never borrow a friends used tissues. [4]Touching doorknobs or chairs can spread germs, as can handling a co-workers coffee mug. [5]If you use someone elses computer, you can pick up a virus left on the keyboard or mouse. [6]A desks surface is also packed with germs. [7]Wash your hands with soap after using the restroom, and try to wash up after shaking hands, too. [8]Soaps action removes germs that can make people ill. [9]Even though you might end up with dry skin from washing so often, you'll also enjoy better health.

Simple plurals are found in the following sentences.

Sentence 1: _____

Sentence 2: _____ _____ _____ _____

_____

Sentence 3: _____

Sentence 4: _____ _____ _____

Sentence 6: _____

Sentence 7: _____ _____

Sentence 8: _____

EDITING PRACTICE 1

In the following paragraph, cross out the words that require apostrophes and write the correct form of each word above it. The first word has been done for you.

AIDS in Perspective

AIDS stands for *acquired immune deficiency syndrome*. ~~Its~~ It's one of the worst illnesses a person can get. Though AIDS is a deadly virus, mens and womens chances of catching it can be lowered. First, though AIDS is contagious, it isnt spread through casual contact. No ones been known to catch AIDS from saliva or from tears. However, contact with someones bodily fluids—blood, semen, vaginal fluids, or breast milk—can spread the disease. Without such contact, the average persons chance of getting AIDS is small. Second, though its fatal in many cases, AIDS does not kill its victims instantly. In fact, some individuals lives hardly change for years. The early symptoms of AIDS are much like flu symptoms: fever, headache, sore muscles and joints, stomachache, swollen lymph glands, or a skin rash. Even after peoples symptoms appear, some patients live normally for years.

EDITING PRACTICE 2

In the blanks for each word, write the singular possessive, plural, and plural possessive forms. Then, on a separate piece of paper, write a paragraph using at least five of the words in the completed list. Your paragraph does not need to be serious.

	Singular Possessive	Plural	Plural Possessive
1. cold	_____	_____	_____
2. eye	_____	_____	_____
3. ear	_____	_____	_____
4. child	_____	_____	_____
5. tummy	_____	_____	_____
6. cough	_____	_____	_____
7. doctor	_____	_____	_____
8. symptom	_____	_____	_____
9. virus	_____	_____	_____
10. medicine	_____	_____	_____
11. effect	_____	_____	_____
12. friend	_____	_____	_____

WRITING PRACTICE

What is the worst illness you've seen someone get? Write a paragraph describing the symptoms of the illness that someone you know has contracted. Check your writing for correct apostrophe usage.

MyWritingLab & Lab Activity 46

mywritinglab For additional help with apostrophes, go to **www.mywritinglab.com** or complete **Lab Activity 46** in the separate *Resources for Writers* Lab Manual.

Quotation Marks

Culture Note

FEMINISM AND GLORIA STEINEM

Although women still push for equal pay and equal opportunities in the workplace, their abilities and contributions are taken far more seriously than they were in the 1960s. Much of the progress women have made can be attributed to the work of the feminist Gloria Steinem. Through her drive, perseverance, and charisma, Steinem made huge strides for women.

UNDERSTANDING QUOTATION MARKS

Quotation marks are used to set off specific words, expressions, or titles, signaling that what follows demands special attention. Quotation marks have three major functions.

- Setting off direct quotations
- Setting off titles of short works
- Setting off special words or expressions

SETTING OFF DIRECT QUOTATIONS

Use quotation marks to indicate that certain words are being spoken by a specific person.

Gloria Steinem

SURF THE NET With brains, beauty, and political brawn, Gloria Steinem paved the way for women in the workforce. Search the Internet for information about Gloria Steinem. Write a few sentences summarizing your findings.
Responding to Images. *What can you tell about Gloria Steinem based on the photo above? Does she appear kind, wise, prosperous, or serious, for instance. Explain.*

Gloria Steinem said, "A woman without a man is like a fish without a bicycle." (Quotation marks set off Steinem's exact words.)

"Most women," said Steinem, "are one man away from welfare." (The quotation is split up, so two pairs of quotation marks are needed to show exactly what Steinem said.)

One of my favorite quotations from Gloria Steinem says, "Without leaps of imagination, or dreaming, we lose the excitement of possibilities. Dreaming, after all, is a form of planning." (A quotation of more than one sentence needs only one set of quotation marks.)

Keep the following rules in mind when you use quotations.

- Unless a quotation begins a sentence, it should usually be introduced by a comma.
- A quotation begins with a capital letter.
- Commas and periods at the end of a quotation go *inside* the quotation marks.

EXERCISE 1 Using Quotation Marks Correctly

In the following sentences, add quotation marks where necessary for the underlined quotations.

1. My boyfriend always says, <u>Gloria Steinem has hurt men.</u>

2. I like to disagree with him, asserting, <u>She hasn't hurt men, but she has helped women.</u>

3. When we disagree, we ask our instructor. He repeats, <u>Gloria Steinem is one of the most important women of the twentieth century.</u>

4. My boyfriend usually claims, <u>I don't have anything against Gloria Steinem. I just don't know enough about her.</u>

5. <u>Why don't you learn about her,</u> I ask my boyfriend, <u>so that you can argue with me some more?</u>

6. The result of these debates is that my boyfriend has found a number of favorite Gloria Steinem quotations. One is, <u>It is more rewarding to watch money change the world than watch it accumulate.</u>

7. Another of his favorite quotations deals with what's right. <u>Law and justice,</u> Steinem wrote, <u>are not always the same.</u>

8. As one Steinem quotation advises, <u>Power can be taken, but not given. The process of the taking is empowerment in itself.</u>

9. I've taught my boyfriend one of my favorites. It reads, <u>We can tell our values by looking at our checkbook stubs.</u>

10. <u>The truth will set you free,</u> my boyfriend loves to quote, <u>but first it will piss you off.</u>

EXERCISE 2 Using Quotation Marks for Conversation

Write down a short conversation using quotation marks to identify who is speaking. Include at least three quotations from each speaker. An example is done for you.

My boss said, "You have done a great job lately, so I'm thinking of promoting you."

I replied, "I'm happy that you appreciate my work, but I'm not sure I want to take on more responsibility."

"This is a good opportunity for you," she answered.

"Thanks for thinking of me," I responded, "but can I think about it for a few days?"

"Take your time and get back to me," she said.

"I will. Thank you again," I said.

Using Parts of Quotations

Sometimes you will want to quote only part of what someone said. In these cases, simply place the part that has actually been said in quotation marks.

Quotation:	Gloria Steinem said, "A pedestal is as much a prison as any small, confined space."
Part of quotation:	In Steinem's view, being on "a pedestal" is like being in "a prison." (Steinem used the specific words *a pedestal* and *a prison*, so the writer places them in quotation marks.)
Quotation:	Gloria Steinem says, "Without leaps of imagination, or dreaming, we lose the excitement of possibilities. Dreaming, after all, is a form of planning."
Part of quotation:	Gloria Steinem gives great value to dreaming, calling it "a form of planning." (Only the words said by Steinem are in quotation marks.)

Indirect Quotations

Often you may want to communicate what someone meant without setting off his or her exact words. Repeating other people's ideas without quoting them word for word is called **paraphrasing.** In these cases, you should not use quotation marks. Make sure, however, to tell who actually made the original statement.

Direct:	My history professor says, "Feminists have largely been misunderstood." (The writer is relating the exact words of a history professor.)
Indirect:	My history professor says that many people have not understood feminists. (The words of the indirect quotation differ from the words of the direct quotation; thus, the writer should not use quotation marks.)
Direct:	Wanda's letter to her mother said, "I am going to be a writer like Gloria Steinem." (The writer is relating Wanda's exact words.)

Indirect: Wanda's wrote a letter to her mother saying that she wants to be a writer like Gloria Steinem. (The writer does not use Wanda's exact words, so no quotation marks are needed.)

EXERCISE 3   Using Indirect Quotations

Revise the following sentences to change the direct quotations into indirect quotations. An example is done for you.

Direct: My mother told me, "You need to grow up so you can take care of a family just as I did."

Indirect: _My mother told me that I need to grow up so I can take care of a family just as she did._

1. Direct: However, I explained, "I want to do something else with my life."

Indirect: _____

2. Direct: She asked, "What could be more important than a family?"

Indirect: _____

3. Direct: I answered, "Making my own decisions is most important to me."

Indirect: _____

4. Direct: I explained, "I don't want to feel like a failure if I decide not to get married and have children."

Indirect: _____

5. Direct: My mother finally agreed and said, "You're right. You should do what makes you happy."

Indirect: _____

SETTING OFF TITLES OF SHORT WORKS

Use quotation marks to indicate the titles of short works such as the following:

- Essays
- Book chapters

- Newspaper and magazine articles
  Magazine article: "A Bunny's Tale" was one of Gloria Steinem's first
  published articles.
- Poems
- Songs
  Helen Reddy's hit "I Am Woman" could easily be interpreted as a
  feminist song.

The titles of longer works are indicated by underlining or italics.

- Newspapers
  New York Times, Christian Science Monitor
- Magazines
  Time, Newsweek, People
- Books
  Water for Elephants, Pompeii, Holes
- Albums and CDs
  Hotel California, Come Away with Me, Nice and Easy
- Movies
  Atonement, There Will Be Blood, Enchanted

Look at how quotation marks, italics, and underlining are used in the
following sentences. *Note:* With a computer, you can use either italics or
underlining for the titles of longer works. Ask your instructor for his or
her preference.

The poem "For My Lover, Returning to His Wife" is in *The Collected
Works of Ann Sexton*. (The poem title is set off by quotation marks
while the book title is italicized.)

The article "Who Will Heed the Warnings of the Population Bomb?"
from the *Los Angeles Times* deals with an important issue. (The article
title is set off by quotation marks while the newspaper title is italicized.)

I love the song "Heart of Glass" from Blondie's *Parallel Lines*. (The song
title is set off by quotation marks while the album title is italicized).

Did you see the episode "Mr. Monk Is on the Run" on the television
show <u>Monk</u>? (The episode title is set off by quotation marks while
the show title is underlined. The underlined title could also have
been italicized, as in the preceding examples.)

EXERCISE 4 Using Quotation Marks for Titles

Add quotation marks or underlining as necessary in the following sentences.

1. Gloria Steinem wrote a number of books, one of which is titled The Thousand Indias.

2. Her article A Bunny's Tale came out the same year as her work The Beach Book.

3. Among her other accomplishments, Steinem co-founded New York magazine and Ms. magazine.

4. Gloria Steinem has been widely interviewed in newspapers such as the Miami Herald and magazines such as Modern Maturity.

5. She was also interviewed on CNN's online program CNN Access.

SETTING OFF SPECIAL WORDS OR EXPRESSIONS

Use quotation marks to set off words used in a specific sense or expressions of particular importance.

Some people think that the term "feminist" has a negative undertone.

Other people, however, claim that "feminist" actions can also include "feminine" women.

SINGLE QUOTATION MARKS

Use single quotation marks to indicate a quotation within a quotation.

My friend Julie said yesterday, "I loved reading 'A Bunny's Tale' years after it was published."

This sentence contains an article title, which requires quotation marks. The regular quotation marks (" ") indicate that someone is speaking, and the single quotation marks (' ') surround the article title.

EXERCISE 5 Using Quotation Marks in Your Writing

Read a paragraph in one of your textbooks. Then, write down a quotation from that book. Be sure to use quotation marks to set off the quotation, as in the following example.

Original: Some raps celebrate their sisters for "getting over" on men, rather than touting self-reliance and honesty.

—Tricia Rose, "Black Sistas," in *Black Noise: Rap Music and Black Culture in Contemporary America*

Quotation: In her essay "Bad Sistas" from her book <u>Black Noise: Rap Music and Black Culture in Contemporary America</u>, Tricia Rose writes, "Some raps celebrate their sisters for 'getting over' on men, rather than touting self-reliance and honesty."

EDITING PRACTICE

Add quotation marks and underlining where necessary in the following paragraph.

Gloria's Message for Me

Few people have had a greater influence on me than Gloria Steinem. My family comes from a country where men make all the decisions. Also, because my mother died when I was young, I was raised in a household with all men: four brothers, an uncle, and a father. They expected me to do all the household work, telling me, A woman's place is in the home. I went to school even though my father constantly said, School is a waste of time when all you'll do is find a man to marry. When I was a senior in high school, I learned about Gloria Steinem in my sociology class. My teacher told me that when Ms. Steinem applied for a job, the magazine editor told her, We don't want a pretty girl. We want a writer. What impressed me most was that Ms. Steinem published all kinds of articles, for example, After Black Power, Women's Liberation and The Disarmament of Betty Coed. She also helped found two magazines: New York magazine and Ms. magazine. She was engaged to her college boyfriend, so she could have gotten married young, but she chose to fight for women. This made me think that I should fight for my life, too. I told my father that women can do more than take care of men. I want to go to college, I said. At first, my father said, No way. However, he came back later and said, I'm very proud that you want to educate yourself. Go to college with my blessing. On top of that, he's helping me pay my tuition. Gloria Steinem helped me see that I have more options than I thought.

WRITING PRACTICE

Write a paragraph discussing how a woman has played an important role in your life. You do not need to choose someone famous. Be sure to include particularly inspiring statements from this person, and check your work for correct quotation usage.

MyWritingLab & Lab Activity 47

mywritinglab

For additional help with quotation marks, go to **www.mywritinglab.com** or complete **Lab Activity 47** in the separate *Resources for Writers* Lab Manual.

Other Punctuation Marks:
Colons and Semicolons,
Parentheses, Dashes,
and Hyphens

Culture Note

MARILYN MONROE, AN AMERICAN ICON

A sex symbol of the 1960s who became an American icon, Marilyn Monroe radiated a ditzy beauty. Partly because of her movie roles and partly because of her suicide at age thirty-six, Marilyn Monroe has had a great effect on America's ideas of femininity.

Marilyn Monroe

PLAN AN INTERVIEW
Known for her platinum-haired appeal, Marilyn Monroe strove to be taken seriously as an actress. Interview two people about their reactions to Marilyn Monroe. Write a few sentences about what you learn.

Responding to Images. *What mood or attitude does the woman in the photo project? Write a few sentences explaining your conclusions.*

UNDERSTANDING OTHER PUNCTUATION MARKS

Commas, quotation marks, and apostrophes are very common punctuation marks. Some other forms of punctuation that are used less often also serve special functions.

- Semicolons
- Hyphens
- Parentheses
- Colons
- Dashes

Knowing how to use these forms of punctuation effectively can help you write a variety of sentences.

SEMICOLONS ;

Use a **semicolon** to join two independent clauses.

> Marilyn Monroe played the role of a blond bombshell; she also played more serious roles.

> Marilyn Monroe experienced great success as a blond beauty; however, she wanted to be taken seriously as an actress in other roles.

A less common but still important use of the semicolon is to separate items in a series where the individual items contain commas. A **series** is two or more items in a row.

> Marilyn Monroe had several identities. She was Norma Jean, the small-town girl; Marilyn Monroe, the movie star; Marilyn, the sex symbol; and Marilyn, wife of three husbands.

> Some biographies of Marilyn Monroe are *Marilyn Monroe: The Biography*, by Donald Spoto; *Marilyn Monroe and the Camera*, by Jane Russell; and *The Ultimate Marilyn*, by Ernest W. Cunningham.

EXERCISE 1 Using Semicolons Correctly

Add semicolons where necessary.

1. Some of Marilyn Monroe's most famous movies are *All About Eve*, in which she first gained attention as a real star *Some Like It Hot*, where she plays a woman named Sugar Kane and *Niagara*, in which she plays an unfaithful wife who plots to kill her husband.

2. Marilyn Monroe had three husbands: James Dougherty, a man she met in an aircraft plant Joe DiMaggio, the baseball star and Arthur Miller, the playwright.

3. Marilyn Monroe is known for many things her sex appeal is just one of them.

4. Marilyn Monroe has been paid tribute by many singers Madonna, the American pop star, dressed like Marilyn Monroe in a music video.

5. Elton John, an English singer and composer, wrote the song "Candle in the Wind" as a tribute to Marilyn Monroe its popularity was due in part to Marilyn Monroe's fame.

COLONS

Colons tell the reader to pay attention to what's coming. Use a colon for these purposes.

- To introduce a list
- To introduce a quotation of more than one sentence
- To call attention to words that follow
- To separate the hour and minutes in telling time

I've often heard that three of Marilyn Monroe's movies are her best: *Niagara, Bus Stop,* and *Some Like It Hot.* (The colon introduces the list of movies.)

Marilyn Monroe describes this experience in one of her biographies: "Sometimes I've been to a party where no one spoke to me for a whole evening. The . . . ladies would gang up in a corner and discuss my dangerous character." (The colon follows an independent clause and introduces a quotation longer than one sentence.)

Now that you've waited for her to come, here she is: Marilyn Monroe. (The colon calls attention to the name that follows.)

Marilyn Monroe has fans even at 5:00 a.m. on a Saturday. (The colon separates the hour from the minutes.)

EXERCISE 2 Using Colons Correctly

Add colons where necessary in the following sentences.

1. One statement of Marilyn Monroe's that I love is this "All little girls should be told they're pretty, even if they're not."

2. Marilyn Monroe is one thing above all a star.

3. At 7 30 p.m., my friends and I will watch *The River of No Return* starring Marilyn Monroe.

4. Marilyn Monroe is known for many traits bleached blond hair, voluptuous figure, soft voice, and pouty lips.

5. Another quotation of Marilyn Monroe's is as follows "It's not true I had nothing on. I had the radio on."

HYPHENS

Use a **hyphen** to join two or more words working together to communicate one concept.

Marilyn Monroe was never considered one of the high-and-mighty actresses of her time.

One of the most talked-about movies that Marilyn Monroe made was *Some Like It Hot*.

Hyphens are also used to split a word at the end of a line. To divide a word at the end of a line, make the break between syllables. One-syllable words should never be hyphenated, and no word should be divided unless absolutely necessary. *Hint:* If you're not sure of syllable breaks, check the dictionary.

At the end of her career, Marilyn Monroe starred in a movie that her husband Arthur Miller wrote for her, *The Misfits*. (The hyphen indicates that the word *husband* continues on the next line.)

Tip: Many word processors and computers automatically keep whole words on one line; you will rarely need to use hyphens to divide single words.

EXERCISE 3 Using Hyphens Correctly

Add hyphens where necessary.

1. Starstudded casts of actors often accompanied Marilyn Monroe in her movies.

2. Though successful in her blond bombshell roles, she took acting classes purely for selfimprovement.

3. Monroe made a name for herself as a serious actress, but fans prefer her as a wideeyed, sexy airhead.

4. Although many people believe that Monroe's death was an accident, others think the star was strung out on drugs.

5. The early death of a wellknown entertainer always makes the news.

DASHES

Use **dashes** to set off remarks that interrupt the flow of a sentence. The interruption signaled by a dash is longer and more pronounced than one set off by two commas. Sometimes the interruption is a complete clause. Dashes are made by typing two hyphens in a row. If you are writing dashes by hand, make them as long as two letters.

Marilyn Monroe's real name—Norma Jean Baker—became more familiar to the public with the popularity of Elton John's song "Candle in the Wind."

Because Marilyn Monroe wanted to be viewed as a serious actress—not just as the blond bombshell she played so well—she took acting lessons.

EXERCISE 4 Using Dashes Correctly

Add dashes where necessary.

1. Marilyn memorabilia photos, books, and calendars, for starters are available on eBay.

2. However, some stores these are usually vintage shops that carry unusual fashions also carry items with Marilyn's image.

3. I often dress up like Marilyn Monroe for Halloween and other parties, of course in a bubble-gum pink gown like the one she wore in *How to Marry a Millionaire*.

4. The woman who cuts my hair Sharrona Scissors, I call her covers the walls of her salon with Marilyn Monroe prints.

5. People often ask Sharrona if they can have her prints which seems rude to me but she always says no.

PARENTHESES

Parentheses also set off information that interrupts the flow of a sentence. Usually, however, the information in parentheses is interesting but not essential to understand the sentence. Common information set off in parentheses includes dates and page numbers.

In a biography of Marilyn Monroe's life (page 153), the writer praises the actress for owning more than 200 books.

Marilyn Monroe (1926–1962) lived a very short life.

Tip: Any comma should go *after* parentheses, as illustrated in the first example above.

EXERCISE 5 Using Parentheses Correctly

Add parentheses where necessary.

1. Did you know that Madonna my mother's favorite pop singer dressed like Marilyn Monroe in one of her early videos?

2. Though Madonna's image is very different from Marilyn Monroe's Madonna is more independent, both women have made a mark in the world.

3. Some people even think that Madonna was smart not to have imitated Marilyn Monroe too closely who *could* impersonate Marilyn?, since no one could ever replace the real Marilyn.

4. In a collector's edition of a Hollywood magazine page 32, Marilyn Monroe is featured.

5. Marilyn Monroe's second husband Joe DiMaggio 1914–1999 was a professional baseball player.

EDITING PRACTICE

Add the correct punctuation marks (colon, semicolon, hyphen, dash, or parentheses) where necessary in the following paragraph. You will need to add four hyphens, a pair of dashes, two colons, three semicolons, and one pair of parentheses.

Marvelous Marilyn

Marilyn Monroe 1926–1962 made her mark in many ways. First, she was a regular girl who "made it" as a movie star. She overcame hardship living with a mother who was mentally ill, living in foster homes, working as a child for horrible wages and became a symbol of how "average" people could rise to the top. Second, Marilyn Monroe made her mark as a beauty. Though today people value the skin and bones look as beautiful, Marilyn let herself look womanly with full curves. Even fans of the starved look appreciate Marilyn's feminine appearance. Marilyn Monroe was quoted as saying this "I don't mind living in a man's world as long as I can be a woman in it." Finally, Marilyn Monroe made her mark as someone whose fame made her unhappy. She was loved on the screen for her performances as a sexy, single upstairs neighbor in *The Seven Year Itch* as a flask wielding member of an all girl band in *Some Like It Hot* and as a faithless wife in *Niagara*. However, Marilyn Monroe still felt she needed to prove herself she enrolled in acting classes. Even her attempts to improve herself left her feeling empty she committed suicide in 1962.

WRITING PRACTICE

Marilyn Monroe became most famous for her portrayal of one type of character: the beautiful, sexy airhead. Write a paragraph discussing another type of character often seen in movies or on television: the tough cop, loyal friend, crooked lawyer, or devoted mother, to name some.

MyWritingLab & Lab Activity 48

mywritinglab For additional help with other punctuation marks, go to **www.mywritinglab. com** or complete **Lab Activity 48** in the separate *Resources for Writers* Lab Manual.

Capitalization

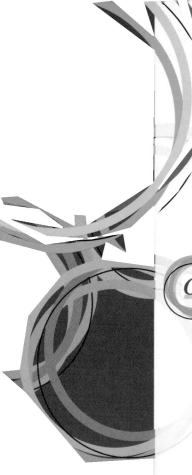

MAIN USES OF CAPITAL LETTERS

Understanding the rules of capitalization can aid you greatly in your writing courses. Keep in mind that not all academic disciplines have the same conventions or rules for capitalization. For instance, some words may be capitalized in science classes but not in humanities courses. When in doubt about what should be capitalized, consult the dictionary. Capital letters are required for many common types of words.

- **Names of people and the pronoun *I*.**

  Yolanda, **F**rank, and **I** planned a big trip.

- **Names of specific places.** Capitalize the names of cities, states, countries, regions, lakes, parks, and mountains. Do not capitalize directions (north, west, etc.).

  I'm from **Y**akima, **W**ashington, in the **N**orthwest.

  We drove to **S**alt **L**ake **C**ity, **U**tah, where we saw the **G**reat **S**alt **L**ake.

Victoria Falls

CRITICAL THINKING Forming the world's largest sheet of falling water, Victoria Falls churns the Zambezi River in Zimbabwe. The residents near Victoria Falls fear that increased tourism will spoil the environment. Write a few sentences discussing whether or not tourism should be limited to preserve the environment.
Responding to Images. Write a few sentences describing in very specific detail the photo above.

- **Names of institutions.** Capitalize the names of government offices, businesses, and academic institutions.

  Department of the **T**reasury
  St. John's **H**ospital
  University of **M**innesota

- **Names of holidays, months, and days of the week.** Capitalize the names of religious and secular holidays, the names of months, and the days of the week. Do not capitalize the names of the seasons of the year: spring, summer, fall, winter.

  I think that **V**alentine's **D**ay comes on a **F**riday this winter, but I know that it's February 14.

- **Brand names of products.** Capitalize the *name* of the product, but not the *type* of product.

Brand Name	Product
Goodyear	tires
Hershey's	chocolate
Nike	shoes
Perdue	chicken

I donated my old **F**ord **T**aurus to a charity.

Names of Places to Be Capitalized

Cities:	Paris, Tulsa, San Diego
States:	West Virginia, Delaware, Montana
Countries:	United Kingdom, Pakistan, People's Republic of China
Regions:	New England, Old South

- **Titles of written or performed works.** Capitalize the first, last, and main words in the titles of articles, books, magazines, newspapers, poems, stories, movies, songs, television shows, and your own papers. The following words usually do not require capitalization.

Articles	a, an, the	*Silence of the Lambs*
Prepositions	*in, of, to,* etc.	"Come Fly with Me"
Coordinating conjunctions	*for, and, nor, but, or, yet, so*	*Romeo and Juliet*

Aaron Copland's symphony ***Appalachian Spring*** is on my ***Best American Composers*** CD.

An article titled "**T**he **W**onder of the **S**even **W**onders" in *National Geographic* told about the seven wonders of the natural world.

Then, I read a poem by John Barton called "**S**unrise, **G**rand **C**anyon," which made me really want to visit Arizona.

- **First word in a sentence or direct quotation.**

Our trip to Mount Everest was a dream that we couldn't afford.

Devon exclaimed, "Let's go to Rio de Janeiro instead!"

EXERCISE 1 Correct Capitalization

Change small letters to capital letters where necessary. You will need to correct thirty-four letters in all. An example is done for you.

> I
> i saw a television special called "the seven natural wonders of the
> *The Seven Natural Wonders*
>
> World
> World" and wanted to see at least one of them before going to
>
> American River College
> american river college in the fall.

1. *Capitalize five words*: my friend john and i want to see victoria falls.

2. *Capitalize six words*: after all, it can't be that far to victoria, british columbia, from where we're starting in portland, oregon.

3. *Capitalize six words*: We had packed our bags from l. l. bean, loaded the honda civic, and filled the tank with chevron gas before John said, "maybe we should look at a michelin map."

4. *Capitalize eight words*: i thought this was crazy since i had seen a movie called *Victoria,* read about queen victoria, and read an article in *via* magazine about victoria falls, so I was sure I knew everything about it already.

5. *Capitalize seven words*: john insisted, saying, "we can't be too careful." it's a good thing i listened because victoria falls turned out to be in africa.

ADDITIONAL USES OF CAPITAL LETTERS

Capital letters are necessary in other cases as well.

- **Titles before a person's name.** Capitalize titles that come directly before a name.

My neighbor **Mr.** Curtis recommends his dentist, **Dr.** Chun.

My neighbor recommends his dentist, Amanda Chun.

Common Titles

Mr.	Dr.
Mrs.	Professor
Ms.	

- **Names showing family relationships.** Capitalize any name you might call a family member.

  I love **Auntie R**ose, and **Uncle D**ave is a favorite, too.

  I asked **G**randma when she learned to ride horses.

  If you place a possessive pronoun in front of a family name, do not capitalize the name.

  I asked my grandma when she learned to ride horses. (The word *my* is a possessive pronoun, so *grandma* is not capitalized.)

- **Names of groups.** Capitalize names of groups with specific affiliations, such as races and nationalities, religions, political groups, companies, unions, and clubs and other associations.

  Buildings in our national parks are often modeled after **N**ative **A**merican themes. The **F**red **H**arvey **C**ompany hired the gifted architect Mary E. J. Colter to design buildings at the Grand Canyon.

  Later, the company was sold to **A**mfac. (The word *company* is not capitalized when it is not part of a name.)

  The most recent group of Grand Canyon tourists includes the **L**utheran **B**rotherhood management team, the **J**unior **L**eague of **T**allahassee, and leaders of the **A**merican **Y**outh **S**occer **O**rganization.

- **Names of school courses.**

  I took **C**hemistry 101, **B**iology 103, and **B**otany 203 last semester.

  I have also taken many other **s**cience classes. (Do not capitalize the names of general subjects.)

- **Historical periods, events, and documents.**

the **C**ivil **W**ar	the **R**enaissance
World **W**ar II	the **M**iddle **A**ges
the **V**ietnam **W**ar	the **G**reat **D**epression
the **T**reaty of **V**ersailles	the **C**onstitution

EXERCISE 2 Using Capital Letters Correctly

Change small letters to capital letters where necessary. Twenty-five words require capitalization.

The great barrier reef is another natural wonder I have always wanted to visit. My neighbor, mr. Burns (a world war II veteran), has been there and says it is magnificent. However, mother and father and everyone at the methodist Church worry that I will get into trouble. Part of their worry is that the reef is so far away, along the queensland coast of australia. My parents also worry that I won't speak the language. They think that people speak chinese or hindi or some other language in australia. What they don't realize is that in australia, people speak english! I'll be fine, I tell them. Last semester I took marine biology 30 from professor Diver in order to learn about the reef. Also, if I travel that far, I could see the aborigines, the original inhabitants of australia. The great barrier reef has been designated a national marine park by the australian government, so it's probably even educational. I would love to go snorkeling and see the reef's huge variety of plant and animal life.

UNNECESSARY CAPITALIZATION

Do not use capital letters where they are not needed.

Words that serve as general labels, like *city, river, artist, company, lawyer,* and *airport,* are not capitalized unless they are part of a name. Note that the underlined letters are not capitalized because they are general terms.

The _artist Thomas Eakins painted grand American _landscapes of _rivers and _mountains.

Last _summer we took an old-fashioned _paddleboat, the *Sea Sprite,* down the Mississippi River. I was surprised by how interesting the river was. (The noun *river* is capitalized only when it is part of a name, *Mississippi River.*)

When we went hiking in the <u>m</u>ountains (the Rockies), I made sure to wear my trusty L. L. Bean <u>h</u>iking <u>b</u>oots. (The noun *mountains* is not capitalized because it is not part of a name; *hiking boots* is not capitalized even though it comes right after a brand name.)

EXERCISE 3 Correcting Errors in Capitalization

Rewrite each incorrectly capitalized word below to begin with a small letter.

1. The City of Rio de Janeiro sits on steep Hillsides that meet the sea.

2. Portugese Explorers were the first Europeans to see the Bay in 1502, when the Area was occupied by Tupi Indians.

3. The explorers thought they had found a huge River, so they called the bay Rio de Janeiro, meaning "River of January," in Honor of the Month they arrived.

4. European Settlement didn't take place on the bay until sixty years later when the Portuguese built a Fort to keep out French Traders.

5. Today, Rio's harbor and Beaches are crowded, but the Natural Beauty of Brazil's mountains by the Bay is unquestionable.

EDITING PRACTICE

Change small letters to capital letters where necessary. Twenty-two words require capitalization.

1. one of the seven wonders of the natural world is the aurora borealis, also known as the northern lights.

2. According to mother and aunt Parker, who used to live in alaska, the northern lights are caused by a reaction in the atmosphere near the north pole.

3. Our old german friend in new york, dr. frank, used to be a scientist

back in heidelberg, germany, so he knows about the lights.

4. he says that people have seen the lights as far south as the northern

united states, and alaska residents see them often.

5. Our friend dr. frank says, "though the lights can be explained by

science, they are still amazing to see."

WRITING PRACTICE

Write a paragraph describing a nature-based location—such as a park or garden—that you find amazing or attractive in some way. Check your writing for correct capitalization.

MyWritingLab & Lab Activity 49

For additional help with capitalization, go to **www.mywritinglab.com** or complete **Lab Activity 49** in the separate *Resources for Writers* Lab Manual.

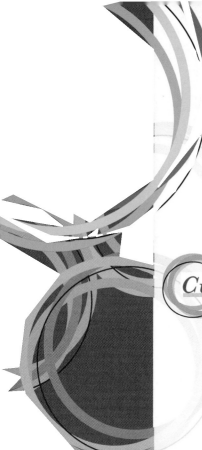

Numbers and Abbreviations

Culture Note

THE BATTLE OF THE LITTLE BIG HORN

Also known as Custer's Last Stand, the Battle of the Little Big Horn proved to be the last great victory of the Native Americans. Fighting without adequate knowledge of his opponents or his route, Custer led his men to their downfall.

USING NUMBERS

Depending on the nature or discipline of the paper you're writing, abbreviations may be acceptable. Rules also vary regarding spelling out numbers versus using numerals. For instance, in nontechnical writing—where the reader is not having to perform calculations while reading—numbers should be spelled out. For many math, science, and engineering courses, however, numerals and other abbreviations save time and space. While this chapter covers some rules for basic usage of abbreviations and numerals, always ask your course instructors what conventions they want you to follow.

Spelling Out Numbers

In nontechnical writing, spell out numbers that can be written in one or two words.

Spelled Out	Numerals
fifteen videos	106 children
twenty-five books	5,735 bonus points
two hundred years	25,697,005 entrants

Using Numerals for Everyday Information

Use numerals to express dates, times, page numbers, book sections, addresses, and percentages.

> June 25, 1876
>
> 12:00 a.m.
>
> page 5
>
> chapter 1
>
> 1633 Broadway, New York, NY 10019

EXERCISE 1 Using Numerals Correctly

Cross out the errors in numbers in the following sentences and write the correction above each one.

1. Crazy Horse (eighteen forty two –1877) was a forceful Sioux leader in the Battle of the Little Big Horn.

2. He led warriors from 5 different Native American tribes: Sioux, Cheyenne, Crow, Arikara, and Arapaho.

3. The Little Big Horn battlefield became a national monument on March 22, nineteen forty six.

4. After the Battle of the Little Big Horn, Chief Sitting Bull was arrested in Canada and held for 2 years.

5. On his release, he hoped to influence his people 1 last time through the Ghost Dance movement.

USING ABBREVIATIONS

In general, you should avoid using abbreviations in formal writing.

Incorrect: I go to class on <u>Wed.</u> and <u>Fri.</u>

Correct: I go to class on <u>Wednesday</u> and <u>Friday</u>.

Incorrect:	Alisha's mom is a <u>dr.</u>
Correct:	Alisha's mom is a <u>doctor</u>.

However, a few types of abbreviations are commonly used.

- **People's titles.** Abbreviate the following titles when they are used with proper names: *Mr., Ms., Mrs., Dr., Jr.,* and *Sr.* (Note that the title *Miss* is not an abbreviation.) Follow an initial in a person's name with a period.

  My history professor, *Dr.* Arrow, is an expert on the Battle of the Little Big Horn. (Do not abbreviate *professor* before a name: Professor Hector Romeis.)

  James T. Arrow, *Jr.*, my history professor's son, also knows a lot about the battle. (When commas are used with *Jr.*, place them before and after the title.)

- **Organizations and items known by their initials.** Many companies, government agencies, and other groups, as well as some common items, are known by their initials. Do not use periods with these abbreviations.

ATM automatic teller machine	CIA Central Intelligence Agency
CD compact disc	NBC National Broadcasting Corporation

- **References to time.** Use numerals when references to time are abbreviated. When using A.D., remember to write that designation *before* the year: A.D. 32.

a.m. or A.M.	350 B.C.
p.m. or P.M.	A.D. 100

  Tip: Spell out *noon* and *midnight* to avoid confusion between 12 P.M. and 12 A.M.

EXERCISE 2 Eliminating Unnecessary Abbreviations

Cross out the errors in abbreviations and write the correction above each one. There are sixteen words to correct in all.

1. At the U. of Mont., many stud. read about the Battle of the Little Big Horn.

2. Stats. can give beginning psych. students a lot of probs.

3. Students in poli. sci. love to discuss ideas with their profs.

4. Next Tues., I will have to explain my ideas about Custer at the mtg.

of Am. Hist. teachers.

5. The meeting is at the new library on Fourth St. in Charlotte,

NC.

EDITING PRACTICE

Find the fourteen errors in numbers and abbreviations in the following paragraph. Cross out each mistake and write the correction above it.

A Last Stand for Many

To force the large Native American army back to the reservations, the army dispatched 3 columns in a coordinated attack, 1 of which contained Lieutenant Colonel Geo. Armstrong Custer and the 7th Cavalry. Spotting the Sioux village about 15 miles away along the Rosebud River on June twenty-fifth, Custer also found a nearby group of about 40 warriors. Ignoring orders to wait, he attacked. He did not realize that the warriors in the village numbered 3 times his strength. Dividing his forces in 3rds, Custer sent troops under Captain Frederick Benteen to prevent the warriors' escape through the upper valley of the Little Bighorn River. Major Marcus Reno's squadron of one hundred seventy five soldiers was to attack the northern end. However, Reno had to retreat, pursued by 2 groups of Cheyenne and Sioux warriors. Just as they finished driving Reno's men out, the Native Americans found roughly two hundred ten of Custer's men coming toward the other end of the village and forced the soldiers back. Meanwhile, a Sioux force under Crazy Horse moved downstream and then doubled back in a sweeping arc, closing in on Custer and his men in a pincer move. The Sioux forces began pouring in gunfire and arrows. In less than 1 hour, Custer and his men were killed in the worst U.S. military disaster to that time. Many of the two hundred sixty men under Custer's command were scalped, but Custer was not.

WRITING PRACTICE

Write a paragraph discussing a time when you made a mistake that had consequences. Check your writing for proper number and abbreviation usage.

MyWritingLab & Lab Activity 50

mywritinglab For additional help with numbers and abbreviations, go to **www. mywritinglab.com** or complete **Lab Activity 50** in the separate *Resources for Writers* Lab Manual.

Words That Look and Sound Alike

UNDERSTANDING HOMONYMS

Many words sound like other words but have different spellings and different meanings. These words are called **homonyms.** Read the word groups that follow, paying attention to how the words differ from each other. Then, fill in each blank with a word from that group.

all ready   completely prepared
already   before; previously

I was _____ to go to Los Angeles with my brother when

he called to say he had _____ left.

brake   to stop; a device that stops a vehicle
break   to damage or cause to come apart; a pause or rest

If you're not prepared to _____ a lot in Los Angeles traffic, you'd better take a long _____ before getting into and out of your car.

buy   to purchase
by   near; of; before

If you plan to _____ something on Rodeo Drive, you had better do it _____ finding something very, very small.

coarse   rough
course   school subject; a route; part of a meal

When I studied Los Angeles as part of my sociology _____,

I learned that people with _____ behavior live there in addition to people with nice manners.

hear   to experience sounds
here   in this place

If you live _____ in Los Angeles, you'd better be ready to

_____ all about the Lakers and the Dodgers.

hole   place where nothing is
whole   complete; entire

Once I drove the _____ way from my home to Los Angeles with

a _____ in the door of my car.

its   belonging to *it*
it's   contraction of *it is* or *it has*

_____easy to daydream about Los Angeles; _____ stars, stores, and beaches are fantastic.

knew   past tense of *know*
new   fresh, unused; opposite of old

I _____that I should get a _____ swimsuit before hitting the beaches.

know   to have knowledge about; to understand
no   a negative

What I didn't _____ was that I had _____ idea where to buy a cute swimsuit.

pair   set of two
pare   trim away excess
pear   type of fruit

When I found a suit with a _____ and apples design, I bought a

_____ of bikinis in the same fabric. Now I must _____

down my figure to look good in it!

passed   past tense of *pass*
past   already happened

When I _____ the police car, I was afraid my clean driving record

would soon be a thing of the _____.

peace   calmness; tranquillity
piece   part or section

The officer gave me a _____ of his mind about driving too fast, but

he didn't give me a ticket. He left me in _____.

plain   simple, unadorned
plane   aircraft

An impressive aircraft, the *Spruce Goose* is the biggest _____ ever

built. It is made of wood and covered in fabric, but the _____ fact is that it's impressive because it's so big.

principal   the head administrator of a school; most important, conse-
quential, or influential; a sum of money that gains interest
principle   a rule or law

A guiding _____ of any high school _____ in Los Angeles
is that a diverse student population must be respected and appreciated.

right opposite of left; correct; a privilege or power that someone has a just claim to

rite the form or manner used for performing a ceremony

write to print or mark words on paper

One _____ of passage in California is going to the ocean. If you're
facing south in California, the ocean will be to your _____. However,
to avoid getting lost, you'd be wise to _____ down directions.

cite to call upon officially or quote

sight something seen

site the spatial location of an actual or planned structure or event

To _____ a great self-proclaimed expert (my brother), in L.A. one
_____ to see is Dodger Stadium. It is also the _____ of
many historic baseball moments.

than used to compare

then at that time

Someday I want to shop on Rodeo Drive rather _____ at flea
markets. Until _____, I'm off to the sale racks.

their belonging to *them*

there at that place; word used with verbs like *is, are, was, were,
had,* and *have*

they're contraction of *they are*

Residents of Los Angeles are proud of _____ city's wide range of
entertainment. Living _____, these residents think that
_____ the envy of people who don't live near the ocean.

threw   past tense of *throw*

through   passing from one side to another; all done

I _____ the frisbee, hoping my dog would catch it.

However, he missed it, so the frisbee sailed _____ the air.

to   toward (They went *to* Los Angeles); part of an infinitive (*to go*)

too   more than enough (There's *too* much to do in Los Angeles); in addition (I'm going to Los Angeles, *too*.)

two   the number 2

In _____ minutes, I am going _____ the beach. Do you

want to come, _____?

were   past tense of *be*

wear   to have on

where   in what place

_____ are you going in that outfit? Why would you _____

that? I wouldn't if I _____ you.

weather   atmospheric conditions

whether   if; in case

_____ it's January or June in Los Angeles, the _____ is
always lovely.

whose   belonging to *whom*

who's   contraction of *who is*

_____ job is it to plan our next beach trip? I want to know

_____ in charge.

your   belonging to *you*

you're   contraction of *you are*

If _____ ready, you can clean up _____ sandy footprints
and go back to the beach.

EXERCISE 1 Recognizing Homonyms

For each sentence below, write the correct word in the blank. Review the definitions on the previous pages if you need help.

1. its, it's

Los Angeles contains many famous landmarks. One of _____ most famous sights is Olvera Street.

Olvera Street

WRITE A PARAGRAPH Revealing a different style from the beaches of Southern California, the Mexican market on Olvera Street offers an enticing selection of authentic goods. Los Angeles, California, offers great cultural diversity. What kind of diversity exists where you live? Write a paragraph describing the cultures in your home, neighborhood, or city. Note that diversity may include differences in race, religion, gender, age, sexual orientation, or interests.

Responding to Images. *Write a few sentences explaining how the photo above is consistent or inconsistent with your ideas of Los Angeles.*

2. right, write   Olvera Street is one of the oldest streets in Los Angeles, running downtown _____ through El Pueblo de Los Angeles.

3. know, no   _____ other thoroughfare in Los Angeles boasts of more than thirty historic buildings or a Mexican marketplace that is full of food and craft stalls.

4. wear, where   Olvera Street is _____ people can gain a sense of historic Los Angeles, before it became the second-largest city in the United States.

5. to, too, two   The Santa Monica Pier, _____, is a wonderful place to visit.

6. passed, past   If you walk on the beach you'll be _____ by skaters, bicyclists, and joggers alike.

7. their, there, they're   Once _____, on the pier itself, you can visit Pacific Park, an amusement park.

8. all ready, already   Best of all, your visit to the pier will seem as if it's _____ paid for because it's free.

9. here, hear   If you ask about sights that are not free, you may _____ about Rodeo Drive shops.

10. weather, whether   _____ you buy anything in the shops or not, strolling down Rodeo Drive will make you feel as if you're spending money.

OTHER COMMONLY CONFUSED WORDS

Aside from homonyms, a number of other words look or sound enough alike to be confusing. As you did with homonyms, read the confusing word groups that follow, paying attention to how the words differ from each other. Then, fill in each blank with a word from that group.

a, an   Both *a* and *an* are generally used before other words to mean "one." Use *an* before words beginning with a vowel (*a, e, i, o, u*).

an ocean   **an** experience   **an** orange   **an** itch   **an** eyesore

Use *a* before words beginning with consonants (all other letters).

a beach   **a** visit   **a** yellow flower   **a** star   **a** great man

My friends and I had _____ urge to visit _____ museum in Los Angeles.

accept   to receive; to agree to
except   but; to exclude

I have seen most of the museums _____ the Getty Center in

Brentwood. I may have to _____ the fact that a visit there must wait.

advice   noun meaning "opinion"
advise   verb meaning "to give advice" or "to counsel"

My mother would _____ me to visit the Museum of Contemporary

Art (MOCA), but I rarely took her _____.

affect   verb meaning "to influence" or "to change"
effect   noun meaning "result"; verb meaning "to cause"

My mother's views don't usually _____ me, but I want to see the

_____ of so much contemporary art in one place.

among   implies three or more
between   implies two

It was hard to choose _____ all the museums in Los Angeles.

_____ MOCA and the La Brea tar pits, I chose the tar pits.

beside   next to
besides   in addition to

Standing _____ the tar pits, I noticed a strong smell.

_____ that, I felt that I was too near the tar.

desert   stretch of dry land; to leave one's job or station
dessert   final course of a meal

The tar pits seemed as though they could still "eat" living creatures; I felt that I could be _____. Additionally, I kept feeling warm, as if I were in the hot _____.

| **fewer** | used to show smaller amount among things that can be counted |
| **less** | used to show smaller amount, degree, or value |

I stayed at the tar pits _____ than an hour and saw _____ than a dozen fossils in the museum.

| **lay** | to put or place something (*Note:* The past tense of *lay* is *laid*.) |
| **lie** | to be prone (*Note:* The past tense of *lie* is *lay*.) |

When I got home, I _____ my tar pits brochure on the counter and decided to _____ down for a while.

| **loose** | not tight; not restrained |
| **lose** | opposite of *win*; to misplace |

I was afraid I might _____ my desire to see more museums, but I wanted to rest in _____, comfortable sweats.

| **quiet** | free from noise; peaceful |
| **quite** | very; completely |

After a nice _____ nap, I was _____ ready to visit another museum.

| **raise** | to lift an object; to grow or increase |
| **rise** | to get up by one's own power |

I was now ready to _____ my standards and _____ to the challenge of visiting the Getty Center.

| **though** | although; despite |
| **thought** | past tense of *think*; an idea |

_____ going to important museums still makes me nervous, the _____ of *not* going to them is scarier still.

EXERCISE 2 Understanding Commonly Confused Words

For each sentence below, write the correct word in the blank. Review the definitions on the previous pages if you need help.

1. among, between   _____ the Dodgers, the Lakers, and the Mighty Ducks, my favorite sports team is the Lakers.

2. beside, besides   Sitting _____ the basketball court at the Staples Center gives me chills.

3. quiet, quite   The entire arena is hushed and _____ when the Lakers shoot a free throw.

4. loose, lose   Some players _____ their concentration in the silent arena and miss the shot.

5. though, thought   I never _____ I would like the basketball team, originally started in Minneapolis–St. Paul. However, I guess everyone loves a winner!

6. buy, by   Before I _____ Lakers tickets, though, I check out the hockey schedule.

7. less, fewer   Although _____ Californians than Minnesotans grow up playing hockey, it's still popular on the West Coast.

8. hole, whole   People used to expect the Mighty Ducks to lose throughout the _____ season.

9. raise, rise   The players showed that they can _____ their level of play high enough to make the playoffs.

10. knew, new   While hockey may be a relatively _____ sport to California, it's gaining fans all the time.

EDITING PRACTICE

Correct the fifteen errors in word choice in the following paragraph.

The Magic Kingdom

Back in the early 1950s, when Anaheim was a small, quite town surrounded by orange groves, Walt Disney, an illustrator and filmmaker, bought more then 160 acres and began building his Magic Kingdom. No one new weather the park would be a success, but it certainly was expensive. Threw the building process, the cost rose to $17 million. It was 1955 before the park was already to open. The original park consisted of five "lands": Main Street, Fantasyland, Adventureland, Frontierland, and Tomorrowland, to. Many of the rides were not finished. Adventureland's only ride was the Jungle Cruise, and Tomorrowland had more exhibits then rides. Of coarse, many Disneyland sites did not exist in 1955; neither the Matterhorn nor the Monorail had been built yet. Some rides and exhibits that where their have long since been gone: the Aluminum Hall of Fame, Rocket to the Moon, a 20,000 Leagues Under the Sea exhibit, Space Station X-1 in Tomorrowland, and stagecoach rides in Frontierland. In fact, we rarely even here about those exhibits now. Fantasyland had rides that are still open today: Snow White's Adventures, Dumbo, and Mr. Toad's Wild Ride. The Autopia didn't arrive until 1956, and "It's a Small World" came in 1966. Throughout it's development, Disneyland has had a profound affect on Southern California.

WRITING PRACTICE

Write a paragraph explaining how a place you know well—your home, school, or church, for instance—has changed over time. Check your writing for correct word choice.

MyWritinglab & Lab Activity 51

mywritinglab For additional help with words that look alike and sound alike, go to **www.mywritinglab.com** or complete **Lab Activity 51** in the separate *Resources for Writers* Lab Manual.

Sentence Variation

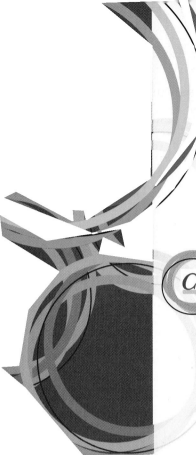

RECOGNIZING YOUR WRITING STYLE

The **style** of writing is what makes people like to read it. You may not realize it, but your writing has a style. It may be short, direct, and to the point, or it may be flowery, descriptive, and wandering. Whatever your style is, it's yours alone. If your words flow together seamlessly, and if your words and sentences are balanced between short and long ones, your writing will be more interesting to read.

Read the Culture Note about Dr. Seuss again, and then read the paragraph below. Which one is more enjoyable to read?

Theodore Geisel is admired for his wordplay. His wordplay is wacky. Theodore Geisel is also admired for his characters. The characters are inventive. Geisel is better known by his pen name, Dr. Seuss. Theodore Geisel uses rhythm and rhyme in children's books. He has made the use of rhythm and rhyme an art. Theodore Geisel's characters are imaginative. His characters take risks. The risks are outlandish. Theodore Geisel's characters learn lessons. The lessons are important. The lessons are in the name of education and entertainment.

No doubt, you noticed that the writing in the Culture Note is more interesting. Even though both paragraphs use the same words, the first version has greater **sentence variety,** mainly because it connects ideas with conjunctions and dependent words.

This chapter explores techniques you can use to make your writing more balanced and varied. Specifically, you can use three strategies to make your sentences more interesting.

- Adding equally important ideas (coordination)
- Adding less important ideas (subordination)
- Combining your sentences for brevity and variety

COORDINATION: ADDING EQUALLY IMPORTANT IDEAS

Coordination involves joining two complete, equally important ideas to form one sentence. If the sentences in a paragraph are all short, they begin to sound the same even though their content is different. For instance, read the following sentences, which are variations of lines in *Green Eggs and Ham*, a children's book by Dr. Seuss.

I am Sam.

I like green eggs and ham.

I like them in a house.

I like them with a mouse.

You probably have no trouble understanding these sentences. Each is a simple, correct sentence that communicates a single idea. Many developing writers write in simple sentences to avoid making errors. While this strategy makes sense, the result is boring for an adult audience. To make your writing more interesting, you can add a second simple sentence to the first. By doing so, you create a **compound sentence,** which joins two independent clauses. Remember that combining two complete ideas requires a comma and a coordinating conjunction (one of the FANBOYS: *for, and, nor, but, or, yet, so*). Here are two examples.

I am Sam, <u>and</u> I like green eggs and ham.

I like them in a house, <u>but</u> I never eat them with rodents.

EXERCISE 1 Coordination—Adding Another Idea to a Simple Sentence

Add another complete idea to each simple sentence below, using a comma and a coordinating conjunction (*for, and, nor, but, or, yet, so*). An example is done for you.

Sentence: Today is your day.

Revised: Today is your day, and you deserve it!

1. Sentence: Doing your homework can be tiring.

Revised: _____

2. Sentence: I enjoy comedies.

Revised: _____ . _____

3. Sentence: My writing is improving.

Revised: _____

4. Sentence: I want to wake up early tomorrow.

Revised: _____

5. Sentence: You're on your own.

Revised: _____

6. Sentence: The new Mexican restaurant is inexpensive.

Revised: _____

7. Sentence: I need a vacation.

Revised: _____

8. Sentence: The computers in the school library are always crowded.

Revised: _____

9. Sentence: People are easily confused by maps.

Revised: _____

10. Sentence: I waited in line for twelve hours for concert tickets.

Revised: _____

EXERCISE 2 Coordination—Combining Two Equally Important Ideas

Combine each pair of sentences into a single sentence, using a comma and a coordinating conjunction (*for, and, nor, but, or, yet, so*). An example is done for you.

Sentences: Dr. Seuss is known for his original stories. His books teach important lessons.

Combined: Dr. Seuss is known for his original stories, and his books

teach important lessons.

1. Sentences: In *Green Eggs and Ham,* one character does not want to try a new food. He puts up a great fight.

Combined: _____

_____

2. Sentences: The character tries and likes the new food. The moral of that story is to keep an open mind.

Combined: _____

_____

3. Sentences: Another story has a serious message. In this story, the main character is an elephant named Horton.

Combined: _____

_____

4. Sentences: Horton agrees to sit on an egg for Maizie, a lazy bird. He is "faithful, one hundred percent."

Combined: _____

_____

5. Sentences: An elephant bird hatches out of the egg. Horton is rewarded for his efforts.

Combined: _____

_____

SUBORDINATION: ADDING LESS IMPORTANT IDEAS

Another technique to vary your sentences is **subordination,** which is the process of joining two ideas, but making one of them less important than the other. Specifically, subordination involves making one idea an independent clause and the other a **dependent clause** (a group of words having a subject, a verb, and a **dependent word** such as *although, because, since*, or *until*.) Though dependent clauses have a subject and a verb, they do not make sense all by themselves. Thus, they are less important than independent clauses in the same sentence.

See how subordination is used to vary some simple sentences.

I am Sam *even though I've always wanted to be named Harry*.

I like green eggs and ham *because my mother made them for me every day of my childhood*.

The writer has added a dependent clause—a group of words (written in italics, above) having a subject, a verb, and a dependent word—for variety. The writer could also have placed the dependent clause before the independent clause.

Even though I've always wanted to be named Harry, I am Sam.

Because my mother made them for me every day of my childhood, I like green eggs and ham.

Remember to add a comma after the dependent clause if you put it first.

Common Dependent Words

after	before	since	until
although	even though	though	when
because	if	unless	while

EXERCISE 3 Subordination—Adding a Less Important
Idea to a Simple Sentence

Add a dependent clause to each of the following sentences. Remember to put a comma after the dependent clause if it comes first. An example is done for you.

Sentence: Tom went to the store.

Revised: *Tom went to the store because he was out of milk.*

1. Sentence: Karen's husband had an accident.

Revised: _____

2. Sentence: The girls fell asleep immediately.

Revised: _____

3. Sentence: Tomatoes are a healthy food.

Revised: _____

4. Sentence: Riding a bicycle can be a challenge.

Revised: _____

5. Sentence: Telling someone the truth can be difficult.

Revised: _____

6. Sentence: Listening to classical music is a great way to relax.

Revised: _____

7. Sentence: Palm reading has become popular.

Revised: _____

8. Sentence: Exercising regularly has many benefits.

Revised: _____

9. Sentence: Moving into a new home can be stressful.

Revised: _____

10. Sentence: Volunteering for a nonprofit organization can be very rewarding.

Revised: _____

EXERCISE 4 Combining Two Ideas Using Subordination

Add dependent words to one simple sentence in each pair to make it a dependent clause. Then combine the sentences into a single sentence. Be sure to use a comma between the clauses if you place the dependent clause first. An example is done for you.

Sentences: One of Dr. Seuss's most beloved stories is *The Sneetches*. It sends a message of open-mindedness.

Revised: *Because it sends a message of open-mindedness, one of*

Dr. Seuss's most beloved stories is The Sneetches.

1. Sentences: The story successfully addresses the sensitive issue of prejudice. It uses humor to make its point.

Combined: _____

_____

2. Sentences: The two kinds of Sneetches are almost exactly alike. The Sneetches with stars on their bellies think they are better than the Sneetches without stars.

Combined: _____

_____

3. Sentences: The Sneetches without stars want to have stars. The star-bellied Sneetches are unkind to them.

Combined: _____

_____

4. Sentences: A stranger named Sylvester McMonkey McBean offers hope to the Sneetches without stars. He has a star-adding machine.

Combined: _____

_____

5. Sentences: The star machine is very expensive. The Sneetches without stars pay to get stars.

Combined: _____

_____

6. Sentences: The original star-bellied Sneetches are unhappy. They see the new star-bellied Sneetches.

Combined: _____

_____

7. Sentences: Sylvester McMonkey McBean offers to help the original star-bellied Sneetches. He also has a star-removal machine.

Combined: _____

_____

8. Sentences: The original star-bellied Sneetches pay to have their stars removed. The star-removal machine is also expensive.

Combined: _____

_____

9. Sentences: All the Sneetches begin adding and removing stars constantly. They can't tell each other apart.

Combined: _____

_____

10. Sentences: The Sneetches discover that their stars make very little difference. Sylvester McMonkey McBean becomes very rich.

Combined: _____

_____

COMBINING SENTENCES FOR BREVITY AND VARIETY

In addition to simply making short sentences longer, sentence combining can alter the way your sentences flow together. Alternating your short sentences with longer ones or starting a longer sentence with a dependent clause can make your writing more interesting.

Combining Sentences to Avoid Repetition

Near the beginning of this chapter, you read a paragraph about Dr. Seuss that started like this:

> Theodore Geisel is admired for his wordplay. His wordplay is wacky.

Look at the sentences again and notice which words are used in both. When you see a term repeated in consecutive sentences, you can often combine them. In this case, combining the two sentences results in a shorter sentence.

> Theodore Geisel is admired for his wacky wordplay.

You have not changed the meaning, but you've omitted three words: *his, wordplay,* and *is.* If you can omit several words from every few sentences, your writing will be more compact.

Sometimes you can combine several sentences into a single sentence, as in the following example.

> Original: Theodore Geisel's characters are imaginative. His characters take risks. The risks are outlandish.

> Combined: Theodore Geisel's imaginative characters take outlandish risks.

> Omitted words: *are, His characters, The risks are*

EXERCISE 5 Combining Sentences to Avoid Repetition

Combine each pair of sentences to form a single one. You may need to add or change some words to combine sentences logically. An example is done for you.

Sentences: Dr. Seuss addresses adult themes in his stories. The themes are prejudice, war, and relationships.

Combined: Dr. Seuss addresses the adult themes of prejudice, war, and relationships in his stories.

1. Sentences: Dr. Seuss's stories combine elements. The elements are from classic tales and fables.

   Combined: _____

2. Sentences: Fables usually contain animals. The animals are the main characters.

   Combined: _____

3. Sentences: Dr. Seuss's stories are like fables. Dr. Seuss's stories contain animals.

   Combined: _____

4. Sentences: Fables often teach a lesson. The lesson is called a moral.

   Combined: _____

5. Sentences: Dr. Seuss's stories contain morals. The morals come from what the characters learn.

   Combined: _____

6. Sentences: The star-bellied Sneetches learn a lesson. The lesson is that appearances don't matter.

   Combined: _____

7. Sentences: Classic tales often have tragic heroes. Tragic heroes have one fatal flaw.

   Combined: _____

8. Sentences: Dr. Seuss's animals often display one significant characteristic. The characteristic can be positive or negative.

   Combined: _____

9. Sentences: Horton the elephant, for instance, displays a characteristic. His characteristic is faithfulness.

Combined: _____

10. Sentences: Maizie the bird, however, displays a characteristic. Her characteristic is laziness.

Combined: _____

Combining Sentences for Variety

In addition to purging your sentences of unnecessary words, combining sentences can spice up your writing style. Read the following two paragraphs. Which one is more interesting? Why?

How Is Butter Better?

The Butter Battle Book is written in classic Dr. Seuss fashion. It is a book about political tensions. The book examines the mentality of the arms race. The book also examines how minor differences between people can lead to misunderstanding and conflict. This story is of the Zooks and the Yooks. The story exposes the darker side of human nature. The story offers entertainment for children. Dr. Seuss started out as a political cartoonist. This book captures Dr. Seuss's views of the Cold War. The book makes people take sides based on their answer to the question "Do you eat your bread butter side up or down?"

The Butter Battle

In classic Dr. Seuss fashion, *The Butter Battle Book*—a book about political tensions—examines the mentality of the arms race and how minor differences between people can lead to misunderstanding and conflict. This story of the Zooks and the Yooks exposes the darker side of human nature while still offering entertainment for children. Written by a man who started out as a political cartoonist, this book captures Dr. Seuss's views of the Cold War and makes people take sides based on their answer to the question "Do you eat your bread butter side up or down?"

The second paragraph, "The Butter Battle," is more interesting because its sentences are more varied. The first paragraph is clear and informative, but every sentence begins the same way, with a subject followed closely by a verb. Writing similar sentences is not incorrect, but it does not make for entertaining reading.

Look at the way sentences from the first paragraph are combined in "The Butter Battle."

Original: This story is of the Zooks and the Yooks. The story exposes the darker side of human nature. The story offers entertainment for children.

Combined: This story of the Zooks and the Yooks exposes the darker side of human nature while still offering entertainment for children.

The writer changed *offers* to *offering* and added the dependent word *while*, linking the sentences in the order in which they appeared in the first paragraph. You can add variety in many other ways as well, as these examples show.

Original: *The Butter Battle Book* is written in classic Dr. Seuss fashion. It is a book about political tensions.

Combined: *The Butter Battle Book*—a book about political tensions—is written in classic Dr. Seuss fashion. (The information from the second sentence is inserted into the middle of the first sentence and enclosed by dashes.)

Combined: A book about political tensions, *The Butter Battle Book* is written in classic Dr. Seuss fashion. (The information from the second sentence is placed at the beginning of the first sentence and followed by a comma.)

EXERCISE 6 Combining Sentences for Variety

Combine the following pairs of sentences by moving the underlined information to the beginning or the middle of the resulting sentence. You may have to change the form of some words to combine the sentences logically. An example is done for you.

Sentences: *How the Grinch Stole Christmas* tells the story of an unhappy creature. *How the Grinch Stole Christmas* is <u>one of Dr. Seuss's most popular tales</u>.

Combined: *How the Grinch Stole Christmas, one of Dr. Seuss's most*

popular tales, tells the story of an unhappy creature.

1. Sentences: The Grinch looks down from his cave and watches the Whos, who live below him. The Whos are <u>a happy group who fully enjoy the Christmas season</u>.

   Combined: _____

   _____

2. Sentences: The Whos' joy bothers the Grinch. The Whos' joy <u>is expressed in hand-holding and singing</u>.

   Combined: _____

3. Sentences: He decides to make them feel as bad as he does. He decides to <u>steal the Whos' Christmas</u>.

   Combined: _____

   _____

4. Sentences: The Grinch dresses up as Santa Claus and creeps into Whoville, where the Whos live. He goes <u>on Christmas Eve</u>.

   Combined: _____

   _____

5. Sentences: The Grinch quietly takes down every sign of Christmas from every home in Whoville. The Grinch takes down <u>every ornament, tree, gift, and morsel of food</u>.

   Combined: _____

   _____

6. Sentences: He even lies to a very little Who about taking her Christmas tree. He lies to <u>Cindy Lou Who</u>.

   Combined: _____

   _____

7. Sentences: The Grinch wakes up early expecting to hear the Whos sobbing with disappointment. The Grinch wakes up <u>the next morning</u>.

Combined: _____

_____

8. Sentences: The <u>Whos wake up</u>. However, they are simply happy to celebrate Christmas together.

Combined: _____

_____

9. Sentences: <u>He hears the Whos sing</u>. The Grinch feels his heart expand, and he reloads all the Whos' gifts and returns them to Whoville.

Combined: _____

_____

10. Sentences: The Whos are so pleased <u>with the Ginch</u>. The Whos invite him to stay and feast with them.

Combined: _____

_____

EDITING PRACTICE

Rewrite the following paragraph on a separate piece of paper, combining sentences to avoid repetition and add variety.

Dr. Seuss's last book was published in 1990. Dr. Seuss's last book is called *Oh, The Places You'll Go!* It is a wonderfully encouraging tale. It is a tale about life. Dr. Seuss encourages children. Dr. Seuss reminds children that they have brains. Dr. Seuss reminds children that they have the means to make changes. Dr. Seuss points out the various choices people make. He discusses these choices through zany, upbeat illustrations and rhyme. He talks about how hitting bottom is something that happens to everyone. Dr. Seuss says that people will certainly pull out of it. Dr. Seuss also discusses temptation.

Dr. Seuss discusses how temptation draws people and tries to lure them away from safety. Dr. Seuss discusses how temptation tries to lure people away from what they know. In the end, though, the story simply reinforces people's self-confidence. The story reminds people that taking a first step is progress.

WRITING PRACTICE

Write a paragraph explaining how a story from your childhood influenced you in some way. The story may be from a book, a movie, a television program, or a person (such as a grandparent). Use strategies from this chapter to make your sentences as varied as possible.

MyWritingLab & Lab Activity 52

mywritinglab For additional help with sentence combining, go to **www.mywritinglab. com** or complete **Lab Activity 52** in the separate *Resources for Writers* Lab Manual.

Tips for Second-Language Writers

Culture Note

FOOTBALL

Considered by many to be the most "American" sport, football involves strength, speed, agility, and strategy. One of the few sports that includes separate teams for offense and defense, football teams include a range of players from highly specialized kickers to an assortment of "backs," or players who run and block other players.

UNDERSTANDING ESL NEEDS

If you learned another language before you learned English, you have a tremendous advantage. Not only can you communicate in two languages, but you have the choice of using words and expressions from two languages in considering and developing your ideas. Writing English, however, presents certain challenges. English grammar is complex, and many rules have exceptions. **English as a second language (ESL)** students need to make sure they use the following elements correctly.

- Subjects
- Verbs
- Prepositions
- Articles
- Adjectives

USING SUBJECTS CORRECTLY

A group of words cannot be a sentence unless it has a subject. When writing English sentences, follow these rules.

- Include a subject in each clause.
- Make every noun a subject or an object.
- Avoid extra or unnecessary pronoun subjects.

Including a Subject in Each Clause

Every sentence must have a subject and a verb. Leaving out a subject results in a sentence fragment. In the examples that follow, the underlined word groups lack a subject.

Incorrect:	Football players get hurt often. <u>Get many injuries</u>. (The writer probably means "*They* get many injuries.")

(fragment marked over "Get many injuries")

Some sentences use a placeholder subject, such as *here, there,* or *it*.

Incorrect:	Are many fans in the stadium.
Correct:	<u>There</u> are many fans in the stadium.
Incorrect:	Is the program for the football game.
Correct:	<u>Here</u> is the program for the football game.
Incorrect:	Some football teams play in the snow. Is very cold.
Correct:	Some football teams play in the snow. <u>It</u> is very cold.

A sentence may require more than one subject. For instance, the following sentence has two **clauses** (groups of related words having a subject and a verb that work together to communicate an idea).

Football <u>fans</u> love to cheer even if <u>they</u> have never played the game.

Because this sentence has two clauses, it requires two subjects: *fans* and *they*. Omitting one of the subjects would result in a sentence error.

Incorrect:	Although the football season is short, is intense.
Correct:	Although the football season is short, <u>it</u> is intense.
Incorrect:	Because football players are often injured, wear protective pads.
Correct:	Because football players are often injured, <u>they</u> wear protective pads.

Making Every Noun a Subject or an Object

In some languages, a word or phrase with no grammatical connection to the sentence announces what the sentence is about. This kind of structure is incorrect in English.

Incorrect: Football dream I want to be a quarterback.

The term *football dream* has no grammatical connection to the rest of the sentence; it serves as neither a subject nor an object. Even though *football dream* appears early in the sentence—a typical place for the subject—it is not the subject because it does not go with the verb, *want*. The sentence subject is *I*. Furthermore, *football dream* is not an object of the verb *want* or of a preposition. You can revise this sentence in two ways.

■ Make the phrase a subject.

        ┌─ subject ─┐
Correct: My <u>football dream</u> is to be a quarterback.

■ Make the phrase an object.

     ┌prepositional phrase ┐
Correct: In my <u>football dream</u>, I am a quarterback.
           object

(*Football dream* is the object of a preposition. Notice that other words also had to be changed so that the sentence makes sense.)

Avoiding Extra or Unnecessary Pronoun Subjects

English does not permit a sentence to have repeated subjects for the same verb. Don't follow the subject with a pronoun that refers to that subject.

               subject
Incorrect: My <u>teacher</u> *she* loves to root for the Buffalo Bills.

Correct: My <u>teacher</u> loves to root for the Buffalo Bills.

Correct: <u>She</u> loves to root for the Buffalo Bills.

               subject
Incorrect: This <u>class</u> *it* does not discuss football often.

Correct: This <u>class</u> does not discuss football often.

Correct: <u>It</u> does not discuss football often.

Even if the subject is separated from the verb by several words, do not repeat the subject with a pronoun.

Incorrect: The <u>players</u> who stand on the line of scrimmage *they* are called the linemen.

Correct: The <u>players</u> who stand on the line of scrimmage are called the linemen.

EXERCISE 1 Using Subjects Correctly

Place a "C" in front of the correct sentence in each pair and an "X" in front of the incorrect sentence. An example is done for you.

   C   It was raining during the halftime show.

   X   Was raining during the halftime show.

_____ **1.** Football players need to take care of themselves because get hurt a lot.

_____ Football players need to take care of themselves because they get hurt a lot.

_____ **2.** Even when my brothers watch football, act as if they're playing it.

_____ Even when my brothers watch football, they act as if they're playing it.

_____ **3.** My favorite activity is watching professional football.

_____ My favorite activity I like to watch professional football.

_____ **4.** My goal it is to become a football coach.

_____ My goal is to become a football coach.

_____ **5.** My mother thinks football is too violent.

_____ My mother she thinks football is too violent.

USING ARTICLES CORRECTLY

Articles signal that a noun will follow. The **indefinite articles,** *a* and *an,* introduce a noun that cannot yet be specifically identified. Use *an* with a word that begins with a vowel (*a, e, i, o, u*) or a vowel sound.

a ball	a coach	a field	a sport	a player

an error	an injury	an ice pack	an elbow	an hour

These items could be *any* ball, coach, field, and so on. In using *a* or *an*, the writer does not identify any item in particular.

Tip: Even though *hour* begins with *h*, it takes *an* because the *h* is silent. The word *uniform* takes an *a* because it begins with a *y* sound.

The **definite article,** *the*, introduces a noun that refers to a specific, identifiable item.

the ball	the coach	the field	the error	the injury	the hour

In writing *the ball*, the writer has in mind a *particular* ball.

An article may come directly in front of a noun, or it can be separated from the noun by modifiers.

a new brown football

an exciting game

the experienced, overpaid coach

Using Articles with Nonspecific Nouns

A noun is **nonspecific** if the reader doesn't know its exact identity. Use *a* or *an* to introduce nonspecific nouns.

A football player is not allowed to bite his opponents. (The rule against biting refers to any football player, not one in particular.)

Using Articles with Specific Nouns

If a noun is **specific**—referring to something that can be identified in particular—use *the*. Here are some ways to identify a specific noun.

■ From other information in the sentence.

Watch me run into the middle of the football field during halftime. (*The* indicates that the "middle" is in the football field.)

■ From other information in another sentence.

I saw an exciting play on television. The play involved the quarterback and a wide receiver. (The play is the one mentioned in the previous sentence.)

- From general information.

  The force of gravity keeps us on the earth. (Here, *the* refers to "gravity" and "earth" because the reader can be expected to know what these are.)

- Before the superlative form of an adjective.

  the best day, the longest run

- Before numbers indicating sequence or order.

  the second step, the first time

Using Articles with Count and Noncount Nouns

Understanding count and noncount nouns helps you know when to use articles and what kind to use. **Count nouns** are nouns that identify people, places, things, or ideas that can be numbered or counted and made plural.

five balls   three fields   two players

Determiners

Determiners are adjectives that *identify* rather than *modify* nouns.

Articles	a, an, the
Demonstrative pronouns	this, that, these, those
Possessive pronouns	my, our, your, his, her, its, their, mine, yours, hers, ours, theirs
Possessive nouns	Joe's, my mom's
Amounts	a few, a little, all, any, both, each, either, enough, every, few, little, many, much, neither, several, some, amount
Numerals	one, first, second, third, etc.

Noncount nouns refer to things that cannot be counted. For example, you cannot have *one* sunburn or *three* sweats.

sunburn   sweat   blood   fatigue

Noncount nouns cannot be given specific numbers to indicate amounts. However, their amounts can be described by using words that indicate nonspecific amounts.

Examples of Noncount Nouns

Concepts and feelings	happiness, competition, ferocity, intelligence, athleticism
Activities	playing, cooking, watching, eating
Foods and drinks	meat, milk, chocolate, tea, water, lasagna
School courses	mathematics, English, French
Bulk materials	lumber, steel, concrete, grain, soil, wheat, flour
Weather	snow, sleet, hail, wind, thunder

a bit   a little   a part of   a piece of   a section of   more   some

In the examples that follow, the modifiers are italicized, and the noncount nouns are underlined.

Tony felt *a bit of* <u>hunger</u> after playing football all day.

During the winter, we received *more* <u>rain</u> than usual.

Only *a part of* the <u>class</u> wanted to study for the exam.

Some nouns can serve as both count and noncount nouns.

My mother uses different <u>flours</u> to make whole wheat bread. (*Flours* refers to individual types of flour, so it is a count noun).

<u>Flour</u> is an essential ingredient in my mother's bread. (*Flour* refers to a general concept; thus, it cannot be counted.)

Omitting Articles

Do not use articles with nonspecific plural nouns or nonspecific noncount nouns. (Plural nouns and noncount nouns are nonspecific when they indicate something in general.)

Nonspecific	**Specific**
<u>Plays</u> take place during the game.	*The* <u>plays</u> they made were tricky.
<u>Water</u> must be on hand for thirsty players.	*The* <u>water</u> is safe to drink.
<u>Coaches</u> in the NFL are fired and hired regularly.	*The* <u>coaches</u> for the Jaguars have experience.

Using Articles with Proper Nouns

Proper nouns—specific names of people, places, things, or ideas—are always capitalized. Most proper nouns do not require articles, but the following types use *the*.

- Plural proper nouns
  the Rockefellers   the Sawtooth Mountains
- Names of significant geographic areas
  the Sahara   the Southwest   the Pacific Ocean   the Seine River

Do not use *the* before the following types of nouns.

- Names of people and animals
  Joe Montana   Sparky
- Names of most places on land
  Europe   Florida   New York   Freeport Way   McKinley Park
- Names of most countries
  Canada   Vietnam   Mexico
  Exception: the United States
- Names of most bodies of water
  Lake Norman   Niagara Falls   Folsom Lake

EXERCISE 2 Choosing the Correct Article

Circle the correct answer from the words in parentheses.

1. The most necessary piece of equipment for the game of football is (the football, a football) itself.

2. (The pair of cleats, A pair of cleats) sat in my brother's closet for months until he bought a ball.

3. In colder parts of (the country, country), players must play in snow and freezing winds.

4. Playing in these conditions gives home teams in (the Wisconsin, Wisconsin) an advantage over warm-weather opponents.

5. Players must have (the good attitude, a good attitude) no matter where they play.

USING VERBS CORRECTLY

Every sentence must have a verb that is right for the sentence. In your writing, follow these guidelines.

- Include verbs in all sentences.
- Use the correct verb tense.
- Use the progressive verb tense correctly.

Including Verbs in All Sentences

Every sentence must have a verb. Remember not to omit the *be* verbs (*am, is, are, was, were*).

Incorrect:	Joe Montana's pass very good.	I a good wide receiver.
Correct:	Joe Montana's pass <u>was</u> very good.	I <u>am</u> a good wide receiver.

Using the Correct Verb Tense

Verbs tell when the action of the sentence takes place. However, other words can also indicate time. Make sure that the verb tense makes sense with the rest of the sentence.

Incorrect:	Last week, I <u>see</u> a football game.
Correct:	Last week, I <u>saw</u> a football game. (The past tense verb *saw* is consistent with the time indicator *last week*.)
Incorrect:	Tomorrow I <u>played</u> catch with my brother. (The past tense verb *played* is inconsistent with the word *tomorrow*.)
Correct:	Tomorrow I <u>will play</u> catch with my brother.

Using the Progressive Verb Tense

The **progressive verb tense** consists of forms of the verb *be* and the *-ing* form (present participle) of the main verb. This tense indicates actions still occurring at a certain time.

Peyton Manning probably *will be* <u>playing</u> football for years.

Verbs for the five senses, mental states, possession, and inclusion are not generally used in the progressive tense.

Incorrect: I <u>am wishing</u> I could be a football player.

Correct: I <u>wish</u> I could be a football player. (The word *wish* refers to a mental activity.)

Verbs Not Used in the Progressive Tense

Mental states	agree, believe, hate, imagine, know, like, love, prefer, think, understand, want, wish
Five senses	feel, hear, see, smell, taste, touch
Possession	belong, have, own, possess
Other verbs	be, contain, cost, have, include, mean, need, weigh

EXERCISE 3 Using Correct Verbs

Circle the correct verb form in each sentence.

1. Even after the game was over, I (hear, heard) the referee's whistle.

2. I (am seeing, see) football games on television every week.

3. The Super Bowl (is my favorite, my favorite) game of the year.

4. Someday, my brother (wants, is wanting) to play quarterback.

5. Yesterday, I (watched, watch) my favorite team lose a big game.

USING ADJECTIVES CORRECTLY

Adjectives—words that describe nouns or pronouns—and other modifiers usually come directly before or after nouns. Some modifiers need to be put in a specific order when they appear in a series.

- **Articles and determiners** always come first in a series of adjectives.

  <u>the</u> big strong football player

  <u>a</u> brilliant coaching maneuver

  <u>an</u> obvious mental error

■ **Nouns acting as adjectives** must come last in a series of adjectives.

the big strong <u>football</u> player (*Football* is an adjective describing *player*.)

a dark <u>coat</u> closet (*Coat* is an adjective describing *closet*.)

an enormous <u>shoe</u> size (*Shoe* is an adjective describing *size*.)

Other adjectives come between these two end points, typically in the following order.

1. **Attitude, judgment, or opinion:** lovely, difficult, kind, sweet, tough, beautiful, brutal
2. **Size:** big, small, gargantuan, Lilliputian, large, microscopic
3. **Shape:** oblong, cylindrical, rectangular, triangular, tall
4. **Age:** young, old, teenaged, preteen, adolescent, elderly
5. **Color:** red, white, blue, purple, pink
6. **Nationality:** German, Vietnamese, Russian, Cuban
7. **Religion:** Lutheran, Jewish, Buddhist, Catholic

Here are some examples of correctly ordered adjectives.

The <u>excellent young American football</u> *coach* was immediately successful.

He worked hard to recruit the <u>tough young high school</u> *players* for his team.

The coach wore <u>the striking orange nylon</u> *uniform* of his team.

EXERCISE 4 Placing Adjectives in Order

Circle the correct choice in each sentence.

1. My family used to live behind (an old concrete football, a concrete football old) stadium.

2. We could hear (the large noisy, the noisy large) crowd cheering.

3. I appreciated the excitement that came from behind (the tall gray, the gray tall) walls of the stadium.

4. I sneaked out my window—down (a wooden long, a long wooden) ladder—to go watch some games.

5. Though my (stern Italian, Italian stern) grandmother got mad at me, seeing the games was worth getting into trouble.

EXERCISE 5 Writing Adjectives in Correct Order

In each sentence below, fill in the blank with three adjectives in the correct order. An example is done for you.

The small young _____ boy wanted to play on the high school football team.

1. He spent hours watching _____ players practicing their plays.

2. He finally worked up the courage to ask _____ coach if he could try out for the team.

3. The coach gave the boy _____ look.

4. Then the coach muttered _____ answer.

5. _____ member of the football team vowed to work as hard as he could to become a useful player.

USING PREPOSITIONS CORRECTLY

From meaning alone, it can be hard to determine the correct preposition to use. Follow these guidelines for using the prepositions *at*, *in*, and *on*.

- *At* can specify a certain point in time or space.

  The game begins <u>at</u> 6:00 p.m., so please be <u>at</u> the gate early.
- *In* can specify stretches of time or space.

  I played football <u>in</u> high school <u>in</u> the 1990s.
- *On* is used with names of streets (excluding precise addresses) and with days of the week or of the month. *On* is also used to show an item's placement.

  When I lived <u>on</u> Mulberry Street, I placed a rocking chair <u>on</u> the front porch every year <u>on</u> July 4 to watch the fireworks.

EXERCISE 6 Using Prepositions

Circle the correct preposition in each sentence.

1. Whenever I watch football, I put my helmet (at, on) my head.

2. I did this a lot (in, at) the 1990s.

3. My brother said the game started (at, on) 7:00 p.m.

4. I watched the game (at, on) my friend's house.

5. My friend's house is (in, on) another street.

EDITING PRACTICE

Correct the underlined errors in the following paragraph.

Many plays have made <u>football American</u> history. One of the most famous plays is "the Catch." It took place at San Francisco's Candlestick Park <u>in</u> January 10, 1982. The San Francisco Forty-Niners <u>trail</u> the Dallas Cowboys 27 to 21 in a championship game. Joe Montana, <u>medium-sized, wily</u> quarterback for the Forty-Niners, threw a pass that appeared to be heading for the stands. Wide receiver Dwight Clark, however, knew the ball was being thrown to him in the back of the end zone. The <u>experienced, tall</u> Clark leaped as high as he could and, to his own amazement, made the catch. <u>Montana stunned</u>, too. With the Catch, and the extra point, the Forty-Niners beat the Cowboys 28 to 27 and went on to beat the Cincinnati Bengals 26 to 21 in Super Bowl XVI. It was the first of four Super Bowl victories the Forty-Niners achieved <u>at</u> the 1980s. Historically, this game transformed the Forty-Niners into the great team who won five Super Bowl championships. <u>It where</u> the legend really began. What few people consider is that the Forty-Niners <u>have</u> good teams before 1981. It was just <u>that Cowboys</u> denied them chances at Super Bowl glory. So "the Catch" not only symbolized the beginning of a great championship run but also marked the defeat of another great team, the Cowboys.

WRITING PRACTICE

Write a paragraph explaining how to play a game you played in your childhood. The game does not need to be a sport. Check your writing for non-standard English usage.

MyWritingLab & Lab Activity 53

mywritinglab For additional help with tips for ESL writers, go to **www.mywritinglab.com** or complete **Lab Activity 53** in the separate *Resources for Writers* Lab Manual.

PART NINE
Readings
for Informed Writing

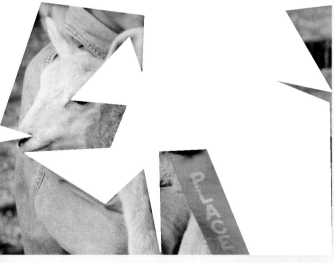

CRITICAL THINKING Many aspects of American society, even recreational areas, contain an element of competition. How positive or negative is competition in different activities? Explain.

Responding to Images. How does the girl in the photo feel about her lamb? How can you tell? Explain.

HOW WE LEARN

Tips for Reading Critically

Without realizing it, you have probably already engaged in critical reading. Every time you question a writer's credibility, you are reading critically. Critical reading is an essential skill that requires you to evaluate the information placed before you. The following suggestions can help you develop your critical reading skills.

1. **Read all titles, beginnings, and endings.** Such information gives you a preview of the upcoming section.

   - The title of a work gives a sense of the writer's tone and the scope of the information to follow.
   - Headings preview the main points and give a sense of the overall organization.
   - The first and last paragraphs often contain the main ideas.
   - Biographical or bibliographical material, which often appears at the end, reveals the context of the piece: when it was written, for whom it was written, why it was written.

2. **Prewrite.** Once you have a sense of where the writer is headed, spend a few minutes writing as quickly as you can about any ideas or questions that come to mind. What do you expect to learn from the material? What conclusions do you think the writer will reach? How relevant is the writer's message for you?

3. **Ask questions as you read.** After surveying the material, plunge in and read it from start to finish, keeping your prewriting ideas and questions in mind. What is the writer's primary argument? How is the writer developing his or her points? Is the writer fulfilling your expectations? How could the writer have been more persuasive?

4. **Ask how this reading relates to other material you've read.** Think about ideas that you have read or encountered before in your life, in other classes, and in other readings. Make notes in the margins so

that when you write a paragraph or essay based on a reading, you'll have clues about connections to outside material.

5. **Take notes as you read.** Use sticky notes, underline, or otherwise highlight key words, phrases, and ideas in the reading. Mark sentences that you think best reveal the writer's thesis, and identify examples that illustrate the main ideas. Make note of any questions that occur to you as you read. Identify words you are unfamiliar with and look them up in the dictionary later.

6. **Reread and rethink.** Just as you reread your own essays when you revise and clarify meaning, you should reread others' writings to make sure you fully understand the main ideas. A second reading can fill in any gaps in understanding.

7. **Write after you finish reading.** Summarize the main points, and ask yourself questions that will help you evaluate the content. Were your expectations fulfilled? Did the writer convince you of his or her point? What, if anything, made the writer's case most convincing? (Keep in mind that the strengths and weaknesses you note in others' writing can help you improve your own.)

8. **Talk it over.** Discuss the material with your classmates or friends. Talk about your impressions of the writer's argument. Share what you did or did not like or agree with in the piece, and then move on to how you formed those opinions. As you gather viewpoints, you may decide to revise or defend your own position.

How We Learn

One of the most important decisions we can make is how we plan to educate ourselves. Some people opt for formal education and spend years in school accumulating knowledge. The essays "Education" and "All I Really Need to Know I Learned in Kindergarten" explore the realm of formal education. Other people choose to learn a hands-on trade, such as plumbing or carpentry. In these cases, people must learn to work with their hands, often forgoing the classroom for the shop or the workroom. "A Homemade Education" and "What Is Intelligence, Anyway?" explain how lessons learned from real life are every bit as valuable as those learned in school. Finally, within education, several issues rear their heads as students attempt to sort out what they need to learn. "The Joy of Boredom" and "How to Write with Style" address the choices we make in relation to our education.

READINGS IN THIS SECTION

ROBERT FULGHUM

From *All I Really Need to Know I Learned in Kindergarten*

Robert Fulghum describes himself as a philosopher. Over the course of his life he has held many jobs, ranging from cowboy to IBM salesman. He has also published essays and written for the theater. In this excerpt from *All I Really Need to Know I Learned in Kindergarten*, Fulghum distills his personal credo down into several simple rules that apply to all aspects of life.

BEFORE YOU READ

Think about the following questions. Write your responses on a separate sheet or in your journal.

- Make a list of any lessons or rules you learned as a young child that you think are still relevant today. Who taught you these rules?
- What about these rules made them relevant for you when you learned them?
- What makes them relevant for you now?

VOCABULARY DEVELOPMENT

Look up the following words in a dictionary. Write down their meanings on a separate sheet or in your journal.

credo (paragraph 1)   cynical (paragraph 2)

naïve (paragraph 2)   idealism (paragraph 2)

brevity (paragraph 3)   existential (paragraph 3)

extrapolate (paragraph 7)

All I Really Need to Know I Learned in Kindergarten

1   Each spring, for many years, I have set myself the task of writing a personal statement of belief: a Credo. When I was younger, the statement ran for many pages, trying to cover every base, with no loose ends. It sounded like a Supreme Court brief, as if words could resolve all conflicts about the meaning of existence.

2   The Credo has grown shorter in recent years—sometimes cynical, sometimes comical, sometimes bland—but I keep working at it. Recently I set out to get the statement of personal belief down to one page in simple terms, fully understanding the naïve idealism that implied.

3   The inspiration for brevity came to me at a gasoline station. I managed to fill an old car's tank with super-deluxe high-octane go-juice. My old hoopy

couldn't handle it and got the willies—kept sputtering out at intersections and belching going downhill. I understood. My mind and my spirit get like that from time to time. Too much high-content information, and *I* get the existential willies—keep sputtering out at intersections where life choices must be made and I either know too much or not enough. The examined life is no picnic.

4   I realized then that I already know most of what's necessary to live a meaningful life—that it isn't all that complicated. *I know it.* And have known it for a long, long time. Living it—well, that's another matter, yes? Here's my Credo:

5   All I really need to know about how to live and what to do and how to be I learned in kindergarten. Wisdom was not at the top of the graduate-school mountain, but there in the sandpile at Sunday School. These are the things I learned:

Share everything.
Play fair.
Don't hit people.
Put things back where you found them.
Clean up your own mess.
Don't take things that aren't yours.
Say you're sorry when you hurt somebody.
Wash your hands before you eat.
Flush.
Warm cookies and cold milk are good for you.
Live a balanced life—learn some and think some and draw and paint and sing and dance and play and work every day some.
Take a nap every afternoon.
When you go out into the world, watch out for traffic, hold hands, and stick together.
Be aware of wonder. Remember the little seed in the Styrofoam cup: The roots go down and the plant goes up and nobody really knows how or why, but we are all like that.
Goldfish and hamsters and white mice and even the little seed in the Styrofoam cup—they all die. So do we.
And then remember the Dick-and-Jane books and the first word you learned—the biggest word of all—LOOK.

6   Everything you need to know is in there somewhere. The Golden Rule and love and basic sanitation. Ecology and politics and equality and sane living.

7   Take any one of those items and extrapolate it into sophisticated adult terms and apply it to your family life or your work or your government or your world and it holds true and clear and firm. Think what a better world it would be if we all—the whole world—had cookies and milk about three

o'clock every afternoon and then lay down with our blankies for a nap. Or if all governments had as a basic policy to always put things back where they found them and clean up their own mess.

8   And it is still true, no matter how old you are—when you go out into the world, it is best to hold hands and stick together.

AFTER YOU READ

Vocabulary Practice

1. Choose at least three words from the Vocabulary Development list on page 710 and write sentences using those words. You may write one sentence using all three words if you wish.

2. What word from the Vocabulary Development list means "believing that people are motivated in all their actions only by selfishness"? Use the word in a sentence that clearly shows its meaning.

3. Fulghum claims that his kindergarten-learned lessons are important, yet his language targets an audience of people who are not children. Choose at least three words or phrases from the essay and explain in a few sentences how these terms reveal Fulghum's intended audience.

Comprehension

Circle the correct answer.

1. Fulghum writes his credo every
    a. fall.   b. winter.
    c. spring.   d. summer.

2. Fulghum defines his credo as
    a. a personal statement of belief.
    b. a personal statement of goals.
    c. a personal list of complaints.
    d. a personal list of blessings.

3. The inspiration for Fulghum's latest credo came from his
    a. house.   b. office.
    c. bicycle.   d. car.

4. Which one of these rules is not part of Fulghum's credo?
    a. Play fair.
    b. Dont't hit people.
    c. Feel proud of yourself for good deeds.
    d. Take a nap every afternoon.

5. What does Fulghum say is "the first word you learned—the biggest word of all"?

    a. Wait   b. Love

    c. Forgive   d. Look

Content

1. How often does Fulghum write his personal credo?
2. What changes has his credo undergone over the years?
3. What are at least three lessons in Fulghum's credo?

Style and Structure

1. What is Fulghum's purpose in writing this essay?
2. Whom is Fulghum writing his essay for? How can you tell?
3. Fulghum uses "the sandpile at Sunday School" to illustrate one of his ideas. What other specific details does Fulghum use? Why do you think he chooses such familiar images? Explain.

Working Together

1. Make a chart showing the most important lesson or skill you learned in every grade of your formal education thus far. You might write "reading" for first or second grade, for example, or "how to avoid bullies" in fourth grade. Which lessons are most valuable? Discuss and summarize your findings for the class.
2. Does every lesson require a teacher? Discuss the types of "lessons" you have learned in your life—from school, from home, from experience—and decide which ones are best learned from another person. Summarize your findings for the class.

Writing Assignments

1. Fulghum claims that all he really needs to know he learned in kindergarten. Do you agree with him? *Write a paragraph agreeing or disagreeing with the idea that kindergarten has taught you the most important lessons of your life.* Be sure to use examples from your life to support your ideas.
2. What person or situation has taught you the most valuable lessons? *Write a paragraph explaining how a specific person or situation has taught you a valuable lesson.* Use details from your experience and observations to illustrate your ideas.
3. Although many lessons may be learned from teachers or parents, must some be learned through experience? What are these? *Write an essay explaining how some lessons must be learned through experience.* (If you believe that all lessons can be learned from teachers or parents, explain which lessons are easiest for teachers or parents to teach children.) Use specific details from your experience and observations to support your ideas.

MALCOLM X

"A Homemade Education" from *The Autobiography of Malcolm X*

When Malcolm X was born in Omaha, Nebraska, in 1925, his name was Malcolm Little. His father was a minister, and he spent his early years in middle America. When his father died, Malcolm X became involved in street life and was sent to prison for burglary. His prison time, however, was a turning point in his life. Malcolm X began corresponding with Elijah Muhammad, leader of the Black Muslim movement. Eventually, he became a militant leader of the Black Revolution, rejecting the surname "Little" as his slave name and calling himself "Malcolm X." His assertion that African-Americans must gain their rights "by any means necessary" became one of his defining statements. Malcolm X was assassinated in 1965.

BEFORE YOU READ

Think about the following questions. Write your responses on a separate sheet or in your journal.

- What kinds of educational experiences have you had? What have your parents, friends, or other acquaintances taught you? What kinds of formal schooling have you had?
- What lessons have proved to be the most valuable to you? How did you learn them?
- What type of education is more valuable to you: formal (in school) or informal (friends, family, and work, for instance)? Explain.

VOCABULARY DEVELOPMENT

Look up the following words in a dictionary. Write down their meanings on a separate sheet or in your journal.

stumble (paragraph 3)   acquire (paragraph 4)

convey (paragraph 6)   emulate (paragraph 6)

immensely (paragraph 10)

A Homemade Education

1   It was because of my letters that I happened to stumble upon starting to acquire some kind of homemade education.

2   I became increasingly frustrated at not being able to express what I wanted to convey in letters that I wrote, especially those to Mr. Elijah Muhammad. In the street, I had been the most articulate hustler out there—I had commanded attention when I said something. But now, trying to write simple English, I not only wasn't articulate, I wasn't even functional. How would I sound writing in slang, the way I would *say* it, something such as, "Look, daddy, let me pull your coat about a cat, Elijah Muhammad—"

3   Many who today hear me somewhere in person, or on television, or those who read something I've said, will think I went to school far beyond the eighth grade. This impression is due entirely to my prison studies.

4   It had really begun back in Charlestown Prison, when Bimbi first made me feel envy of his stock of knowledge. Bimbi had always taken charge of any conversation he was in, and I had tried to emulate him. But every book I picked up had few sentences which didn't contain anywhere from one to nearly all of the words that might as well have been in Chinese. When I just skipped those words, of course, I really ended up with little idea of what the book said. So I had come to the Norfolk Prison Colony still going through only book-reading motions. Pretty soon, I would have quit even these motions unless I had received the motivation that I did.

5   I saw that the best thing I could do was get hold of a dictionary—to study to learn some words. I was lucky enough to reason also that I should try to improve my penmanship. It was sad. I couldn't even write in a straight line. It was both ideas together that moved me to request a dictionary along with some tablets and pencils from the Norfolk Prison Colony school.

6   I spent two days just riffling uncertainly through the dictionary's pages. I'd never realized so many words existed! I didn't know *which* words I needed to learn. Finally, just to start some kind of action, I began copying.

7   In my slow, painstaking, ragged handwriting, I copied into my tablet everything printed on that first page, down to the punctuation marks.

8   I believe it took me a day. Then, aloud, I read back, to myself, everything I'd written on the tablet. Over and over, aloud, to myself, I read my own handwriting.

9   I woke up the next morning, thinking about those words—immensely proud to realize that not only had I written so much at one time, but I'd written words that I never knew were in the world. Moreover, with a little effort, I also could remember what many of these words meant. I reviewed the words whose meanings I didn't remember. Funny thing, from the dictionary's first page right now, that "aardvark" springs to my mind. The dictionary had a picture of it, a long-tailed, long-eared, burrowing African mammal, which lives off termites caught by sticking out its tongue as an anteater does for ants.

10   I was so fascinated that I went on—I copied the dictionary's next page. And the same experience came when I studied that. With every succeeding page, I also learned of people and places and events from history. Actually the dictionary is like a miniature encyclopedia. Finally the dictionary's A section had filled a whole tablet—and I went on into the B's. That was the way I started copying what eventually became the entire dictionary. It went a lot faster after so much practice helped me to pick up handwriting speed. Between what I wrote in my tablet, and writing letters, during the rest of my time in prison I would guess I wrote a million words.

11   I suppose it was inevitable that as my word-base broadened, I could for the first time pick up a book and read and now begin to understand what the book was saying. Anyone who has read a great deal can imagine the new world that opened. Let me tell you something: from then until I left that prison, in every free moment I had, if I was not reading in the library, I was reading on my bunk. You couldn't have gotten me out of books with a wedge. Between Mr. Muhammad's teachings, my correspondence, my visitors—usually Ella and Reginald—and my reading of books, months passed without my even thinking about being imprisoned. In fact, up to then, I had never been so truly free in my life.

AFTER YOU READ

Vocabulary Practice

1. Choose at least three words from the Vocabulary Development list on page 714 and write sentences using those words. You may write one sentence using all three words if you wish.

2. Which word on the Vocabulary Development list means "to try to equal or surpass"? Use this word in a sentence that shows clearly what the word means.

3. What does the expression "Look, daddy, let me pull your coat about a cat, Elijah Muhammad—" indicate about Malcolm X's language? What kind of education does this expression reveal?

Comprehension

Circle the correct answer.

1. Where was Malcolm X when he first decided to improve his reading and writing?

    a. In church   b. At home

    c. In prison   d. On the street

2. In order to improve his reading skills, Malcolm X began to read

    a. the Bible.   b. a dictionary.

    c. an encyclopedia.   d. letters from Bimbi.

3. Another skill Malcolm X practiced as he read was

    a. his penmanship.   b. his pronunciation.

    c. his facial expressions.   d. his posture.

4. Besides copying words, Malcolm X also wrote

    a. poetry.   b. songs.

    c. letters.   d. stories.

5. Malcolm X spent much of his free time
   a. praying.   b. speaking.
   c. singing.   d. reading.

Content

1. What were the initial problems that Malcolm X had with reading? How did these problems lead him to improve his vocabulary?

2. What steps did Malcolm X take to improve his vocabulary? What other improvements occurred as a result of his vocabulary improvement efforts?

3. How did Malcolm X feel after he had copied the first full page of the dictionary? After reading extensively?

Style and Structure

1. What is the main idea of Malcolm X's essay? Restate his main idea in your own words.

2. What transitions does Malcolm X use to lead the reader from step to step in his educational process? Look particularly closely in paragraphs 4, 9, and 10 for examples of specific transitions.

3. What words or expressions does Malcolm X use that suggest that he is educated? What elements suggest that he is being informal, or conversational, in his writing?

Working Together

1. Make a list of the lessons or skills you have somehow learned on your own. Your list may include hands-on techniques such as fixing a leaky faucet, or they may include interpersonal skills such as making friends or quieting a baby. Which lessons lend themselves to self-teaching, as opposed to being taught by someone else? Discuss and share your findings with the class.

2. What steps have you taken to improve your academic success? Which steps have been more effective? Discuss the specific means by which you have become a better student, from attending tutoring or study sessions to organizing your academic schedule, for instance. Share your findings with the class.

Writing Assignments

1. Malcolm X writes that until he began understanding what he read, he "had never been so truly free" even though he was still in prison. *Write a paragraph in which you explain how reading, or any kind of intellectual activity, can make you "free."* Be sure to use examples from your own life in order to illustrate your points.

2. Think about the ways you have taken responsibility for your own education. *Then, write an essay explaining the steps you have taken to improve yourself as a student.* Consider your study habits, your writing habits, your social habits, your sleep habits, and any other habits that affect you as a student. Use details from your own experiences and observations to clearly present all the steps in your process.

3. Malcolm X writes that people who heard him speak often thought he had completed more formal education than he had. *Write a short essay in which you explain what qualities make a person seem "educated."* Be sure to define what you mean by *educated* and then use your own experiences and observations in order to give proof for your ideas.

ISAAC ASIMOV

What Is Intelligence, Anyway?

One of the most prolific writers of all time, Isaac Asimov is best known for his science fiction works. Asimov was considered a man of science, working as a professor of biochemistry, but his novels—which totaled more than five hundred, including those he edited—appealed to greatly varied audiences. In "What Is Intelligence, Anyway?" Asimov considers book learning and common sense.

BEFORE YOU READ

Think about the following questions. Write your responses on a separate piece of paper or in your journal.

- In what areas are you most intelligent or talented?
- To what extent has your intelligence or knowledge increased over the course of your life? Explain.
- Who is someone you consider to be very intelligent? What makes you think so?

VOCABULARY DEVELOPMENT

Look up the following words in a dictionary. Write down their meanings on a separate sheet or in your journal.

aptitude (paragraph 1)   complacent (paragraph 2)
worthy (paragraph 2)   hastened (paragraph 3)
oracles (paragraph 3)   devised (paragraph 4)
verbal (paragraph 4)   intricate (paragraph 4)
arbiter (paragraph 4)   indulgently (paragraph 6)
raucously (paragraph 6)

What Is Intelligence, Anyway?

1   What is intelligence, anyway? When I was in the army I received a kind of aptitude test that all soldiers took and, against a normal of 100, scored 160. No one at the base had ever seen a figure like that, and for two hours they made a big fuss over me. (It didn't mean anything. The next day I was still a buck private with KP as my highest duty.)

2   All my life I've been registering scores like that, so that I have the complacent feeling that I'm highly intelligent, and I expect other people to think so, too. Actually, though, don't such scores simply mean that I am very good at answering the type of academic questions that are considered worthy of answers by the people who make up the intelligence tests—people with intellectual bents similar to mine?

3   For instance, I had an auto-repair man once, who, on these intelligence tests, could not possibly have scored more than 80, by my estimate. I always took it for granted that I was far more intelligent than he was. Yet, when anything went wrong with my car I hastened to him with it, watched him anxiously as he explored its vitals, and listened to his pronouncements as though they were divine oracles—and he always fixed my car.

4   Well, then, suppose my auto-repair man devised questions for an intelligence test. Or suppose a carpenter did, or a farmer, or, indeed, almost anyone but an academician. By every one of those tests, I'd prove myself a moron. And I'd *be* a moron, too. In a world where I could not use my academic training and my verbal talents but had to do something intricate or hard, working with my hands, I would do poorly. My intelligence, then, is not absolute but is a function of the society I live in and of the fact that a small subsection of that society has managed to foist itself on the rest as an arbiter of such matters.

5   Consider my auto-repair man, again. He had a habit of telling me jokes whenever he saw me. One time he raised his head from under the automobile hood to say: "Doc, a deaf-and-dumb guy went into a hardware store to ask for some nails. He put two fingers together on the counter and made hammering motions with the other hand. The clerk brought him a hammer. He shook his head and pointed to the two fingers he was hammering. The clerk brought him nails. He picked out the sizes he wanted, and left. Well, doc, the next guy who came in was a blind man. He wanted scissors. How do you suppose he asked for them?"

6   Indulgently, I lifted my right hand and made scissoring motions with my first two fingers. Whereupon my auto-repair man laughed raucously and said, "Why, you dumb jerk, he used his voice and asked for them." Then he said, smugly, "I've been trying that on all my customers today." "Did you catch many?" I asked. "Quite a few," he said, "but I knew for sure I'd catch you." "Why is that?" I asked. "Because you're so goddamned educated, doc, I *knew* you couldn't be very smart."

7   And I have an uneasy feeling he had something there.

Vocabulary Practice

1. Choose at least three words from the Vocabulary Development list on page 718 and write sentences using those words. You may write one sentence using all three words if you wish.

2. Which word on the Vocabulary Development list means "disagreeably harshly"? Use the word in a sentence that shows the word's meaning clearly.

3. What are some terms Asimov uses to discuss different aspects of intelligence and learning? What do these terms—and the fact that there are so many—say about people's attitudes toward intelligence?

Comprehension

Circle the correct answer.

1. How was Asimov's intelligence identified in the army?
    a. By how well he performed KP
    b. By how well he performed on an aptitude test
    c. By how well he remembered orders
    d. By how well he followed orders

2. How intelligent does Asimov think he is?
    a. Highly intelligent   b. Moderately intelligent
    c. Intelligent in specific areas d. Not very intelligent

3. To whom does Asimov compare himself in this essay?
    a. His plumber   b. His electrician
    c. His car-repair man   d. His gardener

4. How did Asimov respond when he heard a joke set in a hardware store?
    a. He answered incorrectly.
    b. He guessed the correct answer.
    c. He answered correctly.
    d. He asked someone else for the correct answer.

5. Why did the man who told the joke assume that Asimov "couldn't be very smart"?
    a. Because Asimov didn't know how to fix a toilet
    b. Because Asimov answered the joke correctly
    c. Because Asimov was always reading
    d. Because Asimov was so educated

Content

1. To what extent does Asimov think his own type of intelligence is superior to that of, say, a mechanic?

2. What, really, does Asimov say his success on aptitude tests means?

3. Why does Asimov think his mechanic might be right when he says that Asimov is so educated that he can't be very smart?

Style and Structure

1. What is Asimov's point? Rewrite his main idea in your own words.

2. What examples does Asimov use to illustrate different kinds of intelligence?

3. What purpose does Asimov's opening question serve?

4. What transitional words or expressions does Asimov use in the first lines of paragraphs 3 and 5?

Working Together

1. Devise an intelligence test that you think would be fair to everyone. You do not need to make up actual test questions; just indicate the type, such as a language question, math question, practical skills question, or common sense question.

2. Make a list of different kinds of intelligence. As a group, rank the types of intelligence in terms of their value to society, explaining your reasons for placing certain types of intelligence at certain points. Be prepared to defend your choices to the class.

Writing Assignments

1. Asimov writes that he thinks of himself (and expects others to think of him) as intelligent. How do you think of yourself in terms of intelligence? *Write a paragraph in which you explain how intelligent you are in some area.* Your type of intelligence does not need to be the same as Asimov's. Use examples from your own experiences to illustrate your ideas.

2. Asimov writes about situations such as taking aptitude tests that made him feel intelligent, as well as other situations such as the one with his mechanic that lead him to doubt his abilities. What situations cause you to feel most or least intelligent? *Write a paragraph explaining how certain situations do or do not lead you to feel intelligent.* Use examples and illustrations from your own life to support your ideas.

3. Asimov writes about different kinds of intelligence: people who score well on tests and people who work with their hands. What others kinds of intelligence are there? *Write an essay in which you explain, using examples, at least three different kinds of intelligence.* Be sure to use examples from your own life for support.

CAROLYN Y. JOHNSON

The Joy of Boredom

In "The Joy of Boredom," Carolyn Y. Johnson explores various benefits of the boredom we have largely lost. From creativity to simple "down-time," Johnson—a staff writer for the *Boston Globe*—explains that so many of our boredom-combatting devices do not dispense with boredom. Instead, they barely keep it at bay.

BEFORE YOU READ

Think about the following questions. Write your responses on a separate sheet or in your journal.

- How often are you bored?
- What situations are most likely to cause you to be bored?
- What steps, if any, do you take to end your boredom?

VOCABULARY DEVELOPMENT

Look up the following words in a dictionary. Write down their meanings on a separate sheet or in your journal.

doldrums (paragraph 2)	primordial (paragraph 2)
quintessentially (paragraph 2)	ruminations (paragraph 2)
lolling (paragraph 6)	epiphany (paragraph 6)
abhorred (paragraph 8)	advent (paragraph 12)
alleviate (paragraph 15)	elixirs (paragraph 16)
proliferated (paragraph 29)	

The Joy of Boredom

1   A decade ago, those monotonous minutes were just a fact of life: time ticking away as you gazed idly into space, stood in line or sat in bumper-to-bumper traffic.

2   Boredom's doldrums were unavoidable, yet also a primordial soup for some of life's most quintessentially human moments. Jostled by a stranger's cart in the express checkout line, thoughts of a loved one might come to mind. A long drive home after a frustrating day could force ruminations. A pang of homesickness at the start of a plane ride might put a journey in perspective.

3   Increasingly, these empty moments are being saturated with productivity, communication and the digital distractions offered by an ever-expanding array of slick mobile devices. A few years ago, cell-phone maker Motorola even began using the word "microboredom" to describe

the ever-smaller slices of free time from which new mobile technology offers an escape.

4   "Mobisodes," two-minute-long television episodes of everything from *Lost* to *Prison Break* made for the cell-phone screen, are perfectly tailored for the microbored. Cell-phone games are often designed to last just minutes—simple, snack-size diversions like "Snake," solitaire and "Tetris." Social networks like Twitter and Facebook turn every mundane moment between activities into a chance to broadcast feelings and thoughts, even if it is just to triple-tap a keypad with the words "I am bored."

5   But are we too busy twirling through the songs on our iPods—while checking e-mail, while changing lanes on the highway—to consider whether we are giving up a good thing? We are most human when we feel dull.

6   Lolling around in a state of restlessness is one of life's greatest luxuries—one not available to creatures that spend all their time pursuing mere survival. To be bored is to stop reacting to the external world and to explore the internal one. It is in these times of reflection that people often discover something new, whether it is an epiphany about a relationship or a new theory about the way the universe works.

7   Granted, many people emerge from boredom feeling that they have accomplished nothing. But is accomplishment really the point of life? There is a strong argument that boredom—so often parodied as a glassy-eyed drooling state of nothingness—is an essential human emotion that underlies art, literature, philosophy, science and even love.

8   "If you think of boredom as the prelude to creativity, and loneliness as the prelude to engagement of the imagination, then they are good things," said Dr. Edward Hallowell, a Sudbury, Massachusetts, psychiatrist and author of the book *CrazyBusy*. "They are doorways to something better, as opposed to something to be abhorred and eradicated immediately."

9   Public health officials often bemoan the obesity epidemic, the unintended consequence of a modern lifestyle that allows easy access to calories.

10   Technology seems to offer a similar proposition: a wide array of distractions that offer the boon of connection, but at a cost.

11   Already, mobile technology has shaped the way people interact and communicate.

12   Perhaps nothing illuminates the speed of social change better than the new fear of disconnection. People driving a car or standing at a bus stop or waiting in a doctor's office by themselves always have had some distractions available to them, from the radio to *National Geographic*. But until the advent of connected devices, they were still, fundamentally, alone in some way.

13   Today, there is a growing fear of the prospect of being untethered in the world without the security blanket of a cell phone. In the time scale of human inventions, the mobile phone is still new, but it is already a crucial part

of the trinity of things people fear to forget when they leave the house—keys, wallet, and phone.

14   "There is this hyper-anxiety over feeling lonely or disconnected," said Kathleen Cumiskey, a professor of psychology and women's studies at the College of Staten Island who says her stepdaughter sleeps with her cell phone at arm's length and considers turning the device off unthinkable.

15   "Our society is perpetually anxious, and a way to alleviate the anxiety is to delve into something that's very within our control, pleasurable, and fun . . . It feels like it has all the makings of addiction."

16   In a way, the entrepreneurs looking to capitalize on the small moments of spare time that are sprinkled through modern life parallel the pharmaceutical industry. A growing chorus of mental health specialists has begun to question whether normal sadness and social anxiety are being transformed into disorders that people believe need to be cured—by the companies offering elixirs. The tech industry may be doing the same thing with disconnection.

17   Many of the original arguments for having a cell phone—safety, security, emergencies—never figure into the advertisements. Like the commercials that show frowning people transformed into smiling, kitten-cuddling normality, technology companies project a happy world of connection where to intentionally disconnect seems freakish, questionable, undeniably an ailment.

18   Society has accepted connection so well that it takes a step back to see exactly how far things have come. Instead of carrying their entire social universe in a pocket, people used to walk out of their houses and into the world. Today, not picking up the phone for an hour is an act of defiance.

19   Perhaps understandably, boredom has never caught the attention of the psychological world. Emotions like anxiety, fear and anger have been subjected to a much more thorough examination than merely feeling drab, according to Richard Ralley, a lecturer in psychology at Edge Hill University in England.

20   "What's gone wrong with the psychology of emotion is that the ones that are easy to do are the ones that have been researched: fear, threat, fear, threat, again and again and again," Ralley said. "A lot of other emotions that really make us human—pride, for instance—we kind of avoid."

21   So, Ralley set out to examine boredom more closely, with the idea that the feeling must have a purpose. Just looking around, it was evident that children quell boredom quite naturally, with creativity—even to the point of taking the packaging around a gift and playing with it for hours.

22   But as people get older, anxious parents and cranky children demand more and more specific stimuli, whether it is a video game or a hot new phone.

23   As Ralley studied boredom, it came to make a kind of sense: If people are slogging away at an activity with little reward, they get annoyed and find themselves feeling bored. If something more engaging comes along, they move on. If nothing does, they may be motivated enough to think of something new themselves. The most creative people, he said, are known to have the greatest toleration for long periods of uncertainty and boredom.

24   Connectivity, of course, has serious advantages. Parents can check in with their kids. Friends separated by hundreds of miles can have a conversation almost as if they were walking side by side. People feel safer.

25   Still, there has been surprisingly little public discussion of the broad sociological and psychological impact the technology will have.

26   Like much change, it has crept up on people and radically changed behavior and expectations in ways few people could have predicted. At one time, the car was a novelty—things like getting gas and driving on good roads were difficult to do. Today, the modern world is built around an automotive infrastructure, and is almost impossible to navigate without one.

27   "We set up a society that functions that way, and the mobile phone is starting to work in that way," said Rich Ling, a researcher at the Norwegian telecom firm Telenor and author of *New Tech, New Ties*.

28   But as it becomes more difficult to imagine a world without constant connectivity, the very concept of "microboredom" may begin to lower people's tolerance for even a second of empty time.

29   Paradoxically, as cures for boredom have proliferated, people do not seem to feel less bored; they simply flee it with more energy, flitting from one activity to the next. Ralley has noticed a kind of placid look among his students over the past few years, a "laptop culture" that he finds perplexing. They have more channels to be social; there are always things to do. And yet people seem oddly numb. They are not quite bored, but not really interested.

AFTER YOU READ

Vocabulary Practice

1. Choose at least three words from the Vocabulary Development list on page 722 and write sentences using those words. You may write one sentence using all three words if you wish.

2. Which word on the Vocabulary Development list means "to make more bearable"? Use the word in a sentence that shows the word's meaning clearly.

3. What are some terms Johnson uses to describe boredom? What do such expressions communicate about boredom?

Comprehension

Circle the correct answer.

1. How long ago does Johnson say that boredom was "just a fact of life"?
   a. A century ago   b. An eon ago
   c. A decade ago   d. A year ago

2. What are our "empty moments . . . being saturated with," according to Johnson?
   a. Productivity   b. Pleasure
   c. Rest   d. Connection

3. What does Johnson say is "one of life's greatest luxuries"?
   a. Lying around with a bag of potato chips
   b. Living beside a neighbor with a smaller car
   c. Leaving behind a job for a vacation
   d. Lolling around in a state of restlessness

4. What does Johnson say most people feel they've accomplished during boredom?
   a. Everything   b. Nothing
   c. Anything   d. Something

5. What does Johnson say make up "the trinity of things people fear to forget"?
   a. Keys, wallet, and phone b. Pager, sunglasses, cash
   c. Backpack, lunch, binder d. Credit card, jacket, hat

Content

1. In paragraph 2, what examples does Johnson give of how positive results might come from boredom?

2. What does Johnson say there's a strong argument for in regard to boredom?

3. What does Johnson say is "a growing fear"?

Style and Structure

1. What is Johnson's point? Rewrite her main idea in your own words.

2. What kinds of examples does Johnson use to illustrate her ideas?

3. What is a cause of so many new boredom-fighting devices? What is an effect of these devices?

Working Together

1. Discuss how often you are bored now compared to earlier in your life. Why do you think you are more or less bored now than you once were? Explain, and give a brief summary to the class.

2. As a group, discuss how important electronic devices such as cell phones are in your life. Give examples from your experiences and observations to illustrate your points, and give a brief summary to the class.

Writing Assignments

1. Johnson writes, "It is in these times of reflection that people often discover something new." What do you think? *Write a paragraph in which you discuss a time when boredom led you to discover something.* Your discovery may have been that you couldn't work at your job one more second or that you had to find a new place to live. If boredom has never led you to discover anything, then write about what you do to counter boredom. Use examples from your own experiences to illustrate your ideas.

2. Lecturer Richard Ralley says of students with electronic distractions, "They are not quite bored, but not really interested." What does being "interested" mean to you? *Write a paragraph in which you explain what you do when you're interested in something.* You might write about how you talk to others about it, read to learn about it, or think about it often. Use specific examples from your life to illustrate your ideas.

3. Johnson writes that "as people get older, [they] demand more and more specific stimuli, whether it is a video game or a hot new phone." Do you agree? *Write an essay in which you discuss whether or not people need more stimuli as they get older.* Think about the role that games, music, and phones play in your lives, for instance. Use examples and illustrations from your own life to support your ideas.

E. B. WHITE

Education

A well-known essayist and contributing editor to *The New Yorker*, E. B. White authored many works. Some of his best-known and most loved works are the children's tales *Stuart Little* and *Charlotte's Web*. He also revised William Strunk's work *The Elements of Style* and wrote the satire *Is Sex Necessary?* with James Thurber.

BEFORE YOU READ

Think about the following questions. Write your responses on a separate sheet or in your journal.

- What does it mean to be educated? Who determines whether or not a person is educated?
- What are some ways people can be educated?
- What experience or situation was the most educational for you? Explain.

VOCABULARY DEVELOPMENT

Look up the following words in a dictionary. Write down their meanings on a separate sheet or in your journal.

Augean (paragraph 1)	bias (paragraph 2)
regimented (paragraph 2)	seminary (paragraph 3)
sallied (paragraph 3)	punctual (paragraph 3)
incubation (paragraph 3)	esoteric (paragraph 4)
apprehensive (paragraph 6)	laconic (paragraph 6)

Education

1   I have an increasing admiration for the teacher in the country school where we have a third-grade scholar in attendance. She not only undertakes to instruct her charges in all the subjects of the first three grades, but she manages to function quietly and effectively as a guardian of their health, their clothes, their habits, their mothers, and their snowball engagements. She has been doing this sort of Augean task for twenty years, and is both kind and wise. She cooks for the children on the stove that heats the room, and she can cool their passions or warm their soup with equal competence. She conceives their costumes, cleans up their messes, and shares their confidences. My boy already regards his teacher as his great friend, and I think tells her a great deal more than he tells us.

2   The shift from city school to country school was something we worried about quietly all last summer. I have always rather favored public school over private school, if only because in public school you meet a greater variety of children. This bias of mine, I suspect, is partly an attempt to justify my own past (I never knew anything but public schools) and partly an involuntary defense against getting kicked in the shins by a young ceramist on his way to the kiln. My wife was unacquainted with public schools, never having been exposed (in her early life) to anything more public than the washroom of Miss Winsor's. Regardless of our backgrounds, we both knew that the change in schools was something that concerned not us but the scholar himself. We hoped it would work out all right. In New York our son went to a medium-priced private institution with semi-progressive ideas of education, and modern plumbing. He learned fast, kept well, and we were satisfied. It was an electric, colorful, regimented existence with moments of pleasurable pause and giddy incident. The day the Christmas angel fainted and had to be carried out by one of the Wise Men was education in the highest sense of the term. Our scholar gave imitations of it around the house for weeks afterward, and I doubt if it ever goes completely out of his mind.

3   His days were rich in formal experience. Wearing overalls and an old sweater (the accepted uniform of the private seminary), he sallied forth at morn accompanied by a nurse or a parent and walked (or was pulled) two blocks to a corner where the school bus made a flag stop. This flashy vehicle was as punctual as death: seeing us waiting at the cold curb, it would sweep to a halt, open its mouth, suck the boy in, and spring away with an angry growl. It was a good deal like a train picking up a bag of mail. At school the scholar was worked on for six or seven hours by half a dozen teachers and a nurse, and was revived on orange juice in mid-morning. In a cinder court he played games supervised by an athletic instructor, and in a cafeteria he ate lunch worked out by a dietitian. He soon learned to read with gratifying facility and discernment and to make Indian weapons of a semi-deadly nature. Whenever one of his classmates fell low of a fever the news was put on the wires and there were breathless phone calls to physicians, discussing periods of incubation and allied magic.

4   In the country all one can say is that the situation is different, and somehow more casual. Dressed in corduroys, sweatshirt, and short rubber boots, and carrying a tin dinner-pail, our scholar departs at the crack of dawn for the village school, two and a half miles down the road, next to the cemetery. When the road is open and the car will start, he makes the journey by motor, courtesy of his old man. When the snow is deep or the motor is dead or both, he makes it on the hoof. In the afternoons he walks or hitches all or part of the way home in fair weather, gets transported in foul. The schoolhouse is a two-room frame building, bungalow type, shingles stained a burnt brown with weather-resistant stain. It has a chemical toilet in the basement and two teachers above the stairs. One takes the first three grades, the other the fourth, fifth, and sixth. They have little or no time for individual instruction, and no time at all for the esoteric. They teach what they know themselves, just as fast and as hard as they can manage. The pupils sit still at their desks in class, and do their milling around outdoors during recess.

5   There is no supervised play. They play cops and robbers (only they call it "Jail") and throw things at one another—snowballs in winter, rose hips in fall. It seems to satisfy them. They also construct darts, pinwheels, and "pick-up sticks" (jackstraws), and the school itself does a brisk trade in penny candy, which is for sale right in the classroom and which contains "surprises." The most highly prized surprise is a fake cigarette, made of cardboard, fiendishly lifelike.

6   The memory of how apprehensive we were at the beginning is still strong. The boy was nervous about the change too. The tension, on that first fair morning in September when we drove him to school, almost blew the windows out of the sedan. And when later we picked him up on the road, wandering along with his little blue lunch-pail, and got his laconic report

"All right" in answer to our inquiry about how the day had gone, our relief was vast. Now, after almost a year of it, the only difference we can discover in the two school experiences is that in the country he sleeps better at night—and *that* probably is more the air than the education. When grilled on the subject of school-in-country vs. school-in-city, he replied that the chief difference is that the day seems to go so much quicker in the country. "Just like lightning," he reported.

AFTER YOU READ

Vocabulary Practice

1. Choose at least three words from the Vocabulary Development list on page 728 and write sentences using those words. You may write one sentence using all three words if you wish.

2. Which word on the Vocabulary Development list means "brief or terse in speech"? Use the word in a sentence that clearly shows its meaning.

3. White uses the terms "punctual as death," "with an angry growl," "picking up a bag of mail," and "the scholar was worked on" to describe aspects of his son's private school experience. On the basis of these terms, what do you think White's view of the school is?

Comprehension

Circle the correct answer.

1. White opens his essay with a description of
   a. his son's teacher.   b. his own childhood teacher.
   c. himself as a teacher.   d. his son.

2. What is White's attitude toward his son's teacher?
   a. He thinks she is lazy.   b. He thinks she is unintelligent.
   c. He admires her.   d. He thinks she is attractive.

3. Why does White say he favors public school?
   a. His wife attended public school.
   b. He was a teacher at a public school.
   c. Students meet a greater variety of children in public school.
   d. Students have more freedom at a public school.

4. Which one of the following aspects of city and country schools is not a subject of comparison in White's essay?
   a. Plumbing
   b. Mode of transportation to get to school

c. Cost

d. Formality of student attire

5. White's son claims that his day at the country public school goes

a. just like lightning.   b. just like molasses.

c. just like a cheetah.   d. just like mud.

Content

1. What change for his son is White worried about?

2. White claims his son's days at the private school are "rich in formal experience." Is this statement positive or negative? How can you tell?

3. What details does White use to help the reader understand the differences between his son's schools?

Style and Structure

1. What is the main idea of White's essay? Write his argument in your own words.

2. What is the topic sentence of paragraph 3? How does White support this topic sentence?

3. What transitions does White use to indicate the passing of time? Look particularly closely in paragraphs 3, 4, and 6 for examples.

Working Together

1. As a group, make a ranked list of the elements of school—teachers, facilities, books, computers, etc.—that you think contribute to a student's academic experience. Discuss which items are at the top of the list and why. Summarize your findings for the class.

2. Discuss which type of learning environment is best for you. Consider whether an instructor who is nurturing and patient—as opposed to one who is strict and demanding—brings out your best as a student. Summarize your findings and present to the class.

Writing Assignments

1. White clearly favors one of his son's schools over the other. *Write a paragraph in which you compare or contrast two schools or classes that you have attended.* Use examples from your own experiences to illustrate your ideas.

2. Think about a time when you have changed schools, even moving from middle school to high school. *Write a paragraph describing yourself as a new student.* Use examples from your own experiences to illustrate your ideas.

3. White favors the public country school over the private city school. *Write an essay describing a class or school that you either liked or disliked very much.* Be sure to use examples from your own life for support.

KURT VONNEGUT, JR.

How to Write with Style

Best known for his novel *Slaughterhouse Five*, in which his personal experience as a prisoner during World War II is recounted, Kurt Vonnegut is also recognized for his dark humor and biting wit. Vonnegut's other novels include *Cat's Cradle* (1963) and *Breakfast of Champions* (1973). In "How to Write with Style," Vonnegut encourages students to find their own voices by centering their writing on subjects that matter to them.

BEFORE YOU READ

Think about the following questions. Write your responses on a separate sheet or in your journal.

- What writing styles—humorous, serious, descriptive, concise, for instance—do you enjoy reading?
- How would you best describe your own writing style?
- What kinds of writing would you most like to be able to do?

VOCABULARY DEVELOPMENT

Look up the following words in a dictionary. Write down their meanings on a separate sheet or in your journal.

unintentional (paragraph 1)	egomaniac (paragraph 3)
compelling (paragraph 6)	profound (paragraph 9)
eloquence (paragraph 11)	piquant (paragraph 12)
locutions (paragraph 13)	dialect (paragraph 13)
vehemently (paragraph 15)	unambiguously (paragraph 16)

How to Write with Style

1   Newspaper reporters and technical writers are trained to reveal almost nothing about themselves in their writings. This makes them freaks in the world of writers, since almost all of the other ink-stained wretches in that world reveal a lot about themselves to readers. We call these revelations, accidental and unintentional, elements of style.

2   These revelations tell us as readers what sort of person it is with whom we are spending time. Does the writer sound ignorant or informed, stupid or bright, crooked or honest, humorless or playful—? And on and on.

3   Why should you examine your writing style with the idea of improving it? Do so as a mark of your respect for your readers, whatever you're writing. If you scribble your thoughts any which way, your readers will surely

feel that you care nothing about them. They will mark you down as an ego-maniac or a chowderhead—or worse, they will stop reading you.

4   The most damning revelation you can make about yourself is that you do not know what is interesting and what is not. Don't you yourself like or dislike writers mainly for what they choose to show you or make you think about? Did you ever admire an empty-headed writer for his or her mastery of the language? No.

5   So your own winning style must begin with ideas in your head.

1. Find a Subject You Care About

6   Find a subject you care about and which you in your heart feel others should care about. It is this genuine caring, and not your games with language, which will be the most compelling and seductive element in your style.

7   I am not urging you to write a novel, by the way—although I would not be sorry if you wrote one, provided you genuinely cared about something. A petition to the mayor about a pothole in front of your house or a love letter to the girl next door will do.

2. Do Not Ramble, Though

8   I won't ramble on about that.

3. Keep It Simple

9   As for the use of language: Remember that two great masters of language, William Shakespeare and James Joyce, wrote sentences which were almost childlike when their subjects were most profound. "To be or not to be?" asks Shakespeare's Hamlet. The longest word is three letters long. Joyce, when he was frisky, could put together a sentence as intricate and glittering as a necklace for Cleopatra, but my favorite sentence in his short story "Eveline" is this one: "She was tired." At that point in the story, no other words could break the heart of a reader as those three words do.

10   Simplicity of language is not only reputable, but perhaps even sacred. The *Bible* opens with a sentence well within the writing skills of a lively fourteen-year-old: "In the beginning God created the heaven and the earth."

4. Have the Guts to Cut

11   It may be that you, too, are capable of making necklaces for Cleopatra, so to speak. But your eloquence should be the servant of the ideas in your head. Your rule might be this: If a sentence, no matter how excellent, does not illuminate your subject in some new and useful way, scratch it out.

5. Sound Like Yourself

12   The writing style which is most natural for you is bound to echo the speech you heard when you were a child. English was the novelist Joseph

Conrad's third language, and much that seems piquant in his use of English was no doubt colored by his first language, which was Polish. And lucky indeed is the writer who has grown up in Ireland, for the English spoken there is so amusing and musical. I myself grew up in Indianapolis, where common speech sounds like a band saw cutting galvanized tin, and employs a vocabulary as unornamental as a monkey wrench.

13   In some of the more remote hollows of Appalachia, children still grow up hearing songs and locutions of Elizabethan times. Yes, and many Americans grow up hearing a language other than English, or an English dialect a majority of Americans cannot understand.

14   All these varieties of speech are beautiful, just as the varieties of butterflies are beautiful. No matter what your first language, you should treasure it all your life. If it happens not to be standard English, and it shows itself when you write standard English, the result is usually delightful, like a very pretty girl with one eye that is green and one that is blue.

15   I myself find that I trust my own writing most, and others seem to trust it most, too, when I sound most like a person from Indianapolis, which is what I am. What alternatives do I have? The one most vehemently recommended by teachers has no doubt been pressed on you, as well: to write like cultivated Englishmen of a century or more ago.

6. Say What You Mean to Say

16   I used to be exasperated by such teachers, but am no more. I understand now that all those antique essays and stories with which I was to compare my own work were not magnificent for their datedness or foreignness, but for saying precisely what their authors meant them to say. My teachers wished me to write accurately, always selecting the most effective words, and relating the words to one another unambiguously, rigidly, like parts of a machine. The teachers did not want to turn me into an Englishman after all. They hoped that I would become understandable—and therefore understood. And there went my dream of doing with words what Pablo Picasso did with paint or what any number of jazz idols did with music. If I broke all the rules of punctuation, had words mean whatever I wanted them to mean, and strung them together higgledy-piggledy, I would simply not be understood. So you, too, had better avoid Picasso-style or jazz-style writing, if you have something worth saying and wish to be understood.

17   Readers want our pages to look very much like pages they have seen before. Why? This is because they themselves have a tough job to do, and they need all the help they can get from us.

7. Pity the Readers

18   They have to identify thousands of little marks on paper, and make sense of them immediately. They have to *read*, an art so difficult that most

people don't really master it even after having studied it all through grade school and high school—twelve long years.

19   So this discussion must finally acknowledge that our stylistic options as writers are neither numerous nor glamorous, since our readers are bound to be such imperfect artists. Our audience requires us to be sympathetic and patient teachers, ever willing to simplify and clarify—whereas we would rather soar high above the crowd, singing like nightingales.

20   That is the bad news. The good news is that we Americans are governed under a unique Constitution, which allows us to write whatever we please without fear of punishment. So the most meaningful aspect of our styles, which is what we choose to write about, is utterly unlimited.

8. For Really Detailed Advice

21   For a discussion of literary style in a narrower sense, in a more technical sense, I commend to your attention *The Elements of Style*, by William Strunk, Jr., and E. B. White [the most recent edition is published by Longman, 2000]. E. B. White is, of course, one of the most admirable literary stylists this country has so far produced.

22   You should realize, too, that no one would care how well or badly Mr. White expressed himself, if he did not have perfectly enchanting things to say.

AFTER YOU READ

Vocabulary Practice

1. Choose at least three words from the Vocabulary Development list on page 732 and write sentences using those words. You may write one sentence using all three words if you wish.

2. Which word on the Vocabulary Development list means "clear or precise"? Use the word in a sentence that shows the word's meaning clearly.

3. What are some words or expressions that you found surprising or funny in Vonnegut's writing? What effect do these expressions have on your reading of the essay? Explain.

Comprehension

Circle the correct answer.

1. What does Vonnegut say newspaper reporters and technical writers are trained to reveal?

   a. Everything they can about themselves in their writing

   b. The most interesting parts of themselves in their writing

   c. Subtle hints of themselves in their writing

   d. Almost nothing about themselves in their writing

2. What are the revelations that writers give about themselves called?

    a. Elements of style   b. Elements of honesty

    c. Moments of style   d. Moments of character

3. Where does Vonnegut say that "your own winning style must begin"?

    a. With divine inspiration.

    b. With ideas in your head.

    c. With ideas from your experiences.

    d. With ideas from other people's experiences.

4. What does Vonnegut say of simplicity in language?

    a. It's not only difficult to achieve, but unworthy.

    b. It's not only a waste of time, but it's boring.

    c. It's not only reputable, but perhaps even sacred.

    d. It's not only wonderful, but it's descriptive.

5. How does Vonnegut say people should view their first language?

    a. They should make sure they understand it.

    b. They should make every effort to forget it.

    c. They should treasure it all their lives.

    d. They should teach it to someone else.

Content

1. What does Vonnegut say is "the most damning revelation you can make about yourself"?

2. Which two writers does Vonnegut offer as excellent examples of simple writing?

3. Which writers does Vonnegut say are the luckiest in terms of where they grew up?

Style and Structure

1. What is Vonnegut's main idea? Rewrite his main idea in your own words.

2. Vonnegut uses specific language and examples to illustrate his ideas. Find two or three expressions or illustrations that you find particularly vivid.

3. How does Vonnegut organize his ideas in this essay? How effective is this method?

Working Together

1. Which items in Vonnegut's essay do you think are most important? Why? Discuss as a group and compare your findings with those of other groups.

2. Working in small groups, write a description of something familiar on your college campus. You may choose an object, a person, or a place. Follow Vonnegut's tips as best you can to make your writing interesting, and be prepared to read your description to the class.

Writing Assignments

1. Vonnegut lists eight tips for writing with style. What steps do you follow when you write? *Write a paragraph in which you explain your own writing process, step by step.* Use examples from times you've had to write paragraphs for this or another class to illustrate each step.

2. Vonnegut urges his readers to "find a subject you care about." What matters to you? *Write a letter about something you care about.* You may decide whom to write to as well as the subject matter of your letter. Consider, for instance, writing to your boss about how well you're doing at work or writing to a family member about how supportive he or she has been. Use examples and illustrations from your own life to support your ideas.

3. Vonnegut says that your natural writing style is likely to "echo the speech you heard when you were a child." In what ways has your childhood shaped you as a writer? Has it made you thoughtful, shy, sensitive, assertive, descriptive, or concise, for instance? *Write an essay in which you explain two or three ways in which your childhood affected you as a writer.* For example, if your parents became impatient with you for not getting to the point quickly, you could write that you became a direct writer, or that your family's willingness to listen to you made you a descriptive writer. Be sure to use examples from your own life for support.

What We Value

S eemingly every day on television or in the newspaper, we learn about people whose values appear to have been compromised: people allow cameras into their personal lives for fame, sue each other over trivial injuries, and allow their children to watch or take part in overtly violent entertainment. The question arises: What is important to us, as a society? The essays "Money for Morality" and "The Ways We Lie" explore how we view honesty and responsibility, while "Fatso" and "Manners Matter" discuss how our own actions and attitudes as well as those of others can profoundly affect us throughout our lives. Finally, "The Difference Between Male and Female Friendships" calls attention to our habits in relationships and the effects of those relationships.

READINGS IN THIS SECTION

RICHARD RODRIGUEZ

"Blaxicans" and Other Reinvented Americans

Raised in California, Richard Rodriguez is an editor at Pacific News Service and an essayist for PBS's *News Hour.* He is the author of *Brown: The Last Discovery of*

America, the final book in his series about the intersection of his personal and public life. In this essay, Rodriguez examines race relations in a twenty-first century light, one which is no longer limited primarily to two groups.

BEFORE YOU READ

Think about the following questions. Write your response on a separate sheet or in your journal.

- What does the expression *race relations* mean to you? To what extent does it include specific races?
- Do people from different ethnic groups live with or near you? How many groups? How do these groups get along?
- To what extent is your life a mixture of cultures? What cultural influences other than your family's have you encountered? Explain.

VOCABULARY DEVELOPMENT

Look up the following words in a dictionary. Write down their meanings on a separate sheet or in your journal.

unsettling (paragraph 1)	ascendancy (paragraph 12)
peerless (paragraph 2)	denoting (paragraph 13)
dialectic (paragraph 5)	assimilation (paragraph 14)
surname (paragraph 6)	bombast (paragraph 17)
gringo (paragraph 10)	multiplicity (paragraph 19)

"Blaxicans" and Other Reinvented Americans

1   There is something unsettling about immigrants because . . . well, because they chatter incomprehensibly, and they get in everyone's way. Immigrants seem to be bent on undoing America. Just when Americans think we know who we are—we are Protestants, culled from Western Europe, are we not?—then new immigrants appear from Southern Europe or from Eastern Europe. We—we who are already here—we don't know exactly what the latest comers will mean to our community. How will they fit in with us? Thus we—we who were here first—we begin to question our own identity.

2   After a generation or two, the grandchildren or the great-grandchildren of immigrants to the United States and the grandchildren of those who tried to keep immigrants out of the United States will romanticize the immigrant, will begin to see the immigrant as the figure who teaches us most about what it means to be an American. The immigrant, in mythic terms, travels from the outermost rind of America to the very center of American mythology. None of this, of course, can we admit to the Vietnamese immigrant who

served us our breakfast at the hotel this morning. In another 40 years, we will be prepared to say to the Vietnamese immigrant that he, with his breakfast tray, with his intuition for travel, with his memory of tragedy, with his recognition of peerless freedoms, he fulfills the meaning of America.

3   In 1997, Gallup conducted a survey on race relations in America, but the poll was concerned only with white and black Americans. No question was put to the aforementioned Vietnamese man. There was certainly no question for the Chinese grocer, none for the Guatemalan barber, none for the tribe of Mexican Indians who reroofed your neighbor's house.

4   The American conversation about race has always been a black-and-white conversation, but the conversation has become as bloodless as badminton.

5   I have listened to the black-and-white conversation for most of my life. I was supposed to attach myself to one side or the other, without asking the obvious questions: What is this perpetual dialectic between Europe and Africa? Why does it admit so little reference to anyone else?

6   I am speaking to you in American English that was taught me by Irish nuns—immigrant women. I wear an Indian face; I answer to a Spanish surname as well as this California first name, Richard. You might wonder about the complexity of historical factors, the collision of centuries, that creates Richard Rodriguez. My brownness is the illustration of that collision, or the bland memorial of it. I stand before you as an Impure-American, an Ambiguous-American.

· · ·

7   Race mixture has not been a point of pride in America. Americans speak more easily about "diversity" than we do about the fact that I might marry your daughter; you might become we; we might become us. America has so readily adopted the Canadian notion of multiculturalism because it preserves our preference for thinking ourselves separate—our elbows need not touch, thank you. I would prefer that table. I can remain Mexican, whatever that means, in the United States of America.

8   I would propose that instead of adopting the Canadian model of multiculturalism, America might begin to imagine the Mexican alternative—that of a mestizaje society.

9   Because of colonial Mexico, I am mestizo. But I was reinvented by President Richard Nixon. In the early 1970s, Nixon instructed the Office of Management and Budget to identify the major racial and ethnic groups in the United States. OMB came up with five major ethnic or racial groups. The groups are white, black, Asian/Pacific Islander, American Indian/Eskimo, and Hispanic.

10   It's what I learned to do when I was in college: to call myself a Hispanic. At my university we even had separate cafeteria tables and "theme houses,"

where the children of Nixon could gather—of a feather. Native Americans united. African-Americans. Casa Hispanic.

11   The interesting thing about Hispanics is that you will never meet us in Latin America. You may meet Chileans and Peruvians and Mexicans. You will not meet Hispanics. If you inquire in Lima or Bogotá about Hispanics, you will be referred to Dallas. For "Hispanic" is a gringo contrivance, a definition of the world according to European patterns of colonization. Such a definition suggests I have more in common with Argentine-Italians than with American Indians; that there is an ineffable union between the white Cuban and the mulatto Puerto Rican because of Spain. Nixon's conclusion has become the basis for the way we now organize and understand American society.

12   The Census Bureau foretold that by the year 2003, Hispanics would outnumber blacks to become the largest minority in the United States. And, indeed, the year 2003 has arrived and the proclamation of Hispanic ascendancy has been published far and wide. While I admit a competition has existed—does exist—in America between Hispanic and black people, I insist that the comparison of Hispanics with blacks will lead, ultimately, to complete nonsense. For there is no such thing as a Hispanic race. In Latin America, one sees every race of the world. One sees white Hispanics, one sees black Hispanics, one sees brown Hispanics who are Indians, many of whom do not speak Spanish because they resist Spain. One sees Asian-Hispanics. To compare blacks and Hispanics, therefore, is to construct a fallacious equation.

13   Some Hispanics have accepted the fiction. Some Hispanics have too easily accustomed themselves to impersonating a third race, a great new third race in America. But Hispanic is an ethnic term. It is a term denoting culture. So when the Census Bureau says by the year 2060 one-third of all Americans will identify themselves as Hispanic, the Census Bureau is not speculating in pigment or quantifying according to actual historical narratives, but rather is predicting how by the year 2060 one-third of all Americans will identify themselves culturally. For a country that traditionally has taken its understandings of community from blood and color, the new circumstance of so large a group of Americans identifying themselves by virtue of language or fashion or cuisine or literature is an extraordinary change, and a revolutionary one.

. . .

14   I was on a British Broadcasting Corporation interview show, and a woman introduced me as being, "in favor" of assimilation. I am not in favor of assimilation any more than I am in favor of the Pacific Ocean or clement weather. If I had a bumper sticker on the subject, it might read something like ASSIMILATION HAPPENS.

. . .

15   I am in favor of assimilation. I am not in favor of assimilation. I recognize assimilation. A few years ago, I was in Merced, California—a town of about 75,000 people in the Central Valley where the two largest immigrant groups at that time (California is so fluid, I believe this is no longer the case) were Laotian Hmong and Mexicans. Laotians have never in the history of the world, as far as I know, lived next to Mexicans. But there they were in Merced, and living next to Mexicans. They don't like each other. I was talking to the Laotian kids about why they don't like the Mexican kids. They were telling me that the Mexicans do this and the Mexicans don't do that, when I suddenly realized that they were speaking English with a Spanish accent.

16   On his interview show, Bill Moyers once asked me how I thought of myself. As an American? Or Hispanic? I answered that I am Chinese, and that is because I live in a Chinese city and because I want to be Chinese. Well, why not? Some Chinese-American people in the Richmond and Sunset districts of San Francisco sometimes paint their houses (so many qualifiers!) in colors I would once have described as garish: lime greens, rose reds, pumpkin. But I have lived in a Chinese city for so long that my eye has taken on that palette, has come to prefer lime greens and rose reds and all the inventions of this Chinese Mediterranean. I see photographs in magazines or documentary footage of China, especially rural China, and I see what I recognize as home. Isn't that odd?

17   I do think distinctions exist. I'm not talking about an America tomorrow in which we're going to find that black and white are no longer the distinguishing marks of separateness. But many young people I meet tell me they feel like Victorians when they identify themselves as black or white. They don't think of themselves in those terms. And they're already moving into a world in which tattoo or ornament or movement or commune or sexuality or drug or rave or electronic bombast are the organizing principles of their identity. The notion that they are white or black simply doesn't occur.

18   And increasingly, of course, one meets children who really don't know how to say what they are. They simply are too many things. I met a young girl in San Diego at a convention of mixed-race children, among whom the common habit is to define one parent over the other—black over white, for example. But this girl said that her mother was Mexican and her father was African. The girl said "Blaxican." By reinventing language, she is reinventing America.

19   America does not have a vocabulary like the vocabulary the Spanish empire evolved to describe the multiplicity of racial possibilities in the New World. The conversation, the interior monologue of America cannot rely on the old vocabulary—black, white. We are no longer a black-white nation.

20   So, what myth do we tell ourselves? The person who got closest to it was Karl Marx. Marx predicted that the discovery of gold in California would be

a more central event to the Americas than the discovery of the Americas by Columbus—which was only the meeting of two tribes, essentially, the European and the Indian. But when gold was discovered in California in the 1840s, the entire world met. For the first time in human history, all of the known world gathered. The Malaysian stood in the gold fields alongside the African, alongside the Chinese, alongside the Australian, alongside the Yankee.

21   That was an event without parallel in world history and the beginning of modern California—why California today provides the mythological structure for understanding how we might talk about the American experience: not as biracial, but as the re-creation of the known world in the New World.

22   Sometimes truly revolutionary things happen without regard. I mean, we may wake up one morning and there is no black race. There is no white race either. There are mythologies, and—as I am in the business, insofar as I am in any business at all, of demythologizing such identities as black and white—I come to you as a man of many cultures. I come to you as Chinese. Unless you understand that I am Chinese, then you have not understood anything I have said.

AFTER YOU READ

Vocabulary Practice

1. Choose at least three words from the Vocabulary Development list on page 739 and write sentences using those words. You may write one sentence using all three words if you wish.

2. What word from the Vocabulary Development list means "the quality or state of being multiple or various"? Use the word in a sentence that clearly shows its meaning.

3. What are some ethnic or racial groups Rodriguez identifies in his article? Why doesn't he just use *black, white,* and *brown* to describe these groups?

Comprehension

Circle the correct answer.

1. How does Rodriguez open his article?
    a. With a statement about foreigners
    b. With a statement about Americans
    c. With a statement about immigrants
    d. With a statement about illegal aliens

2. How does Rodriguez say the great-grandchildren of today's immigrants will view their great-grandparents?
    a. They will romanticize the great-grandparents.
    b. They will criticize the great-grandparents.

    c. They will idolize the great-grandparents.

    d. They will eulogize the great-grandparents.

3. What question does Rodriguez have about the black-and-white conversation?

    a. Why doesn't it solve any problems?

    b. Why doesn't it admit anyone else?

    c. Why doesn't it ever stop?

    d. Why doesn't it get to the point?

4. What does Rodriguez notice about Laotian Hmong children who dislike Mexican children?

    a. They eat, and enjoy, Mexican food.

    b. They participate in salsa dancing.

    c. They admire Latino baseball players.

    d. They speak English with a Spanish accent.

5. Based on where he lives, what ethnicity does Rodriguez claim he is?

    a. Chinese   b. Japanese

    c. Mexican   d. Spanish

Content

1. What does the term *Blaxican* mean? Who uses the term in Rodriguez's article?

2. In terms of ethnic and cultural mixing, why was the California Gold Rush so important?

3. Why did Rodriguez identify himself as "Hispanic" when he was in college?

Style and Structure

1. What is Rodriguez's point? Write his argument in your own words.

2. What kinds of examples does Rodriguez use to show how people are "reinventing" themselves?

3. Rodriguez uses questions throughout his essay (paragraphs 1, 5, 15, 19). What effect do his questions have on your reading of the article?

Working Together

1. How do you identify yourself racially? Discuss what races or ethnicities make up your family tree and, then, discuss why you or your family has chosen a certain race or ethnicity with which to identify. If your family identifies itself according to a single race or ethnicity, explain what differences exist within that group, such as religious or caste differences. Share your findings with the class.

2. How different are you from your grandparents? What types of factors—such as education, living situation, or age, to name some—account for these differences? To what extent do you think your grandparents would agree with the reasons for the differences between you? Discuss, summarize, and share your findings with the class.

Writing Assignments

1. Rodriguez says that he identifies himself as Chinese because of the city he lives in. How do you identify yourself? *Write a paragraph in which you explain how you identify yourself.* Some factors you might consider in identifying yourself: your parents' races or ethnicities, where you live, how you were raised. Use examples from your own experiences to illustrate your ideas.

2. Rodriguez mentions several ways that people identify themselves: through their parents, by means of made-up categories on a census form, through their cities. How do you think most people identify themselves? *Write a paragraph explaining how certain factors—such as where a person lives or who a person's parents are—determine a person's identity.* Use examples and illustrations from your own life to support your ideas.

3. Rodriguez writes of one girl who describes herself as "Blaxican" because her parents were African and Mexican. What is a term that identifies you? *Write an essay in which you "reinvent" yourself—giving yourself a new name, such as* Blaxican—*and describing yourself in terms of your culture.* Some aspects of your culture you may want to explain in your essay are language, food, entertainment, and religion. Be sure to use examples from your own life for support.

═══ MARY ARGUELLES

Money for Morality

Mary Arguelles is a freelance writer whose articles have appeared in *New Mother, Baby Talk,* and *Reader's Digest.* Ms. Arguelles has also produced and hosted *Twigs,* a local parenting education program in Reading, Pennsylvania. Her essay first appeared in the "My Turn" section of *Newsweek* in 1991.

BEFORE YOU READ

Think about the following questions. Write your responses on a separate sheet or in your journal.

■ How would you define a good deed?

■ What were the circumstances of your last good deed? Why did you do it? Did you expect a reward?

■ Do you think people should be rewarded for good deeds? Explain.

VOCABULARY DEVELOPMENT

Look up the following words in a dictionary. Write down their meanings on a separate sheet or in your journal.

mandatory (paragraph 2)   sufficient (paragraph 2)
ubiquitous (paragraph 3)   collateral (paragraph 3)
mercenary (paragraph 3)   catapulted (paragraph 3)
elicit (paragraph 4)   kowtowing (paragraphs 5, 6)

Money for Morality

1   I recently read a newspaper article about an 8-year-old boy who found an envelope containing more than $600 and returned it to the bank whose name appeared on the envelope. The bank traced the money to its rightful owner and returned it to him. God's in his heaven and all's right with the world. Right? Wrong.

2   As a reward, the man who lost the money gave the boy $3. Not a lot, but a token of his appreciation nonetheless and not mandatory. After all, returning money should not be considered extraordinary. A simple "thank you" is adequate. But some of the teachers at the boy's school felt a reward was not only appropriate, but required. Outraged at the apparent stinginess of the person who lost the cash, these teachers took up a collection for the boy. About a week or so later, they presented the good Samaritan with $150 savings bond, explaining they felt his honesty should be recognized. Evidently the virtues of honesty and kindness have become commodities that, like everything else, have succumbed to inflation. I can't help but wonder what dollar amount these teachers would have deemed a sufficient reward. Certainly they didn't expect the individual who lost the money to give the child $150. Would $25 have been respectable? How about $10? Suppose that lost money had to cover mortgage, utilities and food for the week. In light of that, perhaps $3 was generous. A reward is a gift; any gift should at least be met with the presumption of genuine gratitude on the part of the giver.

3   What does this episode say about our society? It seems the role models our children look up to these days—in this case, teachers—are more confused and misguided about values than their young charges. A young boy, obviously well guided by his parents, finds money that does not belong to him and he returns it. He did the right thing. Yet doing the right thing seems to be insufficient motivation for action in our materialistic world. The legacy of the '80s has left us with the ubiquitous question: what's in it for me? The promise of the golden rule—that someone might do a good turn for you—has become worthless collateral for the social interactions of the mercenary and fast-paced '90s. It is in fact this fast pace that is, in part, a source of the problem. Modern communication has catapulted us into an instant world. Television makes history of events before any of us has even had a chance to absorb them in the first place. An ad for major-league baseball entices

viewers with the reassurance that "the memories are waiting"; an event that has yet to occur has already been packaged as the past. With the world racing by us, we have no patience for a rain check on good deeds.

4   Misplaced virtues are rampant through our culture. I don't know how many times my 13-year-old son has told me about classmates who received $10 for each A they receive on their report cards—hinting that I should do the same for him should he ever receive an A (or maybe he was working on $5 for a B). Whenever he approaches me on this subject, I give him the same reply: "Doing well is its own reward. The A just confirms that." In other words, forget it! This is not to say that I would never praise my son for doing well in school. But my praise is not meant to reward or elicit future achievements, but rather to express my genuine delight in the satisfaction he feels at having done his best. Throwing $10 at that sends out the message that the feeling alone isn't good enough.

Kowtowing to Ice Cream

5   As a society, we seem to be losing a grip on our internal control—the ethical thermostat that guides our actions and feelings toward ourselves, others, and the world around us. Instead, we rely on external "stuff" as a measure of our worth. We pass this message to our children. We offer them money for honesty and good grades. Pizza is given as a reward for reading. In fact, in one national reading program, a pizza party awaits the entire class if each child reads a certain amount of books within a four-month period. We call these incentives, telling ourselves that if we can just reel them in and get them hooked, then the built-in rewards will follow. I recently saw a television program where unmarried, teenaged mothers were featured as the participants in a parenting program that offers a $10 a week "incentive" if these young women don't get pregnant again. Isn't the daily struggle of being a single, teenaged mother enough of a deterrent? No, it isn't, because we as a society won't allow it to be. Nothing is permitted to succeed or fail on its own merits anymore.

6   I remember when I was pregnant with my son I read countless child-care books that offered the same advice: don't bribe your child with ice cream to get him to eat spinach; it makes the spinach look bad. While some may say spinach doesn't need any help looking bad, I submit it's from years of kowtowing to ice cream. Similarly, our moral taste buds have been dulled by an endless onslaught of artificial sweeteners. A steady diet of candy bars and banana splits makes an ordinary apple or orange seem sour. So too does an endless parade of incentives make us incapable of feeling a genuine sense of inner peace (or inner turmoil).

7   The simple virtues of honesty, kindness and integrity suffer from an image problem and are in desperate need of a makeover. One way to do this is by example. If my son sees me feeling happy after I've helped out a friend,

then he may do likewise. If my daughter sees me spending a rainy afternoon curled up with a book instead of spending money at the mall, she may get the message that there are some simple pleasures that don't require a purchase. I fear that in our so-called upwardly mobile world we are on a downward spiral toward moral bankruptcy. Like pre–World War II Germany, where the basket holding the money was more valuable than the money itself, we too may render ourselves internally worthless while desperately clinging to a shell of appearances.

AFTER YOU READ

Vocabulary Practice

1. Choose at least three words from the Vocabulary Development list on page 746 and write sentences using those words. You may write one sentence using all three words if you wish.

2. Which word on the Vocabulary Development list means "working or done for payment only; motivated by a desire for money or other gain"? Use the word in a sentence that clearly shows its meaning.

3. Arguelles uses terms such as *commodities, inflation,* and *savings bond.* What kinds of terms are these? What do they refer to? Why do you think Arguelles uses these terms?

Comprehension

Circle the correct answer.

1. What good deed does Arguelles use to open her essay?
   a. A boy returns a wallet to its owner.
   b. A boy returns money to a bank.
   c. A boy tackles a thief who has stolen a woman's purse.
   d. A boy returns an envelope that he has stolen.

2. How does the owner of the money reward the boy?
   a. By giving him $10
   b. By giving him a handshake
   c. By giving him a pat on the head
   d. By giving him $3

3. How do the boy's teachers respond to his good deed?
   a. They give him a cake.
   b. They give him a class party.
   c. They give him a savings bond.
   d. They give him a check.

4. Arguelles claims that the "legacy of the '80s" is

    a. "Why me?"   b. "What's in it for me?"

    c. "Why should I?"   d. "What if I don't?"

5. Arguelles claims that offering ice cream as a reward for eating spinach

    a. makes spinach look bad.   b. makes children overeat.

    c. makes ice cream taste bad.   d. makes children sick.

Content

1. What situation first caused Arguelles to think about good deeds and rewards in our society?

2. How does Arguelles feel about the role models in society—specifically, the boy's teachers?

3. How does Arguelles feel about offering students money for good grades?

Style and Structure

1. What is the main point of Arguelles's essay? Put her main idea into your own words.

2. What examples does Arguelles use to support her main idea?

3. What words or expressions does Arguelles use to indicate that money has a strong influence on people's values?

Working Together

1. Make a graph or chart of actions that reflect some degree of selflessness or courtesy. You might, for example, place giving someone your place in line at the grocery store lower than returning someone's wallet. At what point, if any, do you think people should be rewarded for their consideration? When does responsibility become optional? Discuss and summarize your findings for the class.

2. Discuss the extent to which people are motivated by the prospect of reward to do the right thing. For instance, how much does a potential reward factor into the actions of someone who returns a lost pet — or lost cell phone — to its owner? Discuss and summarize for the class.

Writing Assignments

1. Arguelles is critical of people who reward scholarly performance with money. What do you think? *Write a paragraph in which you argue for or against the practice of rewarding scholarly performance.* Use details from the text and from your own experience to illustrate your ideas.

2. Arguelles argues, "Misplaced virtues are rampant through our culture." Is she right? *Write a paragraph either agreeing or disagreeing with the idea that society's values—as presented by Arguelles—are "misplaced."* Be sure to use experiences from your own life for support.

3. Think about why money is so important in society today. *Write an essay explaining the reasons money is a vital part of our lives.* Use clear support points and specific examples to make your ideas clear.

STEPHANIE ERICSSON

The Ways We Lie

As the author of *Companion Through Darkness: Dialogues on Grief* and *Companion into Dawn: Inner Dialogues on Loving,* Stephanie Ericsson addresses the ways we attempt to fool ourselves and others with dishonesty as well as the consequences of such acts. Her essay was compiled from her notes for her book *Companion into Dawn* in 1997.

BEFORE YOU READ

Think about the following questions. Write your responses on a separate sheet or in your journal.

■ What is your definition of a lie?

■ What kinds of lies, if any, do you tell regularly? What are your usual reasons for telling lies?

■ How harmful do you think society considers lying? How harmful do you consider lying?

VOCABULARY DEVELOPMENT

Look up the following words in a dictionary. Write down their meanings on a separate sheet or in your journal.

minimize (paragraph 3)	keels over (paragraph 4)
travails (paragraph 4)	penance (paragraph 6)
misdemeanors (paragraph 6)	facades (paragraph 10)
plethora (paragraph 11)	irreparable (paragraph 13)
indignantly (paragraph 16)	sleight of hand (paragraph 26)
methodical (paragraph 29)	reticent (paragraph 35)

The Ways We Lie

1   The bank called today and I told them my deposit was in the mail, even though I hadn't written a check yet. It'd been a rough day. The baby I'm pregnant with decided to do aerobics on my lungs for two hours, our three-year-old daughter painted the living-room couch with lipstick, the IRS put me on hold for an hour, and I was late to a business meeting because I was tired.

2   I told my client the traffic had been bad. When my partner came home, his haggard face told me his day hadn't gone any better than mine, so when he asked, "How was your day?" I said, "Oh, fine," knowing that one more

straw might break his back. A friend called and wanted to take me to lunch. I said I was busy. Four lies in the course of a day, none of which I felt the least bit guilty about.

3   We lie. We all do. We exaggerate, we minimize, we avoid confrontation, we spare people's feelings, we conveniently forget, we keep secrets, we justify lying to the big-guy institutions. Like most people, I indulge myself in small falsehoods and still think of myself as an honest person. Sure I lie, but it doesn't hurt anything. Or does it?

4   I once tried going a whole week without telling a lie, and it was paralyzing. I discovered that telling the truth all the time is nearly impossible. It means living with some serious consequences: The bank charges me $60 in overdraft fees, my partner keels over when I tell him about my travails, my client fires me for telling her I didn't feel like being on time, and my friend takes it personally when I say I am not hungry. There must be some merit to lying.

5   But if I justify lying, what makes me different from slick politicians or the corporate robbers who raided the S & L industry?[1] Saying it's okay to lie one way and not the other is hedging. I cannot seem to escape the voice deep inside me that tells me: When someone lies, someone loses.

6   What far-reaching consequences will I, or others, pay as a result of my lie? Will someone's trust be destroyed? Will someone else pay *my* penance because I ducked out? We must consider the *meaning of our actions*. Deception, lies, capital crimes, and misdemeanors all carry meanings. *Webster's* definition of a *lie* is specific: *1: a false statement or action especially made with the intent to deceive; 2: anything that gives or is meant to give a false impression*.

7   A definition like this implies that there are many, many ways to tell a lie. Here are just a few.

8   **The White Lie:** The white lie assumes that the truth will cause more damage than a simple, harmless untruth. Telling a friend he looks great when he looks like hell can be based on a decision that the friend needs a compliment more than a frank opinion. But, in effect, it is the liar deciding what is best for the lied to. Ultimately, it is a vote of no confidence. It is an act of subtle arrogance for anyone to decide what is best for someone else.

9   Yet not all circumstances are quite so cut-and-dried. Take, for instance, the sergeant in Vietnam who knew one of his men was killed in action but listed him as missing so that the man's family would receive indefinite compensation instead of the lump-sum pittance the military gives widows and children. His intent was honorable. Yet for twenty years this family kept their hopes alive, unable to move on to a new life.

---

[1]In the 1980s, corrupt financiers who worked for savings and loan banks (S & Ls) defrauded thousands of people by selling them savings bonds of little or no value.

10   **Facades:** We all put up facades to one degree or another. When I put on a suit to go to see a client, I feel as though I am putting on another face, obeying the expectation that serious businesspeople wear suits rather than sweatpants. But I'm a writer. Normally, I get up, get the kid off to school, and sit at my computer in my pajamas until four in the afternoon. When I answer the phone, the caller thinks I'm wearing a suit (though the UPS man knows better).

11   But facades can be dangerous because they are used to seduce others into an illusion. For instance, I recently realized that a former friend was a liar. He presented himself with all the right looks and right words and offered lots of new consciousness theories, fabulous books to read, and fascinating insights. Then I did some business with him, and the time came to pay me. He turned out to be all talk and no walk. I heard a plethora of reasonable excuses, including in-depth descriptions of the big break around the corner. In six months of work, I saw less than a hundred bucks. When I confronted him, he raised both eyebrows and tried to convince me that I'd heard him wrong, that he'd made no commitment to me. A simple investigation into his past revealed a crowded graveyard of disenchanted former friends.

12   **Ignoring the Plain Facts:** In the '60s, the Catholic Church in Massachusetts began hearing complaints that Father James Porter was sexually molesting children. Rather than relieving him of his duties, the ecclesiastical authorities simply moved him from one parish to another between 1960 and 1967, actually providing him with a fresh supply of unsuspecting families and innocent children to abuse. After treatment in 1967 for pedophilia, he went back to work, this time in Minnesota. The new diocese was aware of Father Porter's obsession with children, but they needed priests and recklessly believed treatment had cured him. More children were abused until he was relieved of his duties a year later. By his own admission, Porter may have abused as many as a hundred children.

13   Ignoring the facts may not in and of itself be a form of lying, but consider the context of the situation. If a lie is a false action done with the intent to deceive, then the Catholic Church's conscious covering for Porter created irreparable consequences. The church became a coperpetrator with Porter.

14   **Deflecting:** I've discovered that I can keep anyone from seeing the true me by being selectively blatant. I set a precedent of being up-front about intimate issues, but I never bring up the things I truly want to hide; I just let people assume I'm revealing everything. It's an effective way of hiding.

15   Any good liar knows that the way to perpetuate an untruth is to deflect attention from it. When Clarence Thomas[2] exploded with accusations that the Senate hearings were a "high-tech lynching," he simply switched the

---

[2]African-American judge accused of sexual harassment, nominated by President George H. W. Bush to the U.S. Supreme Court in 1991.

focus from a highly charged subject to a radioactive subject. Rather than defending himself, he took the offensive and accused the country of racism. It was a brilliant maneuver. Racism is now politically incorrect in official circles—unlike sexual harassment, which still rewards those who can get away with it.

16   Some of the most skillful deflectors are passive-aggressive[3] people who, when accused of inappropriate behavior, refuse to respond to the accusations. This you-don't-exist stance infuriates the accuser, who, understandably, screams something obscene out of frustration. The trap is sprung and the act of deflection successful, because now the passive-aggressive person can indignantly say, "Who can talk to someone as unreasonable as you?" The real issue is forgotten and the sins of the original victim become the focus. Feeling guilty of name-calling, the victim is fully tamed and crawls into a hole, ashamed. I have watched this fighting technique work thousands of times in disputes between men and women, and what I've learned is that the real culprit is not necessarily the one who swears the loudest.

17   **Omission:** Omission involves telling most of the truth minus one or two key facts whose absence changes the story completely. You break a pair of glasses that are guaranteed under normal use and get a new pair, without mentioning that the first pair broke during a rowdy game of basketball. Who hasn't tried something like that? But what about the omission of information that could make a difference in how a person lives his or her life?

18   For instance, one day I found out that rabbinical legends tell of another woman in the Garden of Eden before Eve. I was stunned. The omission of the Sumerian goddess Lilith from Genesis—as well as her demonization by ancient misogynists as an embodiment of female evil—felt like spiritual robbery. I felt like I'd just found out my mother was really my stepmother. To take seriously the tradition that Adam was created out of the same mud as his equal counterpart, Lilith, redefines all of Judeo-Christian history.

19   Some renegade Catholic feminists introduced me to a view of Lilith that has been suppressed during the many centuries when this strong goddess was seen only as a spirit of evil. Lilith was a proud goddess who defied Adam's need to control her, attempted negotiations, and when this failed, said adios and left the Garden of Eden.

20   This omission of Lilith from the Bible was a patriarchal strategy to keep women weak. Omitting the strong-women archetype of Lilith from Western religions and starting the story with Eve the Rib helped keep Christian and Jewish women believing they were the lesser sex for thousands of years.

21   **Stereotypes and Clichés:** Stereotype and cliché serve a purpose as a form of shorthand. Our need for vast amounts of information in nanoseconds has made the stereotype vital to modern communication. Unfortunately,

---

[3]A psychological term applying to behavior that is hostile but not openly confrontational.

it often shuts down original thinking, giving those hungry for the truth a candy bar of misinformation instead of a balanced meal. The stereotype explains a situation with just enough truth to seem unquestionable. All the "isms"—racism, sexism, ageism, et al.—are founded on and fueled by the stereotype and the cliché, which are lies of exaggeration, omission, and ignorance. They are always dangerous. They take a single tree and make it a landscape. They destroy curiosity. They close minds and separate people. The single mother on welfare is assumed to be cheating. Any black male could tell you how much of his identity is obliterated daily by stereotypes. Fat people, ugly people, beautiful people, old people, large-breasted women, short men, the mentally ill, and the homeless all could tell you how much more they are like us than we want to think. I once admitted to a group of people that I had a mouth like a truck driver. Much to my surprise, a man stood up and said. "I'm a truck driver, and I never cuss." Needless to say, I was humbled.

22   **Groupthink:** Irving Janis, in *Victims of Group Think*, defines this sort of lie as a psychological phenomenon within decision-making groups in which loyalty to the group has become more important than any other value, with the result that dissent and the appraisal of alternatives are suppressed. If you've ever worked on a committee or in a corporation, you've encountered groupthink. It requires a combination of other forms of lying—ignorance of facts, selective memory, omission, and denial, to name a few.

23   The textbook example of groupthink came on December 7, 1941. From as early as the fall of 1941, the warnings came in, one after another, that Japan was preparing for a massive military operation. The Navy command in Hawaii assumed Pearl Harbor was invulnerable—the Japanese weren't stupid enough to attack the United States' most important base. On the other hand, racist stereotypes said the Japanese weren't smart enough to invent a torpedo effective in less than 60 feet of water (the fleet was docked in 30 feet); after all, U.S. technology hadn't been able to do it.

24   On Friday, December 5, normal weekend leave was granted to all the commanders at Pearl Harbor, even though the Japanese consulate in Hawaii was busy burning papers. Within the tight, good-ole-boy cohesiveness of the U.S. command in Hawaii, the myth of invulnerability stayed well entrenched. No one in the group considered the alternatives. The rest is history.

25   **Out-and-Out Lies:** Of all the ways to lie, I like this one the best, probably because I get tired of trying to figure out the real meanings behind things. At least I can trust the bald-faced lie. I once asked my five-year-old nephew, "Who broke the fence?" (I had seen him do it.) He answered, "The murderers." Who could argue?

26   At least when this sort of lie is told it can be easily confronted. As the person who is lied to, I know where I stand. The bald-faced lie doesn't toy with my perceptions—it argues with them. It doesn't try to refashion reality,

it tries to refute it. *Read my lips* . . . No sleight of hand. No guessing. If this were the only form of lying, there would be no such thing as floating anxiety or the adult-children-of-alcoholics movement.

27   **Dismissal:** Dismissal is perhaps the slipperiest of all lies. Dismissing feelings, perceptions, or even the raw facts of a situation ranks as a kind of lie that can do as much damage to a person as any other kind of lie.

28   The roots of many mental disorders can be traced back to the dismissal of reality. Imagine that a person is told from the time she is a tot that her perceptions are inaccurate: *"Mommie, I'm scared."* "No you're not, darling." *"I don't like that man next door, he makes me feel icky."* "Johnny, that's a terrible thing to say, of course you like him. You go over there right now and be nice to him."

29   I've often mused over the idea that madness is actually a sane reaction to an insane world. Psychologist R. D. Laing supports this hypothesis in *Sanity, Madness, and the Family*, an account of his investigation into the families of schizophrenics . . .

30   Dismissal runs the gamut. Mild dismissal can be quite handy for forgiving the foibles of others in our day-to-day lives. Toddlers who have just learned to manipulate their parents' attention sometimes are dismissed out of necessity. Absolute attention from the parents would require so much energy that no one would get to eat dinner. But we must be careful and attentive about how far we take our "necessary" dismissals. Dismissal is a dangerous tool, because it's nothing less than a lie.

31   **Delusion:** I could write a book on this one. Delusion, a cousin of dismissal, is the tendency to see excuses as facts. It's a powerful lying tool because it filters out information that contradicts what we want to believe. Alcoholics who believe the problems in their lives are legitimate reasons for drinking rather than results of the drinking offer the classic example of deluded thinking. Delusion uses the mind's ability to see things in myriad ways to support what it wants to be the truth.

32   But delusion is also a survival mechanism we all use. If we were to fully contemplate the consequences of our stockpiles of nuclear weapons or global warming, we could hardly function on a day-to-day level. We don't want to incorporate that much reality into our lives because to do so would be paralyzing.

33   Delusion works as an adhesive to keep the status quo intact. It shamelessly employs dismissal, omission, and amnesia, among other sorts of lies. Its most cunning defense is that it cannot see itself.

34   These are only a few of the ways we lie. Or are lied to. As I said earlier, it's not easy to entirely eliminate lies in our daily lives. No matter how pious we may try to be, we will still embellish, hedge, and omit to lubricate the daily machinery of living. But there is a world of difference between telling functional lies and living a lie. Martin Buber[4] once said, "The lie is the spirit

---

[4]Jewish theologian and philosopher.

committing treason against itself." Our acceptance of lies becomes a cultural cancer that eventually shrouds and reorders reality until moral garbage becomes as invisible to us as water is to a fish.

35   How much do we tolerate before we become sick and tired of being sick and tired? When will we stand up and declare our *right* to trust? When do we stop accepting that the real truth is in the fine print? Whose lips do we read this year when we vote for president? When will we stop being so reticent about making judgments? When do we stop turning over our personal power and responsibility to liars?

36   Maybe if I don't tell the bank the check's in the mail, I'll be less tolerant of the lies told me every day. A country song I once heard said it all for me: "You've got to stand for something or you'll fall for anything."

AFTER YOU READ

Vocabulary Practice

1. Choose at least three words from the Vocabulary Development list on page 750 and write sentences using those words. You may write one sentence using all three words if you wish.

2. What word from the Vocabulary Development list means "hard work; toil"? Use the word in a sentence that clearly shows its meaning.

3. What does the word *reticent* mean in the following sentence? "When do we stop accepting that the real truth is in the fine print? . . . When will we stop being so reticent about making judgments?"

    a. Silent   b. Obnoxious

    c. Funny   d. Immature

Comprehension

Circle the correct answer.

1. In her opening anecdote, to whom does Ericsson not tell a lie?

    a. The bank   b. Her client

    c. Her partner   d. Her daughter

2. How does Ericsson feel when she tries to go a whole week without lying?

    a. Paralyzed   b. Energized

    c. Proud   d. Defeated

3. The white lie assumes that the truth will

    a. make a bad situation worse.

    b. make the person telling the lie look bad.

    c. cause more damage than an untruth would.

    d. unburden whoever is telling the lie.

4. Omission involves telling
   a. none of the truth.   b. most of the truth.
   c. very little of the truth.   d. all of the truth.
5. What kind of lie does Ericsson "like" the most?
   a. Delusion   b. Omission
   c. The out-and-out lie   d. Dismissal

Content

1. What does Ericsson mean when she says, "When someone lies, someone loses"? To what extent do you agree with her?

2. Why does Ericsson say we lie? What other reasons can you think of?

3. What lie does Ericsson say she likes best? Why?

Style and Structure

1. What is the main point of Ericsson's essay? Restate her main idea in your own words.

2. How well do Ericsson's examples illustrate her main idea? Do you agree with her main idea? Explain.

3. What can you tell about Ericsson's audience? How do her vocabulary and examples target her audience?

Working Together

1. Rank the lies that Ericsson lists in terms of most or least harmful, both according to what Ericsson thinks and to what you think. Then, explain how some lies are more harmful than others. Summarize your findings for the class.

2. List some other types of lies that Ericsson does not mention and explain how the lies you list are more or less harmful than the ones Ericsson describes. Summarize your findings for the class.

Writing Assignments

1. *Write a paragraph in which you assume the opposite stance from Ericsson and argue that lying is necessary, even beneficial.* You may use some of Ericsson's own examples to support your argument, but be sure to use your own experiences and observations, too.

2. At what point do you think children should be told the truth, regardless of its brutality or unpleasantness? *In a well-developed paragraph, explain when children should be told the truth,* offering examples from your life and from Ericsson's essay for support.

3. Think about your habits of telling the truth. Does lying really solve problems? *Write an essay arguing that telling a lie is or is not the easiest way to deal with a problem.* Use specific examples to illustrate your ideas.

JUDITH MARTIN

Manners Matter

Widely known for her syndicated "Miss Manners" column, Judith Martin reigns as an expert on contemporary etiquette and has written several etiquette-oriented books, such as *Miss Manners Saves Civilization.* In "Manners Matter," Martin contrasts the law with etiquette, stating that each performs necessary functions in society, though etiquette often addresses conflicts before they escalate to the level where law must intercede.

BEFORE YOU READ

Think about the following questions. Write your responses on a separate sheet or in your journal.

■ Make a list of the manners you use daily. Your list may include such items as saying "please" or "thank you," and it may include more active forms of behavior such as letting a driver enter your lane ahead of you.

■ What kinds of people or situations cause you to use good manners?

■ How important do you think manners are?

VOCABULARY DEVELOPMENT

Look up the following words in a dictionary. Write down their meanings on a separate sheet or in your journal.

etiquette (paragraph 1)   repressive (paragraph 1)

trivial (paragraph 2)   impulses (paragraph 5)

pillage (paragraph 5)   provocations (paragraph 6)

presiding (paragraph 8)   deduce (paragraph 2)

Manners Matter

1   Society's condemnation of etiquette for being artificial and repressive stems from an idealistic if hopelessly naive belief in what we might call Original Innocence—the idea that people are born naturally good but corrupted by civilization. This is a very sweet idea, but it bears no relation to human nature. Yes, we're born adorable, or our parents would strangle us in our cribs. But we are not born good; that has to be learned. And if it is not learned, when we grow up and are not quite so cuddly, even our parents can't stand us. . . .

2   Administering etiquette, like administering law, is more than just knowing a set of rules. Even the most apparently trivial etiquette rules are dictated by principles of manners which are related to, and sometimes overlap with, moral principles. Respect and dignity, for example, are two big principles of manners from which a lot of etiquette rules are derived. This does not mean that you can simply deduce your rules of behavior from first principles. There are things you just have to know, like whether a man is supposed to show respect by taking his hat off as in church, or putting a hat on, as in a synagogue.

3   Moral people who understand these principles still figure that civility is not a top-priority virtue. First, they're going to fix the world, and then on the seventh day they're going to introduce civility. Deep in their hearts, they think etiquette is best applied to activities that don't really matter much, like eating or getting married.

4   But the absence of manners is a cause of some of our most serious social problems. For instance, our school systems have broken down from what is called lack of discipline. What does that mean? It means that such etiquette rules as sitting still, listening to others, taking turns, and not hitting others have not been taught. A great deal of crime begins with the short tempers people develop from being treated rudely all the time, and from perceived forms of disrespect. Getting "dissed," as it's called in the streets, is one of today's leading motivations for murder.

5   Nor will the business of government be done well, or sometimes done at all, by people who can't work together in civil, statesman-like ways. That is why we have all those highly artificial forms of speech for use in legislatures and courtrooms. Even in a courtroom where freedom of speech is being defended, there is no freedom to speak rudely. In legislatures we have phrases like "my distinguished colleague seems to be sadly mistaken"— because if we spoke freely and frankly, people would be punching each other out instead of airing arguments. We have a legal system that bars us from acting on natural human impulses to pillage, assault, and so forth. Whether we appreciate it or not, we also have an extra-legal system, called etiquette, that does many of the same things.

6   Law is supposed to address itself to the serious and dangerous impulses that endanger life, limb, and property. Etiquette addresses provocations that are minor but can grow serious if unchecked. Etiquette has some very handy conflict resolution systems—such as the apology, sending flowers in the morning, saying "I don't know what I was thinking"—that help settle things before they have to go through the legal system. But as we've seen in the past few decades, when people refuse to comply with etiquette the law has to step in. A classic example is smoking. We've had to use the law to explain such simple etiquette rules as: You don't blow smoke in other people's faces, and you don't blow insults into other people's faces pretending

it's health advice. Sexual harassment is another example that had to be turned over to the law because those in a position of power refused to obey basic values as "Keep your hands to yourself."

7   It's a dangerous idea to keep asking the law to do etiquette's job. Not that I wouldn't love to have a squad of tough cops who would go around and roust people who don't answer invitations and write thank-you notes. But when we have to enlarge the scope of law to enforce manners, it really does threaten freedom. Even I think people should have a legal right to be obnoxious. I don't think they should exercise it. And I do think people should be prepared to take the consequences. If you stomp on the flag, some people will not want to listen to your opinions. If you disrupt and spoil activities for other people who want to participate, they're going to throw you out. Those are the mild little sanctions of etiquette, but they work.

8   Trying to live by law alone does not work. Every little nasty remark is labeled a slander and taken to court; meanness gets dressed up as "mental cruelty"; and everything else that's annoying is declared a public health hazard. That's why we need the little extra-legal system over which I have the honor of presiding.

AFTER YOU READ

Vocabulary Practice

1. Choose at least three words from the Vocabulary Development list on page 758 and write sentences using those words. You may write one sentence using all three words if you wish.

2. What word from the Vocabulary Development list means "keeping down, or holding back"? Use the word in a sentence that clearly shows the meaning of the word.

3. Martin gives many examples of poor manners, from not taking a hat off in church to sexual harassment, some of which are not only poor manners, but also illegal acts. What kinds of words does Martin use to discuss various breaches in behavior? List at least three terms Martin uses and write sentences showing their meanings.

Comprehension

Circle the correct answer.

1. Martin opens her essay with a discussion of

    a. Original Sin.   b. Original Innocence.

    c. Original Truth.   d. Original Behavior.

2. Martin says that society condemns etiquette for being

    a. artificial and repressive.

    b. stale and old-fashioned.

c. energized and in vogue.

d. difficult and unnecessary.

3. Martin says that many forms of manners are related to

    a. lawful actions.   b. kind behavior.

    c. moral principles.   d. childlike innocence.

4. Which one of the following does Martin not specify as a problem stemming from poor manners?

    a. Sexual harassment   b. Murder

    c. Slander   d. Road rage

5. Besides etiquette, what other code of conduct does Martin say ensures that people do not treat each other horribly?

    a. The Ten Commandments   b. The law

    c. The Koran   d. People's natural instincts

Content

1. According to Martin, why are we "born adorable"?

2. What two things does Martin say, in paragraph 2, that people need to understand in order to practice good manners?

3. In what areas does Martin say people have developed "highly artificial forms of speech"? Why does she say we need them?

Style and Structure

1. What is Martin's argument? State her main idea in your own words.

2. What examples does Martin give to support her main idea?

3. Who is Martin's audience? How can you tell? Cite examples from the text to illustrate your ideas.

Working Together

1. Draw a spectrum upon which you plot various types of etiquette: using a particular fork at dinner, for example, or giving someone the right of way in traffic. Then, discuss why you plotted certain acts at certain points on the spectrum. What factors play a role in your decision-making process? Summarize your findings for the class.

2. To what extent does anonymity play in determining people's actions? Explain whether you think people are more or less likely to be courteous to someone they know. Give examples and summarize your findings for the class.

Writing Assignments

1. Martin claims, "We are not born good; that has to be learned." What do you think? *Write a paragraph agreeing or disagreeing with the idea that people are not born good.* Give examples from the text and from your own life in order to illustrate your ideas.

2. Martin writes, "Etiquette addresses provocations that are minor but can grow serious if unchecked." *Using Martin's definition of "etiquette" as a starting point, write a paragraph illustrating that idea.* Use examples from different areas of life to clarify Martin's definition. Some possible examples to explore follow: using your car blinker to signal that you'd like to merge rather than simply forcing your way in; shouting only positive comments at a sports event rather than disparaging another team.

3. Think about the role that manners play in your life. *Then, write an essay arguing that manners are important in a specific area of life.* Some possible areas of your life to focus on are school, work, family relationships, nonfamily personal relationships, daily living, travel, politics, and entertainment (going to the movies or some type of performance or sports activity, for instance). Use specific details from your experience and observations to illustrate your ideas.

CHERYL PECK

Fatso

A lifelong resident of Michigan, Cheryl Peck has written stories and essays nearly all her life. Author of *Fat Girls and Lawn Chairs* (2004) and *Revenge of the Paste Eaters: Memoirs of a Misfit* (2005), Peck strives to write "the Great American Novel." In "Fatso," Peck uses sarcastic humor to examine the hurtful assumptions made about "people of substance."

BEFORE YOU READ

Think about the following questions. Write your responses on a separate sheet or in your journal.

- How important is your weight to you?
- What is your attitude toward people of differing body types? To what extent are you drawn to people who are built a certain way? Explain.
- Have you ever been discriminated against because of any aspect of your appearance? Explain.

VOCABULARY DEVELOPMENT

Look up the following words in a dictionary. Write down their meanings on a separate sheet or in your journal.

register (paragraph 1)	snubbed (paragraph 3)
debilitate (paragraph 3)	crude (paragraph 5)
prone (paragraph 7)	asexual (paragraph 8)
demeanor (paragraph 9)	unparalleled (paragraph 9)
gauging (paragraph 9)	presumption (paragraph 10)

Fatso

1   My friend Annie and I were having lunch and we fell into a discussion of people of size. She told me she had gone to the fair with a friend of hers who is a young man of substance, and while he was standing in the midway, thinking about his elephant ear,[1] someone walked past him, said, "You don't need to eat that," and kept on walking away. Gone before he could register what had been said, much less formulate a stunning retort.

2   And that person was probably right: he did not need to eat that elephant ear. Given what they are made of, the question then becomes: Who *does* need to eat an elephant ear? And to what benefit? Are elephant ears inherently better for thin people than for fat ones? Do we suppose that that one particular elephant ear will somehow alter the course of this man's life in some way that all of the elephant ears before it, or all of the elephant ears to follow, might not? And last but not least, what qualifies any of us for the mission of telling other people what they should or should not eat?

3   I have probably spent most of my life listening to other people tell me that as a middle-class white person, I have no idea what it is like to be discriminated against. I have never experienced the look that tells me I am not welcome, I have never been treated rudely on a bus, I have never been reminded to keep my place, I have never been laughed at, ridiculed, threatened, snubbed, not waited on, or received well-meaning service I would just as soon have done without. I have never had to choose which streets I will walk down and which streets I will avoid. I have never been told that my needs cannot be met in this store. I have never experienced that lack of social status that can debilitate the soul.

4   My feelings were not hurt when I was twelve years old and the shoe salesman measured my feet and said he had no women's shoes large enough for me, but perhaps I could wear the boxes.

5   I have never been called crude names, like "fatso" or "lardbucket." . . . My nickname on the school bus was never "Bismarck," as in the famous battleship. No one ever assumed I was totally inept in all sports except those that involved hitting things because—and everyone knows—the more weight you can put behind it, the farther you can kick or bat or just bully the ball.

6   I have never picked up a magazine with the photograph of a naked woman of substance on the cover, to read, in the following issue, thirty letters to the editor addressing sizism, including the one that said, "She should be ashamed of herself. She should go on a diet immediately and demonstrate some self-control. She is going to develop diabetes, arthritis, hypertension, and stroke, she will die an ugly death at an early age and she will take down the entire American health system with her." And that would, of course, be

---

[1]Fried dough. [Editor's note.]

the only letter I remember. I would not need some other calm voice to say, "You don't know that—and you don't know that the same fate would not befall a thin woman."

7   No one has ever assumed I am lazy, undisciplined, prone to self-pity, and emotionally unstable purely based on my size. No one has ever told me all I need is a little self-discipline and I too could be thin, pretty—a knock-out, probably, because I have a "pretty face"—probably very popular because I have a "good personality." My mother never told me boys would never pay any attention to me because I'm fat.

8   I have never assumed an admirer would never pay any attention to me because I'm fat. I have never mishandled a sexual situation because I have been trained to think of myself as asexual. Unattractive. Repugnant.

9   Total strangers have never walked up to me in the street and started to tell me about weight loss programs their second cousin in Tulsa tried with incredible results, nor would they ever do so with the manner and demeanor of someone doing me a nearly unparalleled favor. I have never walked across a parking lot to have a herd of young men break into song about loving women with big butts. When I walk down the street or ride my bicycle, no one has ever hung out the car window to yell crude insults. When I walk into the houses of friends I have never been directed to the "safe" chairs as if I just woke up this morning this size and am incapable of gauging for myself what will or will not hold me.

10   I have never internalized any of this nonexistent presumption of who I am or what I feel. I would never discriminate against another woman of substance. I would never look at a heavy person and think, "self-pitying, undisciplined tub of lard." I would never admit that while I admire beautiful bodies, I rarely give the inhabitants the same attention and respect I would a soul mate because I do not expect they would ever become a soul mate. I would never tell you that I was probably thirty years old before I realized you really *can* be too small or too thin, or that the condition causes real emotional pain.

11   I have never skipped a high school reunion until I "lose a few pounds." I have never hesitated to reconnect with an old friend. I will appear anywhere in a bathing suit. If my pants split, I assume—and I assume everyone assumes—it was caused by poor materials.

12   I have always understood why attractive women are offended when men whistle at them.

13   I have never felt self-conscious standing next to my male friend who is five foot ten and weighs 145 pounds.

14   I am not angry about any of this.

AFTER YOU READ

Vocabulary Practice

1. Choose at least three words from the Vocabulary Development list on page 762 and write sentences using those words. You may write one sentence using all three words if you wish.

2. Which word on the Vocabulary Development list means "devoid of sexuality"? Use the word in a sentence that shows the word's meaning clearly.

3. What kinds of terms does Peck use in reference to overweight people? To what extent are these terms positive or negative?

Comprehension

Circle the correct answer.

1. What did someone say to "a young man of substance" who was about to eat an elephant ear?

    a. You should eat something healthier.

    b. You don't need to eat that.

    c. You should throw that away.

    d. You should give that to me.

2. What did a salesman tell Peck she might be able to wear on her feet instead of shoes?

    a. Socks   b. Slippers

    c. Bags   d. Boxes

3. What sports does Peck say people assumed she could play?

    a. Those that involved hitting things

    b. Those that involved throwing things

    c. Those that involved lifting things

    d. Those that involved shooting things

4. What does Peck say she would never do to another "woman of substance"?

    a. Laugh at her   b. Befriend her

    c. Discriminate against her   d. Introduce a friend to her

5. What did Peck realize when she "was probably thirty years old"?

    a. That you *can* be too intelligent

    b. That you *can* be too beautiful

    c. That you *can* be too small or too thin

    d. That you *can* be too tall or too kind

Content Questions

1. What situation does Peck begin her essay by relating?

2. Why, according to Peck, have people always assumed she was good at sports that required hitting things?

3. Around whom does Peck feel self-conscious?

Style and Structure

1. What is Peck's point? Rewrite her main idea in your own words.

2. What kinds of examples does Peck use to illustrate her ideas?

3. What is Peck contrasting in her essay?

4. Why does Peck put her arguments in the negative? Why doesn't she simply say she *was* hurt or offended?

Working Together

1. Peck refers to numerous situations and comments that have proved hurtful to her. Do you think people are just insensitive and don't know when they're being hurtful, or do you think they simply don't care whether they're hurtful? Give examples from your experiences and observations to illustrate your points, and give a brief summary to the class.

2. Which characteristics—such as race, gender, appearance, or beliefs—do you think people are most likely to make fun of in someone else? Do the characteristics change with circumstances? For instance, Peck writes about how people were unkind to her as a child and how, even in adulthood, some people treat her rudely. Write up your results in a brief summary and present them to the class.

Writing Assignments

1. Peck writes that she has been "trained" to think of herself as asexual. How have you been trained? *Write a paragraph in which you explain how a person—a parent, teacher, or minister, to name some—trained you in some way*. For instance, if your mother taught you to pick up after yourself and clean, you could write that your mother trained you to be tidy. Use examples from your own experiences to illustrate your ideas.

2. Peck writes that people tell her that she has "no idea what it is like to be discriminated against." Have you ever felt that someone discriminated against you? *Write a paragraph*

in which you discuss a time when you were treated unfairly. Use specific examples from your life to illustrate your ideas.

3. Peck writes, "While I admire beautiful bodies, I rarely give the inhabitants the same attention and respect I would a soul mate." How is your behavior toward someone you greatly respect similar to or different from your behavior toward someone you respect less? *Write an essay in which you compare or contrast your behavior toward two different people.* Explain how you talk to a teacher, for instance, versus how you talk to a younger sibling. You may find that your behavior is consistent with different people. Use examples and illustrations from your own life to support your ideas.

ELLEN GOODMAN AND PATRICIA O'BRIEN

The Difference Between Male and Female Friendships

A writer for the *Boston Globe* since 1967, Ellen Goodman has written numerous books in addition to her syndicated column. In her book with her good friend Patricia O'Brien, *I Know Just What You Mean: The Power of Friendship in Women's Lives*, Goodman and O'Brien explore both friendship as it relates to gender and people's lives.

BEFORE YOU READ

Think about the following questions. Write your responses on a separate sheet or in your journal.

■ What qualities do you most value in a friend?

■ In what situations—celebrations, tragedies, everyday activities—do you most value your friends? Explain.

■ To what extent do you have friends of the opposite sex? Why?

VOCABULARY DEVELOPMENT

Look up the following words in a dictionary. Write down their meanings on a separate sheet or in your journal.

obvious (paragraph 1)	distinct (paragraph 5)
subtext (paragraph 5)	contradictory (paragraph 6)
allotted (paragraph 9)	simplistic (paragraph 11)
retort (paragraph 11)	counterweight (paragraph 16)
sustenance (paragraph 18)	fervently (paragraph 20)

From *I Know Just What You Mean: The Power of Friendship in Women's Lives* (Reprinted in *Interactions*)

The Difference Between
Male and Female Friendships

1   Why do men and women, on the topic of friendship, puzzle each other so much? Let us start with the obvious: women do friendship differently than men. Among women, friendship is conducted face-to-face. But as Carolyn Heilbrun once wrote, "Male friends do not always face each other: they stand side by side, facing the world." While women tend to *be* together, men tend to *do* together.

2   We have thought about this friendship divide ever since [the] . . . time when sex differences were just beginning to go under an intense cultural microscope. We know that men's feelings of closeness and connection are real; that painting a house or watching a ball game together can be an act of friendship. But we also know we would feel lonely if we couldn't talk to each other about everything, through good and bad times.

3   The two of us have wondered over the years just what is going on between men. And the truth is, we have disagreed with each other about whether men are missing something so central to friendship that it amounts to almost a fatal flaw, or whether they are handling friendship just fine—in their own, mysterious way. Do men, as Letty Pogrebin wrote in *Among Friends*, deserve "Incompletes" in the subject of friendship? Are women in the business of grading?

4   "What on earth do you have to say to each other?" men ask. Women have their own counterquestion for male friends: "You spent all day together on the golf course and never told him you were worried about your job?"

5   When we first began telling people that we were writing about women and friendship, the second or third question would invariably be, "What about men? Are you writing about them, too?" Sometimes it was asked with a smile or a teasing challenge; sometimes defensively. We could hear a distinct subtext: if you're writing only about women, are you saying your friendships are better than ours?

6   We answered that we were writing about women because, if you write about what you know, what we know are women's friendships. We would leave it to men to write about their own friendships. The contradictory, complex differences between the two sexes in a time of such change is a topic for a different kind of book. Yet here we are, looking across the gender divide with curiosity and sometimes bewilderment.

7   Let's give comedian Rob Becker the first take on this subject. Becker plays Darwin to the sexes in the theatrical hit, *Defending the Caveman*. He announces to his audiences at one point that—at last—he has the gender-friendship gap all figured out.

8   So, here's how it works, he says. Men were the hunters, see? They were required to stand side by side without talking for fear they'd scare off the

prey. Women? They were gatherers, out there foraging in the jungle for food. So they *had* to talk while they worked, for safety.

9   You get the picture? "If a woman goes for very long without hearing the voice of another woman, she knows she's been eaten by an animal," Becker announces. So women are genetically allotted some five thousand words a day, while men are allotted only two thousand. No wonder women talk more, he triumphantly concludes.

10   Well, hunters and gatherers aside, if there is one prototypical image of women sharing friendship, it's that of two friends sitting across a table from each other, clutching their coffee cups, talking feelings. If there is a similar image of men, it is of buddies sitting together watching television, talking football.

11   We know these images are simplistic and women and men are both guilty of stretching them to make assumptions about each other's friendships that range from the stereotypic to the bizarre. Men never talk about anything but sports, women say in frustration. Women talk only about clothes, men retort. Both sexes get trapped in vast generalizations. But the differences between the same-sex friendships of men and women are real. Decades of research can't be ignored.

12   A long list of studies tell men and women what they already know: men and women talk about different things in different ways. Men are less likely to talk about personal subjects with other men than women are with other women. As Pogrebin summed it up, "The average man's idea of an intimate exchange is the average woman's idea of a casual conversation."

13   What else do the researchers show? Men's friendships are based on shared activities, women's on shared feelings. Men who do things together, paint that house, change that tire, feel close; women who share secrets, troubles, relationships, feel close.

14   If you had a camera you could videotape the gender gap. Women literally touch each other more; they sit closer together, focus on one-to-one sharing. But when men talk about what they do with their friends, you get a different portrait: men doing things together in groups.

15   The research list goes on. Men do not criticize their friends as much as women, but neither do they communicate the kind of acceptance women count on from their friends. Men put shared interests highest among the reasons they bond with a friend, while women first want friends who share their values. And even men tend to view their friendships with women as closer and more intimate than those with other men.

16   And yet—here's the counterweight—at least among grade school boys, a study shows that a relative lack of intimacy and affection doesn't affect the importance or the satisfaction boys get from their friends.

17   Every friendship is as different as the people involved, and not all men are caveman hunters and not all women are cavewoman gatherers. But differences between male and female friendships have remained constant and

consistent. What has shifted are the values placed on those differences. What's striking now is that the culture has gone from seeing men's friendships as superior to seeing women's friendships as superior. Is that just a swing of the pendulum?

18   It's not surprising that philosophers in the past routinely dismissed women as incapable of true friendship. They were certain that, because women led more "trivial" lives, they had limited capacity for elevated feelings. The classical idea of friendship was heroic, and the greatest thing a man could give a friend was his courage and loyalty. Montaigne once wrote in a spirit of superior regret, "To speak truly, the usual capacity of women is not equal to the demands of the communion and intercourse which is the sustenance of that sacred bond; nor do their minds seem firm enough to sustain the pressure of so hard and so lasting a knot."

19   Women, on the other hand, often idealized their relationships with each other. Historian Nancy Cott describes how educated women in the nineteenth century passionately poured out their feelings, often expressing their firm belief in the superiority of female relationships. "I do not feel that men can ever feel so pure an enthusiasm for women as we can feel for one another," wrote one woman to another. "Ours is nearest to the love of angels."

20   The idea that friendship is defined by intimacy has become, in our time, less fervently defined—but more solidly understood. As a result, the gender gap has been focused on the intimacy gap. And men's friendships are indeed often given an "incomplete" grade.

AFTER YOU READ

Vocabulary Practice

1. Choose at least three words from the Vocabulary Development list on page 767 and write sentences using those words. You may write one sentence using all three words if you wish.

2. Which word on the Vocabulary Development list means "to pay or hurl back"? Use the word in a sentence that shows the word's meaning clearly.

3. What are some words Goodman and O'Brien use in discussing friendship in their article? What do these expressions say about friendships? Explain.

Comprehension

Circle the correct answer.

1. How do Goodman and O'Brien say women conduct friendship?

   a. Side by side   b. Mouth-to-ear

   c. Face-to-face   d. Head-to-toe

2. What "grade" do the writers consider giving to men for their friendships?

   a. Incomplete   b. A+

   c. F   d. Credit

3. Why does comedian Rob Becker say women talk more than men?

   a. Women like to explain things multiple ways.

   b. Women don't like sports.

   c. Women were genetically allotted more words than men.

   d. Women are still secretly afraid of being eaten by a wild animal.

4. What does research say men's friendships are based on?

   a. Shared responsibilities   b. Shared activities

   c. Shared enemies   d. Shared feelings

5. Why did philosophers once think that women were incapable of true friendship?

   a. Women had limited interest in relationships other than marriage.

   b. Women had limited mental abilities to understand friendship.

   c. Women had limited physical abilities for bond-forming activities.

   d. Women had limited capacity for elevated feelings.

Content

1. What are the stereotypical subjects that men and women discuss?

2. What do men and women put first in terms of how they bond with friends?

3. How, according to Goodman and O'Brien, has culture's evaluation of men's and women's friendships changed?

Style and Structure

1. What is Goodman's and O'Brien's main idea? Rewrite their main idea in your own words.

2. What kinds of examples do the writers offer to illustrate the natures of men's and women's friendships? Find two or three examples that you find particularly effective.

3. Do the writers integrate examples and discussion of both genders' friendships, or do they keep the examples apart? How effective is this organizational method?

Working Together

1. Make a grading scale for friendship, and give grades to men's, women's, and double-gender (between a man and a woman) friendships. Which type of friendship receives the

highest grade? Why? Upon what factors (such as shared interest or sensitivity) do you base your grades? Discuss your grades as a group, and compare your ideas with those of other groups.

2. Talk about friendships depicted in your favorite movies or television shows. What characteristics seem most prevalent in men's and women's friendships? Be prepared to present your results to the class.

Writing Assignments

1. Goodman and O'Brien write, "While women tend to *be* together, men tend to *do* together." Do you agree? *Write a paragraph in which you contrast women's and men's friendships.* Use examples from the essay and from your own experiences to illustrate your ideas.

2. Goodman and O'Brien write, "Men do not criticize their friends as much as women." What role does criticism play in your relationships? *Write a paragraph explaining the role of criticism in your friendship with one person.* Consider, for instance, how much advice you give each other, or whether one of you redoes the other's work (which some would say is a form of criticism). Use examples and illustrations from your own life to support your ideas.

3. The authors write that "even men tend to view their friendships with women as closer and more intimate than those with other men." Are women's friendships more intimate than men's? In what ways is closeness, or intimacy, demonstrated in friendships? *Write an essay in which you explain how friendship with men or women is more intimate.* Be sure to use examples from your own experiences and observations for support.

Challenges We Face

Perhaps more significant than what we choose to learn or what we choose to believe is how we address the challenges that life sets before us. In "My Mother's English" Amy Tan explores how people deal with changes in their lives, such as living in a different culture or under a different set of circumstances. Other challenges come from the decisions we make daily, as "Working with Difficult People" presents. Finally, sometimes the most severe challenges come out of nowhere and are not our fault. In "The Santa Ana," "The Plot Against People," and "The Price We Pay," writers seek to make sense of circumstances which are beyond our control, from the effects of weather and the frustrations of nonfunctioning objects to the threat of terrorism on our own soil.

READINGS IN THIS SECTION

AMY TAN

My Mother's English

Best known as the author of the novels *The Joy Luck Club*, *The Kitchen God's Wife*, and *The Bonesetter's Daughter*, Amy Tan received her master's degree in linguistics from San Jose State University before working as a language specialist with developmentally disabled children and then as a writer. In "My Mother's English," Tan explores the power or weakness that people possess as a result of their perceived language mastery, and she reveals how her mother's English-speaking skills often caused her to be treated with less respect than she deserved.

BEFORE YOU READ

Think about the following questions. Write your responses on a separate sheet or in your journal.

- What kind of speaking skills do you possess? Make a list of the various groups you interact with, such as friends, family, co-workers, and teachers.
- How does your speech differ from one group of your acquaintances, such as your friends, to others, such as those you listed in the previous question?
- How do people's reactions to you change depending on your speech?

VOCABULARY DEVELOPMENT

Look up the following words in a dictionary. Write down their meanings on a separate sheet or in your journal.

aspect (paragraph 2)	wrought (paragraph 2)
nominalized (paragraph 2)	self-conscious (paragraph 3)
transcribed (paragraph 4)	imagery (paragraph 6)
fractured (paragraph 6)	empirical (paragraph 7)
regrettable (paragraph 9)	insular (paragraph 10)

My Mother's English

1   As you know, I am a writer and by that definition I am someone who has always loved language. I think that is first and foremost with almost every writer I know. I'm fascinated by language in daily life. I spend a great deal of time thinking about the power of language—the way it can evoke an emotion, a visual image, a complex idea or a simple truth. As a writer, language is the tool of my trade and I use them all, all the Englishes I grew up with.

2   A few months back, I was made keenly aware of the Englishes I do use. I was giving a talk to a large group of people, the same talk I had given many times before and also with notes. And the nature of the talk was about my writing, my life, and my book, *The Joy Luck Club*. The talk was going along well enough until I remembered one major difference that made the whole thing seem wrong. My mother was in the room, and it was perhaps the first time she had heard me give a lengthy speech, using a kind of English I had never used with her. I was saying things like "the intersection of memory and imagination," and "there is an aspect of my fiction that relates to this and thus." A speech filled with carefully wrought grammatical sentences, burdened to me it seemed with nominalized forms, past perfect tenses, conditional

phrases, all the forms of standard English that I had learned in school and through books, a form of English I did not use at home or with my mother.

3   Shortly after that I was walking down the street with my mother and my husband and I became self-conscious of the English I was using, the English that I do use with her. We were talking about the price of new and used furniture and I heard myself saying to her, "Not waste money that way." My husband was with me as well, and he didn't notice any switch in my English. And then I realized why: because over the twenty years that we've been together he's often used that English with me and I've used that with him. It is sort of the English that is our language of intimacy, the English that relates to family talk, the English that I grew up with.

4   I'd like to give you some idea what my family talk sounds like and I'll do that by quoting what my mother said during a recent conversation which I videotaped and then transcribed. During this conversation, my mother was talking about a political gangster who had the same last name as her family, Du, and how the gangster in his early years wanted to be adopted by her family which was by comparison very rich. Later the gangster became more rich, more powerful than my mother's family and one day showed up at my mother's wedding to pay his respects. And here's what she said about that, in part, "Du You Sung having business like food stand, like off the street kind; he's Du like Du Zong but not Tsung-ming Island people. The local people call him Du, from the river east side. He belong to that side, local people. That man want to ask Du Zong father take him in become like own family. Du Zong father look down on him but don't take seriously until that man becoming big like, become a Mafia. Now important person, very hard inviting him. Chinese way: come only to show respect, don't stay for dinner. Respect for making big celebration; he shows up. Means gives lots of respect, Chinese custom. Chinese social life that way—if too important, won't have to stay too long. He come to my wedding; I didn't see it I heard it. I gone to boy's side. They have YMCA dinner; Chinese age I was nineteen."

5   You should know that my mother's expressive command of English belies how much she actually understands. She reads the *Forbes Report*, listens to *Wall Street Week*, converses daily with her stockbroker, reads all of Shirley MacLaine's books with ease, all kinds of things I can't begin to understand. Yet some of my friends tell me that they understand 50 percent of what my mother says. Some say maybe they understand maybe 80 percent. Some say they understand almost nothing at all. As a case in point, a television station recently interviewed my mother and I didn't see this program when it was first aired, but my mother did. She was telling me what happened. She said that everything she said, which was in English, was subtitled in English, as if she had been speaking in pure Chinese. She was understandably puzzled and upset. Recently a friend gave me that

tape and I saw that same interview and I watched. And sure enough—subtitles—and I was puzzled because listening to that tape it seemed to me that my mother's English sounded perfectly clear and perfectly natural. Of course, I realize that my mother's English is what I grew up with. It is literally my mother tongue, not Chinese, not standard English, but my mother's English which I later found out is almost a direct translation of Chinese.

6   Her language as I hear it is vivid and direct, full of observation and imagery. That was the language that helped shape the way that I saw things, expressed things, made sense of the world. Lately I've been giving more thought to the kind of English that my mother speaks. Like others I have described it to people as broken or fractured English, but I wince when I say that. It has always bothered me that I can think of no other way to describe it than broken, as it if were damaged or needed to be fixed, that it lacked a certain wholeness or soundness to it. I've heard other terms used, "Limited English" for example. But they seem just as bad, as if everything is limited including people's perceptions of the Limited English speaker.

7   I know this for a fact, because when I was growing up my mother's limited English limited my perception of her. I was ashamed of her English. I believed that her English reflected the quality of what she had to say. That is, because she expressed it imperfectly, her thoughts were imperfect as well. And I had plenty of empirical evidence to support me: The fact that people in department stores, at banks, at supermarkets, at restaurants did not take her as seriously, did not give her good service, pretended not to understand her, or even acted as if they did not hear her.

8   My mother has long realized the limitations of her English as well. When I was fifteen she used to have me call people on the phone to pretend I was she. In this guise, I was forced to ask for information or oftentimes to complain and yell at people that had been rude to her. One time it was a call to her stockbroker in New York. She had cashed out her small portfolio and it just so happened that we were going to New York the next week, our very first trip outside of California. I had to get on the phone and say in my adolescent voice, which was not very convincing, "This is Mrs. Tan." And my mother was in the back whispering loudly, "Why don't he send me check already? Two weeks late. So mad he lie to me, losing me money." Then I said in perfect English, "Yes, I'm getting rather concerned. You had agreed to send the check two weeks ago, but it hasn't arrived." And she began to talk more loudly, "What you want—I come to New York, tell him front of his boss you cheating me?" And I was trying to calm her down, making her be quiet, while telling this stockbroker, "I can't tolerate any more excuses. If I don't receive the check immediately I'm going to have to speak to your manager when I arrive in New York." And sure enough the following week, there we were in front of this astonished stockbroker. And

there I was, red-faced and quiet, and my mother the real Mrs. Tan was shouting at his boss in her impeccable broken English.

9   We used a similar routine a few months ago for a situation that was actually far less humorous. My mother had gone to the hospital for an appointment to find out about a benign brain tumor a CAT scan had revealed a month ago. And she had spoken very good English she said—her best English, no mistakes. Still she said the hospital had not apologized when they said they had lost the CAT scan and she had come for nothing. She said that they did not seem to have any sympathy when she told them she was anxious to know the exact diagnosis since her husband and son had both died of brain tumors. She said they would not give her any more information until the next time; she would have to make another appointment for that, so she said she would not leave until the doctor called her daughter. She wouldn't budge, and when the doctor finally called her daughter, me, who spoke in perfect English, lo-and-behold, we had assurances the CAT scan would be found, they promised a conference call on Monday, and apologies were given for any suffering my mother had gone through for a most regrettable mistake. By the way, apart from the distress of that episode, my mother is fine.

10   But it has continued to disturb me how much my mother's English still limits people's perceptions of her. I think my mother's English almost had an effect on limiting my possibilities as well. Sociologists and linguists will probably tell you that a person's developing language skills are more influenced by peers. But I do think the language spoken by the family, especially immigrant families, which are more insular, plays a large role in shaping the language of the child. . . . While this may be true, I always wanted to capture what language ability tests can never reveal—her intent, her passion, her imagery, the rhythms of her speech, and the nature of her thoughts. Apart from what any critic had to say about my writing, I knew I had succeeded where it counted when my mother finished reading my first book and gave me her verdict. "So easy to read."

AFTER YOU READ

Vocabulary Practice

1. Choose at least three words from the Vocabulary Development list on page 774 and write sentences using those words. You may write one sentence using all three words if you wish.

2. Which word on the Vocabulary Development list means "formed or fashioned"? Use the word in a sentence that shows the word's meaning clearly.

3. Though Tan's mother makes herself understood, Tan described her mother's English as "broken" or "fractured." Why do you think nonstandard English is often given such negative descriptions? Explain.

Comprehension

Circle the correct answer.

1. Amy Tan says she speaks
   a. several distinct versions of the English language.
   b. several languages besides English.
   c. English only.
   d. Chinese only.

2. Which of the following is not mentioned as something Tan's mother understands?
   a. *Forbes*   b. *Wall Street Week*
   c. Amy Tan's books   d. The *San Francisco Chronicle*

3. Tan's mother's English has been described as
   a. poetic, pretty, and descriptive.
   b. childish, silly, and funny.
   c. broken, fractured, and limited.
   d. dirty, vulgar, and slimy.

4. With which of the following professionals has Tan served as translator for her mother?
   a. A dentist   b. A stockbroker
   c. An accountant   d. A lawyer

5. Tan's mother's English is
   a. a direct translation from Vietnamese.
   b. a direct translation from Japanese.
   c. a direct translation from Hmong.
   d. a direct translation from Chinese.

Content

1. What does Tan mean when she mentions "all the Englishes I grew up with"?
2. Why doesn't Tan like the terms "broken English" or "Limited English"? What does she say they imply about the speaker?
3. How is Tan's mother treated by the hospital staff? By her stockbroker? What is her mother's response to such treatment?

Style and Structure

1. What is Tan's main point? Write her main idea in your own words.
2. How does Tan show that other people have difficulty understanding her mother?

3. For whom is Tan writing her essay? What assumptions can you make about her audience?

Working Together

1. Make a list of your own languages—either different forms of English or any other languages or dialects you speak—and evaluate the situations in which you use each one. Which forms are the most versatile? The most limiting? Why? Share your results with the class.

2. Make a list of the ways you make yourself understood to others. For instance, you may speak more slowly or use hand gestures in talking to your grandparents, or you may be sure to use slang in speaking with your friends. Which communication strategies help you make your point most effectively? Discuss and share your results with the class.

Writing Assignments

1. How powerful is spoken language? *Write a paragraph showing how your language—or the language of someone you know—has influenced others.* Give specific details from your life, or someone else's, to illustrate your ideas.

2. Have you ever had trouble being understood? *Write a paragraph explaining how you felt when you couldn't make yourself understood.* Use specific details from your life to support your ideas.

3. Tan writes about "all the Englishes" she grew up with. How does your language change when you're with different groups? *Write an essay illustrating how your language changes from one group, such as your family, to another, such as your friends or classmates.* Use your own experiences and observations to support your ideas.

RUSSELL BAKER

The Plot Against People

A two-time Pulitzer prize winner for his *New York Times* column and his autobiographical novel *Growing Up*, Russell Baker was known for his wit and humor in addressing topics familiar to many. In "The Plot Against People," Baker discusses the challenge humanity struggles daily to meet: dealing successfully with inanimate objects designed to help us.

BEFORE YOU READ

Think about the following questions. Write your responses on a separate sheet or in your journal.

- Have you ever lost your temper with an inanimate object? What happened to make you lose your temper?

- Why do you think people become angry with things that cannot move or think or speak?

- What solutions, if any, can you offer to people who lose their temper with inanimate objects?

VOCABULARY DEVELOPMENT

Look up the following words in a dictionary. Write down their meanings on a separate sheet or in your journal.

cunning (paragraph 3)   plausible (paragraph 6)
locomotion (paragraph 6)   burrow (paragraph 7)
virtually (paragraph 8)   invariably (paragraph 8)
constitutes (paragraph 9)   conciliatory (paragraph 10)
baffled (paragraph 13)   aspire (paragraph 13)

The Plot Against People

1   Inanimate objects are classified scientifically into three major categories—those that break down, those that get lost, and those that don't work.

2   The goal of all inanimate objects is to resist man and ultimately to defeat him, and the three major classifications are based on the method each object uses to achieve its purpose. As a general rule, any object capable of breaking down at the moment when it is most needed will do so. The automobile is typical of the category.

3   With the cunning peculiar to its breed, the automobile never breaks down while entering a filling station which has a large staff of idle mechanics. It waits until it reaches a downtown intersection in the middle of the rush hour, or until it is fully loaded with family and luggage on the Ohio Turnpike. Thus it creates maximum inconvenience, frustration, and irritability, thereby reducing its owner's lifespan.

4   Washing machines, garbage disposals, lawn mowers, furnaces, TV sets, tape recorders, slide projectors—all are in league with the automobile to take their turn at breaking down whenever life threatens to flow smoothly for their enemies.

5   Many inanimate objects, of course, find it extremely difficult to break down. Pliers, for example, and gloves and keys are almost totally incapable of breaking down. Therefore, they have had to evolve a different technique for resisting man.

6   They get lost. Science has still not solved the mystery of how they do it, and no man has ever caught one of them in the act. The most plausible theory is that they have developed a secret method of locomotion which they are able to conceal from human eyes.

7   It is not uncommon for a pair of pliers to climb all the way from the cellar to the attic in its single-minded determination to raise its owner's blood pressure. Keys have been known to burrow three feet under mattresses. Women's purses, despite their great weight, frequently travel through six or seven rooms to find hiding space under a couch.

8   Scientists have been struck by the fact that things that break down virtually never get lost, while things that get lost hardly ever break down. A furnace, for example, will invariably break down at the depth of the first winter cold wave, but it will never get lost. A woman's purse hardly ever breaks down; it almost invariably chooses to get lost.

9   Some persons believe this constitutes evidence that inanimate objects are not entirely hostile to man. After all, they point out, a furnace could infuriate a man even more thoroughly by getting lost than by breaking down, just as a glove could upset him far more by breaking down than by getting lost.

10   Not everyone agrees, however, that this indicates a conciliatory attitude. Many say it merely proves that furnaces, gloves and pliers are incredibly stupid.

11   The third class of objects—those that don't work—is the most curious of all. These include such objects as barometers, car clocks, cigarette lighters, flashlights and toy-train locomotives. It is inaccurate, of course, to say that they *never* work. They work once, usually for the first few hours after being brought home, and then quit. Thereafter, they never work again.

12   In fact, it is widely assumed that they are built for the purpose of not working. Some people have reached advanced ages without ever seeing some of these objects—barometers, for example—in working order.

13   Science is utterly baffled by the entire category. There are many theories about it. The most interesting holds that the things that don't work have attained the highest state possible for an inanimate object, the state to which things that break down and things that get lost can still only aspire.

14   They have truly defeated man by conditioning him never to expect anything of them. When his cigarette lighter won't light or his flashlight fails to illuminate, it does not raise his blood pressure. Objects that don't work have given man the only peace he receives from inanimate society.

Russell Baker, "The Plot Against People." Originally published in *The New York Times*, June 18, 1968. Copyright © 1968 by The New York Times Co. Reprinted by permission.

AFTER YOU READ

Vocabulary Practice

1. Choose at least three words from the Vocabulary Development list on page 780 and write sentences using those words. You may write one sentence using all three words if you wish.

2. What word from the Vocabulary Development list means "confused or puzzled"? Use the word in a sentence to show clearly what it means.

3. Baker describes inanimate objects as having human feelings and thoughts. List at least three instances in which Baker endows objects with human characteristics. Then, write a few sentences explaining why you think he does this.

Comprehension

Circle the correct answer.

1. Which of the following is not a category that inanimate objects fall into?

   a. Things that break down

   b. Things that lose parts

   c. Things that get lost

   d. Things that don't work

2. When will an object capable of breaking down do so, as a general rule?

   a. When no one's looking

   b. When it is most needed

   c. When it arrives from the store

   d. When you're showing it to your friends

3. Which one of the following is not given as an example of something that rarely breaks down?

   a. Pliers   b. Gloves

   c. Keys   d. Sunglasses

4. The fact that inanimate objects thwart humans in only one way each proves, according to some, that these objects are

   a. unimaginative.   b. lazy.

   c. stupid.   d. bored.

5. What is considered the "highest state possible" for inanimate objects?

   a. The state of not working

   b. The state of being lost

   c. The state of having dead batteries

   d. The state of being unscrewed

Content

1. How does Baker classify inanimate objects?

2. What does Baker say is "the goal of all inanimate objects"?

3. What proof does Baker offer for the idea that inanimate objects are "not entirely hostile to man"?

Style and Structure

1. Does Baker have a serious point? What is it?

2. What audience is Baker addressing? What clues does he give you as to when this article was written, and for whom?

3. What examples does Baker give of the way inanimate objects thwart people?

Working Together

1. Make a ranked list of all inanimate objects that frustrate you. Which items are at the top of the list? Why? Discuss your findings and present them to the class.

2. Write a step-by-step description of how to deal with a non-working inanimate object such as a cell phone, printer, or car. Your description may include unnecessary but real steps such as, "kick car tire in frustration." Share your results with the class.

Writing Assignments

1. Baker lists many objects that frustrate people. *Write a paragraph arguing that one object in particular is the most frustrating of all inanimate objects.* Be sure to use examples from your own experiences in order to illustrate your ideas. You do not need to choose an object that Baker uses in his essay.

2. Baker's essay was written before computers were widely used, so he has no examples associated with modern technology. *Write a paragraph classifying objects of one type—communications devices, for instance—according to how helpful or frustrating they are.* You may use humor if you like, but you do not have to. Be sure to use specific details from your own experience and observations in order to illustrate your ideas.

3. Think about machines or other inanimate objects that we rely on. *Write an essay classifying inanimate objects according to how much we need them.* For instance, you may classify them according to how often we use them or according to how important they are. A flashlight, for instance, is something you may not need very often, but it's very important when you do need it. Use examples from your own life and observations to illustrate your ideas.

JOAN DIDION

The Santa Ana

A fifth-generation Californian, Joan Didion has paid close attention to the people, places, and styles of the American West. Writing for many publications, Didion has published five novels of her own, and she has also written movie screenplays—including *A Star is Born* (1976) and *Up Close and Personal* (1996)—as well as nonfiction. Her most recent book, *The Year of Magical Thinking*, details her emotions in the year following her husband's death.

BEFORE YOU READ

Think about the following questions. Write your responses on a separate sheet or in your journal.

- What about your local weather is noteworthy or unusual?
- To what extent does the weather affect your mood or behavior? Explain.
- How reasonable is it for people to blame the weather for their moods or actions? Explain.

VOCABULARY DEVELOPMENT

Look up the following words in a dictionary. Write down their meanings on a separate sheet or in your journal.

mechanistic (paragraph 1)   ominously (paragraph 2)

surreal (paragraph 2)   malevolent (paragraph 3)

leeward (paragraph 3)   ions (paragraph 3)

relentlessly (paragraph 4)   incendiary (paragraph 4)

accentuate (paragraph 6)   impermanence (paragraph 6)

The Santa Ana

1   There is something uneasy in the Los Angeles air this afternoon, some unnatural stillness, some tension. What it means is that tonight a Santa Ana will begin to blow, a hot wind from the northeast whining down through the Cajon and San Gorgonio Passes, blowing up sandstorms out along Route 66, drying the hills and the nerves to the flash point. For a few days now we will see smoke back in the canyons, and hear sirens in the night. I have neither heard nor read that a Santa Ana is due, but I know it, and almost everyone I have seen today knows it too. We know it because we feel it. The baby frets. The maid sulks. I rekindle a waning argument with the telephone company, then cut my losses and lie down, given over to whatever it is in the air. To live with the Santa Ana is to accept, consciously or unconsciously, a deeply mechanistic view of human behavior.

2   I recall being told, when I first moved to Los Angeles and was living on an isolated beach, that the Indians would throw themselves into the sea when the bad wind blew. I could see why. The Pacific turned ominously glossy during a Santa Ana period, and one woke in the night troubled not only by the peacocks screaming in the olive trees but by the eerie absence of surf. The heat was surreal. The sky had a yellow cast, the kind of light sometimes called "earthquake weather." My only neighbor would not come out of her house for days, and there were no lights at night, and her

husband roamed the place with a machete. One day he would tell me that he had heard a trespasser, the next a rattlesnake.

3   "On nights like that," Raymond Chandler once wrote about the Santa Ana, "every booze party ends in a fight. Meek little wives feel the edge of the carving knife and study their husbands' necks. Anything can happen." That was the kind of wind it was. I did not know then that there was any basis for the effect it had on all of us, but it turns out to be another of those cases in which science bears out folk wisdom. The Santa Ana, which is named for one of the canyons it rushes through, is a *foehn* wind, like the *foehn* of Austria and Switzerland and the *hamsin* of Israel. There are a number of persistent malevolent winds, perhaps the best known of which are the mistral of France and the Mediterranean sirocco, but a *foehn* wind has distinct characteristics: it occurs on the leeward slope of a mountain range and, although the air begins as a cold mass, it is warmed as it comes down the mountain and appears finally as a hot dry wind. . . . A few years ago an Israeli physicist discovered that not only during such winds, but for the ten or twelve hours which precede them, the air carries an unusually high ratio of positive to negative ions. No one seems to know exactly why that should be; some talk about friction and others suggest solar disturbances. In any case the positive ions are there, and what an excess of positive ions does, in the simplest terms, is make people unhappy. One cannot get much more mechanistic than that.

4   Easterners commonly complain that there is no "weather" at all in Southern California, that the days and the seasons slip by relentlessly, numbingly bland. That is quite misleading. In fact the climate is characterized by infrequent but violent extremes: two periods of torrential subtropical rains which continue for weeks and wash out the hills and send subdivisions sliding toward the sea; about twenty scattered days a year of the Santa Ana, which, with its incendiary dryness, invariably means fire. At the first prediction of a Santa Ana, the Forest Service flies men and equipment from northern California into the southern forests, and the Los Angeles Fire Department cancels its ordinary non-firefighting routines. The Santa Ana caused Malibu to burn the way it did in 1956, and Bel Air in 1961, and Santa Barbara in 1964. In the winter of 1966–67 eleven men were killed fighting a Santa Ana fire that spread through the San Gabriel Mountains.

5   Just to watch the front-page news out of Los Angeles during a Santa Ana is to get very close to what it is about the place. The longest single Santa Ana period in recent years was in 1957, and it lasted not the usual three or four days but fourteen days, from November 21 until December 4. On the first day 25,000 acres of the San Gabriel Mountains were burning, with gusts reaching 100 miles an hour. In town, the wind reached Force 12, or hurricane force, on the Beaufort Scale; oil derricks were toppled and people ordered off the downtown streets to avoid injury from flying objects. . . .

6   It is hard for people who have not lived in Los Angeles to realize how radically the Santa Ana figures in the local imagination. The city burning is Los Angeles's deepest image of itself: Nathanael West perceived that, in *The Day of the Locust*; and at the time of the 1965 Watts riots what struck the imagination most indelibly were the fires. For days one could drive the Harbor Freeway and see the city on fire, just as we had always known it would be in the end. Los Angeles weather is the weather of catastrophe, of apocalypse, and, just as the reliably long and bitter winters of New England determine the way life is lived there, so the violence and the unpredictability of the Santa Ana affect the entire quality of life in Los Angeles, accentuate its impermanence, its unreliability. The wind shows us how close to the edge we are.

AFTER YOU READ

Vocabulary Practice

1. Choose at least three words from the Vocabulary Development list on page 784 and write sentences using those words. You may write one sentence using all three words if you wish.

2. Which word on the Vocabulary Development list means "tending to inflame or excite"? Use the word in a sentence that shows the word's meaning clearly.

3. Make a list of words that Didion uses to show her attitude toward the Santa Ana wind. What effect does this wide array of language have in terms of your understanding the Santa Ana? Explain.

Comprehension

Circle the correct answer.

1. How does Didion say she knows a Santa Ana is coming?
   a. The weather forecaster predicted it.
   b. She feels it.
   c. The sky turns cloudy.
   d. Her husband is grouchy.

2. Which of the following is *not* a type of "malevolent wind"?
   a. The *foehn* of Austria
   b. The mistral of France
   c. The sirocco of the Mediterranean
   d. The tornado of Kansas

3. What does the air carry before and during a Santa Ana wind?

   a. A lot of dust

   b. An usually high ratio of positive to negative ions

   c. The screams of a big cat

   d. Smoke from fires

4. What weather extremes does Didion say Southern California experiences?

   a. Blinding fog and sleet

   b. Choking dust storms and hail

   c. Torrential rain and dry winds

   d. Blistering heat and humidity

5. According to the essay, how long did the longest Santa Ana wind last?

   a. Fourteen days   b. Fourteen weeks

   c. Four days   d. Four weeks

Content

1. What are the characteristics of a Santa Ana?

2. What are some ways the Santa Ana wind affects people?

3. What image, according to Didion, is the Santa Ana wind connected with in people's minds?

Style and Structure

1. What is Didion's main idea? Rewrite the main idea in your own words.

2. What examples does Didion offer of how the wind affects people? List two or three examples that you find particularly effective.

3. What are some words or expressions that show how Didion feels about the Santa Ana wind? How do they help her communicate her point?

Working Together

1. Individually, make a ranked list of weather, from your most to your least favorite. Compare your list with group members. In what ways are your lists similar? Different? Discuss your lists as a group, and compare your findings with those of other groups.

2. How does the weather affect your moods or behavior? Discuss with your group and present findings to the class.

Writing Assignments

1. Didion writes about the Santa Ana's coming, "We know it because we feel it." Similarly, some people claim that they feel snow "in their bones" or smell a tornado coming. To what extent can you "feel" weather coming? *Write a paragraph in which you explain the degree to which you can tell when a certain type of weather is coming.* Use examples from "The Santa Ana" and from your own experiences to illustrate your ideas.

2. Didion writes that "Los Angeles weather is the weather of catastrophe." What kind of weather do you think is "catastrophic" (violently destructive)? *Write a paragraph explaining how certain weather is catastrophic.* If you cannot think of weather which is that bad, write about the worst weather you have lived through. Use weather you are familiar with as well as examples and illustrations from your own life to support your ideas.

3. Didion writes about the effects of a Santa Ana wind on people in Los Angeles. How much does weather affect people's behavior? *Write an essay in which you explain how much weather affects people's actions.* Be sure to use examples from your own experiences and observations for support.

CONSTANCE FAYE MUDORE

Working with Difficult People

Widely published on a number of different topics, Constance Faye Mudore has also served as editor of *Counting on Your Fingers Is Not Immoral*. In "Working with Difficult People," Mudore describes different types of hard-to-handle co-workers and gives readers tips as to how to deal with them.

BEFORE YOU READ

Think about the following questions. Write your responses on a separate sheet or in your journal.

■ What is the most difficult job you've ever had? Why?

■ What role do co-workers play in terms of making a job more or less difficult?

■ What kind of co-worker are you? To what extent do you help others as opposed to keeping to yourself? Explain.

VOCABULARY DEVELOPMENT

Look up the following words in a dictionary. Write down their meanings on a separate sheet or in your journal.

friction (paragraph 1)	dampen (paragraph 4)
cope (paragraph 5)	hostile (paragraph 7)
humiliate (paragraph 11)	potential (paragraph 13)
assumption (paragraph 19)	monologue (paragraph 21)
indefinitely (paragraph 22)	cubicle (paragraph 24)

Working with Difficult People

1   Friction on the job is a fact of life. With the right know-how, it doesn't have to get the better of you.

2   Travis waited tables on weekends at a popular restaurant. He had worked there for more than a year and liked the job. But his feelings toward work changed after Helene, an assistant manager, was hired. This was because Helene often exploded at Travis in front of customers.

3   He complained to the manager, who only made excuses for Helene. Travis wondered how much longer he could work with such a difficult person.

4   Difficult people are the folks who frustrate and dampen the spirits of the people who work with them. While we can all be difficult at times, difficult people are seen as problems by most of the people around them most of the time. Worst of all, they tend to be reluctant to change their ways.

5   The good news is that there are ways to cope with difficult people. But make no mistake. Coping has nothing to do with changing someone else. The only person's behavior you can change is your own. It also has nothing to do with winning or losing battles with others. Coping requires that you learn ways to help you and the difficult person function together at work as effectively as possible.

6   What follows is a guide to dealing with three difficult personality types you're likely to meet on the job: Helen Hostile, Walter Whiner, and Corey Clam.

Rx for Hostiles

7   Helen Hostile gets her way at work by bullying others. Hostiles usually have strong opinions about how others "should" behave. When they sense a lack of confidence in others, they attack. When their targets run from them, they become even more aggressive.

8   Dr. Robert Bramson, a business management consultant and author of *Coping with Difficult People in Business and in Life*, says, "The first rule of coping with anyone aggressive is that you stand up to that person." But, Bramson emphasizes, you must stand up to them without fighting.

9   Why? Hostiles are good at fighting. If you become aggressive toward them, they'll probably become even more aggressive toward you. You are likely to lose. And even if you do win a particular battle, by becoming aggressive yourself, you damage your own reputation at work.

10   How do you stand up for yourself without fighting? Bramson suggests that you give Hostiles time to run down. Then, get their attention and state your opinions firmly.

11   Travis says, "I figured I had nothing to lose since I was ready to quit anyway. So the next time she blew up at me—which was the next time I worked

with her—I let her vent a little. I was nervous, but I looked her in the eye and said, 'Helene, you have the right to discuss my work. But you don't have the right to humiliate me.'"

12   "She looked at me like she'd never seen me before and walked away. I've worked with her since then. She still explodes, but not at me."

The Silent Treatment

13   Corey Clam volunteers little information, typically answering questions with one word, if he responds at all. A clam's most comfortable response to new information or potential conflict is to shut down.

14   Take Laura. She needed Corey's approval to begin a plan to train employees more effectively. She scheduled a meeting with him and enthusiastically laid out her ideas. At the conclusion, she expected him to comment. He said nothing. Confused, she asked, "Do you need more information?" He said no and indicated that he had another appointment.

15   Laura felt like she had had the wind knocked out of her. She didn't know how to interpret his silence. But if her plan was to proceed, she had to draw him out.

16   How do you get clams to tell you what they think? Ask open-ended questions. These are questions that can't be answered with one word. Instead of asking, "Do you need more information?" Laura should have asked, "What's your reaction to what I'm proposing?"

17   It's also important to give clams time to answer. This might mean you have to get comfortable with long silences. At such times, Bramson suggests "friendly, silent staring," preferably focusing your eyes on the clam's chin. (Direct eye contact can be threatening to clams.) Friendly staring communicates that you're expecting the clam to start speaking at any moment.

18   If the clam still doesn't talk, comment on what's happening by saying, "I'm noticing that you're not commenting. What does that mean?" If none of this works, let the clam know that you will make another appointment to discuss the issue.

19   Laura went back to see her boss and got him to open up. She says, "Corey liked my plan. When I left his office after our first meeting, I was sure that his silence meant he hated it. I'm glad I checked out that assumption."

Warning: Whiners at Work

20   Walter Whiner is another difficult person on the work scene. Whiners complain about problems on the job, but don't do anything to improve things. They tend to believe that it is someone else's responsibility to "fix it."

21   The employees at the bank where Walter works avoid him when he starts complaining about the bank being mismanaged. Missy, who works there after school, says, "I groan inside when Walter comes over to talk to

me. I know I'm in for a long monologue of gripes. Sometimes, he even blames me. To top it off, he never tries any of the things I suggest."

22   How to cope? Listen to what whiners have to say, Bramson says, but put a time limit on it. This allows them to let off steam, but doesn't lock you into having to listen indefinitely. Let them know that you heard what they said by restating their complaints. Don't agree or apologize for any of the things they may be dumping on you as "your fault." And try to get them to problem solve.

23   Here's what Missy did. "The next time Walter came over, I listened to what he said for several minutes. He was complaining about the office manager because she gets to work late every day.

24   "I let him know that I could tell he was frustrated with the manager. But I also let him know that the manager was always available when I needed help. I asked him to think about whether there was anything he could do about the situation and to get back to me. Then I told him I had some work to finish before I left for the day. He went back to his cubicle. Walter still complains a lot, but I don't feel so helpless in dealing with him."

Wishing Doesn't Work

25   Wishing that a difficult person were different is a waste of time. It's only by developing our own interpersonal and problem-solving skills that we can cope with them. Viewed positively, difficult people are some of the best teachers we will ever have.

AFTER YOU READ

Vocabulary Practice

1. Choose at least three words from the Vocabulary Development list on page 788 and write sentences using those words. You may write one sentence using all three words if you wish.

2. Which word on the Vocabulary Development list means "existing in possibility"? Use the word in a sentence that shows the word's meaning clearly.

3. What words or expressions does Mudore use to describe workers' feelings toward difficult people? What do these expressions say about Mudore's overall message?

Comprehension

Circle the correct answer.

1. In the opening example, why doesn't Travis like Helene?
   a. She explodes at him in front of customers.
   b. She never praises him.

    c. She constantly underestimates him.

    d. She is nice to him only when others are present.

2. How does Mudore describe difficult people?

    a. Those who turn on each other easily

    b. Those who never follow through

    c. Those who frustrate and dampen the spirit

    d. Those who claim to want to help but don't

3. How do hostile people get their way at work?

    a. By crushing people's spirits

    b. By bullying others

    c. By spreading rumors about people

    d. By lying to the boss

4. How do "clams" deal with people at work?

    a. By volunteering little information

    b. By trying to control every situation

    c. By losing control at work

    d. By complaining about every little thing

5. How do whiners make life difficult for co-workers?

    a. By trying to fix everyone else's problems but their own

    b. By being absent whenever a big problem arises

    c. By making mistakes in their work

    d. By complaining but doing nothing to help

Content

1. Who does Mudore say is the only one people can change?

2. What, according to Mudore, does coping involve?

3. Why does Mudore focus on only the hostile, clam, and whiner personality types?

Style and Structure

1. What is Mudore's point? Rewrite her main idea in your own words.

2. What three examples does Mudore offer to illustrate what she means by "difficult" people? What do these types have in common?

3. Does Mudore spend equal time discussing each type? What does the development tell you about which type is most or least important to her?

Working Together

1. Discuss which type of person, based on your experiences, is most difficult to deal with. Draw a visual representation of your findings—a chart, graph, or picture—to show which type is most difficult. Make a brief presentation to the class using your drawing as a visual aid.

2. What other types of people make work difficult? Use your experiences to come up with other types of difficult co-workers. Give each type a name, as Mudore does, and give a few examples showing how difficult this type of person is. Write up your ideas in a brief summary and present it to the class.

Writing Assignments

1. Mudore writes, "Viewed positively, difficult people are some of the best teachers we will ever have." Do you agree? *Write a paragraph in which you discuss a time when you learned from a negative situation.* For instance, you might discuss how working with an unreliable person caused you to pay extra attention to detail and, thus, do a better job. Use examples from your own experiences to illustrate your ideas.

2. Mudore writes, "The only person's behavior you can change is your own." How easy or difficult is it to change? *Write a paragraph in which you discuss a time when you tried— successfully or unsuccessfully—to change.* What, specifically, did you try to change? Over what period of time did you try? What were your results? Consider these questions and use specific examples from your life to illustrate your ideas.

3. Mudore writes about three different types of difficult people at work. What other areas of life contain difficult people or situations? *Write an essay in which you discuss difficult people, or difficult situations, in one area of your life.* Explain how people can be difficult in family situations or other personal relationships—you could describe your problems with an irritating older sibling, a competitive younger sibling, or a grouchy grandparent. Use examples and illustrations from your own life to support your ideas.

ADAM MAYBLUM

The Price We Pay

When the World Trade Center in New York City was attacked on September 11, 2001, people quickly condemned terrorists for their violence. However, Adam Mayblum claims that the attacks came as a result of "America" as a concept, the freedoms we enjoy, and the lifestyle we lead. In his essay, Mayblum details the events of September 11 as he experienced them from inside Tower 1, the first tower to be hit, until his escape later that morning.

BEFORE YOU READ

Think about the following questions. Write your responses on a separate sheet or in your journal.

- What was your reaction to the World Trade Center attacks?

- How did your reaction to the World Trace Center attacks compare to your reaction to tragedies in other parts of the world? What accounted for the similarities or differences in the feelings you experienced?

- What events have affected you? Describe a time when an occurrence beyond your control had an impact on your life.

VOCABULARY DEVELOPMENT

Look up the following words in a dictionary. Write down their meanings on a separate sheet or in your journal.

emerge (paragraph 1)	lurched (paragraph 2)
wits (paragraph 2)	cramped (paragraph 8)
fallout (paragraph 9)	debris (paragraph 9)
engulfed (paragraph 10)	democracy (paragraph 11)
concept (paragraph 11)	unite (paragraph 11)

The Price We Pay

1   My name is Adam Mayblum. I am alive today. I am committing this to "paper" so I never forget. So we never forget. I am sure that this is one of thousands of stories that will emerge over the next several days and weeks.

2   I arrived, as usual, a little before eight A.M. My office was on the eighty-seventh floor of 1 World Trade Center, aka Tower 1, aka the North Tower. Most of my associates were in by eight-thirty A.M. We were standing around, joking around, eating breakfast, checking e-mails, and getting set for the day when the first plane hit just a few stories above us. I must stress that we did not know that it was a plane. The building lurched violently and shook as if it were an earthquake. People screamed. I watched out my window as the building seemed to move ten to twenty feet in each direction. It rumbled and shook long enough for me to get my wits about myself and grab a coworker and seek shelter under a doorway. Light fixtures and parts of the ceiling collapsed. The kitchen was destroyed. We were certain that it was a bomb. . . .

3   We did not panic. I can only assume that we thought that the worst was over. The building was standing and we were shaken but alive. We checked the halls. The smoke was thick and white and did not smell like I imagined smoke should smell. Not like your BBQ or your fireplace or even a bonfire. The phones were working. . . . And we all started moving to the staircase. One of my dearest friends said that he was staying until the police or firemen came to get him. In the halls there were tiny fires and sparks. The

ceiling had collapsed in the men's bathroom. It was gone along with anyone who may have been in there. We did not go in to look. . . . Once in the staircase we picked up fire extinguishers just in case. On the eighty-fifth floor a brave associate of mine and I headed back up to our office to drag out my partner who stayed behind. . . . I headed into the stairwell with two friends.

4   We were moving down very orderly in stairwell A. Very slowly. No panic. At least not overt panic. My legs could not stop shaking. My heart was pounding. Some nervous jokes and laughter. I made a crack about ruining a brand-new pair of Merrell's. Even still, they were right, my feet felt great. We all laughed. We checked our cell phones. Surprisingly, there was a very good signal, but the Sprint network was jammed. . . . By now the second plane had struck Tower 2. We were so deep into the middle of our building that we did not hear or feel anything. We had no idea what was really going on. We kept making way for wounded to go down ahead of us. Not many of them, just a few. No one seemed seriously wounded. Just some cuts and scrapes. Everyone cooperated. Everyone was a hero yesterday. No questions asked. I had coworkers in another office on the seventy-seventh floor. I tried dozens of times to get them on their cell phones or office lines. It was futile. Later I found that they were alive. One of the many miracles on a day of tragedy.

5   On the fifty-third floor we came across a very heavyset man sitting on the stairs. I asked if he needed help or was he just resting. He needed help. I knew I would have trouble carrying him because I have a very bad back. But my friend and I offered anyway. . . . He hesitated, I don't know why. I said do you want to come or do you want us to send help for you. He chose for help. I told him he was on the fifty-third floor in stairwell A and that's what I would tell the rescue workers. He said OK and we left.

6   Starting around [the forty-fourth] floor the firemen, policemen, WTC K-9 units without the dogs, anyone with a badge, started coming up as we were heading down. . . .

7   On the thirty-third floor I spoke with a man who somehow knew most of the details. He said two small planes hit the building. Now we all started talking about which terrorist group it was. . . . The overwhelming but uninformed opinion was Islamic fanatics. Regardless, we now knew that it was not a bomb and there were potentially more planes coming. We understood.

8   On the third floor the lights went out and we heard and felt this rumbling coming towards us from above. I thought the staircase was collapsing upon itself. It was ten A.M. now and that was Tower 2 collapsing next door. We did not know that. Someone had a flashlight. We passed it forward and left the stairwell and headed down a dark and cramped corridor to an exit. We could not see at all. I recommended that everyone place a hand on the shoulder of the person in front of them and call out if they hit an obstacle so others would know to avoid it. They did. It worked perfectly. We reached another stairwell and saw a female officer emerge soaking wet and

covered in soot. She said we could not go that way, it was blocked. Go up to four and use the other exit. Just as we started up she said it was OK to go down instead. There was water everywhere. . . . She stayed behind instructing people to do that. I do not know what happened to her.

9   We emerged into an enormous room. It was light but filled with smoke. I commented to a friend that it must be under construction. Then we realized where we were. It was the second floor. The one that overlooks the lobby. We were ushered out into the courtyard, the one where the fountain used to be. My first thought was of a TV movie I saw once about nuclear winter and fallout. I could not understand where all of the debris came from. There was at least five inches of this gray pasty dusty drywall soot on the ground as well as a thickness of it in the air. Twisted steel and wires. I heard there were bodies and body parts as well, but I did not look. It was bad enough. We hid under the remaining overhangs and moved out to the street. We were told to keep walking toward Houston Street. . . .

10   We came upon a post office several blocks away. We stopped and looked up. Our building, exactly where our office is (was), was engulfed in flame and smoke. A postal worker said that Tower 2 had fallen down. I looked again and sure enough it was gone. My heart was racing. We kept trying to call our families. I could not get in touch with my wife. Finally I got through to my parents. Relieved is not the word to explain their feelings. They got through to my wife, thank G-d, and let her know I was alive. We sat down. A girl on a bike offered us some water. Just as she took the cap off her bottle we heard a rumble. We looked up and our building, Tower 1, collapsed. I did not note the time, but I am told it was ten-thirty A.M. We had been out less than fifteen minutes.

11   Today the images that people around the world equate with power and democracy are gone, but "America" is not an image, it is a concept. That concept is only strengthened by our pulling together as a team. If you want to kill us, leave us alone because we will do it by ourselves. If you want to make us stronger, attack and we unite. This is the ultimate failure of terrorism against the United States and the ultimate price we pay to be free, to decide where we want to work, what we want to eat, and when and where we want to go on vacation. The very moment the first plane was hijacked, democracy won.

AFTER YOU READ

Vocabulary Practice

1. Choose at least three words from the Vocabulary Development list on page 794 and write sentences using those words. You may write one sentence using all three words if you wish.

2. Which word on the Vocabulary Development list means "flowed over and enclosed"? Use the word in a sentence that shows the word's meaning clearly.

3. In general, how would you describe the level of language Mayblum uses in this essay? Why do you think he writes at this level? Explain.

Comprehension

Circle the correct answer.

1. Why does Mayblum write this essay?

   a. So we will get revenge.   b. So we will never forget.

   c. So we will understand.   d. So we will forgive.

2. When the first plane hit, what did people think it was?

   a. A tunnel collapse   b. A huge celebration

   c. A crash   d. A bomb

3. How did Mayblum get out of the building?

   a. By climbing out a window

   b. By taking the elevator

   c. By walking down the stairs

   d. By riding an escalator

4. Did Mayblum's cell phone work after the attack?

   a. Yes   b. No

5. What happened "the very moment the first plane was hijacked," according to Mayblum?

   a. Terrorists won.   b. American lost.

   c. Democracy won.   d. Democracy lost.

Content

1. How do people initially react to the first plane attack? How does Mayblum explain this reaction?

2. When Mayblum emerges into the second-floor lobby, of what is he reminded?

3. How does Mayblum say the concept of "America" is strengthened?

Style and Structure

1. What is Mayblum's point? Rewrite his main idea in your own words.

2. What kinds of examples does Mayblum use to illustrate his "journey" out of the building? Why do you think he focuses on these types of objects and situations?

3. How does Mayblum organize his essay? What signals does he give to keep the reader on track? Give examples from the text to support your answer.

Working Together

1. Discuss how you reacted to the attacks. To what extent have your feelings changed over time? To what extent has this essay caused you to feel more or less strongly about the attacks? Discuss your reactions and present a brief summary of them to the class.

2. Mayblum writes, "Everyone was a hero." What qualities or actions make up a hero? As a group, discuss what defines a hero. Write up your results in a brief summary, and present them to the class.

Writing Assignments

1. Mayblum writes of his step-by-step journey out of Tower 1 after it had been hit. What is a significant journey that you have made? *Write a paragraph in which you explain, step by step, a trip you have taken.* For instance, you might discuss your first walk or ride to college, a ride to an event (such as sports or music) where you participated, or the journey to give someone news (either good or bad). Do your best to make your reason for choosing this particular trip clear as Mayblum does when he explains why he's writing his essay. Use examples from your own experiences to make each step in your journey clear.

2. Mayblum writes, "Everyone was a hero yesterday." At what times are people more "heroic" than others? Do we necessarily need tragedy to bring out our best? *Write a paragraph explaining how a negative situation does or does not bring out the best in someone you know.* Describe, for instance, a friend of yours who misses free throws in a casual basketball game but never misses them in a real one, or explain how a co-worker who is usually reliable "cracks" under pressure and makes mistakes. Use examples and illustrations from Mayblum's essay and from your own life to support your ideas.

3. Mayblum writes, "If you want to make us stronger, attack and we unite." How true is this idea for an area of your life? *Write an essay in which you explain how a group in your life—family, friends, team, co-workers, to name some—do or do not pull together in times of trouble.* Be sure to use examples from your own life for support.

Credits

Literary Credits

Mary Arguelles, "Money for Morality." First published in *Newsweek* (My Turn), 1991. Reprinted by permission of the author.

Isaac Asimov, "What Is Intelligence Anyway?" Published by permission of the Estate of Isaac Asimov c/o Ralph M. Vicinanza, Ltd.

Russell Baker, "The Plot Against People." From The New York Times, 6/18 © 1968 The New York Times. All rights reserved. Used by permission and protected by the Copyright Laws of the United States. The printing, copying, redistribution, or retransmission of the Material without express written permission is prohibited.

Joan Didion, "The Santa Ana." Excerpt from "Los Angeles Notebook" from *Slouching Towards Bethlehem* by Joan Didion. Copyright © 1966, 1968. Renewed 1996 by Joan Didion. Reprinted by permission of Farrar, Straus, and Giroux LLC.

Stephanie Ericsson, "The Ways We Lie." Copyright © 1992 by Stephanie Ericsson. Originally published by *The Utne Reader*. Reprinted by the permissions of Dunham Literary as agents for the author.

Robert Fulghum, from *All I Really Need to Know I Learned in Kindergarten* by Robert L. Fulghum. Copyright © 1986, 1988 by Robert L. Fulghum. Reprinted by permission of the author.

Ellen Goodman and Patricia O'Brien, "The Difference Between Male and Female Friendships." Reprinted with permission of Simon & Schuster Adult Publishing Group, from *I Know Just What You Mean: The Power of Friendship in Women's Lives* by Ellen Goodman and Patricia O'Brien. Copyright © 2000 by Ellen Goodman and Patricia O'Brien. All rights reserved.

Carolyn Y. Johnson, "The Joy of Boredom." Copyright © 2008. Reprinted with permission of Globe Newspaper Company.

Malcolm X, "A Homemade Education," copyright © 1964 by Alex Haley and Malcolm X.

Copyright © 1965 by Alex Haley and Betty Shabazz, from *The Autobiography of Malcolm X* by Malcolm X and Alex Haley. Used by permission of Random House, Inc.

Judith Martin, "Manners Matter" from *The American Enterprise*, August 15, 1999. Reprinted with permission of The American Enterprise. On the web at www.TAEmag.com.

Adam Mayblum, "The Price We Pay." Reprinted by permission of the author.

Constance Faye Mudore, "Working with Difficult People." Special permission granted by Weekly Reader, published and copyrighted by Weekly Reader Corporation. All rights reserved.

Cheryl Peck, "Fatso." From *Revenge of the Pasta Eaters* by Cheryl Peck. Copyright © 2005 by Cheryl Peck. By permission of Grand Central Publishing. All rights reserved.

Richard Rodriguez, "'Blaxicans' and Other Reinvented Americans." Copyright © 2003 by Richard Rodriguez (Originally appeared in *The Chronicle of Higher Education*, September 12, 2003). Reprinted by permission of Georges Borchardt, Inc. on behalf of the author.

Amy Tan, "My Mother's English." Copyright © 1990 by Amy Tan. From speech delivered at the California Association of Teachers of English 1990 Conference. Reprinted by permission of the author and the Sandra Dijkstra Literary Agency.

Kurt Vonnegut, "How to Write with Style." Reprinted by permission of Farber Literary Agency Inc.

E. B. White, "Education" from *One Man's Meat*. Text copyright © 1939 by E. B. White. Reprinted by permission of the author.

Photo Credits

1: Diehm/Stone/Getty Images Inc; **14**: Ace Stock Limited/Alamy Images; **19**: Alamy Images; **35**: Bob Daemmrich/The Image Works; **43**: David Madison/Stone/Getty Images Inc.; **47**: Underwood & Underwood/Corbis;

Index